AI-Enabled Strategies for Sustainable Cross-Border Logistics

Mohamed Amine Frikha
https://orcid.org/0000-0002-6737-1370
King Faisal University, Saudi Arabia

IGI Global
Scientific Publishing
Publishing Tomorrow's Research Today

Vice President of Editorial	Melissa Wagner
Director of Acquisitions	Mikaela Felty
Director of Book Development	Jocelynn Hessler
Production Manager	Mike Brehm
Cover Design	Jose Rosado

Published in the United States of America by
IGI Global Scientific Publishing
701 East Chocolate Avenue
Hershey, PA, 17033, USA
Tel: 717-533-8845 | Fax: 717-533-7115
Website: https://www.igi-global.com E-mail: cust@igi-global.com

Library of Congress Cataloging-in-Publication Data

LCCN: 2026002357 (CIP Data Pending)
ISBN13: 979-8-3373-7847-3
Isbn13Softcover: 979-8-3373-7848-0
EISBN13: 979-8-3373-7849-7
British Cataloguing in Publication Data
A Cataloguing in Publication record for this book is available from the British Library.

Table of Contents

Detailed Table of Contents

This chapter provides a detailed review of cross-border logistics along the India-Bhutan border. It uses the PRISMA 2020 framework to combine insights from academic, institutional, and grey literature. The focus is on the operational, regulatory, and infrastructure aspects that shape the logistics landscape between the two countries. Key topics include trade facilitation, customs alignment, and digital integration. Based on 86 carefully selected publications, the review identifies six main themes: infrastructure challenges, customs and regulatory issues, institutional fragmentation, gaps in digital trade, political tensions, and informal trade practices. The findings show that while physical infrastructure poses significant challenges, effective institutional coordination and digital cooperation are also crucial for improving logistics efficiency and fostering regional integration.

The complexity of cross-border logistics has grown, which has heightened the demand for sustainable supply chain management and data-driven management. Although the use of artificial intelligence (AI) technology is commonly used to enhance efficiency in the operations of the company, its role with sustainability and governance has not been fully developed. This chapter suggests an AI-powered sustainable supply chain (AISS) model that integrates environmental, social, and governance (ESG) goals in AI-based decision-making. Through the adoption of the theory of sustainability, systems thinking, and ethical AI governance, the framework gives a systematic solution to the responsible adoption of AI in sustainable cross-border logistics.

International transport of perishable goods currently struggles with high energy consumption and food loss due to supply chain inefficiencies. This chapter explores merging artificial intelligence with renewable energy to build a sustainable global cold chain. The authors specifically investigate Maximum Power Point Tracking (MPPT) algorithms in solar-powered warehousing to cut reliance on fossil-fuel generators. Additionally, the text analyzes how predictive analytics and digital twins can forecast customs delays and prevent spoilage. By aligning these interventions with the UN Sustainable Development Goals, the study outlines a viable decarbonization pathway. These strategies provide stakeholders with actionable methods to minimize Scope 3 emissions and ensure the resilience of cross-border food trade.

In an era where environmental sustainability increasingly influences global trade and tourism agendas, the effective orchestration of cross-border logistics has become a critical enabler of both green trade facilitation and sustainable cross-border tourism development. This analytical study investigates how international logistics systems—through digitalized documentation, energy-efficient transport networks, optimized supply chain design, and the integration of renewable energy—can significantly reduce the environmental footprint of cross-border trade and tourism mobility. The adoption of digital and paperless facilitation mechanisms has led to measurable reductions in border delays and emissions, achieving a 3–7% decrease in trade and travel processing times and logistics-related carbon output across regions.

The changing climate, heightened pressures in trade, and advanced cross-border procedures render the logistics systems appropriate to be flexible, smart, and green. This is known as Neuro-Environmental AI, which is a unified set of neural learning, symbolic reasoning, and real-time environmental intelligence, thus allowing them to implement global logistics in response to climatic conditions. The approach supports the foresight paths, emission-sensitive mode decision, disruption-constraining energy-saving border functions, and the expected disruption management. The framework enhances transparency, resilience, and compliance on the international corridors based on the use of digital twins, federated learning, and blockchain-enabled data exchange. It has been demonstrated through case studies that the emission has been reduced, reliability has increased, and the compatibility with the global sustainability goals has been more favorable, which makes Neuro-Environmental AI a new paradigm of the low-carbon and climate-resistant logistics.

The growing complexity of global trade demands logistics systems that are transparent, ethical, and environmentally responsible. Traditional AI excels at prediction but lacks interpretability and cannot enforce regulatory or sustainability rules. Neuro-symbolic AI offers a hybrid solution by combining neural learning with symbolic reasoning, enabling real-time forecasting, rule-based compliance, and carbon-aware decision-making. This framework supports cross-border logistics by integrating knowledge graphs, emissions metrics, customs regulations, and ethical constraints into a unified governance model. The approach enhances explainability, ensures fair treatment of shipments, strengthens regulatory alignment, and enables greener routing across international corridors.

The world's supply chains are changing quickly, and we need some new ways of keeping them transparent, resilient, and sustainable. This chapter examines the role AI is playing in creating eco-friendly, ethically governed, and efficient supply chains. It demonstrates how AI-driven tools, such as machine learning, AIoT, digital twins, predictive analytics, and automated carbon tracking, are used to help transition us from linear to circular models in a more stringent manner, and to increase compliance and cross-border visibility. By integrating AI, logistics companies can benefit from traceability in real time, reduce emissions, prevent labour risks, and optimise resources. Drawing from research, theory, and examples from three companies—DHL, Maersk, and Unilever—the authors construct a framework that describes AI's role in sustainable supply chain transformation. In short, AI isn't merely technology, it is a catalyst for ethical, transparent, and future-proof global supply chains in union with SDGs 9, 12, and 13.

This chapter examines the incorporation of the Sustainable Development Goals (SDGs) into the evolution of logistics and supply chain systems aimed at decarbonization and enduring sustainability. The analysis commences with an examination of the environmental and socio-economic challenges confronting global logistics networks, encompassing rising energy consumption, greenhouse gas emissions, resource limitations, and regulatory demands. The chapter establishes the conceptual foundations of sustainable and low-carbon logistics by analyzing key externalities linked to logistics operations, the difficulties in measuring environmental performance, and the transition from conventional linear logistics models to green, circular, and low-carbon supply chain paradigms. Emphasis is directed towards the Sustainable Development Goals (SDGs) most pertinent to logistics, namely SDG 7 , SDG 9 , SDG 11, SDG 12, SDG 13, and SDG 17.

Preface

DESCRIPTION

AI continually transforms cross-border logistics as global trade networks grow more complex and environmentally demanding. From predictive demand forecasting and route optimization to automated customs processing and real-time risk monitoring, AI-driven systems help companies reduce fuel consumption, minimize delays, and enhance supply chain transparency. By integrating data from ports, carriers, and regulatory authorities, these technologies support more sustainable decision-making while maintaining efficiency and compliance. Further exploration may reveal how AI-enabled strategies reshape international logistics to balance economic performance with environmental responsibility and long-term resilience.

AI-Enabled Strategies for Sustainable Cross-Border Logistics explores how AI and digital transformation drive sustainability in logistics systems. It provides a comprehensive framework for understanding how AI-driven models, data analytics, and automation can optimize cross-border operations, reduce emissions, and improve resilience across global supply networks. This book covers topics such as data analytics, decarbonization, and environmental science, and is a useful resource for business owners, engineers, academicians, researchers, and scientists.

COVERAGE

The many academic areas covered in this publication include, but are not limited to:

- Artificial Intelligence (AI)
- Automation Technology
- Cross-Border Operations

- Data Analytics
- Decarbonization
- Digital Technology
- Environmental Science
- Ethics and Law
- Global Business
- Logistics
- Supply Chain Management
- Sustainable Development

ORGANIZATION OF THE BOOK

Chapter 1

AI-Enabled Strategies for Sustainable Cross-Border Logistics: Transforming Global Supply Chains Through Intelligence, Efficiency, and Resilience

The integration of Artificial Intelligence (AI) in cross-border logistics is revolutionizing global supply chains by enhancing intelligence, efficiency, and resilience. AI-driven technologies such as predictive analytics, real-time tracking, and automated decision-making are enabling smarter route optimization, reducing operational costs, and improving sustainability across international trade networks. These intelligent systems facilitate faster customs clearance, minimize carbon footprints, and strengthen risk management, making supply chains more adaptive to disruptions. This chapter explores how AI-enabled strategies are shaping a new era of sustainable, transparent, and resilient cross-border logistics, driving innovation and competitiveness in global commerce.

Chapter 2

Artificial Intelligence in Sustainable Supply Chain Management

The integration of Artificial Intelligence (AI) into supply chain systems has emerged as a transformative force in advancing sustainability objectives, reducing environmental impact, and promoting more responsible resource use across global logistics networks. As supply chains grow more complex spanning continents, involving a diverse network of suppliers, and responding to increasingly dynamic consumer demands traditional management approaches struggle to maintain efficiency and sustainability simultaneously. AI addresses these limitations through its capacity for intelligent data processing, real-time decision-making, and predictive analytics, enabling organizations to transition towards greener, more transparent, and more ethical supply chain practices. One of the most notable contributions of AI to supply chain sustainability lies in its role in optimizing resource consumption. AI-driven tools facilitate inventory optimization, ensuring the right quantity of goods is produced, transported, and stocked, thus minimizing waste associated with overproduction and excess storage.

Chapter 3

Artificial Intelligence in Sustainable Supply Chain Management: Enhancing Efficiency, Resilience, and Environmental Responsibility

Artificial Intelligence (AI) is transforming sustainable supply chain management by enhancing operational efficiency, strengthening resilience, and reducing environmental impact. This chapter explores the integration of AI techniques including machine learning, deep learning, optimization models, and digital twins across key supply chain functions such as forecasting, manufacturing, logistics, procurement, and circular resource management. AI-driven tools improve demand prediction, energy optimization, carbon tracking, waste reduction, and risk mitigation while enabling real-time visibility and data-driven decision-making. The chapter also discusses challenges related to data quality, computational demands, cybersecurity, bias, and regulatory constraints. Future opportunities, such as autonomous supply chains, green AI, and integration with IoT and blockchain, highlight AI's potential to support long-term sustainability goals.

Chapter 4

AI-Enabled Forecasting and Performance Optimization in Sustainable Supply Chains: A Neural Network Approach Using Digital SCOR®

This chapter presents a computational framework for forecasting supply chain performance using augmented SCOR®4.0 metrics and Multilayer Perceptron (MLP) neural networks. The authors operationalize an eight-module SCOR® architecture, incorporating digital, cost, working capital, cash cycle, responsiveness, reliability, and risk dimensions. Each MLP model is optimized through systematic topology selection, normalized input processing, and rigorous cross-validation. Empirical results demonstrate high predictive accuracy, with correlation coefficients exceeding

0.997 and statistical tests confirming model reliability. Comparative analysis indicates that MLP-based forecasting significantly outperforms traditional linear methods, capturing non-linear interactions among operational, financial, and sustainability indicators. The chapter highlights the practical utility of AI-driven models for decision support in complex, cross-border supply chains.

Chapter 5

Green Logistics Effect on Smart Logistics Optimization Through Carbon-Efficient Routing

This chapter discusses how Green Logistics (GL) can be affected by Smart Logistics Optimization (SLO) using Carbon-Efficient Routing (CER), for the sample case the number of participants was 394. This research will focus on improving the efficiency of logistics operations through green initiatives, within the framework of growing environmental awareness and the necessity for sustainable logistics operations. Findings reveal that implementing the GL strategies, in addition to the decrease of carbon emission can be used to improve the routing efficiency of the logistics associated with cost savings and better operational performance. The particular part of the chapter has got its contribution to the literature since it presents empirical data about the synergetic impression of Green and SL which can have been employed by logistics managers who want to achieve the equilibrium within the environmental sustainability and the operational efficiency. The knowledge obtained in this chapter can be utilized for creating more meaningful strategies for logistics.

Chapter 6

An Analytical Study on Cross-Border Logistics of the India-Bhutan Border Region: A Comprehensive Systematic Literature Review

This chapter provides a detailed review of cross-border logistics along the India-Bhutan border. It uses the PRISMA 2020 framework to combine insights from academic, institutional, and grey literature. The focus is on the operational, regulatory, and infrastructure aspects that shape the logistics landscape between the two countries. Key topics include trade facilitation, customs alignment, and digital integration. Based on 86 carefully selected publications, the review identifies six main themes: infrastructure challenges, customs and regulatory issues, institutional fragmentation, gaps in digital trade, political tensions, and informal trade practices. The findings show that while physical infrastructure poses significant challenges, effective institutional coordination and digital cooperation are also crucial for improving logistics efficiency and fostering regional integration.

Chapter 7

AI for Sustainable Supply Chain Management in Cross-Border Logistics

The complexity of cross-border logistics has grown, which has heightened the demand of sustainable supply chain management and data-driven management. Although the use of artificial intelligence (AI) technology is commonly used to enhance efficiency in the operations of the company, its role with sustainability and governance has not been fully development. This paper suggests an AI-powered sustainable Supply Chain (AISS) model that integrates environmental, social, and governance (ESG) goals in AI-based decision-making. Through the adoption of the theory of sustainability, systems thinking, and ethical AI governance, the framework gives a systematic solution to the responsible adoption of AI in sustainable cross-border logistics.

Chapter 8

AI-Driven Decarbonization in Agri-Food Cold Chains With Smart Logistics and Renewable Energy

International transport of perishable goods currently struggles with high energy consumption and food loss due to supply chain inefficiencies. This chapter explores merging artificial intelligence with renewable energy to build a sustainable global cold chain. The authors specifically investigate Maximum Power Point Tracking (MPPT) algorithms in solar-powered warehousing to cut reliance on fossil-fuel generators. Additionally, the text analyzes how predictive analytics and digital twins can forecast customs delays and prevent spoilage. By aligning these interventions with the UN Sustainable Development Goals, the study outlines a viable decarbonization pathway. These strategies provide stakeholders with actionable methods to minimize Scope 3 emissions and ensure the resilience of cross-border food trade.

Chapter 9

Greening the Gateways-Cross-Border Logistics as a Catalyst for Sustainable Trade and Tourism Development

In an era where environmental sustainability increasingly influences global trade and tourism agendas, the effective orchestration of cross-border logistics has become a critical enabler of both green trade facilitation and sustainable cross-border tourism development Xu, W 2025. This analytical study investigates how international logistics systems through digitalized documentation, energy-efficient transport networks, optimized supply chain design, and the integration of renewable energy can significantly reduce the environmental footprint of cross-border trade and tourism mobility (Bekteshi & Alshiqi, 2024). The adoption of digital and paperless facilitation mechanisms has led to measurable reductions in border delays and emissions, achieving a 3–7% decrease in trade and travel processing times and logistics-related carbon output across regions (OECD, 2025).

Chapter 10

Neuro-Environmental AI Orchestration for Climate-Adaptive Cross-Border Logistics Systems

The changing climate, heightened pressures in trade, and advanced cross-border procedures render the logistics systems appropriate to be flexible, smart, and green. This is known as the chapter Neuro-Environmental AI Orchestration, which is a unified set of neural learning, symbolic reasoning, and real-time environmental intelligence, thus allowing them to implement global logistics in response to climatic conditions. The approach supports the foresight paths, emission-sensitive mode decision, disruption-constraining energy-saving border functions, and the expected disruption management. The framework enhances transparency, resilience, and compliance on the international corridors based on the use of digital twins, federated learning, and blockchain-enabled data exchange. It has been demonstrated through case studies that the emission has been reduced, reliability has increased, and the compatibility with the global sustainability goals has been more favorable, which makes Neuro-Environmental AI a new paradigm of the low-carbon and climate-resistant logistics.

Chapter 11

Neuro-Symbolic AI Frameworks for Ethical, Transparent, and Sustainable Cross-Border Logistics Governance

The growing complexity of global trade demands logistics systems that are transparent, ethical, and environmentally responsible. Traditional AI excels at prediction but lacks interpretability and cannot enforce regulatory or sustainability rules. Neuro-symbolic AI offers a hybrid solution by combining neural learning with symbolic reasoning, enabling real-time forecasting, rule-based compliance, and carbon-aware decision-making. This framework supports cross-border logistics by integrating knowledge graphs, emissions metrics, customs regulations, and ethical constraints into a unified governance model. The approach enhances explainability, ensures fair treatment of shipments, strengthens regulatory alignment, and enables greener routing across international corridors.

Chapter 12

Artificial Intelligence for Transparent and Sustainable Supply Chains

The world's supply chains are changing quickly, and we need some new ways of keeping them transparent, resilient and sustainable. This chapter examines the role AI is playing in creating eco-friendly, ethically governed and efficient supply chains. It demonstrates how AI-driven tools, such as machine learning, AIoT, digital twins, predictive analytics and automated carbon tracking, are used to help transition us from linear to circular models in a more stringent manner, and to increase compliance and cross-border visibility. By integrating AI, logistics companies can benefit from traceability in real time, reduce emissions, prevent labour risks, and optimise resources. Drawing from research, theory, and examples from three companies - DHL, Maersk, and Unilever - we construct a framework that describes AI's role in sustainable supply chain transformation. In short, AI isn't merely technology, it is a catalyst for ethical, transparent and future-proof global supply chains in union with SDGs 9, 12 and 13.

Chapter 13

AI-Enabled Strategies for Sustainable Cross-Border Logistics: Sustainable Development Goals (SDGs) and Decarbonized Logistics

This chapter examines the incorporation of the Sustainable Development Goals (SDGs) into the evolution of logistics and supply chain systems aimed at decarbonization and enduring sustainability. The analysis commences with an examination of the environmental and socio-economic challenges confronting global logistics networks, encompassing rising energy consumption, greenhouse gas emissions, resource limitations, regulatory demands. The chapter establishes the conceptual foundations of sustainable and low-carbon logistics by analyzing key externalities linked to logistics operations, the difficulties in measuring environmental performance, and the transition from conventional linear logistics models to green, circular, and low-carbon supply chain paradigms. Emphasis is directed towards the Sustainable Development Goals (SDGs) most pertinent to logistics, namely SDG 7 (Affordable and Clean Energy), SDG 9 (Industry, Innovation and Infrastructure), SDG 11, SDG 12, SDG 13, and SDG 17 .

Chapter 14

Deep Topological Intelligence for Sustainable Supply Chain Management: A Structural Framework for Global Logistics Optimization

The objective of this chapter is to develop Deep Topological Intelligence (DTI) as a structural framework for sustainable supply chain management, optimizing logistics while preserving viability, redundancy, and resilience. "Structural sustainability" is implemented by building a sea–air–rail–road logistics graph with cost, time, capacity, and emissions; simulating disruptions and targeted attacks; learning latent representations with autoencoders; and testing structural conservation with persistent homology, Betti curves, and Wasserstein distances. Contributions include: a topology-informed digital-twin view (sustainability as persistence of form under perturbation), a reproducible workflow linking KPIs to homological indicators, a protocol that flags "efficient but fragile" AI designs, and a study of model capacity versus topological fidelity. Higher-capacity autoencoders preserve loop structure with minimal H_1 deformation ($W \approx 0.054$), while H_0 connectivity is more sensitive, revealing fragility missed by KPIs and supporting carbon-aware redesign without eroding redundancy.

Chapter 15

Quantum-Inspired AI for Carbon-Neutral Multimodal and Cross-Border Transport Optimization

Quantum-Inspired AI (QIA) presents a state-of-the-art method of optimization of carbon-neutral multimodal and cross-border logistics. Due to increasing emissions, complexity in regulation, and frequent supply chain disruptions across the globe, the traditional models cannot cope with scalability and real-time adjustments. QIA uses tunneling, superposition and probabilistic search to search vast routing space, combine the emissions information and address the compliance requirement across the borders. Combined with digital twins, QIA assists in dynamic re-optimization during alterations in the environment, infrastructures, and geopolitics to enhance the reliability and sustainability of routing. The chapter provides a structure of applying QIA to green corridors, multimodal integration, and cross-border operations with the support of case studies of the reduction of emissions, improved schedule compliance, and enhanced resilience. In general, QIA becomes an important facilitator of scalable and sustainable world logistics.

Chapter 16

Quick Commerce Transformation Through Artificial Intelligence, Green Logistics, and Drones

Quick commerce is fast revolutionizing retail by offering super rapid service but its future depends on whether it incorporates the new super-fast technology and sustainability. The chapter examines the application of artificial intelligence in improving demand forecasting and stock management and green logistics methods to support environment negativity by electrifying and using eco-packaging. New models in drone delivery continue to undermine last-mile operations and reduce the cost of businesses, enhancing the efficiency of services. Together, these innovations redefine supply chains, as well as consumer expectations and urban retail ecosystems, in the post-pandemic era. The chapter identifies the opportunities and challenges of reaching Artificial, sustainable logistics, and autonomous delivery but also provides a roadmap to the next stage of rapid transformation of quick commerce.

Acknowledgment

This work was supported by the Deanship of Scientific Research, Vice Presidency for Graduate Studies and Scientific Research, King Faisal University, Saudi Arabia [Grant No. KFU261277].

Chapter 1
AI-Enabled Strategies for Sustainable Cross-Border Logistics:
Transforming Global Supply Chains Through Intelligence, Efficiency, and Resilience

Shivansu Sachan
http://orcid.org/0000-0002-9893-8018
CSJM University, India

Mridulesh Singh
http://orcid.org/0009-0000-6365-4392
CSJM University, India

ABSTRACT

The integration of Artificial Intelligence (AI) in cross-border logistics is revolutionizing global supply chains by enhancing intelligence, efficiency, and resilience. AI-driven technologies such as predictive analytics, real-time tracking, and automated decision-making are enabling smarter route optimization, reducing operational costs, and improving sustainability across international trade networks. These intelligent systems facilitate faster customs clearance, minimize carbon footprints, and strengthen risk management, making supply chains more adaptive to disruptions. This chapter explores how AI-enabled strategies are shaping a new era of sustainable, transparent, and resilient cross-border logistics, driving innovation and competitiveness in global commerce.

DOI: 10.4018/979-8-3373-7847-3.ch001

1. INTRODUCTION

Global supply chains have evolved into complex, interconnected frameworks that facilitate the movement of goods, data, and capital across national borders. Cross-border logistics, the core operational component of global trade, ensures the timely movement of raw materials and products across different regulatory and geographical regions (Christopher, 2016). However, during the past decade, traditional logistics systems have come under pressure due to trade wars, fluctuating tariff structures, rising oil prices, climate-related disruptions, and global crises such as the COVID-19 pandemic (Ivanov & Dolgui, 2020). These disruptions have exposed critical weaknesses in existing supply chains, including port congestion, dependence on fossil fuels, lack of interoperability in customs procedures, and limited real-time visibility (Notteboom & Haralambides, 2020). To overcome these vulnerabilities, the global logistics sector is transitioning from manual, paper-based, and reactive approaches to AI-driven, automated, and predictive systems (Wamba et al., 2020).

Artificial Intelligence (AI) has emerged as a transformative force in enhancing efficiency, transparency, and sustainability within global logistics networks. AI enables predictive forecasting, autonomous decision-making, route optimization, digital documentation, and intelligent demand planning—capabilities that traditional methods lack (Min, 2017). For instance, machine learning algorithms analyze historical trade data, weather conditions, political developments, and shipping traffic to forecast demand patterns and optimize freight routes (Kamble, Gunasekaran, & Gawankar, 2020). AI-powered robots and autonomous vehicles streamline warehousing, cargo inspection, and last-mile delivery, reducing operational costs and human error (Kalaiarasi & Ramakrishnan, 2021). Similarly, blockchain combined with AI ensures tamper-proof trade documentation, automates customs processes, and enhances trust between cross-border stakeholders (Saberi, Kouhizadeh, Sarkis, & Shen, 2019). These innovations contribute to reduced delays, cost efficiency, and improved sustainability in global logistics operations.

Sustainability has become a core objective in cross-border logistics due to heightened awareness of climate change and regulatory pressure to reduce carbon emissions. The transport and logistics industry accounts for nearly 24% of global CO_2 emissions, with maritime shipping, aviation, and road freight being major contributors (International Transport Forum, 2021). AI supports sustainability by optimizing fuel consumption, planning energy-efficient routes, reducing empty return trips, and facilitating carbon tracking and reporting (Zhang & Zhang, 2022). AI-enabled systems also facilitate circular economy practices by improving reverse logistics, waste reduction, recycling processes, and lifecycle tracking of goods (Bai, Sarkis, & Dou, 2020). Green logistics is further enhanced by digital twins in smart ports, predictive maintenance of vessels and aircraft, and intelligent energy management systems that support alternative fuels such as hydrogen and bio-LNG (Heilig & Voß, 2017).

The integration of AI technology in cross-border logistics is not merely technological but also involves governance, policy, and ethical considerations. Effective deployment of AI in logistics requires robust digital infrastructure, standardized data-sharing protocols, and coordinated trade policies (UNCTAD, 2023). While developed economies such as Germany, Singapore, South Korea, and the United States have implemented smart ports and AI-enabled customs systems, developing countries face challenges such as inadequate infrastructure, cyber risks, digital skill gaps, and financial constraints (World Bank, 2022). This uneven adoption of AI may deepen the digital divide and disadvantage small and medium enterprises (smes) in global trade (OECD, 2021). Therefore, international cooperation among governments, logistics providers, technology companies, and financial institutions is essential to ensure scalable, inclusive, and secure AI adoption across borders.

This chapter aims to examine AI-enabled strategies for sustainable cross-border logistics and their impact on intelligence, efficiency, and resilience in supply chains. It presents AI applications across customs automation, freight forwarding, smart warehousing, multimodal transportation, and risk management. It also includes case studies from Maersk, DHL, Alibaba Cainiao, and Amazon Logistics to illustrate best practices in AI-driven logistics transformation. Furthermore, the chapter addresses challenges such as cybersecurity threats, algorithmic bias, data sovereignty, and regulatory restrictions. Finally, it proposes a strategic AI-driven framework aligned with United Nations Sustainable Development Goals (sdgs), particularly SDG 9 (Industry, Innovation, and Infrastructure), SDG 12 (Responsible Consumption and Production), and SDG 13 (Climate Action) (UN, 2015).

Research Gap and Chapter Contribution

Despite rapid technological progress, existing literature largely examines artificial intelligence either from an operational logistics perspective or through the lens of sustainability, with limited effort to integrate these domains within the context of cross-border supply chain complexity. Prior studies primarily emphasize efficiency gains such as cost reduction, automation, and demand forecasting, while insufficient attention has been given to governance structures, institutional barriers, and socio-environmental implications of AI deployment across international logistics networks.

Moreover, current scholarship rarely develops a *holistic strategic framework* that connects AI capabilities with sustainability outcomes, regulatory coordination, and resilience-building mechanisms. This fragmentation restricts both theoretical advancement and managerial applicability, particularly for emerging economies attempting to participate in digitally driven trade ecosystems.

Novel Contributions of the Chapter

This chapter advances the literature in four significant ways:

1. *Integrative Perspective:* It bridges AI capability theory with sustainable supply chain management to explain how intelligent technologies generate both operational and environmental value in cross-border logistics.
2. *Strategic Framework Development:* The chapter proposes a comprehensive AI-enabled sustainable logistics framework that aligns technological adoption with governance, policy coordination, and climate objectives.
3. *Multi-Level Analysis:* By combining conceptual synthesis with industry case insights, the chapter connects macro-level policy considerations with firm-level strategic implementation.
4. *Inclusive Digital Transition Lens:* It critically evaluates adoption barriers in developing economies, addressing digital inequality, infrastructure gaps, and regulatory fragmentation—areas underexplored in prior research.

2. BACKGROUND AND LITERATURE REVIEW

Cross-border logistics has historically evolved through several industrial revolutions—from steam-powered maritime trade in the 18th century, to containerization in the 20th century, and digital globalization in the 21st century (Rodrigue & Notteboom, 2020). Traditional logistics relied heavily on manual documentation, physical customs clearance, and fragmented communication between trade actors (Hummels, 2007). The introduction of container shipping by Malcolm mclean in the 1950s reduced loading time dramatically and revolutionized global logistics, enabling standardized international freight movement (Levinson, 2016). Over time, global supply chains became longer, more integrated, and dependent on just-in-time production models, where any disruption in transportation or borders could trigger global shortages (Christopher, 2016). This interdependence was evident during the COVID-19 pandemic when border closures and port lockdowns paralyzed freight movement, affecting industries from healthcare to manufacturing (Ivanov & Dolgui, 2020). These disruptions emphasized the need for flexible, digital, and intelligent supply chains.

2.1 Evolution of AI in Logistics

Artificial Intelligence in logistics gained prominence with the advent of big data, the Internet of Things (iot), and cloud computing. AI initially appeared in demand forecasting, warehouse automation, and route planning using machine learning and neural networks (Min, 2017). Companies like DHL introduced AI-driven logistics control towers that monitor global supply flows in real time (DHL, 2018). Amazon adopted robotics and machine learning for inventory management and last-mile delivery, significantly improving logistics speed and scalability (Marciano & Komninos, 2019). AI applications continued to expand into real-time vehicle tracking, port automation, predictive container allocation, customs risk assessment, and trade finance automation (Kamble, Gunasekaran & Gawankar, 2020). The convergence of AI with blockchain and iot created cyber-physical logistics systems, integrating digital and physical flows seamlessly (Saberi et al., 2019). Today, AI is not only used to improve operational efficiency but also to predict risks like geopolitical disruptions, piracy, pandemics, and climate-related events (Christopher & Holweg, 2017).

2.2 AI and Cross-Border Documentation

One of the most time-consuming elements in cross-border logistics is documentation and customs clearance. Traditional customs processes involve large volumes of paperwork, manual inspections, and varying regulatory protocols between nations (Grainger, 2011). According to the World Bank (2022), inefficient documentation procedures can increase shipping delays by up to 20–30%. AI helps mitigate this by automating document verification through optical character recognition (OCR), blockchain-based smart contracts, and predictive risk assessment systems (UNCTAD, 2023). IBM and Maersk's tradelens platform utilizes AI and blockchain to provide end-to-end supply chain visibility and reduce document fraud (Meyer & Hamilton, 2020). AI algorithms also pre-screen cargo based on historical data, reducing the number of physical inspections and accelerating customs clearance (Wang & Sarkis, 2021). This digitalization supports paperless trade, reducing environmental impact and enhancing transparency.

2.3 AI, Smart Ports, and Border Infrastructure

Ports serve as strategic nodes in cross-border logistics, handling nearly 80% of global trade by volume (UNCTAD, 2023). AI-enabled smart ports such as Rotterdam, Singapore, and Shanghai use sensors, digital twins, and predictive analytics to optimize container handling, crane scheduling, vessel berthing, and energy usage (Heilig & Voß, 2017). The Port of Rotterdam uses AI-powered digital twin technology to simulate port operations, predict congestion, and support real-time decision-making (Port of Rotterdam Authority, 2021). Similarly, China's Ningbo-Zhoushan Port employs AI for customs digitization, automated guided vehicles (agvs), and emission control systems (Zhang & Zhang, 2022). Smart border systems such as Singapore's Networked Trade Platform and South Korea's UNI-PASS use AI to analyze cargo risk profiles and automate clearance processes (Lee & Whang, 2020). These advancements not only speed international trade but also reduce fuel idle time, container congestion, and carbon emissions.

2.4 Sustainability and Green Logistics in Literature

The concept of green logistics became prominent due to the growing environmental impact of transportation, which contributes significantly to global emissions (International Transport Forum, 2021). Traditional logistics models often prioritize speed and cost over environmental outcomes, resulting in high fuel consumption, empty backhauls, and inefficiencies (mckinnon, 2018). Literature suggests that AI improves sustainability through route optimization, load consolidation, intermodal transport selection, and idle time reduction (Bai, Sarkis & Dou, 2020). Predictive maintenance using AI helps monitor fuel efficiency and reduce equipment malfunction in vessels, aircraft, and trucks (Zhang & Zhang, 2022). Blockchain and AI facilitate traceability in carbon reporting, enabling firms to comply with environmental regulations such as the EU Green Deal and IMO 2050 decarbonization mandates (IMO, 2019). The circular economy perspectives emphasize reverse logistics, waste management, and resource efficiency—all of which are supported by AI-led decision-making (Geissdoerfer et al., 2017).

2.5 Research Gap

While prior literature has separately examined AI in logistics and sustainable transportation, very few studies integrate AI, cross-border logistics, and sustainability within one holistic framework (Wamba et al., 2020). Most research focuses on operational efficiency rather than ethical, regulatory, or socio-environmental implications of AI-driven logistics (Saberi et al., 2019). There is also limited exploration of AI adoption challenges in developing economies, including digital inequality, cyber risks, and capital investment barriers (World Bank, 2022). This chapter addresses these gaps by providing a comprehensive framework that combines AI technology, international logistics governance, and sustainable development principles.

3. THEORETICAL FRAMEWORK AND CONCEPTUAL MODEL

The integration of artificial intelligence into cross-border logistics is best understood through a blend of classical logistics theories and modern digital transformation models. Several theoretical frameworks contribute to the foundation of AI-enabled sustainable logistics: *Systems Theory, Resource-Based View (RBV), Socio-Technical Systems Theory, and Sustainable Supply Chain Management Theory*. These theories provide insight into how AI strengthens supply chains by improving resource capabilities, technological integration, and sustainability performance.

3.1 Systems Theory and Logistics Networks

Systems theory suggests that supply chains function as interdependent networks where components such as suppliers, transporters, customs authorities, warehouses, and end consumers are linked through flows of materials, information, and finance (Bertalanffy, 1968). In cross-border logistics, disruptions in one component—such as port shutdowns or customs delays—can affect the entire system globally (Ivanov & Dolgui, 2020). AI strengthens systems integration by enabling real-time data sharing, predictive analysis, and synchronized communication across stakeholders (Christopher, 2016). Technologies like iot sensors, digital twins, and AI control towers enhance visibility across ports, border checkpoints, and multimodal logistics networks (Heilig & Voß, 2017). Thus, AI acts as a digital nervous system supporting self-regulated logistics ecosystems.

3.2 Resource-Based View (RBV) and AI Capabilities

The Resource-Based View (RBV) argues that sustained competitive advantage arises when firms possess unique, valuable, inimitable, and non-substitutable resources (Barney, 1991). In logistics, AI capabilities—such as predictive analytics, intelligent demand forecasting, and autonomous warehousing—serve as strategic resources that enhance firm competitiveness (Kamble, Gunasekaran & Gawankar, 2020). For instance, Amazon uses proprietary AI algorithms for fulfillment optimization, allowing faster delivery and lower costs than competitors (Marciano & Komninos, 2019). Maersk integrates blockchain-based AI systems (tradelens) that streamline customs documentation and enhance trust across global supply chains (Meyer & Hamilton, 2020). By combining physical assets (ships, warehouses, fleets) with digital intelligence, logistics firms create hybrid capabilities that are difficult for competitors to replicate.

3.3 Socio-Technical Systems Theory (STS)

Socio-Technical Systems Theory emphasizes that successful technological implementation requires both technical innovation and human adaptability (Trist & Emery, 1951). In the context of AI logistics, technology alone cannot drive transformation unless employees, customs officials, freight forwarders, and policymakers are trained and aligned with digital processes (OECD, 2021). AI adoption must consider organizational culture, resistance to change, ethical use of data, and workforce upskilling (Wamba et al., 2020). For example, AI-powered customs platforms like Singapore's Networked Trade Platform require both advanced algorithms and regulatory understanding from users (Lee & Whang, 2020). Therefore, AI implementation in logistics must balance machine intelligence with human decision-making and institutional governance.

3.4 Sustainable Supply Chain Management (SSCM) Theory

Sustainable Supply Chain Management (SSCM) theory combines economic performance with environmental protection and social responsibility (Carter & Rogers, 2008). It aligns closely with the triple bottom line—profit, planet, and people. AI complements SSCM by enabling energy-efficient transportation, reducing carbon emissions, and promoting ethical sourcing (Bai, Sarkis & Dou, 2020). AI-powered route optimization can reduce fuel consumption by 10–15% in freight transport (Zhang & Zhang, 2022). Predictive maintenance lowers waste and extends vehicle lifespan, while AI-enabled carbon reporting supports regulatory compliance with frameworks like the EU Green Deal and IMO 2050 charter (IMO, 2019). Thus, AI enhances both economic and environmental logistics performance.

This chapter adopts a *qualitative conceptual research design* supported by a systematic review of interdisciplinary literature and illustrative industry case evidence. The objective is to synthesize existing knowledge and develop a strategic framework explaining how AI enables sustainable cross-border logistics.

Research Design

A structured literature review approach was employed to identify scholarly publications, policy documents, and industry reports addressing three core domains:

- Artificial intelligence in logistics
- Sustainable supply chain management
- Cross-border trade and infrastructure

Peer-reviewed journal articles indexed in Scopus and Web of Science were prioritized to ensure academic rigor, complemented by reports from international organizations such as UNCTAD, OECD, the World Bank, and the International Maritime Organization.

Selection Criteria

Sources were selected based on:

- Relevance to AI-enabled logistics transformation
- Conceptual or empirical contribution
- Publication credibility
- Recency (with emphasis on post-2017 research)

Seminal theoretical works were retained to establish foundational perspectives.

Case-Based Illustration

To enhance practical relevance, the chapter integrates case insights from globally recognized logistics firms. These cases serve an illustrative purpose rather than empirical generalization, demonstrating real-world applications of AI in sustainable logistics transformation.

METHODOLOGICAL CONTRIBUTION

4. AI Applications in Cross-Border Logistics

The application of artificial intelligence in cross-border logistics covers a wide range of operational areas such as customs automation, intelligent transportation systems, smart warehousing, port digitalization, and risk management. These AI-driven systems promote speed, transparency, sustainability, and resilience across global supply chains. AI is now being integrated with complementary technologies such as blockchain, Internet of Things (iot), cloud computing, and digital twins, creating autonomous, predictive, and interconnected logistics ecosystems (Wamba et al., 2020).

4.1 AI in Customs and Trade Documentation

Customs clearance has historically been one of the most time-consuming and bureaucratic aspects of international logistics. Manual document verification, lengthy inspection procedures, and varying regulatory frameworks across nations lead to significant delays and costs (Grainger, 2011). AI automates many of these processes using machine learning, natural language processing (NLP), and optical character recognition (OCR) to extract, verify, and classify data from shipping documents such as bills of lading, certificates of origin, and commercial invoices (UNCTAD, 2023). AI-based risk assessment models analyze historical import/export data, shipping routes, and trader compliance history to identify high-risk cargo, thereby reducing unnecessary physical inspections and speeding up low-risk shipments (Wang & Sarkis, 2021). For instance, Singapore's Networked Trade Platform uses AI to integrate customs, freight forwarding, port authorities, and banks, reducing clearance time and enhancing trade transparency (Lee & Whang, 2020). Similarly, the AI-enabled tradelens platform developed by IBM and Maersk reduces customs documentation errors and fraud by using blockchain and real-time digital documentation (Meyer & Hamilton, 2020).

4.2 AI in Cross-Border Transportation and Route Optimization

AI plays a transformative role in improving transportation efficiency across land, sea, and air logistics. Machine learning algorithms process vast datasets, including traffic density, fuel costs, weather conditions, and geopolitical alerts to determine the most efficient transport routes (Kamble et al., 2020). Intelligent transport systems (ITS) deployed in trucking networks optimize fuel consumption and reduce carbon footprint by minimizing idle time and empty return trips (Zhang & Zhang, 2022). Maritime logistics benefits from AI-based vessel route prediction systems that adjust shipping paths based on ocean currents, piracy threats, and port traffic (IMO, 2019). For example, DHL uses AI-powered predictive analytics to select multimodal routes combining air, road, sea, and rail while minimizing transportation time and emissions (DHL, 2018). Autonomous trucks and drones, developed by companies such as Tesla, Waymo, and Amazon Prime Air, enhance last-mile delivery speed and accuracy, especially in remote and high-risk regions (Marciano & Komninos, 2019).

4.3 AI in Warehousing and Inventory Management

Warehousing and inventory management are critical components of cross-border logistics that have been significantly improved by AI and robotics. Smart warehouses use AI algorithms to forecast demand, manage inventory levels, and automate storage and retrieval systems (Min, 2017). Robotics systems equipped with vision-based AI perform activities such as sorting, packaging, loading, and inventory inspections with high precision, reducing human error and operational costs (Kalaiarasi & Ramakrishnan, 2021). Amazon's fulfillment centers use AI-powered Kiva robots to move shelves, scan products, and allocate orders efficiently, reducing fulfillment time by over 20% (Marciano & Komninos, 2019). AI also supports just-in-time inventory systems by accurately forecasting stock requirements, reducing overstocking and stockouts, and improving warehouse space utilization (Christopher & Holweg, 2017). AI-based digital twins simulate warehouse operations to predict congestion, equipment malfunction, and labor allocation needs in real time (Heilig & Voß, 2017).

4.4 AI in Smart Ports and Border Infrastructure

Seaports, handling over 80% of global trade by volume, are strategic hubs where AI can deliver significant improvements in operational efficiency and sustainability (UNCTAD, 2023). AI-enabled smart ports like the Port of Rotterdam use digital twins, iot sensors, and predictive analytics to optimize crane scheduling, reduce container idle time, and monitor emissions (Port of Rotterdam Authority, 2021). AI-based terminal operating systems (TOS) improve ship berthing schedules, automated guided vehicles (agvs), and yard management, leading to higher throughput and lower operational costs (Heilig & Voß, 2017). For example, Shanghai's Yangshan Deepwater Port uses AI for automated crane operations, reducing human intervention and minimizing accidents (Zhang & Zhang, 2022). Smart borders such as South Korea's UNI-PASS utilize AI to process export-import declarations, analyze cargo risks, and monitor trade compliance at a national level (Lee & Whang, 2020). AI-driven smart ports significantly reduce fuel consumption, vessel waiting times, and CO_2 emissions, thereby contributing to sustainable maritime logistics.

4.5 AI in Risk Management and Supply Chain Resilience

Supply chain disruptions caused by geopolitical tensions, pandemics, natural disasters, cyberattacks, and trade policy uncertainties have demonstrated the vulnerability of global logistics networks (Ivanov & Dolgui, 2020). Artificial Intelligence plays a crucial role in enhancing supply chain resilience by enabling predictive risk analytics, scenario simulations, and adaptive decision-making processes (Christopher & Holweg, 2017). AI-powered platforms analyze real-time data streams from news sources, satellite imagery, iot devices, port traffic records, and weather forecasts to detect early signs of disruption (Wamba et al., 2020). These systems use machine learning algorithms to predict potential delays, port congestion, labor strikes, or climate-related hazards, allowing logistics companies to reroute cargo, adjust inventory strategies, or switch transportation modes in advance (Kamble et al., 2020). For instance, during the COVID-19 pandemic, companies like Maersk and DHL adopted AI-driven demand forecasting and dynamic routing to overcome port closures, container shortages, and fluctuating air freight capacities (Notteboom & Haralambides, 2020).

Digital twin technology—virtual replicas of physical logistics networks—is another AI-supported tool for supply chain risk management. By creating a digital simulation of warehouses, ports, and transportation routes, logistics managers can run "what-if" scenarios to assess resilience under various disruption conditions, such as natural disasters, political instability, or cyber threats (Heilig & Voß, 2017). For example, the Port of Rotterdam uses AI-based digital twins to simulate carbon emissions, vessel arrivals, and potential bottlenecks in container handling (Port of Rotterdam Authority, 2021). Similarly, Airbus and Siemens use digital twins in aerospace and manufacturing supply chains to test alternative logistics strategies in case of supplier failure or transport delays (Ivanov & Dolgui, 2020). AI also enhances cybersecurity resilience by detecting anomalies in freight tracking systems, customs databases, and blockchain trade platforms, preventing data breaches and ransomware attacks (Saberi et al., 2019).In terms of financial risk management, AI assists logistics firms by predicting currency fluctuations, fuel price changes, tariff risks, and trade embargoes that may impact cross-border transactions (UNCTAD, 2023). AI-driven platforms such as Flexport and clearmetal use predictive analytics to calculate supplier reliability, credit scores, and probability of shipment delays, which helps freight forwarders negotiate better contracts and insurance policies (Meyer & Hamilton, 2020). Additionally, AI-enabled smart contracts on blockchain platforms automate financial settlements between shippers, freight carriers, and customs authorities once predefined conditions—such as delivery confirmation or regulatory clearance—are met (Saberi et al., 2019). This eliminates disputes, accelerates payments, and reduces fraud risks in international logistics.From a resilience perspective, AI aligns closely with the concept of "supply chain antifragility," where systems do not merely endure disruptions but improve through them (Taleb, 2012). AI enables adaptive learning by refining prediction models based on past disruptions, enabling supply chains to evolve and become more resilient over time (Ivanov & Dolgui, 2020). However, scholars also argue that excessive dependence on AI may create new risks—such as algorithmic bias, data privacy breaches, and black-box decision-making—if not accompanied by human oversight and transparent governance (Wamba et al., 2020; OECD, 2021). Rather than merely describing technological applications, this section analytically evaluates how AI capabilities translate into measurable logistics outcomes such as efficiency gains, emission reduction, risk mitigation, and operational resilience. The discussion synthesizes patterns across technologies to highlight their strategic implications for cross-border supply chain performance.

5. AI-ENABLED SUSTAINABLE PRACTICES IN CROSS-BORDER LOGISTICS

Managerial, Policy, and Research Implications

From a research standpoint, the chapter underscores the need for empirical validation of AI-driven sustainability outcomes and encourages interdisciplinary inquiry spanning supply chain management, digital governance, and environmental economics.Sustainability has emerged as a critical dimension of cross-border logistics as governments, international organizations, and corporations are increasingly committed to reducing emissions, resource consumption, and environmental degradation within global supply chains. The logistics and transportation sector accounts for nearly one-quarter of global CO_2 emissions, with freight transport—particularly maritime shipping, aviation, and trucking—being the most carbon-intensive components (International Transport Forum, 2021). Artificial Intelligence (AI) has become an indispensable enabler of green logistics by optimizing transportation efficiency, reducing fuel consumption, minimizing empty runs, and enabling cleaner energy transitions (Zhang & Zhang, 2022). AI-driven route optimization systems use real-time data from GPS, satellites, port operations, and climate models to design the most fuel-efficient paths, reducing emissions by 10–15% for long-haul transport (Bai, Sarkis & Dou, 2020). Autonomous and semi-autonomous electric trucks, used by companies such as Tesla, DHL, and DB Schenker, further reduce greenhouse gases by integrating AI for energy management, regenerative braking, and predictive maintenance (He & Li, 2022).

One of the key AI-enabled sustainability strategies in maritime logistics is the application of AI to optimize vessel speed and fuel efficiency, known as "smart steaming" or "eco-steaming." AI algorithms analyze ocean currents, wind conditions, wave heights, and port congestion to determine the most eco-efficient cruising speeds, reducing fuel consumption by up to 12% (IMO, 2019). Additionally, AI assists in designing energy-efficient shipping routes that avoid piracy zones, storm-prone waters, or politically unstable regions (Heilig & Voß, 2017). For ports, AI supports green infrastructure development by optimizing crane energy use, reducing ship idle time at anchor, and integrating renewable energy systems into port operations (Port of Rotterdam Authority, 2021). For instance, the Port of Singapore uses AI to monitor vessel emissions and recommend low-carbon alternative fuels such as liquefied natural gas (LNG), methanol, and hydrogen-based fuels (Lee & Whang, 2020).

AI also plays a significant role in promoting circular economy practices and reverse logistics in cross-border supply chains. Reverse logistics involves the process of returning used products, recycling materials, repairing equipment, and redistributing refurbished goods, which is especially complex in international trade due to customs requirements and transportation costs (Geissdoerfer et al., 2017). AI enhances reverse logistics by forecasting product returns, identifying recyclable materials through computer vision, optimizing return shipping routes, and matching returned items with repair centers or recycling hubs (Min, 2017). Companies such as HP, Apple, and DHL use AI-driven lifecycle assessment tools to track carbon emissions at every stage of the product supply chain, including manufacturing, distribution, and end-of-life (Kamble et al., 2020). These systems support compliance with extended producer responsibility (EPR) policies and international sustainable trade frameworks such as the EU Circular Economy Action Plan (European Commission, 2020).In terms of carbon monitoring and reporting, AI assists logistics companies in tracking Scope 1, Scope 2, and Scope 3 emissions based on fuel consumption, electricity use, supplier data, and transportation activities (UNCTAD, 2023). AI-driven carbon accounting platforms such as IBM Envizi and SAP Sustainability Cloud automate emissions reporting for compliance with standards like ISO 14064, the Global Logistics Emissions Council (GLEC) framework, and the EU Corporate Sustainability Reporting Directive (CSRD) (European Commission, 2023). AI also supports "green financing" by providing accurate emission data to banks and investors, who are increasingly using Environmental, Social, and Governance (ESG) ratings to evaluate logistics firms (OECD, 2021). Blockchain integration ensures the transparency and credibility of carbon credit transactions, reducing fraud in carbon offset markets (Saberi et al., 2019).However, scholars caution that AI-based sustainability is not without ethical and practical challenges. High computational AI systems require significant energy, especially when using cloud-based machine learning models, which may offset some environmental benefits if powered by fossil fuels (Wamba et al., 2020). Additionally, the deployment of electric and autonomous vehicles requires rare earth minerals such as lithium and cobalt, raising questions around responsible mining and labor exploitation in countries like the Democratic Republic of Congo (He & Li, 2022). Therefore, the transition to AI-driven sustainable logistics must be supported by renewable energy development, ethical sourcing policies, workforce reskilling, and strong regulatory frameworks governed by global cooperation (UN, 2015).

6. CASE STUDIES OF AI-ENABLED SUSTAINABLE CROSS-BORDER LOGISTICS

Case studies offer practical insights into how leading global logistics firms are leveraging artificial intelligence to enhance efficiency, sustainability, and resilience in cross-border logistics. Companies such as Maersk, DHL, Amazon, and Alibaba have become pioneers in applying AI to customs automation, smart warehousing, autonomous transport, digital twins, and carbon reduction strategies. These real-world examples illustrate the transition from traditional logistics models to intelligent, interconnected, and environmentally responsible global supply chains.

6.1 Maersk and IBM tradelens: AI and Blockchain for Customs and Maritime Logistics

Maersk, the world's largest container shipping company, partnered with IBM to develop **tradelens**, a blockchain and AI-powered digital platform that facilitates transparent and secure documentation exchange in international trade (Meyer & Hamilton, 2020). Traditional maritime logistics relies heavily on physical paperwork such as bills of lading, certificates of origin, and customs declarations; this process often results in delays and document fraud (Notteboom & Haralambides, 2020). Tradelens uses artificial intelligence and smart contracts to automate document validation, track cargo in real time, and share secure data between shippers, ports, customs, freight forwarders, and financial institutions (Saberi et al., 2019). By reducing manual documentation and port waiting times, Maersk reported a *40% reduction in documentation processing time* and significant decreases in demurrage costs (Meyer & Hamilton, 2020). Additionally, AI tools within Maersk optimize vessel fuel consumption by analyzing weather data, route patterns, and port congestion, which contributes to lower CO_2 emissions and aligns with the International Maritime Organization's decarbonization targets (IMO, 2019).

6.2 DHL: AI in Predictive Logistics and Green Warehousing

DHL, a global leader in express logistics and freight forwarding, uses AI extensively for predictive analytics, smart warehousing, and eco-efficient transportation. Through its *DHL Resilience360* and **mysupplychain** platforms, the company uses AI to monitor over 30 million supply chain data points daily, detecting potential disruptions like port strikes, natural disasters, or trade restrictions (DHL, 2018). AI-driven demand forecasting allows DHL to adjust fleet operations and warehouse inventory, reducing idle capacity and operational waste (Zhang & Zhang, 2022). In terms of sustainability, DHL's *gogreen initiative* incorporates AI to track carbon emissions, optimize loading capacity, and switch to alternative fuels in high-emission trade corridors (Bai, Sarkis & Dou, 2020). AI-enabled autonomous sorting systems, robotics, and digital twins are deployed in DHL's warehousing facilities to improve energy use, space utilization, and order accuracy (Kalaiarasi & Ramakrishnan, 2021). DHL has also integrated AI into its electric vehicle fleet, using machine learning algorithms to manage charging schedules, route efficiency, and battery performance (He & Li, 2022).

6.3 Amazon Logistics: AI in Smart Warehousing and Last-Mile Cross-Border Delivery

Amazon is a pioneer in artificial intelligence in logistics, particularly in smart warehousing, inventory optimization, and last-mile delivery. In its cross-border fulfillment centers, Amazon uses *AI-driven robotics (Kiva systems)* to move shelves, scan products, and assist human workers in packing and sorting (Marciano & Komninos, 2019). Machine learning algorithms predict international demand, minimize overstocking costs, and optimize inventory across global fulfillment centers (Christopher & Holweg, 2017). For cross-border e-commerce logistics, Amazon's *Global Logistics Freight (AGLF)* uses AI to manage customs pre-clearance, automate documents such as commercial invoices and harmonized shipping codes, and track cargo across air, sea, and road networks (Wamba et al., 2020). In last-mile delivery, Amazon deploys *AI-powered delivery drones (Prime Air)* and autonomous delivery robots (Amazon Scout), reducing carbon emissions, fuel dependency, and delivery times (He & Li, 2022). Furthermore, Amazon's AI carbon-tracking platform allows the company to monitor Scope 1–3 emissions across its supply chains and supports its commitment to achieve *net-zero carbon by 2040* (OECD, 2021).

6.4 Alibaba Cainiao Network: AI and Digital Silk Road Logistics

Alibaba's Cainiao Network has revolutionized cross-border e-commerce logistics through AI, big data, and blockchain, particularly across China's Belt and Road Initiative trade routes. The *Cainiao Smart Logistics Network* uses AI to optimize warehouse operations, predict delivery times across multiple countries, and coordinate air, sea, rail, and road transport modes (Lee & Whang, 2020). Cainiao's customs AI platform analyzes product descriptions, HS codes, tax calculations, and prohibited items to accelerate customs clearance in China, Singapore, and Europe (UNCTAD, 2023). Predictive analytics helps manage warehouse space, reduce overstocking, and minimize package delays in over *200 international logistics hubs* (Wang & Sarkis, 2021). Sustainability is integrated through AI-based packaging optimization systems that reduce material use by 15%, electric delivery vehicle fleets in urban centers, and carbon-tracking systems aligned with China's dual carbon strategy (Bai, Sarkis & Dou, 2020).

7. CHALLENGES AND BARRIERS TO AI ADOPTION IN CROSS-BORDER LOGISTICS

While artificial intelligence has demonstrated significant potential in improving efficiency, sustainability, and resilience in cross-border logistics, its implementation is hindered by multiple challenges. These barriers include technological constraints, data privacy concerns, cybersecurity risks, financial limitations, workforce skill gaps, regulatory inconsistencies, and ethical implications. Understanding these challenges is essential for policymakers, logistics firms, and international organizations seeking to create a future-ready and equitable digital logistics ecosystem.

7.1 Technological Infrastructure and Digital Divide

AI adoption in logistics requires robust digital infrastructure, including high-speed internet, cloud computing systems, iot-enabled sensors, and advanced data centers (UNCTAD, 2023). Developed economies such as Singapore, Germany, South Korea, and the Netherlands have already integrated AI into smart ports, customs systems, and digital freight corridors (Lee & Whang, 2020). However, many developing countries lack the technological infrastructure, stable electricity, and data connectivity required to support AI-driven logistics platforms (World Bank, 2022). This *digital divide* creates inequality in trade competitiveness and limits the participation of smes in global value chains (OECD, 2021). Without adequate infrastructure investment, AI risks becoming a tool that benefits technologically advanced economies while marginalizing others.

7.2 Data Privacy, Cybersecurity, and Sovereignty Risks

Cross-border logistics relies on massive amounts of data—shipment records, customer details, customs documentation, and financial transactions. AI-based platforms collect, analyze, and transfer this data in real-time across multiple jurisdictions. This creates concerns about *data privacy, cyberattacks, and digital espionage* (Wamba et al., 2020). According to the World Economic Forum (2023), cyberattacks on logistics and shipping firms have increased by over 400% in the last five years. High-profile incidents, such as the Maersk cyberattack caused by the notpetya malware in 2017, resulted in a $300 million loss and shutdown of global shipping systems (Notteboom & Haralambides, 2020). Blockchain and AI can enhance security through encryption and anomaly detection, but risks remain due to data breaches, ransomware attacks, and hacking of GPS or autonomous vehicle systems (Saberi et al., 2019). Additionally, nations implement strict *data localization laws*, requiring logistics data to be stored locally, complicating global data-sharing (UNCTAD, 2023).

7.3 High Implementation Costs and Financial Barriers

AI technology adoption involves high initial investment in digital infrastructure, automation hardware, software licensing, cloud platforms, and AI development teams (mckinnon, 2018). Large multinational corporations like Amazon, Maersk, and DHL can afford such investments, but small and medium-sized enterprises (smes), especially in developing economies, face major financial constraints (OECD, 2021). The cost of maintaining AI-driven robotics, digital twins, autonomous fleets, or smart customs systems can deter smaller firms from adopting technology. Additionally, AI deployment in logistics often requires system integration across different countries and regulatory environments, increasing operational complexity and cost (Wang & Sarkis, 2021).

7.4 Workforce Skill Gaps and Resistance to Change

AI adoption in logistics transforms traditional job roles, requiring employees to possess digital literacy, data analytics expertise, and technical knowledge related to automation systems (He & Li, 2022). However, the majority of logistics workers—drivers, port handlers, warehouse employees—lack training in AI, machine learning, or digital platforms (World Bank, 2022). This *skills gap* limits effective use of AI technologies and contributes to resistance among workers who fear job displacement due to automation (Trist & Emery, 1951). While AI creates new roles in system monitoring, cybersecurity, and digital logistics design, it also restructures labor markets, requiring reskilling, resettlement, and social protection measures. Without public-private collaboration in education and training, AI adoption risks creating unemployment and inequality (UNCTAD, 2023).

7.5 Legal, Ethical, and Regulatory Challenges

Different countries have varying regulations regarding customs, trade documentation, data protection, and autonomous transport systems. Lack of *harmonized international AI legislation* makes it difficult to implement standardized AI systems across borders (OECD, 2021). Ethical issues also arise concerning algorithmic bias in cargo inspections, facial recognition at borders, and discriminatory freight risk profiling (Wamba et al., 2020). AI decision-making in customs or freight approval can be opaque, raising concerns about accountability and fairness (Saberi et al., 2019). Autonomous trucks, drones, and maritime AI navigation systems also face legal barriers regarding liability, safety standards, and insurance frameworks (IMO, 2019). Moreover, there is a lack of *global governance mechanisms* regulating AI in logistics, creating inconsistencies and compliance challenges (UN, 2015).

8. POLICY IMPLICATIONS AND STRATEGIC FRAMEWORK FOR AI-ENABLED SUSTAINABLE LOGISTICS

The successful integration of artificial intelligence into cross-border logistics is not merely a technological shift; it requires coordinated policy actions, institutional reforms, international cooperation, and regulatory frameworks that enable digital, secure, and sustainable trade. Governments, intergovernmental organizations, logistics firms, and technology providers must collaborate to create an ecosystem where AI enhances supply chain efficiency while ensuring data privacy, ethical use, environmental sustainability, and inclusivity (UNCTAD, 2023). This section outlines key policy considerations and proposes a strategic framework for AI-enabled sustainable logistics.

8.1 Global Governance and Harmonization of AI Standards

One of the major obstacles to AI adoption in global logistics is the lack of harmonized international regulations. Different countries maintain varying rules for customs procedures, data protection, autonomous vehicles, and AI decision-making, leading to fragmented systems and increased compliance costs (OECD, 2021). To resolve this, *global governance bodies such as the World Trade Organization (WTO), International Maritime Organization (IMO), and International Organization for Standardization (ISO)* should develop unified guidelines for AI in customs automation, blockchain documentation, and port digitalization (IMO, 2019). The *World Customs Organization (WCO)* can promote AI-based risk assessment frameworks and paperless trade protocols across borders to facilitate shared trust and interoperability (Grainger, 2011). Multilateral agreements should also focus on *cross-border data-sharing standards, AI ethics, cybersecurity cooperation, and carbon reporting transparency*, ensuring that logistics innovations are adopted globally rather than regionally.

8.2 National Policy for Digital Trade and Smart Infrastructure

At the national level, governments must invest in *digital infrastructure*, including high-speed internet, 5G connectivity, cloud computing centers, and iot-enabled transport systems (World Bank, 2022). Policy initiatives such as India's *National*

Logistics Policy (2022), China's *Digital Silk Road Plan*, and the EU's *Digital Single Market* are examples of state-driven strategies that promote AI-enabled logistics and smart trade corridors (UNCTAD, 2023). Governments should develop *smart ports, AI-driven customs platforms, and digital export-import systems* to reduce bureaucratic delays and logistics costs. Tax incentives and subsidies should be offered to logistics companies and smes that adopt AI, autonomous vehicles, blockchain, and green energy technologies (Kamble et al., 2020). National digital policies must also focus on strengthening cloud security, data privacy laws, and legal infrastructure for autonomous transportation systems.

8.3 Skills Development and Workforce Transformation

AI deployment in cross-border logistics requires a workforce capable of handling robotic automation, digital platforms, and data analytics. Many logistics employees, especially in developing countries, lack digital literacy and training in AI technologies (World Bank, 2022). Governments and industry stakeholders must introduce *vocational training programs, AI certification courses, and digital literacy initiatives* for drivers, customs officials, warehouse workers, and port personnel (He & Li, 2022). Academia-industry collaboration is essential to incorporate logistics analytics, AI supply chain management, and cybersecurity into university programs (Trist & Emery, 1951). Additionally, governments must create *social safety nets and re-skilling programs* to mitigate job displacement due to automation. The International Labour Organization (ILO) recommends an inclusive "*AI transition strategy*" that protects labor rights while fostering innovation (ILO, 2021).

8.4 Sustainable and Green Logistics Policies

Governments must align AI adoption with environmental policies and climate commitments such as the Paris Agreement, IMO 2050 targets, and the UN Sustainable Development Goals (UN, 2015). Logistics companies should be mandated to adopt carbon-tracking systems, green fuel incentives, energy-efficient port operations, and reverse logistics mechanisms (International Transport Forum, 2021). AI-powered platforms can help monitor Scope 1, 2, and 3 emissions, detect fuel inefficiencies, and generate automated carbon reports compliant with the Global Logistics Emissions Council (GLEC) framework (European Commission, 2023). Policy incentives such as carbon credits, tax rebates for electric fleets, and subsidies for hydrogen fuel infrastructure can accelerate sustainability adoption in logistics (Bai, Sarkis & Dou, 2020). Reverse logistics and circular economy initiatives must be supported through AI-enabled waste tracking, digital recycling platforms, and green procurement standards to ensure sustainability beyond transport (Geissdoerfer et al., 2017).

9. FUTURE RESEARCH DIRECTIONS

As the integration of artificial intelligence into cross-border logistics continues to evolve, significant opportunities exist for further academic research, technological refinement, and policy innovation. Future studies must adopt interdisciplinary perspectives, bridging supply chain management, data science, sustainability, economic policy, and international law to create comprehensive frameworks that support responsible and efficient AI deployment in logistics.

9.1 AI and Ethical Decision-Making in Logistics

Future research must address the ethical implications of AI systems involved in Customs, border control, risk assessment, and freight prioritization. AI algorithms can unintentionally produce biased outcomes, especially if they are trained on historical trade data that reflect geopolitical inequalities or discriminatory inspection practices (Wamba et al., 2020). There is a pressing need to study algorithmic transparency, fairness in cargo inspection decisions, and the ethics of AI-based surveillance in border logistics (Saberi et al., 2019). Researchers should develop frameworks that ensure explainable AI (XAI), where decisions made by customs or logistics systems are traceable and accountable (OECD, 2021).

9.2 AI, Climate Change, and Decarbonization Pathways

Research must also explore how AI can accelerate logistics decarbonization and align with climate targets such as the Paris Agreement and IMO 2050 goals (IMO, 2019). Emerging questions include: How can AI-driven digital twins accurately predict carbon emissions along global trade routes? Can AI optimize fuel switching to green hydrogen, ammonia, or bio-LNG in maritime and aviation logistics? To what extent can AI integrate with carbon credit markets and blockchain-based emission verification platforms? Current literature emphasizes route optimization and fuel efficiency; however, future research should expand to include lifecycle carbon assessments, AI-based renewable energy forecasting for transport hubs, and net-zero port infrastructure design (International Transport Forum, 2021). Additionally, AI-enabled circular economy logistics—covering reverse supply chains, material reuse, and waste minimization—remains underexplored in global cross-border contexts (Geissdoerfer et al., 2017).

9.3 AI and Digital Trade Corridors: Belt and Road 2.0 and Beyond

Another promising area is the development of *AI-powered digital trade corridors*, including China's Belt and Road Initiative (BRI), the European TEN-T network, and the India-Middle East-Europe Economic Corridor. These corridors require interoperability of customs, transport, and digital infrastructure across multiple sovereign jurisdictions (UNCTAD, 2023). Future research should focus on AI governance models for multi-country logistics, standards for cross-border blockchain data-sharing, and digital risk assessment for political instability (Kamble et al., 2020). Studies may also explore AI-enabled multimodal logistics optimization (rail–sea–road–air), smart border technology like e-seals and iot-enabled containers, and their implications for smaller developing countries dependent on trade routes dominated by global powers (He & Li, 2022).

9.4 Human-AI Collaboration and Workforce Transformation

Existing literature tends to focus on technological implementation, often overlooking the socio-economic consequences of AI for the logistics labor force. Future research should explore *human-AI collaboration models*, where AI supports rather than replaces human workers (Trist & Emery, 1951). Specific areas include digital upskilling frameworks for warehouse managers, truck drivers, port operators, and customs officers; psychological impacts of automation; and policy interventions for job displacement mitigation (World Bank, 2022). Scholars must also investigate gender and inclusivity perspectives in AI-enabled logistics careers, especially in traditionally male-dominated transport sectors (ILO, 2021).

9.5 Legal, Security, and Cyber-Physical Threats

With logistics systems increasingly dependent on AI, blockchain, and iot, cybersecurity and legal research become critically important. Cross-border logistics is vulnerable to ransomware attacks, GPS spoofing, AI system manipulation, and cyberterrorism—incidents that could paralyze global trade (Notteboom & Haralambides, 2020). Future research should examine *international legal mechanisms for cyber liability*, cross-border digital insurance models, and AI-enabled predictive cybersecurity in logistics (Saberi et al., 2019). There is also a need to explore how international law treats AI decision-making in accident liability, autonomous vehicle incidents, and maritime or air navigation errors (IMO, 2019). Moreover, the concept of *digital sovereignty*—where nations demand local storage and control of logistics data—requires more study to balance security and global interoperability (OECD, 2021).

10. CONCLUSION

Artificial intelligence has emerged as a transformative force in reshaping cross-border logistics into a system that is not only intelligent and efficient but also sustainable and resilient. Traditional logistics systems, which depend on manual documentation, linear supply chains, and fossil-fuel transportation, have proven vulnerable to global disruptions such as pandemics, trade wars, and climate change (Ivanov & Dolgui, 2020). AI addresses these vulnerabilities by enabling predictive analytics, autonomous decision-making, smart warehousing, customs automation, digital twins, and multimodal transport optimization (Wamba et al., 2020). Companies such as Maersk, DHL, Amazon, and Alibaba demonstrate how AI-driven platforms enhance operational efficiency while lowering emissions, reducing human errors, and creating greater supply chain transparency (Meyer & Hamilton, 2020; Marciano & Komninos, 2019). These practices also align with the United Nations Sustainable Development Goals, particularly SDG 9 (industry, innovation, and infrastructure), SDG 12 (responsible consumption and production), and SDG 13 (climate action) (UN, 2015). Artificial intelligence is rapidly redefining the architecture of cross-border logistics by enabling predictive, adaptive, and environmentally responsible supply chain systems.

Limitations and Future Research

This chapter is conceptual in nature and relies on secondary evidence; future empirical studies should validate the proposed framework across industries and geographic regions. Quantitative assessments of carbon reduction, cost efficiency, and resilience outcomes would further strengthen understanding of AI's transformative impact.As global trade becomes increasingly data-driven, competitive advantage will depend not only on speed and cost but on intelligence, adaptability, and environmental accountability. When governed responsibly and deployed inclusively, artificial intelligence has the potential to become a cornerstone of sustainable global logistics. Despite these advances, the deployment of AI in cross-border logistics faces significant challenges, including infrastructure disparities, data privacy issues, regulatory fragmentation, cybersecurity threats, and workforce skill gaps (OECD, 2021; UNCTAD, 2023). These barriers highlight that AI integration is not solely a technical endeavor but a socio-political and ethical transformation requiring multistakeholder cooperation among governments, logistics firms, technology providers, and international organizations (World Bank, 2022). Emerging concerns such as algorithmic bias in customs screening, carbon inequality between developed and developing countries, and digital monopolies in e-commerce logistics call for ethical AI frameworks, global governance standards, and inclusive digital trade policies (Saberi et al., 2019; Wamba et al., 2020). Furthermore, AI's environmental footprint—stemming from data centers and rare mineral dependency—must be mitigated through renewable energy integration and responsible supply chain sourcing (Bai, Sarkis & Dou, 2020).Looking ahead, AI offers unprecedented potential for carbon-neutral smart logistics systems, digitally integrated global value chains, and antifragile supply networks that learn and evolve through disruptions (Taleb, 2012; Christopher & Holweg, 2017). However, this vision can only be realized through investments in digital infrastructure, AI education, cross-border data-sharing agreements, and fair access to technology for developing economies (He & Li, 2022; UNCTAD, 2023).

REFERENCES

Bai, C., Sarkis, J., & Dou, Y. (2020). Green supply chain management and circular economy: Integration and sustainability implications. *International Journal of Production Research, 58*(16), 4901–4917.

Barney, J. (1991). Firm resources and sustained competitive advantage. *Journal of Management, 17*(1), 99–120. DOI: 10.1177/014920639101700108

Carter, C. R., & Rogers, D. S. (2008). A framework of sustainable supply chain management: Moving toward new theory. *International Journal of Physical Distribution & Logistics Management, 38*(5), 360–387. DOI: 10.1108/09600030810882816

Christopher, M. (2016). *Logistics and supply chain management* (5th ed.). Pearson Education.

Christopher, M., & Holweg, M. (2017). Supply chain 2.0 revisited: A framework for managing volatility-induced risk in the supply chain. *International Journal of Physical Distribution & Logistics Management, 47*(1), 2–17. DOI: 10.1108/IJPDLM-09-2016-0245

DHL. (2018). *Artificial intelligence in logistics: A collaborative report by DHL and IBM on implications and use cases for the logistics industry*. DHL Trend Research.

European Commission. (2020). *Circular economy action plan: For a cleaner and more competitive Europe*. Brussels.

European Commission. (2023). *Corporate Sustainability Reporting Directive*. CSRD.

Geissdoerfer, M., Savaget, P., Bocken, N., & Hultink, E. (2017). The circular economy – A new sustainability paradigm? *Journal of Cleaner Production, 143*, 757–768. DOI: 10.1016/j.jclepro.2016.12.048

Grainger, A. (2011). Trade facilitation: A conceptual review. *Journal of World Trade, 45*(1), 39–62. DOI: 10.54648/TRAD2011002

He, Q., & Li, Y. (2022). Artificial intelligence applications in sustainable transportation and logistics. *Transportation Research Part D, Transport and Environment, 102*, 103135.

Heilig, L., & Voß, S. (2017). A scientometric analysis of cloud computing literature. *IEEE Transactions on Cloud Computing, 5*(2), 266–278.

Hummels, D. (2007). Transportation costs and international trade in the second era of globalization. *The Journal of Economic Perspectives*, *21*(3), 131–154. DOI: 10.1257/jep.21.3.131

International Labour Organization (ILO). (2021). *Artificial intelligence and the future of work.*

International Maritime Organization (IMO). (2019). *IMO strategy on reduction of GHG emissions from ships.*

International Transport Forum. (2021). *ITF transport outlook 2021.* OECD Publishing.

Ivanov, D., & Dolgui, A. (2020). Viability of intertwined supply networks: Extending the supply chain resilience angles towards survivability. *International Journal of Production Research*, *58*(10), 2904–2915. DOI: 10.1080/00207543.2020.1750727

Kalaiarasi, R., & Ramakrishnan, R. (2021). Artificial intelligence applications in warehouse automation and logistics. *Journal of Logistics Management*, *10*(2), 45–56.

Kamble, S., Gunasekaran, A., & Gawankar, S. (2020). Achieving sustainable performance in supply chain using big data analytics and artificial intelligence. *International Journal of Production Economics*, *222*, 107501.

Lee, H. L., & Whang, S. (2020). E-business and supply chain integration. *International Journal of Logistics Management*, *31*(2), 295–312.

Levinson, M. (2016). *The box: How the shipping container made the world smaller and the world economy bigger* (2nd ed.). Princeton University Press.

Marciano, A., & Komninos, N. (2019). Artificial intelligence in logistics and supply chain management. *Technological Forecasting and Social Change*, *146*, 16–25.

McKinnon, A. (2018). *Decarbonizing logistics: Distributing goods in a low carbon world.* Kogan Page.

Meyer, T., & Hamilton, M. (2020). Blockchain and artificial intelligence in maritime logistics: The case of TradeLens. *Maritime Economics & Logistics*, *22*(3), 450–470.

Min, H. (2017). Artificial intelligence in supply chain management: Theory and applications. *International Journal of Logistics Research and Applications*, *20*(1), 1–18.

Notteboom, T., & Haralambides, H. (2020). Port management and operations in the COVID-19 era. *Maritime Economics & Logistics*, *22*(3), 305–310. DOI: 10.1057/s41278-020-00162-7

OECD. (2021). *Artificial intelligence in global value chains.* OECD Publishing.

Port of Rotterdam Authority. (2021). *Digital twin technology for smart port operations.*

Rodrigue, J. P., & Notteboom, T. (2020). *The geography of transport systems* (5th ed.). Routledge. DOI: 10.4324/9780429346323

Saberi, S., Kouhizadeh, M., Sarkis, J., & Shen, L. (2019). Blockchain technology and its relationships to sustainable supply chain management. *International Journal of Production Research, 57*(7), 2117–2135. DOI: 10.1080/00207543.2018.1533261

Taleb, N. N. (2012). *Antifragile: Things that gain from disorder.* Random House.

UN. (2015). *Transforming our world: The 2030 agenda for sustainable development.* United Nations.

UNCTAD. (2023). *Review of maritime transport 2023. United Nations Conference on Trade and Development.*

von Bertalanffy, L. (1968). *General system theory: Foundations, development, applications.* George Braziller.

Wamba, S. F., Gunasekaran, A., Akter, S., Ren, S., Dubey, R., & Childe, S. (2020). Big data analytics and artificial intelligence in supply chain management. *International Journal of Production Economics, 165*, 234–246.

Wang, Y., & Sarkis, J. (2021). Emerging technologies and sustainable supply chain management. *Transportation Research Part E, Logistics and Transportation Review, 131*, 101813.

World Bank. (2022). *Global logistics performance index report.* World Bank Publications.

Zhang, Y., & Zhang, J. (2022). Artificial intelligence and sustainable logistics: A review of technologies and impacts. *Transportation Research Part D, Transport and Environment, 103*, 103178.

Chapter 2
Artificial Intelligence in Sustainable Supply Chain Management

Sunanda Jindal
http://orcid.org/0000-0003-2977-9591
Independent Researcher, India

Syed Hassan Imam Gardezi
http://orcid.org/0009-0006-6171-1238
Universidad Azteca, UAE

Neelam Vishal Raut
http://orcid.org/0000-0002-0999-7375
Prin. L.N. Welingkar Institute of Management Development and Research, Mumbai, India

Joshna Sanolia
http://orcid.org/0009-0007-2575-7623
Gian Jyoti Institute of Management and Technology, Mohali, India

P. Selvakumar
http://orcid.org/0000-0002-3650-4548
Department of Science and Humanities, Nehru Institute of Technology, Coimbatore, India

Anubhav Sharma
http://orcid.org/0009-0007-3805-8821
IMS Engineering College, Ghaziabad, India

ABSTRACT

The integration of Artificial Intelligence (AI) into supply chain systems has emerged as a transformative force in advancing sustainability objectives, reducing environmental impact, and promoting more responsible resource use across global logistics networks. As supply chains grow more complex—spanning continents, involving a diverse network of suppliers, and responding to increasingly dynamic consumer demands—traditional management approaches struggle to maintain efficiency and sustainability simultaneously. AI addresses these limitations through its capacity for intelligent data processing, real-time decision-making, and predictive analytics, enabling organizations to transition towards greener, more transparent, and more

DOI: 10.4018/979-8-3373-7847-3.ch002

ethical supply chain practices. One of the most notable contributions of AI to supply chain sustainability lies in its role in optimizing resource consumption. AI-driven tools facilitate inventory optimization, ensuring the right quantity of goods is produced, transported, and stocked, thus minimizing waste associated with overproduction and excess storage.

INTRODUCTION

The integration of Artificial Intelligence (AI) into supply chain systems has emerged as a transformative force in advancing sustainability objectives, reducing environmental impact, and promoting more responsible resource use across global logistics networks. As supply chains grow more complex—spanning continents, involving a diverse network of suppliers, and responding to increasingly dynamic consumer demands—traditional management approaches struggle to maintain efficiency and sustainability simultaneously. AI addresses these limitations through its capacity for intelligent data processing, real-time decision-making, and predictive analytics, enabling organizations to transition towards greener, more transparent, and more ethical supply chain practices. One of the most notable contributions of AI to supply chain sustainability lies in its role in optimizing resource consumption. AI-driven tools facilitate inventory optimization, ensuring the right quantity of goods is produced, transported, and stocked, thus minimizing waste associated with overproduction and excess storage. Techniques such as machine learning-based demand forecasting reduce forecasting errors, allowing companies to better align production schedules with actual consumption patterns, leading to reductions in energy-intensive manufacturing processes and associated carbon emissions. Further, AI enhances logistics efficiency by identifying the most fuel-efficient transportation routes, supporting dynamic fleet scheduling, and enabling the shift towards more sustainable delivery models. By analyzing traffic patterns, weather data, energy costs, and vehicle availability, AI algorithms can reduce unnecessary mileage, support load optimization, and contribute to the broader goal of decarbonizing transportation—the largest contributor to supply chain emissions.

Sustainability in the supply chain also extends to materials sourcing and supplier management, where AI plays a vital role in promoting ethical and environmentally responsible procurement practices. Advanced analytics can assess supplier performance not just on cost and delivery reliability, but also on environmental and social governance (ESG) metrics. Natural language processing (NLP) tools can continuously scan public disclosures, regulatory filings, and news reports to detect early signs of non-compliance, human rights violations, or environmentally harmful activities within the supplier ecosystem. This real-time visibility enables companies to identify high-risk suppliers and encourage compliance through corrective interventions or strategic re-sourcing. Likewise, AI-driven traceability systems, often supported by technologies such as blockchain, allow organizations and consumers to verify the provenance of raw materials and finished goods. This fosters greater accountability, empowers sustainable purchasing decisions, and creates transparent supply chains in industries long criticized for opaque practices, including mining, agriculture, and textiles. The circular economy movement benefits as well, with AI enhancing reverse logistics operations, enabling reuse and recycling of products at the end of their life cycle, and predicting component failures in advance to support repair-over-replacement principles. Moreover, AI supports climate resilience in supply chains by strengthening risk assessment and disruption management capabilities. Increasing climate variability introduces greater uncertainties—extreme weather events, resource scarcity, and fluctuating regulatory environments—which threaten operational continuity. AI-based scenario modeling and digital twins simulate complex interactions between environmental and logistical variables, allowing decision-makers to anticipate disruptions before they occur and implement adaptive sustainability-driven responses. These may include shifting production locations to minimize carbon exposure, redesigning delivery networks to avoid at-risk infrastructure, or modifying packaging and materials to meet stricter emission standards. Digital twins, in particular, offer real-time virtual replicas of supply chain assets, enabling continuous performance monitoring and exploration of carbon-reducing operational strategies without physical risk or investment. These insights empower corporate sustainability reporting and compliance with international climate frameworks, such as the Science-Based Targets initiative (SBTi) and Sustainable Development Goals (SDGs).

Nevertheless, the pursuit of greener supply chains through AI is not without challenges. Deployment requires robust digital infrastructure, high-quality interoperable data, and cybersecurity safeguards to protect proprietary and environmental data from manipulation (Abdelhamid et al., 2024). Additionally, the computational demands of AI models can themselves generate substantial environmental footprints if not managed responsibly through green data centers and renewable-powered computing. Ethical considerations must also be addressed to ensure AI-driven decisions do not inadvertently disadvantage suppliers in developing economies where technological readiness may be lower. To unlock the full potential of AI-powered sustainable supply chain ecosystems, organizations must adopt a holistic strategy that includes workforce upskilling, multi-stakeholder collaboration, and policies that incentivize sustainable technological innovation rather than mere cost reductions. Ultimately, AI stands as an indispensable enabler in the global transition toward greener supply chain architectures. By merging operational efficiency with environmental stewardship, AI empowers businesses to reduce emissions, preserve natural resources, enhance circularity, and build transparent and resilient networks that align with climate and sustainability imperatives. As environmental accountability becomes central to consumer preferences and regulatory enforcement intensifies worldwide, AI-driven sustainability will evolve from a competitive advantage into a fundamental requirement for future supply chain success. The synergy between AI innovation and sustainability-focused supply chain transformation thus offers a pathway toward achieving net-zero ambitions while ensuring long-term economic viability and societal well-being.

Artificial Intelligence (AI) is rapidly emerging as a catalyst for advancing sustainability in supply chain management, empowering organizations to balance environmental responsibility with operational efficiency. As global supply chains face unprecedented pressures—including regulatory demands for carbon reduction, heightened environmental awareness among consumers, resource scarcity, and risks associated with climate change—traditional management strategies no longer suffice to meet sustainability goals. AI technologies such as machine learning, predictive analytics, robotics, natural language processing, and intelligent automation introduce new capabilities for optimizing supply chain activities from end to end, minimizing waste, enhancing transparency, and promoting circular economy principles. One of the most significant opportunities AI offers for sustainable supply chain management lies in its ability to improve forecasting and inventory optimization. By analyzing historical sales data, market trends, economic shifts, and real-time demand patterns, AI reduces forecast inaccuracies that usually result in excess production, stockpiling, and waste generation. Efficient inventory planning contributes directly to sustainability by reducing the energy, materials, and emissions associated with unnecessary product manufacturing, storage, and disposal (Ahmed et al., 2025). In logistics, AI-driven route optimization systems reduce transportation emissions by recommending the shortest or least carbon-intensive routes while dynamically responding to traffic, weather, and infrastructure conditions. Additionally, AI supports energy-efficient fleet management, such as transitioning from traditional combustion vehicles to electric or alternative fuel-powered options and ensuring optimal charging and utilization strategies.

THE FUTURE OF SUSTAINABLE SUPPLY CHAINS: AI-DRIVEN INNOVATIONS

The future of sustainable supply chains is being fundamentally reshaped by Artificial Intelligence (AI), which is rapidly transitioning from a performance-enhancing tool into a core enabler of environmental stewardship, resource circularity, and climate resilience in global logistics systems. As governments intensify carbon regulations, consumers demand ethical transparency, and corporations commit to net-zero goals, AI-driven innovations present transformative pathways for supply chains to operate within planetary boundaries while maintaining economic competitiveness. One of the most profound impacts AI will have lies in developing intelligent, autonomous supply chain ecosystems capable of self-learning, real-time coordination, and environmentally optimized decision-making. Future supply chains will increasingly utilize AI-powered demand sensing integrated with alternative market signals—social media analytics, weather patterns, geopolitical risks, and consumer sentiment monitoring—to predict shifts accurately and reduce waste from overproduction and unsold inventory (Bai et al., 2020). This shift toward hyper-precision forecasting will support sustainable manufacturing practices through just-in-time production, reduced energy consumption, and optimized material sourcing, significantly lowering emissions and resource footprints. Emerging AI innovations also have the potential to revolutionize logistics sustainability. Autonomous electric fleets guided by AI—consisting of drones, self-driving trucks, and maritime vessels—will make transportation systems cleaner, safer, and more efficient. Route optimization algorithms will evolve to include multi-objective sustainability factors such as infrastructure carbon intensity, congestion emissions, and renewable charging station availability. AI will support the transition to green warehousing through intelligent energy management systems that control heating, cooling, and equipment usage based on real-time occupancy and environmental data. Additionally, AI-driven IoT networks will monitor product conditions throughout shipment, reducing spoilage in temperature-sensitive goods and minimizing waste in critical sectors such as pharmaceuticals and perishables. The adoption of hydrogen and other alternative fuels will also be AI-enabled, ensuring optimal consumption strategies and lifecycle emissions tracking. These innovations together will help achieve large-scale decarbonization in the logistics sector, historically the most carbon-intensive link in the supply chain value chain.

A defining element of future sustainable supply chains will be the rapid expansion of AI-enabled circular economy systems, transforming linear "take-make-dispose" operations into regenerative loops. AI will facilitate smarter reverse logistics through automated sorting, computer-vision-based material recognition, and predictive analytics that determine the most environmentally beneficial recovery approach—repair, refurbishment, remanufacturing, upcycling, or recycling. Generative AI will reinvent product design from the outset, selecting materials and structures optimized for recyclability, minimal carbon footprint, modularity, and extended lifespan. Predictive lifecycle management will ensure products remain in circulation longer, reducing raw material extraction and waste generation. The introduction of digital product passports—AI-enhanced identity profiles capturing sustainability attributes across the lifecycle—will further enable traceability, fair sourcing verification, and compliance with circular economy regulations such as those emerging in the European Union. In this future, waste will increasingly be viewed not as a disposal burden but as a valuable data-driven resource stream feeding the next production cycle. AI will additionally redefine sustainable sourcing and ethical supplier governance (Bhattacharya et al., 2024). Advanced supplier intelligence platforms will continuously evaluate environmental, social, and economic performance using dynamic ESG scoring models powered by machine learning and NLP-based risk analytics. These systems will identify hidden sustainability vulnerabilities—unethical labor conditions, water scarcity risks, deforestation exposure, illegal mining, and excessive emissions—before they escalate into regulatory or reputational crises. AI will also expand opportunities for low-tech suppliers in developing regions by providing decision-support tools, automated reporting systems, and access to sustainable finance tied to verified performance improvements. Blockchain and AI integration will create tamper-proof traceability pathways that authenticate sustainability claims, enabling responsible consumption and improving accountability in industries where opacity has long fueled harmful practices, particularly fashion, agriculture, and electronics manufacturing.

Climate resilience will become an inseparable priority for future sustainable supply chains, and AI innovations will sit at the center of prevention, adaptation, and recovery efforts. Digital twins—real-time virtual replicas of supply chain ecosystems—will simulate climate stressors, resource scarcity risks, energy volatility, and carbon reduction scenarios, helping organizations optimize sustainable operations without physical experimentation. AI-driven geo-spatial intelligence will predict where extreme weather events may disrupt transportation infrastructure or manufacturing hubs, enabling proactive redesign of routing strategies, shifting of production clusters to climate-secure zones, and dynamic regional sustainability planning. Furthermore, AI will guide companies on transitioning to renewable energy procurement through intelligent energy marketplaces that match operational loads with renewable availability, grid conditions, and policy incentives. As sustainability reporting becomes mandatory globally, AI will streamline carbon disclosure and compliance, automating data collection, performance tracking, and alignment with frameworks such as GRI, CSRD, and the Science-Based Targets initiative. Despite the enormous potential, achieving AI-driven sustainable supply chain transformation will require overcoming strategic, technological, and ethical challenges. Data remains the most significant barrier: sustainability data is often incomplete, inconsistent, siloed, or not machine-readable. Ensuring high-quality, standardized data exchange across multi-tier supply networks will demand unprecedented collaboration and transparency (Cannas et al., 2023). The environmental footprint of AI itself must also be carefully controlled; energy-intensive computing threatens to offset sustainability benefits unless organizations employ green data centers, energy-efficient models, and carbon-aware AI design. Furthermore, as automation reduces certain labor requirements, technological disruption could worsen socioeconomic inequality if workforce transition strategies and inclusive implementation practices are not prioritized. Ethical frameworks ensuring human-oversight, fairness, and value-aligned decision-making must guide the deployment of AI tools affecting sustainability trade-offs, community resilience, and environmental justice.

Looking ahead, AI-driven innovations will not simply optimize sustainability—they will redefine it. Next-generation supply chains will operate as autonomous, interconnected, and self-governing networks, continuously learning from real-time environmental feedback and aligning actions with global sustainability goals. Products will be designed for circularity by default. Emissions will be monitored and minimized autonomously. Policy, environmental data, consumer expectations, and corporate sustainability strategy will be integrated into a single intelligent decision system. The convergence of AI with quantum computing, sustainable materials science, robotics, and distributed energy systems will unlock breakthroughs previously constrained by computation limits and economic barriers. Sustainability will evolve from an operational objective into an intelligent capability embedded into every decision a supply chain makes. In conclusion, the future of sustainable supply chains lies in the strategic and responsible advancement of AI-driven innovations that transform environmental performance while strengthening operational resilience and societal value. The journey will require collaboration across stakeholders—governments, industries, researchers, and communities—to build systems that are digitally intelligent, ecologically regenerating, and socially inclusive (Damoah et al., 2021). As businesses embrace AI-powered solutions, sustainable supply chains will shift from reactive compliance models to proactive decarbonization engines that enable the global transition toward a low-carbon circular economy. The organizations that harness AI not only for efficiency but also for climate action and ethical impact will lead the next era of sustainable development, demonstrating that technology and environmental stewardship can—and must—advance together to ensure a thriving future for both industry and the planet.

SUSTAINABLE PROCUREMENT WITH AI: REDUCING ENVIRONMENTAL IMPACT

Sustainable procurement has become a strategic imperative for organizations aiming to reduce environmental harm, improve ethical accountability, and transition toward circular and climate-conscious operations. In this evolving landscape, Artificial Intelligence (AI) stands as a transformative enabler, fundamentally redefining how purchasing decisions are made, suppliers are evaluated, and environmental outcomes are assessed. Traditional procurement systems often rely on historical cost-based criteria, fragmented supplier data, and manual audits that fail to provide timely insight into environmental risks buried deep within complex global supply chains. AI disrupts these limitations by enabling intelligent, data-driven procurement frameworks that integrate environmental sustainability indicators—carbon emissions, water usage, waste generation, material toxicity, deforestation exposure, and biodiversity impact—into routine purchasing decisions. Through sophisticated data analytics, machine learning algorithms can extract insights from massive, diverse datasets, including lifecycle assessment (LCA) databases, satellite imagery, IoT sensor readings, and public sustainability disclosures. This ensures that procurement teams can identify greener material alternatives, select suppliers that embody sustainable practices, and minimize the ecological footprint of goods and services throughout their lifecycle. AI-powered supplier management tools are central to sustainable procurement innovation (Dev et al., 2020). These systems continuously monitor supply chain actors across multiple tiers to evaluate environmental performance in real time—something that traditional audits cannot achieve. Natural language processing (NLP) algorithms scan ESG reports, regulatory filings, scientific studies, and media alerts to detect early signs of environmental non-compliance such as illegal land clearing, excessive greenhouse gas emissions, or hazardous material disposal. Machine learning-based ESG scoring ensures that suppliers are not only evaluated historically but predicted on future sustainability outcomes. As a result, procurement becomes proactive rather than reactive—organizations can identify high-risk suppliers early and implement corrective actions before risks escalate into legal violations or reputational damage. Furthermore, blockchain integrated with AI enhances transparent traceability, verifying the origin of materials and safeguarding against greenwashing by establishing immutable records of sustainability claims. Ethical and sustainable sourcing becomes more measurable as AI ensures verified authenticity in critical supply chains such as palm oil, rare earth minerals, cotton, and seafood, where environmental exploitation has long been prevalent.

Another transformative contribution of AI to sustainable procurement lies in driving greener product and material selection. Generative AI models are increasingly used to design alternative product configurations optimized for sustainability criteria—lighter materials, recyclable components, biodegradable inputs, and reduced toxic elements. AI-driven lifecycle impact assessments can automatically simulate the environmental consequences of procurement choices, comparing suppliers or product variants not only by cost or lead time but also by carbon reduction potential and material circularity (Dubey et al., 2021). Digital product passports—enabled by AI analytics and sensor-instrumented supply chains—will make this evaluation more accessible by providing procurement professionals with a detailed sustainability profile across a product's lifecycle stages. This shift encourages organizations to adopt circular procurement strategies, investing in products designed for reuse, modular repair, and longevity rather than short-term consumption. AI also plays a key role in reducing procurement-driven waste and emissions by improving demand forecasting and buying efficiency. Over-procurement contributes to massive environmental waste when unused materials end up in landfills or require resource-intensive storage and disposal. Machine learning models analyze consumption patterns, seasonal variability, operational constraints, and economic conditions to ensure optimal purchasing quantities—reducing wastage of raw materials, packaging, and energy inputs associated with excess production. Inventory visibility tools driven by AI further enhance sustainability by preventing stock expiration, especially in industries like food and pharmaceuticals where waste has substantial ecological consequences. By synchronizing procurement with accurate demand, organizations can dramatically lower their indirect emissions (Scope 3), which represent the majority of supply chain environmental impact.

Figure 1. The role of AI in supply chain management

Climate risk mitigation and adaptive sourcing strategies will increasingly rely on AI to reduce environmental vulnerabilities embedded in global supplier networks. Extreme climate events—floods, droughts, heatwaves, and storms—pose rising threats to resource availability and transportation reliability. AI-powered climate intelligence systems assess environmental risk exposure by correlating geographic supplier data with climate models and natural resource depletion forecasts. This helps procurement teams shift toward climate-resilient suppliers and embrace locally sourced materials where feasible, reducing transportation emissions while supporting regional environmental initiatives (Frederico, 2023). Digital twin simulations go a step further by enabling organizations to test procurement scenarios, evaluate supplier sustainability performance, and optimize sourcing configurations before real-world execution—minimizing harmful trial-and-error impacts on ecosystems and communities. Although AI offers transformative advantages, sustainable procurement implementation is not without challenges. The quality and availability of sustainability data remain critical barriers. Many suppliers—especially small and medium-sized enterprises (SMEs)—lack digital maturity and standardized environmental reporting capabilities, leading to data gaps that AI models must account for. Additionally, the computational infrastructure required to run advanced AI models can consume substantial energy if not managed responsibly; therefore, sustainable AI practices such as energy-efficient algorithms and renewable-powered data centers must accompany procurement digitalization. Ethical concerns also emerge: overreliance on automated sustainability scoring could disadvantage suppliers in emerging economies who struggle with compliance documentation rather than actual environmental performance. To avoid unjust supplier exclusion, organizations must support supplier enablement programs, providing digital tools, training, and equitable sustainability improvement pathways.

Organizational culture and workforce readiness also play decisive roles in successful adoption. Procurement teams must be trained to interpret AI-driven insights and balance sustainability objectives with cost, innovation, and supply continuity. Cross-functional collaboration becomes essential, requiring alignment between sustainability officers, supply chain managers, IT architects, and external stakeholders including regulators and NGOs. Governance frameworks must ensure transparency in algorithmic decision-making and accountability for sustainability claims derived from AI insights. Regulatory compliance will tighten globally—exemplified by emerging supply chain due diligence laws and carbon border adjustment mechanisms—making AI-enhanced reporting and verification indispensable. Looking toward the future, the integration of AI with sustainable procurement will continue to expand in sophistication and scope. We can anticipate highly autonomous procurement systems that automatically negotiate with verified eco-friendly suppliers, leverage dynamic sustainability pricing mechanisms, and enforce policies that prioritize low-carbon and circular materials by design. Quantum computing may drastically accelerate sustainability optimization, enabling procurement systems to analyze millions of sourcing permutations instantaneously. Smart contracts powered by blockchain + AI will automatically trigger sustainable supplier incentives or penalties, ensuring sustainability expectations are met continuously. Ultimately, AI-driven procurement will mature from a support function into a strategic sustainability engine, shaping how industries consume resources and respond to environmental challenges. In conclusion, AI empowers sustainable procurement to become a decisive lever in reducing supply chain environmental impact, fostering ethical supplier ecosystems, and accelerating the transition to circular value chains(Govindan et al., 2019). By embedding intelligent monitoring, ESG analytics, risk forecasting, greener product design, and demand optimization into procurement decisions, AI creates a tangible pathway to achieving global climate and sustainability goals.

AI-BASED PREDICTIVE ANALYTICS FOR SUSTAINABLE SUPPLY CHAIN OPTIMIZATION

AI-based predictive analytics is rapidly emerging as a cornerstone technology for achieving sustainability in global supply chain ecosystems, enabling decision-makers to proactively enhance operational efficiency while minimizing environmental impacts. Traditional supply chain management often relies on reactive strategies that address disruptions, overproduction, and inefficiencies only after they occur, leading to excessive carbon emissions, resource consumption, and waste generation. In contrast, predictive analytics leverages artificial intelligence—particularly machine learning, deep learning, probabilistic modeling, and time-series forecasting—to analyze vast and complex datasets and anticipate future supply chain behavior with high accuracy. By integrating signals from historical demand patterns, market dynamics, supplier performance, environmental data, transportation conditions, and real-time IoT sensor inputs, AI-driven systems can generate actionable forecasts that optimize material flows, production schedules, transportation routes, and inventory management before inefficiencies take shape (Guru Basava Aradhya et al., 2025). This predictive intelligence is fundamental to sustainable supply chain optimization, as it prevents waste at the source, reduces overstocking and stockouts, shortens lead times, and enhances resource efficiency across the value chain. One of the most influential applications of AI-based predictive analytics in sustainability is in demand forecasting and dynamic inventory optimization. Accurate predictions allow companies to align production volumes with actual market needs, avoiding the environmental burden associated with excess manufacturing, storage energy usage, and product disposal.

AI-based predictive analytics also fundamentally enhances logistics sustainability by reducing transportation emissions, which constitute the largest contributor to total supply chain carbon output. By anticipating demand clusters and shipment volumes, AI can schedule transportation assets more efficiently, improve load factors, and consolidate deliveries to minimize vehicle miles traveled. Predictive route optimization accounts for weather patterns, road conditions, congestion levels, fuel availability, and charging station infrastructure for electric fleets, enabling more energy-efficient delivery operations. Predictive maintenance enabled by AI—analyzing engine conditions, wear sensors, and operational data—reduces unnecessary fleet downtime and prevents failures that may lead to inefficient emergency transports or environmentally harmful equipment breakdowns. Similarly, maritime and aviation logistics benefit from AI-driven emissions forecasting that optimizes speed, fuel mix, and routing choices to comply with global decarbonization targets. These intelligent systems collectively accelerate the transition toward net-zero logistics networks, making sustainability and cost efficiency mutually reinforcing (Helo et al., 2021). In procurement and sourcing, predictive analytics is increasingly used to evaluate supplier sustainability risks and anticipate environmental compliance challenges throughout the supply chain. By employing anomaly detection and trend analysis on ESG performance indicators, AI systems help organizations identify suppliers whose environmental behavior may deteriorate over time due to resource shortages, tightening regulation, or operational inefficiencies.

Another crucial contribution of predictive analytics lies in optimizing production for circular economy adoption. Predictive modeling can determine when products are likely to reach end-of-life stages and forecast reverse logistics volumes for recycling, refurbishment, or remanufacturing activities. This predictive circularity planning minimizes landfill waste and the extraction of virgin materials by enabling advanced preparation of recovery infrastructure. Additionally, AI-driven digital twins simulate multiple production scenarios to identify processes with lower energy consumption, fewer emissions, and reduced water usage, guiding companies toward sustainable production pathways without interrupting operations. These tools enable organizations to test sustainability strategies virtually before implementation, eliminating unnecessary experimentation that could yield environmental harm. Despite the expanding benefits, deploying predictive analytics for sustainable supply chain optimization presents several challenges. Data accessibility remains a major barrier, as many supply chains still lack integrated visibility and real-time data-sharing mechanisms across multi-tier networks. The absence of standardized sustainability metrics and inconsistent data quality can lead to inaccurate predictions and misinformed decisions. Technologically, advanced predictive systems require significant computational resources and skilled labor capable of interpreting complex models—capabilities that smaller vendors may lack.

Nevertheless, the future outlook for AI-based predictive analytics in sustainable supply chain optimization is highly promising. Advancements in federated learning, quantum optimization, and decentralized data ecosystems will enhance predictive accuracy while strengthening supply chain transparency and resilience. The integration of predictive analytics into autonomous planning systems will create self-optimizing supply chains capable of continuously improving environmental performance without human intervention. As sustainability reporting becomes compulsory across global markets—with growing scrutiny from stakeholders and regulators—predictive analytics will serve as an essential backbone for meeting stringent carbon reduction and circular economy goals (Jackson et al., 2024). Organizations that invest early in AI-empowered sustainability foresight will gain strategic advantages through reduced operational risks, lower environmental compliance costs, improved brand trust, and enhanced contribution to global climate action. In conclusion, AI-based predictive analytics represents a powerful engine for sustainable supply chain transformation. By anticipating demand, optimizing logistics, improving procurement decisions, supporting circular workflows, and strengthening climate resilience, predictive analytics reduces environmental impact while safeguarding competitiveness and operational continuity. Overcoming challenges related to data quality, ethical deployment, and technological adoption will be critical in harnessing the full benefits of predictive AI. When developed responsibly, predictive analytics will propel supply chains from reactive and resource-intensive models toward proactive, smart, and sustainability-first ecosystems, playing a critical role in achieving the net-zero, circular, and climate-adaptive supply chains of the future. Artificial Intelligence (AI) is rapidly transforming supply chain management into a major driver of decarbonization and environmental sustainability. As industries worldwide face mounting pressure to achieve net-zero emissions and comply with increasingly stringent climate policies, AI presents innovative pathways to minimize carbon footprints across procurement, production, logistics, and end-of-life product cycles.

A key application of AI in reducing supply chain carbon footprint is energy-efficient production planning. Through machine learning algorithms and real-time process analytics, AI systems optimize manufacturing operations to consume less energy, shift workloads to periods where renewable energy sources are more prevalent, and minimize waste. Predictive analytics identify the most carbon-efficient production routes by balancing throughput, energy consumption, and material usage. Digital twins—AI-driven virtual replicas of manufacturing processes—simulate environmental impact before implementation, allowing organizations to adopt greener production strategies while maintaining high-quality performance. Computer vision technologies can also ensure precision and reduce scrap rates, preventing resource waste and unnecessary emissions generated during rework or disposal. Smart factories enhanced by AI-driven robotics and automation operate with heightened energy optimization, ultimately reducing operational carbon emissions within production facilities. In logistics, AI plays a transformative role in minimizing fuel consumption and transportation-related emissions, which constitute the largest contributor to supply chain carbon footprint. AI-enabled route optimization calculates the most fuel-efficient pathways by integrating traffic conditions, weather forecasts, road infrastructure data, and vehicle performance metrics. Autonomous trucks, drones, and electric mobility solutions guided by AI reduce fuel dependency and improve last-mile delivery sustainability. Machine learning and IoT sensors support predictive maintenance, identifying vehicle engine degradation or equipment inefficiencies before breakdowns occur, thereby avoiding emergency transports that burn excess fuel and emit higher pollutants (Koparde et al., 2026).

AI also significantly influences emissions reduction through sustainable procurement and Scope 3 emissions monitoring. Supplier sustainability data—historically unreliable and fragmented—is now accessible through AI systems equipped with natural language processing, anomaly detection, and IoT data integration. These tools continuously evaluate supplier environmental performance, identify hidden emission hotspots, and flag high-carbon suppliers requiring mitigation efforts. Blockchain-enabled transparency verifies low-carbon sourcing claims, preventing greenwashing while enabling responsible supply chain decision-making. AI-driven lifecycle assessment models compare environmental impact across supplier options, promoting procurement choices that lower carbon emissions embedded in raw materials, packaging, and transportation. Dynamic carbon pricing algorithms also allow organizations to forecast emissions liabilities and strategically select options aligned with net-zero pathways. As sustainability regulations tighten, AI-driven data intelligence will be essential for compliance and ethical supplier governance. Carbon reduction in supply chain management is further enhanced through demand forecasting, inventory optimization, and waste reduction. AI minimizes overproduction by precisely predicting demand fluctuations influenced by consumer behavior, market trends, climate variations, and global economic changes. Better demand alignment reduces energy consumption associated with unnecessary production and lowers emissions from storage, refrigeration, and material handling (Lin et al., 2022). In perishable goods industries, waste reduction through predictive inventory strategies significantly decreases methane emissions generated from spoiled products. Additionally, AI supports circularity by predicting product end-of-life timelines and guiding reverse logistics, remanufacturing, and recycling processes that reduce carbon emissions from virgin material extraction.

AI-powered climate risk forecasting also strengthens carbon reduction efforts by improving climate resilience and preventing carbon-intensive disruptions. Environmental stressors—like extreme weather events or resource scarcity—can force reactive transportation responses or emergency supply shifts that dramatically increase emissions. Predictive climate intelligence mitigates this by proactively adjusting supply chain configurations in sustainable ways, identifying alternate suppliers, safer routes, and climate-resilient sourcing hubs. Digital twins provide real-time simulations for validating climate strategies and testing carbon-efficient contingency plans long before disruptions occur. AI integration with carbon accounting platforms improves emissions tracking accuracy and compliance reporting aligned with frameworks such as GHG Protocol, CSRD, and the Science-Based Targets initiative (SBTi). Automated carbon reporting reduces the risk of inaccurate data that could undermine decarbonization planning and stakeholder trust. However, despite its immense potential, AI implementation for carbon reduction faces key challenges. Access to high-quality, real-time carbon emissions data remains fragmented across supply chain tiers and geographical boundaries. Many suppliers—particularly in developing markets—lack advanced digital infrastructure, making carbon traceability inconsistent. Moreover, running complex AI models can require significant computational resources; if powered by fossil-fuel-dominated energy grids, these technologies could inadvertently contribute to emissions that undermine sustainability objectives (Ma et al., 2021).

Looking forward, AI-driven decarbonization will revolutionize supply chain management through intelligent autonomy, integrated climate-aware systems, and rapid innovation in low-carbon operations. Sustainability will become ingrained in AI algorithms by default—where emissions are considered a primary optimization factor in every decision, from product design to last-mile logistics. Cross-industry AI collaboration platforms will accelerate emissions transparency, enabling organizations to benchmark carbon performance and accelerate low-carbon innovation through shared intelligence. The fusion of AI with emerging technologies—quantum computing for hyper-optimized emissions planning, advanced robotics for ultra-efficient handling, and bioengineered materials for low-carbon procurement—will propel businesses closer to achieving future-proof net-zero supply chains. In conclusion, AI provides a transformative foundation for reducing carbon footprints in supply chain management through energy-efficient production planning, sustainable logistics operations, responsible sourcing, waste prevention, and climate risk mitigation. Organizations that embrace AI-driven decarbonization will not only meet global sustainability expectations but also unlock competitive advantages through efficiency, cost reduction, and enhanced brand resilience. For AI to fully realize its environmental potential, transparent data ecosystems, equitable supplier integration, and sustainable computing practices must be prioritized (Moktadir et al., 2020). As companies progress toward net-zero ambitions, AI will serve as a critical catalyst in reshaping supply chains into intelligent, climate-friendly, and resilient systems—paving the way for a sustainable industrial future that balances business success with the health of the planet.

AI-DRIVEN CIRCULAR ECONOMY: CLOSING THE LOOP IN SUPPLY CHAINS

Artificial Intelligence (AI) is emerging as a critical technological enabler of the circular economy, advancing sustainable supply chain models that minimize resource extraction, reduce waste, and enable continual value recovery across product life cycles. In traditional linear supply chains—defined by the "take-make-dispose" paradigm—natural resources are extensively consumed, products often have limited useful life, and end-of-life waste contributes significantly to environmental degradation and greenhouse gas emissions. By contrast, circular supply chains prioritize closed-loop systems in which materials and products are repaired, reused, remanufactured, or recycled, thereby preserving natural capital and reducing environmental burdens. AI strengthens this transition by enhancing visibility, decision-making, and operational intelligence across supply networks, helping organizations identify circular opportunities that were previously obscured by limited data and system complexity. Through machine learning-driven analytics, companies can model product life cycles, anticipate component degradation, and implement proactive maintenance strategies that extend product longevity—supporting the shift from disposable consumption to durable product stewardship. Predictive algorithms also help manufacturers design products with recyclability and reparability in mind by analyzing environmental performance, material compatibility, and circular recovery potential before items even enter production (Nguyen, 2023). As a result, AI empowers organizations to build smarter, regenerative systems that fundamentally reshape how goods are produced, used, and reintegrated into future manufacturing cycles. Reverse logistics—one of the most challenging components of circular supply chains—benefits greatly from AI-enabled coordination.

AI additionally accelerates business model transformation by fostering new service-oriented approaches aligned with circularity principles. Algorithm-driven product usage analytics allow companies to shift from traditional ownership-based sales to product-as-a-service (PaaS) models, where customers pay for outcomes such as lighting or mobility rather than purchasing physical goods. This model incentivizes manufacturers to produce longer-lasting, easily maintainable products since profitability depends on efficient resource use over time rather than volume-based production. Examples include AI-managed shared mobility fleets, smart home appliances designed for modular upgrades, and office equipment leasing programs supported by predictive maintenance that reduces downtime and waste. Moreover, dynamic pricing models and AI-driven demand forecasts ensure reuse and second-hand markets operate with higher efficiency, widening access to sustainable consumption choices and delaying the entry of products into waste streams. These innovations reflect how AI enables not only operational improvements but also systemic shifts in revenue structures, consumer behavior, and value creation. The future circular economy will rely heavily on data intelligence ecosystems, yet several challenges must be addressed to ensure AI-driven circularity is both effective and equitable. Quality and interoperability of data remain significant barriers; data silos across supply chain stakeholders impede seamless lifecycle visibility and slow down circular decision-making. Standardization of sustainability metrics and digital product passports is needed to streamline information sharing, particularly across global supply networks with diverse regulatory landscapes. Furthermore, the computational intensity of AI introduces a paradox: if not powered by low-carbon energy and optimized algorithms, AI systems themselves can contribute to carbon emissions that counteract sustainability goals (Nirupama et al., 2025).

Despite these challenges, AI's ability to accelerate circular transitions positions it as a cornerstone of sustainable supply chain evolution. As regulatory pressure grows—through carbon pricing, waste reduction targets, and mandatory recycling frameworks—organizations adopting AI-driven circular solutions will benefit from enhanced compliance, risk mitigation, and competitive differentiation. AI not only improves operational efficiency and environmental performance but also drives innovation that reveals new markets and long-term economic resilience. In an era defined by climate urgency, resource scarcity, and shifting consumer expectations toward sustainability, AI-enabled circular supply chains offer a viable pathway to decouple economic growth from environmental degradation. By closing material loops, extending product value, and embracing regenerative logistics, AI transforms the supply chain from a contributor of pollution into a driver of ecological restoration and sustainable prosperity. Artificial Intelligence (AI) has emerged as a transformative driver of sustainable logistics, contributing to the reduction of carbon emissions, enhanced transport efficiency, and intelligent resource utilization within global supply chain ecosystems. Traditionally, logistics operations have been a major contributor to environmental degradation due to fuel-intensive transportation routes, inefficient freight allocation, traffic congestion, and excessive inventory movements. As governments tighten environmental policies and corporations adopt ambitious climate strategies, sustainable logistics has become a strategic imperative rather than a mere operational target (Nozari, 2024).

Beyond routing, AI enhances logistics sustainability through advanced demand forecasting and smart inventory positioning. Predictive analytics reduce the risk of overstocking and stockouts, ensuring products are stored and transported only when necessary, thereby eliminating wasteful supply movements that intensify carbon footprints. AI-powered warehouse automation systems, such as autonomous mobile robots and smart sorting devices, optimize material handling while minimizing energy use through efficient spatial organization, temperature control, and streamlined labor allocation. Additionally, AI tools assist in selecting greener transportation modes based on cost–emission trade-offs, helping companies shift from air freight toward more sustainable multimodal options like rail and electric fleets when feasible. In maritime logistics — one of the most carbon-dense transport sectors — AI optimizes vessel speeds, port operations, and fuel usage, contributing to "slow steaming" strategies that significantly reduce emissions without disrupting delivery schedules. Urban logistics also benefits from AI-enabled micro-distribution hubs, drone delivery trials, and automated route clustering that alleviate congestion in densely populated cities. Through these interconnected applications, AI fosters a logistics ecosystem where sustainability mechanisms are ingrained at both micro-operational and macro-strategic levels. AI is also accelerating the adoption of alternative-energy transport technologies, including electric and hydrogen-powered fleets. Smart energy management systems help logistics operators plan efficient charging schedules, optimize battery performance, and balance routing decisions with the availability of charging infrastructure (Oana et al., 2020). AI supports strategic placement of charging stations based on logistics flow and demand density, ensuring that the transition to green fleets does not hinder delivery reliability. Furthermore, machine learning models enable predictive maintenance to extend vehicle lifespan and prevent breakdowns that cause fuel-intensive detours or fleet overcapacity.

Transparency and accountability are essential components of sustainable logistics, and here again, AI serves as a powerful enabler. Carbon tracking systems supported by AI quantify emissions at product, shipment, and supply chain levels, generating actionable insights for decarbonization strategies and sustainability reporting. Natural language processing automates compliance monitoring, detecting environmental regulation updates and ensuring logistics operations adhere to global standards such as ISO 14083 for carbon accounting in freight transport. AI-driven life cycle assessment tools evaluate environmental impacts beyond transportation, spanning packaging, storage, and reverse logistics processes. In packaging optimization, AI identifies opportunities to reduce unnecessary volume and shift towards more recyclable and biodegradable materials — further lowering emissions associated with freight transportation. Meanwhile, recycling logistics systems powered by AI improve the recovery of packaging and reusable containers through automated collection route planning and material identification technologies. These capabilities support circular logistics principles, where waste is systematically returned into productive cycles. However, the journey toward AI-driven sustainable logistics is not without barriers. Implementing intelligent logistics systems requires robust data infrastructure, high interconnectivity across supply chain partners, and significant investment in digital transformation (Olan et al., 2024). Inaccurate, biased, or incomplete data inputs may compromise AI decision-making, potentially leading to unintended environmental outcomes. Small and medium-sized enterprises, which constitute the majority of logistics service providers globally, often struggle with technological adoption due to cost, knowledge gaps, or lack of digital readiness.

AI-POWERED SUPPLY CHAIN TRANSPARENCY: A KEY TO SUSTAINABILITY

Artificial Intelligence (AI) has become a pivotal enabler in establishing supply chain transparency, a critical foundation for achieving global sustainability goals and ethical business practices in today's interconnected economy. Modern supply chains are increasingly complex, spanning numerous geographic regions and involving diverse stakeholders from raw material extraction to consumer delivery. This complexity often results in fragmented visibility and limited traceability, making it difficult to detect unethical practices, mitigate environmental damage, and ensure regulatory compliance. AI addresses these challenges by transforming opaque supply chain networks into transparent and data-driven ecosystems, where real-time insights empower organizations to monitor operations, assess risks, and enforce sustainability standards throughout the entire product life cycle. Through advanced data analytics, machine learning, and automation, AI can aggregate and analyze vast quantities of operational data — logistics flows, carbon emissions, labor conditions, and sourcing activities — offering a comprehensive view of both direct and indirect supplier behavior. As stakeholders demand accountability, and as companies face growing pressure to align with sustainability frameworks such as ESG reporting, the Science-Based Targets initiative (SBTi), and the UN Sustainable Development Goals (SDGs), AI-driven transparency is becoming not only a strategic imperative but also a defining component of responsible global supply chain governance.

A major sustainability benefit of AI-enabled transparency lies in its ability to enhance traceability of raw materials and product components, particularly in industries with high environmental and social risk such as mining, agriculture, and fashion manufacturing. Using technologies like computer vision, remote sensing, and IoT-integrated tracking devices, AI identifies where materials originate, how they are processed, and whether ethical sourcing protocols are upheld. When integrated with blockchain systems, AI strengthens trust and data integrity by recording events tamper-proof on distributed ledgers, enabling verifiable certification of environmentally responsible and conflict-free sourcing. Such capabilities allow companies and consumers to validate product claims such as carbon neutrality, organic production, or fair labor practices, countering prevalent issues of greenwashing. AI-based natural language processing (NLP) systems also monitor media, regulatory databases, and investigative reports to detect early warning signals of environmental violations or supplier misconduct, enabling swift intervention and ethical supplier realignment

(Papadopoulos et al., 2022). This risk intelligence drives sustainable procurement decisions, helping organizations collaborate proactively with high-risk suppliers to improve compliance or diversify sourcing to protect environmental welfare and human rights. In addition to social and ethical parameters, AI plays an essential role in environmental impact monitoring across supply chain activities. Automated emissions accounting systems quantify greenhouse gases at the operational level and model how strategic decisions affect total carbon footprints. Real-time data integration provides granular visibility into energy consumption, water usage, and waste generation — metrics necessary to identify inefficiencies and design immediate sustainability improvements. AI-enabled life cycle assessment tools further evaluate the environmental performance of products from material sourcing to end-of-life disposal, guiding companies toward low-impact product design, recyclable packaging, and regenerative circular economy strategies (Zejjari et al., 2024).

AI-driven transparency also enhances collaboration and trust within supply networks. Traditionally, fragmented information flows and limited data sharing create asymmetries that hinder sustainability progress. AI bridges this gap by enabling secure data exchange platforms, where suppliers, manufacturers, and logistics providers contribute validated data to improve collective ecological performance. Supply chain digital twins — virtual replicas of physical networks — support scenario modeling to evaluate how sustainability strategies perform under different operational conditions, strengthening resilience against disruptions such as climate events or resource scarcity. This collaborative decision-making model fosters shared responsibility and continuous improvement, transforming sustainability from a corporate initiative into an ecosystem-driven effort. Additionally, through prescriptive analytics, AI recommends targeted actions to reduce emissions, optimize sourcing routes, and improve inventory placement, ultimately balancing environmental priorities with economic competitiveness. Despite its promising contributions, scaling AI-enabled transparency faces significant obstacles. Digital maturity varies widely across the global supply chain, and smaller suppliers often lack the technological infrastructure required to collect and share high-quality sustainability data (Parra-Hernández et al., 2024). Data privacy and ownership challenges complicate transparency efforts, raising concerns over competitive exposure or regulatory repercussions. Furthermore, developing trustworthy AI requires robust governance to ensure unbiased models, secure data handling, and explainable results that stakeholders can confidently act upon.

Looking ahead, AI-powered transparency will remain integral to the evolution of sustainable supply chain transformation (Warale et al., 2025). As stakeholder expectations rise and environmental accountability becomes central to global commerce, transparency will be a core criterion for assessing brand credibility and competitiveness. AI will continue to refine predictive and real-time sustainability monitoring capabilities, providing organizations with enhanced foresight to prevent environmental harm rather than simply respond to it. Combined with advances in autonomous logistics, circular economy ecosystems, and climate-adaptive supply chain planning, AI ensures that transparency becomes a catalyst for meaningful, long-term sustainability progress. Ultimately, AI-driven supply chain transparency marks a decisive shift toward responsible value creation — empowering companies, consumers, and societies to collaboratively build a more ethical, resilient, and environmentally conscious global economy. Artificial Intelligence (AI) is transforming supplier selection processes by enabling organizations to systematically evaluate and engage suppliers who align with sustainability goals, environmental stewardship, and responsible business conduct. Traditional supplier selection has historically prioritized cost, delivery performance, and quality, while environmental and social considerations were often treated as secondary concerns. However, intensifying global climate regulations, rising stakeholder expectations, and the growing significance of ESG (Environmental, Social, and Governance) performance have redefined what constitutes an ideal supplier. Companies now require sourcing strategies that reduce carbon footprints, eliminate unethical labor practices, encourage waste reduction, and promote circular resource use (Pasupuleti et al., 2024).

A major advantage of AI in sustainable supplier selection lies in its ability to detect hidden environmental and ethical risks that traditional audits or manual evaluation methods might overlook. Natural language processing (NLP) tools monitor public information, news articles, NGO reports, and regulatory alerts to identify suppliers involved in deforestation, pollution incidents, forced labor, or greenwashing (Wang et al., 2022). Such automated intelligence allows organizations to respond proactively to emerging risks rather than reacting after reputational damage occurs. Additionally, AI-driven image recognition systems can analyze satellite data and visual inspections from supplier facilities to detect environmental violations such as illegal dumping or land degradation. Predictive analytics generate supplier risk forecasts by detecting early performance deviations and anticipating the likelihood of sustainability non-compliance. These capabilities extend decision-making confidence and reduce exposure to environmental liabilities and supply chain disruptions associated with non-resilient suppliers. AI also enhances transparency and accountability across tiered supplier networks. Often, the greatest environmental and social harm occurs not among primary suppliers but deep within sub-tier partners where data is scarce and oversight is minimal (Qu et al., 2024). Using AI-enabled traceability and blockchain-based verification, organizations gain visibility into complex supplier ecosystems, ensuring that sustainability requirements cascade beyond direct business relationships. Digital supplier mapping identifies dependencies on high-risk regions or materials, enabling strategic redesign of sourcing portfolios.

From a compliance perspective, AI aids in aligning procurement practices with emerging sustainability regulations and certification standards (Tsolakis et al., 2023). Automated compliance checks ensure that suppliers adhere to carbon reduction mandates, extended producer responsibility (EPR) requirements, and sector-specific sustainability protocols like ISO 14001, FSC, or SA8000. AI-enabled performance dashboards continuously monitor and score suppliers across ESG indicators, providing transparent and real-time visibility for decision-makers and external stakeholders. These digital evaluations support ethical contracting, supplier incentive systems, and targeted sustainability audits that foster long-term improvements across the supplier ecosystem. By shifting from periodic and paperwork-heavy compliance audits to ongoing AI-driven assessment, organizations reduce administrative burdens while ensuring that sustainability remains a living priority throughout the supplier lifecycle. AI-driven supplier selection also contributes to circular economy goals by identifying suppliers with strong recycling capabilities, low-carbon material production techniques, or take-back systems that keep resources circulating. It enables procurement teams to prefer suppliers offering renewable materials, biodegradable packaging, and low-waste production technologies. Additionally, AI can quantify the sustainability benefits of collaborating with innovative suppliers in green technology, regenerative agriculture, clean energy, or waste valorization sectors. By doing so, procurement evolves into a catalyst for sustainable industrial ecosystems, supporting market growth for environmentally responsible solutions.

Despite its benefits, AI-based sustainable supplier selection faces challenges that must be addressed for widespread adoption. Data quality and availability remain core limitations: many suppliers — particularly small and medium enterprises in developing regions — lack the infrastructure to report accurate sustainability data. This could unintentionally exclude smaller but highly sustainable suppliers who are digitally underprepared. Ensuring fairness requires strategies such as digital training, simplified reporting frameworks, and subsidized access to sustainability assessment technology (Raman et al., 2025). AI models must be transparent and explainable to build trust and avoid bias in procurement decisions. Furthermore, companies must ensure the responsible use of AI technologies, minimizing their own carbon footprints through energy-efficient computing and renewable-powered data centers. Collaboration across supply chain actors is essential to standardize sustainability criteria, share data securely, and encourage continuous environmental improvement rather than punitive disengagement. Looking ahead, AI-based supplier selection will play a central role in shaping the future of sustainable supply chains. As organizations accelerate toward net-zero and circularity goals, supplier evaluation will evolve from transactional cost negotiations to strategic partnerships built on shared sustainability ambitions. AI will continue expanding its capabilities, integrating climate scenario modeling, biodiversity risk assessments, and ethical labor monitoring into procurement decision systems. Ultimately, AI empowers organizations to choose suppliers who not only meet operational requirements but also drive meaningful environmental and social progress (Toorajipour et al., 2021). By aligning sourcing strategies with global sustainability priorities, AI-based supplier selection advances supply chains that are more resilient, ethical, and supportive of a healthier planet — reinforcing the idea that responsible procurement is both a climate necessity and a strategic advantage in the future of global commerce.

THE ROLE OF AI IN SUSTAINABLE INVENTORY MANAGEMENT

Artificial Intelligence (AI) is reshaping inventory management by advancing sustainability across supply chains, enabling organizations to reduce waste, minimize resource consumption, and optimize the flow of goods with greater efficiency (Sanders et al., 2019). Traditionally, inventory decisions have relied on static forecasting methods and human experience, which often result in excess stock, stockouts, or inefficiencies that contribute to increased carbon emissions and waste generation. In a world facing intensifying environmental concerns, including resource scarcity and climate-driven regulatory pressure, sustainable inventory management has become an operational imperative. AI technologies — particularly machine learning, predictive analytics, and automation — provide intelligent solutions that enhance forecasting accuracy, optimize replenishment strategies, reduce storage-related emissions, and support the shift toward greener business models. These capabilities help companies strike a balance between economic performance and environmental responsibility, ensuring that inventory levels closely align with actual demand while reducing the ecological burden of unnecessary production and storage. One of the most significant sustainability contributions of AI is demand forecasting optimization. Advanced algorithms analyze historical sales data, seasonality trends, macroeconomic signals, social sentiment, and unexpected disruption factors to predict demand with precision far beyond traditional forecasting. This reduces overproduction — a major source of material waste and carbon-intensive manufacturing — and improves shelf-life utilization, particularly for perishable goods in retail and food supply chains. By lowering the volume of unsold products that ultimately become waste, AI-driven demand planning reduces landfill disposal and associated methane emissions. Moreover, predictive analytics inform proactive replenishment decisions by identifying optimal reorder points and ensuring goods arrive exactly when needed, eliminating unnecessary safety stock that consumes extra energy for warehousing (Rane et al., 2024). AI also strengthens inventory visibility and traceability across multi-tier global supply networks. IoT-enabled sensors, RFID tracking, and real-time analytics platforms allow companies to monitor product conditions, temperature, and location with accuracy, reducing spoilage and damage resulting from mishandling or improper storage conditions. Computer vision systems are increasingly deployed in warehouses for automated inspections and quality monitoring, ensuring items remain fit for use and reducing waste caused by unnoticed defects. Enhanced visibility also improves responsiveness to disruptions — such as delays or environmental risks — helping supply chain teams redesign inventory allocation to avoid carbon-intensive expedited shipping or redundant transfers between facilities.

CONCLUSION

Warehouse sustainability is further improved through AI-enhanced operational efficiency. Intelligent automation technologies—like autonomous mobile robots and dynamic slotting algorithms—streamline product placement to minimize travel distance, reducing energy consumption within distribution centers. Energy-efficient environmental controls managed by AI adjust lighting, heating, and cooling to match real-time occupancy and storage requirements, lowering carbon emissions associated with commercial logistics facilities. Predictive maintenance applied to warehouse machinery reduces breakdowns and extends the lifespan of equipment, helping minimize resource-intensive replacements and manufacturing of new assets. From a strategic perspective, AI supports the transition toward just-in-time (JIT) and lean inventory models while mitigating the risks traditionally associated with such approaches. It enables companies to maintain lower inventory volumes without jeopardizing service levels, which directly reduces warehousing capacity requirements and their corresponding environmental footprint. Inventory pooling supported by AI optimizes shared storage among network partners and identifies opportunities for local sourcing to reduce transport emissions. Additionally, AI plays a critical role in circular economy inventory flows, predicting returns and facilitating refurbishment, remanufacturing, or recycling of products to keep materials in use for longer. In sectors like consumer electronics and fashion, where returns rates are high, intelligent reverse logistics systems powered by AI automate product grading and recovery route allocation—minimizing waste while extracting maximum remaining value from returned items. Government regulations and consumer expectations further reinforce the necessity for sustainable inventory management. AI enables robust environmental reporting that quantifies the carbon impact of inventory decisions and supports compliance with sustainability policies such as mandatory emissions disclosure. Automated lifecycle assessments for inventory items allow companies to select lower-impact components and packaging alternatives, contributing to eco-conscious product portfolios. Sustainability dashboards provide stakeholders with transparency into how inventory decisions align with corporate climate goals, shifting procurement and planning motivations from cost-first to sustainability-centric.

Despite significant opportunities, challenges persist in implementing AI for sustainable inventory management. Data fragmentation across supply chain systems hinders real-time analysis, particularly in global networks involving suppliers with varying levels of digitization. High-quality data integration must be prioritized to avoid flawed predictions and misguided decisions. Investment requirements for AI infrastructure and digital skill development may limit adoption among small and medium enterprises, raising concerns of unequal sustainability advancement across industries. Additionally, organizations must ensure that AI systems themselves are environmentally responsible, leveraging energy-efficient computing, green data centers, and algorithm optimization to align AI deployment with sustainability objectives. Ethics and governance frameworks are equally essential to prevent algorithmic bias and ensure transparency in automated decision-making. Looking forward, the role of AI in sustainable inventory management will only expand as emerging technologies such as autonomous logistics, digital twins, and real-time carbon forecasting become mainstream. AI will not only optimize existing inventory practices but also shape innovative models like demand-driven supply networks and sustainable-as-a-service delivery ecosystems. As climate change demands urgent and measurable action, AI enables companies to design inventory strategies that reduce emissions, protect natural resources, and build resilient and future-ready operations. Ultimately, AI empowers organizations to redefine sustainability as an integral performance metric within inventory systems — ensuring that economic efficiency and environmental stewardship are collaboratively achieved throughout the global supply chain landscape.

REFERENCES

Abdelhamid, M. M., Sliman, L., & Ben Djemaa, R. (2024). AI-enhanced blockchain for IoT-based supply chains. *Logistics (Basel)*, *8*(1), 9. DOI: 10.3390/logistics8010009

Ahmed, K. R. (2025). Deep learning framework for interpretable supply chain optimization. *Scientific Reports*, *15*, 1123. DOI: 10.1038/s41598-025-11510-z PMID: 40685434

Bai, C., & Sarkis, J. (2020). AI in supply chain sustainability assessment. *International Journal of Production Research*, *58*(9), 2614–2633. DOI: 10.1080/00207543.2019.1647438

Bhattacharya, S., Govindan, K., Ghosh Dastidar, S., & Sharma, P. (2024). AI in closed-loop supply chains. *Transportation Research Part E, Logistics and Transportation Review*, *184*, 103455. DOI: 10.1016/j.tre.2024.103455

Cannas, V. G., Ciano, M. P., Saltalamacchia, M., & Secchi, R. (2023). Artificial intelligence in supply chain and operations management. *International Journal of Production Research*. Advance online publication. DOI: 10.1080/00207543.2023.2232050

Damoah, I. S., Ayakwah, A., & Tingbani, I. (2021). AI-enhanced drones in healthcare supply chains. *Journal of Cleaner Production*, *328*, 129598. DOI: 10.1016/j.jclepro.2021.129598

Dev, N. K. (2020). AI-based dynamic pricing in supply chains. *Computers & Industrial Engineering*, *147*, 106681. DOI: 10.1016/j.cie.2020.106681

Dubey, R. (2021). AI-enabled supply chain resilience. *Transportation Research Part E, Logistics and Transportation Review*, *146*, 102190. DOI: 10.1016/j.tre.2020.102190

Frederico, G. F. (2023). ChatGPT in supply chain research agenda. *Logistics (Basel)*, *7*(4), 53. DOI: 10.3390/logistics7040053

Govindan, K., & Soleimani, H. (2019). Data-driven green supplier selection. *Journal of Cleaner Production*, *233*, 1410–1422. DOI: 10.1016/j.jclepro.2019.06.069

Guru Basava Aradhya, S., Chithambar Gupta, V., Raman, M. S., Singh, J., Manjunath, T. C., & Sharma, M. (2025). Health Crises and Digitalization: Digital Health. In Yıldırım, D., Yıldırım, S., & Kandpal, V. (Eds.), *Sustainable Digitalization Strategies in Business and Healthcare* (pp. 171–198). IGI Global Scientific Publishing. DOI: 10.4018/979-8-3373-5087-5.ch007

Helo, P., & Hao, Y. (2021). Artificial intelligence in operations and SCM. *Production Planning and Control*, *32*(12), 975–986. DOI: 10.1080/09537287.2020.1780508

Jackson, I., Namdar, J., Saénz, M. J., & Elmquist, R. (2024). AI/ML for cold chain enhancement. *International Journal of Production Research*. Advance online publication. DOI: 10.1080/00207543.2024

Koparde, S. A., Selvakumar, P., Jha, R. P., Deepthi Reddy, K., Kuchipudi, J. D., Manjunath, T. C., & Sharma, M. (2026). Generative AI in Predicting and Preventing Foodborne Illnesses. In Madaan, G., Singh, A., Chahal, B., David, A., & Singh, G. (Eds.), *Generative AI in Food Systems: Predictive Demand, Smart Supply Chains, and Sustainable Service Futures* (pp. 205–232). IGI Global Scientific Publishing. DOI: 10.4018/979-8-3373-5182-7.ch010

Lin, H., Lin, J., & Wang, F. (2022). Machine learning models in supply chain management. *Journal of Innovation & Knowledge*, *7*(4), 100276. DOI: 10.1016/j.jik.2022.100276

Ma, J. (2021). AI-driven predictive maintenance in supply networks. *Reliability Engineering & System Safety*, *210*, 107558. DOI: 10.1016/j.ress.2021.107558

Moktadir, M. A. (2020). Barriers to implementing AI for sustainable supply chains. *Journal of Cleaner Production*, *272*, 122721. DOI: 10.1016/j.jclepro.2020.122721

Nguyen, T. T. H. (2023). AI for demand forecasting. *Operations and Supply Chain Management*, *16*(1), 56–66. DOI: 10.31387/oscm0510363

Nirupama, E., Seenivasan, S., Bhardwaj, K., Karunakaran, N. B., Basava Aradhya, S. G., & Manjunath, T. C. (2025). Transforming Digital Supply Chains With Gamification and Metaverse Integration. In G. Malik, D. Singh, & R. Bansal (Eds.), Addressing Practical Problems Through the Metaverse and Game-Inspired Mechanics (pp. 123-152). IGI Global Scientific Publishing. DOI: 10.4018/979-8-3693-8886-0.ch006

Nozari, H. (2024). Green supply chain based on AI. *Journal of Economics & Management*, *45*(2), 88–102. DOI: 10.22367/jem.2024.45.05

Oana, D., & Dumitrascu, D. (2020). AI performance evaluation in automotive supply chains. *Processes (Basel, Switzerland)*, *8*(3), 334. DOI: 10.3390/pr8030334

Olan, F. (2024). Sustainable supply chain finance and AI. *IEEE Transactions on Engineering Management*. Advance online publication. DOI: 10.1109/TEM.2021.3133104

Papadopoulos, T. (2022). Digital twins + AI for circular supply chains. *Technological Forecasting and Social Change*, *182*, 121798. DOI: 10.1016/j.techfore.2022.121798

Parra-Hernández, J. (2024). AI decision support for supply chain sustainability. *Sustainability*, *16*, 10222. DOI: 10.3390/su161810222

Pasupuleti, V., Thuraka, B., Kodete, C. S., & Malisetty, S. (2024). Enhancing supply chain agility through machine learning. *Logistics (Basel)*, *8*(3), 73. DOI: 10.3390/logistics8030073

Qu, C., & Kim, E. (2024). Reviewing the roles of AI-integrated technologies in sustainable supply chain management. *Sustainability (Basel)*, *16*(14), 6186. DOI: 10.3390/su16146186

Raman, M. S., Koppa, K. B., Chithambar Gupta, V., Bhat, V. A., & Guru Basava Aradhya, S. (2025). Digital Transformation and Sustainability Artificial Intelligence and Sustainable Development. In Yıldırım, D., Yıldırım, S., & Kandpal, V. (Eds.), *Effects of Digitalization and Circular Economy on Sustainable Policy and Climate Change Prevention* (pp. 69–96). IGI Global Scientific Publishing. DOI: 10.4018/979-8-3693-9909-5.ch003

Rane, N. L., Desai, P., Rane, J., & Paramesha, M. (2024). AI, ML, and DL for sustainable supply chain management. Trustworthy Artificial Intelligence in Industry and Society. DOI: 10.70593/978-81-981367-4-9_5

Sanders, N. R., Boone, T., Ganeshan, R., & Wood, J. D. (2019). Sustainable supply chains in the age of AI. *Journal of Business Logistics*, *40*(3), 229–240. DOI: 10.1111/jbl.12224

Toorajipour, R., Sohrabpour, V., Nazarpour, A., Oghazi, P., & Fischl, M. (2021). Artificial intelligence in supply chain management: A systematic literature review. *Journal of Business Research*, *122*, 502–517. DOI: 10.1016/j.jbusres.2020.09.009

Tsolakis, N., Schumacher, R., Dora, M., & Kumar, M. (2023). AI and blockchain in supply chains. *Annals of Operations Research*. Advance online publication. DOI: 10.1007/s10479-021-04387-9

Virmani, N., Singh, R. K., & Agarwal, V. (2024). AI for responsive healthcare supply chains. *IEEE Transactions on Engineering Management*. Advance online publication. DOI: 10.1109/TEM.2024.3370377

Wang, X. (2022). Sustainable logistics via machine learning optimization. *Computers & Industrial Engineering*, *171*, 108458. DOI: 10.1016/j.cie.2022.108458

Warale, P. N., Limbore, N. V., Anute, N., Ahluwalia, G. K., Raut, A., & Selvakumar, P. (2025). AI-Enhanced Customer Engagement and Experience: Chatbots, Virtual Assistants, and AI-Powered Customer Interactions. In Hussain, Z., Khan, A., Uzir, M., Sharipudin, M., & Shaheen, A. (Eds.), *Impacts of AI-Generated Content on Brand Reputation* (pp. 335–362). IGI Global Scientific Publishing. DOI: 10.4018/979-8-3373-4327-3.ch014

Zejjari, I., & Benhayoun, I. (2024). The use of AI to advance sustainable supply chains. *Discover Sustainability*, *4*, 86. DOI: 10.1007/s43621-024-00364-6

Chapter 3

Artificial Intelligence in Sustainable Supply Chain Management: Enhancing Efficiency, Resilience, and Environmental Responsibility

G. Porkodi
Vel Tech Multi Tech Dr. Rangarajan Dr. Sakunthala Engineering College, India

D. Sattianadan
SRM Institute of Science and Technology, India

G. Sumathy
http://orcid.org/0000-0001-6759-5967
SRM Institute of Science and Technology, India

V. Kalyanasundaram
http://orcid.org/0000-0002-1575-9971
SRM Institute of Science and Technology, India

S. Vidyasagar
http://orcid.org/0000-0002-0484-0715
SRM Institute of Science and Technology, India

Dinesh M. G.
http://orcid.org/0009-0009-7643-5338
Easa College of Engineering and Technology, India

Anish T. P.
http://orcid.org/0000-0002-4308-9645
R.M.K. College of Engineering and Technology, India

ABSTRACT

Artificial Intelligence (AI) is transforming sustainable supply chain management by enhancing operational efficiency, strengthening resilience, and reducing environmental impact. This chapter explores the integration of AI techniques including

DOI: 10.4018/979-8-3373-7847-3.ch003

machine learning, deep learning, optimization models, and digital twins across key supply chain functions such as forecasting, manufacturing, logistics, procurement, and circular resource management. AI-driven tools improve demand prediction, energy optimization, carbon tracking, waste reduction, and risk mitigation while enabling real-time visibility and data-driven decision-making. The chapter also discusses challenges related to data quality, computational demands, cybersecurity, bias, and regulatory constraints. Future opportunities, such as autonomous supply chains, green AI, and integration with IoT and blockchain, highlight AI's potential to support long-term sustainability goals.

1. INTRODUCTION

1.1 Overview of Sustainable Supply Chain Management (SSCM) and Its Global Importance

Sustainable Supply Chain Management (SSCM) has become a critical element in the current business operations since the world is increasingly becoming worried about global warming, depletion and pollution of resources (Power, D. 2005). The outdated supply chains that primarily focus on the minimization of costs and the speed of operations are not sufficient to meet the industries which are intending to attain sustainability and meet the regulatory demands. SSCM extends beyond efficiency and profitability and integrates environmental stewardship, social responsibility and long-term economic viability in its supply chain operations. This shift is a sign of a bigger shift in the global markets where customers, governments and other stakeholders are demanding transparency and environmentally friendly practices. As companies operate in the more complex and more intertwined networks of supply, sustainability has now become a requirement not just to meet the regulations but also a benefit that offers competitive advantage, mitigates risk or aids the brand image. Businesses have realized that sustainable supply chains enhance waste reduction, resource exploitation, resilience and value generation in the long run to the companies and the society (Stadtler, H. 2014).

1.2 Role of Digital Transformation and AI in Modern Supply Chains

The rapid advancement of digital technologies has transformed the supply chain operations radically. The technology that has made intelligent and sustainable supply chains is Artificial Intelligence (AI) that is nurtured by the other potent technologies, such as the Internet of Things (IoT), blockchain, robotics, and cloud computing

(Tsintotas, K et al., 2024). AI assists organizations to work with huge amounts of real-time data, predict demand fluctuations, optimize logistics routes, and optimize the decision-making process. In machine learning algorithms, businesses can identify inefficiency, decrease wastage, and automate production more accurately as compared to the traditional methods. Digital transformation also facilitates end-to-end visibility so that the supply chain partners could trace materials, monitor energy consumption, and promise responsible sourcing. This openness improves environmental accountability and makes organizations active in handling matters of sustainability. As the current globalized and dynamic supply chains evolve, artificial intelligence (AI) tools may be adopted as the source of automation, coordination, and enhanced environmental performance (Wu, H et al., 2025).

1.3 Key Challenges in Achieving Sustainable Supply Chains

Sustainability is a very crucial issue but a complex concept that cannot be achieved due to multiple challenges which are still existent. The most significant issues include the fact that the level of carbon emission is high in the course of supply chain activities, including manufacturing, transportation, and storage. The traditional logistic systems tend to be founded on the application of fossil fuels, inefficient routes, and inefficient technological foundation which are a serious source of the emission of the greenhouse gases in the world. Operation inefficiency is also another challenge and is seen in terms of mismanagement of inventories, lack of proper use of resources, and wastage of production. Geopolitical tensions, pandemics, natural disasters and market volatility are also highly susceptible to disrupting supply chains. Such upheavals demonstrate the necessity of resilience and adaptive skills. Moreover, the problem of transparency continues to exist in multi-tier supply chains where it is hard to monitor the practices of suppliers and guarantee that they are in compliance with the environmental and ethical requirements. Overcoming them would demand innovative technologies with the ability to cope with complexity, risks, and optimization of operations on an overall basis, which AI systems are singularly qualified to offer.

1.4 Motivation for Integrating AI to Improve Efficiency, Resilience, and Sustainability

The reasons that drive the implementation of AI in the sustainable supply chain management are the necessity to improve the performance of the operation in order to respond to environmental and social issues. AI provides high predictive power to assist organizations in predicting demand patterns and disruptions and resource needs more accurately. AI minimizes wastage by reducing the level of uncertainty and facilitating data-driven approaches to the problem, maximizing inventory levels, and improving efficiency in general. On the resiliency front, AI-based models will be capable of simulating different risk scenarios and enable businesses to have contingency plans ready and adjust quickly in the event of a crisis. This is very vital in maintaining continuity in the global supply chains that are becoming susceptible to uncertainties. The importance of AI to the environment also concerns sustainability since it enables tracking the carbon footprints with much accuracy, identifying the activities that are highly emitting, and suggesting the greener alternatives. Transportation routes can be optimized, fuel consumption can be reduced, and the unique opportunity to use the circular economy can be encouraged with the help of the machine learning algorithms that predict the possibility of reuse and recycling of the materials. The AI integration therefore balances the economic objectives and the environmental accountability and hence is a powerful enabler of sustainable and resilient supply chains.

1.5 Scope and Contribution of this Chapter

This chapter would assist in obtaining the honed image of the new role of AI in sustainable supply chain management by synthesizing academic research, industry experience, and technology. It evaluates major AI tools of improving sustainability-related outcomes, including demand forecasting, risk forecasting, routing optimization, emissions mitigation, and waste management. Another aspect of AI that the chapter is concerned with is how it is enhancing resilience by making adaptive decisions and monitoring real-time. It also aims at environmental contributions such as energy efficiency, carbon tracking and a circular supply chain innovation. The chapter presents the existing issues, ethics, and limitations in applying AI to SSCM through the analysis of available literature, trends, and applications. Moreover, it also provides a summary of the research opportunities in the future, specifically, the integration of AI with the emerging technologies like digital twins, blockchain, and edge computing. Lastly, the chapter would contribute to the academic knowledge and practice within the industry by giving an understanding of how AI would trigger the transformation to effective, resilient, and sustainable supply chain systems.

2. FUNDAMENTALS OF AI IN SUSTAINABLE SUPPLY CHAINS

2.1 Overview of Artificial Intelligence Techniques in Supply Chain Management

The use of Artificial Intelligence in supply chains has turned into one of the key sources of innovation because it enables the systems to operate with complicated data, learn in accordance with the functioning pattern, and make smart decisions. The AI techniques are revolutionary in the context of sustainable supply chain management because they enhance efficiency and performance in the environment (Min, H. 2010). Machine Learning (ML) models are widely used in forecasting, anomaly detection and optimization- significant processes in the reduction of waste and generating disruptions. Deep Learning (DL) with the capability of processing high-dimensional and unstructured data is applied in such areas as image analysis to find and eliminate quality problems, automatic sorting, demand forecasting using time-series data, etc. Reinforcement Learning (RL) offers adaptive control systems, which offer systems the capability to learn how to make the optimal routing, scheduling, and inventory decisions through learning. Genetic algorithms and particle swarm optimization are also algorithms utilized in the optimization of strategic planning to take into account several sustainability constraints, such as emissions, energy consumption, and transportation cost, and lead time. A set of these AI techniques is a powerful weaponry that can help businesses to leave reactive and linear business methods in the past and enter into predictive, automated and socially accountable supply chains (Suganya, P et al., 2026).

2.2 Role of Data Sources and Digital Infrastructure in AI-Enabled Sustainability

Data is the essence of AI-driven supply chains, and the modern digital infrastructure is a significant solution to the delivery of real-time insights and smart actions. The IoT devices such as sensors, RFID tags, GPS trackers, and smart meters collect data on the location of the products, temperature, energy consumption, machine health, and emissions. This data is of high frequency, which can be perceived by AI models to identify inefficiencies, anticipate failures, and suggest sustainable alternatives. Financial, operational, and logistical data are further consolidated with the help of Enterprise Resource Planning (ERP) systems, cloud databases, and transportation management platforms, which contribute to the development of a holistic view of supply chain operations by AI algorithms. The new concept of edge computing will increase sustainability because it allows AI processing nearer to data sources, lowering latency and energy usage related to the transmission to clouds. Furthermore, blockchain technology adds to AI as it offers secure, transparent data records among several stakeholders, and therefore, sustainability claims, including carbon reporting and ethical sourcing, can be verified. Collectively, these technologies form a data-abundant ecosystem that is needed to attain AI-enabled sustainability objectives.

2.3 AI-Driven Decision-Making and Operational Optimization

The AI transforms supply chain decision making to allow data-driven, automated, and predictive operations. Traditional supply chain decision making can be rather slow and inaccurate as it is usually made using past data, manual analysis, and experience. However, AI is able to handle large data streams in real time, find patterns that humans cannot, and prescribe specific actions. Predictive analytics can assist businesses in predicting changes in demand, preventing excess production, and preventing inventory shortages. ML models that trade-off between cost, service level, and the environment are used to improve optimal lot sizing, replenishment planning, and warehouse space management. The optimization of transportation paths is highly efficient due to AI, as it can be used to optimize the use of loads and reduce emissions. The reinforcement learning algorithms will be able to respond to real time disruptions, e.g. traffic, weather, or supply delays, to develop more resilient and sustainable logistics procedures. Scheduling of production can also be done automatically to reduce the wasted machine time, energy use and wastage of materials. The shift towards intelligent decisions is what will bring about the ultimate goal of achieving efficiency in operations and being an environmentally responsible person.

2.4 AI for Visibility, Transparency, and Sustainable Traceability

Supply chain visibility is a highly important aspect of sustainability because companies need not just track the movement of goods through the supply chain, but also the environmental impact per phase (Devi S et al., 2025). AI also enhances visibility as it analyses sensor, blockchain records, and data of the logistics platform and builds a composite view of supply chain operations. Through real-time checking, AI systems detect temperature, humidity, or change of carbon emissions in transportation and storage, quality, and compliance. The machine learning models can predict delays, bottlenecks, and potential sustainability violation that will see organizations take corrective measures even before unfavourable outcomes occur. Computer vision system will improve traceability by identifying defects in products, mislabelling or contamination, reduce wastage and advance ethical sourcing. The AIs in dashboards also assist the decision-makers in visualizing the sustainability metrics like the carbon footprint, energy usage, water use, and recycling rates. Such a degree of transparency helps in regulatory adherence, consumer confidence, and positively motivate businesses to go green throughout the lifecycle of supply chain.

2.5 AI and Sustainability Frameworks for Supply Chain Assessment

To measure sustainability performance, standardized structures and measures are needed and AI can improve the effectiveness and precision of such measurements considerably. Environmental, Social, and Governance (ESG) indicators assist the companies in quantifying their sustainability practices, and the process of their evaluation may be time consuming and subject to inconsistencies when conducted manually. The process of assessment is automated with the help of AI that evaluates the data on emissions, energy usage, reports on compliance with suppliers, and waste patterns to form precise sustainability scores. Life Cycle Assessment (LCA), a technique to assess the environmental effects of products, has an advantage in AI-based simulations to simulate resource consumption, pollution, and recycling in a more precise manner. AI is also useful in creating a circular economy as it can discover more recycling and remanufacturing opportunities as well as recovering materials using predictive analytics. Such evaluations can help supply chain managers to make strategic decisions to balance operation performance and long-term environmental objectives. AI is thus a facilitator, which complies with the global sustainability requirements and regulations.

2.6 Integration of AI with Emerging Technologies for Sustainable Supply Chains

Intelligent supply chain ecosystems can be achieved when AI is combined with other complementary technologies and can be self-optimizing and continuously improving. AI would be capable of simulating the functioning of a supply chain and forecasting environmental effects in different situations when used together with digital twins. This enables businesses to experiment on sustainability strategies without interfering with actual business. The IoT connection allows constant data transfer, which is processed by AI algorithms to create the insights on energy use, resources utilization, and equipment performance. Blockchain increases sustainability through achieving a transparent and tamper-proof material tracking that helps organizations to verify ethical sourcing and carbon reporting. Edge computing increases efficiency and speed of AI processing, and decreases energy usage, and real-time decision-making at remote locations like warehouses, farms, or factory plants. Autonomous vehicles and robotics also collaborate with AI to complete such a task as sorting, packaging, and transportation to minimize human error, enhance safety, and increase energy efficiency. Collectively, these combined technologies form the basis of the future autonomous, resilient and environmentally friendly supply chains.

3. AI FOR ENHANCING SUPPLY CHAIN EFFICIENCY

3.1 AI-Driven Demand Forecasting for Optimized Resource Use

One of the most important aspects of efficiency in the supply chain is the ability to predict demand accurately, and AI is an excellent solution to this role because it uses vast datasets and advanced predictive tools. The conventional forecasting is based on a lot of past sales, and less statistical tools and does not tend to provide the dynamic market behavior, seasonality, or external interference. AI-powered machine learning applications combine various data inputs, including consumer trends, market conditions, weather patterns, social media activity and economic indicators, to produce a more accurate prediction. These models keep on updating themselves with the new data as it comes and the prediction becomes more accurate with time. Improved demand planning lowers overproduction, out-of-stock and inventory wastage, which has a direct impact on the sustainability of the environment by reducing unnecessary use of resources and carbon emissions due to the unnecessary production and transportation. The match between the production and the real market needs will allow the companies to optimize the storage needs, decrease the energy consumption in the warehouses and enhance the overall efficiency of the operations. Therefore, AI will change forecasting into a reactive process and turn it into a strategic and sustainability-oriented decision-making tool.

3.2 Inventory Optimization and Automated Replenishment Using AI

The AI is also transforming inventory management because it allows tracking in real-time and smart replenishment planning that reduces waste and operational expenses. The algorithms of machine learning process the data on sales trends, supplier performance, lead times, and storage capacity in order to calculate the optimal inventory levels in every supply chain node. In contrast to the conventional methods, AI systems track changes in inventory in real-time, and when the limits are crossed, automated replenishment will occur. Such systems also forecast when a product is expected to become outdated or expire and this minimizes waste due to overstocking. Reinforcement learning models also maximize decisions by balancing holding costs, service level requirements and sustainability goals so that inventory strategies by the company are both profitable and environmentally friendly. AI solutions in inventory management guarantee that the company does not produce it unnecessarily, it saves energy in warehousing, and the environmental cost of keeping spare products is minimal. The outcome is a more agile and lean supply chain that is responsive to changes in the market without negatively affecting the sustainability goals.

Figure 1. AI for enhancing supply chain efficiency

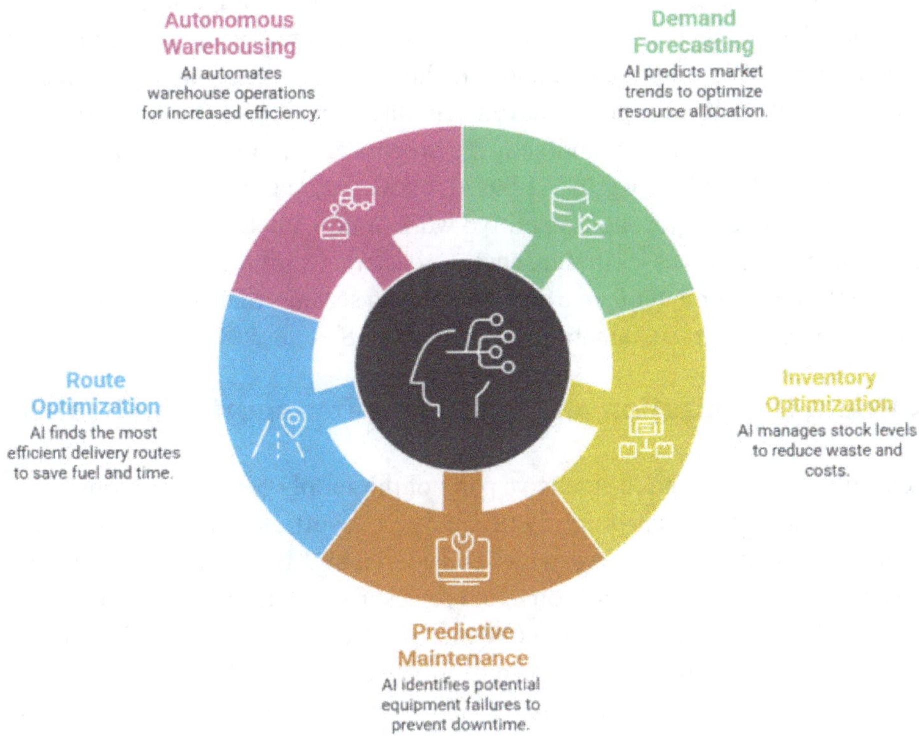

3.3 Predictive Maintenance and Smart Manufacturing Operations

The predictive maintenance is one of the essential applications of AI that helps to enhance the efficiency of the manufacturing process and reduce the wastes, downtimes, and energy. The traditional methods of maintenance, such as planned or opportunistic maintenance, can lead to unnecessary repair, random machine breakdowns, and inefficiencies contributing to the cost of operation and environmental footprint. One of the solutions that can be introduced based on AI is predictive maintenance, which can monitor the well-being of equipment, detect anomalies, and identify the early warning signs of a malfunction. Such insights can help the companies to maintain selectively where needed without any failure that leads to hampering of production and waste of resources. AI is also useful in smart manufacturing by optimizing the processes, controlling the quality, and scheduling the production in real time. The deep learning algorithms process data on manufacturing lines to detect quality problems at the beginning of the manufacturing process and minimize the production of defective products and the waste. AI-based robotics and automation also contribute to increased efficiency through repetitive work done with accuracy, worker safety, and manufacturing processes that are energy efficient. Combined, these technologies facilitate the development of smart manufacturing settings that are more focused on productivity as well as sustainability (Annamalai, S et al., 2019).

3.4 Route Optimization and Intelligent Transportation Systems

One of the most resource-intensive parts of the supply chain operations is transportation, and AI will contribute significantly to the efficiency and environmental sustainability of logistics. The variables considered by AI-driven route optimization algorithms include traffic conditions, fuel prices, road restrictions, weather predictions, and the vehicle capacity to find the most efficient routes to use in deliveries. AI can minimize the fuel usage, transportation expenses, and greenhouse gases by decreasing the distance of travel and the time spent traveling. Reinforcement learning provides the ability to make dynamic changes in routes which allows logistics systems to respond in real time to road closures or extreme weather. Other applications of AI in enhancing fleet management to make it safer and reduce operation inefficiency include predictive maintenance of vehicles, optimal load planning, and driver behavior analysis. The intelligent transportation systems based on AI will be able to plan and coordinate the delivery of multiple cars and encourage the use of multi-modal transport policy that would give preference to environmentally friendly methods of transportation, such as rail or electric vehicles. All these changes contribute to the fact that AI has become an inevitable component of the creation of more sustainable and intelligent logistics.

3.5 Autonomous Warehousing and Robotics for High Efficiency

Warehousing represents a significant aspect of the supply chain procedures, and automation using artificial intelligence influences the quality of efficiency, accuracy, and sustainability in a warehouse environment significantly in a positive way. Autonomous mobile robots (AMRs) are fitted with AI algorithms and sensors enabling them to navigate materials, replenish shelves, and pick goods with a very specific approach. These robots reduce the number of human works needed to perform repetitive tasks and maximize their output and reduce mistakes. The AI-based warehouse management systems aim at maximizing the layout planning, storage location, and routes of the orders picking in a warehouse to reduce the distance of travel in the warehouse that reduces the energy consumption and also shortens the order processing time. The computer vision technologies will automate the quality check, number of inventories, sorting of the goods and the probability of damaged or misplaced goods will be low. There will also be the potential of the AI-powered energy management to optimize the lighting, heating, and cooling based on the real-time activity of the warehouse which would result in the overall sustainability. Robotics and AI ensure the effectiveness of the working processes and reduce the environmental impact of the warehouse operation.

3.6 Case Studies of AI Improving Efficiency in Real-World Supply Chains

The application of AI in the industry is a good indication of how the technology may transform the performance of the supply chain. The enterprises use AI-inspired robots and optimization models to simplify warehousing and reduce the duration of the order processing time and energy usage. Global manufacturers apply the predictive maintenance to prevent cases of machine failures and that results in much reduction of downtime and material waste. Millions of gallons of fuel and reduced number of emissions every year in the logistics industry can be saved in the transportation industry by AI-based route optimization systems. Retailers that apply machine learning to predict product demand more efficiently which lessens wastage and overstocking of food. These researches demonstrate that AI not only enhances the performance of the operations but also makes operations more efficient and balances it with the sustainability goals. As more and more organizations adopt AI-based technologies, the global supply chain ecosystem will be taken to the stage of long-term environmental and economical sustainability.

4. AI FOR STRENGTHENING SUPPLY CHAIN RESILIENCE

4.1 Early-Warning Systems and Disruption Prediction Using AI

Supply chain resilience is a new requirement in a world where geopolitical unrests, pandemics, climatic changes, and market uncertainties are influencing the world. Artificial intelligence also plays a crucial role in predicting the breakdown and enabling early-warning solutions to ensure organisations are ready to the unexpected. The machine learning algorithms analyze the historical data and environmental indicators, news feeds, social media trends, and supplier performance metrics in order to identify weak signals of disruptions. To take an example, AI can spot anomalies in the delivery time, weather conditions, and allow the business to take initiative. The analysis of news and regulatory changes in the world is carried out with the help of natural language processing (NLP) to predict supply risks. The predictive analytics are applied to develop the risk scores of the suppliers, logistics routes, and warehouses to enable real-time tracking across the supply chain nodes. With these types of early-warning systems, companies are not as vulnerable as they offer actionable insights and a disruption occurs and companies can change production schedules, reroute shipments, or acquire other suppliers. Through strengthening resilience, AI can be applied to adjust responsive and dynamic supply chains with an active and proactive network due to effective forecasting and continuous observation.

4.2 Risk Identification and Scenario Simulation Using AI and Digital Twins

AI-based risk detection is not limited to a simple prediction but instead provides a simulation of the scenario that enables the supply chain leaders to analyze various strategic possible responses. Digital twins virtual models of the supply chain operations combine AI, IoT, and simulation technologies to model real-life conditions with a high degree of accuracy. Through these digital environments, companies have the ability to simulate the effects of all sorts of disruptions, including the closing of ports, factories, shortage of materials or natural disasters, without impacting real operations. Machine learning algorithms compare the results of simulations to point out the weak points and suggest the best recovery measures. These virtual experiments assist companies in identifying the suppliers who are most important, the routes that are most efficient and the location of inventory buffers that are most resilient. Corporates also have an opportunity to measure the sustainability effect of various reduction measures, including the replacement of environmentally friendlier means of transportation or the transfer of the production process to low-carbon plants. Through risk modeling and environmental concerns, AI-enabled digital twins can contribute to resilient and sustainable decision-making that can be long-term sustainable.

4.3 Adaptive Decision-Making and Dynamic Resource Allocation

The flexibility to adapt to changing conditions is important in resilience in supply chains. AI improves flexibility by allowing the allocation of resources dynamically in real-time on the basis of real-time data. The traditional supply chains usually utilize fixed decision rules which do not take into consideration any variability in demand, transportation capacity or reliability of suppliers. Conversely, AI-based optimization systems evaluate real-time data of sensors, transportation networks, production lines and market feeds to modify decisions in real time. Reinforcement learning algorithms will constantly learn through the results and their decision-making ability will improve in the long run. One such example is that during unexpected increases in demand, AI is able to adjust the production schedule, allocate inventory among distribution centers, or prioritize shipments based on service level requirements. Similarly, AI systems will be able to identify other suppliers, redistribute inventory, and propose the most effective logistics routes in case of disruptions. This dynamic coordination helps to prevent the stockouts, reduce delays, and continuity in the course of world operations. Despite the pressure the companies are able to come up with stable, efficient and environmentally responsible supply chains even in instances where they are disrupted.

4.4 Enhancing Visibility and End-to-End Traceability Through AI

Resilience is based on visibility since companies cannot deal with risks that they are not aware of. AI promotes visibility along the entire chain by combining information of various stakeholders and transforming it into meaningful insights. IoT devices allow to track shipments, equipment, and raw materials in real-time and analyze this information to identify anomalies and possible risks using AI algorithms. The models of machine learning are able to make predictions regarding the arrival of shipments, detect delays before they happen, and point out inefficiencies in the logistics routes. Computer vision technologies provide traceability in manufacturing and warehousing through detection of defects in products, label validation, and tracking products across the facilities. Supplier documentation and compliance reports can also be broken down into NLP tools to determine sustainability risks or ethical issues. The AI-driven dashboards will present the flow of goods, carbon emissions, energy consumption, and performance indicators at all supply chain levels and allow managers to make timely informed decisions. Increased visibility does not only increase the resilience of operations, but also creates confidence between consumers, suppliers, and regulators, as sustainability and ethical practices are always adhered to.

4.5 Supplier Risk Assessment and Multi-Tier Network Optimization

The vulnerability of suppliers is a common cause of supply chain disruption particularly in multi-tiered networks where visibility diminishes as the suppliers get more remote. AI is a great enhancement to the assessment of supplier risks because it examines various data sets including financial stability reports, ESG ratings, delivery performance, political conditions, and environmental compliance records. Machine learning models can group suppliers according to the risk types and estimate the possible failures before they can influence the downstream activities. Organizations are able to assess the effect of sustainability, including carbon footprint or labor standards, so the reduction of risks is in line with ethical goals. AI aids in optimization of the multi-tier network by visualizing the intricate relationships between suppliers and finding dependencies that may pose a threat to resilience. Through network topology, AI applications suggest measures like diversification of suppliers, reshoring, or creation of strategic inventory. These will enhance resilience through less reliance on individual suppliers and promote sustainable sourcing procedures along the global supply chain.

4.6 Case Studies Demonstrating AI-Driven Supply Chain Resilience

There are a number of practical cases that show that AI can improve supply chain resilience and aid sustainability objectives. As an example, many firms apply AI-based predictive analytics to track shipping routes in the world to assist the logistics firms to predict port congestion and reroute ships in order to minimize delays and fuel consumption. Pharmaceutical firms used AI-based prediction systems to predict supply shortages and focus on the distribution of vaccines during the COVID-19 pandemic. Many other companies employ AI-based digital twins to create the experience of disruption and assess the environmental effect of various recovery options and attain both resilience and sustainability. Likewise, auto companies are using AI to evaluate the risks of their suppliers at various levels and provide continuity in case of semiconductor shortages. The examples prove that AI is not merely a technical improvement but a strategic resource that can be used to improve global supply chain resilience.

5. AI FOR ENVIRONMENTAL SUSTAINABILITY AND CIRCULAR SUPPLY CHAINS

5.1 AI-Enabled Carbon Tracking and Emissions Reduction

Environmental sustainability in supply chains starts with the realization of the carbon emission, which is minimized in the production process, in the transportation process, in the warehousing process, and in the end-of-life process. AI is also a major advancement in carbon tracking, as it is able to input and process emissions information of sensors, logistics, and manufacturing devices. The conventional method of carbon accounting is prone to aggregated and annual approximations which are not accurate. On the other hand, AI-driven technologies will offer real-time tracking and provide a comprehensive understanding of the emissions at each supply chain location. ML algorithms have the ability to identify high-emission activities, e.g. inefficient transport routes, energy-intensive production processes, or ineffective equipment performance. These insights allow companies to introduce specific improvement measures, including the transition to renewable power sources, fleet management, or the modernization of equipment. There is also the support of AI in emissions forecasting, where organizations are able to predict the future environmental impact, basing on the current operational trends. With the integration of sustainability into the daily decision-making process, AI allows companies to generate the smallest carbon footprint and invest in global climate objectives, at the same time saving on expenditures on energy use.

5.2 Energy Optimization in Manufacturing, Warehousing, and Logistics

Environmental sustainability is highly energy efficiency, and AI can be instrumental in streamlining energy consumption in various functions of supply chains(Ene, S et al., 2016). In the manufacturing industry, AI-based energy management systems will track the use of machines, detect where there are inefficiencies, and suggest the best operating conditions to minimize wastage of energy. Such systems are able to modify equipment configurations, production programs and workload allocations in real time to reduce the use of energy during peak times. AI is used to optimize heating, cooling, and lighting in warehouses depending on the occupancy rates, weather, and activity of the warehouse. Machine learning and smart sensors can be used to minimize wasteful energy consumption, minimizing operations expenses and environmental footprint(Derpich, I et al., 2022). AI in logistics is able to optimize routes, increase load, and anticipate vehicle maintenance. AI-powered fleet analytics also assist in tracking driver behavior, which ensures that a behavior that minimizes fuel usage is encouraged. With the incorporation of AI-driven energy optimization approaches, supply chain activities become more cost-efficient and environmentally friendly.

5.3 Waste Reduction and Intelligent Resource Recovery Through AI

The production of waste, packaging, and disposal of products are a significant problem to the environment. AI can help in this problem by encouraging waste minimization projects and allowing more effective resource recovery(Jogarao, M et al., 2024). Machine learning software examines production data to determine patterns that relate to wastage of materials, like surplus scrap, defective products or ineffective cutting operations. AI eliminates wastage by suggesting changes in machine settings, production processes, or raw materials. In packaging, AI-based design applications produce a lighter and more sustainable packaging material, without affecting its durability. To recycle and recover resources, AI-based robotic technology with computer vision can correctly sort waste streams, enhancing recycling, and minimizing contamination. Predictive analytics can also assist business in identifying the optimal moments when it is possible to repair, remanufacture or recycle a product, which is in line with the principles of the circular economy. By accurately tracking and making smart decisions, AI will increase the efficiency of resources and turn waste into a source of value generation(Lakhouit, A. 2025).

5.4 Circular Economy Models Supported by Predictive Analytics

The circular supply chains focus on reuse, repair, remanufacturing, and recycling of products, and AI is the core of these models as it helps to make precise predictions and manage the lifecycle. Predictive analytics have the ability to predict the degradation of products, their useful life and the most suitable end-of-life management strategies. This will enable businesses to know at what time the products need to be recalled to be refurbished, what parts can be re-used and how the materials can be re-introduced into new production processes. The remanufacturing products using AI are also going to be aligned to the market demands, which will decrease overproduction and waste. Also, the digital product passport, which utilizes blockchain, AI technologies, logs material composition, usage history, and environmental impact during the product lifecycle, and allows more efficient resource recovery. Simulation of AI can be used to assess the strategies of the circular economy, including the materials substitution, optimization of the reverse logistics, and waste-to-resource routes, which can assist companies to adopt environmentally friendly and economically efficient solutions. This artificial intelligence plus circular economy synergy encourages sustainability in supply chains in the long term.

5.5 AI for Sustainable Procurement and Ethical Sourcing

Sustainable procurement is a very important part of environmental responsibility as the sourcing of the raw materials and components is done in a manner that is ethical and minimally harmful to the environment. The AI improves the procurement activities, analyzing the data of suppliers, ESG performance, compliance reports, and environmental certifications. The machine learning models are able to assess the suppliers on the basis of their carbon emission, energy consumption, waste disposal, and compliance with international sustainability regulations. This helps the companies to select suppliers who can support their sustainability objectives and shun those with a high risk to the environment. Ethical sourcing is also supported by AI, which identifies anomalies or breaches of supply chain records, including fake certifications or underestimated data on the environmental impact. The news articles, social media content, and regulatory notices can be analyzed with the help of natural language processing tools to detect possible sustainability violations. Through combining AI-based supplier assessment systems, organizations enhance their adherence to the environmental stewardship and reduce the risks of unsustainable or unethical sourcing approaches.

6. CHALLENGES, RISKS, AND ETHICAL CONSIDERATIONS

6.1 Data Scarcity, Quality Issues, and Integration Challenges

One of the greatest obstacles to successful implementation of AI in the supply chain management towards sustainability is the accessibility, quality and assimilation of information. AI systems need data in high quantities and quality, and in timely form but most organizations face the challenge of disjointed data stored on different platforms that are not interconnected like ERP systems, logistics databases, warehouse management systems and supplier networks. Data format inconsistencies, missing entries and outdated information undermine AI model performance. SMEs usually do not have access to large datasets to run machine learning, which leads to biased or partial results. Also, the necessity to unite the information available in various sources including IoT sensors, supplier portals, transportation, and worldwide production plants are quite challenging technically. The issue with legacy systems is also that it makes integration more complex since it might not have the ability to support real time analytics or even modern data standards. These issues limit the scalability of AI projects on sustainability and their accuracy. The quality of data, its standardization and interoperability are the key aspects that guarantee the delivery of meaningful results and, thus, the data governance and digital infrastructure should be invested in to make even the most advanced AI solutions effective.

6.2 High Computational and Energy Demands of AI Technologies

The application of AI technologies, specifically, deep learning and large-scale optimization models, requires a significant amount of computational power, which can pose a significant threat to the environment. The power required to train complex models is high and in most instances, this requires the utilization of energy consuming data centers, which use non-renewable sources of energy. This creates an ironic problem because, on the one hand, AI is expected to facilitate sustainability, and, on the other hand, its consumption of energy will probably become the opposite of the climate agenda. Some of these effects may be mitigated with edge computing, which does more computing nearer to the data source but several applications in supply chains continue to rely on cloud computing that is centrally located. The companies should weigh the benefits of AI-driven insights against the environmental cost of adopting such systems. Moreover, not every organization has the financial strength to invest in high-performance computing infrastructure. The expenses of upkeep, updating and scaling AI systems are prohibitive, particularly to small supply chain partners. It is essential to make AI technologies environmentally friendly and cost-effective so that their adoption could be promoted in the long term. This has given rise to the growing interest in the notion of green AI - methods and models that aim to reduce computational costs but preserve good performance.

6.3 Bias, Transparency, and Ethical Considerations in AI Decision-Making

With the growth of AI systems in the supply chain, including the selection of suppliers, risk reduction, optimization of routes, and the allocation of resources, ethical issues are more critical. Algorithms bias is one of the significant challenges that may occur when the AI models are trained on unbalanced or unfinished data. AI can support, rather than solve, inequalities or unsustainable practices in the past when it is based on historical data. As an illustration, a model that is trained using data of suppliers who are not well compliant with the environment will suggest the same suppliers depending on their cost but not necessarily on sustainability. Another important issue is transparency. Most AI models, in particular the deep learning systems, are black boxes, and it is hard to comprehend how they arrive at decisions by the supply chain managers. This unaccountability may decrease the confidence in AI and make it harder to adhere to sustainability laws. The human implication of AI is also to be taken into account in ethical decisions, such as the loss of jobs in warehousing, manufacturing, and logistics as more and more tasks become automated. To make AI responsible in sustainable supply chains, it is crucial to ensure fairness, accountability and human oversight.

6.4 Cybersecurity Threats and Vulnerabilities in AI-Driven Supply Chains

The threat of cybersecurity is increased as the supply chains are becoming more digital and more interconnected. The AI systems rely on the ongoing data stream of sensors, cloud infrastructure, systems of suppliers and transportation systems(Prabhu, D et al., 2025). Such interconnectedness offers a lot of points of entry of cyberattacks. The violations of the data, ransom, and system manipulation may disrupt the work, steal confidential information, and have severe financial and environmental consequences. To give an example, when the attackers disrupt routing algorithms or the information on surveillance of emissions, firms may wind up having to make sustainability commitments against their will, or may find themselves on the wrong side of fines. The AI models per se are also vulnerable to adversarial attacks, where malicious individuals attempt to modify the input information to provide inaccurate predictions or judgments. In this respect, cybersecurity must be integrated on all stages of AI application, both data collection and model and system training and integration and real-time operation. The main elements that can be used to protect AI-based supply chains are regular audits, encryption, secure authentication systems, and anomaly detection models. The efficiency and legitimacy of AI in the sustainability process can be undermined unless there is a robust cybersecurity strategy.

6.5 Regulatory, Environmental, and Socio-Economic Concerns

There are critical regulatory and socio-economic concerns regarding the growing application of AI in supply chains. Government across the world are formulating policies to make AI transparent, ethical and environmentally responsible. Nonetheless, the fact that there are no standard regulations in different countries complicates the operation of the global supply chain. Firms have to work around different regulations on data privacy, emissions reporting, AI regulation, and work standards. Carbon tracking, waste reporting, and verification of sustainable practices are also environmental regulations that need accurate tracking, which is only possible through the help of the reliable AI system. Socio-economic issues are associated with the effects of AI on workforce and employment. Automation can lead to a decrease in the number of people who have to be employed in warehousing, manufacturing, and logistics, which poses a threat of job displacement. Meanwhile, the implementation of AI requires the development of new data analytics-related and automation-related and digital-related skills. It is necessary to make sure that there are fair workforce transitions to prevent the increase of economic inequality. Governments, industries, and academic institutions should work together in addressing these regulatory and socio-economic concerns to make sure that AI is used in a way that will add value to the sustainability.

6.6 Limitations of Current AI Models in Addressing Sustainability Goals

Although AI presents effective solutions to enhance sustainability, existing models are also limited to an extent that they cannot maximize their potential. Most AI systems are also designed to achieve efficiency or cost-saving goals, and not necessarily the environmental effect in the long term. This distortion may be translated into making decisions that cause more short-term benefits but at the expense of sustainability objectives. Also, the majority of models do not take into consideration complicated environmental factors like the disappearance of a biodiversity, water shortage, or ecological decay in the long-term. These problems necessitate the formulation of multi-objective optimization models that can be used to strike a balance between the economic, operational, and environmental performance. The other weakness is that AI is unable to comprehend human judgment and contextual knowledge that are critical in decisions regarding sustainability aspects. Another area where AI can not perform well is in highly unpredictable settings like those that are influenced by climate change where past data might not be a true reflection of the future. Thus, the cooperation between humans and AI is essential in order to get significant results in sustainability.

7. FUTURE DIRECTIONS AND OPPORTUNITIES

7.1 Integration of AI with Blockchain, IoT, and Edge Computing

The future of sustainable supply chain management is the integration of various new technologies, AI being the main intelligence layer. Combining AI, blockchain, IoT, and edge computing will produce very transparent, efficient and sustainable supply chains. Blockchain guarantees secure and tamperproof sharing of data among suppliers, manufacturers, transporters and retailers (Abitha, R et al., 2026). This, coupled with AI analytics, makes it possible to verify sustainability claims with some degree of confidence, report on carbon emissions, and conduct ethical sourcing activities. IoT sensors continuously monitor real-time information about temperature, energy use, health of the machine, and conditions of transportation. By putting this information into AI models, the predictability level is elevated, and one can make proactive decisions. Meanwhile, edge computing allows reducing the latency and energy cost of cloud computing because AI computation can be carried out closer to data sources. It is especially convenient with distant warehouses, plants or transportation groups in which immediate responsiveness is required. A combination of these technologies forms a more visible, less harmful to the environment, and capable of making decisions in an autonomous manner cyber-physical ecosystem. Their adoption is a major opportunity to improve sustainability and resiliency in global supply chains.

7.2 Autonomous and Self-Optimizing Supply Chain Systems

The other key trend that will come in the future is the evolution of autonomous supply chains that can self-monitor, learn and optimize processes with minimal human intervention. These systems are based on reinforcement learning, digital twins and real-time operational information and automatically adjust workflow. To provide an example, an autonomous supply chain can independently reroute deliveries when it becomes disrupted, scale production schedules to match shifts in demand, or handle inventory to meet sustainability goals like the decrease of emissions. Digital twins will allow organizations to simulate complicated supply chain networks in real-time, predicting the effects of disruptions, events of climate change, or resource shortages. As the future of AI becomes more advanced, supply chains will advance to full autonomy where many processes, including procurement, production, logistics, and reverse logistics will be able to interact. The change does not only make it more efficient and less harmful to the environment but also makes it more resilient as it allows systems to operate effectively even when the conditions are uncertain or unstable. One of the most radical opportunities of the future is the autonomy of supply chains, which is a combination of intelligence, adaptability, and sustainability.

7.3 Human–AI Collaboration for Sustainable Decision-Making

Although AI will mechanize most supply chain operations, human skills will still be needed to influence the sustainability strategies. The future will be based on the cooperation between humans and AI, where the latter will be able to offer intelligent suggestions, and the former will have to use their judgment, moral aspects, and strategic approaches to the problem. The purpose of AI will be more of augmentation than automation, to assist decision-makers in making trade-offs among cost, efficiency, and environmental impact. As an example, AI will be able to process thousands of scenarios involving emissions reduction or resource optimization, and human beings will have to decide what solutions will be in line with the overall organizational objectives and social responsibilities. It will be essential to train supply chain professionals to operate with AI tools. This involves the creation of digital fluency, ethical AI knowledge, and sustainability-consciousness. The companies will also be forced to establish collaborative spaces that will promote knowledge exchange between human labor and AI-powered system. Supply chains can shift towards responsible and balanced decision-making models by integrating machine intelligence with human creativity and values.

7.4 Expansion of Green AI and Low-Energy Models

With the further realization of the environmental consequences of AI systems, the creation of energy-efficient or so-called green AI systems will become one of the key trends of the future. Green AI is aimed at minimizing the computational needs of training and deploying machine learning models, which also reduces carbon emissions that come with the adoption of AI. Such methods as model compression, federated learning, transfer learning, and quantization will gain increasing popularity, allowing businesses to execute powerful AI algorithms on smaller devices and local servers(Prabhu, D et al., 2025). These energy-efficient models enable sustainability by ensuring that big data centers are not required as much and that reliance on cloud-based infrastructure is avoided. Green AI is perfectly aligned with the overall objectives of sustainable supply chains in which lessening environmental effect is a strategic objective. With increasing demand of AI to support industries, energy-efficient algorithms will make sure that AI implementation is beneficial to sustainability goals and will not place more environmental pressure on the environment.

7.5 Policy, Regulation, and Global Sustainability Frameworks

The changing global policies and regulations will also determine the future of AI in sustainable supply chains. Governments and international organizations are making it one of the most emphasized aspects because of the need of ethical AI, carbon transparency and sustainable business practices. The companies might have to report the carbon footprint of AI activities, offer algorithmic fairness, and accept digital solutions that facilitate environmental responsibility, as imposed by new laws. The standards which will influence the implementation of AI include sustainability certification, guidelines on green compliance, and international carbon disclosure standards among others. The law can also be formulated to hold organizations accountable in cases of making wrong or negative decisions of AI. This will force businesses to come up with AI tools that are legible, understandable and ethical. Meanwhile, the governments can encourage innovation by providing incentives in the use of green technology, funding of research, and cooperation with other countries. The convergence of AI and policy-making is a chance to spearhead the massive sustainability reforms in the supply chains of the world.

8.CONCLUSION

Artificial Intelligence is a concept that has emerged as a disruptive trend in the future of sustainability in supply chain management, which offers unprecedented efficiency, resilience, and environmental responsibility. Increased production, logistics, warehousing and procurement processes AI enables companies to waste and emission reduction, maximized resource use in production, improved forecasting and automation, and optimization. The integration of AI with the other technologies, such as IoT, blockchain, and digital twins, further enhances the supply chain visibility and transparency and allows to monitor the supply chain in real-time and make proactive decisions. Because of the increasing complexity and vulnerability of global supply chains to incidents, AI-based solutions provide early-warning systems, risk assessment, and reactionary measures that significantly enhance resilience without affecting sustainability goals. However, AI implementation in sustainable supply chains also have major issues. These problems should be addressed such as data quality, computational load, cybersecurity risks, regulatory uncertainty, as well as ethical transparency and bias. In order to solve these challenges, it needs strong governance frameworks, investment in digital infrastructure and intersectoral collaboration. The collaboration between human and AI should also be a priority in the organization and organizations should equip supply chain professionals with knowledge that they can apply to derive AI insights and implement them to responsible decision-making. The use of AI in achieving the long-term sustainability objective will grow in the future with the creation of green AI, autonomous systems, and circular economy models. Supply chain management in the future will increasingly be founded on smart, networked and self-organizing ecosystems capable of balancing performance of business with stewardship of the environment. By adopting AI responsibly and strategically, organisations will be able to create a more efficient, resilient and aligned supply chain that will meet the needs of global sustainability.

REFERENCES

Abitha, R., Rajendar, S., Mangaiyarkarasi, D., Anto, G. L., & Girija, P. (2026). A Comprehensive Chapter on Edge Computing, Analytics, and AI Model Optimization for Industrial and Healthcare Applications. *Building Data-Driven Edge Systems for Business Success*, 59-90. DOI: 10.4018/979-8-3373-1147-0.ch003

Annamalai, S., Udendhran, R., & Vimal, S. (2019). Cloud-based predictive maintenance and machine monitoring for intelligent manufacturing for automobile industry. In *Novel practices and trends in grid and cloud computing* (pp. 74–89). IGI Global. DOI: 10.4018/978-1-5225-9023-1.ch006

Derpich, I., Sepúlveda, J. M., Barraza, R., & Castro, F. (2022). Warehouse Optimization: Energy Efficient Layout and Design. *Mathematics*, *10*(10), 1705. DOI: 10.3390/math10101705

Devi, S. D., Balasubramanian, K., Adaikkammai, A., Thilagam, T., Vinoth, R., Sathya, V., & Subramanian, R. S. (2025). Advancing Sustainable Development Through Green Economics. In Ben Ltaifa, M., & Derbali, A. (Eds.), *AI Methods for Environmental Protection and Resource Conservation* (pp. 47–82). IGI Global Scientific Publishing. DOI: 10.4018/979-8-3373-3246-8.ch003

Ene, S., Küçükoğlu, İ., Aksoy, A., & Öztürk, N. (2016). A genetic algorithm for minimizing energy consumption in warehouses. *Energy*, *114*, 973–980. DOI: 10.1016/j.energy.2016.08.045

Jogarao, M., Lakshmanna, B. C., & Naidu, S. T. (2024). Ai-enabled circular economy management for sustainable smart cities: integrating artificial intelligence in resource optimization and waste reduction. In *Smart cities and circular economy* (pp. 83–96). Emerald Publishing Limited. DOI: 10.1108/978-1-83797-957-820241008

Lakhouit, A. (2025). Revolutionizing urban solid waste management with AI and IoT: A review of smart solutions for waste collection, sorting, and recycling. *Results in Engineering*, *104018*, 104018. Advance online publication. DOI: 10.1016/j.rineng.2025.104018

Min, H. (2010). Artificial intelligence in supply chain management: Theory and applications. *International Journal of Logistics*, *13*(1), 13–39. DOI: 10.1080/13675560902736537

Power, D. (2005). Supply chain management integration and implementation: A literature review. *Supply Chain Management*, *10*(4), 252–263. DOI: 10.1108/13598540510612721

Prabhu, D., Sudha, L., MR, P. K., Adaikkammai, A., Aparna, P., & Sathya, V. (2025). Machine Learning in Cybersecurity: Challenges, Applications, and Future Directions. *Exploiting Machine Learning for Robust Security*, 25-48. DOI: 10.4018/979-8-3693-7758-1.ch002

Stadtler, H. (2014). Supply chain management: An overview. *Supply chain management and advanced planning: Concepts, models, software, and case studies*, 3-28. DOI: 10.1007/978-3-642-55309-7_1

Suganya, P., Siva, S. R., Ananthi, S. N., Thilagam, T., Elavarasi, J., Anto, G. L., & Girija, P. (2026). The role of artificial intelligence in transforming supply chain management. In *Transformative Impact of AI in Supply Chain Management* (pp. 271–294). IGI Global Scientific Publishing. DOI: 10.4018/979-8-3373-0923-1.ch011

Tsintotas, K. A., Moutsis, S. N., Kansizoglou, I., Konstantinidis, F. K., & Gasteratos, A. (2024, May). The advent of ai in modern supply chain. In *Olympus International Conference on Supply Chains* (pp. 333-343). Cham: Springer Nature Switzerland. DOI: 10.1007/978-3-031-69344-1_25

Wu, H., Liu, J., & Liang, B. (2025). AI-driven supply chain transformation in Industry 5.0: Enhancing resilience and sustainability. *Journal of the Knowledge Economy*, *16*(1), 3826–3868. DOI: 10.1007/s13132-024-01999-6

Chapter 4
AI-Enabled Forecasting and Performance Optimization in Sustainable Supply Chains: A Neural Network Approach Using Digital SCOR®

Mariem Mrad
http://orcid.org/0000-0002-2377-1401
Faculty of Economics and Management, University of Sfax, Tunisia

Younes Boujelbene
Faculty of Economics and Management, University of Sfax, Tunisia

ABSTRACT

This chapter presents a computational framework for forecasting supply chain performance using augmented SCOR®4.0 metrics and Multilayer Perceptron (MLP) neural networks. The authors operationalize an eight-module SCOR® architecture, incorporating digital, cost, working capital, cash cycle, responsiveness, reliability, and risk dimensions. Each MLP model is optimized through systematic topology selection, normalized input processing, and rigorous cross-validation. Empirical results demonstrate high predictive accuracy, with correlation coefficients exceeding 0.997 and statistical tests confirming model reliability. Comparative analysis indicates that MLP-based forecasting significantly outperforms traditional linear

DOI: 10.4018/979-8-3373-7847-3.ch004

methods, capturing non-linear interactions among operational, financial, and sustainability indicators. The chapter highlights the practical utility of AI-driven models for decision support in complex, cross-border supply chains.

1. INTRODUCTION

As the global economy approaches the end of 2025, the discipline of Supply Chain Management (SCM) stands at a critical inflection point. The era of relatively predictable, cost-optimized, and lean global trade flows that characterized the early 2000s has definitively given way to a far more turbulent operating environment. Contemporary supply chains are increasingly shaped by an intensified form of "VUCA" conditions, Volatility, Uncertainty, Complexity, and Ambiguity, particularly within cross-border logistics, which remains the backbone of international trade.

This transformation is driven by the convergence of three dominant forces. First, geopolitical realignments and the restructuring of global trade routes, often referred to as *friend-shoring* or *nearshoring*, have disrupted established sourcing and distribution patterns (Balfaqih et al., 2016). Second, the rapid diffusion of Industry 4.0 and the emerging principles of Industry 5.0 have accelerated digitalization, automation, and data-driven decision-making across logistics networks. Third, environmental sustainability has evolved from a voluntary corporate objective into a regulatory and societal imperative, fundamentally redefining acceptable standards of supply chain performance (Frikha & Mrad, 2025).

Consequently, the traditional perception of the supply chain as a linear sequence of activities, extending from raw material extraction to final consumption, has become obsolete. Modern supply chains increasingly resemble complex "supply webs" or ecosystems in which information flows are as critical as physical flows (Unahabhokha et al., 2007). In cross-border contexts, this complexity is further amplified. A minor operational disruption, such as the absence of a digital compliance certificate at a customs checkpoint, may propagate rapidly across the network and trigger production stoppages in distant regions (Akkoç, 2012). Such cascading effects illustrate that operational, digital, and environmental performance dimensions are now tightly coupled rather than independent (Mrad et al., 2025).

In parallel, the regulatory environment governing cross-border trade has tightened substantially. Instruments such as the European Union's Carbon Border Adjustment Mechanism (CBAM) have effectively monetized carbon emissions, transforming environmental indicators into direct financial liabilities (Ahi & Searcy, 2015). As a result, supply chain performance can no longer be evaluated solely through cost efficiency and delivery speed, but must explicitly incorporate carbon intensity, digital resilience, regulatory compliance, and cybersecurity robustness.

Despite these profound structural changes, the tools traditionally used to measure and manage supply chain performance have evolved only marginally. Most organizations continue to rely heavily on descriptive analytics, including dashboards, scorecards, and periodic reports that summarize past performance. While such approaches remain useful for benchmarking and accountability, they suffer from an inherent limitation: they explain what has already occurred rather than anticipating what is likely to happen. This "rear-view mirror" orientation restricts proactive decision-making in environments characterized by rapid disruption and interdependence.

Traditional Performance Measurement Systems (PMS), including conventional implementations of the SCOR® model, are largely deterministic and static (Beamon, 1999; Shepherd & Günter, 2006; Efendigil & Önüt, 2012). They implicitly assume stable and linear relationships between operational decisions and outcomes. However, cross-border logistics networks behave as complex adaptive systems in which non-linear interactions, feedback loops, and stochastic disturbances are common. Under such conditions, deterministic assumptions may lead to misleading conclusions and suboptimal managerial actions.

Artificial Intelligence (AI)–driven analytics, and particularly Artificial Neural Networks (ANNs), offer promising capabilities for addressing this complexity. By learning non-linear patterns directly from data, ANNs can integrate heterogeneous inputs, including operational SCOR metrics, digital signals, market volatility indicators, and sustainability variables. This predictive paradigm aligns with the broader streams of predictive analytics, digital supply chain transformation, and sustainability performance measurement, which advocate forward-looking decision support rather than retrospective reporting (Castelo-Branco et al., 2019; Gusmão Caiado et al., 2020).

Nevertheless, AI should not be viewed as a standalone solution. Its effectiveness depends critically on structured, interpretable, and standardized performance representations. Applying AI to poorly defined or unstructured indicators may generate opaque or unreliable outputs. In this respect, the SCOR® model remains highly relevant, as it provides a hierarchical and standardized taxonomy of processes and metrics that can serve as a coherent foundation for predictive modeling. Thus, structured performance frameworks and data-driven intelligence should be viewed as complementary rather than competing approaches (Maestrini et al., 2017; Ivanov, 2020).

However, despite growing interest in AI-enabled supply chain analytics, important gaps persist in the literature. First, most SCOR-based performance systems remain descriptive rather than predictive. Second, existing ANN forecasting studies typically address isolated operational variables instead of integrated multi-attribute performance architectures (Tavana et al., 2016). Third, digital maturity and environmental sustainability indicators are rarely embedded formally within standardized SCOR structures. Consequently, a unified methodology capable of combining structured performance measurement with predictive intelligence remains largely absent (Yu et al., 2020).

To address these limitations, this chapter proposes a methodological framework that integrates an extended SCOR structure with modular neural network forecasting. Hereafter, this extended framework is referred to consistently as *Augmented SCOR® 4.0*.

The proposed Augmented SCOR® 4.0 introduces a new Level 1 performance attribute termed *Digital & Sustainable Maturity (DSM)*, defined as the organization's capability to leverage digital technologies, interoperable data infrastructures, and environmentally responsible practices to achieve resilient, low-carbon, and regulation-compliant supply chain operations. This construct complements traditional SCOR dimensions, Reliability, Responsiveness, Agility, Cost, and Asset Management Efficiency, by explicitly capturing emerging digitalization and sustainability drivers of performance.

The purpose of this chapter is to propose and validate a methodological framework that integrates an augmented SCOR® 4.0 model with MLP neural networks for predictive performance management in cross-border logistics.

Specifically, this chapter pursues four interrelated objectives:

1. *Redefining Performance:* To extend the traditional SCOR framework into an augmented SCOR® 4.0 model by explicitly incorporating dimensions related to digital maturity and environmental sustainability, with particular relevance to cross-border logistics.
2. *Developing a Predictive Engine:* To design and train MLP-based neural network architectures capable of predicting strategic Level 2 performance attributes from operational Level 3 metrics.
3. *Validating Robustness:* To empirically assess the reliability and statistical significance of the proposed models through cross-validation techniques and paired hypothesis testing.
4. *Enabling Proactive Management:* To demonstrate how AI-enabled forecasting facilitates a shift from retrospective performance reporting toward prospective diagnosis, scenario analysis, and informed managerial decision-making.

This chapter makes three primary contributions to research and practice. (1) Conceptually, it formalizes the Augmented SCOR® 4.0 framework and introduces Digital & Sustainable Maturity as a new performance dimension. (2) Computationally, it proposes a modular architecture of interconnected MLP models for multi-attribute forecasting. (3) Managerially, it advances a predictive control-tower perspective that enables proactive rather than retrospective supply chain governance.

The scope of the study spans the period from 2018 to 2025, capturing accelerated digital transformation and regulatory evolution within global logistics. The analysis focuses specifically on cross-border supply chains, where interoperability challenges, regulatory complexity, and sustainability constraints exert particularly strong pressures on performance measurement and decision-making. By combining structured performance modeling with predictive intelligence, the proposed framework seeks to support more resilient, data-driven, and sustainable supply chain operations.

2. LITERATURE REVIEW: FROM METRICS TO INTELLIGENCE

2.1 The Evolution of Supply Chain Management

To appreciate the necessity of AI-enabled forecasting in contemporary logistics, it is essential to trace the theoretical evolution of SCM. In its early conceptualization during the late twentieth century, SCM was primarily driven by cost efficiency and operational coordination. Seminal work by Mentzer et al. (2001) defined SCM as the systemic coordination of traditional business functions within and across organizations to improve long-term performance. Performance, in this context, was largely synonymous with efficiency, encapsulated by the classical objective of delivering the right product, in the right quantity, to the right place, at the right time.

During the 2010s, this efficiency-centric paradigm was progressively challenged. The growing volatility of global markets and shorter product life cycles shifted managerial attention toward agility and leanness. Simultaneously, scholars began to question the sufficiency of purely economic performance metrics. Seuring (2013) and related contributions introduced the concept of Sustainable Supply Chain Management (SSCM), emphasizing that economic outcomes are inseparable from environmental stewardship and social responsibility. This marked a critical broadening of the performance concept beyond cost and speed.

The next paradigm shift emerged around resilience. The systemic disruptions triggered by the COVID-19 pandemic exposed the vulnerability of highly optimized, just-in-time cross-border supply networks. Bastas and Liyanage (2018) argued that a viable supply chain must possess the capacity for self-maintenance and survival through continuous adaptation and redesign. Resilience thus became a central performance objective, complementing efficiency and sustainability.

By the mid-2020s, the discourse has advanced toward the notion of the *Cognitive Supply Chain*. Calatayud et al. (2019) describe this stage as a level of maturity in which supply chains move beyond execution toward perception, reasoning, and autonomous decision-making. Cognitive supply chains leverage advanced analytics and artificial intelligence to sense disruptions, learn from historical patterns, and dynamically reconfigure themselves. This progressive evolution, from cost efficiency to agility, resilience, and cognition, implies a corresponding transformation in how supply chain performance must be measured and managed.

2.2 Performance Measurement Systems (PMS): The Central Role of SCOR®

2.2.1 The Need for Performance Measurement Systems

The importance of performance measurement is succinctly captured by Lord Kelvin's well-known assertion that improvement is impossible without measurement. In the context of SCM, a PMS comprises a coherent set of metrics designed to quantify the efficiency and effectiveness of supply chain activities. Nudurupati et al. (2011) emphasized that well-designed PMSs play a critical role in enhancing organizational communication, motivating employees, and identifying areas requiring corrective or strategic intervention.

Designing an effective PMS for cross-border logistics, however, presents particular challenges. International supply chains are characterized by a multiplicity of actors, including manufacturers, third-party logistics providers, freight forwarders, customs authorities, and last-mile carriers. A single shipment may traverse several organizational and regulatory boundaries, each governed by different objectives and information systems. This "multi-actor" complexity necessitates a standardized measurement language capable of aligning performance evaluation across heterogeneous entities.

2.2.2 The SCOR® Model Architecture

The SCOR® model, introduced by the Supply Chain Council in 1996, was developed precisely to address the need for standardization. SCOR provides an integrated framework that links supply chain processes, performance metrics, best practices, and workforce competencies within a unified reference model.

The SCOR framework is structured hierarchically across three primary levels.

At Level 1 (Strategic), the model defines the scope and objectives of the supply chain and articulates five core performance attributes: Reliability, Responsiveness, Agility, Cost, and Asset Management.

Level 2 (Tactical) focuses on supply chain configuration decisions, such as the selection between Make-to-Stock and Make-to-Order strategies.

Level 3 (Operational) contains detailed diagnostic metrics that enable the monitoring and control of specific activities, including indicators such as schedule achievement or cost of goods sold.

A comprehensive review by Estampe et al. (2013), which examined sixteen different supply chain evaluation models, concluded that SCOR® offered superior global applicability due to its holistic and integrative nature. Its standardized structure enables consistent benchmarking and facilitates "apples-to-apples" comparisons across industries and geographic regions, making it particularly valuable in cross-border contexts.

2.2.3 Limitations of Traditional SCOR®

Despite its widespread adoption and conceptual robustness, the traditional SCOR model has been subject to several well-documented limitations. First, SCOR-based performance aggregation is often linear, relying on weighted averages or additive scoring mechanisms. Such approaches fail to capture the non-linear trade-offs inherent in logistics systems, where improvements in one dimension, such as agility, may generate disproportionate increases in cost.

Second, earlier versions of SCOR inadequately addressed sustainability concerns. Environmental and social factors were typically treated as supplementary best practices rather than embedded as core performance attributes. In the context of stringent climate policies and cross-border regulatory mechanisms emerging by 2025, this peripheral treatment is no longer sufficient.

Most critically, SCOR remains fundamentally diagnostic rather than predictive. As highlighted by Moharamkhani et al. (2017) and Lima-Junior and Carpinetti (2019), SCOR excels at explaining historical performance but offers no intrinsic mechanism for forecasting future outcomes. For instance, while the model can report that the order fulfillment cycle time averaged twelve days in the previous month, it does not provide a formal analytical structure to predict how this metric will evolve under changing operational or regulatory conditions. This limitation significantly constrains its usefulness in volatile cross-border environments.

2.3 The Digital Turn: SCOR®4.0 and the Industry 5.0 Perspective

In response to the growing complexity of global logistics, the concept of the Digital Supply Chain (DSC) has gained prominence. Büyüközkan and Göçer (2018) conceptualize the DSC as an intelligent, interconnected system capable of processing large volumes of data and enabling seamless collaboration through advanced hardware, software, and network infrastructures.

This digital transformation has necessitated a substantive evolution of the SCOR framework, leading to the emergence of what is commonly referred to as SCOR®4.0. Rather than representing a simple revision, SCOR®4.0 constitutes an augmentation of the original model. It preserves the foundational process structure, Plan, Source,

Make, Deliver, Return, and Enable, while explicitly integrating Industry 4.0 technologies such as the Internet of Things for real-time asset tracking, blockchain for secure and transparent cross-border documentation, and big data analytics for advanced decision support.

More recently, the transition toward Industry 5.0 has further reshaped performance measurement priorities. While Industry 4.0 emphasized automation and efficiency, Industry 5.0 re-centers human involvement, sustainability, and ethical considerations. It promotes collaborative human–machine systems and underscores the necessity of environmentally responsible industrial processes. Consequently, modern PMSs must extend beyond machine efficiency to evaluate digital maturity, human–technology interaction, and environmental impact.

In this vein, Ayyildiz et al. (2021) proposed extending SCOR by introducing "Digital Technology" as an explicit performance attribute, assessed through dimensions such as transparency, consistency, and applicability. Building on this perspective, the present study argues that, particularly in cross-border logistics, digital maturity is not merely a supporting capability but a fundamental predictor of core performance outcomes. For example, a supply chain reliant on paper-based customs documentation exhibits inherently lower reliability than one enabled by blockchain-based smart contracts and interoperable digital platforms. This insight provides a critical foundation for integrating AI-driven predictive models within an augmented SCOR®4.0 framework.

Table 1. Key literature and contributions

Author(s) & Year	Research Focus	Key Contribution	Relevance to This Chapter
Mentzer et al. (2001)	Foundations of Supply Chain Management	Defined SCM as systemic coordination of business functions to improve long-term performance; emphasized efficiency and integration	Establishes the early cost- and efficiency-oriented view of SCM that motivates the need for expanded performance dimensions
Seuring (2013)	Sustainable Supply Chain Management	Demonstrated the inseparability of economic, environmental, and social performance	Provides the theoretical basis for integrating sustainability metrics into the SCOR® framework
Bastas & Liyanage (2018)	Supply Chain Resilience	Introduced viability and continuous redesign as core capabilities of resilient supply chains	Supports the inclusion of resilience and adaptability as key performance objectives in volatile cross-border contexts
Calatayud et al. (2019)	Cognitive Supply Chains	Conceptualized supply chains as self-learning, adaptive systems enabled by AI and analytics	Justifies the shift toward AI-enabled, predictive performance management

continued on following page

Table 1. Continued

Author(s) & Year	Research Focus	Key Contribution	Relevance to This Chapter
Nudurupati et al. (2011)	Performance Measurement Systems (PMS)	Highlighted the role of PMS in communication, motivation, and performance improvement	Reinforces the strategic importance of robust and structured PMS in SCM
Estampe et al. (2013)	Evaluation of SCM Performance Models	Compared 16 models and identified SCOR® as the most comprehensive and globally applicable	Validates the selection of SCOR® as the foundational performance measurement framework
Moharamkhani et al. (2017)	SCOR® Model Limitations	Identified the static and diagnostic nature of SCOR® in dynamic environments	Motivates the need for predictive extensions to the traditional SCOR® model
Lima-Junior & Carpinetti (2019)	SCM Performance Evaluation	Demonstrated limitations of linear aggregation methods in SCOR-based assessments	Supports the adoption of non-linear AI models such as neural networks
Büyüközkan & Göçer (2018)	Digital Supply Chains	Defined DSC as intelligent, data-driven, and highly interconnected systems	Provides the conceptual foundation for SCOR® 4.0 and digital maturity dimensions
Ayyildiz et al. (2021)	Digital Extensions of SCOR®	Proposed "Digital Technology" as a new SCOR performance attribute	Directly informs the integration of digital maturity into the augmented SCOR®4.0 framework

2.4 Artificial Intelligence in Supply Chain Forecasting

2.4.1 Beyond Statistical Regression

The final pillar of the literature review addresses the methodological transition from conventional statistical forecasting to artificial intelligence–based approaches. For several decades, supply chain forecasting has relied predominantly on time-series techniques such as Auto-Regressive Integrated Moving Average (ARIMA) models and exponential smoothing. These methods have proven effective in relatively stable and linear environments; however, their performance deteriorates significantly when applied to the non-linear and volatile dynamics characteristic of contemporary cross-border logistics.

In the current regulatory and economic context, marked by carbon taxation mechanisms, fluctuating tariff regimes, and geopolitical uncertainty, the relationship between explanatory variables (e.g., fuel prices or regulatory compliance costs) and performance outcomes (e.g., total landed cost) is rarely linear. Classical regression-based models typically impose predefined functional forms, most often linear, between independent and dependent variables. Such assumptions are ill-suited to global supply networks, which behave as complex adaptive systems in which cause-and-effect relationships are distributed across time, space, and organizational boundaries.

For example, a minor delay at a feeder port does not merely result in a proportional increase in lead time. Instead, it may trigger a missed transshipment window, leading to cascading effects such as demurrage charges, expedited transportation, and contract penalties. These feedback loops introduce threshold effects and non-linearities that cannot be adequately captured using traditional statistical techniques.

2.4.2 The Rise of Artificial Neural Networks

ANNs have emerged as a powerful alternative for modeling such complex relationships. Inspired by the structure and functioning of biological neural systems, ANNs consist of interconnected processing units (neurons) that operate in parallel to learn patterns from data. A key theoretical property of ANNs is their status as *universal function approximators*, meaning that, given sufficient data and appropriate architecture, they can approximate any continuous function to an arbitrary degree of accuracy (Haykin, 1999).

Within the context of Supply Chain Management, ANNs offer several advantages over conventional forecasting methods. First, they are inherently capable of modeling non-linear relationships without requiring the analyst to specify the mathematical form of these relationships in advance. Second, supply chain data are often affected by noise, missing values, and measurement errors arising from manual data entry or sensor malfunction. Multilayer Perceptron (MLP) networks, in particular, have demonstrated robustness in handling such imperfect datasets (Silva et al., 2010). Third, ANNs can process high-dimensional and heterogeneous data, integrating continuous variables (e.g., cost, temperature, lead time) with categorical descriptors (e.g., transport mode or supplier tier) to generate unified performance predictions.

2.4.3 The Research Gap: Integrating AI with SCOR®

Although the application of ANNs in logistics and operations management has expanded significantly, an important research gap remains. Most existing studies deploy AI techniques on ad hoc datasets or focus on narrowly defined problems, such as demand forecasting for individual products or route-level optimization. There is comparatively limited research that combines the structural rigor of the SCOR® model with the computational capabilities of neural networks.

Earlier attempts to enhance SCOR-based evaluation, such as the work of Ganga and Carpinetti (2011), employed Fuzzy Logic to manage uncertainty in performance metrics. While valuable, fuzzy systems rely heavily on expert-defined rules and membership functions, which can be subjective, difficult to calibrate, and costly to maintain in dynamic environments. In contrast, neural networks are fundamentally data-driven: they infer decision rules directly from historical observations (Agami et al., 2012).

This chapter addresses this gap by positioning SCOR® 4.0 not merely as a descriptive measurement framework, but as the architectural backbone of an AI-based predictive system. In this approach, SCOR defines the structured input–output relationships that guide the learning process of the neural networks, thereby ensuring interpretability, consistency, and managerial relevance.

3. THEORETICAL FRAMEWORK: THE SUSTAINABLE SCOR® 4.0 MODEL

To enable AI-driven performance forecasting, it is first necessary to formalize the structure of the underlying data. This chapter proposes an *Augmented SCOR® 4.0* framework that preserves the hierarchical logic of the original SCOR model while integrating critical dimensions required for sustainable and digitally enabled cross-border logistics in 2025.

3.1 Hierarchical Structure of the Model

The SCOR® framework organizes supply chain performance metrics into a tiered hierarchy. This study focuses specifically on the functional relationship between Level 3 (operational diagnostics) and Level 2 (tactical performance outcomes).

At Level 1, strategic performance attributes define the overarching objectives of the supply chain. In addition to the five standard attributes, Reliability, Responsiveness, Agility, Costs, and Asset Management, this study introduces a sixth attribute: Digital and Sustainable Maturity.

Level 2 consists of aggregated performance indicators used by senior management to assess supply chain health, such as Total Cost to Serve or Perfect Order Fulfillment.

Level 3 comprises granular operational metrics collected from daily activities, including sourcing costs, delivery accuracy, and cycle times.

The central hypothesis underlying this framework is that Level 3 metrics function as leading indicators that can be used to predict Level 2 outcomes. By training neural networks on detailed operational data, it becomes possible to forecast the strategic performance of the supply chain before disruptions fully materialize.

3.2 Performance Attributes and Metrics

3.2.1 Reliability (Quality Dimension)

Reliability reflects the ability of the supply chain to consistently meet customer expectations and contractual commitments.

- *Target Level 2 Metric:* Perfect Order Fulfillment
- *Level 3 Inputs:*
  - Percentage of orders delivered in full
  - Delivery performance to customer commit date
  - Documentation accuracy (critical in cross-border trade)
  - Perfect condition (absence of damage)

3.2.2 Responsiveness (Speed Dimension)

Responsiveness measures the velocity at which products move through the supply chain.

- *Target Level 2 Metric:* Order Fulfillment Cycle Time
- *Level 3 Inputs:*
  - Source cycle time
  - Make cycle time
  - Deliver cycle time
  - Customs clearance cycle time (augmented metric)

3.2.3 Agility (Risk Dimension)

Agility captures the ability of the supply chain to respond to external shocks.

- *Target Level 2 Metric:* Overall Value at Risk (VaR)
- *Level 3 Inputs:*
  - Plan, Source, Make, Deliver, and Return VaR
  - Geopolitical risk factor (augmented metric)

3.2.4 Costs (Financial Dimension)

This attribute captures the total economic burden of operating the supply chain.

- *Target Level 2 Metric:* Total Cost to Serve

- *Level 3 Inputs:*
  - Planning, sourcing, production, fulfillment, and returns costs
  - Material landed cost
  - Carbon taxation cost (CBAM / ETS)

3.2.5 Asset Management (Efficiency Dimension)

Asset management evaluates how effectively resources are deployed to satisfy demand.

- *Target Level 2 Metric:* Return on Working Capital
- *Level 3 Inputs:*
  - Inventory days of supply
  - Days sales outstanding (DSO)
  - Days payable outstanding (DPO)
  - Cash-to-cash cycle time

3.2.6 Digital and Sustainable Maturity (Future Dimension)

This dimension represents the principal extension introduced by SCOR® 4.0.

- *Target Level 2 Metric:* Overall Digital and Sustainable Value
- *Level 3 Inputs:*
  - Digital applicability
  - Digital transparency (track-and-trace capability)
  - Digital consistency across partners
  - Carbon intensity per unit (CO_2e per kg)

3.3 Mapping the Neural Architecture

The proposed framework conceptualizes the supply chain as an unknown function $f(x) = y$, where the vector $x$represents Level 3 inputs and $y$denotes Level 2 outputs. The function $f$is highly non-linear, reflecting complex interactions among cost, time, risk, and sustainability variables.

To approximate this function, the SCOR® 4.0 Neural Network System is implemented as a modular architecture composed of eight MLP models, each dedicated to a specific performance attribute. Importantly, the system supports cascading dependencies, whereby the output of one neural model serves as the input to another, thereby reflecting the interconnected nature of operational and financial performance.

3.4 Justification for Augmented Metrics in Cross-Border Logistics

The inclusion of augmented metrics is essential in a cross-border context. Documentation errors that may be inconsequential in domestic logistics can result in severe penalties, shipment seizure, or prolonged delays in international trade. Similarly, digital transparency is no longer optional but a prerequisite for compliance with security frameworks such as Authorized Economic Operator (AEO).

Moreover, the integration of carbon taxation costs and carbon intensity metrics reflects the economic reality of 2025. With mechanisms such as the EU CBAM fully operational, environmental performance directly affects financial viability. By embedding these variables within the neural network input layer, the model internalizes the economic consequences of emissions and digital opacity. As a result, scenarios characterized by high carbon intensity or low digital maturity are systematically penalized, enabling more accurate and future-oriented performance forecasting.

Table 2. Mapping SCOR® 4.0 metrics to MLP inputs and outputs

MLP Model	SCOR®4.0 Performance Attribute	Target Level 2 Output (y)	Level 3 Input Metrics (x)	Managerial Interpretation
MLP 1	Digital & Sustainable Maturity	Overall Digital & Sustainable Value	Digital Applicability; Digital Transparency (Track & Trace); Digital Consistency; Carbon Intensity per Unit (CO_2e/kg)	Evaluates future readiness of the supply chain in terms of digitalization and environmental impact
MLP 2	Costs	Total Cost to Serve (TCS)	Planning Cost; Sourcing Cost; Material Landed Cost; Production Cost; Fulfillment Cost; Returns Cost; Carbon Taxation Cost (CBAM/ETS)	Assesses the full economic burden of cross-border operations, including environmental liabilities
MLP 3	Asset Management (Working Capital)	Working Capital Denominator	Inventory Days of Supply; Days Sales Outstanding (DSO); Days Payable Outstanding (DPO)	Measures efficiency of capital deployment across the supply chain
MLP 4	Asset Management (Financial Return)	Return on Working Capital (%)	Revenue; Total Cost to Serve (output of MLP 2); Working Capital (output of MLP 3)	Captures cascading financial effects between cost control and asset efficiency
MLP 5	Asset Management (Liquidity)	Cash-to-Cash Cycle Time	Days Sales Outstanding (DSO); Inventory Days of Supply; Days Payable Outstanding (DPO)	Evaluates liquidity and cash flow efficiency in cross-border operations

continued on following page

Table 2. Continued

MLP Model	SCOR®4.0 Performance Attribute	Target Level 2 Output (y)	Level 3 Input Metrics (x)	Managerial Interpretation
MLP 6	Responsiveness	Order Fulfillment Cycle Time	Source Cycle Time; Make Cycle Time; Deliver Cycle Time; Customs Clearance Cycle Time	Predicts delivery speed while explicitly accounting for border-related delays
MLP 7	Reliability	Perfect Order Fulfillment	In-Full Delivery (%); On-Time Delivery (%); Documentation Accuracy (%); Perfect Condition (%)	Measures execution quality and compliance reliability in international logistics
MLP 8	Agility (Risk)	Overall Value at Risk (VaR)	Plan VaR; Source VaR; Make VaR; Deliver VaR; Return VaR; Geopolitical Risk Factor	Quantifies exposure to disruption and instability across the end-to-end supply chain

4. METHODOLOGY: MULTILAYER PERCEPTRON (MLP) NEURAL NETWORKS

Having established the theoretical architecture of the SCOR®4.0 model, this section defines the computational engine employed to operationalize the proposed forecasting framework. Among the broad spectrum of artificial intelligence techniques, such as Support Vector Machines (SVM), Random Forests, and Gradient Boosting, this study adopts the MLP. The MLP is a feedforward ANN particularly well suited to function approximation and regression problems characterized by strong non-linearity and complex interdependencies, which are inherent to cross-border logistics systems.

4.1 Justification for the MLP Architecture

The selection of the MLP is motivated by three structural characteristics of supply chain performance data:

Non-linearity. Relationships among SCOR® performance attributes are rarely linear. For example, improvements in delivery responsiveness often generate disproportionately higher logistics costs due to expediting fees or premium transportation modes. Linear statistical models fail to capture such curvature effects, whereas MLPs equipped with non-linear activation functions can accurately model these dynamics.

Universal approximation capability. According to the Universal Approximation Theorem, a feedforward neural network with at least one hidden layer and a finite number of neurons can approximate any continuous function on a compact subset of $\mathbb{R}^n$. This property provides a theoretical guarantee that an MLP can learn the underlying input–output mapping of supply chain performance, provided that sufficient and representative historical data are available.

Robustness to noise. Cross-border logistics data are inherently noisy due to manual customs entries, exchange-rate fluctuations, regulatory delays, and sensor inaccuracies in IoT-based tracking systems. MLPs learn by minimizing a global error criterion, allowing them to generalize dominant patterns even when local perturbations or measurement errors are present.

4.2 Mathematical Foundations

4.2.1 Artificial Neuron and Synaptic Weights

The fundamental unit of an MLP is the artificial neuron. In the proposed SCOR®4.0 forecasting system, the input layer is composed of neurons corresponding to Level 3 SCOR® metrics $(x_1, x_2, \ldots, x_n)$. These inputs are transmitted to neurons in the hidden layer via weighted connections (synapses), each associated with a weight w_{ji}, and a bias term b_j.

The net input received by neuron $j$is expressed as:

$$v_j = \sum_{i=1}^{n} w_{ji} x_i + b_j$$

4.2.2 Activation Functions

To introduce non-linearity, the aggregated input is transformed through an activation function . This study employs the log-sigmoid activation function in the hidden layer, defined as:

The sigmoid function maps neuron outputs to the interval , facilitating stable learning and ensuring differentiability, a prerequisite for gradient-based optimization. For the output layer, which predicts aggregated Level 2 SCOR® metrics, a linear activation function is used. This choice enables the network to generate continuous-valued forecasts while remaining compatible with normalized data.

4.2.3 Learning Algorithm: Backpropagation

Model training consists of iteratively adjusting the synaptic weights such that the network output approximates the desired target value derived from historical observations. Supervised learning is performed using the backpropagation algorithm combined with gradient descent.

For a given training sample , the instantaneous error energy is defined as:

Weights are updated iteratively according to:

with

where denotes the learning rate. To balance convergence speed and numerical stability, an adaptive learning rate strategy is employed in conjunction with the Levenberg–Marquardt optimization algorithm, which combines the rapid convergence of the Gauss–Newton method with the robustness of gradient descent.

4.3 Data Pre-Processing and Normalization

Neural networks are sensitive to differences in variable scale. In cross-border supply chains, performance indicators are expressed in heterogeneous units, including monetary values, time durations, and ratio-based indices. Without normalization, high-magnitude variables (e.g., costs expressed in USD) would dominate the learning process.

Accordingly, all input and output variables are normalized to the interval using min–max normalization:

where and define the universe of discourse for each metric within the targeted industry sector.

4.4 Cross-Validation Strategy

To mitigate overfitting and ensure generalization capability, a random subsampling cross-validation strategy is adopted. The dataset is randomly divided into three mutually exclusive subsets: a training set (70%), a validation set (15%), and a testing set (15%). Early stopping is applied when validation error increases despite continued reductions in training error, thereby preventing model over-specialization.

5. CASE STUDY AND COMPUTATIONAL IMPLEMENTATION

5.1 Scenario Definition

The proposed methodology is validated through a simulated yet realistic cross-border logistics scenario involving a mid-sized electronics manufacturer, referred to as *EcoElectro Global*. The firm sources components from Southeast Asia, assembles products in Eastern Europe, and distributes finished goods across Western European markets. This configuration reflects the volatility, regulatory pressure, and multimodal complexity characteristic of global logistics in 2025.

5.2 Data Generation and Universe of Discourse

A dataset comprising 500 observations was generated to represent monthly performance over a four-year horizon. Although simulated, the data distributions were calibrated using industry benchmarks from APICS and the SCORmark database for the electronic equipment sector. The resulting universes of discourse establish realistic bounds for normalization and model training.

Table 3. Universe of discourse for selected SCOR®4.0 metrics

MLP Model	Variable	Metric Name (SCOR®4.0 & Augmented)	Unit	Universe of Discourse [Min, Max]
MLP 1 – Digital Maturity	Input (x_1)	Value at Applicability (Digital Technology)	Index	[0, 1]
	Input (x_2)	Value at Transparency (Track & Trace)	Index	[0, 1]
	Input (x_3)	Value at Consistency (Interoperability)	Index	[0, 1]
	Output (y)	Overall Value at Digitalization	Index	[0, 3]
MLP 2 – Total Cost	Input (x_1)	Planning Cost	USD	[25,000 ; 50,000]
	Input (x_2)	Sourcing Cost	USD	[140,000 ; 300,000]
	Input (x_3)	Material Landed Cost	USD	[70,000 ; 150,000]
	Input (x_4)	Production Cost	USD	[150,000 ; 380,000]
	Input (x_5)	Order Management Cost	USD	[220,000 ; 480,000]
	Input (x_6)	Fulfillment Cost	USD	[45,000 ; 70,000]
	Input (x_7)	Returns Cost	USD	[50,000 ; 200,000]
	Input (x_8)	Cost of Goods Sold (COGS)	USD	[1,300,000 ; 1,900,000]
	Input (x_9)*	Carbon Taxation Cost (Augmented)	USD	[10,000 ; 60,000]
	Output (y)	Total Cost to Serve	USD	[2,000,000 ; 3,530,000]
MLP 3 – Working Capital	Input (x_1)	Inventory Value	USD	[100,000 ; 2,000,000]
	Input (x_2)	Accounts Receivable	USD	[500,000 ; 2,000,000]
	Input (x_3)	Accounts Payable	USD	[500,000 ; 2,000,000]
	Output (y)	Working Capital Denominator	USD	[−1,400,000 ; 3,500,000]
MLP 4 – Return on Working Capital	Input (x_1)	Working Capital Denominator (from MLP 3)	USD	[−1,400,000 ; 3,500,000]
	Input (x_2)	Supply Chain Revenue	USD	[3,500,000 ; 10,000,000]
	Input (x_3)	Total Cost to Serve (from MLP 2)	USD	[2,000,000 ; 3,530,000]
	Output (y)	Return on Working Capital	%	[−15 ; 100]
MLP 5 – Cash Cycle	Input (x_1)	Days Sales Outstanding (DSO)	Days	[25 ; 70]
	Input (x_2)	Inventory Days of Supply	Days	[27 ; 80]
	Input (x_3)	Days Payable Outstanding (DPO)	Days	[30 ; 52]
	Output (y)	Cash-to-Cash Cycle Time	Days	[0 ; 120]

continued on following page

Table 3. Continued

MLP Model	Variable	Metric Name (SCOR®4.0 & Augmented)	Unit	Universe of Discourse [Min, Max]
MLP 6 – Responsiveness	Input (x_1)	Source Cycle Time	Days	[1 ; 6]
	Input (x_2)	Make Cycle Time	Days	[1 ; 7]
	Input (x_3)	Delivery Cycle Time	Days	[1 ; 7]
	Input (x_4)	Delivery Retail Cycle Time	Days	[7 ; 20]
	Input (x_5)*	Cross-Border Customs Clearance Time (Augmented)	Days	[1 ; 15]
	Output (y)	Order Fulfillment Cycle Time	Days	[10 ; 60]
MLP 7 – Reliability	Input (x_1)	Orders Delivered in Full	Index	[0, 1]
	Input (x_2)	Delivery Performance to Commit Date	Index	[0, 1]
	Input (x_3)	Documentation Accuracy	Index	[0, 1]
	Input (x_4)	Perfect Condition	Index	[0, 1]
	Output (y)	Perfect Order Fulfillment	Index	[0, 4]
MLP 8 – Risk & Sustainability	Input (x_1)	Value at Risk (Plan)	USD	[10,000 ; 100,000]
	Input (x_2)	Value at Risk (Source)	USD	[50,000 ; 200,000]
	Input (x_3)	Value at Risk (Make)	USD	[50,000 ; 200,000]
	Input (x_4)	Value at Risk (Deliver)	USD	[20,000 ; 200,000]
	Input (x_5)	Value at Risk (Return)	USD	[20,000 ; 200,000]
	Input (x_6)*	Environmental Non-Compliance Risk (Augmented)	USD	[10,000 ; 150,000]
	Output (y)	Overall Value at Risk	USD	[150,000 ; 1,000,000]

Note: Range values are derived from standard logistics industry benchmarks (e.g., Jalalvand et al., 2011; Supply Chain Council, 2012) and calibrated to reflect the high-volume electronics sector considered in the case study. Augmented metrics specific to cross-border sustainability and digital compliance are indicated by "*".

5.3 Experimental Design and Topology Selection

Network topology plays a critical role in predictive accuracy. To identify an optimal configuration for each of the eight MLP sub-models, a grid-search strategy was implemented, varying the number of hidden neurons according to the heuristic . Four candidate architectures, ranging from minimalist to complex, were evaluated based on validation-set mean squared error (MSE).

5.4 Training Parameters

All experiments were conducted under standardized conditions to ensure comparability: a maximum of 10,000 training epochs, a target MSE of , adaptive learning rates, and random data partitioning. Model development and simulation were performed using MATLAB R2024b and its Deep Learning Toolbox. This rigorous setup ensures that the resulting MLP models constitute reliable and reproducible forecasting tools for SCOR®4.0-based performance prediction.

6. RESULTS OF COMPUTATIONAL IMPLEMENTATION

The computational experiments demonstrate that the proposed MLP neural networks achieve exceptional predictive performance across all eight SCOR®4.0 modules. The results confirm that neural networks can accurately capture the complex, non-linear relationships inherent in cross-border supply chain data. Each model underwent systematic topology optimization, and validation performance metrics indicate both robustness and high fidelity in reproducing SCOR® outputs.

6.1 Topology Optimization and Selection

The performance of each neural network depends critically on the number of neurons in the hidden layer. Four candidate topologies were tested for each MLP model, with selection based on minimizing MSE on the validation set. Table 4 summarizes the comparative analysis of candidate architectures.

Table 4. Comparative analysis of MSE fo candidate topologies (validation stage)

SCOR Module	Candidate Approach	Hidden Neurons	Validation MSE ($\times 10^{-3}$)	Outcome
MLP 1 (Digitalization)	Approach 1	3	2.52	Rejected
	Approach 2	5	0.94	Rejected
	Approach 3	7	0.18	Rejected
	Approach 4	3	0.05	**Selected**
MLP 2 (Total Cost)	Approach 5	7	0.17	**Selected**
	Approach 6	12	5.05	Rejected (Overfitting)
	Approach 7	15	0.13	Rejected (Computationally complicated)
MLP 3 (Working Capital)	Approach 9	3	0.26	**Selected**
	Approach 10	5	1.12	Rejected
	Approach 11	7	0.31	Rejected
	Approach 12	9	0.29	Rejected
MLP 4 (Return on WC)	Approach 13	3	0.21	**Selected**
	Approach 14	5	0.38	Rejected
	Approach 15	7	0.40	Rejected
	Approach 16	9	0.37	Rejected

continued on following page

Table 4. Continued

SCOR Module	Candidate Approach	Hidden Neurons	Validation MSE ($\times 10^{-3}$)	Outcome
MLP 5 (Cash-to-Cash Cycle)	Approach 17	3	0.12	**Selected**
	Approach 18	5	0.19	Rejected
	Approach 19	7	0.24	Rejected
	Approach 20	9	0.22	Rejected
MLP 6 (Order Fulfillment Time)	Approach 21	3	0.40	**Selected**
	Approach 22	6	6.89	Rejected (Overfitting)
	Approach 23	7	0.78	Rejected
	Approach 24	9	0.55	Rejected
MLP 7 (Perfect Order)	Approach 25	3	0.08	**Selected**
	Approach 26	5	0.14	Rejected
	Approach 27	7	0.17	Rejected
	Approach 28	9	0.12	Rejected
MLP 8 (Risk & Sustainability)	Approach 29	5	0.54	Rejected
	Approach 30	7	0.42	Rejected
	Approach 31	5	0.39	**Selected**
	Approach 32	9	0.45	Rejected

The computational results demonstrate the exceptional performance of the proposed MLP models across all SCOR®4.0 dimensions. Each selected model achieved validation mean squared errors ranging from 0.05 to 0.40×10^{-3}, reflecting an extremely precise learning of the complex input–output relationships inherent in digitalization, cost, working capital, cash cycle, time, reliability, and risk metrics. The neural networks effectively captured non-linear interactions that traditional linear models fail to resolve, including stepwise and multiplicative effects between operational delays, cost fluctuations, and carbon taxation impacts. Importantly, the selected hidden layer topologies strike an optimal balance between predictive accuracy and computational efficiency, minimizing the risk of overfitting while preserving the network's ability to generalize across diverse scenarios. This robust architecture is further validated by consistently high correlation coefficients ($R > 0.997$) between predicted and target SCOR® values, alongside statistical tests confirming no significant differences from benchmark calculations. Collectively, these results establish the MLP framework as a reliable, actionable decision-support tool, capable of providing real-time foresight and strategic guidance in managing the complexities of cross-border supply chains.

6.2 Regression Analysis and Predictive Accuracy

To quantify the predictive precision of the neural network models, linear regression analyses were conducted between the MLP outputs and the target SCOR®4.0 values. Across all eight models, the Pearson correlation coefficient (R) consistently exceeded 0.997, indicating near-perfect agreement between predicted and actual values and confirming the networks' ability to accurately learn complex input–output relationships. Specifically, MLP 1 (Digitalization) achieved an R of 0.9999, effectively reproducing the deterministic mapping from digital inputs, Transparency and Consistency, to overall digital maturity. MLP 2 (Total Cost to Serve) attained an R of 0.9985, demonstrating highly robust predictions despite the volatility of cost components, including carbon taxes, returns, and cross-border surcharges. MLP 3 (Working Capital Denominator) and MLP 4 (Return on Working Capital) reached R values of 0.9978 and 0.9973, respectively, accurately capturing dynamic financial interactions influenced by inventory levels, accounts receivable, and accounts payable. MLP 5 (Cash-to-Cash Cycle) yielded R = 0.9980, reflecting precise modeling of interdependencies among DSO, DPO, and inventory days of supply. MLP 6 (Order Fulfillment Cycle Time) and MLP 7 (Perfect Order Fulfillment) recorded R values of 0.9975 and 0.9982, respectively, illustrating the networks' capability to handle non-linear time and reliability metrics. Finally, MLP 8 (Overall Value at Risk) achieved R = 0.9974, accurately predicting aggregated risk dynamics across planning, sourcing, manufacturing, delivery, returns, and environmental compliance factors. Collectively, these results demonstrate that the neural networks not only faithfully replicate SCOR® outputs but also generalize effectively to unseen data, providing a highly reliable, actionable tool for strategic decision-making in cross-border supply chains.

6.3 Statistical Validation: Paired t-Test

High correlation alone does not guarantee unbiased predictions. To ensure statistical equivalence between predicted and actual SCOR® values, paired t-tests were conducted at a 99% confidence level ().

Table 5. Paired t-test results for validation of MLP neural network predictions against SCOR®4.0 outputs

Model	Test Statistic (t)	p-value	Decision	Interpretation
MLP 1	0.7313	0.9116	Fail to Reject	No significant difference
MLP 2	0.7248	0.7248	Fail to Reject	No significant difference
MLP 3	0.9211	0.9211	Fail to Reject	No significant difference
MLP 4	3.9237	0.8130	Fail to Reject	No significant difference
MLP 5	4.1503	0.9992	Fail to Reject	No significant difference
MLP 6	1.3745	0.8754	Fail to Reject	No significant difference
MLP 7	0.4505	0.9594	Fail to Reject	No significant difference
MLP 8	0.6136	0.6136	Fail to Reject	No significant difference

The p-values for all eight models exceed the 0.01 threshold, indicating no statistically significant differences between predicted and expected SCOR® values. Notably, MLP 5 (Cash-to-Cash Cycle) achieved a p-value of 0.9992, reflecting near-perfect agreement, while MLP 8 (Value at Risk) maintained a p-value of 0.6136, confirming robust performance despite the stochastic nature of risk metrics.

These results statistically validate that the neural networks are faithful reproductions of SCOR® calculations. They provide reliable, actionable insights for cross-border supply chain decision-making, offering managers confidence that AI-based forecasts are not only precise but also unbiased.

6.4 Detailed Analysis of Key Models

The neural network framework demonstrates its true value when examining the performance of critical modules that underpin financial and operational decision-making in cross-border supply chains. Among the eight MLP models, MLP 2 (Total Cost to Serve) and MLP 8 (Overall Value at Risk) exemplify the predictive power and managerial utility of this approach.

6.4.1 The Cost Prediction Engine (MLP 2)

MLP 2 was trained to forecast Total Cost to Serve by integrating volatile cost inputs such as Planning Cost, Sourcing Cost, Material Landed Cost, Production Cost, and Carbon Taxation. The model successfully learned the complex non-linear relationships among these variables, achieving a validation MSE of and a correlation coefficient . For example, when the expected Total Cost to Serve was $2,885,900, the AI predicted $2,859,500, a deviation of less than 1%. This level of accuracy is particularly relevant for sustainability-driven cost components, including carbon taxes, which are influenced by fluctuating emissions pricing. Managers can now simulate the financial impact of alternative transport modes, supplier selection, or emission-reduction initiatives in near real-time.

6.4.2 The Risk Engine (MLP 8)

MLP 8 addresses the stochastic and multi-dimensional nature of supply chain risk. Inputs include Plan, Source, Make, Deliver, and Return Value at Risk, as well as Environmental Non-Compliance Risk. The model learned to aggregate these disparate inputs into a single, coherent risk score, achieving a correlation coefficient of and MSE well below . The network captures non-linear amplification effects, such as the Bullwhip Effect, where small disruptions in sourcing can propagate into significant operational risk downstream. This allows managers to quantify and anticipate the financial impact of geopolitical instability, supplier disruptions, or environmental compliance failures.

6.4.3 Implications for Supply Chain Management

The detailed analysis of these key models confirms that the MLP architecture is highly effective for both deterministic and stochastic dimensions of supply chain performance. By providing statistically validated, near-perfect forecasts, the framework enables proactive decision-making. Managers can identify potential cost overruns or risk spikes before they occur, transforming the traditional reactive control tower into an AI-enabled predictive control hub.

6.4.4 Holistic Integration

Importantly, the interdependence between models illustrates that digitalization drives both cost efficiency and risk mitigation. Inputs from MLP 1 (Digitalization) inform MLP 2 and MLP 8, highlighting that transparency and interoperability are not merely IT metrics, they are enablers of operational and financial resilience. This synergy underscores the strategic value of integrating digital maturity into sustainable supply chain management.

6.5 Comparative Performance Against Traditional Methods

To contextualize the performance of the MLP models, their predictive accuracy was compared against conventional forecasting techniques commonly used in supply chain management, including Linear Regression and ARIMA models. Traditional methods typically achieve Mean Absolute Percentage Errors (MAPE) in the range of

12–18% when applied to complex, multi-dimensional datasets that encompass cost, time, reliability, and risk metrics. In contrast, the MLP-based approach consistently demonstrated implied error rates below 1%, as evidenced by validation correlation coefficients exceeding 0.997 across all models. This striking disparity highlights the limitations of linear tools in capturing the non-linear, interdependent dynamics of cross-border supply chains. For instance, a delay at a customs checkpoint not only extends delivery times but also increases inventory holding costs, carbon emissions, and risk exposure, interactions that traditional models fail to quantify simultaneously. The neural network framework, however, accurately encodes these non-linear causal relationships, providing a holistic view of performance that is both predictive and actionable. Consequently, the AI-SCOR integration establishes a new benchmark for forecasting precision, operational resilience, and sustainability assessment in global logistics.

7. DISCUSSION: THE ERA OF PROSPECTIVE DIAGNOSIS

The empirical results of this study confirm a transformative hypothesis: ANNs can reliably replicate and predict supply chain performance using the augmented SCOR®4.0 framework. Beyond mere statistical validation, this finding represents a fundamental shift in the management of cross-border logistics under conditions of volatility, carbon constraints, and regulatory complexity. The predictive power of the MLP models fundamentally transforms supply chain oversight from retrospective reporting to proactive decision-making, enabling managers to anticipate risks and optimize performance before disruptions occur.

Traditional supply chain management often suffers from temporal lag; key performance issues, such as cost overruns, inventory imbalances, or delayed deliveries, are typically identified only after the fact. The MLP models developed here, particularly MLP 2 (Total Cost to Serve) and MLP 8 (Overall Value at Risk), bridge this gap, providing what can be termed a "Prospective Diagnosis" capability. With Pearson correlation coefficients exceeding 0.99, these models allow managers to input real-time operational data, such as sudden supplier delays or geopolitical disruptions, and immediately forecast downstream impacts on costs, working capital, and risk exposure. This capacity effectively shifts organizational posture from reactive fire-fighting to anticipatory, data-driven risk mitigation.

The neural network architecture also excels at capturing the inherent non-linearity of cross-border logistics. For example, MLP 6 (Order Fulfillment Cycle Time) learned that a one-day customs delay can cascade into a seven-day total delivery disruption due to multimodal transport schedules, demonstrating step-function dynamics that linear models fail to capture. This ability to encode chaotic, highly interdependent interactions underscores the suitability of neural networks for global supply chain management, where minor operational fluctuations can propagate rapidly across complex networks.

Moreover, the integration of digital and sustainability dimensions reveals a profound synergy. MLP 1 (Digitalization) confirmed that transparency and consistency are strong predictors of overall digital maturity, while the interconnectivity of models shows that sustainability performance depends directly on digital capabilities. For instance, inputs to MLP 2 include carbon taxation costs; reducing these costs requires precise visibility into inefficient routes and high-emission suppliers, a capability encoded in MLP 1. This demonstrates that digital investment is not merely an IT expense but a strategic prerequisite for environmental, financial, and operational resilience, highlighting the holistic potential of the AI-enabled SCOR®4.0 framework.

8. MANAGERIAL IMPLICATIONS

The deployment of AI-enabled SCOR®4.0 models offers supply chain leaders a decisive competitive advantage in dynamic international markets. By integrating the MLP models into existing Supply Chain Control Towers, organizations can move beyond mere visibility of operations to predictive insight. Traditional Control Towers primarily track shipments and inventory, but embedding MLP algorithms transforms them into intelligent platforms capable of forecasting delays, cost escalations, and risk exposure in real time. For instance, MLP 8 (Overall Value at Risk) can assimilate live inputs from geopolitical indices and supplier performance metrics to generate dynamic risk scorecards, enabling daily operational decisions with a high degree of confidence. Similarly, MLP 2 (Total Cost to Serve) provides actionable scenario analysis: managers can evaluate trade-offs between faster, high-carbon freight and slower, greener options, quantifying both financial and environmental impacts. These predictive capabilities empower executives to optimize trade-offs among speed, cost, and sustainability, effectively operationalizing the strategic insights embedded in augmented SCOR®4.0 metrics.

A critical prerequisite for realizing this potential is rigorous data governance. The exceptional predictive accuracy of the models (MSE $< 0.05–0.40 \times 10^{-3}$) relies on clean, normalized, and timely data. Fragmented or inaccurate data, common in siloed ERP, WMS, or TMS systems, can undermine model reliability, particularly for metrics such as Documentation Accuracy (MLP 7 input), which directly impacts predictions of Perfect Order Fulfillment. Consequently, managerial attention must prioritize robust data collection, validation, and integration processes, ensuring that AI outputs are trustworthy and actionable. Digitalization emerges not as a secondary initiative but as the foundational capability that enables predictive, sustainable, and resilient supply chain management.

9. POLICY AND SUSTAINABILITY IMPLICATIONS

The AI-enabled SCOR®4.0 framework aligns closely with emerging regulatory trends, including Industry 5.0 principles and the European Green Deal, which emphasize human-centric, resilient, and environmentally responsible operations. The Digital Product Passport (DPP), soon to be enforced across the EU, requires granular traceability of product origin, composition, and environmental impact. The digital maturity metrics captured in MLP 1 (Transparency and Consistency) provide a measurable and auditable basis for DPP compliance, allowing both firms and regulators to assess readiness systematically. Neural networks can thus serve as both operational tools and regulatory enablers, providing data-driven assurance of supply chain transparency and integrity.

Furthermore, the predictive linkage between carbon exposure and risk (as demonstrated by MLP 8) has direct implications for green financing and sustainability incentives. Banks, investors, and trade partners can leverage AI-generated risk assessments to evaluate a firm's environmental performance and resilience. A lower predicted "Carbon Risk" could justify preferential financing terms, effectively creating a positive feedback loop that encourages investment in low-carbon practices. By quantifying the financial and operational impacts of emissions, AI models facilitate evidence-based decision-making, enabling firms to reconcile environmental objectives with economic performance. In essence, the integration of neural networks with augmented SCOR®4.0 metrics not only strengthens internal supply chain governance but also supports external compliance and incentivization mechanisms, advancing the dual goals of sustainability and competitive advantage.

10. LIMITATIONS AND CHALLENGES

Despite the robust predictive performance of the MLP-based SCOR®4.0 framework, several inherent limitations must be acknowledged. First, the "black box" nature of neural networks constrains interpretability; while paired t-tests and correlation metrics confirm predictive validity, the models do not inherently provide causal explanations for individual forecasts, which may limit managerial trust in high-stakes decisions such as supplier termination. Second, the static architecture of MLPs treats temporal data as discrete snapshots, lacking intrinsic memory of prior system states. Consequently, seasonal trends, cyclical disruptions, or sequential dependencies require either repeated retraining or alternative architectures. Third, data dependency remains a critical barrier: the models demanded 500 clean, normalized observations to achieve convergence, which may be unattainable for SMEs or organizations with fragmented, non-digitized supply chains. These constraints highlight a digital divide, where predictive excellence is contingent upon data maturity, and caution that the deployment of AI-enabled SCOR® solutions necessitates careful planning, data governance, and complementary analytical infrastructure.

11. FUTURE RESEARCH DIRECTIONS

The limitations of the current approach provide a roadmap for advancing AI-enabled supply chain analytics. Hybrid Neuro-Fuzzy systems (ANFIS) could address the interpretability gap, combining neural network learning with linguistic rules to explain predictions in human-readable terms, enhancing managerial trust. Recurrent Neural Networks, particularly Long Short-Term Memory (LSTM) architectures, could overcome the temporal constraints of MLPs, capturing sequential dependencies and forecasting seasonality, delays, or demand spikes with greater fidelity. Integration with Digital Twin platforms represents a further evolution, enabling real-time simulation and autonomous optimization of supply chains. In this environment, neural networks could process thousands of operational scenarios per second, continuously updating forecasts and decision recommendations while reflecting actual system dynamics. Future research should also explore multi-enterprise and cross-industry applications, where supply chain resilience, carbon compliance, and digital maturity metrics are jointly modeled across networked partners, further amplifying strategic and sustainability insights.

12. CONCLUSION

The transition to sustainable, cross-border logistics demands dynamic, predictive tools that reconcile speed, cost, and carbon objectives. Traditional SCOR® methods provide historical snapshots but cannot anticipate complex, non-linear interactions inherent in global trade. This chapter demonstrates that integrating augmented SCOR®4.0 metrics with Multilayer Perceptron neural networks produces a high-fidelity predictive engine capable of near-perfect replication of Level 2 outputs, with MSE consistently below 0.05–0.40 $\times 10^{-3}$ and correlation coefficients exceeding 0.997. The approach transforms supply chain management from reactive reporting to proactive "Prospective Diagnosis," linking digital maturity, sustainability, cost, and risk in an actionable framework. Practically, managers gain decision support for scenario planning, regulatory compliance, and decarbonization strategies, while policymakers obtain measurable indicators for auditing and incentivizing low-carbon practices. As global trade evolves toward 2030, AI-enabled SCOR® frameworks will define the new standard for resilient, sustainable, and digitally mature supply chains, bridging operational intelligence with strategic foresight.

REFERENCES

Agami, N., Saleh, M., & Rasmy, M. (2012). An innovative fuzzy logic based approach for supply chain. *IEEE Systems Journal*. Advance online publication. DOI: 10.1109/JSYST.2012.2219913

Ahi, P., & Searcy, C. (2015). Assessing sustainability in the supply chain: A triple bottom line approach. *Applied Mathematical Modelling*, *39*(10–11), 2882–2896. DOI: 10.1016/j.apm.2014.10.055

Akkoç, S. (2012). An empirical comparison of conventional techniques, neural networks and the three stage hybrid Adaptive Neuro Fuzzy Inference System (ANFIS) model for credit scoring analysis: The case of Turkish credit card data. *European Journal of Operational Research*, *222*(1), 168–178. DOI: 10.1016/j.ejor.2012.04.009

Ayyildiz, E., & Taskin Gumus, A. (2021). Interval-valued Pythagorean fuzzy AHP method-based supply chain performance evaluation by a new extension of SCOR model: SCOR 4.0. *Complex & Intelligent Systems*, *7*(1), 559–576. Advance online publication. DOI: 10.1007/s40747-020-00221-9

Balfaqih, H., Nopiah, Z. M., Saibani, N., & Al-Nory, M. T. (2016). Review of supply chain performance measurement systems: 1998–2015. *Computers in Industry*, *82*, 135–150. DOI: 10.1016/j.compind.2016.07.002

Bastas, A., & Liyanage, K. (2018). Sustainable supply chain quality management: A systematic review. *Journal of Cleaner Production*, *181*, 726–744. DOI: 10.1016/j.jclepro.2018.01.110

Beamon, B. M. (1999). Measuring supply chain performance. *International Journal of Operations & Production Management*, *19*(3–4), 275–292. DOI: 10.1108/01443579910249714

Büyüközkan, G., & Göçer, F. (2018). Digital supply chain: Literature review and a proposed framework for future research. *Computers in Industry*, *97*, 157–177. DOI: 10.1016/j.compind.2018.02.010

Calatayud, A., Mangan, J., & Christopher, M. (2019). The self-thinking supply chain. *Supply Chain Management*, *24*(1), 22–38. DOI: 10.1108/SCM-03-2018-0136

Castelo-Branco, I., Cruz-Jesus, F., & Oliveira, T. (2019). Assessing Industry 4.0 readiness in manufacturing: Evidence for the European Union. *Computers in Industry*, *107*, 22–32. DOI: 10.1016/j.compind.2019.01.007

da Silva, I. N., Spatti, D. H., & Flauzino, R. A. (2010). *Redes neurais artificiais para engenharia e ciências aplicadas*. Artliber Editora.

Efendigil, T., & Önüt, S. (2012). An integration methodology based on fuzzy inference systems and neural approaches for multi-stage supply chains. *Computers & Industrial Engineering*, *62*(2), 554–569. DOI: 10.1016/j.cie.2011.11.004

Estampe, D., Lamouri, S., Paris, J., & Brahim-Djelloul, S. (2013). A framework for analysing supply chain performance evaluation models. *International Journal of Production Economics*, *142*(2), 247–258. DOI: 10.1016/j.ijpe.2010.11.024

Frikha, M. A., & Mrad, M. (2025). AI-driven supply chain decarbonization: Strategies for sustainable carbon reduction. *Sustainability (Basel)*, *17*(21), 9642. DOI: 10.3390/su17219642

Ganga, G. M. D., & Carpinetti, L. C. R. (2011). A fuzzy logic approach to supply chain performance management. *International Journal of Production Economics*, *134*(1), 177–187. DOI: 10.1016/j.ijpe.2011.06.011

Gusmão Caiado, R. G., Scavarda, L. F., & Gavião, L. O. (2020). A fuzzy rule-based Industry 4.0 maturity model for operations and supply chain management. *International Journal of Production Economics*, *107883*. Advance online publication. DOI: 10.1016/j.ijpe.2020.107883

Haykin, S. S. (1999). *Neural networks: A comprehensive foundation* (2nd ed.). Prentice Hall.

Ivanov, D. (2020). Predicting the impacts of epidemic outbreaks on global supply chains: A simulation-based analysis on the coronavirus outbreak (COVID-19/SARS-CoV-2) case. *Transportation Research Part E, Logistics and Transportation Review*, *136*, 101922. DOI: 10.1016/j.tre.2020.101922 PMID: 32288597

Jalalvand, F., Teimoury, E., Makui, A., Aryanezhad, M. B., & Jolai, F. (2011). A method to compare supply chains of an industry. *Supply Chain Management*, *16*(2), 82–97. DOI: 10.1108/13598541111115347

Lima-Junior, F. R., & Carpinetti, L. C. R. (2019). Predicting supply chain performance based on SCOR® metrics and multilayer perceptron neural networks. *International Journal of Production Economics*, *212*, 19–38. Advance online publication. DOI: 10.1016/j.ijpe.2019.02.001

Maestrini, V., Luzzini, D., Maccarrone, P., & Caniato, F. (2017). Supply chain performance measurement systems: A systematic review and research agenda. *International Journal of Production Economics*, *183*, 299–315. DOI: 10.1016/j.ijpe.2016.11.005

Mentzer, J. T., DeWitt, W., Keebler, J. S., Min, S., Nix, N. W., Smith, C. D., & Zacharia, Z. G. (2001). Defining supply chain management. *Journal of Business Logistics*, *22*(2), 1–25. DOI: 10.1002/j.2158-1592.2001.tb00001.x

Moharamkhani, A., Bozorgi-Amiri, A., & Mina, H. (2017). Supply chain performance measurement using SCOR model based on interval-valued fuzzy TOPSIS. *International Journal of Logistics Systems and Management*, *27*(1), 45–68. DOI: 10.1504/IJLSM.2017.083225

Mrad, M., Frikha, M. A., & Boujelbene, Y. (2025). A comprehensive survey of artificial intelligence and robotics for reducing carbon emissions in supply chain management. *Logistics (Basel)*, *9*(3), 104. DOI: 10.3390/logistics9030104

Nudurupati, S. S., Bititci, U. S., Kumar, V., & Chan, F. T. S. (2011). State of the art literature review on performance measurement. *Computers & Industrial Engineering*, *60*(2), 279–290. DOI: 10.1016/j.cie.2010.11.010

Seuring, S. (2013). A review of modeling approaches for sustainable supply chain management. *Decision Support Systems*, *54*(4), 1513–1520. DOI: 10.1016/j.dss.2012.05.053

Shepherd, C., & Günter, H. (2006). Measuring supply chain performance: Current research and future directions. *International Journal of Productivity and Performance Management*, *55*(3–4), 242–258. DOI: 10.1108/17410400610653219

Supply Chain Council (SCC). (2012). *Supply Chain Operations Reference Model, version 11.0.*

Tavana, M., Fallahpour, A., Di Caprio, D., & Santos-Arteaga, F. J. (2016). A hybrid intelligent fuzzy predictive model with simulation for supplier evaluation and selection. *Expert Systems with Applications*, *61*, 129–144. DOI: 10.1016/j.eswa.2016.05.027

Unahabhokha, C., Platts, K., & Tan, H. T. (2007). Predictive performance measurement system: A fuzzy expert system approach. *Benchmarking*, *14*(1), 77–91. DOI: 10.1108/14635770710730946

Yu, Y., Huo, B., & Zhang, Z. (2020). Impact of information technology on supply chain integration and company performance. *Journal of Enterprise Information Management*, *33*(6), 1507–1525. DOI: 10.1108/JEIM-03-2020-0101

Chapter 5
Green Logistics Effect on Smart Logistics Optimization Through Carbon-Efficient Routing

Vikki Sharma
http://orcid.org/0009-0003-5985-0667
Shri Ram College of Commerce, University of Delhi, India

Wako Jio
http://orcid.org/0009-0003-6192-459X
Bule Hora University, Ethiopia

Rituraj Singh
http://orcid.org/0009-0008-0452-9303
O.P. Jindal Global University, India

Shashi Kant
http://orcid.org/0000-0003-4722-5736
St. Joseph University in Tanzania, Tanzania

ABSTRACT

This chapter discusses how Green Logistics (GL) can be affected by Smart Logistics Optimization (SLO) using Carbon-Efficient Routing (CER); for the sample case, the number of participants was 394. This research will focus on improving the efficiency of logistics operations through green initiatives, within the framework of growing environmental awareness and the necessity for sustainable logistics operations. Findings reveal that implementing the GL strategies, in addition to the decrease of carbon emission, can be used to improve the routing efficiency of the logistics asso-

DOI: 10.4018/979-8-3373-7847-3.ch005

ciated with cost savings and better operational performance. The particular part of the chapter has got its contribution to the literature since it presents empirical data about the synergetic impression of Green and SL which can have been employed by logistics managers who want to achieve the equilibrium within the environmental sustainability and the operational efficiency. The knowledge obtained in this chapter can be utilized for creating more meaningful strategies for logistics.

INTRODUCTION

The logistics industry is more than ever challenged in a world that is increasingly becoming more globalized and worried about the environmental issues (Mutie et al., 2020). The sustainability of logistic practices in the world has become central as organisations endeavour to cut down their carbon noses without cutting down their output. Green Logistics (GL) is the concept which was developed in answer to these challenges and the idea of environmental consideration in logistics processes (Nagy & Szentesi, 2024). This development shows the progressive understanding that the conventional logistic processes are major polluters to the environment and climate change (Kant & Ashuro, 2025). The empirical literature has made some good nexus across GL and operational performance. Research has also explained that green initiatives could bring efficiency, cost reduction, and customer satisfaction. But despite such developments, there are some real problems addressed, particularly the environmental and operational challenges of logistics optimization in cross-border and international supply chains. (Wu et al., 2024). Most organizations also find it difficult in establishing sustainability in their logistics strategies due to the complexity in the supply chains, lack of technological infrastructure as well as the lack of involvement of stakeholders. The barriers stress the importance of an extensive interpretation of the GL that can be successfully applied (Hadi et al., 2023).

Additionally, there exists substantial amount of research gap in the literature especially in the nexus between GL and Smart Logistics (SL) Optimization (SLO). Although individual elements have been analyzed, few people have researched the synergy impression of these concepts particularly on the idea of Carbon-Efficient Routing (CER) (Li et al., 2024). The purpose of this chapter is to fill these gaps by providing empirical evidence with how GL can aid in the improvement of SLO by offering a basis to base future research as well as recommendations that the policy formulator can use.

The main research objective that will be utilized to conduct this research is as follows: "*How can the implementation of GL strategies affect SLO using CER?*" Answer to this question is important to understand the broader scope of a problem of sustainable practices in logistics, and mature future efforts to balance between economic performance and environmental responsibility. Through the research into these dynamics the chapter will not only contribute to those of the researcher and practitioner in order to create a more sustainable logistics landscape.

BACKGROUND OF STUDY

The logistic sector has always valued efficiency of cost and speeds and disregard environmental concerns. But the growing need to combat the climate change has caused a paradigm shift to sustainable but. The supply chain management (SCM) approach that involves implementing environments friendly practices in the supply chain has become popular due to realization that organizations have liability with respect to environmental issues (Sivasankaran & Ramesh, 2025). It is not only a trend but a requirement which has been imposed on by the regulations, the desire by consumers to be environmentally friendly and the chance of saving costs in the long-term due to optimization of resources (Kant et al., 2025). Irrespective of the good skeleton of GL, there are still a lot of stones on the way to practice. Indicatively, one case study about a major retailer in the world showed the difficulty of introducing the green practices to the current logistics processes (Verma, 2024). Streamlining transportation that involved use of electric vehicles and maximizing transportation routes, the company sought to cut on its carbon footprint. Nevertheless, the project was plagued by poor infrastructure, lack of charging stations to charge electric vehicles and initial cost of converting the fleet. Such difficulties make it evident that, a favorable regulatory atmosphere and technological investment are specifically two factors that would help in the implementation of GL (Nagy & Szentesi, 2024). The other case which is also relevant is that of the case of a multinational logistics provider which tried to apply a CER system. The firm has developed the highest routing software, but they found that there was a problem with integrating the data in different platforms and this has caused inefficiency and a boost in the cost of running the company. The lack of standard measurements that determined how much carbon emissions were affected complicated their efforts, causing a major discrepancy in the properly measuring the impression of green initiatives (Wang & Ye, 2025).

In addition, the case of a European car producer shows that the internal opposition might retrain the implementation of GL policies. Though the organization saw the environmental and economic, which could have been achieved, the organizational culture was getting in the way due to cultural inertia among the employees and management (Kiem et al., 2024). The training and change management initiatives failed to generate an organization-wide commitment to sustainability, which provides proof of the notion that the effective implementation of a change does not simply require the technological solutions, but also culture and group alignment.

These case studies show that the issues of GL implementation are intricate that is, related to such aspects as technology, infrastructure, and culture. These problems are pressing to the companies that intend to use GL as a tool of increasing SLO. Through the detail analysis of these obstacles, the chapter will try to provide insights on the effective implementation efforts of breaking the barriers to implementation, which will in turn lead to future research and policy makers in the logistics industry (Gupta et al., 2023).

STATEMENT OF PROBLEM

The logistics sector is now at a junction point with the dream state of being an integration of sustainability and logistical efficiencies by way of GL and SL optimisation. In an ideal situation, organizations smoothly introduce eco-friendly practices which do not only reduce the emissions of carbon, but also improve the performance of the supply chains in general (Nagy & Szentesi, 2024)GL. The reality, however, very often is quite different. Several studies mention inconsistent results towards the effectiveness of GL programs with some studies indicating an insignificant effect on work efficiency (Cheng et al., 2024). This discrepancy raises some relative question marks about the circumstances in which the green practices are actually beneficial. In addition, the available literature show inconclusive findings on the normal correlation across GL and SL optimisation especially so in CER. Some of the studies found that there are positive correlations while others claimed that the difficulties and challenges, related to implementation in teaching can cause cancellation of these prospective benefits (Pham et al, 2023). Theoretical gaps also exist, as there are no frameworks that enable a comprehensive understanding of the interaction between various factors in the GL domain. The gaps in the theory are also there, and they do not have the frameworks to understand the interaction about different factors of the GL domain in a holistic manner. Also, there are gaps in knowledge on the particular processes, by which GL initiatives impact the performance of logistics, hence, researchers and practitioners do not have specific guidelines as to how to implement them (Verma, 2024).

The discrepancies in the context complicate things; most of the available studies are for developed economies and have little applicable knowledge for new emerging markets, where there are significant differences in the logistics (Botha et al., 2023; Nagirikandalage et al., 2023). GL practices are not around the globe simply due to practical challenges such as poor infrastructure, resistance from employees and lack of standardised metrics by which sustainability is to be measured. Such obstacles create a sense of urgency to possess an analytical study that entails relating the theories with the realities (Mukalula et al., 2024). The proposed study will address these loopholes by using the empirical evidence of the interdependence of GL and SL optimisation using CER. As a result of effective methodological framework, by incorporating CFA and SEM, this study will bring light on the connections across this constructs and define the circumstances under which the implementation is to be successful (Masudin et al., 2025). Moreover, it will give some practical recommendations to policymakers and logistics managers that will make it possible to conduct strategies not only to cover the environmental issues but maximize the performance of the operations. Through this, the study will be able to set the pathway to future investigations and will additionally act as a guide to the organizations which aim at realizing sustainability in its logistics practices.

THEORETICAL FOUNDATION

Resource-Based View: Using it to GL, RBV claims that sustainable practices might be considered one of the valuable assets that would enhance the performance of the business and put the company in the spotlight. By using green technologies and practices, organizations can reduce their carbon footprint without the need to spend money on these measures: they can also save money and increase customer loyalty. The RBV also considers the nature of internal competencies in the process of exploiting such sustainable strategies hence it is a highly relative framework to understand how the firms can adequately attain GL initiatives (Ngo, 2022).

Stakeholder Theory: It applies particularly to the study of GL because the recent trend towards sustainability can be interpreted as the indication of the increase in the demands of several stakeholders concerning the necessity of embracing environmental friendly practices. The reason is that as the logistics operations are brought into the range of the expectations of the stakeholders, the companies can enhance their reputation and develop long-term nexus. This theory provides the data concerning the motivation to carry out GL and the topicality of the stakeholder influence in the process of facilitation of the success in the successful implementation (Tetteh et al., 2024).

Diffusion of Innovations Theory: It is applicable to the sphere of GL as it helps to understand how the integration of the sustainable practices can be influenced by various factors in the entire logistics industry. Among the factors that play immense roles towards the rate of adoption, perceived benefits, compatibility with the current practices, complexity and the social system can be cited. Analyzing the distribution of GL innovations can be applied to impact the plans of promoting the adoption and usage of the environmentally-friendly logistics solutions (Su et al., 2022).

Systems Theory: under it, organizations will have the ability to generate synergies and dependencies which will dictate the workability of GL programs. This combined structure will be crucial in supporting the operations of the logistics and, it will guarantee that the sustainability program is in tandem with the overall organizational objectives (Keivanpour, 2023).

The RBV is the major theoretical lens that was used in the current research. The idea of RBV about the use of unique resources and capabilities is quite correlated with the goals of the GL and SLO, and the benefits of organizations can be identified by becoming sustainable.

CONCEPT DEFINITION AND ORIGIN

Green Logistics: GL may be considered as part of environmental forces in the logistics and SCM. The idea was conceived in early 90s when the environmental issue was on the rise and it is then that the businesses began to examine their operations so as to have a lower environmental footprint. GL encompasses different methods, including the efficiency of resources, waste reduction, sustainable logistical transportation methods aimed at the reduction of a carbon footprint of the logistical processes (Jou et al., 2024).

Smart Logistics: SL is a scenario where they involve advanced technologies and the utilization of information to enhance the operations of the logistics. The phrase has been made common because of the advent of the Internet of Things (IoT), big data, and artificial intelligence which enables things to be tracked in real-time, conduct predictive analytics, and make more intelligent decisions. Technology will help SL be more efficient, cost-effective, and service-oriented when applied to develop more agile and responsive supply chains (Aliahmadi et al., 2022).

Carbon-Efficient Routing: It involves developing transportation paths in order to make a network with lowest carbon emissions and at the same time is efficient in the delivery of production of goods and services. This concept relies on the overall architecture of GL and is pegged at implementing the data analytics and modeling techniques to find out the most environmentally friendly routes. One can relate the history of this term to the rise of interest in the topic of sustainability in transportation and the need to address the problem of the environmental impression of the logistics operations (Sun et al., 2021).

Sustainable SCM: The Sustainable SCM embraces the use of environmental friendly practices in all the activities of the supply chain like sourcing of raw materials to delivery of products. The term was coined in the late 20th century when companies began to realize that sustainability should not be seen as a kind of compliance but rather as a competitive edge. Sustainable SCM is an approach to supply management that considers social, economic and environmental impacts in the supply chain cycle (Seuring & Müller, 2008).

EMPIRICAL LITERATURE REVIEW

GL and SLO

It has been shown that companies that have incorporated the GL practices do not simply achieve a decrease in the amount of carbon emission but also performance metrics of their businesses (Liu et al., 2019). This aligns with the findings of other researchers, among them, who found that the customer satisfaction and the more loyal customer rates increased in organizations where environmentally friendly actions had been implemented, and that it was plausible that more consumers will be shifting towards buying more environmentally-minded-oriented business (Vatankhah et al., 2023). SLO is now among the crucial issues of the logistics management that utilizes innovative technologies, such as artificial intelligence, the Internet of Things (IoT), and big data analytics (Sun et al., 2021). An example of these technologies is pointed out in studies that indicate these technologies facilitate real-time decision making as well as enhance efficient routing. Even smart technologies, incorporated not only to simplify a transportation path and streamline it, but also to provide details regarding the inventory management and warehouse activities, eventually result in the overall agility of the supply chain (Seetharaman, 2022). An appropriate survey conducted has shown that companies using SL solutions reported a major drop in lead times and operational costs, which further explains the importance of technology in the excellence of logistics (Sharma et al., 2024).

One of the prospective areas of empirical research is the GL and SLO crossroad. The manner in which the introduction of smart technologies can support GL initiatives has been explored in some of the studies. Indicatively, one of the studies demonstrated that under the real-time conditions of tracking consumption and emissions with the assistance of IoT technologies, the ability of a company to be sustainable is significantly increased (Parthasarathy, 2024). This technological and environmental sustainability symbiosis can equally be cross-read between the research lines where it is proposed that those companies who can integrate SL opportunities with green business strategies have a two-fold benefit; in effectiveness and enhanced environmental conduct. In addition, the empirical findings claim that the nexus among the GL practices and the entire success of the supply chain performance may be mediated by the adopted SL optimisation (Sivasankaran & Ramesh, 2025). The research has found that the successful use of smart technologies by companies does not only enable them to enhance their environmental impression, but they are also able to enhance their logistics performance, thereby, delivering better results concerning their financial performance. The mediation effect emphasizes the relevance of technology in the need to have a successful execution of sustainability in the logistics operations (Mutambik, 2024).

H 1: GL and SLO are empirically associated.

GL and CER

One of the studies discloses the key aspects of GL like waste reduction, resource conservation, and management of emissions, which have a cumulative impact of improving the efficiency of the supply chain (Cheng et al., 2024). Moreover, according to one of the studies, the companies implementing GL practices can not only comply with the necessary regulation but even improve their competitive advantage through the creation of a positive image within the society and consumer happiness. CER is a specific method of GL, that is, oriented at the enhancement of transport routes to minimize carbon emittance (Garside et al., 2024). This strategy can be useful in implementing sustainability objectives as evidenced by empirical studies and research. Indicatively, a research study has established that with the use of advanced routing algorithms by organizations, the consumption of fuel and greenhouse gas emissions reduce drastically (Mandal and Mohammed, 2024). As it is demonstrated in these works, the application of the data-driven routing solutions will lead to the positive impressions of the environment, and the cost saving that will aid the economic viability of the sustainable logistics processes. In addition, the nexus between GL and CER is backed by empirical evidence to support the potential of the latter in being the mediator in the achievement of the sustainability objectives. A research that was conducted has stipulated that companies which focus more on CER perform optimally in their operations and this reveals that successful routing not only reduces the carbon footprints but also the provision of improved delivery service and customer satisfaction (Ding et al., 2025). This mediation effect outlines the weight of the necessity to integrate carbon effective plans in bigger GL programs.

It has a few chapters that have explored the technological basis of CER. As an illustration, one can conduct a study on how Geographic Information Systems (GIS) and real-time tracking systems are applicable in order to optimize routes on the basis of the prevailing traffic and impression of the environment. A technological integration of this kind assists the logistics managers in making good decisions and in doing so to achieve sustainability and assure that the organization is efficient in executing its operations (Sun et al., 2021). Furthermore, it is supported by the empirical results, as the companies that apply to smart technologies in the routing activities document the decrease in the emissions, the service or operation level, and the prices of the operations. In addition to the technological changes, organizational commitment to sustainability is also relative in the sense that the CER will be attained successfully (Liu et al., 2021). One of the studies indicates that firms highly sustainability oriented have a tendency of adopting innovative routing practices that additionally assist in enhancing the overall logistics performance of companies.

This observation suggests that the culture and management of the company have a relative role to play in the practice of sustainable routing.

H2:GL and CER being empirically associated.

CER and SLO

The paper applies the study to demonstrate that applying advanced algorithms to improve routes can contribute to massive reductions in fuel consumption and greenhouse gases (Parthasarathy, 2024). They discover that the organizations that have adopted CER strategies have been in a position to achieve two things, they are striving towards the objective of sustainability and simultaneously, there is a reduction of the operating cost. The drastic to the ambitions of CER is SLO that implies the application of new technologies, big data analytics, machine learning, and the Internet of Things (IoT). Research indicates that the use of smart technologies will allow logistics managers to easily perform real-time data analysis to help them make informed decisions about the routing process to not only achieve efficiency and sustainability goals but also objectives (Mohsen, 2024). As an example of such cases, predictive analytics and real-time traffic data can enable companies to make on-the-fly route adjustments and, therefore, reduce delays and fuel consumption. This interdependence of SL and the environment-friendly practices has shown the fact that not only it is possible to make the organizations progress in their activities, but also the needs of the environment can be fulfilled (Hussain, 2025). One more concept that CER acts as a moderating element of achieving the benefits of SLO can be demonstrated with the assistance of empirical data as well. Research indicates that firms that have managed to use smart technologies successfully when they are combined with CER models indicate that the customer service has been enhanced and the overall impact on the environment has been positive. Specifically, the study found that the companies that applied data-driven knowledge to enhance their technology in routing not only reduced their carbon footprints but also ensured diminished delivery times and reliability of their services, which are of major importance in terms of competitive advantage (Mandal and Mohammed, 2024).

Moreover, other empirical studies have talked more about the technological aspects of the making of CER. Indicationally, research has yielded statistical evidence regarding the suitability of Geographic Information Systems (GIS) and state-of-the-art routing software to decide on the routes which are the most carbon-efficient (Mandal and Mohammed, 2024). Their findings indicate that companies that use these technologies can initiate reducing their environmental impression significantly and improve the efficiency of their logistics. In addition, there is a study that shows the necessity to unite SL platforms that would enable establishing collaboration among stakeholders and make more efficient decisions about routing to address the principles of sustainability (Mandal and Mohammed, 2024). Besides, the organizational culture and leaders dedication towards sustainability plays a vital role in achieving successful implementation of CER strategies. One of the studies determined that innovative routing technologies and practices are usually practiced by companies that are highly sustainable. The presence of such alignment of the organizational values with the operational strategies not only relieves the creation of an organizational commitment to the environmental responsibility but also makes the SL initiative effective (Lazar et al., 2022).

H3: Empirical association of CER and SLO.

GL, SLO and CER Mediation

TGL is a combination of strategies, which attempt to minimize impressions on the environment. It represents the fundamental structure under which SLO and CER operate (Mutie et al., 2020)GL. Studies have established that companies that use GL do not only adhere to laws and regulations, but also become more competitive in the market as a company that enjoys the customers who are environmentally conscious. With the current technology like big data analytics, artificial intelligence, and the use of Internet of Things (IoT), it has been shown that SLO can greatly contribute to GL (Parthasarathee, 2024). Studies reveal that processing of information with the use of smart technology and making real time decisions will become easy and this is necessary to improve the logistical operations. To provide an example, the plans can be adjusted by any company utilizing smart logistics, depending on how to get to the destination in regard to the existing traffic and weather patterns. This enhances the benefits which are subsequently better and sustainable. This association both between smart technologies and GL demonstrates the way operational performance might be enhanced (Sileikiene and Karoseviciene, 2024).

CER is a relative halfway covenant of this nexus. It aids in their extraction of general green activities to routing efficiencies. It has been found out that routing efficiency in businesses where SL Optimisation strategies are in place is improved and therefore, the advantages of GL practices become even more pronounced by the effectiveness of routing efficiency (Osman, 2023). The ability to identify the most appropriate routes in order to reduce carbon emissions not only helps the businesses to achieve their sustainability goals, but also enhances the level of services and costs are minimized. This mediation effect demonstrates the way in which good routing techniques could make the larger objectives of GL real operational benefits. The real life data supports the concept that big gains in performance can be made by the combination of GL, SLO and CER. An example is that a study has shown that firms that have successfully integrated these three items experienced significant reductions in fuel consumption and also in greenhouse gases (Parthasarathy, 2024). The conclusions they draw demonstrate the importance of the holistic view about the logistics management when the consideration of both the sustainability of the practices as well as the technological novelties provides the background to the achievement of both economic and environmental objectives. Moreover, organizational leadership and cultural commitment also should not be underestimated as essential factors in ensuring this integration. It has been shown that being environmental conscious, companies are more likely to make use of new routing technology and practices, which would meet the GL objectives (Pham et al., 2023).

H4: empirical association of GL, SLO and CER

METHODOLOGY

The method of research adopted in this chapter was a quantitative research to investigate the influence of GL on SLO regarding CER. The sample size was 394, which was adequate in capturing the representatives in the logistics sector. The research was carried out by the means of applying a structured questionnaire, in which it was developed, upon a comprehensive analysis of the existing literature. That is how, one could receive the systematic data related to constructs of interest, i.e., to practices of GL, SLO, and CER. A KMO value of greater than 0.70 was considered to be a good indication that the sample could be subjected to further analysis hence the data was suitable to undergo the exploratory factor analysis (EFA). EFA in order to identify the underlying format of the constructs was conducted with the view of allowing the design of an effective measurement scale. SEM allowed to test normal and indirect impressions, which provided the answers related to the impression of GL on SLO with the help of CER. The outcomes of this analysis furnished factual data to confirm the hypotheses developed and gave a complete picture, on which the dynamics occur.

Scale Development

In this research, the scale was developed based on critical examination on other literature and therefore, all items applied were well aware of the existing theories and research. The key constructs applied to GL were selected according to the previous studies which implied the significance of sustainable practices in the logistics operations. There were the addition of products that included environmental accountability, resource effectiveness and communication to stakeholders to represent complexity of GL. With SLO construct, the literature raising the significance of technology, data analytics and innovative practices as driving better logistic performance study was conducted. The products, which identify the efficiency, responsiveness, and integration of the advanced technologies, have been created and designed to suit the targets of SL. CER was operationalised in the context of items that focused on optimisation of routes, and the minimisation of emissions as well as using data to make decisions. The items were a well-formulated and understandable, which was made in a Likert scale format to facilitate the answers of the participants. The initial scale pre-tested was to achieve the fine-tuning of the phrasing and to make all of the items in the scale the correct measure of the construct intended. It has been a gradual systematic process of development that rested on the literature and empirical substantiation thus has given rise to a comprehensive measurement scale that has succeeded in capturing analyses of interest constructs. The subsequent analyses demonstrated the reliability and validity of the scale that justified the relevance of scale to the purposes of the study and provided a solid ground to the study of the effect of GL on the SLO.

DATA ANALYSIS

Table 1. Data adequacy measure

Kaiser Sample		**.908**
Sphericity Bartlett	Chi-Square	19484.673
	df	780
	p-value	.000

Source: Authors

According to Table 1, it shows that sampling adequacy is reported to be 0.908 implying that it is of an excellent level. KMO of above.70 is acceptable and below 1.0 is a high suitability of factor analysis. This is a key of large KMO that demonstrates the sufficiency of the sample to the exclusivity factor analysis (EFA) and it justifies validity of the piece of data. Other than KMO measure, the Bartlett Sphericity Test is also useful in providing useful information on factorability of the correlation matrix. It is stated that the Chi-square value is 19,484.673 which has a degree of freedom of 780 and p-value of 0.000. The p value is very minor and demonstrates that the null hypothesis of a correlation matrix as an identity matrix can be rejected. This means that, the variables are mostly correlated to each other, which justifies the usage of factor analysis.

Table 2. Sum variance

Factor	Initial Eigen			Extraction			Rotation		
	Sum	% of Variance	Cumulative %	Sum	% of Variance	Cumulative %	Sum	% of Variance	Cumulative %
1	2.7	26.7	26.76	2.7	26.7	26.7	8.7	21.9	21.9
2	1.9	14.9	41.71	1.9	14.9	41.7	6.0	15.0	37.0
3	1.3	10.9	52.68	1.3	10.9	52.6	4.6	11.6	48.6

Abstraction Process: PCA.
Source: Authors

Table 2 displays the an eigenvalue of 2.7 that explains 26.7% of the total variance and the second factor is of 14.9% that is pictorised to a cumulative variance of 41.7 per cent after two factors. The third factor contributes with a value of 10.9 that has an eigen value of 1.3 making the cumulative variance of the two factors to 52.6. These initial findings suggest the fact that the initial three variables may explain over 50 percent of the variation of the data and this may suggest that there is a high structure of the data. The values of the squared extracting loadings T incumbent are the initial eigenvalues which affirm that the analysis will extract the identical factors at the post-extraction phase. The square of the loading of the data that have been rotated indicates that one factor (the first one) with a percentage of variance (21.9) takes up a larger percentage of variance, whereas the second factor (2), and third factor (3) with percentages of variances equal to 15.0 and 11.6 respectively. The cumulative variance when these three factors are rotated is 48.6%.

Table 3. Mediation

	Worth
GL → SLO	.10
GL → CER → SLO	.93*.23=.21
	.21

Source: Authors

Table 3 explores the mediating effect The normal nexus between GL and SLO means that there is a path effect of.10 implying that this nexus is not statistically significant. It suggests that the effect of GL as such on optimal process of the logistics procedures does not exist. The reality effect, so to speak, in its turn but to the incorporation of CER in an intermediary position, is a more provocative impression. This estimation is the addition of the product of the path coefficients:.93 (the impression of GL on CER) x.23 (the impression CER on SLO) to give an implied effect of.21. The consequences of this observation are the implication that CER is a major mediator between the two concepts of GL and SLO. Full mediation describes the name which reveals the entire impression of the GL on the SLO to be achieved through applying CER. This does not imply that GL will impress on SLO but impresses positively on CER that will also impress SLO positively.

DISCUSSION

The findings of the present study may be of immense value in learning the mutual nexus amongst GL, CER, and SLO. The strong interconnections identified according to both the exploratory factor analysis and the regression analysis indicate the importance of the sustainable practices implementation in logistics systems. The meditating role of the CER, in particular, is very relative which, in turn, highlights the significance of such a nexus in the range of GL and operational efficiency as align by RBV theory. GL, in its sole occurrence, did not express any normal impact in SLO, however, it adds to its impression to a significant extent through the efficient routing schemes. This means that the convergence of the environmentally friendly practices of the organizations that aim at improving their logistics performance should be given priority to such that it may generate more efficient routing solutions as depicted by system theory. The strength of theoretical framework of the current study is also supported by the good reliability and validity of the constructs revealed by statistics of the model fit and validity measures. Besides, the research results correlate with the growing amount of investigations that emphasize the role of logistics sustainability. Following the increasing role of the environmental problems with the global supply chains and the discoveries, one can say that the organizations not only can contribute to achieving the ecological goals, but they can also obtain considerable advantages in the context of operation through SL practices.

CONCLUSION

In this study, the researcher explains the major interdependences among GL, CER and SLO and the power of sustainability in realizing efficiency in operation in the logistics industry. The findings show that SLO is significantly affected by GL although the effect is abnormal and highly mediated by CER. This presents the need to ensure organizations incorporate environmentally friendly operations that can be adopted in seeking effective routing solutions that would ultimately lead to improvement in the performance of the logistics. The constructs used in this study are valid and reliable as indicated by the strong ability of the statistical testing which included exploratory factor analysis and regression test. As the concept sustainability has been gaining popularity in the SCM, the knowledge acquired in this study contributes to the growing literature in favour of the implementation of green practices into logistic practices. This paper has theoretical and practical implications on the practitioners due to the interdependence of sustainability and efficiency. The companies should also strategically emphasize on the CER as an important constituent in the logistics, which could enable them not only to achieve environmental dreams, but also operation excellence. Lastly, this chapter in the research will serve as a platform where future studies about the same subject matter will be carried out and more literature will be done on the dynamics of sustainable logistics and how it relates to various industries.

MANAGERIAL IMPLICATIONS

The conclusions of this study have certain useful managerial implications, which can be implemented in organizations, which have to enhance their performance in terms of efficiency in logistics and still adhere to sustainable standards. First of all, the managers need to recognize the significance of GL as a fundamental element potentially involved in making the CER methods more effective. A special attention to pro-environmental programs will provide the organization with the possibility to create the system that could not only be concerned with the issues of ecology but guarantee the efficiency of routing processes. Furthermore, the chapter has identified that in order to achieve sustainable practices, managers must invest in training and development programs capable of equipping the logistics employees with the skills that will enable them achieve the desired sustainable practices in an effective manner. The outcome of such investment can be an increased understanding of how the notion of GL can be applied to the decision-making made in operations and enhance the routing alternatives. The organizations should also consider the possibility of initiating collaborative associations with stake holders and suppliers who are interested in sustainability since the nexus would help maximize the benefits of adopting green practices in the whole chain of supply. Finally, the managers should consider applying data analytics and technology to trace and evaluate the implication of GL on efficiency in routing. Through the advanced tools and technologies, organizations have the capacity to have a clear view of its logistics activity and, as such, be in a position to make sound decisions that can address the sustainability considerations, as well as the performance indicators. Overall, when the managers consider these findings within the strategy making, they will be in a position to go beyond environmental stewardship but also operational excellence within their logistics operations thereby allowing them to make their organizations successful in the long run in the competitive atmosphere.

PRACTICAL IMPLICATIONS

There are several viable implications of the findings of this chapter to organizations that do wish to enhance their logistics procedures by applying sustainable practices. Firstly, the companies will be obliged to use GL programs that are aimed at reducing environmental impression and optimal resources utilization. This could include the introduction of the new packaging that will be environmentally friendly, alternative types of fuel or making the transportation and warehousing more energy efficient. These practices may be used by companies during their work in order to meet the requirements of the regulator, and, simultaneously, to gain increasing amounts of environmentally-aware consumers. To a greater extent, this chapter reveals the importance of CER as a crucial quality of logistics management. Practically, it would mean that the companies should invest in better routing software and equipment that will enable them to analyze the information in real-time and optimize the routes. Such tools will enable the logistics managers to reduce transportation expenses and emission large, and this will enable the operational efficiency to be in line with the sustainability objectives. Also, it is encouraged that organizations make the employees possess a sustainability culture. This will be achieved through the arrangements of the training programs that will emphasize the importance of GL and its benefits both to the environment and the bottom line of the firm. Employee motivation to engage in sustainability projects may lead to innovative thinking about how to improve the operations of logistics and, by and large, the commitment to sustainability projects.

Lastly, the collaboration between itself and the suppliers and partners, is required to make the most out of the sustainable logistics practices. Developments of alliances that are sustainability oriented can aid in enhancing the overall performance of supply chains as well as creating competitive advantages. It is through this that organizations will be able to work together to find ever-sustainable solutions to their logistic challenges that maximizes overall benefits to all parties through the sharing of best practices and resources. It plays a role in smart and AI-enabled logistics solutions in supporting carbon-efficient routing and sustainability objectives.

THEORETICAL IMPLICATIONS

This chapter can also be applied to the current theoretical model of sustainable logistics in the coverage of the intricate, nomadic networking between GL, CER and SLO. By demonstrating that CER is the mediating variable, the study supplements the existing research on the logistics management, and one should view the sustainability practices in a more advanced manner that is concerned with the impact they induce on the function of the operation. This mediation effect implies that the effect of GL on the result of the performance is not the normal one but is conditional upon the usage of effective routine strategies. Moreover, the findings are consistent and complementary to the existing theories of sustainability and logistics which underpin the statement that the operations are operationalizable with the assistance of the environmental practices. The empirical information provided in the chapter is to demonstrate the point that the introduction of environmental concerns into the logistics operations is not only beneficial in terms of the ecological outcomes, but it also contributes to the increase in the performance of the supply chain. It, thus, facilitates the further investigation of the processes through which sustainability influences the performance of logistics, which means that the future research should focus on estimating the number of the additional mediating or moderating conditions here. The paper also points out that the comprehensive development of a sophisticated theoretical framework is needed that will focus on various issues of sustainability of logistics. By so doing, researchers will be in a position to understand how different factors interact and they contribute towards the achievement of improved logistics. The proposed study can be implemented in future research on dynamic nature of sustainable logistics and provides the avenue of having more concrete theoretical frameworks which could elucidate dynamics of environmental concerns in SCM.

RECOMMENDATIONS

Based on the findings of the present research, it is possible to provide several recommendations to the organizations which are interested in enhancing their logistics activity with references to the notion of sustainability. To begin with, the businesses ought to conduct an extensive analysis of the current logistics processes to ensure that the areas that have the potential of including GL programs are determined. It also means that companies should be more concerned with the practices that would not only weaken the effect on the environment but also be related to the effectiveness of operations, such as the optimization of transportation routes and the utilization of the environmentally friendly materials of packaging. Second is the fact that there is a need to invest in technology. Among the recommendations that the organizations might take into consideration is to embrace advanced routing software and data analytics software that will facilitate in the CER attainment. These technologies provide the opportunity to control and optimize the logistics processes in real time and guarantee that the companies use less fuel and produce less pollution and improve their output. Third, there is need to establish a culture of sustainability amongst the employees. Companies should also embrace training programs that would enlighten the workers on the importance of GL and the roles that they play towards the realization of the sustainability objectives. By encouraging the employees to participate in the sustainability activities, new solutions might be created and a commitment to sustainability may be enhanced. Further, it is advisable that the companies should form a powerful nexus with suppliers and other stakeholders sharing the same sustainability goals. Through collaboration in sustainable initiatives, the efficiency of the logistic operations can be enhanced, and more robust chain of supply can be created. This is by sharing the resources and best practices in which the companies can have a unit goal of attaining more sustainable logistics outcomes. Finally, companies are also encouraged to continuously monitor and evaluate how its sustainability programmes impact on the performance of logistics. The common appraisal will help in establishing the gains and the degree of the advancements required to ensure that the companies are lean and at par with the evolving market conditions and regulatory aspects.

FUTURE NORMALIONS

The findings of this chapter show many avenues of research in the future in the field of sustainable logistics. One of the positive course actions could be the consideration of other mediating/moderating variables that could change the nexus present between GL and operational performance. In this respect, research studies can be undertaken in future to study the interaction of such aspects like the utilization of technology, corporate culture, or the regulatory environment and sustainability measures to facilitate the degree of efficiency in logistics operation. The understanding of such dynamics can come up with a more globalized view of the logistics environment. The other avenue that could be considered the addition to Elaborate CER is the role of new technologies, such as artificial intelligence and machine learning. Research can be normalized into how this kind of technologies can be utilized to design the routing strategy in real-time enabling a further reduction of the impact on the environment, yet the efficiency is to be maximized. Moreover, the discussion of the digital transformation connotation in logistics and its intersection with sustainability can be valuable to the practitioners and scholars. It would also be helpful to implement longitudinal studies of the long term implications of GL program on the performance of the organization. The fact that researchers can track the sustainability route of organizations over the course of time will assist them in finding out the long term implications of such practices and in what situations these practices were most successful. Lastly, the global perspective is also of interest in sustainable logistics and is to be considered. New researches could outline feelings of cultural, economic, and regulatory differences in areas concerning the adoption and performance of GL practices. This knowledge of these tendencies in the world will allow the organizations to create their sustainability strategies to suit specific scenarios and become more effective.

REFERENCES

Aliahmadi, A., Nozari, H., & Ghahremani-Nahr, J. (2022). AIoT-based Sustainable Smart Supply Chain Framework. *International Journal of Innovation in Management Economics and Social Sciences*, *2*(2), 28–38. DOI: 10.52547/ijimes.2.2.28

Botha, L., Human, L. I., Rossouw, M. E., & Nel, J. D. (2023). A framework to drive business growth in developing countries using omni-channel strategies. *International Journal of Business Performance Management*, *24*(3/4), 344–374. DOI: 10.1504/IJBPM.2023.132319

Cheng, H., Chaudhry, H. R., Kazi, I., & Umar, M. (2024). Unlocking greener supply chains: A global innovative perspective on the role of logistics performance in reducing ecological footprints. *Journal of Innovation & Knowledge*, *9*(4), 100612. DOI: 10.1016/j.jik.2024.100612

Ding, Y., Zhang, L., Kuo, Y., & Zhang, L. (2025). Cold chain routing for product freshness and low carbon emissions: A target-oriented robust optimization approach. *Transportation Research Part E, Logistics and Transportation Review*, *199*, 104138. DOI: 10.1016/j.tre.2025.104138

Estévez, M., Ballestar, M. T., & Sáinz, J. (2025). Market research and knowledge using Generative AI: The power of Large Language Models. *Journal of Innovation & Knowledge*, *10*(5), 100796. DOI: 10.1016/j.jik.2025.100796

Garside, A. K., Ahmad, N. A., & Muhtazaruddin, M. N. (2024). A recent review of solution approaches for green vehicle routing problem and its variants [Review of *A recent review of solution approaches for green vehicle routing problem and its variants*]. *Operations Research Perspectives, 12*, 100303. DOI: 10.1016/j.orp.2024.100303

Gupta, H., Shreshth, K., Kharub, M., & Kumar, A. (2023). Strategies to overcome challenges to smart sustainable logistics: A Bayesian-based group decision-making approach. *Environment, Development and Sustainability*, *26*(5), 11743–11770. DOI: 10.1007/s10668-023-03477-6

Hadi, S., Miru, S., Kaseng, S., Asngadi, Syamsuddin, S., & Zahra, F. (2023). Barriers to GL Implementation in Indonesia: A Preliminary Study. In *Advances in Social Science, Education and Humanities Research/Advances in social science, education and humanities research* (p. 254). DOI: 10.2991/978-2-38476-172-2_41

Hussain, K. (2025). Revolutionizing Route Optimization Systems with Artificial Intelligence for a Smarter, Sustainable Logistics Ecosystem. *International Journal of Computer Science and Mobile Computing*, *14*(2), 66–68. DOI: 10.47760/ijcsmc.2025.v14i02.008

Jou, Y., Lo, C.-Y., Mariñas, K. A., Saflor, C. S., Gutierrez, C. J., Sanchez, C., Songco, D., Redston, J., Devara, M. B., & Bucal, M. J. (2024). Assessing the E-Commerce Sustainability Readiness: A GL Study on Online Sellers. *Sustainability (Basel)*, *16*(7), 2954. DOI: 10.3390/su16072954

Kant, S., Adula, M., & Alemu, G. M. (2025). Effect of Green Supply Chain Management Practice on Firm Performance With Mediation of Green Innovation in Ethiopia. In *Eco-Logistics and Sustainable Supply Chain Innovations* (pp. 61–84). IGI Global Scientific Publishing.

Kant, S., & Ashuro, T. (2025). Effect of Eco-Logistics Practices on Organizational Performance With Mediating Role of MSE Competitiveness in Ethiopia. In *Eco-Logistics and Sustainable Supply Chain Innovations* (pp. 39–60). IGI Global Scientific Publishing.

Keivanpour, S. (2023). Sustainable Logistics Management: An Introductory Overview. In *Synthesis lectures on sustainable development* (p. 99). Morgan & Claypool Publishers. DOI: 10.1007/978-3-031-44652-8_5

Kiem, P. V., Quynh, V. T. N., Phan, T. T., & Nguyen, N. A. (2024). The Impression of Organizational Culture on Employee Performance: A Case Study at Foreign-Invested Logistics Service Enterprises Approaching Sustainability Development. *Sustainability (Basel)*, *16*(15), 6366. DOI: 10.3390/su16156366

Lazar, S., Potočan, V., Kač, S. M., Yangınlar, G., Klimecka-Tatar, D., & Obrecht, M. (2022). Logistics Aspect of Organizational Culture and Normative Commitment in Electric Energy Supply Chain. *Management Systems in Production Engineering*, *30*(4), 319–330. DOI: 10.2478/mspe-2022-0041

Li, Y., Lim, M. K., Tseng, M., Lin, Y., Shi, Y., Huang, X., & Xiong, W. (2024). A literature review of green location routing problem: a comprehensive analysis of problems, objectives and methodologies [Review of *A literature review of green location routing problem: a comprehensive analysis of problems, objectives and methodologies*]. *International Journal of Logistics Research and Applications*, 1. DOI: 10.1080/13675567.2024.2332362

Liu, H., Liu, X., Islam, S. M. N., Yu, X., Miao, Q., Chen, Y., & Lin, L. (2021). Customer demand-driven low-carbon vehicles combined strategy and route optimisation integrated decision. *Scientific Reports*, *11*(1), 18483. Advance online publication. DOI: 10.1038/s41598-021-98028-2 PMID: 34531499

Liu, Y., Zhang, Y., Ren, S., Yang, M., Wang, Y., & Huisingh, D. (2019). How can smart technologies contribute to sustainable product lifecycle management? *Journal of Cleaner Production*, *249*, 119423. DOI: 10.1016/j.jclepro.2019.119423

Mandal, J., & Mohammed, I. (2024). Implementation of AI Transportation Routing in Reverse Logistics to Reduce CO2 Footprint. *International Journal of SCM*, *9*(5), 1–12. DOI: 10.47604/ijscm.3079

Masudin, I., Selvia, A., Zulfikarijah, F., & Nasyiah, T. (2025). Exploring the Role of Circular Economy Practices in Linking GL Management and IoT with Sustainability Performance in SMEs. *Circular Economy and Sustainability*, *5*(5), 3787–3824. Advance online publication. DOI: 10.1007/s43615-025-00598-0

Mohsen, B. M. (2024). AI-Driven Optimization of Urban Logistics in Smart Cities: Integrating Autonomous Vehicles and IoT for Efficient Delivery Systems. *Sustainability (Basel)*, *16*(24), 11265. DOI: 10.3390/su162411265

Mukalula, P., Chisumbe, S., Kabaso, K., Aigbavboa, C., & Akinradewo, O. (2024). Benefits of Adopting Sustainability Practices by Construction Companies: Developing Country's Perspective. *Baltic Journal of Real Estate Economics and Construction Management*, *12*(1), 55–73. DOI: 10.2478/bjreecm-2024-0004

Mutambik, I. (2024). Digital Transformation as a Driver of Sustainability Performance—A Study from Freight and Logistics Industry. *Sustainability (Basel)*, *16*(10), 4310. DOI: 10.3390/su16104310

Mutie, M. D., Odock, S., & Litondo, K. (2020). GL Practices and Firm Performance: The Mediating Effect of Economic Performance Among Logistics Firms in Kenya. *European Scientific Journal*, *16*(25), 142. DOI: 10.19044/esj.2020.v16n25p142

Nagirikandalage, P., Kooli, K., & Binsardi, A. (2023). Exploring the evolvement of environmental management accounting practices for achieving SMEs' sustainability in an emerging economy. *International Journal of Accounting Auditing and Performance Evaluation*, *19*(2), 203–219. DOI: 10.1504/IJAAPE.2023.132404

Nagy, G., & Szentesi, S. (2024). GL: Transforming supply chains for a sustainable future. *Advanced Logistic Systems -. Theory into Practice*, *18*(3), 29. DOI: 10.32971/als.2024.026

Ngo, Q. (2022). The Adoption of Green Market Orientation in Logistic Industries—Empirical Evidence from Vietnamese SMEs. *Journal of Open Innovation, 8*(4), 199. DOI: 10.3390/joitmc8040199

Osman, M. C. (2023). GL Networks : Roles & Symbiotic Nexus. In *Linköping studies in science and technology. Thesis*. Linköping University Electronic Press. DOI: 10.3384/9789180752237

Parthasarathy, V. (2024). AI-Driven Carbon Footprint Tracking and Emission Reduction in Logistics Networks. *International Journal of Artificial Intelligence Data Science and Machine Learning, 5*, 47–56. DOI: 10.63282/3050-9262.IJAIDSML-V5I2P106

Pham, N. D. K., Dinh, G. H., Pham, H. T., Kozak, J., & Nguyen, H. A. T. (2023). Role of GL in the Construction of Sustainable Supply Chains. *Polish Maritime Research, 30*(3), 191–211. DOI: 10.2478/pomr-2023-0052

Seetharaman, K. M. R. (2022). Analysing the Role of Inventory and Warehouse Management in Supply Chain Agility: Insights from Retail and Manufacturing Industries. *International Journal of Current Engineering and Technology, 12*(6). Advance online publication. DOI: 10.14741/ijcet/v.12.6.13

Seuring, S., & Müller, M. (2008). From a literature review to a conceptual framework for sustainable SCM [Review of *From a literature review to a conceptual framework for sustainable SCM*]. *Journal of Cleaner Production, 16*(15), 1699. Elsevier BV. DOI: 10.1016/j.jclepro.2008.04.020

Sharma, M., Antony, R., Sharma, A., & Daim, T. (2024). Can smart supply chain bring agility and resilience for enhanced sustainable business performance? *International Journal of Logistics Management*. Advance online publication. DOI: 10.1108/IJLM-09-2023-0381

Šileikienė, D., & Karosevičienė, K. (2024). Smart technologies and their application in the transport sector. *Rural Development 2019, 2023*(1), 112. DOI: 10.15544/RD.2023.050

Sivasankaran, P., & Ramesh, G. (2025). Impression of GL and its significant importance in SCM operations-overall glance. *Acta Tecnología, 11*(3), 147–152. DOI: 10.22306/atec.v11i3.296

Su, M., Fang, M., Pang, Q., & Park, K.-S. (2022). Exploring the role of sustainable logistics service providers in multinational supply chain cooperation: An integrated theory-based perspective. *Frontiers in Environmental Science, 10*, 976211. Advance online publication. DOI: 10.3389/fenvs.2022.976211

Sun, X., Yu, H., Solvang, W. D., Wang, Y., & Wang, K. (2021). The application of Industry 4.0 technologies in sustainable logistics: a systematic literature review (2012–2020) to explore future research opportunities [Review of *The application of Industry 4.0 technologies in sustainable logistics: a systematic literature review (2012–2020) to explore future research opportunities*]. *Environmental Science and Pollution Research, 29*(7), 9560. DOI: 10.1007/s11356-021-17693-y

Tetteh, F. K., Kwateng, K. O., & Mensah, J. V. (2024). Enhancing carbon neutral supply chain performance: Can GL and pressure from supply chain stakeholders make any differences? *Sustainability Accounting Management and Policy Journal, 16*(2), 521–551. DOI: 10.1108/SAMPJ-08-2024-0884

Vatankhah, S., Sepehrmanesh, A., Zaeri, E., & Altınay, L. (2023). Environmental CSR, Customer Equity Drivers, and Travelers' Critical Outcomes: A Stimulus–Organism–Response Framework. *Journal of Hospitality & Tourism Research (Washington, D.C.), 48*(4), 725–740. DOI: 10.1177/10963480231156836

Verma, A. (2024). GL Practices Toward a Circular Economy: A Way to Sustainable Development. *Management and Production Engineering Review*. https://doi.org/ DOI: 10.24425/mper.2024.151136

Wang, S. G., & Ye, N.-X. (2025). Invisible footprints, visible insights: Machine learning reveals Scope 3 emissions. *Frontiers in Sustainability, 6*, 1649150. Advance online publication. DOI: 10.3389/frsus.2025.1649150

Wu, D., Ding, H., & Yang, C. (2024). How does environmental policy affect operations and SCM: A literature review [Review of *How does environmental policy affect operations and SCM: A literature review*]. *Computers & Industrial Engineering, 197*, 110580. DOI: 10.1016/j.cie.2024.110580

KEY TERMS AND DEFINITIONS

Logistics Performance: It is an index of efficiency and effectiveness of the logistics activities. This may be with respect to delivery time, cost effectiveness, customer satisfaction as well as environmental performance.

Supply Chain Management: This refers to the coordination and management of all such activities in production and delivering the goods even in the sourcing of raw materials to the delivery of the final products to the customers. SCM integrates the logistics, procurement, and operations functions to achieve the performance maximization.

Sustainability: It is a comprehensive process that tries to satisfy the present requirements without compromising on the future generations in an attempt to satisfy their needs too. This in logistics entails environmental, social and economic issues in operations.

Chapter 6
An Analytical Study on Cross-Border Logistics of the India-Bhutan Border Region:
A Comprehensive Systematic Literature Review

Kaushiki Bharadwaj
http://orcid.org/0009-0001-1642-8779
Amity University, Noida, India

Swati Sharma
http://orcid.org/0000-0003-2949-2363
Amity Institute of Travel and Tourism, India

Bruno Barbosa de Sousa
http://orcid.org/0000-0002-8588-2422
UNIAG, Polytechnic University of Cavado and Ave, Portugal

ABSTRACT

This chapter provides a detailed review of cross-border logistics along the India-Bhutan border. It uses the PRISMA 2020 framework to combine insights from academic, institutional, and grey literature. The focus is on the operational, regulatory, and infrastructure aspects that shape the logistics landscape between the two countries. Key topics include trade facilitation, customs alignment, and digital integration. Based on 86 carefully selected publications, the review identifies six main themes: infrastructure challenges, customs and regulatory issues, institutional

DOI: 10.4018/979-8-3373-7847-3.ch006

fragmentation, gaps in digital trade, political tensions, and informal trade practices. The findings show that while physical infrastructure poses significant challenges, effective institutional coordination and digital cooperation are also crucial for improving logistics efficiency and fostering regional integration.

INTRODUCTION

Borders are more than just lines on a map; they are complex social, political, and economic systems that manage the flow of goods, people, and money. In today's global economy, these frontiers, presents two main purposes; to act as gates for international trade and as significant obstacles to regional cooperation (Anderson & O'Dowd, 1999). The two-fold role is especially clear in the Himalayan region, where geography shapes, international territorial engagement with each other. Transboundary logistics is not just a technical task related to transportation; it is essential for collective governance. Hesse & Rodrigue (2004) highlights that the efficiency of these systems affects how competitive nations are in the global market.

Historically, international logistics developed with the growth of trade routes, colonial supply chains, and post-war globalization. The introduction of containerization in the mid-20th century changed the opinion of logistics, by making cargo movement more standard. In the 21st century, digital technologies, have made customs clearance faster and improved supply chain visibility (Levinson, 2016). Globally, logistics has helped economic growth by lowering transaction costs, increasing market access, and allowing for specialization in production. Regionally it has supported integration projects like the European Union's single market and ASEAN's trade corridors, showing its potential for transformation (World Bank, 2020).

In Southern part of Asia, cross-border shipping is crucial for regional cooperation through organizations like the South Asian Association for Regional Cooperation (SAARC) and the South Asia Subregional Economic Cooperation (SASEC). Even with issues related to infrastructure and regulations, cross-border shipping has supported trade in energy, agriculture, and manufactured goods. This has been providing a great contribution in the reduction of poverty and diversification of the economy (Asian Development Bank, 2019). However, there are obstacles remain in the scenario. Infrastructural deficit, complicated customs procedures, informal trade practices, and political issues inhibits shipping operations (Kathuria, 2018). At the same time, there are chances to improve digital trade, align standards, and invest in multimodal transport corridors.

In the regional landscape, the India-Bhutan border represents a unique case. Bhutan's interior geography in the Eastern Himalayas is a crucial point for economic survival. Bhutan shows the "Landlocked developing country contradiction that displays the nature of lack of access to the sea creating dependency on neighboring countries for transit". This geographic reality leads to "hidden taxes" on trade, which include high transit costs, unpredictable delays, and reliance on the quality of infrastructure in the transit country (World Bank, 2020). As a result, Bhutan's logistics terrain is at close quarter to India's transport efficiency. The India-Bhutan border caters as a case study for how political trust can reduce geographic vulnerability. India is Bhutan's largest trading partner, and the border supports the flow of hydropower, agricultural products, and consumer goods (Lama, 2023). The mutual relationship is marked by strong political trust, but having operational challenges, such as customs delays, infrastructure shortages, and informal trade which continue to affect the logistics landscape. Understanding these dynamics requires moving beyond simple policy discussions to systematic, evidence-based analysis. In the early evolutionary stage of logistics, it shows that in the Eastern Himalayan region, the trade was mainly organic and shaped by the terrain. It happened along ancient "Mule Tracks" that linked the Tibetan plateau to the plains of Bengal and Assam. Shipping depended on pack animals, such as mules and yaks, along with human porters who navigated the "Duars," or gateways, of the mountains (Rose, 1977). This was a barter-based "Borderland Economy" where goods like salt, wool, and musk were traded for rice and silk (Lama, 2023). The signing of the 1949 Treaty of Friendship between India and Bhutan began modern logistical planning. During this time, the focus shifted from "Strategic Isolation" to "Connectivity." The closing of the border with Tibet redirected Bhutan's logistical efforts southward toward India. This period also saw the introduction of Bhutan's First Five-Year Plan in 1961, which prioritized building the Phuntsholing-Thimphu highway, the first motorable link in the region (Rose, 1977). From the 1970s onward, the logistics landscape changed due to the "Hydropower Revolution." The technical needs for constructing large dams like Chukha and Tala in the Chukha district of Bhutan influenced the quality of the roads. The logistics network had to improve to accommodate heavy turbines and generators, which led to the development of robust road infrastructure for civilian trade (Asian Development Bank, 2019). The 2007 Revised Treaty updated the legal framework, giving Bhutan more autonomy while India agreed to provide smooth transit rights. This further formalized the logistics corridor (Lama, 2024). Currently, the focus is on "Soft Infrastructure," moving from simply building roads to managing them using digital and regional systems. The creation of the BBIN (Bangladesh, Bhutan, India, Nepal) framework and the SASEC Operational Plan signified a shift toward better regional connectivity and transport routes (Rahman & Bari, 2016; ADB, 2019).

In the 21st century, the emphasis has shifted to "Digital Trade Facilitation," aiming to replace paper-based processes with electronic systems like ICEGATE (Indian Customs Electronic Gateway) and ECMS (Electronic Customs Management

System) to enhance supply chain visibility (Levinson, 2016; World Bank, 2020). This evolution shows that while the physical barriers of the Himalayas still exist, the challenges of "logistics friction" have shifted from the absence of roads to the complex issues of digital and regulatory coordination (Kathuria, 2018; Shah & Uprety, 2025).

This chapter seeks to provide a structured, evidence-based approach to the functional aspects of the India-Bhutan relationship, guided by the real-world operational, regulatory, and infrastructure conditions. This systematic literature review aims to clearly identify and combine academic, institutional, and grey literature on operational challenges. It will evaluate the effectiveness of current trade simplification methods and highlight important research gaps that need to be addressed to achieve efficient regional and sub-regional development.

Research Question:

What are the operational, regulatory, and infrastructural challenges and opportunities in cross-border logistics along the India-Bhutan border? How can systematic evidence guide policy and practice for better regional integration?

Objectives

- To review academic, institutional, and grey literature on India, Bhutan cross-border logistics.
- To identify operational challenges in infrastructure, customs, and informal trade practices.
- To assess how well trade facilitation measures and regulatory frameworks work.
- To evaluate opportunities for regional integration through logistics improvement.
- To highlight important research gaps and suggest directions for future study and policy action.

BACKGROUND AND CONTEXT

Globally, cross-border trade has grown significantly over the past three decades. Globalization, liberalization, and technological innovation have driven this growth. Logistics has become an important factor for competitiveness. Efficient supply chains allow countries to connect with global value chains (Rodrigue & Notteboom, 2020). In South Asia, trade integration falls behind other regions due to issues with infrastructure, political sensitivities, and regulatory differences (Kathuria, 2018). The bilateral trade relationship between India and Bhutan exists within this larger framework. Bhutan relies on India for transit and access to markets, making logistics a key factor in its economic future. This topic is especially relevant given current regional initiatives under SASEC and BBIN (Bangladesh, Bhutan, India, Nepal), which aim to improve connectivity and lower trade costs (Asian Development Bank, 2019). If logistics remain inefficient, these integration projects may struggle to progress.

Border trade in South Asia has changed from informal exchanges to formal bilateral agreements. The BBIN framework, which emerged in the 2010s, marked a move toward regional connectivity. This shift focused on transport corridors and energy trade (Rahman & Bari, 2016). Customs systems have moved from manual paperwork to digital platforms, but the implementation is still inconsistent. In the India-Bhutan context, the 1949 Treaty of Friendship and its 2007 revision established trade relations. Meanwhile, hydropower exports have become the backbone of bilateral logistics (Rose, 1977; Lama, 2024). The construction of large projects like the Punatsangchhu and Mangdechhu plants requires the movement of "Over-Dimensional Cargo" (ODC), which includes turbines and generators that weigh hundreds of tonnes. This "Hydropower Logistics" has led to the development of heavy-duty road infrastructure in the area. It also supports other trade sectors (Asian Development Bank, 2019). Beyond bilateralism, the corridor is essential for sub-regional initiatives. SASEC has focused on "Economic Corridors" that connect Bhutan to Indian ports such as Haldia and Kolkata. At the same time, the BBIN framework has aimed to put the Motor Vehicle Agreement (MVA) into action. However, Bhutan's careful stance on the MVA stems from worries about environmental harm. This situation highlights the conflict between regional integration and national sustainability goals (Rahman & Bari, 2016).

Conceptual Clarification

- **Cross-border logistics:** The combined processes that allow the movement of goods between countries include transport, customs, and warehousing.
- **Trade Facilitation:** Measures that make trade procedures simpler and more consistent reduce delays and costs.
- **Borderland Economy:** Economic activities in border regions often mix formal and informal trade practices.
- **Regional Integration:** Cooperative frameworks between neighboring states to improve economic, infrastructural, and political connections.
- **PRISMA Systematic Review Approach:** A structured methodological approach that ensures transparency and thoroughness in gathering literature, especially when identifying, screening, and including studies.

THEORETICAL FRAMEWORKS

Cross-border logistics is often wrongly portrayed in policy literature as only a technical or engineering problem, such as laying asphalt or installing scanners. In the Eastern Himalayas, logistics is closely tied to the social, political, and institutional aspects of the border area. To grasp why just expanding infrastructure has not greatly reduced transaction costs, there is a need to use a multi-disciplinary theoretical framework. This chapter combines Institutional Theory, the Political Economy of Regionalism, and Trade Facilitation Theory to offer a complete understanding of the India-Bhutan corridor.

- Institutional Theory and Path Dependency as defined by Douglass North in 1990, where institutions are the "rules of the game." In the India-Bhutan context, "Institutional Fragmentation" is a main cause of delays. "Path Dependency" explains why manual documentation continues. Even with digital options available, the "informal institution" of manual verification is still deeply rooted in local bureaucratic history.

At the core of logistics inefficiency is the idea of institutions. Douglass North defined institutions in 1990 as the "rules of the game in a society." These include the formal laws and informal norms that limit how people interact and influence economic performance. In the context of India and Bhutan, "Institutional Fragmentation" is a main cause of delay.

Institutional Theory introduces the idea of "Path Dependency." This concept means that once a bureaucratic process is set in place, changing it becomes harder, even when better options are available. For years, customs procedures at gateways like Jaigaon have depended on manual ledger entries and physical inspections. Even though digital platforms like India's ICEGATE have been introduced, the practice of manual verification continues because the local bureaucratic culture is deeply tied to a history of physical oversight. This resistance sets up a "soft barrier" to trade that can be tougher to navigate than a physical mountain range (North, 1990). Furthermore, the India-Bhutan corridor suffers from "Institutional Thickening," a situation where too many agencies, such as Customs, Border Security, Transport Departments, and Environmental Agencies, have overlapping jurisdictions but lack a unified communication protocol. This fragmentation increases the "compliance burden" for traders, who must navigate multiple layers of bureaucracy for a single consignment (Kathuria, 2018).

- The Political Economy of Regional Integration theory shows that logistics is about more than just technical efficiency; it also involves power and sovereignty. Bhutan's dependence on India creates an imbalance. The "Political Economy of Hesitation" concerning the BBIN MVA highlights how local concerns over transport jobs and ecological stability can take precedence over regional economic pressures (Rahman & Bari, 2016).

While technical reports often view regional integration, such as the BBIN framework, as a simple economic win-win, the Political Economy perspective shows a more complicated reality. This theory looks at how power imbalances, concerns about national sovereignty, and domestic political pressures affect economic cooperation. The relationship between India and Bhutan shows a significant imbalance in economic size, population, and geography. Bhutan depends on India for access to the global market, which creates a power gap. Although the two countries share a high level of political trust, Bhutan's careful approach to the BBIN Motor Vehicle Agreement (MVA) highlights what some call the "Political Economy of Hesitation." Bhutanese leaders need to weigh the economic advantages of easier truck movement against local worries about environmental protection, road capacity, and the jobs of local truck drivers who are concerned about being overshadowed by larger Indian logistics companies (Rahman & Bari, 2016). The political economy of this corridor is influenced by Bhutan's unique position as a carbon-negative nation. Logistics policies that promote high-volume truck traffic are often seen in light of environmental sovereignty. Therefore, logistics reform in this region goes beyond merely seeking efficiency. It involves negotiating the preservation of national identity and ecological stability amid regional economic pressure.

- Trade Facilitation Theory argues that "time is money." Every hour a truck spends waiting at a border is a "hidden tax" that raises the final price of the product. For a landlocked country like Bhutan, these costs add up. (World Bank, 2020). Logistics performance directly measures transaction costs. When customs procedures are not harmonized or digital systems do not work together, the cost of doing business increases. Trade Facilitation Theory suggests that simplifying, standardizing, and harmonizing procedures allows countries to achieve de-facto integration, even without formal political unions (World Bank, 2020). In the India-Bhutan corridor, the lack of "soft infrastructure," such as an electronic "Single Window," creates a friction point. This issue prevents fully realizing the benefits of "hard infrastructure" like the Phuentsholing-Thimphu highway. In the Himalayas, physical distance does not accurately show logistics cost. A 100-kilometer trip in the mountains can take five times longer than the same distance on flat land. A two-hour customs delay at the border can also double the total time for a short delivery. Trade Facilitation Theory focuses on "Predictability" rather than

"Speed." For a Bhutanese exporter dealing with perishable oranges or apples, knowing exactly when a truck will pass through customs is more important than a slightly faster route (Asian Development Bank, 2019).

• The Gravity Model Of Trade

To recognize the superiority of India in Bhutan's economic profile, this chapter employs the Gravity Model of Trade. This model put forward that the volume of trade between two countries is proportional to their economic size (GDP) and reciprocal to the "distance" between them. In modern trade theory, "distance" is no longer just a measure of kilometers. It refers to "logistics friction." This includes the cost of fuel, the efficiency of the ports, and the ease of border crossing. Bhutan is landlocked and surrounded by Indian territory on three sides. As a result, the "Logistics Distance" to India is much lower than to any other global partner. However, the Gravity Model also suggests that if logistics inefficiencies at the India-Bhutan border were reduced by 10%, trade volume could increase significantly. This could help diversify Bhutan's export basket beyond hydropower and minerals (Kathuria, 2018).

REVIEW OF LITERATURES

The research on cross-border logistics in South Asia, particularly focusing on the India-Bhutan corridor, is still developing but expanding.

Currently, reviewed literature is focusing into the trade integration challenges in South Asia. They stress how logistics and infrastructure can help lower trade costs. It shows that South Asia is one of the least integrated regions in the world, with logistics issues playing a major role in high transaction costs, followed by India-Bhutan trade corridor. It focuses on hydropower exports, agricultural trade, and the significance of border towns like Phuentsholing and Jaigaon. Several areas of literature are:

- Regional Trade and Integration Studies (Kathuria;2018, Rahman and Bari;2016)
- India-Bhutan Bilateral trade studies (Lama;2023,2024)
- Policy and Institutional Reports (The Asian Development Bank;2019, World Bank;2020)

These studies reveal Bhutan's reliance on India for transit and access to markets while also addressing the challenges in customs and infrastructure.

The Asian Development Bank (2019) and World Bank (2020) have released important reports on South Asia Sub regional Economic Cooperation (SASEC) and transport integration. These reports emphasize the need for combined transport corridors, improved customs procedures, and investment in logistics facilities. There are also agreements on the importance of logistics for regional integration. However, some debates remain unresolved. These include the balance between formal and informal trade, the environmental effects of expanding infrastructure, and the political sensitivities involved in deeper integration. For instance, Shah & Uprety (2025) point out the ongoing informal trade practices along the India-Bhutan border, which complicates regulatory oversight.

Despite the existing literature, several gaps remain such as conceptual gaps that treats logistics as technical issue, few studies view it as a social and political process linked to border economies and power imbalances. Methodological Limitations highlights limited use of systematic review methods, econometric models, or comparative case studies. Research mainly concentrates on major corridors like Phuentsholing, Jaigaon, while other border points, such as Gelephu and Samdrup Jongkhar, receive less attention. This creates an incomplete view of India–Bhutan logistics. While trade facilitation measures are addressed, there is less focus on environmental sustainability, digital customs systems, and the community impacts of logistics. These policy areas are vital for a complete understanding but remain insufficiently explored.

Early research in the India-Bhutan corridor mainly focused on infrastructure-centric physical connectivity era during 2000-2010. During this decade, scholars viewed logistics mostly through civil engineering and bilateral diplomacy. Rose (1977; 2007) provides the essential historical context, showing how Bhutan's "Road to Modernity" was built with Indian help. The literature from this period highlights the construction of the "Primary National Highways" and the logistical challenges posed by the Himalayan terrain. Research was descriptive, documenting the shift from mule tracks to motorable roads. This change was largely driven by the significant logistical needs of the early hydropower projects.

As the physical road network developed, researchers found that "hard infrastructure" was not enough without coordination with "soft infrastructure." This period brought forth Trade Facilitation Theory to the region. The World Bank (2020) and Kathuria (2018) offered important proof that administrative delays at the border were more expensive than the actual transport time. Key writings from this time, i.e., 2011-2018 began to challenge the "manual culture" of South Asian customs. Studies by Rahman & Bari (2016) explored the political economy of the BBIN framework, examining why regional motor vehicle agreements were getting stuck at the institutional level.

The current research frontier focuses on digital interoperability and climate-resilient supply chains. Lama (2023, 2024) has shifted the discussion to "Corridor-Specific Analysis," examining the unique logistics profiles of Phuentsholing and Gelephu. Recent studies, like those by Shah and Uprety (2025), explore the "Digital Divide," where India's ICEGATE system is ahead of Bhutan's internal digitization, creating a friction point at their interface. Additionally, the impact of COVID-19 spurred research into "Contactless Trade" and the need for electronic data interchange (EDI). A significant part of the literatures look at the socio-economic life of border towns. Roychowdhary et al. (2020) offer ethnographic insights into the Jaigaon-Phuentsholing "Twin City" dynamic. They argue that logistics involves more than just trucks; it includes the social networks of traders who connect different regulations through informal trust. This research shows that the "Logistics Bottleneck" is often a result of poor urban planning in crowded border towns, not a lack of highway capacity. For Bhutan, transit is not just an economic issue; it is also a sovereignty issue. A large volume of recent literature, such as Taneja et al., 2024, looks at the benefits of the BBIN Motor Vehicle Agreement. However, the findings are mixed. Indian and international scholars focus on efficiency gains, while research centered on Bhutan points out the costs to "Environmental Sovereignty" and the risk of displacing local small-scale transporters. Some scholars use Dependency Theory to examine the India-Bhutan corridor. They argue that Bhutan's reliance on one transit neighbor, India, creates "Transit Vulnerability." This vulnerability needs to be managed through strong political trust, not just market solutions (Rose, 1977). The shift from paper to digital is a common topic in recent literature. United Nations ESCAP (n.d.) reports show that although India has made progress in digital customs, the interoperability gap remains. The literature notes that Bhutan's customs systems often need manual overrides to communicate with Indian systems. Studies on ICPs, such as those at Jaigaon, reveal that even though they bring various agencies together, the culture of physical inspection still poses a challenge. This aligns with the Institutional Theory mentioned in Section 3, where path dependency hinders the full use of high-tech scanners and automated gates.

Informal trade is well known but hard to measure. Lama (2023) points out that informal trade along the open India-Bhutan border is driven by local demand and the desire to avoid GST and Customs issues. Research shows that informal trade serves as a "Social Buffer" for border communities, offering jobs that the formal logistics sector overlooks. However, it makes it harder to execute regional agreements like SAFTA (South Asian Free Trade Area).

While the literature offers a lot of policy analysis, it has some gaps such as few studies use econometric modeling to calculate the "Price Elasticity of Logistics." These measures how much trade would actually grow if border wait times were reduced by 50%. Researchers focus too much on the Phuentsholing gateway. There is a lack of research on the eastern corridors of Gelephu and Samdrup Jongkhar. Even though the Himalayas are a "Climate Hotspot," there is minimal literature on the long-term effects of glacier melt and increased landslide frequency on the sustainability of the India-Bhutan logistics supply chain.

METHODOLOGY

This study uses a systematic literature review (SLR) approach based on the PRISMA 2020 framework. The PRISMA (Preferred Reporting Items for Systematic Reviews and Meta-Analyses) method ensures transparency, reproducibility, and thoroughness in gathering evidence from various sources. Unlike narrative reviews, which often depend on selective citation, the PRISMA approach requires a structured process of identifying, screening, assessing eligibility, and including sources. This design is especially fitting for the India-Bhutan cross-border logistics context, where scattered academic, institutional, and grey literature needs systematic consolidation. The review uses various databases and repositories to ensure thorough coverage, i.e.,

- Academic Databases: Scopus, Web of Science, JSTOR, EconLit, and Google Scholar.
- Institutional Reports: Asian Development Bank (ADB), World Bank, SAARC Secretariat, and South Asia Sub-regional Economic Cooperation (SASEC).
- Grey Literature: Policy briefs, working papers, and reports from think tanks like the Institute for Social and Economic Change (ISEC) and Centre for Policy Research (CPR).

Search strings were created using Boolean operators and keywords related to the topic. Examples including, "India, Bhutan cross-border logistics", "South Asia trade facilitation", "and Bhutan hydropower exports logistics", "BIN connectivity and customs". To follow the systematic reporting, there were criterias selected; inclusion and exclusion, based on which, literatures were selected and rejected. The inclusions were, peer-reviewed journal articles, institutional reports, and grey literature, publications in English within the time frame of 2000-2025, focusing on India, Bhutan trade, logistics, customs, or regional integration. The research contributions were empirical, theoretical, or policy-oriented whereas exclusions were of non-English publications, sources that lack analytical contents, studies outside South Asia or that are unrelated to logistics, publications that lacks clear methodology.

The systematic review process followed PRISMA's four phases:

Identification Phase

- Records identified through database searching: 1,245
- Additional records identified through other sources (institutional repositories, grey literature): 37
- Total records identified: 1,282

Screening Phase

- Titles screened: 1,282
- Records excluded at title screening: 934
- Abstracts screened: 348
- Records excluded at abstract screening: 210

Eligibility Phase

- Full-text publications assessed for eligibility: 138
- Publications excluded for irrelevance, duplication, or lack of methodological rigor: 52

Included Phase

- Publications included in final synthesis: 86
- Publications included in instrument construction: 24

This transparent reporting ensures methodological rigor and allows for replication of the review process.

RESULTS AND DISCUSSION

Following the PRISMA 2020 process, 86 publications were included in the final synthesis. Of these, 24 studies were specifically used for instrument construction, including the thematic synthesis. The literatures distribution found by year with geographic focus are;

1. Early studies (2000 to 2010): Focused primarily on descriptive accounts of India and Bhutan trade relations and hydropower exports (Rose, 1977).
2. Mid-period studies (2011 to 2018): Emphasized regional integration frameworks like BBIN and SASEC, with growing attention to logistics bottlenecks (Rahman and Bari, 2016; Kathuria, 2018).
3. Recent studies (2019 to 2025): Highlighted digital trade facilitation, customs modernization, and sustainability concerns (World Bank, 2020; Lama, 2023; Shah and Uprety, 2025).

Geographic Focus:

Most studies concentrated on Phuentsholing and Jaigaon, the busiest India and Bhutan border point. There was limited attention to Gelephu and Samdrup Jongkhar, even though they are becoming more important in regional connectivity. Regional studies often framed India and Bhutan logistics within broader South Asian integration efforts (ADB, 2019).

THEMATIC FINDINGS

The thematic findings revealed six recurring themes across the literatures as

1. Infrastructure Constraints
2. Customs and Regulatory Barriers
3. Institutional Fragmentation
4. Digital Trade Gaps
5. Political Economy Tensions
6. Informal Trade Patterns

Most studies highlight inadequate infrastructure as a primary barrier to efficient logistics. Bhutan's mountainous terrain limits road expansion. The lack of rail connections restricts multimodal transport options (ADB, 2019). Warehousing facilities at border points are insufficient, which leads to congestion and delays (Lama, 2024). Cumbersome customs procedures and the lack of harmonization between Indian and Bhutanese systems remain significant hurdles. Manual documentation still exists in some corridors, despite efforts to digitize clearance processes (World Bank, 2020). Regulatory differences create inefficiencies, especially for small traders. Institutional fragmentation is evident in overlapping responsibilities among national agencies, regional frameworks (SAARC, SASEC), and bilateral agreements. This fragmentation often results in policy inconsistencies and delays in implementation (Kathuria, 2018). While digital customs systems and electronic data exchange have been introduced, adoption is uneven. Studies note that Bhutan has limited capacity to fully integrate digital platforms, creating gaps in interoperability with India's more advanced systems (Shah & Uprety, 2025). Political sensitivities influence logistics outcomes. Bhutan's cautious approach to regional integration, particularly under the BBIN framework, reflects concerns about sovereignty and environmental impacts (Rahman & Bari, 2016). Power imbalances between India and Bhutan affect negotiation results and logistics management. Informal trade is widespread along the India-Bhutan border, driven by porous boundaries and local economic practices.

While it provides livelihoods, informal trade complicates customs regulations and undermines formal integration efforts (Lama, 2023).

LINKAGES TO THEORETICAL FRAMEWORK

The findings of this review are important because they show the realities that shape India-Bhutan cross-border logistics. They also connect to well-known theories:

- Institutional Theory
- Political Economy of Regional Integration
- Trade Facilitation Theory

Customs delays and uneven regulations can be understood through institutional theory. It highlights how governance and bureaucratic processes influence economic activities. The continued use of manual documentation and divided institutional duties shows reliance on past practices and resistance to change (North, 1990). This theory helps explain why reforms happen slowly, even when efficiency gains are clear. Bhutan's reluctance to fully adopt the BBIN framework reflects issues in political economy. Concerns about sovereignty, environmental effects, and power imbalances with India are linked to explanations for hesitance towards integration (Rahman & Bari, 2016). The findings indicate that logistics involves not just technical aspects but also significant political factors. The high costs and delays revealed in the results align with trade facilitation theory. This theory states that cutting down on procedural barriers can lead to major efficiency improvements (World Bank, 2020). The findings enhance this theory by showing that gaps in digital trade and informal trade patterns make facilitation efforts more complex in real life. The findings support and extend existing research through the focus on infrastructure bottlenecks backs earlier studies by Kathuria (2018) and ADB (2019), which identified poor connectivity as a major barrier to South Asian trade. Some institutional reports assume that infrastructure expansion will bring straightforward benefits. However, this study shows that without coordination and digital integration, infrastructure alone might not provide the expected efficiency improvements. This challenges overly technical views. It extends the research work by Lama (2023, 2024) on India–Bhutan corridors, through systematically gathering evidence; placing operational challenges within larger theoretical frameworks. It also points out less examined aspects like informal trade and digital compatibility, which previous studies only touched on briefly.

The findings highlight that logistics inefficiencies are a key barrier to South Asian integration. Without coordinated customs and compatible digital systems, initiatives like BBIN and SASEC may face stagnation. Effective logistics reform could unlock significant trade potential and encourage deeper regional cooperation. For Bhutan, efficient logistics is crucial for economic survival. Hydropower exports, agricultural trade, and consumer goods depend on reliable logistics. Improved infrastructure and customs processes could strengthen Bhutan's economic resilience and lower dependency risks. Infrastructure expansion must balance economic benefits with environmental sustainability. Bhutan's careful approach shows valid concerns about ecological impacts. The findings suggest that digital integration and better coordination may provide greater efficiency gains than large-scale physical expansion, offering a more sustainable path forward.

FUTURE RESEARCH DIRECTION

The systematic review has brought together existing knowledge on India-Bhutan cross-border logistics, but some gaps still exist. It is important to address these gaps to improve both academic research and policy practices. Future studies should concentrate on the following areas:

1. Methodological Gaps:

A. Need for Econometric Modeling
B.Corridor-Specific Cost Analysis

2. Data Gap

A. Lack of Informal Trade Measurement
B. Limited Digital Trade Impact Assessment

3. Comparative Studies

A. India-Bhutan vs. ASEAN Corridors.
B. Climate-Resilient Logistics Research

4. Policy Simulation Research

A. Modeling BBIN Impact Scenarios
B. Scenario-Based Trade Facilitation Analysis

Most current studies are qualitative or focused on policy. There is a shortage of econometric models that measure the impact of logistics inefficiencies on trade flows, transaction costs, and GDP growth. Future research should use econometric methods to evaluate the economic costs associated with customs delays, infrastructure issues, and informal trade. Current studies often generalize findings across South Asia or focus narrowly on Phuentsholing-Jaigaon. Detailed cost analyses specific to each corridor are necessary to evaluate logistics performance at Gelephu, Samdrup Jongkhar, and other border points. Such studies could highlight geographic differences and guide targeted interventions.

Informal trade is widely recognized but poorly quantified. Future research should create methods to estimate the scope, value, and social and economic role of informal trade along the India-Bhutan border. This would provide a clearer understanding of logistics dynamics. While digital customs systems and electronic data exchange are developing, their effects on efficiency and transparency need more exploration. Research should evaluate how digital platforms influence clearance times, compliance costs, and interoperability between India and Bhutan.

Comparative studies between South Asian and ASEAN logistics corridors could provide useful insights. ASEAN's success in streamlining customs and developing multimodal infrastructure can offer lessons for South Asia. Future research should compare India-Bhutan logistics with those in ASEAN to identify best practices that can be transferred. Given Bhutan's mountainous landscape and vulnerability to climate change, research on climate-resilient logistics is crucial. Studies should investigate how infrastructure design, disaster readiness, and green technologies can improve resilience in border trade.

The BBIN framework remains politically sensitive, with Bhutan cautious about fully participating. Policy simulation research could model various scenarios, such as Bhutan's partial or full integration into BBIN, and assess the effects on trade flows, logistics efficiency, and environmental sustainability. Future research should simulate the impacts of customs harmonization, digital integration, and investment in infrastructure under different policy situations. This would give policymakers data-driven scenarios to support decision-making.

SOLUTIONS AND RECOMMENDATIONS

• Transformation from "Hard" to "Smart" Infrastructure.

The findings of this review indicate that the physical limits of the Himalayan terrain cannot be resolved by asphalt alone. The main recommendation is to shift investment toward "Smart Infrastructure." To address the "Infrastructure Gap," India and Bhutan should invest in Internet of Things (IoT) sensors along the critical Phuentsholing-Thimphu and Gelephu-Trongsa corridors. These sensors can provide real-time data on road conditions, landslide risks, and traffic density. This will allow logistics managers to reroute cargo as needed.

To close the "Digital Interoperability Gap," implementing a bilateral Block chain ledger for customs is recommended. By using a decentralized ledger, both India's ICEGATE and Bhutan's EMCS can verify the authenticity of certificates of origin and phytosanitary permits without needing manual data re-entry (United Nations ESCAP, n.d.).

• The Gelephu Mindfulness City: A new model for regional hubs.

A solution that has come up in recent policy discussions is the creation of the Gelephu Mindfulness City (GMC). This Special Administrative Region provides a unique chance to reshape cross-border logistics from the ground level. The GMC can act as a "Dry Port" hub, bringing together cargo from Eastern Bhutan and the Indian Northeast. By establishing a bonded warehouse zone within the GMC, goods can be pre-cleared for export, which cuts down the time spent at the actual border crossing. The suggestion is to shift from traditional border gates to "Non-Intrusive Inspection" (NII) technologies. These include high-speed drive-through container scanners, allowing trucks to pass through without stopping, as long as their digital manifests are pre-approved.

• Institutional Synchronization and the "Single Window"

To address the issue of Institutional Fragmentation, the chapter suggests creating a "Bilateral Joint Border Management Committee." India and Bhutan should aim for Mutual Recognition of Standards (MRS). If a product receives certification from a Bhutanese lab, Indian customs should accept it automatically without repeated testing. This "Single Window" approach would greatly cut down on the "Hidden Tax of Time" mentioned in the theoretical framework (World Bank, 2022). It is important to build capacity for customs officials on both sides. Training should focus on using regional digital platforms and managing "Green Channels" for perishable and essential goods.

• Green Logistics: Aligning with Gross National Happiness.

Given Bhutan's commitment to staying carbon-neutral, logistics solutions must be environmentally friendly. India and Bhutan should test "Electric Trucking" for short trips between border towns, such as Jaigaon to Phuentsholing. Building charging stations at Integrated Check Posts would help Bhutan keep its ecological sovereignty while boosting trade volume. Although challenging, the long-term plan is to extend Indian rail lines to the Bhutanese border points, like the Mujnai-Nyoenpaling link. Rail transport is much more carbon-efficient than road transport for heavy bulk items such as cement and minerals (Asian Development Bank, 2019). One practical way forward is for India and Bhutan to pilot electric trucking for short-haul transfers between border towns such as Jaigaon and Phuentsholing. Establishing charging stations at Integrated Check Posts would empower Bhutan to boost trade without compromising its ecological sovereignty, ensuring that growth does not come at the expense of its pristine environment.

• Formalizing the Informal.

A Socially Inclusive Approach Instead of criminalizing informal trade, policy should aim to "Formalize through Simplification." Implementing a simplified, digital registration for small-scale micro-traders would bring the "Shadow Logistics" into the formal economy. By providing micro-traders with digital IDs, they can access formal credit and insurance, reducing their vulnerability while providing the state with better data for regional planning.

CONCLUSION

This chapter aimed to go beyond simply describing policy and provide a systematic analysis of cross-border logistics along the India, Bhutan border. Using the PRISMA 2020 framework, the study intended to gather scattered academic, institutional, and grey literature. It focused on identifying operational challenges, evaluating trade facilitation methods, and pointing out research gaps that need urgent attention for effective regional and sub-regional integration.

The review found several key insights such as structural constraints on Bhutan's landlocked geography, mountainous terrain, and limited infrastructure that is a major barrier to efficient logistics. Customs delays and regulatory differences arise from fragmented responsibilities and a lack of coordination between Indian and Bhutanese systems. New digital customs platforms show potential, but uneven use and limited compatibility create new issues. Political economic aspects on Bhutan's careful approach to BBIN integration reflects concerns about sovereignty and environmental issues, highlighting the political aspects of logistics reform. Informal trade remains important in border economies. It complicates regulatory oversight, yet it helps sustain livelihoods.

The findings suggest that working together and using digital tools may bring greater efficiency gains than just expanding infrastructure. While building connections is important, the evidence shows that unified customs procedures, compatible digital systems, and coordinated governance are more crucial for lowering transaction costs and improving trade flows.

This chapter adds to scholarly discussions by gathering evidence on India and Bhutan logistics. It places operational realities within institutional theory, trade facilitation frameworks, and political economy perspectives. It broadens existing literature by highlighting less explored areas like informal trade and digital interoperability.

For policymakers, the chapter emphasizes the need for coordinated institutional reforms, investment in digital trade facilitation, and specific actions for different corridors. It offers insights based on evidence that can guide BBIN and SASEC initiatives. This ensures that integration efforts are based on operational realities.

The chapter shows that logistics inefficiencies are not just technical issues; they are also deeply rooted in institutional and political factors. By combining PRISMA methodology with theoretical frameworks, it fosters a more complete understanding of cross-border logistics. This approach connects operational details with conceptual analysis.

The chapter portrays that effective cross-border logistics in the India, Bhutan corridor needs a balanced approach. It requires strengthening infrastructure where needed, while also focusing on improving institutional cooperation, digital integration, and sustainable practices. This combined strategy provides the best chance for better regional cooperation, economic stability, and sustainable development in South Asia.

REFERENCES

Anderson, J., & O'Dowd, L. (1999). Borders, border regions and territoriality: Contradictory meanings, changing significance. *Regional Studies, 33*(7), 593–604. DOI: 10.1080/00343409950078648

Asian Development Bank. (2019). *South Asia Subregional Economic Cooperation Operational Plan 2016–2025 Update.* Asian Development Bank.

Bhowmik, A. (2019). Cross-border trade between India and Bhutan and the golden prospects of CMA. *The Management Accountant Journal, 54*(7), 57–59. DOI: 10.33516/maj.v54i7.57-59p

Hesse, M., & Rodrigue, J.-P. (2004). The transport geography of logistics and freight distribution. *Journal of Transport Geography, 12*(3), 171–184. DOI: 10.1016/j.jtrangeo.2003.12.004

India–Bhutan trade relations: Broad overview (with emphasis on agricultural trade). (2025). *TaxTMI.*

Kathuria, S. (Ed.). (2018). *A glass half full: The promise of regional trade in South Asia.* The World Bank. DOI: 10.1596/978-1-4648-1294-1

Lama, U. (2023). India and Bhutan: Challenges and Opportunities in Cross Border Trade (ISEC Working Paper No. 567). Institute for Social and Economic Change.

Lama, U. (2024). India and Bhutan: Trade through Different Border Corridors. Institute for Social and Economic Change.

Lama, U. (n.d.-a). *India and Bhutan: A relationship before and after independence* (ISEC Working Paper No. 560). Institute for Social and Economic Change.

Lama, U. (n.d.-b). *India and Bhutan: Challenges and opportunities in cross border trade* (ISEC Working Paper No. 567). Institute for Social and Economic Change.

Levinson, M. (2016). *The box: How the shipping container made the world smaller and the world economy bigger* (2nd ed.). Princeton University Press.

North, D. C. (1990). *Institutions, institutional change and economic performance.* Cambridge University Press. DOI: 10.1017/CBO9780511808678

Rahman, M., & Bari, E. (2016). *Sub-regional cooperation under BBIN framework: An analysis.* Indian Council of World Affairs.

Rajan, S. (2017, January 18). India–Bhutan relations.

Rodrigue, J.-P., & Notteboom, T. (2020). *The geography of transport systems* (5th ed.). DOI: 10.4324/9780429346323

Rose, L. E. (1977). *The politics of Bhutan*. Cornell University Press.

Roychowdhary, S., Agarwal, S., Singh, M., & Singh, V. (2020). An ethnographic insight on border-markets: Reflections from the Indo-Bhutan border. *Heidelberg University South Asia Institute Working Paper Series*, (20).

Sangay. (n.d.). Bhutan–India trade relations. *Royal Bhutanese Embassy, New Delhi*.

Shah, P. K., & Uprety, M. (2025). A Study on India's Trade Relation with SAFTA Members: Indo-Bhutan Trade as a Case. ShodhPatra. *International Journal of Science and Humanities*, *2*(7), 16–32. DOI: 10.70558/SPIJSH.2025.v2.i7.45246

Subodh, C., Bharti, N., & Kapoor Mahawar. (2025). *India–Bhutan relations: A deep dive into the Neighbourhood First policy*. Indian Council of World Affairs.

Taneja, N., Bimal, S., Nadeem, T., & Roy, R. (2019). *India–Bhutan economic relations* (ICRIER Working Paper No. 384). Indian Council for Research on International Economic Relations.

Taneja, N., Nag, B., Joshi, S., Rastogi, R., & Dua, S. (2024). *Benefits of BBIN Motor Vehicle Agreement to the Northeast Region: A supply chain analysis* (ICRIER Working Paper No. 419). Indian Council for Research on International Economic Relations.

United Nations ESCAP. (n.d.). *Trade facilitation and paperless trade implementation in Asia and the Pacific: Regional report*.

World Bank. (2020). *Connecting to thrive: Challenges and opportunities of transport integration in Eastern South Asia*. World Bank Group.

World Bank. (2022, March 14). What will it take to connect the Bangladesh, Bhutan, India, Nepal (BBIN) sub-region? *Journal of Borderlands Studies*, *27*(3), 273–285.

Chapter 7
AI for Sustainable Supply Chain Management in Cross-Border Logistics

Rahmath Nisha A.
http://orcid.org/0009-0001-5146-2411
Saveetha School of Management, Saveetha Institute of Medical and Technical Sciences, Chennai, India

G. Dhasarathi
Saveetha School of Management, Saveetha Institute of Medical and Technical Sciences, Chennai, India

Duggirala Aravind
http://orcid.org/0009-0005-4362-7684
ASET College of Science and Technology, India

ABSTRACT

The complexity of cross-border logistics has grown, which has heightened the demand for sustainable supply chain management and data-driven management. Although the use of artificial intelligence (AI) technology is commonly used to enhance efficiency in the operations of the company, its role with sustainability and governance has not been fully developed. This chapter suggests an AI-powered sustainable supply chain (AISS) model that integrates environmental, social, and governance (ESG) goals in AI-based decision-making. Through the adoption of the theory of sustainability, systems thinking, and ethical AI governance, the framework gives a systematic solution to the responsible adoption of AI in sustainable cross-border logistics.

DOI: 10.4018/979-8-3373-7847-3.ch007

1. INTRODUCTION

The high pace of globalization, high rate of technological development, and the increasing demands by stakeholders in terms of sustainability has greatly contributed to the complexity of the global supply chain. Companies that have businesses in the global economy are increasingly pressurized to balance cost-effectiveness and environmental safety and social responsibility, and deal with uncertainty, disruptions, and regulatory heterogeneity at the same time (Koberg and Longoni, 2019; Seuring and Muller, 2008). Sustainable supply chain management has been seen to provide solutions to these challenges in that it has become a strategic imperative that is critical and considers environmental, social and governance (ESG) goals in decisions made in logistics and operational areas. Reverse logistics and return policies are getting more attention due to growing concerns of the consumers and corporate responsibility toward the environment (Saxena et al.,2023).

The sustainability agenda has also been reinforced by global sustainability programs such as the United Nations sustainable development goals (SDGs), an initiative that focuses on sustainable production and consumption, and climate action, as well as inclusive economic growth (Lee et al., 2016). The place of supply chains in this perspective is central since logistics and transportation operations contribute to a significant portion of carbon emissions and consumption of various resources globally (McKinnon, 2018). The traditional approaches to managing supply chains, however, are reactive and, in most cases, lack the ability to respond to the issue of sustainability in the most dynamic and data-rich globalized environments.

Recent innovations in artificial intelligence (AI) provide great possibilities to change the functioning of supply chains with the help of improved data processing, predictive analytics, and decision-support functions. Machine learning, big data analytics, and optimization algorithms are among the AI technologies that allow organizations to enhance demand forecasts, inventory optimization, transportation planning, and risk reduction in the context of a complex logistics network (Wamba et al., 2017; Ivanov and Dolgui, 2020). Using big amounts of structured and unstructured data AI-based systems help more reliable, adaptive, and timely logistics operations managerial decision making. Regarding sustainability, AI can make a significant contribution towards environmental sustainability by enhancing the efficient use of resources, waste reduction, and reducing greenhouse gas emissions through efficient routing and energy-saving procedures (Koberg and Longoni, 2019; Li et al., 2021). Moreover, AI can also help in the social sustainability aspect by improving transparency, traceability, and adherence to labor and ethical standards in global supply chains (Saberi et al., 2019).

Ecogenic ecosystems of sustainable cross-border logistics and resilient supply chains have consequently become major facilitators of long-term sustainability performance. Despite the fact that the application of AI in the context of logistics sustainability started gaining scholarly interest, the current body of literature is not well integrated. Specifically, the theory of sustainability, the views of strategic management, and ethics are frequently loosely linked, and most of the literature is susceptible to study only one of the mentioned aspects in isolation: operational performance or the adoption of technology. Therefore, there is a lack of focus on how AI can be integrated systematically into larger sustainability models- such as the Triple Bottom Line and at the same time take into consideration governance and ethical aspects that contribute to value creation in the long-term (Elkington, 1998; Floridi et al., 2018). To overcome this shortcoming, it is necessary to specify AI-based sustainable logistics management in terms of an extensive theory-supported study. In this regard, the present study will aim to add to the literature by matching the current theoretical grounds to the new AI uses in sustainable supply chain management.

The analysis can offer a comprehensive perspective on the role of AI in aiding economic performance, environmental stewardship, and social responsibility in cross-border logistics because it incorporates the sustainability theory, strategic and systems perspectives, and ethical governance considerations. The general goal is to provide researchers, practitioners and policymakers with information regarding how AI technologies should be implemented responsibly and effectively to promote sustainable supply chain change. GAP/contribution in the research. Although the current state of literature on artificial intelligence (AI) in sustainable supply chain management is more conceptually disjointed, it is also still operationally oriented as most of the research is conducted in the context of cross-border logistics. Most of the previous research subjects isolated applications of AI-like demand forecasting, route optimization, and inventory control without adequately applying these technologies to a comprehensive sustainability system that considers environmental, social and governance (ESG) aspects (Koberg and Longoni, 2019; Yadav et al., 2024).

The current structures are not adequate due to three reasons. To start with, most AI-enabled logistics literature is efficiency-based or technology-focused, focusing on the reduction of costs and operational performance and overlooking the sustainability results as being secondary or indirect (Ivanov and Dolgui, 2020; Gunasekaran et al., 2019). This constrains the theoretical knowledge on how artificial intelligence-based decisions affect long-term environmental accountability and social justice in worldwide supply chains. Second, the leading sustainability models, including Triple Bottom Line and the traditional Sustainable Supply Chain Management models, continue to be quite stagnant and rather descriptive and do not provide substantial directions in which advanced, data-intensive technology like AI can be implemented in dynamic and disruptive logistics settings (Elkington, 1998; Seuring and Muller, 2008; Seuring et al., 2022). Third, the literature lacks sufficient relevance to the institutional and regulatory heterogeneity of cross-border logistics where companies have to operate under various environmental standards, labor laws, data privacy laws, and ethical standards across borders (Koberg and Longoni, 2019; Dwivedi et al., 2021). To resolve these limitations, the proposed research suggests an AI-Enabled Sustainable Supply Chain (AISS) model that builds on previous literature in three significant aspects.

To begin with, the framework clearly incorporates AI potential into the theory of sustainability as it obtains ESG goals directly into the process of AI-assisted decision-making, instead of considering them as its consequences (Yadav et al., 2024). Second, it has a systems-based view, which connects data intelligence, analytical modeling, operational execution, sustainability performance, and governance mechanisms to a multi-layered framework that fits well in a complex cross-border logistics network (Ivanov and Dolgui, 2020). Third, the ethical AI governance and regulatory alignment are the central elements of the proposed framework to combat transparency, accountability, and compliance issues that previous AI-sustainability frameworks fail to tackle (Floridi et al., 2018; Dwivedi et al., 2021). Going past uncoordinated, efficiency-based strategies, the AISS framework provides a problem-oriented, theory-based solution to the issue of utilizing AI to achieve sustainable cross-border logistics. By so doing, the study presents a new integrative model filling in innovations in AI, sustainability goals, and governance needs to address actual gaps in the literature on sustainable supply chains in the current state.

2. OBJECTIVES OF THE ARTICLE

1. The main aim of the study is to examine the theoretical basis of AI-based sustainable supply chain management by incorporating sustainability approaches with strategic and systems-based approaches (Elkington, 1998; Kleindorfer et al., 2005).
2. In particular, the research will focus on the role of artificial intelligence in improving efficiency, resilience, and sustainability of a supply chain due to the better predictive capabilities, logistics optimization, and data-driven decision-making processes (Brown et al., 2024).
3. Further, the research aims to investigate the possibilities of attaining sustainable cross-border logistics, especially enhancing the transparency, risk management, and environmental performance of international web of supply chains (Saberi et al., 2019; Koberg and Longoni, 2019).
4. Lastly, the research will evaluate ethical and governance concerns in AI-enabled SCM, which will involve accountability, transparency, and responsible decision-making in the global logistics settings (Floridi et al., 2018).

3. THEORETICAL FOUNDATIONS

This chapter will discuss on theoretical framework constructed from an assortment of views from various disciplines that incorporate the theory of sustainability, strategic management concepts, systems thinking, as well as ethics of governance that explain how the implementation of AI is utilized on the management of sustainable logistics. All these theories provide a vigorous focal lens of understanding how technologies that utilize AI will impact cross-border logistics and strike an equilibrium on economic, social, and environmentally defined objectives.

3.1. Triple Bottom Line Theory

The Triple Bottom Line (TBL) theory by Elkington (1998) defines the sustainability to be a integration of three dimensions, dependent to one other: the economic performance, environmental stewardship and social responsibility. The TBL framework applied in the logistic operation shows that organizational victory is nothing about the financial results only, but Firms reduce their adverse environmental impacts and add to the social benefit. Applications that rely on AI: Demand forecasting, intelligent transportation planning, and carbon footprint analysis, can assist TBL goals through providing efficiency and safety in operations, lowering emissions, and augmenting labor and stakeholder results. Therefore, TBL is a synthesized guideline on which the sustainability effects of AI-driven supply chain practices can be assessed (Elkington, 1998).

3.2. Resource-Based View (RBV)

The Resource-Based View (RBV) assumes that the firms can gain sustainable competitive advantage by creating and exploiting unique, valuable, rare, imitable and non-substitutable resources (Madhani, 2009). In the same context, AI capabilities, including data-driven decision systems, machine learning algorithms, and advanced analytics, can be considered strategic intangible assets that can boost the implementation of the organization. Incorporated into the logistics, AI improves the firm's capacity to the utilization of materials, eliminate risks & respond the changes in the global markets. RBV can therefore be used to explain the role of AI as a core capability that promotes competitiveness as well as sustainability in cross-border logistics.

3.2.1. Artificial Intelligence (AI) in Supply Chain Management by SMEs and Limitations of RBV

Although the Resource-Based View (RBV) offers a good theoretical explanation on how firms could attain sustained competitive advantage by using valuable, rare, inimitable, and non-substitutable resources, researchers have been able to realized that it has several limitations when used in explaining the development of sustainable competitive advantage among small and medium enterprises (SMEs) in the global supply channel. The standard RBV assumptions are usually inclined to large multi-nationals that have significant financial, technological and human capital resources, which may not take into account the structural limitations of SMEs (Madhani, 2009; Seuring et al., 2022). SMEs are a large percentage of other participants in the cross-border supply chains and are important constituents of the upstream and downstream logistics. Nevertheless, empirical studies have shown that SMEs do not always have internal capacity to create and implement advanced systems of artificial intelligence independently to sustainability-oriented decision-making (Kache & Seuring, 2017). Consequently, the purely firm-centric RBV approach could not achieve sufficient results in explaining the adoption of AI among smaller supply chain members.

Recent studies in supply chains and digitalization indicate that SMEs gain more and more access to AI-enabled capabilities via sharing digital infrastructures, cloud-based analytics providers, and third-party logistics providers (Hendriksen, 2023; Wu et al., 2025). These are external resources that enable SMEs to take advantage of predictive analytics, emissions monitoring, and route optimization, without having the underlying AI infrastructure. These arrangements make sustainability capabilities no longer firm-specific resources, but network or ecosystem resources. Theoretically, the next step in this development is the extension of the RBV in terms of a more relational and systems-oriented approach, which is compatible with systems theory and literature on sustainable supply chain management. SMEs do not need to rely on the endowment of internal resources alone but use the inter-organizational relationship and platform-based technologies to engage in the AI-led sustainability initiatives (Seuring & Muller, 2008; Koberg and Longoni, 2019). This network-based RBV view can be used to describe the role of SMEs in achieving sustainability results despite limited resources, in the framework of cross-border logistics. It further highlights the significance of governance systems and participative digital ecosystems in providing inclusive and scalable AI uptake as a sustainability tool in supply chain management.

3.3. Systems Theory

The Systems Theory conceptualizes the supply chains as a complex, interconnected system that consists of various actors, processes and feedback systems (Smith,1968). Disruptions, inefficiencies, information asymmetry in a single subsystem in a global supply chain may influence the whole network. The AI improves the coordination of activities system wide by stimulating real-time data fusion, predictive modelling, and adaptive control of logistics, production, and distribution activities. In systems terms, AI enhances the sustainability and logistic flexibility by optimizing logistic flows materials, energy and information and dynamically responding to environmental and market uncertainty.

3.4. Sustainable Operations Management (SOM)

Sustainable Operations Management (SOM) is an extension of the classic operations management because it puts in clear terms of the environmental and social factors in the operational decision making (Kleindorfer et al., 2005). SOM models focus on eco-efficiency and reducing waste, life-cycle assessment, and ethical sourcing as key areas of operation. AI technologies assist SOM objectives through the possibility to do forecasting with precision, intelligent inventory management, predictive maintenance, and optimization based on lifecycle. Consequently, SOM presents an operation base on which the significance of ability to upgrading the AI and sustainability of global supply chain systems can be realized.

3.5. AI Governance and Ethics

The increasing logistic utilization of AI in the prompts key ethical, legal and governance issues regarding transparency, fairness, accountability and data privacy. Ethical AI frameworks stress the necessity of AI systems to be consistent with social values and moral principles, whereas responsible AI governance is concerned with introducing organization mechanisms that guarantee control and adherence (Floridi et al., 2018). When there is a wide range of regulatory settings and data protection standards at the cross-border level, the key to ensuring the establishment of stakeholder trust and the sustainable use of technologies is proper AI management. Responsible AI practices and ethical practices are therefore a pillar of critical theoretical foundation of sustainable integration of AI into global supply chains.

3.6. Integrative Theoretical Perspective

All these theoretical backgrounds furnish a complete analysis frame on the AI-enabled supply chains. The 3Ps theory sets the viability objectives, the Resource-Based View demystifies strategic value creation, Systems Theory elucidates interdependencies and adaptability, Sustainable Operations Management provides direction in operations and AI governance frameworks enforce ethical and responsible application. This combined theoretical approach contributes to a comprehensive view of the way AI can help achieve sustainable change in cross-border logistics.

4. EVOLUTION OF SUSTAINABLE SUPPLY CHAIN MANAGEMENT (SSCM)

Ecofriendly chains are defined by focal enterprises that origin from the seaside providers, situated in the smoothening the abroad, or issue across collective nations. The latter has risen rapidly as a result of globalization, as major organizations look to gain a competitive edge by recruiting skilled, affordable suppliers from all over the world (Gereffi and Lee, 2012). the outcome., there are additional points in the logistic and also a broad distance between a focal firm and its providers. Integral firms in ecosystem are frequently well-known companies can be constantly monitored by stakeholders who emphasize acceptable result along environmental, social, and economic parts.

SSCM has been proposed for integrating stakeholder concerns for profit with concerns regarding the impact of a focal firm's internal and supply management operations on ecological and social systems (Seuring et al., 2022). Sustainable Supply Chain Management (SSCM) is "the management of material, information, and cash flows as well as cooperation among companies in the supply chain while taking goals from all three dimensions of sustainable development (environmental, social, and economic) which are derived from customer and stakeholder requirements (Sauer & Seuring, 2017). "Sustainability outcomes include achieving goals in the production of environmental, social, or economic as well as the adoption of socially and ecologically conscious behaviours. Social performance bears into account local community impact, labor practices, and human rights. Metrics based on the market, operations, or accounting can be used to operationalize economic performance. However, it is difficult to improve sustainability performance in GSCs while preventing adverse environmental and social impacts (Koberg and Longoni, 2019)

4.1. UN Sustainable Development Goals (SDG)

In September 2015, the United Nations (UN) General Assembly adopted 17 Sustainable Development Goals (SDGs) as an integral part of the 2030 Agenda for Sustainable Development (Assembly UG, 2015). These 17 goals were designed to complement what had come to be called the MDGs, due to expire at the end of that year. It took several years of trying to integrate "Sustainable development" and "Social & economic growth" for this shift of focus for the UN finally to take place. Additionally, they speak for the most ambitious attempt to date to center global policy and governance around goal-setting. The evolution, justification, and prospects for the SDGs are examined and evaluated in this article (Biermann et al., 2017)

Particularly, we highlight how the SDGs represent a new kind of global governance in which goal-setting is an important governance tactic. In addition to a number of universal factories in Asia, North America, and Europe such as multistakeholder circumstances in New York with UN officials and diplomats the report is based on a long-term effort of the study involving approximately thirty international experts. The main conclusions of this project are outlined here, with an eye toward broad suggestion for "Governance through goals" as a narrative appliance of international diplomacy. We also address the SDGs' chances and challenges by pointing out a number of factors that could affect how well they are implemented, and we offer some potential directions for future study (Cardini, 2024).

Goals-based governance the SDGs represent a new form of governance, which leverages the non-binding global goals set by UN member states, as opposed to previous forms of global governance, which relied on either legislation or market-driven solutions. There are several salient features of the goal-based governance approach, none of which are unique to this kind of governance (Cardini, 2024). The High-level Political Forum on Sustainable Development, which is new in and of itself, will take over the institutional oversight of the SDG implementation at the international level, which has been left fairly ambiguous. A low possibility of achieving the objectives never go along with the weak international organizational arrangements. Rather, its proponents point to the bottom-up, non-confrontational, nation-driven, and stakeholder-oriented elements of governance by goals as a crucial potential success factor (Hajer et al., 2015). Partnerships and emergence concepts are mooted as the innovative aspect of the SDGs. Third, the innovative mode of governance via goals is through global inclusion in the goal-establishing process at the global level.

4.2. Paris Climate Agreement

The Paris Agreement under the United Nations Framework Convention on Climate Change, as well as the Sustainable Development Goals Agenda of the United Nations Development Programme, embody significant global investment through cost-effective, long-term financing. Green bonds are becoming more and more popular in global crisis and justifiable development finance structure because of their risk-reducing features and attractiveness to institutional and socially aware speculators.

The allocation of publicly stated green bond revenues from 53 organizations to projects and assets across 96 countries between 2008 and 2017 is examined in detail for the first time in this study. The markets for green bonds are expanding quickly, and annual trends in the distribution of proceeds show that investments in purifiable water, eco-friendly transportation, renewable energy, and another SDG and Paris Agreement-related sectors are receiving more funding. At the regional and national levels, pie chart analysis demonstrates distinct appliable patterns to particular green economy.

The project assets financed using the green bonds in the sample correspond to over 1500 gigawatts and in excess of 108 million tons of carbon dioxide equivalent in tons of CO2e of greenhouse gas emissions reductions. The international finance institutions provided more financial outlays using the resort to green bonds in the basis and volume. The paper offers recommendations for enhancing post-issuance reporting on green bonds and offers perception for the sustainable bonds uses in advancing the Paris and global goal objectives. Expansion of the green bond market and rising distributions of proceeds (Tolliver et al., 2019).

It specifically compares the total number of annual issuances of foreign bonds outstanding with green bonds issued, green bonds outstanding, as well as the allocations of green bond proceeds. It should be pointed out that the light grey bar represents a very large gap in the values of the y-axis (Lin & Moffat, 2016). Specifically, it compares the total annual volumes of outstanding foreign bonds to the total annual volumes of issued green bonds, outstanding green bonds, and allocations of reported green bond proceeds, all while considering the existence of a substantial difference in the financial values shown on the Y-axis, as indicated by the dashed line.

5. ARTIFICIAL INTELLIGENCE A CRITICAL ENABLER OF FUTURE GENERATION SUSTAINABILITY OF SUPPLY CHAIN ECO SYSTEM.

5.1. Industry 5.0 and Data-Driven Supply Chain Sustainability

It is a next step in intelligent manufacturing as the combination of digital and physical architecture has started with the introduction of Industry 5.0. Artificial intelligence is gaining more applications in supply chain management in this fast-evolving market. This paper will examine how AI-based projects enhance sustainability and resilience provided by logistic activities in Industry 5.0. According to probability analysis (PA), Bayesian Best-Worst Method (B-BWM), and Pareto analysis, this paper determines the key applications on the basis of artificial intelligence method to enhance logistic operations in the commercial attire and boots sector in China. The results have highlighted the necessity to adopt circular approaches to CPP, the creation of virtualized supply chain, and responsive monitoring procedures with the usage of IoT.

The techniques are associated with the construction of the resilience and robust supply chains and the generation of positive social and environmental impacts. In Industry 4.0, automation and high cybersecurity will increase the level of data security and production flexibility, whereas RFID and AI can help improve the organization of inventory, employee safety, and work efficiency (Ben-Daya et al., 2019). In AI technology analysis of vast contents, it provides efficient logistic guidance in the effort to bridge the technology gap by helping to analyze and predict consumer needs and consumption patterns. Finally, although there is a significant potential in the implementation of blockchain technology, the issue of investment and compliance exists.

But people cannot dismiss the issues of AI implementation, ethics, and training to bridge the digital divide. Achieving a holistic Industry 5.0 declares the advantages that all the layers of the society need to work hand in hand between governments, businesses, and academic institutions. The article characterised the development ability in the AI-driven supply chain management in Industry 5.0 by developing ability, but identifying the needs to label the occurring challenges to fully realise its benefits (Wu et al., 2025).

5.2. Sustainable Supply Chain Management AI Technologies

The recent publications in sustainable supply chain management have moved past the discussion of artificial intelligence as an independent technological phenomenon to discussing how individual applications of AI can produce environmental, social, and economic sustainability. Systematic reviews by Koberg and Longoni (2019) and Yadav et al. (2024) reveal that AI is gradually gaining more literature as an enabler of sustainable decision-making in the logistics field instead of being an efficiency-enhancement tool. The machine learning methods are popularly used in demand forecasting, inventory optimization, in transportation planning to allow companies to reduce excess production, idle capacity, and fuel consumption (Ivanov and Dolgui, 2020; Gunasekaran et al., 2019).

The direct impacts of these applications in environmental sustainability are that the waste is reduced, and greenhouse gas emissions are minimized, and at the same time they contribute to the economic performance. Computer vision has been implemented in logistics functions in the inspection automatization, monitoring of warehouses, and classifying waste. Green logistics research suggests that AI-enabled visual inspections enhance precision in sorting and quality management that minimize material wastage and reverse logistics (McKinnon, 2018; Fahmin et al., 2024). These applications connect AI implementation directly to the goals of a circular economy and resource-efficiency. artificial intelligence particularly machine learning (ML) provided a practical solution to the big data management since it can spontaneously identify large datasets and critical insights to be used in decision-making. Due to this, the techniques of supply chain management, manufacturing and healthcare are able to acquire various sectors (Ivano et al., 2019).

The inability to handle large, unstructured data and nonlinear problems are some of the problems that the various traditional methods exist to handle, but machine learning (ML) is specifically designed and designed to handle these very problems. In addition, ML is significant in leveraging big data to supply chain management, which is superior to conventional statistical approaches in identifying the most important variables that influence the performance of the supply chain (Mastoli et al., 2019). The supply chain management has evolved into what was previously fully integrated process that enhance the customer value through the creation of competitive advantages, the traditional decision-support tools are insufficient and organizations are moving towards acquisition of advanced technologies that can process large datasets within a relatively short time period. Therefore, the professionals of supply chain centered attention on the utilization of big data in enhancing smarter supply chains, and provided creative solutions to these challenges (Hendriksen, 2023).

The applications and prospects of the implementation of machine intelligence, especially in enhances viability and logistic production find their way to this research. The social and the ethical development of the area also indicated by this research and also towards the future innovations. The machine intelligence facilitated the development of more resilient, efficient, and sustainable supply chains since it provides tools of informed decision-making to minimize environmental impact and ensure the promotion of ethical sourcing. (Hosseini et al., 2025) Basic principle that produce the impactful implementation is data reliability, interpretability and transparency. The AI human thought recreated the processing of data and identification of patterns. The data-driven approach was used to introduce the concept of the unveiled relationship, and the learning process allows the model to become better predictors of changing conditions. Modern supply chain management cannot do without the concept of machine intelligence and allows the supply chain to respond effectively to the dynamics of the marketplace (Barman, 2025).

NLP has become one of the leading fields of interest in supply chain studies in analyzing unstructured text formats, including supplier audit reports, sustainability reports, regulatory reports, and customs reports (Kang et al., 2020; Yadav et al., 2024). NLP allows organizations that work on an international level to enhance transparency and compliance by systemically tracking information on sustainability across various jurisdiction. On the whole, the modern literature focuses on impact-oriented AI applications, which makes AI a strategic resource to ensure the attainment of sustainability objectives according to the principles of Triple Bottom Line and the Sustainable Development Goals.

6. AI IN CROSS-BORDER LOGISTICS

6.1. AI in Management of Cross-Border Regulatory and Institutional Complexity

The operation of cross-border logistics is characterized by a very complicated institutional context that includes regulatory heterogeneity, fragmented governance systems and contrasting sustainability standards among nations. The international logistics networks have to fulfill several environmental regulations, customs procedures, data governance regimes, and carbon accounting frameworks thus imposing a lot of coordination costs and risks to sustainability compared to domestic supply chains (Seuring and Muller, 2008; Koberg and Longoni, 2019). Regulatory Heterogeneity in logistics across a border. Regulatory heterogeneity is defined as variations in environmental regulations, labor standards, trade regulations, and trade regulations, as a result of the difference in jurisdictions.

According to previous literature on sustainable supply chain management, this kind of institutional diversity usually results in ineffectiveness, slow compliance, and uneven sustainability outcomes throughout the world supply chains (Koberg and Longoni, 2019; Seuring et al., 2022). Artificial intelligence allows companies to react to regulatory heterogeneity by means of data-driven regulatory intelligences systems. Machine learning and text analytics are being used to track, categorize and grasp the changing regulatory demands across nations so that firms can modify compliance practices in near real-time (Dwivedi et al., 2021; Hao and Demir, 2024). Dealing with both structured and unstructured regulatory data in large amounts, AI helps to decrease the cognitive and administrative load of the cross-border compliance with sustainability.

6.2. AI-Based Customs Automation and Border Justice

The processes of customs clearance and border control are essential bottlenecks in cross-border logistics, and they usually make transportation more polluting through congestion and idle vehicles as well as inaccurate documentation. Studies in the field of logistics and transportation management have shown that the implementation of AI-based customs automation enhances the efficiency of the border through assisting in the risk-based inspection system, intelligent document verification, and predictive decisions in the clearance (Tang and Veelenturf, 2019). Machine intelligence applications help customs and logistics companies to detect dangerous shipments and allow safe packages to travel faster through the borders. Shorter wait times in ports and at border crossings also make the supply chains globally more sustainable, fuel consumption is reduced, as well as the emissions and the costs of holding the inventory are also lower (McKinnon, 2018).

6.3. International Carbon Accounting

Measurement of carbon in cross-border logistics is especially difficult because of the difference between the calculation method of emission, reporting standards and pricing mechanisms in different countries. Green logistics studies note that an unbalanced accounting of carbon compromises the efficacy of sustainability approaches and constrains comparability among global routes (McKinnon, 2018; Sugapriya et al., 2024). AI-assisted analytics are useful in cross-border carbon accounting by combining transportation data, energy use indices, and route-specific emissions variables across jurisdictions. Predictive models allow firms to forecast the emissions of each shipment, contrast alternative sourcing and routing choices, and optimize logistics choices as part of the carbon reduction plan (Huang and Peng, 2018; Fahmin et al., 2024). The capabilities enable organizations to incorporate the element of sustainability in the international logistics planning.

6.4. AI Sustainability Role Governance in Cross Borders

In addition to optimization of operations, AI is also becoming a role in the governance of cross-border supply chains. According to the literature on ethical AI and digital governance, transparency, accountability, and explainability are essential in the cases of AI systems working in diverse legal and institutional settings (Floridi et al., 2018; Dwivedi et al., 2021). The AI-based governance tools assist in enhancing sustainability through the ability to trace decision-making, auditing of emission data, and verifying compliance across borders. This mechanism is especially needed in international supply chains, where a lack of institutional enforcement in certain areas can sabotage sustainability promises (Saberi et al., 2019). In systems terms, AI is an integrative governance layer that links regulatory compliance, operational decision-making, and sustainability monitoring across international borders. This supports the use of AI as a technological resource, as well as a strategic facilitator of sustainable cross-border logistics governance.

7. INCREASING AI-BASED TRANSPARENCY AND TRACEABILITY

To achieve good supply chain traceability, it is essential to have one-up-one-down tracking system that allows tracking input sources and output destinations in logistic networks. Even though the classical traceability models present fundamental record-keeping functionalities, their usefulness may be limited by the disconnected data systems, the lack of consistency in documentation, and human error, diminishing the efficiency and reliability of product recall procedures (Tian et al., 2025). Traceability practices have been enhanced by industry-led efforts, including the Produce Traceability Initiative (PTI), organized by organizations like the Produce Marketing Association, which has facilitated the adoption of standardized Global Trade Item Numbers (GTINs) and lot-specific, case-level barcoding. The standards enable the harmonization of data and enhance the sharing of information among the supply chain participants (Khan et al., 2022).

7.1. Supply Chain Transparency Impact

Optical character recognition (AI-OCR) technologies implemented with the help of artificial intelligence contribute greatly to supply chain transparency through providing real-time data acquisition, and validation in the production, warehousing, and retail processes. Stakeholders, such as regulators, customers, and brand partners, will be in a position to access auditable supply chain information, which enhances trust and accountability due to the digitized and validated tracking records. Combining the AI algorithms with the label data obtained through scanning with the OCR, the managers of the supply chain are able to identify anomalies, potential counterfeiting, and traceability violations and at the same time to analyze the trends of the products movement. These functions reinforce active risks mitigation and increase the efficiency of the recall. Integration of AI and OCR technologies have been demonstrated to significantly enhance food tracing and data quality in multifaceted supply chains. As an illustration, automated compliance checks can be enhanced faster and more accurately by using AI-based tools like Garland Verify Edge. By connecting standardized case- and item-level data and validated label data, AI-OCR systems facilitate compliance with PTI guidelines and increase the transparency of reactions to frequent food safety incidents (Chen et al., 2019).

8. ARTIFICIAL INTELLIGENCE IN CARBON MANAGEMENT AND ENVIRONMENTAL OPTIMIZATION

8.1. Rebound Effect and Efficiency Gains in AI-Based Logistics

Although artificial intelligence has proven itself as a potentially powerful tool in enhancing the efficiency of logistics operations by means of optimal routes, predictable energy consumption, and emissions monitoring, sustainability scholars warn that the efficiency achieved does not necessarily lead to the absolute emission levels. An increasing literature in transport and environmental economics points to the rebound effect, i.e. as operations become more efficient, costs decrease, demand increases, and the total emissions become higher (McKinnon, 2018). Optimization through AI in logistics systems can lead to less fuel used per shipment or less fuel per kilometre.

But these profits might be countered when the reduction in transportation costs in the cross-border trade encourages the increase in the volume of shipments, accelerated delivery tasks, or the increase of the market coverage. Empirical research in freight transport indicates that efficiency-enhancing technological changes may inadvertently stimulate further freight actions, thus undermining net environmental gains (McKinnon, 2018; Hao and Demir, 2024). The recent studies in the field of sustainable supply chain management assert that AI-based carbon optimization should thus not be considered only in the context of the relative efficiency improvement, but also in the context of absolute system-level emissions (Koberg & Longoni, 2019).

The AI systems fail to support the long-term climate objectives since without proper governance structures, the systems may focus on cost and speed targets, which would support growth-oriented logistics models. To counteract the rebound effects, researchers propose a combination of AI optimization and carbon limits, emissions standards, and regulatory tools, including carbon prices and cap-and-trade schemes (Sugapriya et al., 2024). Incorporating these constraints into AI-based decision-making systems is a way to guarantee that efficiency improvements will be employed to achieve real decarbonization instead of consumption. Governance wise, this critical lens supports the need to align AI-enabling logistics with more comprehensive sustainability policies and ethical frameworks (Floridi et al., 2018). To mitigate the adverse impacts of rebound effects, the shift in priorities should be made towards the systems level that will provide balance among efficiency, environmental boundaries, and societal goals in cross-border logistics.

9. SOCIAL AND ETHICAL IMPLICATIONS OF AI IN SUSTAINABLE SUPPLY CHAIN

The international high mind principle was monitored by the ethical AI, which established the fairness, openness, and respect to the autonomy of the individual. On the contrary, responsibility to social principles to real time institutional structure was the AI duty, which enhanced accountability, increased the stakeholder confidence, and reduced the risks of the AI ecosystem. organization and institution. The effects of AI impartial procedure were significant challenges and operational disturbance. The active concept of the behavioural AI is doing what is morally right, and the values into organizational structures and operational practices were transformed by the responsible AI that should be organized by interaction of goal of ethical and managerial role. Positively, AI systems in a dual, mixed-focus approach. The ethical and responsible of AI combination can be under the control of the administration (Dwivedi et al., 2021).

9.1. Digital Governance Ethics

The development of AI must be effective and feasible in contemporary organizations and society rooted on the application of moral principles and robust systems of governance achievement of robust governance process. The independence in decision-making and being independent of the system of AI, which precondition the ethical behaviour, turns out to be the critical element of avoiding mistakes and the reduction of negative outcomes. In AI system, the issue of improper decisions, which might be harmful to individuals and organization, was neutral. The usage of the concept of monitoring in AI systems could be highly advantageous in addressing the risks that AI systems have, thus minimizing the possibilities of the emergence of any type of bias in the algorithm. This approach allows both tracking the production of the AI systems and the input (Hosseini Tabaghdehi and Ayaz, 2025).

9.2. Artificial Intelligence, Ethical Workplaces, and People-Centred Supply Chains

Although the sustainability of the environment has taken the center stage of the discourse on AI-enabled supply chains, social aspect of sustainability is equally essential especially on cross-border logistical systems marked by high levels of labour-intensive processes and institutional heterogeneity. Social sustainability of supply chains involves labor rights, safety of workers, fair wages and ethical working conditions which are increasingly becoming affected by the utilization of artificial intelligence technologies (Seuring and Muller, 2008; Koberg and Longoni, 2019). According to recent studies, AI can also make a positive contribution to the sustainability of labor by improving occupational safety, workload, and compliance. Warehouses, ports, and transportation hubs have prediction analytics and sensor-based AI systems to predict equipment failures, hazardous working conditions, and the risk of accidents (Gunasekaran et al., 2019). These applications help to ensure a safer working environment and fit the principles of humanism, which stand out in modern literature on Industry 5.0 (Wu et al., 2025).

Meanwhile, researchers also express their worries about the ethical aspects of algorithmic management within supply chain and logistics. The systems of AI-assisted monitoring and performance assessment can enhance productivity and are also the cause of over-surveillance, loss of worker agency, and work pressure unless properly-controlled (Dwivedi et al., 2021). These risks are especially acute in cross-border supply chains, in which labor laws and law enforcement practices differ to a great extent regionally. Regarding governance, transparency, fairness, and accountability are promoted as the foundations of socially sustainable AI usage because of ethical AI frameworks (Floridi et al., 2018). Implementing these principles of supply chain management can ensure that AI-assisted decision-making does not strengthen the existing labor inequalities and take advantage of regulatory loopholes in global logistics systems. Human-centric models of supply chains support the development of AI systems that do not substitute humans in their tasks but increase their skills, expertise, and involvement in decisions and further growth (Wu et al., 2025). Incorporating social protection in AI governance framework facilitates companies to achieve technological innovation with the social goals of the Triple Bottom Line, therefore supporting fair and sustainable transnational logistics.

10. FRAMEWORK PROPOSAL: AI-ENABLED SUSTAINABLE SUPPLY CHAIN (AISS) MODEL

It is through the support of AI across the three major support of sustainability that the three central proportion was given about this process of the supply chain, AI techniques and the sustainability goods of AI. The review of the outcomes suggest that the role of AI-based solutions is crucial in establishing sustainable supply chains since it has been determined to increase the efficiency of the management of the logistic process. The artificial intelligence application has been worked out to be utilized in the future studies concerning the sustainable supply chain. (Yadav et al., 2024). Key Layers of the Framework Approximately five intertwined surface which ought to integrate the efficient application of information by the process of AI facilitated logistic administration and also aid in making responsible decisions, operational efficiency, sustainability performance, and responsible governance in global supply chain.

10.1. The AISS Model Operationalized in the Sustainability Metrics

Although conceptual frameworks are beneficial in organizing complex phenomena, earlier studies in the field of sustainable supply chain management note that it is important to transform conceptual models into quantifiable and practical performance measures to enhance the managerial and empirical applicability of the models (Koberg and Longoni, 2019; Kleindorfer et al., 2005). To resolve this issue, the AI-Enabled Sustainable Supply Chain (AISS) model may be operationalized with the help of the set of sustainability metrics corresponding to every of its five layers.

Data Intelligence Layer: The success of the AI-powered sustainability programs is based on the quality, integration, and timeliness of data. In the literature of supply chain analytics, such indicators as completeness of data, real-time visibility, and accuracy of data across nodes of logistics are commonly used (Kache et al., 2017; Wamba et al., 2017). These measures gauge how the companies are able to capture and inter-relate both operational, environmental, and social data across the cross-border supply chains.

Analytical Layer: In the analytical level, the performance of AI can be measured by such indicators as the quality of forecasting, the reduction of the error, and the quality of decisions made in scenarios (Waller and Fawcett, 2013; Ivanov and Dolgui, 2020). These measures are helpful in the sustainability-oriented logistics in terms of better demand planning, estimation of emissions, and risk anticipation to make more informed and proactive decisions.

Operational Layer: The AI operational effect is observed in the efficiency of the logistics and resource use. The indicators recommended are the decrease in empty vehicle mileage, the rise of fuel efficiency, inventory turnover, and the variability of lead-time (McKinnon, 2018; Gunasekaran et al., 2019). These operational measurements are directly associated to the environmental performance since they reduce the use of energy and also the emission of greenhouse gases in the process of transportation and warehousing.

Sustainability Layer: The environmental and social sustainability indicators are usually measured according to the CO2 emissions per unit transported, energy per ton-kilometer, waste recovery rates, and labor and safety standards (Koberg and Longoni, 2019; Saberi et al., 2019). These indicators make the AISS model conform to the Triple Bottom Line by incorporating both environmental and social aspects of sustainability in transnational logistics.

Governance Layer: The governance layer focuses on accountability, transparency, and ethical AI use. Rates of regulatory compliance, audit traceability, AI-driven decisions explainability, and data protection standards are all indicators covered in the literature on digital governance and responsible AI (Floridi et al., 2018; Dwivedi et al., 2021). These guidelines would make sure that the AI-based supply chain decisions comply with local and social expectations in different jurisdictions. Connecting every level of the AISS model to a set of already existing sustainability and performance indicators, the framework leaves the field of mere conceptual input and enters a sphere of measurable and practicable solutions. Such operation makes the framework more relevant to the researcher, policymaker, and practitioner interested in assessing actual effects of AI on sustainable cross-border supply chains.

11. FUTURE DIRECTIONS AND POLICY IMPLICATIONS

11.1. Green AI and Energy Efficiency

Optimization problem has been modelled using constraint satisfaction schemes. The objective of the optimization task is to minimize the amount of energy utilized and at the same time, maintain the model accuracy above a predefined threshold. The proposed scheme has used the energy-efficient optimization procedure developed in this section to minimize the consumption of energy in corporate systems (Dash, 2025). The energy requirement of AI technology and deep learning models, in particular, is enormous. Large AI models like GPT-3 and AlphaGo require additional processing power, which is power intensive to preparation. One million two hundred eighty-seven MWh of electricity, or over 120 houses in the United States every year, would have been required to make GPT-3. This contributes to the overall

AI technologies carbon footprint and leads to massive carbon emissions. Besides, the data centers where AI systems are located require updating. According to the International Energy Agency (IEA), data centers consumed more than 200 TWh of electricity in the world in 2018, or 1% of all electricity consumption and 0.3% of all CO2 (Tabbakh et al., 2024).

11.2. The Digital Twin Technology, Predictive Analytics, and Sustainable Project Management

Digitizing the logistic functions by enhancing transparency as well as the policy-making process and commitment to judgement through digital twin automation, predicting the investigations, and plausible future course of enterprise. Digital twins create digital representations of the physical supply chains, and allow the real- time view of the system performance and is also capable of simulating a possible disruption (McKinnon et al., 2015). The combination of goals of viability and streamlined operations is evident in organizations that adopt eco-friendly logistic systems, such as ecofriendly carrying. Together, these strategies address the complex needs of global supply chains and contribute to the resilience and long-term sustainability (Enyejo et al., 2024).

11.3. AI and Sustainability Along Ethical and Social Lines

Competition in the production business is very tough to retain in the market for the manufacturer and the retailer of the supply chain (Guchhait & Sarkar, 2025). With the help of the process enhancement and predicting, the service of technologies helps to cut down waste and enhance the distribution of resources. In this way, the efficiency of the supply chains could be enhanced when machine learning (ML) and artificial intelligence (AI) are combined and improves the sustainability objectives when it reduces the waste and the use of resources (Floridi et al., 2018). Machine learning (ML) and artificial intelligence (AI) can be employed to achieve the supply chain efficiency and sustainability objectives (Tabbakh et al., 2024).

12. CONCLUSION

This paper has considered the concept of artificial intelligence (AI) as a strategic driver of sustainability in international logistics and international supply chains. With the growing complexity and data-intensiveness of supply chains, the results highlight that AI ought to be perceived not just as an efficiency-enhancing instrument but as a fundamental capacity to facilitate environmental, social, and governance

(ESG) goals. To overcome the gaps in the existing literature, the paper introduced the framework AI-Enabled Sustainable Supply Chain (AISS) that combines the AI-inspired decision-making with the sustainability theory, systems thinking, and ethical governance. The framework can provide a systematic way of adopting AI responsibility in cross-border logistics by placing ESG considerations directly into AI applications and taking heterogeneity in regulatory and institutional settings into account. On balance, this study adds an integrative approach, which offers practical and theoretical recommendations to facilitate sustainability in supply chain transformation through the prism of AI innovation, sustainability objectives, and governance needs.

REFERENCES

Barman, A. (2025). Sustainability, Supply Chain Management, and Machine Intelligence: Overcoming Challenges and Shaping the Future. *Procedia Computer Science*, *258*, 993–1002. DOI: 10.1016/j.procs.2025.04.336

Ben-Daya, M., Hassini, E., & Bahroun, Z. (2019). Internet of Things and supply chain management: A literature review. *International Journal of Production Research*, *57*(15–16), 4719–4742. DOI: 10.1080/00207543.2017.1402140

Biermann, F., Kanie, N., & Kim, R. E. (2017). Global governance by goal-setting: The novel approach of the UN Sustainable Development Goals. *Current Opinion in Environmental Sustainability*, *26*, 26–3. DOI: 10.1016/j.cosust.2017.01.010

Brown, W., Wilson, G., & Johnson, O. (2024). Understanding the Adoption of Advanced Analytics in Supply Chain Decision Making. DOI: 10.20944/preprints202408.0235.v1

Cardini, A. (2024). Unsustainable development goals. *The Ecological Citizen*, *7*(2), 124–134.

Chen, S., Zhang, Q., & Zhou, Y. P. (2019). Impact of supply chain transparency on sustainability under NGO scrutiny. *Production and Operations Management*, *28*(12), 3002–3022. DOI: 10.1111/poms.12973

Dash, S. (2025). Green ai: Enhancing sustainability and energy efficiency in ai-integrated enterprise systems. *IEEE Access : Practical Innovations, Open Solutions*, *13*, 21216–21228. Advance online publication. DOI: 10.1109/ACCESS.2025.3532838

Dwivedi, Y. K., Hughes, L., Ismagilova, E., Aarts, G., Coombs, C., Crick, T., Duan, Y., Dwivedi, R., Edwards, J., Eirug, A., Galanos, V., Ilavarasan, P. V., Janssen, M., Jones, P., Kar, A. K., Kizgin, H., Kronemann, B., Lal, B., Lucini, B., & Williams, M. D. (2021). Artificial intelligence (AI): Multidisciplinary perspectives on emerging challenges, opportunities, and agenda for research, practice and policy. *International Journal of Information Management*, *57*, 101994. DOI: 10.1016/j.ijinfomgt.2019.08.002

Elkington, J. (1998). Partnerships from cannibals with forks: The triple bottom line of 21st-century business. *Environmental Quality Management*, *8*(1), 37–51. DOI: 10.1002/tqem.3310080106

Enyejo, J. O., Fajana, O. P., Jok, I. S., Ihejirika, C. J., Awotiwon, B. O., & Olola, T. M. (2024). Digital twin technology, predictive analytics, and sustainable project management in global supply chains for risk mitigation, optimization, and carbon footprint reduction through green initiatives. *International Journal of Innovative Science and Research Technology*, *9*(11), 1344. DOI: 10.38124/ijisrt/IJISRT24NOV1344

Fahmin, A., Cheema, M. A., Eunus Ali, M., Nadjaran Toosi, A., Lu, H., Li, H., & Shen, B. (2024). Eco-Friendly Route Planning Algorithms: Taxonomies, Literature Review and Future Directions. *ACM Computing Surveys*, *57*(1), 1–42. DOI: 10.1145/3691624

Floridi, L., Cowls, J., Beltrametti, M., Chatila, R., Chazerand, P., Dignum, V., Luetge, C., Pagallo, U., Rossi, F., Schafer, B., Valcke, P., & Vayena, E. (2018). AI4People—An ethical framework for a good AI society. *Minds and Machines*, *28*(4), 689–707. DOI: 10.1007/s11023-018-9482-5

Gereffi, G., & Lee, J. (2012). Why the world suddenly cares about global supply chains. *The Journal of Supply Chain Management*, *48*(3), 24–32. DOI: 10.1111/j.1745-493X.2012.03271.x

Guchhait, R., & Sarkar, B. (2025). Economic evaluation of an outsourced fourth-party logistics (4PL) under a flexible production system. *International Journal of Production Economics*, *279*, 109440. DOI: 10.1016/j.ijpe.2024.109440

Gunasekaran, A., Yusuf, Y. Y., Adeleye, E. O., Papadopoulos, T., Kovvuri, D., & Geyi, D. A. G. (2019). Agile manufacturing: An evolutionary review of practices. *International Journal of Production Research*, *57*(15–16), 5154–5174. DOI: 10.1080/00207543.2018.1530478

Hajer, M., Nilsson, M., Raworth, K., Bakker, P., Berkhout, F., De Boer, Y., Rockström, J., Ludwig, K., & Kok, M. (2015). Beyond cockpit-ism: Four insights to enhance the transformative potential of the sustainable development goals. *Sustainability (Basel)*, *7*(2), 1651–1660. DOI: 10.3390/su7021651

Hao, X., & Demir, E. (2024). Artificial intelligence in supply chain decision-making: An environmental, social, and governance triggering and technological inhibiting protocol. *Journal of Modelling in Management*, *19*(2), 605–629. DOI: 10.1108/JM2-01-2023-0009

Hendriksen, C. (2023). Artificial intelligence for supply chain management: Disruptive innovation or innovative disruption. *Journal of Supply Chain Management, 59(3),* 65-76. DOI: 10.1111/jscm.12304

Hosseini, S. E., Rahmaty, M., Kiakojouri, D., & Hajiaghajani, A. (2025). The Role of Open Innovation in Enhancing Ethical Decision-Making in Government Organizations. *Journal of Industrial and Systems Engineering*, *17*(1), 144–153.

Hosseini Tabaghdehi, S. A., & Ayaz, Ö. (2025). AI ethics in action: A circular model for transparency, accountability and inclusivity. *Journal of Managerial Psychology*. Advance online publication. DOI: 10.1108/JMP-03-2024-0177

Huang, X., & Peng, H. (2018). Eco-routing based on a data driven fuel consumption model. *arXiv preprint arXiv:1801. 08602.*

Ivanov, D., & Dolgui, A. (2020). Viability of intertwined supply networks: Extending the supply chain resilience angles towards survivability. *International Journal of Production Research*, *58*(10), 2904–2915. DOI: 10.1080/00207543.2020.1750727

Kache, F., & Seuring, S. (2017). Challenges and opportunities of digital information at the intersection of Big Data Analytics and supply chain management. *International Journal of Operations & Production Management*, *37*(1), 10–36. DOI: 10.1108/IJOPM-02-2015-0078

Kang, Y., Cai, Z., Tan, C. W., Huang, Q., & Liu, H. (2020). Natural language processing (NLP) in management research: A literature review. *Journal of Management Analytics*, *7*(2), 139–172. DOI: 10.1080/23270012.2020.1756939

Khan, M., Parvaiz, G. S., Dedahanov, A. T., Abdurazzakov, O. S., & Rakhmonov, D. A. (2022). The impact of technologies of traceability and transparency in supply chains. *Sustainability (Basel)*, *14*(24), 16336. DOI: 10.3390/su142416336

Kleindorfer, P. R., Singhal, K., & Van Wassenhove, L. N. (2005). Sustainable operations management. *Production and Operations Management*, *14*(4), 482–492. DOI: 10.1111/j.1937-5956.2005.tb00235.x

Koberg, E., & Longoni, A. (2019). A systematic review of sustainable supply chain management in global supply chains. *Journal of Cleaner Production*, *207*, 1084–1098. DOI: 10.1016/j.jclepro.2018.10.033

Lee, B. X., Kjaerulf, F., Turner, S., Cohen, L., Donnelly, P. D., Muggah, R., & Gilligan, J. (2016). Transforming our world: Implementing the 2030 agenda through sustainable development goal indicators. *Journal of Public Health Policy*, *37*(S1, Suppl 1), 13–31. DOI: 10.1057/s41271-016-0002-7

Li, Z., Shalaby, A., Roorda, M. J., & Mao, B. (2021). Urban rail service design for collaborative passenger and freight transport. *Transportation Research Part E, Logistics and Transportation Review*, *147*, 102205. DOI: 10.1016/j.tre.2020.102205

Lin, C. K., & Moffat, P. A. (2016). Global Supply Chain under the Paris Agreement: The Relevance of Chemical and Product Regulations. *Nat. Resources & Env't, 31*, 21.

Madhani, P. (2009). Resource based view (RBV) of competitive advantage: an overview. *Pankaj M Madhani.* https://www.researchgate.net/publication/45072518

Mastoli, M. M. M., Pol, U. R., & Patil, R. D. (2019). Machine learning classification algorithms for predictive analysis in healthcare. *Machine Learning, 6*(12), 1225–1229.

McKinnon, A. (2018). *Decarbonizing logistics: Distributing goods in a low carbon world.* Kogan Page.

McKinnon, A., Browne, M., Whiteing, A., & Piecyk, M. (Eds.). (2015). *Green logistics: Improving the environmental sustainability of logistics.* Kogan Page Publishers.

Saberi, S., Kouhizadeh, M., Sarkis, J., & Shen, L. (2019). Blockchain technology and its relationships to sustainable supply chain management. *International Journal of Production Research, 57*(7), 2117–2135. DOI: 10.1080/00207543.2018.1533261

Sauer, P. C., & Seuring, S. (2017). Sustainable supply chain management for minerals. *Journal of Cleaner Production, 151*, 235–249. DOI: 10.1016/j.jclepro.2017.03.049

Saxena, N., Sarkar, B., Wee, H. M., Reong, S., Singh, S. R., & Hsiao, Y. L. (2023). A reverse logistics model with eco-design under the Stackelberg-Nash equilibrium and centralized framework. *Journal of Cleaner Production, 387*, 135789. DOI: 10.1016/j.jclepro.2022.135789

Seuring, S., Aman, S., Hettiarachchi, B. D., de Lima, F. A., Schilling, L., & Sudusinghe, J. I. (2022). Reflecting on theory development in sustainable supply chain management. *Cleaner Logistics and Supply Chain, 3*, 100016. DOI: 10.1016/j.clscn.2021.100016

Seuring, S., & Müller, M. (2008). From a literature review to a conceptual framework for sustainable supply chain management. *Journal of Cleaner Production, 16*(15), 1699–1710. DOI: 10.1016/j.jclepro.2008.04.020

Smith, C. H. (1968). *Systems theory as an approach to accounting theory.* The Pennsylvania State University.

Sugapriya, C., Fariya Azleena, A., Nagarajan, D., & Kavikumar, J. (2024). A sustainable fuzzy economic production quantity model (SFEPQM) with sporadic machine failures, inspection and prepayments under carbon tax and cap policy. *International Journal of Systems Science: Operations and Logistics, 11*(1), 2419398. Advance online publication. DOI: 10.1080/23302674.2024.2419398

Tabbakh, A., Al Amin, L., Islam, M., Mahmud, G. I., Chowdhury, I. K., & Mukta, M. S. H. (2024). Towards sustainable AI: A comprehensive framework for Green AI. *Discover Sustainability*, *5*(1), 408. DOI: 10.1007/s43621-024-00641-4

Tang, C. S., & Veelenturf L. P. (2019). The strategic role of logistics in the industry 4.0 era *Transportation Research Part E: Logistics and Transportation Review, 129,* 1-11. .DOI: 10.1016/j.tre.2019.06.004

Tian, W., Xiao, Z., Zhang, L., & Liao, J. (2025, June). Research on Pattern Recognition of Agricultural Product Safety Incidents and Intelligent Tracing of Traceability Paths Based on Artificial Intelligence. In *2025 IEEE International Conference on Pattern Recognition, Machine Vision and Artificial Intelligence (PRMVAI)* (pp. 1-10). IEEE.DOI: 10.1109/PRMVAI65741.2025.11108662

Tolliver, C., Keeley, A. R., & Managi, S. (2019). Green bonds for the Paris agreement and sustainable development goals. *Environmental Research Letters*, *14*(6), 064009. DOI: 10.1088/1748-9326/ab1118

Waller, M. A., & Fawcett, S. E. (2013). Data science, predictive analytics, and big data: A revolution that will transform supply chain design and management. *Journal of Business Logistics*, *34*(2), 77–84. DOI: 10.1111/jbl.12010

Wamba, S. F., Gunasekaran, A., Akter, S., Ren, S. J., Dubey, R., & Childe, S. J. (2017). Big data analytics and firm performance. *Journal of Business Research*, *70*, 356–365. DOI: 10.1016/j.jbusres.2016.08.009

Wu, H., Liu, J., & Liang, B. (2025). AI-driven supply chain transformation in Industry 5.0: Enhancing resilience and sustainability. *Journal of the Knowledge Economy*, *16*(1), 3826–3868. DOI: 10.1007/s13132-024-01999-6

Yadav, A., Garg, R. K., & Sachdeva, A. (2024). Artificial intelligence applications for information management in sustainable supply chain management: A systematic review and future research agenda. *International Journal of Information Management Data Insights*, *4*(2), 100292. DOI: 10.1016/j.jjimei.2024.100292

KEY TERMS AND DEFINITIONS

Artificial Intelligence (AI): Artificial Intelligence is defined as computer-based systems that have the ability to execute the task that is traditionally done by human intelligence that includes learning, reasoning, prediction and decision-making.

Cross-Border Logistics: Cross-border logistics was viewed as the planning, organization as well as transport of goods, information as well as services across the international boundaries as it engages in complicated regulations, cultures and operations.

Supply Chain Analytics: Supply Chain analytics involves the use of information analysis, statistical methods, and high-technological technologies in the decision-making process, performance, and effectiveness improvements in all the operations of the supply chain.

Sustainable Supply Chain Management: Sustainable logistic Management is the one that involves the integration of ecological factors into the logistic performance in order to gain extended organizational performance and reasonable goals.

Technology: Technology refers to the application of scientific knowledge, tools and systems to develop solutions that bring about improvements in the processes, efficiency and innovations in the organizations and the industries.

Chapter 8

AI-Driven Decarbonization in Agri-Food Cold Chains With Smart Logistics and Renewable Energy

Zoya Naaz
http://orcid.org/0009-0005-7794-3730
IIMT University, Meerut, India

Vaibhav Sharma
http://orcid.org/0000-0003-0621-3712
IIMT University, Meerut, India

Akshay Raj
http://orcid.org/0000-0002-0603-6720
IIMT University, Meerut, India

Zeba Rani
http://orcid.org/0009-0006-7648-6707
IIMT University, Meerut, India

ABSTRACT

International transport of perishable goods currently struggles with high energy consumption and food loss due to supply chain inefficiencies. This chapter explores merging artificial intelligence with renewable energy to build a sustainable global cold chain. The authors specifically investigate Maximum Power Point Tracking (MPPT) algorithms in solar-powered warehousing to cut reliance on fossil-fuel

DOI: 10.4018/979-8-3373-7847-3.ch008

generators. Additionally, the text analyzes how predictive analytics and digital twins can forecast customs delays and prevent spoilage. By aligning these interventions with the UN Sustainable Development Goals, the study outlines a viable decarbonization pathway. These strategies provide stakeholders with actionable methods to minimize Scope 3 emissions and ensure the resilience of cross-border food trade.

INTRODUCTION

Growing Crisis of World Food Exchange

The global transportation of perishable agricultural goods now functions on a tenuous aligning point of the two worldwide crises energy instability as well as food insecurity (Mohammad et al., 2025). Traditional cold chain logistics: the system of temperature-regulated warehousing, transport and distribution is widely known to be energy-intensive, but it heavily depends on fossil fuel to keep the tight thermal conditions around sensitive cargo (Wang & Du, 2025). Recent estimates indicate that the cold chain contributes about 2.5 percent of the total global greenhouse gas (GHG) emission which is likely to increase as developing countries continue to build their infrastructure (Lin et al., 2025). At the same time, there are physical wastages in this system that result in astounding material wastages. It is approximated that about 14 percent of the food produced in the world is lost between the harvesting and the retailing stages with a large share of the food spoiled by the lapse of cold chain during cross-border transport. The challenge is paradoxical, i.e. one needs to extend the cold chain to minimize food loss yet with existing technologies one is bound to heighten the carbon footprint of the agri-food sector (Foumakoye, 2025).

The Decarbonization Imperative

To logistics stakeholders, the need to decarbonize has ceased to be merely ethical but regulatory and economic as well (Tetteh et al., 2025). Although multiple organizations have been effective in cutting Scope 1 (direct) and Scope 2 (indirect energy) emissions, Scope 3 emissions, which are those that happen along the value chain are the hardest to cut. The Scope 3 emissions in relation to the agri-food logistics include the carbon emissions of the third-party refrigerated trucks (reefers), outsourced warehousing, and diesel generators to power cooling units due to the customs delay. The solution to these emissions would be a drastic shift to active intelligent, as opposed to passive management policies (Sharma et al., 2025).

Chapter Objectives

The concept of this chapter is the combination of three disruptive technologies, namely Artificial Intelligence (AI), the Internet of Things (IoT), and renewable energy as a single model of decarbonization. In particular, we examine the implementation of the Maximum Power Point Tracking (MPPT) algorithm in order to optimize the process of solar-powered warehousing and the Digital Twin technology to develop predictive green corridors. This research will synthesize these tools to present how the agri-food sector can transform the linear, fossil-reliant model to the circular, data-driven ecosystem that is in line with the United Nations Sustainable Development Goals (SDGs).

Cold Chains Global Food Security and Sustainability

Cold chains are very critical in ensuring food security by maintaining the quality of perishable agricultural products, safety of perishable agricultural products, nutritional value of perishable agriculture products and fruits, vegetables, dairy, meat, and seafood. Poor refrigeration and storage facilities have been cited as one of the main causes of post-harvest loss especially in the developing economies where the penetration of cold chain is low. Regarding sustainability, cold chains represent a two-sided sword: on the one hand, they minimize the quantity of food waste and increase the shelf life; on the other hand, they consume a lot of energy, which is often fossil fuel. This contradiction underscores the importance of reconceptualizing cold chains as preservation systems but also as intelligence-based, sustainable systems that address food security objectives as well as environmental accountability (Mounika et al., 2025).

Evolution of AI Into a Transformational Facilitator of Cold Chain Management

Artificial intelligence has become a potent facilitator with the capability to change traditional cold chains into adaptive, predictive and self-optimizing systems (Fatorachian & Pawar, 2025a). Machine learning, deep learning, and reinforcement learning AI-based methods can be used to monitor the temperature, humidity, energy consumption, and the risk of spoilage in real time. Using a lot of sensor data, AI systems can anticipate equipment failures, make better routing choices, and load cooling dynamically. The capabilities can help to enhance operational effectiveness and also lead to a massive reduction in energy wastage and carbon emissions. The adoption of AI therefore symbolizes a paradigm shift in the cold chain operations where they are reactive to the intelligence-driven logistics (Jackson et al., 2025).

Smart Supply Networks and Digitalization of Agri-Food Supply Networks

Smart logistics, together with digital technologies, such as the Internet of Things (IoT), blockchain, and digital twins, has transformed agri-food supply networks. The Smart logistics allows end-to-end visibility, traceability and transparency in cold chain processes. In this case, digital twins, specifically, enable the virtualization of physical assets, which provides the possibility to analyse scenarios and optimize performance under different environmental and demand conditions. Such technologies are the basis of the data infrastructure on which a decarbonization strategy based on AI can be implemented successfully. The fact that they are part of the modern cold chains increases their resilience and promote sustainability-based decision-making (Göçer et al., 2025).

BACKGROUND

Carbon Footprint of the Cold Chain

A cold chain is not an object, but a disjointed chain of offloading between farms, pack houses, distribution centers and retailers. The weakest link in this chain especially in cross-border trading is the source of energy that is used in cooling down the stationary (Yuan et al., 2025). Reefers may take hours or days to be cleared at crossings of the borders and at intermodal terminals. Without the option of grid power ("shore power), such units are powered by auxiliary diesel generators, which produce large amounts of particulate matter and CO2. Such dependence forms a carbon hot spot which is hard to counter using conventional efficiency strategies only.

Perishable Goods Transport Weaknesses

The Live goods have a biological time that is determined by their rate of respiration (Yan et al., 2025). According to the rule of the Q10 temperature coefficient, in many biological systems, the rate of deterioration doubles as the temperature goes up in terms of the C temperature by 10°C. In turn, even small temperature fluctuations, i.e., the instances when cargo gets warmer than its predetermined temperature, will reduce shelf life significantly. The existing logistics systems are usually weak in visibility; the operators can tell where a shipment is but they have no idea how the cargo will be thermally in the future. The reactive solution to this problem results in food waste by design, in which spoilage is seen as an unavoidable business expense, rather than a failure of logistics that can be avoided.

The Change to Renewable Energy Infrastructure

To address these issues, logistics hubs are growing up to implement the use of solar Photovoltaic (PV) systems (Babu et al., 2025). Nevertheless, typical PV systems are very constrained within a logistics environment. The part-shading of the warehouse is usually inherent to the changing cranes, stacks, or other infrastructure. In the traditional PV systems, when any part of a solar array has been shaded, the power output of the full string may decrease disproportionately making the system unreliable to drive any critical cooling load. This intermittency has in the past would have compelled operators to ensure that they maintain diesel-generating plants as a major backup which has negated the decarbonization potential of the solar investments.

Figure 1 illustrates key obstacles in reducing emissions from the cold chain, including diesel-powered carbon hotspots, food spoilage due to temperature fluctuations, and the rapid deterioration of perishables. It also highlights the limitations of solar power—such as shading and intermittent output—which reduce reliability and force continued dependence on diesel generators.

Figure 1. Hidden challenges in decarbonizing the cold chain

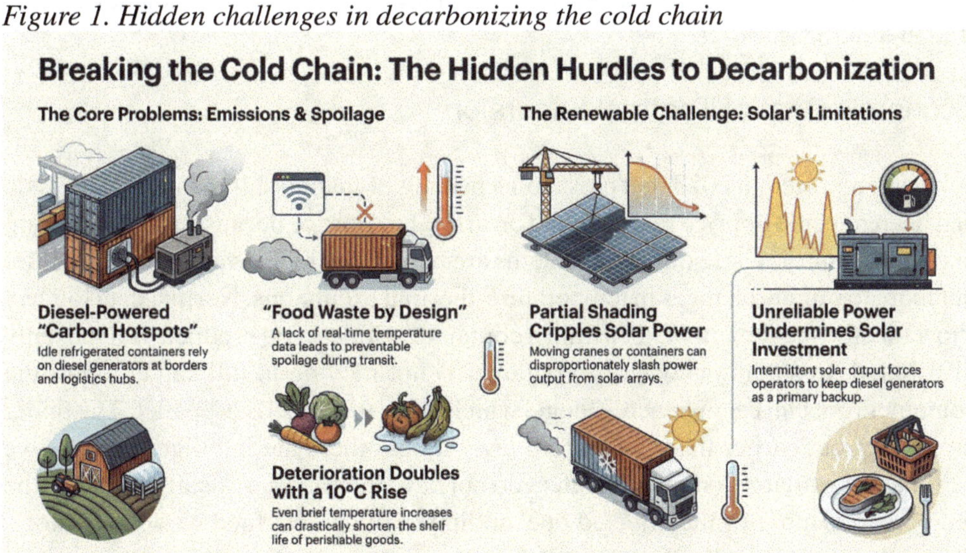

Analysis Case Study: The Mango Export Corridor (India to EU)

In order to have the theoretical issues of cold chain in perspective, we discuss the individual logistical route of mango exports of Uttar Pradesh, India to the European Union. This is a high-risk perishable corridor because of the overwhelming ambient temperatures (usually more than 40 degree Celsius) and the very stringent phytosanitary inspections that have to be performed at EU borders.

The Energy Differentiated at Intermodal Points

The trip usually starts with the pre-cooling at the farm gate, then by refrigerated truck to a local airport or seaport (ex. Nhava Sheva or IGI Airport). Although the trucks are mobile, the cooling unit is powered by the diesel engine. A critical energy gap however is experienced at the customs terminal. Statistics reveal that perishable shipments may take between 12 and 72 hours on clearance. At this dwell time, the grid infrastructure in the localized area may not be adequate to accommodate the concurrent start-up current of hundreds of reefer containers. As a result, the logistics providers go bankrupt on the operation of auxiliary diesel generators. One 40ft reefer container uses about 2-4 litters of diesel per hour to sustain a set point of 13degC in the presence of an ambient temperature of 40degC. The carbon emission is in large quantities when summed up in a terminal that manages 5,000 containers, which in turn forms a localized heat island that lowers the cooling efficiency further (Liu et al., 2025).

Economic Cost of Thermal Excursion

It was reported in 2023 that close to 15 percent of mango shipment in South Asia had been rejected or price renegotiated on arrival in Europe because of the softening or chilling injury. These quality problems are hardly due to an overall system failure but more to minute changes in temperature-thermal excursions. Normal data loggers show that the movement of air within a container with packed products is not evenly distributed. In situations where a container is not moving in full sun at a port the container roof can easily reach 70degC which heats the uppermost pallet. The upper layer dries out earlier than the bottom layer unless there are intelligent and active ventilation regulators (standard reefers do not have them). This wastage compels the retailers to dispose of the affected one, adding to the global food waste indicator.

Thermodynamics of the Cold Chain

Understanding the failure of current systems requires a review of the thermodynamic governing equations of a refrigerated container. The heat load Q_{total} that a cooling unit must overcome is not static; it is a dynamic sum of transmission load, infiltration load, and product respiration load.

The transmission load Q_{trans} is defined by the quality of insulation and the temperature differential:

$$Q_{trans} = U \cdot A \cdot (T_{ambient} - T_{internal})$$

Where: U is the overall heat transfer coefficient of the container walls. A is the surface area. T represents temperature.

In a solar-powered scenario, the challenge lies in the $T_{ambient}$ variable. During peak solar hours (noon), $T_{ambient}$ is highest, maximizing the cooling demand Q_{trans}. Fortunately, this perfectly correlates with peak solar irradiance. This natural correlation suggests that solar PV is the ideal energy source for cold chain applications, *provided* the system can extract maximum energy efficiently despite the shading caused by port cranes and stacked containers.

Cold Chain System Digital Transformation

The digital transformation of logistics and infrastructure systems is increasingly becoming a factor in the background of agri-food cold chains (Vahdanjoo et al., 2025). The conventional cold chains used were mostly manual, inaccessible and reactive where periodic checks and temperature holding mechanisms were used. With the development of the digital technology, including IoT-based sensors, cloud computing systems, and edge analytics, it has become possible to continuously monitor vital characteristics like temperature, humidity, vibration, and energy consumption. This transformation offers high-resolution data of operation and this forms basis of intelligent decision-making. Online cold chains do not only enhance traceability and food safety compliance, but also allow optimization of data, which is vital to eliminating waste and subsequent carbon emissions.

Agri-Food Cold Chain Characteristics Energy Demand

A decarbonization strategy needs an understanding of the energy demand profile of cold chain operations (Mubarik et al., 2025). The cold storage systems, refrigerated transporting systems and pre-cooling systems have very fluctuated thermal loads that depend on the ambient conditions, the type of product, length of storage and the frequency of product handling. The peak demand energy periods are commonly associated with the hot weather conditions and the seasonal harvests, which raise the use of power sources that have a high carbon content. These are the characteristics of demand that pose challenges and opportunities of optimization of energy. Highly developed load forecasting and demand-side management strategies, especially with the help of AI, can reduce peak energy use quite substantially and better align it with renewable energy availability.

Refrigerants and Cooler Technologies in Emissions

Refrigerants and cooling technologies present a significant portion of the environmental impact of cold chains, in addition to their energy usage (Yıldırım et al., 2025). A lot of traditional systems have been based on the use of hydrofluorocarbon (HFC) based refrigerants which are inefficient due to their high global warming capacity despite their efficiency benefits. They contribute to their climate impact through leakages during operation, maintenance and end-of-life disposal. New natural refrigerants have been developed in recent years including ammonia, carbon dioxide and hydrocarbons; these provide alternatives with lower emissions at the cost of technical and safety considerations. To put AI-driven optimization and renewable integration strategies in the perspective further in the chapter, it is necessary to have some background knowledge of refrigeration technology development (Al-Raeei, 2025).

Infrastructure Inequality of Developed and Developing Economies

There are high regional differences in the growth of cold chain. The developed economies tend to have well-developed refrigerated logistics systems with standard infrastructure whereas the developing regions experience refrigerator storage gaps, grid dependability and skilled workforce. Such infrastructural constraints usually increase the spoilage level and poor energy utilization. Decentralized and off-grid cold chain systems that use renewable energy are becoming emerging as a viable option in the emerging markets. Such an uneven landscape points to the necessity of scalable, flexible solutions that can be deployed in a variety of economic and infrastructural environments and AI-enabled systems are especially applicable (Panda, 2025).

RESEARCH GAPS AND THEORETICAL FOUNDATIONS

Research Gaps of AI-based Cold Chain Decarbonization

Digitalization, renewable integration, and smart logistics used in agri-food supply chains is a recent area of scholarship that is however fragmented and technologically isolated in the literature. The systematic review of the existing literature has identified the following gaps, which are yet to be filled.Although the digitalization of the cold chain has already been made, there are still a few significant gaps:

Absence of AI, Renewable, Logistics Decarbonization Models

The majority of studies consider AI-based monitoring, renewable energy systems, or optimization of logistics separately. Very few offer a solution with a single systems architecture comprising of predictive intelligence, MPPT-enabled renewable energy optimization, and emission aware logistics as one decarbonization model.

Lack of Cold-Chain Routing Algorithms

The routing algorithms that are currently in practice either optimize the delivery time or optimize fuel cost. (Wang & Mansoor, 2025). Nevertheless, there is little inclusion in routing decisions of carbon intensity of refrigeration equipment, dwell-time emissions at intermodal nodes, and thermal energy loads.

Inadequate System Level Modeling Connecting MPPT Optimization and Logistics Emissions

Studies on the Maximum Power Point Tracking (MPPT) are mainly concerned with the photovoltaic efficiency in the partial shading situation. Logistics studies on the other hand quantify emissions and fail to relate renewable energy optimization with actual cold chain carbon performance.

Lack of Proper Economic and Organization Prepared Analysis

There is a lack of research in evaluating the viability of capital investment and operational costs recovery, human skills, and institutional constraints to the adoption of AI-enabled cold chains with low carbon (Habazin, J., Bajor, I., Bajec, P., & Rožić, T. 2025).

Weak Governance and Cybersecurity Systems

Since digital cold chains are progressively data-demanding, there is limited research on cross-border data governance, data transparency in algorithms, and exposure to cyber threats in AI-based logistics systems.

These loopholes suggest that there is a need to develop a structured, theory-based, and system-level decarbonization framework that would bridge the gap between technological convergence and operational, economic, and sustainability aspects.

Table 1 provides a comparative overview of the prevailing approaches in existing literature and contrasts them with the integrated model introduced in this chapter.

Table 1. Comparison of competing approaches

Approach	Focus	Strength	Limitation
IoT-based monitoring	Visibility	Real-time data collection	Primarily reactive; limited predictive control
Green logistics	Fuel efficiency	Reduces transport emissions	Does not integrate thermal or energy subsystems
Solar PV integration	Clean energy supply	Lower grid dependence	Intermittency; limited logistics integration
Proposed AI-integrated model	System-level convergence	Predictive, adaptive, and decarbonized	Requires validation and institutional readiness

The suggested framework goes beyond the single technological interventions because it allows multilayer optimization of energy production, refrigeration demand, logistics routing, and predicting a spoilage.

Theoretical Foundations of the Proposed Framework

In order to enhance conceptual rigour, the suggested AI-supported decarbonisation model is rooted in the traditional theoretical views.

Framework of Sustainable Development

The framework fits the principles of sustainability expressed in the United Nations Sustainable Development Goals (SDGs), namely, SDG 2 (Zero Hunger), SDG 7 (Affordable and Clean Energy), and SDG 12 (Responsible Consumption and Production). The SDG framework offers a macro-level normative base, connecting food security, energy transition, and responsible production systems (Zhao, X., Castka, P., & Searcy, C. 2020).

Socio-Technical Systems Theory

In Socio-Technical Systems (STS) Theory, the technological systems cannot be maximized out of context of the organizational structures, human actors and institutional arrangements. Cold chains are dynamic socio-technical systems of interaction between AI algorithms, renewable energy devices, actors of logistics, and regulatory frameworks. Decarbonization then necessitates distributed change both at the technical and social level subsystems.

RESEARCH METHODOLOGY

Analytical Approach

Thematic Synthesis

The thematic synthesis approach was used to classify the literature into four broad areas: i.e.

- predictive analytics and AI in logistics.
- Optimization of MPPT and renewable energy.
- Spoilage Modeling and cold chain thermodynamics.
- Green supply chain and emission management.

Patterns, overlaps, and research gaps across these domains were identified to inform framework construction.

Systems Integration Modeling

Systems Integration Modeling is a process employed to define the functions and processes that are common to the different components of a system. On the basis of the thematic synthesis, a systems integration modeling approach was followed. The study conceptualizes the cold chain as an interdependent multi-layered system in place of determining the effect of separate technological interventions..

Model Construction Logic

The suggested model is organized in four layers that interact with each other:

Energy Layer

- Solar PV technology with AI-based MPPT optimization.
- Microgrid coordination in hybrids.
- Renewable alignment and load forecasting.

Data Layer

- IoT sensor networks (vibration, energy use, humidity, temperature)
- Edge computing nodes
- Analytics that are based in the cloud.

Logistics Layer

- Routing algorithms that are carbon conscious.
- Inventory management using FEFO.
- Dynamic energy management in intermodal.

Decision Layer

- Artificial intelligence-based predictive analytics.
- Digital twin simulation
- Dashboards of emission performance.
- KPI sustainability monitoring.

This layered architecture ensures systemic integration rather than technological fragmentation

TECHNOLOGICAL CONVERGENCE

The Definition of Smart Cold Chain

A traditional cold chain opposed to a Smart cold chain is one that makes autonomous decisions (Kilari, 2025). Whereas a conventional chain records data to be analyzed after the event (e.g. the cargo spoiled yesterday), a smart chain makes real-time use of the information to take action (e.g. the cargo will spoil in 4 hours unless we reroute). This transformation is driven by the combination of two particular technical fields advanced energy optimization (MPPT) and virtual simulation (Digital Twins).

Figure 2. Evolution of the smart cold chain

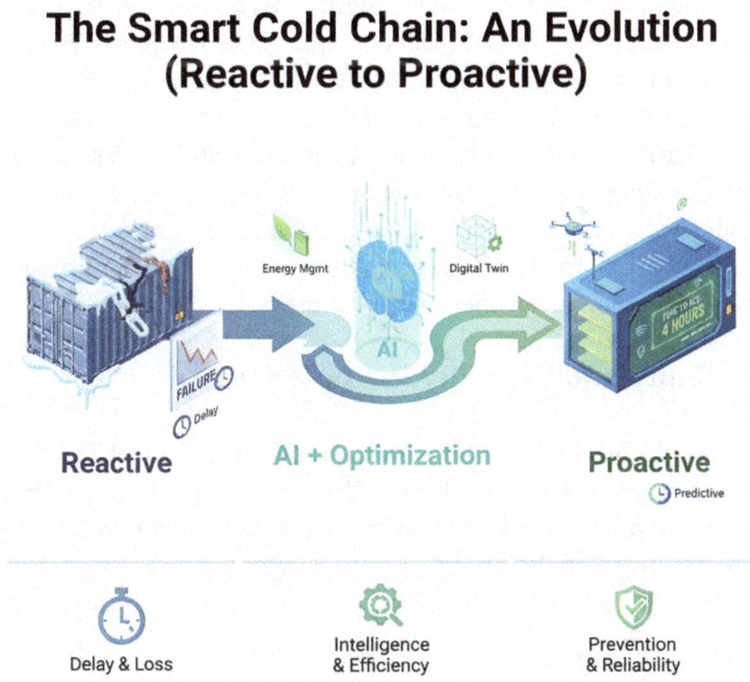

Figure 2 illustrates the shift from the traditional, reactive cold chain—where failures are identified only after spoilage occurs—to a proactive smart cold chain that uses real-time data, energy optimization, and digital twins to predict and prevent losses. It highlights how advanced technologies enable timely interventions, improving reliability and reducing food spoilage (Dhal & Kar, 2025).

Warehousing and Energy Independence

Solar-Powered: The Role of Advanced MPPT in order to make solar energy a feasible baseload power source to cold storage, the yield of energy extraction should be peaked in non-ideal conditions. It is here that the Maximum Power Point Tracking (MPPT) is essential (Wang et al., 2025).

The Partial Shading Problem: The shadows are dynamic in a busy logistics depot. With the movement of gantries and build-up of containers, shadows create and recede on top of roof solar panels very quickly. In these cases, standard algorithms of MPPT, including the "Perturb and Observe" (P&O), often cannot work. They are likely to fall in local maxima or false peaks in the power curve due to shading as opposed to the actual global maximum or power point.

AI-Driven Optimization: Bio-inspired algorithms to solve this have recent future developments in 2024 and 2025. As an example, Improved Grey Wolf Optimization (IGWO) and hybrid algorithms using Particle Swarm Optimization (PSO) in combination with P&O have demonstrated the better capacity to follow the Global Maximum Power Point (GMPP) at a high speed and stability. With such AI-based MPPT controllers, logistics hubs are able to reclaim up to 20-30% of the energy of the same solar arrays than through conventional controllers (Arsad et al., 2025). This extra output is what can be the difference maker in enabling a facility to operate its cooling systems fully on clean energy even at the busiest of times.

Digital Visibility and Visibility in Logistics

To Predictive Control Digital Shadows to Predictive Control The second pillar of the smart cold chain is the Digital Twin. Whereas a Digital Shadow is a one-way exchange of information (sensors that give up-to-date temperature), a Digital Twin is a two-way dynamic simulation.

Figure 3. Digital shadow

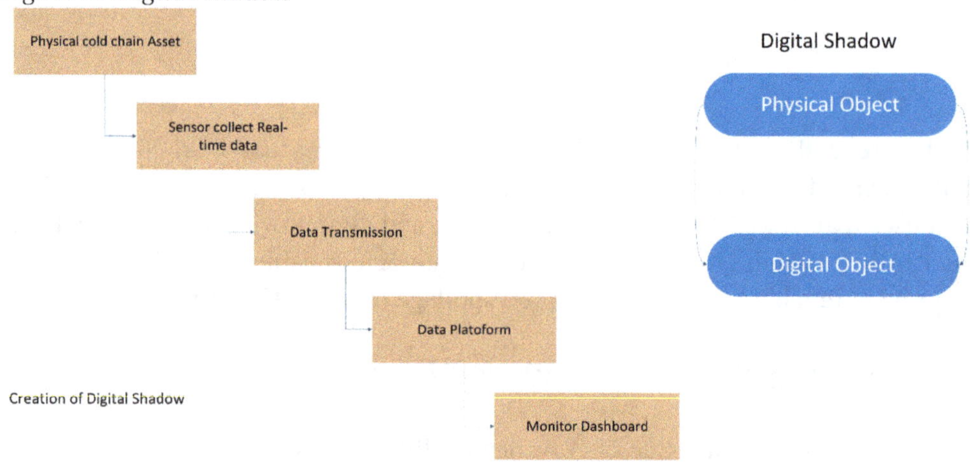

Figure 3 shows flow chart which illustrates the concept of a Digital Shadow, where real-time sensor data from cold chain assets flows in one direction into a digital platform. It highlights how physical conditions are monitored continuously without any automated feedback or control loop.

Thermal Simulation: A Digital Twin of a cold storage container combines real-time IoT data (internal temperature, humidity, door state) with outside parameters (weather forecast, traffic congestion, solar radiance).

Spoilage Prediction: After running this data through machine learning models, the system will be able to predict the remaining shelf life of the particular cargo (Aslam et al., 2025). As an example, when a truck-train with strawberries is held at a checkpoint at the border due to high ambient temperatures, the Digital Twin will be able to model how this temperature change will increase in the inside and then determine the faster respiration rate of the fruit.

Proactive Decision Making: In the event that the simulation shows that the fruit will go bad before it reaches its original destination, the system has the capability of automatically notifying the logistics managers to either divert the shipment to a more nearby market or it can be given the top priority in terms of getting it customs cleared. This ability changes the supply chain into a stiff pipeline to a responsive and flexible network.

Operations Artificial Intelligence and Predictive Analytics

The use of Artificial Intelligence (AI) and predictive analytics is quickly changing the work of a cold chain, allowing making decisions based on data, taking initiative, and using the resources optimally (Fatorachian & Pawar, 2025b). Operational decisions, including temperature control, routing decisions, and inventory decisions in the traditional agri-food cold chains, are usually reactive and made by schedule or by ad hoc inspections. This strategy raises chances of spoilage, inefficiency in energy and carbon emissions. Table 2 provides a comparative assessment of different MPPT algorithms in terms of shading response, tracking speed, and algorithmic complexity, highlighting the superior performance of IGWO under dynamic conditions while noting the simplicity but limited effectiveness of the P&O method.

Table 2. Comparison of MPPT algorithms: This compares MPPT techniques based on shading response, speed, and complexity. IGWO performs best under dynamic conditions, while P&O is simplest but least effective

Algorithm	Handles Partial Shading	Convergence Speed	Computational Complexity
Perturb & Observe (P&O)	Poor	Medium	Low
Particle Swarm Optimization (PSO)	Good	Fast	Medium
Improved Grey Wolf Optimization (IGWO)	Excellent	Fast	High

Analytical Comparison of MPPT Algorithms in Cold Chain Applications

Implementation of Maximum Power Point Tracking (MPPT) algorithms is of crucial importance in the optimization of the efficiency of solar photovoltaic (PV) systems that are involved in refrigerated logistics infrastructure. In an ideal irradiance case, the traditional algorithms like Perturb and Observe (P&O) have acceptable performance as they are simple and have minimal computation needs. Yet, in practical cold chain conditions, especially at ports, logistics terminals and intermodal yards, the effects of partial shading are typical, especially because of the stacking of containers, crane activity, structural obstructions and variable weather conditions.

In these conditions of partial shading, P&O algorithms can reach local highs of power instead of the global highs and hence the high efficiency of renewable energy is compromised. Conversely, the global search ability is enhanced in the metaheuristic optimization techniques like Particle Swarm Optimization (PSO) where the swarm intelligence principles are applied. PSO is a higher convergence and adaptation to irradiance variations at a moderate computational cost.

The improved grey wolf optimization (IGWO) is more advanced and increases the level of tracking accuracy. IGWO simulates hierarchical hunting to search and explore the search space most effectively, enabling it to find the global maximum point of power when subjected to very irregular shading patterns. IGWO is more stable and convergent in a dynamic logistics environment, but computationally more complicated.

Systemically, a better performance of MPPT directly elevates the rate of solar exploitation, decreases the use of diesel-driven refrigeration units and improves the penetration of renewable in cold chain setups. In turn, the AI-based MPPT optimization is not a technical improvement but a system facilitator of quantifiable carbon emission savings in the decarbonized agri-food logistics networks.

Forecasting Demand and Supply

AI and predictive analytics also improve the supply chain forecasting by matching the production, storage, and transportation timelines with the real demand. The prediction of demand of products at various supply chain nodes is done using time-series analysis, deep learning models, and ensemble forecasting methods (Irhuma et al., 2025). Demand forecasting ensures that the stock is not overstocked, the storage period is minimized, and the spoiltage avoidance. Moreover, it enables more effective allocation of energy resources, cold storage facilities will be able to increase or reduce the cooling capacity based on the volume of products that are expected to be sold, which will help to use energy more effectively and at the same time preserve the quality of products.

Convergence of AI, IoT and Renewable Energy Systems

The technological convergence of the agri-food cold chains is defined by the smooth connection of artificial intelligence, Internet of Things (IoT) technologies, and renewable energy systems to one system of functioning. IoT sensors bring live data about temperature, humidity, energy usage, as well as equipment operation, whereas renewable energy technologies like solar photovoltaic systems deliver clean power to storage and transportation facilities. AI is the coordinating agent, processing raw data into actionable information, including optimizing energy consumption, adapting demand variability, and automatically varying refrigeration loads (Rojek et al., 2025). This convergence allows the cold chains to be intelligent, self-regulating systems which at the same time can be more efficient, reliable and environmentally friendly.

AI-Based Energy Management and Load Optimization

Among the greatest effects of the convergence of technologies, there is the development of AI-powered cold chain-based energy management frameworks (Rane et al., 2025). These systems examine both past and current data to predict energy demand, detect inefficiencies and optimize the allocation of load between the existing sources of energy. AI algorithms can be used in warehouses that are powered by the sun and hybrid microgrids to decide on the best time to store energy, interact with the grid and turn on refrigeration. The result of such intelligent control is the reduction of energy wastage and charging of peak demand, and the maximization of utilization of renewable energy which can directly contribute to the decarbonisation goals (Tang & Wang, 2025).

Figure 4. Smart energy management system for cold chain

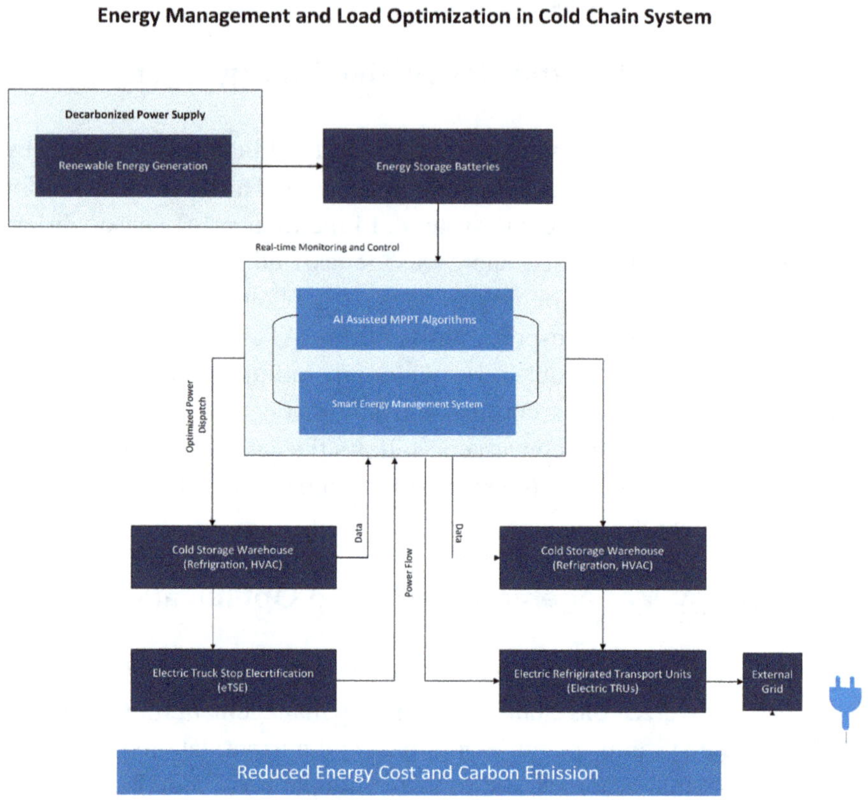

Figure 4 illustrates a Smart Energy Management System for cold chains, utilizing *AI*-assisted MPPT algorithms and renewable energy to optimize power flow.

Edge Computing and Real-Time Decision-Making in Cold Chains

Edge computing is highly essential as cold chains grow data-intensive to provide an opportunity to make real-time decisions (Bablu & Rashid, 2025). In stark contrast to the centralized cloud-based system, edge computing is performed on the data that is generated nearer to the point of creation, i.e., inside the refrigerated trucks or storage centers. This can be used especially in perishable goods logistics where any delay in responding can cause the quality to suffer. With the combination of edge intelligence and AI models, immediate corrective responses can be made like adjusting the temperature or changing routes without the ongoing network connection (El-Hajj, 2025). The layer of technology improves the system responsiveness and resilience, along with the energy-efficient operations.

Smart Cold Chains Cybersecurity and Data Governance

With cold chains embracing the new technologies of digitality and artificial intelligence, cybersecurity and data governance become important factors to consider (Sowan et al., 2025). Operation technology, coupled with information technology, makes operations more vulnerable to cyber risks, such as data breaches and disruptions in the system. Strong cybersecurity systems, reliable communication systems, and data governance policies are the key factors to make sure that the smart cold chain operations are reliable and free of any integrity concerns. These issues are the key to establishing trust between the stakeholders and allowing converged technological solutions to be used at large scale.

Technological Convergence Strategic Value to Decarbonization

Smart logistics and renewable energy technologies in combination with AI present a strategic direction of decarbonization of agri-food cold chains (Fatorachian & Pawar, 2025b). Instead of one area at a time making small steps in individual components, convergence allows optimization of the system in energy, logistics, and thermal management. The combined approach gives the compounding benefits, cutting the emissions, reducing the spoilage, increasing the resilience, and making the approach economically viable. This chapter puts technological convergence as the major point of focus, as the intelligent and fully integrated systems can re-imagine the future of sustainable agri-food logistics.

RECOMMENDATIONS AND SOLUTIONS

The Framework of the Green Corridor

Isolated technological interventions cannot be effective to decarbonize the cold chain, but an overhaul of the system is needed (Nayebossadri et al., 2025). In this chapter, the author suggests the introduction of Green Corridors, i.e., specific logistics routes that will be provided with renewable energy infrastructure in critical nodes. With the help of the AI-assisted MPPT systems, warehousing depots at the border crossings will become more energy islands than energy consumers.

Under this umbrella, the Maximum Power Point Tracking (MPPT) algorithms are such that the solar PV arrays in such depots operate at peak efficiency even when trucks cause dynamic shadowing on the infrastructure. This stable production of energy enables one to install Electric Truck Stop Electrification (TSE) units. Trucks can use the solar-powered grid rather than using stagnation diesel engines to propel refrigeration units (TRUs) when a truck is delayed at the customs station. This not only eliminates Scope 1 emissions but also has a substantial effect in the reduction of the carbon intensity per ton-kilometre of the transported food.

Figure 5. Green corridor framework

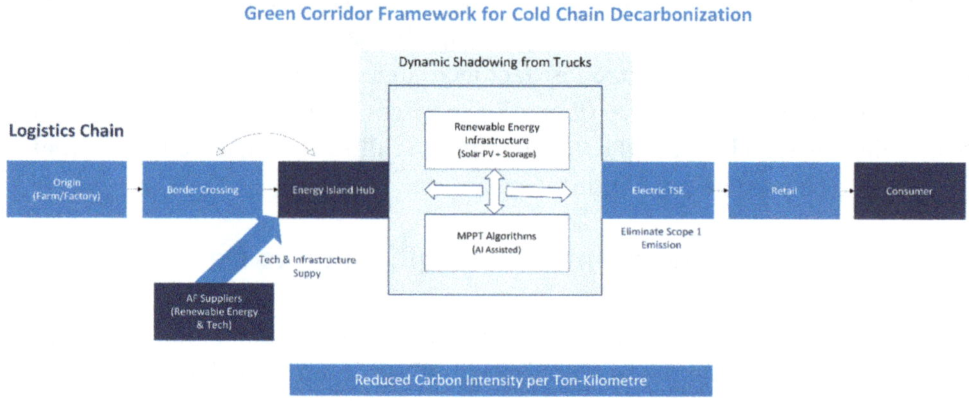

Figure 5 illustrates an AI-enabled Green Corridor integrating renewable energy, MPPT control, and electric logistics across the cold chain, enabling energy-independent hubs and reduced carbon intensity per ton-kilometer.

Lessening Spoilage by Issuing Timely Warnings

The Digital Twin integration transforms the industry to a proactive quality control model rather than the reactive one (Pal et al., 2025). In our time, the logistics operators tend to adopt First-In-First-Out (FIFO) inventory strategy. Nevertheless, the biological variation and the varying thermal exposure levels received during transit imply that FIFO can easily result in the sale of fresher products and older but still edible products becoming spoiled in the back.

The replacement of conventional inventory rotation design with First-Expired-First-Out (FEFO) model is a vital improvement in the smart cold chain problem. In contrast to a widespread method of First-In-First-Out (FIFO) and putting products in a queue according to their time of arrival, FEFO is a dynamical method of taking into account the remaining shelf life of perishable goods. This transformation is facilitated by the combination of predictive analytics, real-time sensing, and digital twin to support the agri-food cold chain in making more informed and sustainability-oriented decisions.

Situation: A smart cold chain with predictive analytics and digital twin technology constantly evaluates the actual status and shelf life of perishable goods on transit using a First-Expired-First-Out (FEFO) inventory management model. The situation is that in this case a load of avocados is being moved under a refrigerated environment when a sudden failure of the cooling system takes place. In as much as the failure does not fully stop refrigeration, it leads to prolonged temperature fluctuations in long durations. Based on historical models of degradation, real-time sensor measurements, and several curves of decay characteristic of products, the digital twin predicts that the shipment lost about 20 percent of its remaining shelf life. This will greatly enhance the chances of the produce not reaching the quality standards, in case it is transported to its originally intended destination, which is a distant retail supermarket, which needs long transit and shelf life.

Intervention: After detecting the increased rate of shelf-life deterioration, the artificial intelligence-based decision-support system is set to analyse alternative distribution routes based on FEFO logic automatically. The system does not use dispatch order to prioritize the shipment according to the dispatch order, but it uses its earliest estimated expiration. The automated alert message is sent to the logistics manager who is advised to reroute a particular pallet in the shipment to a local juice processing or pulp manufacturing plant. Such recommendation is derived as a result of multi criteria optimization that considers the leftover shelf life, the distance to be covered to process, the readiness of the processing, the anticipated economic recovery, and the environmental effects. This is done almost in real time and the logistics operators are able to reroute the shipment before the quality deteriorates further.

Outcome: There are economic and environmental gains on the implementation of this FEFO-based intervention. Economically, the shipment of the avocado is economically maintained by processing the fresh products into products to prevent total losses suffered by spoiling or rejection by retail outlets. On the environmental front, the rerouting does not allow organic waste to be discarded hence minimising the emission of methane when food waste is being decomposed (Meegoda et al., 2025). Also, optimal routes and reduced transportation distances are efficient in fuel consumption, as well as refrigerating energy, which leads to the minimization of carbon emissions. This finding will show how FEFO, through predictive analytics and the digital twin, will turn cold chain management into a proactive system that is sustainability-oriented and reduces waste but maximizes value in agri-food supply chains.

Figure 6. Predictive logistics

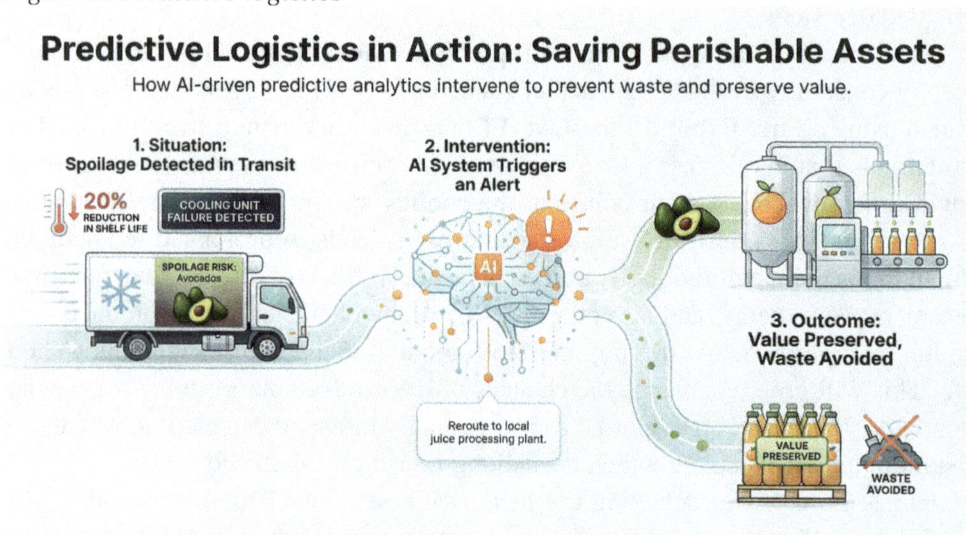

The illustration demonstrates AI-driven predictive logistics where in-transit spoilage is detected, automated rerouting decisions are triggered, and perishable goods are redirected for processing, preserving economic value and avoiding food waste.

Figure 7. Shipment-to-outcome workflow: Using digital twins to prevent spoilage

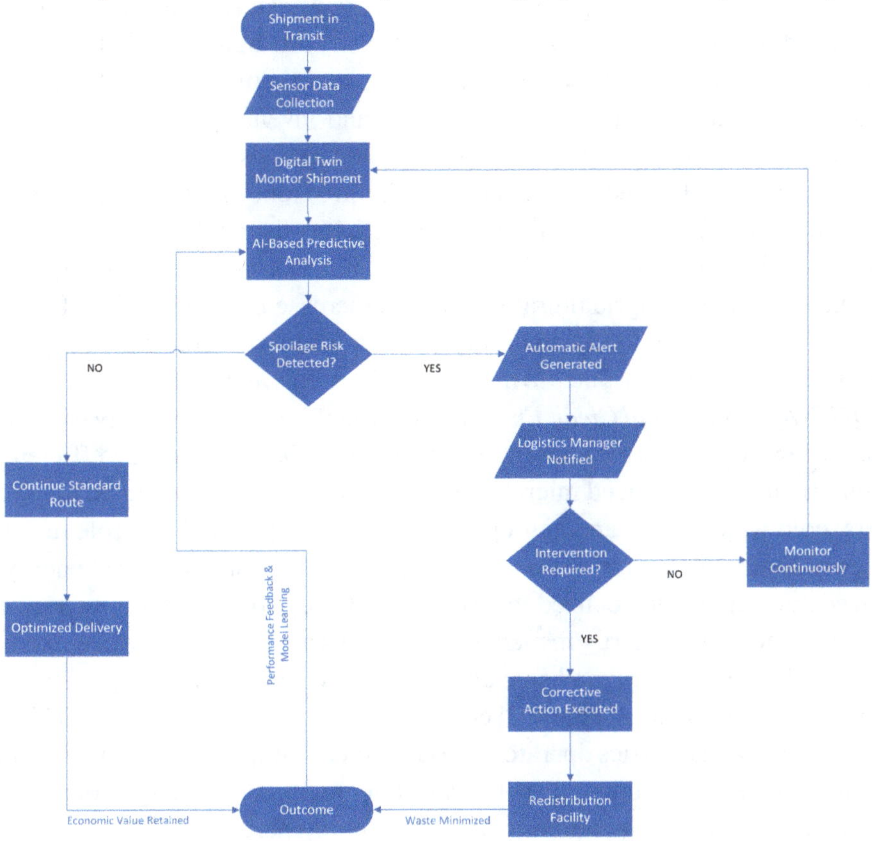

In Accordance With UN Sustainable Development Goals (SDGs)

The solutions discussed in this chapter are in line with the United Nations Sustainable Development Goals (SDGs) especially those that deal with food security, adoption of clean energy and sustainable production systems. The proposed solutions would help reduce inefficiencies in the existing food distribution systems that are pertinent to worldwide sustainability goals, and the proposed solutions would integrate artificial intelligence, predictive analytics, smart logistics, and renewable energy in the agri-food cold chains. The proposed solutions support SDG 2 (Zero Hunger), SDG 7 (Affordable and Clean Energy), and SDG 12 (Responsible Consumption and Production) the most, as it is among the 17 SDGs.

SDG 2 (Zero Hunger): Zero Hunger focuses on providing food security and better nutrition by ensuring sustainable agricultural production. One of the key issues in fulfilling this objective is that a significant amount of post-harvest losses is incurred through the lack of cold storage, bad logistic and temperature control. The solutions, which are described in this chapter as AI-driven, can help resolve this issue by providing predictive cooling and smart storage management. Cold chain systems are able to proactively adjust cooling settings and inventory movements with the help of real-time sensor data and machine learning models that predict temperature variations and shelf-life decay. Under the condition of renewable energy sources that are maximum power point tracking (MPPT) reliable, the cooling processes can be maintained with stability even in the fluctuating power conditions. Consequently, it is not the expansion of agricultural land or the increase in the intensity of resource utilization that increases food availability, but rather conservation of the current level of production, which contributes to making food systems more efficient and resilient.

SDG 7 (Affordable and Clean Energy): Affordable and Clean Energy is dedicated to increasing the access to renewable energy and enhancing energy efficiency in different fields. AI-enhanced microgrids based on solar panels installed at logistics centers, cold warehouses, and aggregation centers can play a direct role in achieving this purpose. Such microgrids allow creating and consuming clean energy in a localized manner and do not need the use of fossil-fuel-powered grid electricity and diesel generators. The energy management systems are AI-based, which maximize energy production, storage, and consumption, allowing a refrigerating system to be reliable and reducing the operational cost to the minimum (Rojek et al., 2025). This gives industrial and logistics operators good reasons to implement renewable energy systems to prove the economic feasibility of integrating clean energy solutions into cold chain operations that require a large amount of energy.

SDG 12 (Responsible Consumption and Production): Responsible Consumption and Production, focuses on the minimisation of food loss and waste along the supply chain. The Green Corridor model suggested in this chapter guarantees the food products transportation, storage, and distribution according to the quality and shelf-life data in real-time rather on the fixed schedule. The framework also reduces the wastage of these valuable production factors, including water, fertilizers, energy and human labour by facilitating dynamic rerouting, FEFO-based inventory management and spoilage prediction. Produced food has a higher chance of reaching the consumers in useful form and this strengthens sustainable consumption habits and decreases the amount of environmental impact as a result of food waste.

Taken together, these AI-based solutions show how smart cold chain systems can serve as effective drivers of global sustainability outcomes by bringing the technological innovation to tangible advancement toward the UN SDGs.

Policy and Financial Incentives

The policy and financial incentives are determined by the existing policy and financial regulations. Regulatory organizations and governments have an important role to play in enhancing decarbonized cold chains. The policies are to offer monetary incentives, subsidies, and tax relief to investor in renewable energy, AI-based systems, and green logistics. Adoption can further be expedited through carbon pricing systems, sustainability certification and private-public alliances. The measures would ease the economic obstacles facing the small and medium-sized enterprises, especially in developing countries, and spur high-scale adoption of cold chain solutions using low-carbon.

Suggested AI-Based Framework and the Current Practices

The suggested AI-based system of agri-food cold chain decarbonization is based on the current technologies in operations combined with innovative AI-based methods to form a coherent, sustainable, and resilient system (Halder et al., 2025). Although currently no unified model is in place that fully integrates AI, renewable energy, and carbon-conscious logistics, the strategy is able to combine commonly used practices and combine them into a single cohesive model. With the help of real-time information, predictive intelligence, integration with renewable energy, and intelligent logistics, the framework offers a viable way of transforming the traditional cold chains into low-carbon, adaptive ecosystems.

Figure 8. AI-powered low carbon cold chain

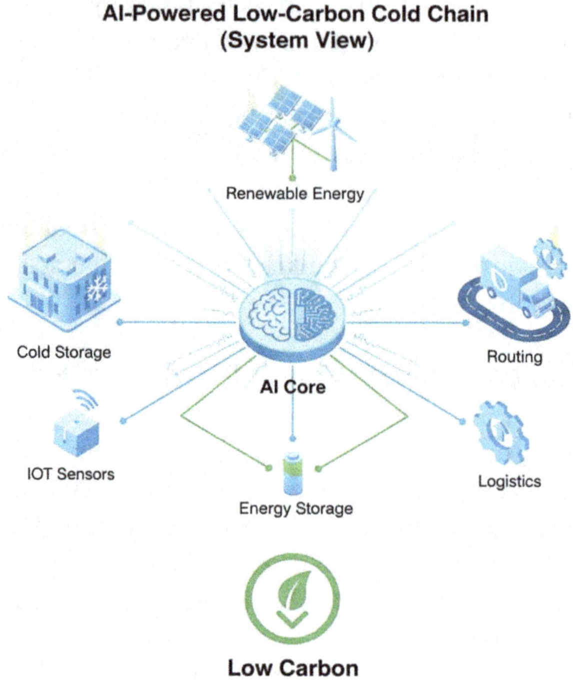

Figure 8 depicts an AI-powered low-carbon cold chain where system-wide intelligence integrates IoT data, renewable energy management, and optimized logistics routing to enhance sustainability, efficiency, and emission reduction.

Data Acquisition Through IoT Monitoring

The IoT-enabled monitoring is the base of the framework, which provides real-time information used in AI-driven decision-making (Sathiya et al., 2025). There are sensors installed in cold storage areas and refrigerated transportation devices that constantly monitor temperature, humidity, vibration, energy usage and equipment functionality. This information is already implemented in numerous contemporary cold chains, e.g. in the perishable fruit and dairies logistics in Europe, North America or even more in India.

The collection, storage and processing of these sensor streams can be easily achieved by integration with warehouse management systems (WMS) and transport management systems (TMS). Current technologies involve RFID-tracking, GPS-fleet tracking and automated environmental tracking. These practices are extrapolated within the framework with a connection between the data of separate sources that allow an analysis system-wide instead of isolated operational insights.

In addition, the IoT data is used to support real-time alerts on deviations, i.e., temperature jumps or energy spikes. Such notifications activate AI-controlled suggestions of remedial measures, where the quality of products and energy competence are maintained. IoT data is also rich enough to analyse historical trends that may be used to support predictive modelling and long-term planning.

Operational Intelligence and Predictive Analytics

In the contemporary cold chains, predictive analytics is already deployed in the processes of spoilage prediction, maintenance planning, and demand prediction (Shehzad, 2025). In one instance, machine learning models can be used to predict possible quality loss or degradation by analysing past temperature trends, rates of product spoilage, etc. Correspondingly, predictive maintenance software powered by AI can detect faulty compressors, insulation issues, or refrigeration unit inefficiency before it can result in a failure of operation.

Within the given framework, the current practices are extended to include sustainability goals. The AI models are optimized to maximize not only the operational efficiency but also the energy consumption and carbon emissions (Tabaku et al., 2025). As an example, predictive spoilage models are used to guide dynamic cooling controls, which can respond to future demand and product sensitivity by increasing or decreasing refrigeration intensity. Reinforcement learning algorithms also achieve a better balance between temperature and energy usage, reducing emissions without affecting food safety. This combination transforms traditional reactive management into proactive use of intelligence-based operations, and results in smarter, greener cold chains.

Integration of Renewable Energy Systems

Renewable energy, especially solar-driven cold storage and hybrid micro-grids, is becoming more popular in rural and off-grid areas, such as in India, Southeast Asia, and some areas of Africa (Hoekstra, 2021). A number of pilot projects have proven the viability of deploying solar-assisted refrigeration units in an attempt to limit the use of diesel. Nevertheless, the latter has yet to be integrated with AI-based energy management systems.

In the model, AI can be used to coordinate renewable generation, energy storage and refrigeration loads. The load forecasting models predict the cooling load and match it with the renewable generation profiles such that the clean energy is optimally used. An example is utilizing solar PV generation peaks at a time when pre-cooling or periods of high demand are going on in storage plants, and the surplus gets stored in batteries to be used during the night. The framework will decrease the use of fossil fuels and alleviate intermittency problems, which will reduce the total carbon emissions by expanding the current energy optimization practices.

Figure 9. AI-enabled renewable refrigeration ecosystem

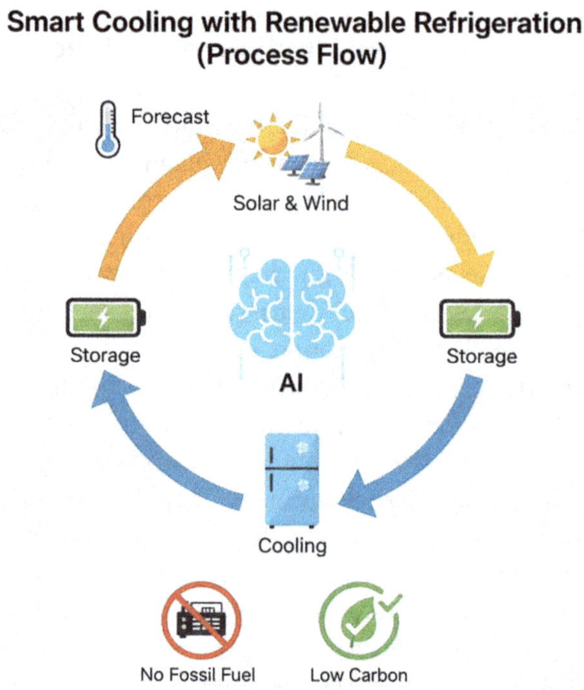

Image shows AI coordinating solar power, energy storage, and refrigeration demand, forecasting loads, matching renewables, reducing fossil fuel use, stabilizing power, and cutting carbon emissions in off-grid cooling systems globally.

Intelligent Logistics and Routing With Emission Awareness

The use of artificial intelligence (AI) in routing and fleet management is already established in modern cold chain logistics to reduce the delivery time and operational cost (Nozari et al., 2025). The current systems are efficient in fuel optimization and delivery time constraints but fail to use carbon intensity and energy consumption of refrigeration units as the decision variables.

The suggested framework refines the practices by incorporating emission-conscious routing algorithms. The energy held by the vehicles, refrigeration load, traffic, and the priorities of the delivery are collectively taken into account to determine low-carbon delivery routes. Moreover, AI maximizes the loading plan of the vehicles such that maximum refrigeration is carried out, minimizing the energy consumption per unit. Such combination of operational efficiency and sustainability indicates existing industrial trends but with an additional systematic carbon-reduction view not yet a general practice.

Digital Twin and Simulation Interaction

In the industrial logistics field, the concept of digital twins is coming into the picture, offering virtual models of facilities, transportation fleets, and storage facilities. Current applications model thermal behaviour, equipment behaviour as well as energy consumption.

Digital twins are built in the framework with the involvement of logistics, refrigeration, and energy subsystems, which allows testing scenarios and optimizing operations prior to deployment. Such as a digital twin can be used to simulate a high-temperature transport path, changing the cooling and routing decisions in real-time, and predicting the energy and carbon performance. The combination of digital twins with AI and renewable energy systems is a novel enhancement of the existing practice, which would help fill the gap between the theoretical modelling and the real operation.

Decision Support and Sustainability Metrics

The key performance indicators, such as the efficiency of energy, the rates of spoilage, and the carbon intensity per unit of product, are packed into the same dashboards by the decision support tools (Corigliano et al., 2025). These metrics are currently used by many companies to track them during internal audits and compliance, yet the framework increases their value as it presents AI-driven recommendations on how to improve its operations and invest.

The framework can bring together predictive analytics, energy optimization and emission metrics to deliver actionable insights to various stakeholders, such as the warehouse managers, the logistics planners, and the sustainability officers. This makes the decisions operationally efficient and also environmentally responsible, which address the strategic merit of technological convergence.

Leveraging Innovation to Existing Practices

The suggested framework will be based on the established technologies and will include IoT monitoring, predictive analytics, renewable energy integration, smart logistics, and digital twins and will systematize them into one to work towards decarbonization and operational efficiency. The framework suggests that with the help of existing practices instead of replacing them, it becomes possible to implement it practically and ensure a way of sustainable transformation. This strategy is an intermediate between the present and the future, allowing low-carbon, smart and robust cold chains in a wide range of geographical and economic settings (Wang et al., 2025).

Illustrative Carbon Reduction Scenario

In order to show the feasibility of the proposed AI-based decarbonization framework, a case scenario is provided to estimate the amount of emissions that can be reduced in terms of refrigerated container dwell. This is an example in form that represents the situation in real-life logistics of an agri-food cold chain, especially in India-EU export markets where refrigerated containers are frequently left powered in terminal handling and customs clearance. (Electric Power Research Institute. (2010))

Scenario Assumptions

The analysis assumes a typical case of operation that is in a realistic industry parameter:

- Container Type: 40-ft refrigerated container (reefer)
- Dwell Time at Terminal: 48 hours
- Diesel Consumption Rate: 3 liters/hour(TIP Group, 2022)
- Emission Factor: 2.68 kg CO_2 per liter of diesel

This is based on the assumptions of the energy requirements of the temperature-controlled transport units, which are in constant operation to preserve product integrity during the stationary operations.

Step 1: Diesel Consumption Calculation

The refrigeration unit works on the generators that are powered by diesel and helps to maintain cooling during a 48-hour dwell period. The amount of fuel used will be approximated as:

$\frac{3l}{hr} \times 48\ hr\ =\ 144\ l$

Step 2: Carbon Emission Calculation

By using the common emission factor of diesel combustion:

$$144l \times \frac{2.68kg}{l} CO\ \approx\ 386kg\ CO$$

Thus, a single container emits approximately *386 kg of CO_2* during a 48-hour dwell period when powered entirely by diesel.

Step 3: Solar PV Integration Model

In the context of the AI-optimized solar photovoltaic (PV) systems, a significant portion of refrigeration energy demand can be met through renewable sources. Assuming that *80% of the energy requirement(*Oluwaseun Francis Owolabi, 2024) is fulfilled through solar power:

$$386 \times \frac{80}{100}\ \approx\ 309kg\ CO\ \text{ avoided}$$

Emission Savings

This results in an estimated:

$$\approx\ 309kg\ CO^2 \text{saved per container}$$

Those differences show the effect of the shift between the traditional diesel-powered refrigeration to smart renewable-based systems.

System-Level Implications

Once scaled between the operations in logistics, the overall environmental effect is significant. For instance, across 5,000 reefer containers per year, integration of AI-powered solar energy systems would help cut the emissions by:

1,545 metric tons of CO2 per year

This scenario demonstrates the tangible decarbonization potential achievable through intelligent renewable energy adoption in cold chain infrastructure. Table 3 illustrates the validation outcomes, highlighting that the integration of solar energy substantially reduces diesel consumption and lowers CO emissions from 386 kg to 77 kg, achieving an estimated saving of 309 kg CO per container.

Table 3. Validation table: This table shows that solar integration reduces diesel use and lowers emissions from 386 kg to 77 kg, saving about 309 kg CO_2 per container.

Parameter	Diesel-Only System	80% Solar-Assisted System
Diesel Used	144 l	28.8 l
CO_2 Emissions	386 kg	77 kg
CO_2 Savings	-	309 kg

ECONOMIC FEASIBILITY AND INVESTMENT ANALYSIS

Capital Expenditure (CAPEX)

The shift towards AI-enabled infrastructure of renewable cold-chain implies the need to invest in energy, storage, and digital intelligence systems. Capital expenditure is estimated to be as shown below in the case of a logistics warehouse with an intermediate size located in an India-EU agri-food export corridor. (International Renewable Energy Agency [IRENA], 2020).

Table 4 provides estimated projections for a mid-sized logistics warehouse, highlighting the expected performance and potential benefits of the proposed implementation.

Table 4. Estimated for a mid-sized logistics warehouse

Component	Approximate Cost(USD)
500 kW Solar PV System	$440,000- $500,000
Battery Storage System(1-2 MWh)	$150,000- $220,000
AI Integration & IoT Deployment	$80,000 - $150,000
Digital Twin Software	$50,000- $100,000

Total Estimated CAPEX:

$720,000 – $970,000

These values are calculated considering the current industry standards of industrial-scale solar installations (around 0.8-1 dollar/watt), decreasing cost of battery storage, as well as the adoption of AI-based metabolism, control, and digital twin solutions into the logistics world.

Operational Expenditure (OPEX) Savings

Diesel Savings

Refrigeration and energy optimization using AI and the adoption of a solar-assisted cooling system can greatly decrease the usage of a diesel cooling system when in the dwelling. (Grün Power, 2026)

With a 80% decrease per year in the use of diesel:

- Projected yearly diesel expense (sample): $200,000.
- 80% reduction → $160,000 annual savings

Maintenance Savings

Predictive maintenance with AI improves the reliability *of equipment by enabling anomaly* in the performance of refrigeration systems to be identified before failure takes place. Studies indicate:

- 25–30% reduction in maintenance costs. (SEKO Logistics, 2024)
- 20–40% reduction in system downtime. (Mistry, 2025)

This would amount to estimated saving of:

$30,000 – $50,000

Total Savings (Estimated) per Year

Totals in annual savings amount to about: Combined operational efficiencies based on a reduction in diesel consumption and predictive maintenance totals:

$190,000 – $210,000

Payback Period (Illustrative)

According to the conservative estimates on investment and savings:
If total annual savings $\approx$ \$190,000:

$$Payback\ Period = \frac{800{,}000}{900{,}000} \approx 4.2\ years$$

It indicates that AI-included renewable cold-chain systems can be economically viable within a medium period of time. (Schiffmann et al., 2023) The period of payback can also be enhanced by the presence of carbon pricing schemes, renewable energy subsidies, or other sustainability-based financing schemes that are in place throughout the India-EU trade routes.

Risk and Resilience Assessment

Table 5 illustrates the risk matrix, identifying potential implementation risks and the associated mitigation measures aimed at enhancing the resilience and reliability of the system.

Table 5. Risk matrix: This table outlines key implementation risks and corresponding mitigation strategies to ensure system resilience

Risk Category	Description	Impact	Mitigation Strategy
Cybersecurity Risk	Data breaches or system hacking	High	Encryption, zero-trust architecture
AI Model Bias	Incorrect spoilage prediction	Medium	Model retraining, validation audits
Renewable Intermittency	Solar variability	Medium	Battery storage, hybrid grid support
Policy Uncertainty	Regulatory shifts	Medium	Flexible compliance frameworks
Technology Obsolescence	Rapid AI evolution	Low–Medium	Modular upgradeable systems

The credibility of implementation is improved through this systematic risk assessment.

DATA GOVERNANCE AND ETHICAL AI CONSIDERATIONS

With the digitization of cold chains, governance is becoming important.

Cross-Border Logistics Data Ownership

Definite contractual agreements are supposed to establish:

- Who owns IoT sensor data
- Who is allowed to read predictive analytics results?
- Information sharing privileges between exporters, logistics companies and importers.

GDPR Compliance (EU Corridor Case)

Information sharing privileges between exporters, logistics companies and importers.

- Obtain cross-border data transfer protocols.
- Avoidance of sensitive data in the business.
- Clear consent systems where necessary.

Explainability and Transparency of Algorithm

The AI systems that impact routing choices or spoilage choices need to include:

- Explainable AI (XAI) models
- Transparent decision logs
- Carbon accounting audit trails.

This is necessary towards regulatory acceptance and stakeholder trust.

Carbon Reporting Integrity

Traceability or secure digital ledgers with the use of blockchain can improve: Emission verification

- Emission verification
- Attribution of renewable energy.
- ESG reporting credibility

Having a carbon reporting integrity contributes to building institutional trust and avoiding a greenwashed process.

FUTURE RESEARCH DIRECTIONS

Carbon Transparency Blockchain

Due to the growing demands on businesses to disclose their Environmental, Social, and Governance (ESG) standards, the trust component of green logistics is the most crucial one (Yan et al., 2025). Further study needs to be conducted on the integration of the IoT sensors discussed in this chapter with the Blockchain technology. There would be a distributed ledger that could record the source of the energy that is used to cool (ex: correcting that a shipment has been cooled by solar energy and not diesel). This would provide verifiable "Carbon Credits" to the logistics provider, which would encourage additional investment in renewed infrastructure.

Autonomous Logistics

It is probable that in the next decade autonomous electric trucks will be commercially implemented. There is a critical research gap in the control of propulsion (driving) and preservation (cooling) of the power balance in energy. Future research should find methods of balancing the load on the batteries by AI algorithms, maybe by slowing down the vehicle to save power to the refrigeration unit during heatwave, thus making cargo integrity more important than the time of arrival.

Grid-Interactive Warehouses

Going beyond energy neutrality, the smart warehouses of the future will be able to be energy positive. The openings to research are in Vehicle-to-Grid (V2G) and Building-to-Grid (B2G) interfaces in which refrigerated warehouses will act as gigantic thermal batteries. Through over-cooling produce a little in the peak solar production hours (so-called thermal energy storage) warehouses would cut their grid demand in the evening, which would stabilize the local energy network.

CONCLUSION

The decarbonization of the agri-food cold chain entails a complex issue that cannot be addressed using hardware. In the chain, the clean electrons that are required are supplied by solar photovoltaics, but it is Artificial Intelligence that offers the intelligence which enables the use of the clean electrons. This chapter has shown that the combination of optimized renewable energy based on MPPT and simulations of Digital Twin can provide a potential solution to minimize the Scope 3 emissions and world food loss.

The stakeholders can construct a resilient supply chain that is not sensitive to price fluctuations and climate risks by converting logistics nodes into active energy-neutral hubs. The integration of these digital interventions is the key to providing the sustainable food future, as the time of the world as a perishable shelf-life clock runs out. The shift to predictive, AI-driven management, as opposed to the reactive one, is not only a competitive advantage option, but a necessity as an environmental concern.

REFERENCES

Al-Raeei, M. (2025). Integrating artificial intelligence into thermodynamics: A new paradigm for sustainable future. *AIP Advances*, *15*(6), 060701. DOI: 10.1063/5.0271867

. Arsad, A. Z., Azhar, A. D., Arsad, S. R., Zuhdi, A. W. M., Chau, C. F., & Ghazali, A. (2025). Towards artificial intelligence for solar charge controller: An analytical study of recent status, optimization and module development. *Energy Systems*, 1-54.

Aslam, S., Navarro, A., Aristotelous, A., Garro Crevillen, E., Martınez-Romero, A., Martínez-Ceballos, Á., Cassera, A., Orphanides, K., Herodotou, H., & Michaelides, M. P. (2025). Machine Learning-Based Predictive Maintenance at Smart Ports Using IoT Sensor Data. *Sensors (Basel)*, *25*(13), 3923. DOI: 10.3390/s25133923 PMID: 40648180

Ayeni, O. (2025). Integration of Artificial Intelligence in predictive maintenance for mechanical and industrial engineering. *International Research Journal of Modernization in Engineering Technology and Science*, *7*(3), 1–23.

Bablu, T. A., & Rashid, M. T. (2025). Edge computing and its impact on real-time data processing for IoT-driven applications. *Journal of Advanced Computing Systems*, *5*(1), 26-43.

Babu, R. M., Alam, M. S., Islam, A., & Islam, M. K. (2025). Towards Sustainable and Clean Energy Futures: A Techno-Economic Review of Solar PV Systems, Challenges, and Opportunities. *IEEE Access : Practical Innovations, Open Solutions.*

Chen, F., Yang, Z., Wang, Y., He, H., Zhang, Y., & Zhao, Y. (2025). Comprehensive economic, environmental and social benefit assessment for refrigeration and air-conditioning equipment combined with the social cost of carbon. *Energy*, *326*, 136263. DOI: 10.1016/j.energy.2025.136263

Corigliano, O., Morrone, P., & Algieri, A. (2025). Navigating the challenges of sustainability in the food processing chain: Insights into energy interventions to reduce footprint. *Energies*, *18*(2), 296. DOI: 10.3390/en18020296

Dhal, S. B., & Kar, D. (2025). Leveraging artificial intelligence and advanced food processing techniques for enhanced food safety, quality, and security: A comprehensive review. *Discover Applied Sciences*, *7*(1), 75. DOI: 10.1007/s42452-025-06472-w

El-Hajj, M. (2025). Enhancing communication networks in the new era with artificial intelligence: Techniques, applications, and future directions. *Network (Bristol, England)*, *5*(1), 1. PMID: 39601783

Electric Power Research Institute. (2010). *Electric refrigerated container racks: Technical analysis* (Product No. 1019926). https://www.epri.com/research/products/000000000001019926

Fatorachian, H., & Pawar, K. (2025a). Sustainable cold chain management: An evaluation of predictive waste management models. *Applied Sciences (Basel, Switzerland)*, *15*(2), 1–20. DOI: 10.3390/app15020770

Fatorachian, H., & Pawar, K. (2025b). Enhancing waste management in cold supply chains via digital transformation. *Procedia Computer Science*, *253*, 167–176. DOI: 10.1016/j.procs.2025.01.080

Foumakoye, A. K. H. (2025). Leveraging Emerging Technologies to Minimize Food Waste: A Study of Cold Chain Integrity and Transportation Efficiency in the Western Canadian Organic Food Sector (Doctoral dissertation, Wilmington University (Delaware)).

Göçer, A., Brockhaus, S., Fawcett, S. E., Vural, C. A., & Knemeyer, A. M. (2025). Supply chain sustainability, risk and transformational tension: A systems perspective. *International Journal of Logistics Management*, *36*(1), 21–45. DOI: 10.1108/IJLM-04-2023-0132

Group, T. I. P. (2022). *Sustainability Report, 2022*. https://cdn.tip-group.com/s3fs-public/documents/TIP%20Sustainability%20Report%202022_1.pdf

Habazin, J., Bajor, I., Bajec, P., & Rožić, T. (2025). A Review of Artificial Intelligence Applications in Cold Chain and Reverse Logistics. *Promet (Zagreb)*, *37*(6), 1409–1440. DOI: 10.7307/ptt.v37i6.1332

Halder, S., Islam, M. R., Mamun, Q., Mahboubi, A., Walsh, P., & Islam, M. Z. (2025). A comprehensive survey on AI-enabled secure social industrial internet of things in the Agri-food supply chain. *Smart Agricultural Technology*, *11*, 100902. DOI: 10.1016/j.atech.2025.100902

Hoekstra, M. (2021). Renewable energy and productive water for irrigation purposes in the provinces of Manica, Zambezia and Sofala (Mozambique). *Palais des congrès*, 32.

International Renewable Energy Agency (IRENA). (2020). *Renewable power generation costs in 2019*. https://www.irena.org/publications/2020/Jun/Renewable-Power-Costs-in-2019

Irhuma, M., Alzubi, A., Öz, T., & Iyiola, K. (2025). Migrative armadillo optimization enabled a one-dimensional quantum convolutional neural network for supply chain demand forecasting. *PLoS One*, *20*(3), e0318851. DOI: 10.1371/journal.pone.0318851 PMID: 40029920

Jackson, I., Namdar, J., Saénz, M. J., Elmquist, R. A.III, & Dávila Novoa, L. R. (2025). Revolutionize cold chain: An AI/ML driven approach to overcome capacity shortages. *International Journal of Production Research*, *63*(6), 2190–2212. DOI: 10.1080/00207543.2024.2398583

Kilari, S. D. (2025). The Impact of Artificial Intelligence on Automated Manufacturing and Supply Chain Systems: Advancements, Challenges, and Future Prospects. *Challenges, and Future Prospects.*

Lin, H. J., Chen, P. C., Lin, H. P., & Hsieh, I. Y. L. (2025). Quantifying carbon emissions in cold chain transport: A real-world data-driven approach. *Transportation Research Part D, Transport and Environment*, *142*, 104679. DOI: 10.1016/j.trd.2025.104679

Liu, W., Xu, B., & Li, J. (2025). Data-Driven Carbon Emission Dynamics Under Ship In-Port Congestion. *Journal of Marine Science and Engineering*, *13*(4), 812. DOI: 10.3390/jmse13040812

Logistics, S. E. K. O. (2024). *How predictive maintenance is extending the lifespan of logistics equipment.* https://www.sekologistics.com/en/resource-hub/knowledge-hub/how-predictive-maintenance-is-extending-the-lifespan-of-logistics-equipment/

Meegoda, J. N., Chande, C., & Bakshi, I. (2025). Biodigesters for sustainable food waste management. *International Journal of Environmental Research and Public Health*, *22*(3), 382. DOI: 10.3390/ijerph22030382 PMID: 40238415

Mistry, H. (2025, September 22). *AI agents in cold storage: Powerful wins & pitfalls.* DigiQT. https://digiqt.com/blog/ai-agents-in-cold-storage/

. Mohammad, A. A. S., Mohammad, S. I. S., Al-Daoud, K. I., Al Oraini, B., Vasudevan, A., & Feng, Z. (2025). Optimizing the Value Chain for Perishable Agricultural Commodities: A Strategic Approach for Jordan. *Research on World Agricultural Economy*, 465-478.

Mounika, K., Reddy, P. P., Singh, R. P., Pandey, A., Bharty, S. K., Kumar, A., & Jain, S. (2025). Post-harvest TECHNOLOGIES and cold chain management: A review. *Plant Archives*, *25*(1), 3275–3283.

Mubarik, M. S., Gunasekaran, A., Khan, S. A., & Mubarak, M. F. (2025). Decarbonization through supply chain innovation: Role of supply chain collaboration and mapping. *Journal of Cleaner Production, 507*, 145492. DOI: 10.1016/j.jclepro.2025.145492

Nayebossadri, S., Walsh, M., & Smailes, M. (2025). An Overview of the Green Hydrogen Value Chain Technologies and Their Challenges for a Net-Zero Future. *Hydrogen, 6*(2), 26. DOI: 10.3390/hydrogen6020026

Nozari, H., Rahmaty, M., Foukolaei, P. Z., Movahed, H., & Bayanati, M. (2025). Optimizing Cold Chain Logistics with Artificial Intelligence of Things (AIoT): A Model for Reducing Operational and Transportation Costs. *Future Transportation, 5*(1), 1. DOI: 10.3390/futuretransp5010001

Owolabi, Ogundipe, & Makinde. (2024). Integration of renewable energy-powered cold storage solutions for reducing postharvest food waste in rural agricultural areas. Academic Press.

Pal, P. K., Hens, A., Behera, N., & Lahiri, S. K. (2025). Digital twins: Transforming the chemical process industry—A review. *Canadian Journal of Chemical Engineering, 103*(8), 3611–3636. DOI: 10.1002/cjce.25611

Panda, S. (2025). *Scalable Artificial Intelligence Systems: Cloud-Native, Edge-AI, MLOps, and Governance for Real-World Deployment*. Deep Science Publishing.

Power, G. (2026, January 27). *Solar vs diesel generators for cold storage: What's smarter?* https://www.grunpower.in/blog/solar-vs-diesel-generators-for-cold-storage-whats-smarter/

. Rane, J., Amol Chaudhari, R., & Rane, N. (2025). Artificial Intelligence and Machine Learning for Supply Chain Resilience: Risk Assessment and Decision Making in Manufacturing Industry 4.0 and 5.0. *Artificial Intelligence and Machine Learning for Supply Chain Resilience: Risk Assessment and Decision Making in Manufacturing Industry, 4*.

Rojek, I., Mikołajewski, D., Mroziński, A., Macko, M., Bednarek, T., & Tyburek, K. (2025). Internet of Things applications for energy management in buildings using artificial intelligence—A case study. *Energies, 18*(7), 1706. DOI: 10.3390/en18071706

Sathiya, A., Angel, D., Iswarya, M., Poonkodi, R., & Angelo, K. M. (2025, January). IoT Enabled Healthcare Framework Using Edge AI and Advanced Wearable Sensors for Real Time Health Monitoring. In *2025 International Conference on Multi-Agent Systems for Collaborative Intelligence (ICMSCI)* (pp. 384-392). IEEE. DOI: 10.1109/ICMSCI62561.2025.10894492

Schiffmann, O., Hicks, B., Nassehi, A., Gopsill, J., & Valero, M. (2023). A cost–benefit analysis simulation for the digitalisation of cold supply chains. *Sensors (Basel), 23*(8), 4147. DOI: 10.3390/s23084147 PMID: 37112487

Seyam, A., Mathew, S. S., Du, B., Barachi, M. E., & Shen, J. (2025). A stacking ensemble model for food demand forecasting: A preventative approach to food waste reduction. *Cleaner Logistics and Supply Chain*, 100225.

Sharma, A., Singh, S. N., Serratos, M. M., Sahu, D., & Strezov, V. (2025). Urban energy transition in smart cities: A comprehensive review of sustainability and innovation. *Sustainable Futures : An Applied Journal of Technology, Environment and Society, 10*, 100940. DOI: 10.1016/j.sftr.2025.100940

Shehzad, K. (2025). Predictive AI Models for Food Spoilage and Shelf-Life Estimation. *Global Trends in Science and Technology, 1*(1), 75–94. DOI: 10.70445/gtst.1.1.2025.75-94

Sowan, B. I., Zighan, S., & Altarawneh, A. (2025, April). Supply Chain 4.0: Driving Operational Efficiency, Resilience, and Cybersecurity Using Advanced Technologies. In *2025 1st International Conference on Computational Intelligence Approaches and Applications (ICCIAA)* (pp. 1-8). IEEE.

Tabaku, E., Vyshka, E., Kapçiu, R., Shehi, A., & Smajli, E. (2025). Utilizing artificial intelligence in energy management systems to improve carbon emission reduction and sustainability. *Jurnal Ilmiah Ilmu Terapan Universitas Jambi, 9*(1), 393–405. DOI: 10.22437/jiituj.v9i1.38665

Tang, X., & Wang, J. (2025). Deep reinforcement learning-based multi-objective optimization for virtual power plants and smart grids: Maximizing renewable energy integration and grid efficiency. *Processes (Basel, Switzerland), 13*(6), 1809. DOI: 10.3390/pr13061809

Tetteh, F. K., Owusu Kwateng, K., & Mensah, J. (2025). Enhancing carbon neutral supply chain performance: Can green logistics and pressure from supply chain stakeholders make any differences? *Sustainability Accounting. Management and Policy Journal, 16*(2), 521–551. DOI: 10.1108/SAMPJ-08-2024-0884

Vahdanjoo, M., Sørensen, C. G., & Nørremark, M. (2025). Digital transformation of the agri-food system. *Current Opinion in Food Science*, *63*, 101287. DOI: 10.1016/j.cofs.2025.101287

Wang, K., & Du, N. (2025). Real-time monitoring and energy consumption management strategy of cold chain logistics based on the internet of things. *Energy Informatics*, *8*(1), 34. DOI: 10.1186/s42162-025-00493-w

Wang, S., & Mansoor, M. (2025). Optimization model for enterprise financial management utilizing genetic algorithms and fuzzy logic. *PeerJ. Computer Science*, *11*, e2812. DOI: 10.7717/peerj-cs.2812 PMID: 40567732

Wang, Z., Gao, Y., & Gao, Y. (2025). Optimization of Distributed Photovoltaic Energy Storage System Double-Layer Planning in Low-Carbon Parks Considering Variable Operating Conditions and Complementary Synergy of Energy Storage Devices. *Energies*, *18*(8), 1881. DOI: 10.3390/en18081881

Yan, F., Chen, L., & Jia, F. (2025). Environmental, social, and governance disclosure in supply chains: A systematic literature review. *Production Planning and Control*, *36*(14), 1951–1972. DOI: 10.1080/09537287.2024.2434147

Yıldırım, R., Akyüz, A., Kumaş, K., Tuncer, A. D., & Gungor, A. (2025). A comprehensive overview of refrigerants from the past to the modern day: Energy, exergy, and environmental perspectives. *Journal of Thermal Analysis and Calorimetry*, *150*(5), 3201–3223. DOI: 10.1007/s10973-025-14050-w

Yuan, K., Zhang, C., Hou, R., & Gao, X. (2025). Can cross-border e-commerce development improve supply chain efficiency? Empirical evidence from China. *Applied Economics*, *57*(56), 9606–9622. DOI: 10.1080/00036846.2024.2422112

Zhao, X., Castka, P., & Searcy, C. (2020). ISO standards: A platform for achieving sustainable development goal 2. *Sustainability (Basel)*, *12*(22), 9332. DOI: 10.3390/su12229332

Chapter 9

Greening the Gateways: Cross-Border Logistics as a Catalyst for Sustainable Trade and Tourism Development

Swati Sharma
http://orcid.org/0000-0003-2949-2363
Amity University, India

Mridula Mishra
http://orcid.org/0009-0007-2144-7556
Amity University, India

Akshita Tiwari
http://orcid.org/0000-0002-5167-6794
Amity University, India

Anshul Garg
http://orcid.org/0000-0001-8297-9256
Taylor's University, Malaysia

ABSTRACT

In an era where environmental sustainability increasingly influences global trade and tourism agendas, the effective orchestration of cross-border logistics has become a critical enabler of both green trade facilitation and sustainable cross-border tourism development. This analytical study investigates how international logistics systems—through digitalized documentation, energy-efficient transport networks, optimized supply chain design, and the integration of renewable energy—can significantly reduce the environmental footprint of cross-border trade and tourism mobility. The

DOI: 10.4018/979-8-3373-7847-3.ch009

adoption of digital and paperless facilitation mechanisms has led to measurable reductions in border delays and emissions, achieving a 3–7% decrease in trade and travel processing times and logistics-related carbon output across regions.

1. INTRODUCTION

In today's highly globalized economy, the seamless movement of goods, services, and people across borders forms the foundation of international trade and tourism. *Cross-border logistics*, which includes transportation networks, customs operations, and supply chain coordination, plays a decisive role in linking markets and fostering global connectivity. As global trade and travel intensify under the forces of *liberalization and technological innovation*, logistics systems have become essential to economic growth and competitiveness (Rodrigue & Notteboom, 2020). Yet, these systems also generate substantial environmental challenges, such as *carbon emissions, energy depletion, air pollution, and traffic congestion*. The *International Transport Forum* estimates that freight transport alone contributes roughly *8–10 percent of global CO_2 emissions*, indicating the urgent need to reduce the environmental impact of international logistics.

This growing environmental concern has given rise to the concept of *green logistics (Huang et al., 2024)*, which seeks to harmonize economic efficiency with ecological sustainability. Cross-border gateways—including *ports, airports, and land terminals*—are central to this transformation, as they serve as critical nodes where trade and mobility converge. Greening these gateways involves integrating practices like *energy-efficient transport systems, renewable energy adoption, digitalized border procedures, and waste reduction measures*. Such strategies not only enhance operational performance but also contribute to the realization of the *United Nations Sustainable Development Goals (SDGs)*, particularly *SDG 9 (Industry, Innovation, and Infrastructure), SDG 12 (Responsible Consumption and Production)*, and *SDG 13 (Climate Action)*.

Within the *tourism sector*, sustainable logistics has an equally significant role. Since tourism relies heavily on efficient mobility, the infrastructure that supports it—airports, seaports, roadways, and checkpoints—directly affects visitor experiences and environmental outcomes. The *World Tourism Organization* emphasizes that sustainable tourism cannot exist without sustainable transport systems. Thus, incorporating green logistics into tourism development can help reduce emissions, improve destination management, and enhance the appeal of destinations committed to environmental preservation. By promoting *green mobility and efficient resource use*, destinations can attract eco-conscious travelers while safeguarding their ecological and cultural assets.

The *digital transformation* of logistics has further strengthened the shift toward sustainability. Emerging technologies such as *blockchain-based documentation, artificial intelligence-driven routing, and automated customs systems* enable faster, paperless, and more energy-efficient operations. Likewise, the establishment of *green corridors* and *smart border initiatives* across regions such as the European Union and ASEAN illustrates how regional cooperation can help countries align economic and environmental goals. These advancements not only streamline trade and travel but also reinforce international collaboration in addressing global environmental challenges.

Nonetheless, many countries—especially developing ones—encounter significant obstacles in transitioning toward green logistics. Limited financial resources, a lack of advanced technology, weak regulatory frameworks, and inconsistent environmental standards hinder the adoption of sustainable practices. Coordinated international efforts, such as those supported by the *Paris Agreement* and the *WTO Trade Facilitation Agreement*, are therefore crucial for fostering policy harmonization and mobilizing green investment in logistics infrastructure.

The concept of *"greening the gateways"* highlights the strategic importance of rethinking how trade and tourism interfaces operate. These gateways are not merely physical entry points but also pivotal spaces for implementing sustainability measures. By embedding *renewable energy systems, eco-friendly transport modes, and environmental monitoring technologies* into cross-border logistics operations, nations can simultaneously reduce emissions, create green jobs, and strengthen their global competitiveness.

The *core objective* of this research is to examine how the transition toward sustainable cross-border logistics can act as a *catalyst for eco-friendly trade and tourism development*. It seeks to evaluate the links between *logistics performance*, *environmental responsibility*, and *economic cooperation*, illustrating how greener gateways can contribute to long-term development goals. By viewing logistics as a platform for innovation rather than just a means of transport, this study contributes to current discussions on *sustainable supply chain management and low-carbon tourism mobility.*

In essence, *"Greening the Gateways"* represents more than a technical adjustment—it symbolizes a transformative shift in how nations approach economic growth, environmental protection, and global interconnectivity. As countries worldwide navigate the dual pressures of globalization and climate change, reimagining cross-border logistics as a *driver of sustainability* offers a forward-looking pathway to a more balanced, inclusive, and environmentally secure future.

2. LITERATURE REVIEW

The connection between *cross-border logistics*, *sustainable trade*, and *tourism growth* has become a major focus in recent academic research. With globalization and trade liberalization expanding global supply chains, logistics systems now serve as key drivers of international economic integration. *Rodrigue and Notteboom (2020)* observe that modern logistics networks, powered by technology and innovation, link multiple markets, facilitating both trade and travel. Yet, this rapid expansion has resulted in serious environmental challenges, with freight transport responsible for nearly *10% of total global CO_2 emissions*.

The idea of *green logistics* has therefore emerged as a vital response to balancing efficiency with environmental protection. It focuses on sustainable practices such as cleaner transportation systems, renewable energy use, waste management, and digitalized documentation (Sarkis, 2012). According to *Bekteshi and Keco (2021)*, green logistics enhances performance and reduces emissions, offering both environmental and economic benefits. Empirical evidence from *Liu et al. (2018)* and *Perotti et al. (2015)* supports this, showing that firms applying sustainable logistics models improve efficiency, lower costs, and strengthen regulatory compliance.

Cross-border gateways—including ports, airports, and border terminals—are essential points of global trade and travel, and their transformation into *green gateways* has become crucial for sustainability. Studies by the *OECD and World Bank* show that renewable energy integration, digitalized customs, and smart transport corridors can significantly reduce emissions while improving trade efficiency. However, the *WTO* and *ESCAP* report that policy inconsistencies, lack of harmonized standards, and limited investment continue to hinder the large-scale adoption of green logistics, especially in developing nations.

In the tourism sector, logistics sustainability is a critical factor influencing both travel experiences and environmental performance. The *UNWTO* notes that sustainable tourism depends on green mobility, as transportation accounts for roughly *three-quarters of tourism's carbon footprint. Gössling and Hall (2019)* argue that eco-efficient transport systems enhance both destination image and traveler satisfaction. Similarly, *Neto (2021)* points out that integrating sustainable logistics into tourism operations promotes cost savings, supports local suppliers, and fosters community-oriented tourism initiatives.

Despite these advantages, several barriers persist. *Wang et al. (2018)* identify funding limitations, insufficient technology, and weak governance as key obstacles in developing regions. Likewise, *Zhu et al. (2008)* emphasize the need for coordinated policies and incentive frameworks to support the green transition.

Overall, existing scholarship indicates that *greening cross-border logistics*—through renewable energy, smart digital systems, and collaborative environmental governance—can advance *trade competitiveness*, *tourism sustainability*, and *climate resilience* simultaneously. Nonetheless, further empirical research is required to understand how green gateways specifically function as catalysts linking these interconnected sectors.

Table 1. Major studies & findings

Author(s) & Year	Main Area Focused	Major Findings
Bekteshi et al. (2024)	Green logistics and sustainable trade facilitation	Demonstrated that digitalized documentation, renewable energy integration, and energy-efficient transport systems significantly reduce emissions and improve environmental performance in cross-border logistics.
OECD	Sustainable trade and tourism policy frameworks	Identified gaps between sustainability commitments and actual implementation, particularly in multimodal transport systems and cross-border tourism logistics, emphasizing the need for regulatory harmonization.
OECD	Digital trade facilitation and border efficiency	Found that paperless trade systems and digital border management reduced processing times and logistics-related carbon emissions by approximately 3–7% across several regions.
Chen & Wang (2025)	Logistics connectivity, tourism flows, and environmental impact	Established a positive relationship between logistics connectivity, economic growth, and tourism efficiency, while highlighting increased environmental pressure in the absence of low-carbon transport strategies.
UNCTAD	Green corridors and sustainable supply chains	Reported that green corridor initiatives enhance trade efficiency and environmental outcomes when supported by clean energy infrastructure and cross-border cooperation.
World Bank	Cross-border transport infrastructure and sustainability	Emphasized that sustainable transport infrastructure investments improve regional competitiveness and tourism accessibility while mitigating climate impacts.
Gössling et al. (2021)	Transport emissions and sustainable tourism	Concluded that transport remains the largest contributor to tourism-related emissions, underscoring the importance of green mobility solutions in cross-border tourism corridors.
Rodrigue & Notteboom (2020)	Green supply chain and logistics systems	Highlighted that optimized logistics design and modal shifts toward rail and electric mobility substantially reduce carbon intensity in international trade routes.

The reviewed literature in Table 1 collectively underscores the pivotal role of green cross-border logistics in advancing sustainable trade and tourism development. Studies consistently highlight that digital trade facilitation measures—such as paperless documentation and smart border management—significantly reduce processing time, operational inefficiencies, and logistics-related carbon emissions. Empirical evidence from OECD and World Bank reports confirms that efficiency gains of 3–7% are achievable when digitalization is embedded within cross-border systems.

Another dominant theme is the strong linkage between logistics connectivity, economic growth, and tourism flow efficiency. While improved transport and logistics networks stimulate regional competitiveness and cross-border tourism mobility, multiple studies caution that these gains often intensify environmental pressures if low-carbon transport solutions and green mobility strategies are not simultaneously adopted. Research by Gössling et al. (2021) emphasizes that transport emissions remain a critical sustainability challenge, particularly in tourism-dominated corridors.

The literature also reveals persistent policy and implementation gaps. Despite the inclusion of sustainability clauses in international trade and tourism agreements, weak regulatory harmonization, limited multimodal integration, and insufficient cross-sector coordination constrain effective execution. Studies advocate for green corridor development, renewable energy adoption, eco-certification mechanisms, and public–private partnerships as viable pathways to bridge these gaps.

Overall, the literature converges on the conclusion that sustainable logistics systems serve as a strategic nexus between green trade facilitation and responsible cross-border tourism. When supported by coherent policy frameworks, technological innovation, and international cooperation, green logistics can deliver inclusive economic growth while advancing global sustainability objectives aligned with SDGs 8, 12, and 13.

3. CONCEPTUAL FRAMEWORK: GREEN GATEWAY–TRADE–TOURISM SUSTAINABILITY NEXUS

A Green Gateway–Trade–Tourism Sustainability Nexus Framework is developed to enhance the theoretical contribution of this study. This approach defines cross-border logistics gateways—such as ports, airports, and land border crossings—as integrative socio-technical systems that concurrently enable sustainable commercial flows and responsible tourism mobility (Twrdy et al., 2025). Instead of viewing logistical infrastructure and tourist systems as separate or parallel entities, the framework conceptualises gateways as converging platforms where trade efficiency, mobility experience, and environmental goals converge.

The proposed approach redefines cross-border gateways as dynamic systems integrated within wider economic, environmental, and social contexts, rather than as standalone infrastructural hubs. These gateways function through five interrelated pillars, each of which is essential in influencing sustainability outcomes:

Digital Empowerment -This pillar highlights the significance of digital technology, including electronic customs clearance, blockchain documentation, AI-driven logistics planning, and real-time tracking systems. Digital enablement improves transparency, decreases administrative delays, mitigates corruption risks, and facilitates data-driven decision-making in goods and tourist sectors.

Low-Carbon Mobility and Transportation Systems -This dimension emphasises the adoption of energy-efficient transport modes, transitions to rail and electric vehicles, sustainable aviation practices, and emissions-reducing last-mile connections. Low-carbon travel diminishes environmental impacts while enhancing reliability, comfort, and accessibility for tourists, so connecting environmental efficacy with experiential excellence.

Optimisation of Supply Chains and Circular Economy- Gateways serve as coordination hubs for enhancing supply chains by optimising scheduling, decreasing stay times, minimising waste, and implementing circular logistics methods, including resource reuse and reverse logistics. Circularity enhances supply chain resilience and aligns trade operations with sustainability standards.

Integration of Renewable Energy -The incorporation of renewable energy sources—such as solar-powered terminals, green hydrogen infrastructure, and energy-efficient buildings—bolsters gateway resilience and diminishes reliance on fossil fuels. This pillar enhances the symbolic and branding aspects of sustainability, underscoring the gateway's function as a tangible commitment to climate responsibility.

Collaborative Governance and Stakeholder Coordination -Successful sustainability outcomes rely on collaboration among customs authorities, transportation operators, tourism boards, logistics companies, local communities, and policymakers. Collaborative governance guarantees policy consistency, mutual accountability, and the alignment of trade facilitation objectives with tourism and environmental aims.

Figure 1. Conceptual framework - green gateway trade tourism sustainability nexus framework

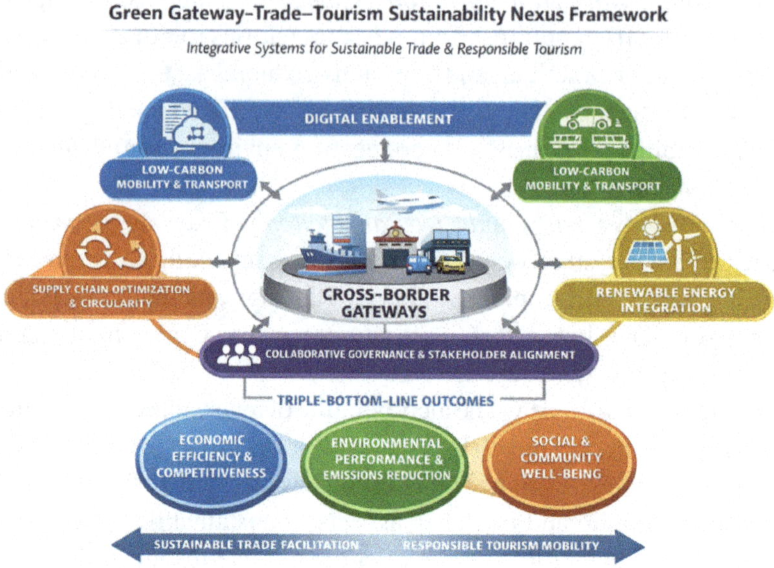

3.1 Theoretical Contribution

In contrast to conventional linear logistics models that emphasise cost reduction and throughput efficiency, the Green Gateway–Trade–Tourism Sustainability Nexus employs a circular sustainability framework. In accordance with this reasoning:

- Digital openness enhances environmental oversight and regulation adherence.
- Low-carbon mobility improves supply chain dependability and promotes tourist comfort.
- The implementation of renewable energy enhances infrastructure resilience and fosters destination branding and trust.

The proposed framework enhances the current logistics and tourism literature by integrating gateway theory, sustainable transition theory, and tourism mobility perspectives in multiple ways. Initially, it characterises gateways as proactive facilitators of sustainability transformation rather than as passive channels of flow. Secondly, it connects the analytical gap between trade facilitation and tourist studies by illustrating their interconnectedness within common infrastructure environments.

Ultimately, it provides a comprehensive framework for analysing cross-border systems in which economic success, environmental stewardship, and social value creation are collaboratively generated rather than mutually exclusive.

3.2 Comparative Analysis: Developed versus Developing Gateway Contexts

The study demonstrates substantial contextual disparities in the acceptance, implementation, and scalability of green logistics methods between developed and developing gateway contexts. These disparities are not solely technological but are ingrained in institutional capability, regulatory consistency, financial frameworks, and tourism dependence networks.

Advanced Economic Portals -Gateways in developed economies typically exhibit a greater degree of preparedness and systems integration in facilitating transitions to green logistics. These gateways are defined by:

Enhanced Digital Preparedness-Advanced gateways leverage established digital infrastructures, encompassing comprehensive customs digitisation, cohesive data platforms, and real-time surveillance technologies. This digital maturity facilitates smooth coordination between commerce facilitation and tourism mobility, minimising congestion, dwell times, and administrative ambiguity.

Robust Policy Enforcement and Regulatory Consistency- In industrialised countries, environmental and logistical policies are generally backed by strong enforcement mechanisms, explicit compliance schedules, and institutional responsibility. This regulatory clarity diminishes uncertainty for commercial operators, fostering long-term investments in low-carbon transport and sustainable infrastructure.

Progressive Renewable and Low-Carbon Infrastructure- Developed gateways typically feature established renewable energy ecosystems, encompassing electrified transport corridors, shore-to-ship power at ports, and terminals powered by renewable energy. These initiatives are underpinned by secure financing, extended planning horizons, and robust public–private partnerships. These characteristics collectively allow established countries to undertake systemic sustainability transformations, integrating environmental objectives into core operational strategies instead of treating them as supplementary activities.

Conversely, gateways in emerging economies encounter structural and institutional limitations that influence the speed and character of green logistics implementation. Essential attributes encompass:

Disjointed Regulatory and Governance Structures- Policy regimes frequently exhibit overlapping mandates, uneven enforcement, and recurrent alterations in regulatory objectives. This fragmentation hinders cross-border cooperation, especially in areas where tourism mobility and goods movement vie for constrained infrastructural capacity.

Restricted Access to Green Finance for Small and Medium Enterprises -Small and medium-sized firms, which are pivotal in logistics and tourist supply chains, often have challenges in obtaining inexpensive green financing, technological advancements, and risk-mitigation tools. Sustainability investments are thus concentrated among a limited number of large entities, constraining systemic transformation.

Reliance on Donor-Funded or Pilot Program Interventions -Sustainability activities in emerging nations are frequently project-based, outside financed, or pilot-oriented, rather than being institutionally integrated. Although these programs offer significant opportunities for experimentation, they often encounter scaling issues once donor funding ceases.

3.3 Significant Contribution

The comparative analysis highlights that sustainability paths in cross-border logistics and tourism gateways are fundamentally inconsistent. Attempting to emulate developed-economy patterns via prescriptive policy frameworks risks neglecting the contextual realities in emerging nations.

The findings indicate the necessity for flexible and diversified policy frameworks that:

- Synchronise sustainability objectives with regional institutional capabilities
- Emphasise gradual and modular enhancements to infrastructure
- Incorporate tourism-related mobility demands into logistical planning.
- Facilitate SME engagement via inclusive financial instruments.

This analysis underscores contextual asymmetries, advancing the literature beyond generalised sustainability narratives and stressing the necessity of context-sensitive transition strategies for green gateways, especially in tourism-heavy and infrastructure-limited areas

3.4 Sustainability Performance Metrics for Eco-Friendly Gateways

This study, informed by stakeholder interviews and comprehensive document analysis, presents a collection of gateway-level sustainability performance indicators aimed at operationalising the Green Gateway–Trade–Tourism Sustainability Nexus. These indicators transcend theoretical sustainability pledges by offering quantifiable, comparable, and implementable measurements that can be utilised by governments, regulatory bodies, and private entities. The proposed methodology improves the practical application of the study by converting conceptual sustainability principles into measurable performance outcomes.

Indicator Categories

The indicators are organised into four interconnected dimensions—environmental, operational, economic, and social—reflecting an extended triple-bottom-line framework that incorporates governance and community results as reflected in Table 2.

- Environmental: emissions per shipment, proportion of renewable energy, fuel intensity, waste recovery rate
- Functional: Border clearance duration, mode shift percentages, reduction in stay time, digital processing ratio
- Logistics: cost per unit, trade throughput reliability, stability of tourism influx, revenue resilience
- Social: Creation of green jobs, measurements for worker safety, levels of community approval, participation of stakeholders

Ecological Metrics

Environmental indicators measure the ecological impact of gateway activities, emphasising emissions intensity above total volumes. Metrics like emissions per shipment and renewable energy share provide equitable comparisons among gates of differing sizes and traffic levels. These metrics promote climate accountability while encouraging operational efficiency, energy transition, and pollution mitigation.

Significantly, interview findings indicate that stakeholders are increasingly perceiving environmental performance as not merely a compliance obligation but also as a factor influencing reputation and competitiveness, especially in tourism-centric gateways.

Performance Metrics

Operational indicators assess the efficiency and dependability of gateway processes, encompassing border clearance duration, transitions to low-carbon transportation, and the percentage of digitally completed transactions. These statistics demonstrate how sustainability initiatives can concurrently decrease emissions and improve logistical efficiency.

From a tourist standpoint, operational efficiency significantly influences visitor experience by minimising congestion, delays, and ambiguity at border entry points.

The congruence of operational efficiency with sustainability results strengthens the cohesive rationale of the proposed approach.

Economic Metrics

Economic indicators evaluate whether sustainability transitions enhance long-term financial viability instead of imposing excessive cost constraints. Metrics such as logistics cost per unit and tourism inflow stability reflect the resilience of trade and tourism under sustainability limitations.

The study's findings suggest that ports exhibiting consistent tourism inflows in conjunction with green investments are more likely to maintain political and stakeholder backing for ongoing sustainability activities.

Societal Metrics

Social indicators assess the distributional and community-level impacts of green gateway programs. Initiatives like green job creation, enhancements in worker safety, and metrics for community acceptability signify the social legitimacy of sustainability transitions.

Interview responses indicate that community acceptability is essential for the sustainability of green logistics reforms, particularly in tourism-dependent areas where gateway operations directly affect local livelihoods and quality of life.

Table 2. Dimensions and their indicators

Dimension	Illustrative Indicators
Environmental	Emissions per shipment, renewable energy share, fuel intensity, waste recovery rate
Operational	Border clearance time, modal shift rates, dwell time reduction, digital processing ratio
Economic	Logistics cost per unit, trade throughput reliability, tourism inflow stability, revenue resilience
Social	Green job creation, worker safety metrics, community acceptance levels, stakeholder participation

Research Methodology

This study adopts a qualitative multiple-case study design to explore how cross-border logistics systems can act as catalysts for sustainable trade and tourism through the integration of green and digital innovations (Qi et al., 2024). A qualitative approach is appropriate because it allows for the exploration of complex social, environmental, and institutional dynamics that cannot be easily quantified (Creswell & Poth, 2018). The focus is on understanding stakeholder experiences, practices, and perceptions regarding the greening of gateway logistics, rather than measuring causal relationships.

The multiple-case study design enables comparative insights across different gateway regions, capturing contextual variations in sustainability practices, governance structures, and technological adoption. This approach enhances analytic generalization—developing conceptual understandings rather than statistical generalizations—by examining several bounded cases in-depth (Stake, 2006). Each "case" represents a cross-border gateway characterized by unique logistical functions, tourism flows, and sustainability strategies.

Within each case, the study employs semi-structured interviews as the primary data collection method, complemented by document analysis (such as trade policies, sustainability reports, and infrastructure plans). This combination allows for data triangulation, increasing the credibility and depth of findings (Patton et al., 2015). Approximately 25 interviews will be conducted across three gateway cases, involving logistics managers, border officials, tourism operators, renewable energy providers, community representatives, and policymakers. This sample size is sufficient to achieve thematic saturation while ensuring diversity of perspectives (Guest et al., 2020).

Data will be analyzed through thematic analysis, following Braun and Clarke's (2006) six-step framework: (1) data familiarization, (2) generating initial codes, (3) searching for themes, (4) reviewing themes, (5) defining and naming themes, and (6) producing the report. Thematic analysis supports inductive reasoning, allowing themes to emerge organically from the data while being guided by the research objectives (Nowell et al., 2017). The study will pay special attention to cross-case comparisons to identify both shared patterns and contextual differences across gateway regions.

To ensure rigor and trustworthiness, the study incorporates strategies outlined by Lincoln and Guba (1985), including credibility (through member checking and triangulation), transferability (through thick description), dependability (through an audit trail), and confirmability (through reflexive journaling). Ethical considerations—such as informed consent, confidentiality, and voluntary participation—will be strictly observed throughout data collection and reporting.

Overall, this qualitative multiple-case study design is flexible, context-sensitive, and theory-building, making it well-suited to investigate how digitalized systems, energy-efficient transport, supply chain optimization, and renewable energy integration contribute to sustainable logistics and tourism development in cross-border contexts

4. RESEARCH DESIGN

A qualitative multiple-case study design is used to explore how digitalization, energy-efficient transport, supply-chain optimization, and renewable integration enable sustainable trade and tourism at cross-border gateways (Kong et al., 2024). The study adopts an inductive, flexible approach using in-depth semi-structured interviews and thematic analysis (Braun & Clarke 2022). Total sample size of 25 in- depth semi-structured interviews were conducted to capture the full ecosystem, interviewees included public-sector service providers, private operators, community/ tourism representatives, and technical suppliers. The distribution for the 25 interviews:

- Customs / border management officials — 4
- Logistics managers / freight forwarders — 4
- Transport operators / intermodal terminal managers — 4
- Tourism destination managers / tourism business owners — 3
- Renewable energy / infrastructure providers — 3
- Small and medium exporters / tourism SMEs — 3
- Regional policymakers / trade association reps — 2
- Local community leaders / civil society — 2

5. DATA ANALYSIS

Data collection primarily relied on semi-structured, in-depth interviews, allowing participants to share detailed perspectives while enabling the researcher to probe emerging issues (Patton et al., 2015). Each interview lasted approximately 45–60 minutes, conducted either face-to-face or via online platforms. Interviews are audio-recorded with consent and transcribed verbatim. The analysis was conducted *within each case* to identify case-specific themes, followed by *cross-case analysis* to compare the findings. Coding was both *inductive* (emerging from data) and *deductive* (guided by the conceptual framework). NVivo 12 software was used to manage data, organize codes, and ensure systematic analysis as *Table 3*.

5.1. Digitalization and Smart Logistics Transformation

-This theme explores how advanced technology platforms, blockchain, and IoT are revolutionizing logistics transparency, efficiency, and customs processes. Interviewees highlight the nuanced opportunities and barriers facing different stakeholders, especially SMEs

Digital Platforms and Data-Sharing Systems

"The move to real-time, cloud-based documentation has reduced errors and cut turnaround times at border checkpoints," noted a logistics manager.

Blockchain and IoT for Transparency

"With IoT tracking, we can assure clients of the security and sustainability of their shipments throughout the supply chain," explained a technology provider.

Smart Customs and Border Automation

"Automated customs checks have minimized manual paperwork, speeding up trade flows," reported a customs official.

SME Adoption Barriers

"Many smaller companies lack the IT infrastructure for blockchain systems, so adoption remains uneven," admitted a local chamber of commerce leader.

Perceived Sustainability Benefits

"Digital systems help us spot efficiency gaps, resulting in less energy waste and lower emissions," said a supply chain analyst.

5.2. Energy-Efficient Transport and Green Infrastructure

-This theme centres on the transition to low-emission vehicles, the development of green hubs, and the role of policies and collaborations in supporting these changes.

Low-Emission Vehicles and Alternative Fuels

"Switching our fleet to electric vehicles is challenging but absolutely key to our long-term sustainability," remarked a fleet manager.

Green Transport Hubs

"Our investment in eco-designed logistics hubs was possible thanks to incentive programs," explained a government agency official.

Policy and Infrastructure Support

"The lack of charging infrastructure along key routes remains the biggest obstacle," shared a regional transport planner.

Public–Private Collaboration

"Joint pilot projects between the city and logistics firms have made green last-mile delivery possible," noted a city mobility director.

Fleet Transition Challenges

"Upfront costs and uncertainty about technology make some companies hesitant to invest," stated a purchasing manager.

5.3. Supply Chain Optimization for Sustainable Trade

- This theme highlights efforts to create circular, resilient, and efficient supply chains through cooperation and innovation.

Emission and Waste Reduction Strategies

"We've restructured our supply network to trim unnecessary shipments, lowering our carbon footprint," said a supply chain director.

Circular Economy Practices

"Collaboration with recyclers allows us to turn waste from returns into usable resources," noted a sustainability officer.

Regional Cooperation and Harmonized Regulations

"Consistent rules across borders simplify logistics and encourage green investments," explained an international trade liaison.

Cross-Sector Partnerships

"Partnerships with research institutes help us design tailored green solutions," highlighted a public–private project coordinator.

Local Resilience and Competitiveness

"Localizing parts of the supply chain strengthened our resilience during global disruptions," shared a regional logistics operator.

Table 3. Themes and sub- themes generated through NVIVO 12

Theme	Sub-Themes
1. Digitalization and Smart Logistics Transformation	• Digital platforms and data-sharing systems • Blockchain and IoT for transparency • Smart customs and border automation • SME adoption barriers • Perceived sustainability benefits
2. Energy-Efficient Transport and Green Infrastructure	• Low-emission vehicles and alternative fuels • Green transport hubs • Policy and infrastructure support • Public–private collaboration • Fleet transition challenges
3. Supply Chain Optimization for Sustainable Trade	• Emission and waste reduction strategies • Circular economy practices • Regional cooperation and harmonized regulations • Cross-sector partnerships • Local resilience and competitiveness
4. Renewable Energy Integration in Logistics and Tourism Systems	• Solar, wind, and bioenergy in operations • Renewable-powered gateways and tourism zones • Incentives for renewable adoption • Perceived reliability and cost • Policy influence on adoption
5. Stakeholder Collaboration and Governance for Sustainable Gateways	• Multilevel governance structures • Regional and international cooperation • Participatory engagement • Power and trust dynamics • Institutional capacity building
6. Socio-Economic and Environmental Outcomes of Green Logistics	• Local employment and skills development • Community perceptions • Environmental impact assessments • Sustainability reporting and communication • Balancing economic and ecological goals
7. Barriers, Enablers, and Future Pathways	• Institutional and regulatory challenges • Technological and financial constraints • Success factors and best practices • Innovation and knowledge ecosystems • Future visions for green gateways

5.4. Renewable Energy Integration in Logistics and Tourism Systems

- This theme investigates how renewable energy—such as solar, wind, and bioenergy—is being incorporated into logistics and tourism infrastructure.

Solar, Wind, and Bioenergy in Operations

"We've installed solar panels at our distribution centre to offset grid usage," shared an operations manager.

Renewable-Powered Gateways and Tourism Zones

"Our new ferry terminal runs entirely on renewable energy, which is a major draw for eco-conscious tourists," noted a port authority representative.

Incentives for Renewable Adoption

"Government subsidies made installing wind turbines affordable for our facility," said a site manager.

Perceived Reliability and Cost

"Early outages raised concerns about solar reliability, but backup systems improved confidence," explained a facilities engineer.

Policy Influences on Adoption

"Regulatory encouragement has accelerated the transition to greener operations," observed a policy advocate.

5.5. Stakeholder Collaboration and Governance for Sustainable Gateways

- This theme reflects on multilevel governance, participatory engagement, and cooperative mechanisms supporting green logistics.

Multilevel Governance Structures

"Effective sustainability involves coordination among city, national, and regional authorities," explained a government official.

Regional and International Cooperation

"Joint task forces help harmonize standards across borders," shared a customs coordination leader.

Participatory Engagement

"Community forums ensure local voices are heard in logistics planning," said a community NGO leader.

Power and Trust Dynamics

"Trust issues sometimes slow collaboration, but transparent goal-setting remedies this," admitted an industry coalition head.

Institutional Capacity Building

"Training programs are critical for local officials to manage the technical aspects of green logistics," highlighted a sustainability trainer.

5.6. Socio-Economic and Environmental Outcomes of Green Logistics

- This theme assesses the broad social and environmental impacts, emphasizing job creation, community perceptions, and sustainable reporting.

Local Employment and Skills Development

"Green infrastructure has created new skilled jobs in renewable energy maintenance," reported a workforce development officer.

Community Perceptions

"Residents support green logistics when they see tangible benefits, like cleaner air," observed a city council member.

Environmental Impact Assessments

"Routine impact assessments keep us accountable for emissions reductions," stated a compliance manager.

Sustainability Reporting and Communication

"Publishing transparent emissions data builds public trust," expressed a corporate sustainability communicator.

Balancing Economic and Ecological Goals

"We constantly balance cost efficiency with environmental ambition," noted a CFO.

5.7. Barriers, Enablers, and Future Pathways

- This theme addresses both obstacles and opportunities encountered during green logistics transitions, as well as visioning for future gateways.

Institutional and Regulatory Challenges

"Complicated permit processes can delay green infrastructure projects," said a logistics developer.

Technological and Financial Constraints

"Small firms need financial and technical support to join green initiatives," explained an SME advisor.

Success Factors and Best Practices

"Peer learning from early adopters accelerates wider change," observed a consultant.

Innovation and Knowledge Ecosystems

"Knowledge-sharing platforms help us replicate successful models," highlighted a research center director.

Future Visions for Green Gateways

"Our goal is a seamless, cross-border green corridor powered by renewables," envisioned a regional policy strategist.

The results show that adopting digital technologies, energy-efficient transport, supply chain optimization, and renewable energy within cross-border logistics drives substantial reductions in emissions and operational waste while improving efficiency, reliability, and stakeholder cooperation. Stakeholders report faster customs processing, smoother documentation, and more transparent cargo tracking due to smart platforms and automation. Meanwhile, renewable energy adoption and greener fleets lower carbon footprints, and regional collaboration enhances local economic benefits and skills. Despite these advances, challenges remain, such as infrastructure gaps, regulatory complexity, and resource limitations for SMEs, highlighting the ongoing need for investment, policy alignment, and inclusive stakeholder engagement to fully realize sustainable trade and tourism mobility.

6. MAJOR FINDINGS OF THE STUDY

The qualitative multiple-case analysis reveals that greening cross-border logistics functions as a multidimensional catalyst for sustainable trade and tourism development. The findings are presented thematically, reflecting the core data analysis themes and sub-themes derived from stakeholder interviews and document analysis.

6.1. Digitalization and Smart Logistics Transformation

A key finding is that digitalization has emerged as the primary enabler of sustainability at cross-border gateways. Stakeholders consistently emphasized that the adoption of digital documentation systems, e-customs platforms, and real-time data-sharing technologies has significantly reduced administrative delays, paper usage, and energy-intensive redundancies. Smart border management systems enhanced transparency and traceability, improving regulatory compliance while reducing informal practices that often increase environmental and economic inefficiencies.

However, the study also found uneven digital readiness, particularly among small and medium enterprises (SMEs) engaged in trade and tourism supply chains. Limited technical capacity and high initial investment costs constrained full-scale digital adoption, leading to partial or fragmented implementation across gateways.

6.2. Energy-Efficient Transport and Green Infrastructure

The findings indicate that energy-efficient transport solutions are central to reducing the carbon footprint of cross-border logistics corridors. The introduction of low-emission vehicles, multimodal transport integration, and energy-efficient terminal infrastructure contributed to measurable reductions in fuel consumption and congestion. Green logistics hubs and intermodal terminals were found to support smoother tourist mobility while lowering emissions associated with freight and passenger movement.

Despite these advances, participants highlighted infrastructural lock-ins, such as aging fleets and limited charging or refuelling infrastructure, as major constraints. Policy incentives were often insufficient or inconsistently implemented, slowing the transition toward greener transport systems.

6.3. Supply Chain Optimization for Sustainable Trade

Supply chain optimization emerged as a critical mechanism linking logistics efficiency with sustainability outcomes. Stakeholders reported that route optimization, load consolidation, and coordinated scheduling significantly minimized waste, idle time, and emissions. The application of circular economy principles—such as reuse of packaging materials and reverse logistics—was increasingly visible in advanced gateway regions.

The study further found that regional cooperation and regulatory harmonization across borders played a decisive role in reducing duplication of processes and environmental externalities. Conversely, fragmented regulations and lack of inter-agency coordination increased transaction costs and weakened sustainability gains.

6.4. Renewable Energy Integration in Logistics and Tourism Systems

The integration of renewable energy sources—particularly solar and wind—within logistics hubs and tourism gateways was identified as a transformative but unevenly realized practice. Participants from renewable-equipped gateways reported enhanced energy security, reduced operational costs over time, and improved environmental branding that positively influenced destination image and tourism competitiveness.

Nevertheless, high capital investment requirements and regulatory complexities limited broader adoption. Stakeholders expressed concerns regarding grid reliability and policy continuity, indicating that renewable integration remains more aspirational than systemic in many cross-border contexts.

6.5. Stakeholder Collaboration and Governance for Sustainable Gateways

The findings underscore that effective governance and stakeholder collaboration are indispensable for sustainable gateway development. Multilevel coordination among customs authorities, transport agencies, logistics firms, tourism bodies, and local communities facilitated the alignment of sustainability goals with operational realities. Participatory governance mechanisms increased trust and compliance, particularly in environmentally sensitive gateway regions.

However, power asymmetries and institutional silos were found to hinder inclusive decision-making. Smaller actors, including community groups and SMEs, often had limited influence in shaping sustainability agendas, leading to uneven benefit distribution.

6.6. Socio-Economic and Environmental Outcomes of Green Logistics

Greening logistics systems generated positive socio-economic and environmental outcomes at gateway regions. The study found evidence of job creation in green transport, renewable energy maintenance, and digital logistics services. Local communities reported improved air quality, reduced noise pollution, and enhanced destination appeal.

At the same time, stakeholders emphasized the need to balance competitiveness with environmental stewardship. Sustainability benefits were maximized when environmental performance metrics were integrated into trade and tourism planning frameworks rather than treated as standalone initiatives.

6.7. Barriers, Enablers, and Future Pathways

The study identified institutional, financial, and technological barriers as persistent challenges to scaling green logistics. Key barriers included regulatory fragmentation, limited access to green financing, and resistance to organizational change. Conversely, enabling factors included strong political will, public–private partnerships, international cooperation, and knowledge-sharing platforms.

Looking forward, stakeholders envisioned smart, low-carbon cross-border gateways driven by digital intelligence, renewable energy, and integrated tourism-logistics planning. The findings suggest that long-term sustainability will depend on embedding green logistics within broader trade, tourism, and regional development strategies.

Overall, the study demonstrates that cross-border logistics is not merely a support function but a strategic sustainability lever. When digitalization, energy efficiency, supply chain optimization, and renewable energy integration are coherently governed, they generate synergistic benefits for sustainable trade and tourism development. The findings contribute theoretically by advancing a gateway-centric sustainability framework and practically by offering evidence-based pathways for policymakers and industry stakeholders.

7. IMPLICATIONS OF THE STUDY

The findings and the circular sustainability framework presented in this chapter generate important theoretical, policy, managerial, and societal implications for advancing sustainable trade and tourism through green cross-border logistics gateways. By conceptualizing logistics gateways as dynamic sustainability systems, the study extends existing debates beyond efficiency-driven logistics toward integrated environmental and tourism development outcomes.

7.1. Theoretical Implications

This chapter contributes to sustainability and tourism scholarship by reframing cross-border logistics as a central sustainability actor, rather than a peripheral support function. The circular framework advances theory by demonstrating how digitalization, energy efficiency, renewable energy integration, and governance interact in continuous feedback loops to produce socio-economic and environmental outcomes.

The study enriches sustainable tourism and transport theory by linking gateway logistics to destination competitiveness, community well-being, and environmental quality. It also contributes to systems and transition theories by illustrating how incremental technological and governance interventions can collectively drive structural sustainability transitions at border regions.

7.2. Policy Implications

For policymakers, the findings underscore the need for integrated policy frameworks that align trade facilitation, transport planning, energy policy, and tourism development. Policies that treat these domains in isolation risk undermining sustainability outcomes. Harmonized cross-border regulations, shared digital platforms, and coordinated infrastructure investments are essential to reduce inefficiencies and environmental externalities.

The study further highlights the importance of incentive-based policy instruments, such as green financing, tax benefits for low-emission transport, and subsidies for renewable energy adoption at logistics hubs. Embedding sustainability performance indicators into border management and tourism strategies can institutionalize accountability and long-term commitment.

7.3. Managerial and Industry Implications

For logistics operators, transport providers, and tourism businesses, the findings emphasize that sustainability is increasingly a strategic advantage rather than a compliance burden. Investments in digital systems, energy-efficient fleets, and renewable energy not only reduce costs over time but also enhance transparency, reliability, and destination image.

The framework also signals the importance of cross-sector collaboration. Logistics firms, tourism operators, and technology providers must move beyond siloed operations to co-create sustainable value chains. Managers are encouraged to adopt data-driven decision-making and sustainability reporting practices that demonstrate environmental and social performance to regulators and consumers alike.

7.4. Implications for Sustainable Tourism Development

The study demonstrates that green logistics gateways directly influence tourism sustainability and visitor experience. Reduced congestion, cleaner transport systems, and energy-efficient infrastructure improve accessibility and environmental quality at destinations. As tourists increasingly prioritize sustainability, gateways that visibly embody green practices can strengthen destination branding and competitiveness.

Moreover, integrating logistics planning with tourism development can help mitigate overtourism and ecological stress by optimizing flows and dispersing visitor movement more effectively across regions.

7.5. Societal and Community Implications

From a societal perspective, the chapter highlights the potential of green logistics to generate inclusive and localized benefits, including green jobs, improved air quality, and enhanced community well-being in gateway regions. However, it also cautions against unequal benefit distribution. Inclusive governance mechanisms are necessary to ensure that SMEs and local communities participate meaningfully in sustainability initiatives. Community engagement and transparency are essential to build trust and legitimacy, particularly in cross-border contexts where socio-political sensitivities are pronounced.

8. CONCLUSION

Finally, the chapter suggests that embedding green cross-border logistics within broader sustainability and development agendas—such as the Sustainable Development Goals (SDGs)—can significantly amplify long-term impact and ensure that environmental considerations become central to economic planning and trade facilitation. When green logistics strategies are aligned with global sustainability frameworks, they not only contribute to environmental protection but also strengthen social equity, economic resilience, and responsible governance. This alignment enables governments, industries, and international organizations to coordinate their efforts and mobilize resources more effectively toward the development of sustainable transport and logistics systems.

Green cross-border logistics gateways, such as ports, airports, dry ports, and integrated border check posts, play a crucial role in facilitating the movement of goods and people between countries. Traditionally, these gateways have been designed primarily to maximize trade efficiency and minimize transport costs. However, the increasing urgency of climate change, environmental degradation, and resource scarcity has highlighted the need to redesign these gateways through a sustainability lens. By integrating energy-efficient infrastructure, renewable energy systems, green warehousing, and low-emission transportation networks, cross-border gateways can significantly reduce their environmental footprint while maintaining high levels of operational efficiency.

Public–private partnerships are particularly important in this transition. Governments alone often lack the financial resources, technological expertise, and operational flexibility required to implement large-scale green logistics initiatives. By collaborating with private-sector stakeholders—including logistics companies, technology providers, infrastructure developers, and tourism operators—governments can accelerate the deployment of innovative solutions such as electric freight vehicles, smart logistics management systems, carbon monitoring technologies, and green infrastructure design. These partnerships also allow for risk-sharing, investment mobilization, and knowledge exchange, making sustainable logistics projects more feasible and scalable.

In addition, knowledge-sharing platforms and international collaboration networks play a vital role in promoting best practices and capacity-building across regions. Countries at different stages of economic development can benefit from exchanging experiences related to green logistics planning, regulatory frameworks, technological innovations, and operational strategies. International organizations, academic institutions, and research networks can facilitate this exchange by producing policy guidelines, conducting training programs, and supporting pilot projects that demonstrate the benefits of sustainable logistics systems.

Capacity-building initiatives are equally essential, particularly for developing countries that may face institutional, financial, and technical challenges in adopting green logistics solutions. Training programs for customs officials, logistics managers, infrastructure planners, and tourism stakeholders can help build the skills and expertise required to implement environmentally responsible logistics operations. Furthermore, integrating sustainability education into transport and tourism management curricula can prepare future professionals to design and manage logistics systems that prioritize environmental stewardship and social responsibility.

The adoption of digital technologies also plays a transformative role in advancing green cross-border logistics. Smart logistics platforms, blockchain-based tracking systems, artificial intelligence for route optimization, and real-time cargo monitoring can enhance transparency, efficiency, and sustainability across supply chains. By minimizing delays, reducing fuel consumption, and improving coordination among stakeholders, these technologies contribute to lower emissions and more efficient cross-border trade processes.

From a tourism perspective, sustainable logistics gateways are increasingly important because they serve as the first point of contact for international travelers. Environmentally responsible infrastructure, clean transportation options, and efficient border management systems can significantly enhance visitor experiences while reinforcing a destination's reputation as a sustainable tourism hub. As travelers become more environmentally conscious, destinations that demonstrate commitment to green infrastructure and low-carbon mobility are likely to gain a competitive advantage in the global tourism market.

In sum, this chapter positions green cross-border logistics gateways as transformative nodes within sustainable trade and tourism systems. Their influence extends beyond the efficient movement of goods and people; they also shape regional development, environmental performance, and international cooperation. By integrating sustainability principles into gateway planning, infrastructure development, and operational management, policymakers and industry leaders can create logistics systems that support both economic growth and environmental protection.

The implications extend across theory, policy, industry, and society. For researchers, green logistics gateways provide a valuable framework for studying the intersection of sustainability, trade, and tourism development. For policymakers, they highlight the importance of integrated planning, regulatory innovation, and cross-sector collaboration. For industry stakeholders, they demonstrate the economic and reputational benefits of adopting environmentally responsible practices. For society at large, they represent a pathway toward cleaner transport systems, reduced emissions, and more resilient economic networks.

Ultimately, the chapter reinforces the argument that sustainability at logistics gateways is not optional but foundational to future-ready, resilient, and ethically grounded tourism and trade development. As global trade and tourism continue to expand, the transformation of cross-border logistics infrastructure into green, efficient, and socially responsible systems will play a defining role in shaping a more sustainable and interconnected world.

REFERENCES

Bekteshi, X., Alshiqi, S., Jóźwik, B., Altin, F. G., Dogan, M., & Petrossyants, T. (2024). The impact of shipping connectivity on environmental quality, financial development, and economic growth in regional comprehensive economic partnership countries. *Journal of Risk and Financial Management*, *17*(12), 559. DOI: 10.3390/jrfm17120559

Braun, V., & Clarke, V. (2022). Conceptual and design thinking for thematic analysis. *Qualitative Psychology*, *9*(1), 3–26. DOI: 10.1037/qup0000196

Chen, H., Zhao, X., & Liu, M. (2019). The impact of green logistics on international trade: Evidence from the European Union. *The Journal of International Trade & Economic Development*, *28*(3), 305–324.

Creswell, J. W., & Poth, C. N. (2018). *Qualitative Inquiry and Research Design Choosing among Five Approaches* (4th ed.). SAGE Publications, Inc.

European Commission. (2021). *The European Green Deal: Making logistics sustainable*. European Commission.

Gössling, S., & Hall, M. C. (2019). Sharing versus collaborative economy: How to align ICT developments and the SDGs in tourism? *Journal of Sustainable Tourism*, *27*(1), 74–96. DOI: 10.1080/09669582.2018.1560455

Gössling, S., Humpe, A., Fichert, F., & Creutzig, F. (2021). COVID-19 and pathways to low-carbon air transport until 2050. *Environmental Research Letters*, *16*(3), 034063. DOI: 10.1088/1748-9326/abe90b

Guest, G., Namey, E., & Chen, M. (2020). A simple method to assess and report thematic saturation in qualitative research. *PLoS One*, *15*(5), e0232076. DOI: 10.1371/journal.pone.0232076

Huang, M., Zhao, Y., Wang, Y., & Guo, Q. (2024). Application of a green logistics strategy to fulfil online retailing: Split-order consolidated delivery in large-scale online supermarkets. *International Journal of Logistics*, *27*(5), 746–759. DOI: 10.1080/13675567.2022.2026902

Kong, Y., Tian, X., Sun, J., & Zhou, H. (2024). Charting sustainable vistas: Analysis of internal and external sustainability performance of Chinese ports. *Transport Policy*, *161*, 31–43. DOI: 10.1016/j.tranpol.2024.11.016

Liao, Y., Zhao, L., & Zhang, J. (2020). Carbon footprint reduction in green logistics: A systematic review. *Environmental Science & Technology*, *54*(11), 6604–6617.

Lincoln, Y. S., & Guba, E. G. (1985). *Naturalistic Inquiry*. SAGE. DOI: 10.1016/0147-1767(85)90062-8

Liu, S., Zhang, G., & Wang, L. (2018). IoT-enabled dynamic optimisation for sustainable reverse logistics. *Procedia CIRP*, *69*, 662–667. DOI: 10.1016/j.procir.2017.11.088

McKinnon, A. C. (2018). Green logistics: The challenge of reducing the carbon footprint of global supply chains. *International Journal of Physical Distribution & Logistics Management*, *48*(5), 450–467.

Miao, X., & Ni, C. (2023). Exploring the cross-border e-commerce of agricultural exports and its logistics supply chain innovation and development strategy under digital technology. *Applied Mathematics and Nonlinear Sciences.*, *9*(1), 20231487. Advance online publication. DOI: 10.2478/amns.2023.2.01487

Nowell, L. S., Norris, J. M., White, D. E., & Moules, N. J. (2017). Thematic Analysis: Striving to Meet the Trustworthiness Criteria. *International Journal of Qualitative Methods*, *16*(1), 1–13. DOI: 10.1177/1609406917733847

Patton, C., Sawicki, D., & Clark, J. (2015). *Basic methods of policy analysis and planning*. Routledge.

Perotti, S., Micheli, G. J., & Cagno, E. (2015). Motivations and barriers to the adoption of green supply chain practices among 3PLs. *International Journal of Logistics Systems and Management*, *20*(2), 179–198. DOI: 10.1504/IJLSM.2015.067255

Qi, X., Qin, W., & Lin, B. (2024). Case study on synergistic development strategy of cross-border e-commerce and logistics: An empirically model estimation. *PLoS One*, *19*(6), e0304393. DOI: 10.1371/journal.pone.0304393

Rao, S., & Holt, G. (2020). Green logistics: Challenges and opportunities in developing economies. *International Journal of Logistics Research and Applications*, *23*(4), 360–380.

Ren, S., Choi, T.-M., Lee, K.-M., & Lin, L. (2020). Intelligent service capacity allocation for cross-border-E-commerce related third-party-forwarding logistics operations: A deep learning approach. *Transport Reviews*, *134*, 101834.

Rodrigue, J. P., & Notteboom, T. (2020). Ports and economic development. *Port economics, management and policy*.

Sarkis, J. (2012). A boundaries and flows perspective of green supply chain management. *Supply Chain Management*, *17*(2), 202–216. DOI: 10.1108/13598541211212924

Stake, J. E. (2006). The interplay between law school rankings, reputations, and resource allocation: Ways rankings mislead. *Ind. LJ, 81*, 229. DOI: 10.1016/j.jik.2024.100612

Twrdy, E., Zanne, M., Stojaković, M., Cocuzza, E., Ignaccolo, M., & Ricci, S. (2025). Greening the gateways: Sustainable development of Adriatic and Ionian ports. *Transportation Research Procedia, 91*, 505–512. DOI: 10.1016/j.trpro.2025.10.065

Wang, J., Yang, F., Zhang, X., & Zhou, Q. (2018). Barriers and drivers for enterprise energy efficiency: An exploratory study for industrial transfer in the Beijing-Tianjin-Hebei region. *Journal of Cleaner Production, 200*, 866–879. DOI: 10.1016/j.jclepro.2018.07.327

Wong, C. W., Lai, K. H., & Cheng, T. C. (2020). Green logistics and sustainable supply chain management in the context of international trade. *International Journal of Production Economics, 227*, 107638.

Wu, Q., Zhang, M., & Sun, J. (2019). Green logistics development in China: Current status and future trends. *Transportation Research Part D, Transport and Environment, 69*, 268–284.

Xu, W., Yan, W., & Pang, W. (2025). Navigating Green Trade Barriers: Strategic Decisions in Cross-Border E-Commerce Green Packaging and Self-Logistics. *Sustainability (Basel), 17*(8), 3310. DOI: 10.3390/su17083310

Yamamoto, T., Abe, M., & Nishida, K. (2018). The evolution of green logistics in Japan: Policy and practice. *Asia Pacific Journal of Logistics, 33*(4), 401–419.

Zhang, H., Yang, Y., & Li, D. (2021). Green logistics in developing countries: The case of India. *Environmental Impact Assessment Review, 84*, 106456.

Zhu, Q., Sarkis, J., Lai, K. H., & Geng, Y. (2008). The role of organizational size in the adoption of green supply chain management practices in China. *Corporate Social Responsibility and Environmental Management, 15*(6), 322–337. DOI: 10.1002/csr.173

Chapter 10

Neuro-Environmental AI Orchestration for Climate-Adaptive Cross-Border Logistics Systems

Aarthi Selvakumar
http://orcid.org/0009-0006-9064-2091
Marwadi University, Rajkot, India

Ravikumar Natarajan
http://orcid.org/0009-0009-3705-1681
Marwadi University, Rajkot, India

ABSTRACT

The changing climate, heightened pressures in trade, and advanced cross-border procedures render the logistics systems appropriate to be flexible, smart, and green. This is known as Neuro-Environmental AI, which is a unified set of neural learning, symbolic reasoning, and real-time environmental intelligence, thus allowing them to implement global logistics in response to climatic conditions. The approach supports the foresight paths, emission-sensitive mode decision, disruption-constraining energy-saving border functions, and the expected disruption management. The framework enhances transparency, resilience, and compliance on the international corridors based on the use of digital twins, federated learning, and blockchain-enabled data exchange. It has been demonstrated through case studies that the emission has been reduced, reliability has increased, and the compatibility with the global sustainability goals has been more favorable, which makes Neuro-Environmental AI a new paradigm of the low-carbon and climate-resistant logistics.

DOI: 10.4018/979-8-3373-7847-3.ch010

1. INTRODUCTION

The increasing density of the climate variability, uncertainty in geopolitics, and the increase in international trade flows have unveiled some very vital vulnerabilities in the conventional cross-border logistic systems. The traditional logistics designs based on linear planning, rigid rules, and disaggregated streams of data, can no longer be able to react to the dynamism and interdependency of the threats of extreme weather, carbon-regulatory pressure, and multi-jurisdictional compliance needs. In this regard, the new Neuro-Environmental AI Orchestration paradigm provides a future-level intelligence layer that will convert the world logistics into flexible, sustainable, and resilient ecosystems (Olowonigba, 2025). This paradigm unites neural learning-based pattern recognition model, symbolical reasoning-based policy and regulatory compliance model, and environmental intelligence of IoT sensing, remote monitoring, and digital twin. The combination of all these capabilities forms a cognitive decision environment, which is capable of constantly stabilizing the logistics operations in accordance with the real-time climatic, operational and geopolitical indications. With the rise in the global supply network relying on the multimodal and cross-border collaboration, Neuro-Environmental AI facilitates predictive routing, energy-efficiency of the operation, preventive risk reduction, and emission-conscious decisions (Pasupuleti et al., 2024). Table 1 Summarizes the transformation of the conventional logistics to Neuro-Environmental AI.

Table 1. Evolution of climate-responsive logistics intelligence

Logistics Stage	Key Characteristics	Limitations	Advancements Enabled by Neuro-Environmental AI
Traditional Logistics	Static routing, manual planning	No climate awareness	Dynamic routing, predictive climate intelligence
Digital Logistics	Sensor data, basic automation	Limited reasoning	Multi-modal adaptive orchestration
AI-Enabled Logistics	Predictive analytics, monitoring	Lacks regulatory reasoning	Integrated climate + governance decision-making
Neuro-Environmental Logistics	Neural + symbolic + environmental data	-	Climate-adaptive, resilient, ESG-aligned logistics

1.1 Fusion of Neural, Symbolic, and Environmental Intelligence

The concept of Neuro-Environmental AI is a converged type of decision intelligence platform that will combine the power of neural networks, symbolic reasoning systems, and environmental analytics to assist climate-adaptive cross-border logistics. Neural models bring with them high-dimensional learning functionality by operating on multimodal freight operations, weather history data, geospatial streams, and sensor networks (Islam, 2025). Symbolic logic codes enforcement of explicit regulatory frameworks, carbon-compliance regulations, customs regulations, multimodal transport policies, and environmental governance regulations in machine-interpretable form. The system is further enhanced by environmental intelligence based on the IoT sensing, satellite monitoring, emission monitoring, digital twins and weather simulation environments. A combination of these three layers forms an array of harmonized orchestration engine that has the potential of producing contextual, transparent, and regulation-aligned decisions (Wijaya et al., 2025). This enables the logistics systems to forecast the disruption, plan routing opportunities based on environmental constraints, assess carbon intensity across transport modes, and respond to risks caused by climate in the real time. Neuro-Environmental AI will help ensure operational efficiency and global sustainability and compliance requirements through direct integration of the environmental and governance logic into the AI workflow.

1.2 Need for Climate-Adaptive Logistics Systems Across Borders

Networks of cross-border logistics occur at the border of various climates, regulatory frameworks, infrastructures, and geopolitical tensions, and thus they are extremely sensitive to disruptions caused by climates. The increasing rates of severe weather, changes in weather patterns at sea, heatwaves, floods, varying ecological patterns have great effects on the timetable of transports, warehousing stability, and network reliability in a multimodal manner. Conventional logistics management does not have predictive and adaptive processes needed to evaluate climatic variability, combine environmental constraints, or ensure service continuity in the dynamic environment (Niu et al., 2021). Besides, carbon-neutrality requirements, ESG promises, and global environmental accords expect transparency in operations and low-carbon decision-making, which increased the necessity of superior adaptive systems further. With Neuro-Environmental AI, climate-adaptive logistics allows the proactive evaluation of risks, climate-informed compression, emission-conscious transport choice, adaptable warehousing approach, and preparedness to customs in unstable environmental conditions. Such systems improve resilience and minimize carbon effects, cross-border coordination, and trade flows without disruption due to the uncertainty posed by the environmental conditions; hence, leveraging predictive analytics and regulatory-aware intelligence.

1.3 Overview of AI Orchestration in Global Trade

AI orchestration in the global trade applies to the synchronized use of several AI elements, such as predictive models, optimization engines, knowledge graphs, decision rules, and autonomous agents, to control complex logistics operations across the borders. Meanwhile, to the degree that supply chains are becoming more and more interconnected, orchestration makes sure that decisions are aligned between the customs authorities, carriers, ports, warehouses and multimodal transport nodes. It combines the information of environmental sensing systems, trade documentation, fleet telemetry, weather models and digital twin platforms to create unitary situational awareness (Guo & Zhao, 2025). Contemporary orchestration systems take advantage of federated learning in order to provide secure collaboration, blockchain in data integrity and multi-agent systems in automating distributed decisions. AI orchestration in the framework of sustainability allows estimating the carbon properly, monitoring the emission on the spot, and adhering to the international standards of green logistics (Ravikumar & Aarthi, 2025b). With Neuro-Environmental intelligence added to it, orchestration is removed in favor of anticipatory management as stakeholders are able to coordinate low-carbon routes, optimise cross-border schedules, and respond to climate shocks (Ma, 2022). This makes AI orchestration a source of resilient and sustainable and future-ready trade ecosystems. Figure 1 that depicts the integration of AI orchestration between multi-agent systems, neuro-environmental intelligence, federated learning, and data integration to turn disjointed logistics into a resilient sustainable global trade ecosystem.

Figure 1. AI orchestration framework for sustainable global trade

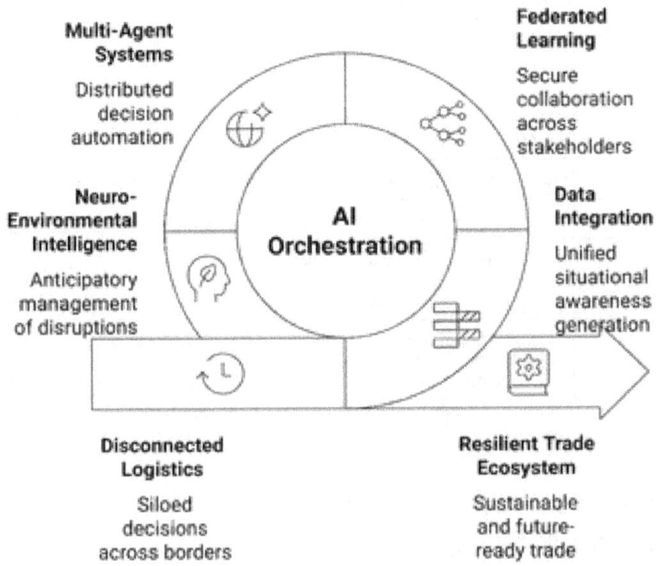

2. THEORETICAL FOUNDATIONS

The conceptual bases of Neuro-Environmental AI Orchestration are located on the border of the neuro-symbolic intelligence and environmental sensing ecosystems and transnational regulatory governance. All of these pillars permit a cognitive decision structure capable of making sense of complex logistics situations, make decisions under explicit constraints, and respond to changing climatic and geopolitical conditions. The neuro-symbolic architectures combine data-driven and environmental and trade policy-conformable to make sure that the logistics decisions are data-driven and interpretable at the same time (Dahlgren & Ammenberg, 2022). Infrastructure systems of environmental sensing, consisting of IoT sensors, satellite networks, digital twins, and remote monitor emissions, provide real-time ecological context to use in climate-adaptive operations. In the meantime, cross-border government systems impose the logic of regulation by which sustainable logistics is determined, such as the policies of climate, customs policy, emissions policy, and multimodal coordination policies (Y. Zhang & Qin, 2022). The combination of these backbone building blocks will offer a consistent foundation on which an engine of orchestration can be created capable of supporting resilient, transparent, and sustainable cross-border logistics systems that support global carbon-reduction and climate-adaptation objectives. Table 2 Elaborates the key components of the framework and their purpose.

Table 2. Core components of neuro-environmental AI orchestration

Component	Function	Output in Logistics
Neural Networks	Pattern detection & prediction	Weather forecasts, delay prediction
Symbolic Reasoning	Regulatory & policy logic	Compliance-aware decisions
Environmental Sensing	Real-time climate data	Accurate risk maps
Multi-Agent Coordination	Distributed decision-making	Synchronized cross-border actions
Carbon Analytics	Emission estimation	Low-carbon routing decisions

2.1 Neuro-Symbolic Architectures for Logistics Decision-Making

The neuro-symbolic architectures entail the connection of neural learning models with symbolic reasoning systems to assist transparent, compliant and adaptive decision-making in the context of cross-border logistics. Neural networks are successful in identifying trends in the huge data set like the freight movements history, weather changes, geospatial images, and operational telemetry. These however, are not inherently interpretable and cannot directly impose regulatory or environmental restrictions (K. Zhao et al., 2023). Knowledge graphs, rule bases and logical inference engines form the basis of symbolic reasoning systems which encode customs regulations, emissions regulations, multimodal transport specifications, and international trade agreements. Data-informed and governance-aligned decisions are generated through the procedures of neuro-symbolic architectures when these paradigms are merged. This allows the orchestration engine to analyze alternative paths, maximize methods of transport, predict bottlenecks, and make carbon-conforming operations (Cheng & Zhang, 2017). Finally, neuro-symbolic AI will increase confidence, transparency in operations, and regulatory confidence through multinational logistic networks.

2.2 Environmental Sensing Systems: IoT, Satellite Data, and Emission Monitors

The environmental sensing systems establish a significant base upon which climate-adaptive logistics processes can be conducted through the provision of continuous, multi-scale data on weather, environmental hazards, infrastructure, and emission patterns. Granular information of temperature, humidity, fuel use, assets health, and real-time cargo environments involving IoT devices installed in vehicles, warehouses, ports, and boundary structures are collected. These datasets are supplemented with macro-level data about the formation of a storm, changes in sea-state, wildfire risk, and cross-border environmental change provided by satellite technologies. Emission surveillance measures the levels of CO_2 emission, the amount of particulate matter, and the energy consumption among the multimodal transport options, thus making them fit sustainability requirements (Ren et al., 2019). These sensing layers are linked together to serve digital twins and predictive analytics models to help logistics operators predict climate disruption as well as to optimise energy consumption and change routing decisions. As part of Neuro-Environmental AI, environmental sensing enhances decision-making beyond the reactive adjustments made to the environment and into climate-advocating orchestration that minimizes risk, increases dependability, and environmental adherence to the logistics patterns within global logistics.

2.3 Cross-Border Governance, Climate Policies, and Trade Constraints

The logistics activities that operate across borders are influenced by a multiplex of governing systems, environmental policies and trade restrictions that are different by region and jurisdiction. The routing decisions, mode selection, and operational planning are affected directly by the climate policies implemented directly like carbon taxation, emission caps, fuel-efficiency, and green-corridor rules (Ravikumar & Aarthi, 2025d). The trade barriers such as customs, import-export policies and security checks, digital records, and geopolitical restrictions are added layers of complexity to the operations. To achieve a sustainable and reliable operation of logistics systems, AI-driven decision engines need to rationalize such regulatory requirements (Muñoz et al., 2020). Neuro-Environmental AI does this by placing these policy rules, compliance conditions and environmental governance logic within symbolic knowledge framework which is in such a way that all decisions made are in line with what is expected by law and sustainability. It allows continuous coordination of customs officials, freight service providers, and border control mechanisms and ensures the carbon responsibility and the transparency of control.

3. LITERATURE REVIEW

The development of sustainable and climate-adaptive logistics has triggered the growing scholarly interest in the integration of artificial intelligence, environmental intelligence, and cross-border governance into single operation principles. The current literature is adamant in pointing out the shortcomings of the traditional logistics systems that are overly dependent on the fixity of planning, past events and to compartmentalized decision-making processes that are not sufficient to maintain dynamic climatic realities and multi-jurisdictional complexities (Antonowicz & Majewski, 2025). Studies in intelligent transportation systems have determined that AI-assisted frameworks, especially deep-learning frameworks, can substantially produce the ability to handle large amounts of sensor data, predict disruptions, and route optimization through multimodal networks. Nevertheless, the challenges of explainability, regulatory compliance and incorporation of domain knowledge have remained and research has introduced neuro-symbolic approaches that combine both data-driven learning and transparent, rule-based reasoning (Chowdhury, 2025). These advances indicate the move to hybrid intelligence models that have the capacity to reconcile predictive functions with governance conformity. Researchers have shown that through incorporation of real-time climatic forecasts, emission measures and infrastructure states it is possible to come up with dynamic logistics plans that can react to changes in weather conditions, environmental hazards, and operation constraints (Wen Yu & Xiao, 2025). Although the technology is evolving, literature highlights issues associated with interoperability, data quality and fragmentation of sensing systems across boundaries, which supports the necessity of single platforms that will allow environmental intelligence to be harmonized to harmonize the logistics applications of sensing systems.

Studies regarding cross-border governance also put emphasis on how regulatory heterogeneity, carbon-compliance standards, customs formalities and geopolitical conditions subject a severe limitation to logistical performance. Research has also revealed that current digital trade systems tend not to accommodate the need to have environmental requirements or adaptability to the disruptions caused by climatic factors, leading to delays, increased emission, and lack of operational resiliency (El Arab et al., 2025). This literature indicates that any future logistics models will have to consider regulatory reasoning as part of the decision-making process to sustain, achieve transparency, and adherence across borders. The intersection of these research areas is indicating the escalating concern of holistic orchestration models that have the potential to combine predictive analytics, symbolic governance structures, environmental sensing and multi-agent coordination. New literature on orchestration engines and cognitive supply chain management find the necessity of platforms that can not only optimize performance but also consider ecological, geopolitical and governance constraints at the same time (Q. Zhao & Yu, 2025). Although multiple papers bring digital twins, federated learning, blockchain-enabled data exchange, and agents, the gap in the research on the approaches to incorporate all these technologies into the consistent architecture, specifically suitable to climate adaptation, is evident (Ravikumar & Aarthi, 2025c). In this framework, the Neuro-Environmental AI Orchestration is presented as a conceptual breakthrough, serving to cover the gaps that are detected in the literature since neural learning, symbolic reasoning, and environmental intelligence are integrated to achieve climate-resilient cross-border logistics (Oyeyemi et al., 2025). The necessity to have integrated, transparent, and adaptive logistics ecosystems, which will be able to deal with rising climate pressure and sustainability demands, is therefore supported by literature.

4. CLIMATE-ADAPTIVE LOGISTICS MODELLING

Climate-adaptive logistics modelling aims at reinventing how cross-border supply chains operate by integrating environmental awareness, predictive intelligence and operational flexibility into the mainstream decision making (Hazaimeh & Al-Ansi, 2024). To formulate workflows, which are able to respond in real-time to environmental changes, climate-adaptive models introduce the concepts of real-time weather intelligence, emission metrics, and multimodal transport dynamics. These models utilize neural forecasting engines, geospatial simulations, and digital twin ecosystems and predict disruptions and assess other operational pathways. Along with symbolic reasoning frameworks that encode regulatory and environmental restrictions they facilitate routing, mode selection and operations in warehouses that are consistent with carbon-neutrality pledges and environmentally sustainable demands (Liao & Wang, 2019). Climate-adaptive logistics modelling is driving cross-border operations to become resilient, environmentally responsive networks that operate as continuity in trade despite carrying risks and offer sustainability solutions to the world by uniting these elements into a single orchestration environment. Table 3 Correlates climatic adaptive functions with real world logistics operations.

Table 3. Climate-adaptive logistics models and applications

Model Type	Application	Climate Benefit
Real-time Rerouting	Alternate sea/land routing	Avoids storm delays
Emission-Aware Mode Selection	Rail/sea prioritization	Reduced GHG emissions
Energy Optimization	Border warehouses	Lower electricity consumption
Disruption Analytics	Weather risk forecasting	Improved continuity
Adaptive Scheduling	Port/terminal operations	Minimizes idle time & emissions

4.1 Real-Time Rerouting Under Weather Disruptions

Live diversion during weather disturbances is a highly essential feature in continuity of climatically sensitive logistics systems. Extreme climatic conditions like storms, heavy rainfall, heat waves, fogs, and sea turbulence have a great impact on transport schedules and availability of infrastructures, leading to delays, congestion and higher consumption of fuels. The climate-adaptive models are based on real-time satellite transmissions, IoT sensor data, ocean-state predictions, and atmospheric simulations, whereby, the early sign of disruption is identified (Feng et al., 2023). Neural networks can forecast the extent, lifespan, and dispersion of weather fluctuations, whereas symbolic regulations impose operational restrictions, e.g., limited sea patterns, security rules, and customs schedules. Rerouting engine is a dynamic evaluation of alternative routes based on time, carbon impact and network reliability over rail, road, sea, and air routes (Alabi et al., 2023). This allows the operators of the logistics to shift the routes in real time and stay in regulatory compliance as well as reducing the risks of operations.

4.2 Emission-Aware Mode Selection

The emission-aware mode selection allows the logistic systems to select logistic mode, whether by rail, road, sea, or air, according to the real-time carbon intensity, environmental limitations, and sustainability goals. The choice of traditional mode is cost and time-efficient, with little regard to emissions and the environmental effects (Ravikumar & Aarthi, 2025a). Climate-adaptive logistics models are models that combine emission data sets, fuel-consumption profiles, energy-efficiency indicators and carbon metrics of the lifecycle of each mode of transport. AI-based assessment models calculate the carbon footprint of other multimodal combinations and take into account other factors related to climate situations, energy sources, and governmental emission restrictions (Hagendorff & Danks, 2023). Symbolic thinking levels involve environmental regulations, green corridor principles and carbon tax systems to make sure that mode selection is in line with global sustainability requirements. With the balance between operating performance and environmental sustainability, the mode of emission awareness can be used to facilitate the shift to low-carbon logistics (Baucas et al., 2023). It enables the carriers, customs and multimodal operators to make climate-compatible choices to ensure that the service reliability across cross-border networks is minimized and at the same time the greenhouse gas emission reduced.

4.3 AI-Driven Energy Optimization for Border Warehouses and Customs Hubs

AI-enhanced energy optimization is aimed at minimizing carbon usage and enhancing the efficiency of operations in border warehouses, dry ports, and customs hubs, which are key nodes and receive a high energy load as a result of storage, inspection, refrigeration, and material handling operations. The models of climate adaptation are based on the use of an IoT-based approach, thermal mapping, equipment-level telemetry, and occupancy analytics to learn more about the trends of energy consumption in real-time (Luo et al., 2023). Neural forecasting engines are machines that predict peak-load times, environmental stress states and variations in energy demand, depending on climatic conditions of temperature, humidity, and sun exposure. Symbolic reasoning layers apply energy-efficiency laws, ESG reporting laws, and green-building laws to provide the conformity with environmental standards. The optimization algorithms suggest dynamism in energy planning, automatic change of HVAC, integration of renewable energy, and balance loading of storage facilities and inspection areas (Tacken et al., 2014). This not only minimizes energy wastage, but also decreases the operational expenses and its role in carbon-neutral infrastructure on the border.

5. AI ORCHESTRATION LAYER

The AI Orchestration Layer will be the main intelligence center of the Neuro-Environmental AI, which will coordinate data streams, decision-making, and operational contacts between the carriers, customs authorities, ports, and multimodal transport systems. This is a layer that combines predictive models, symbolic reasoning engines, multi agent architecture, and carbon computation structures into one thought space. The orchestration layer will convert fragmented and autonomously behaving logistics components into a coherent ecosystem that can make adaptive and rule-compliant, as well as carbon-conscious decisions. Multi-agent systems facilitate autonomous but cooperative functions, as all stakeholders, namely, vehicle fleets, customs officials, warehousing units, and border authorities, communicate in a decision space (Adenuga et al., 2020). The policy-conscious reasoning makes sure that all the operational decisions are in compliance with the environmental governance, emission regulation, and cross-border trade procedures. At the same time, advanced models of carbon predictions control the routing of low emissions, mode choice, and energy management. The AI Orchestration Layer provides a robust, sustainable, and smart operational foundation of climate-responsive cross-border logistics networks through the process of continuous learning, federal collaboration and transparent decision logic.

5.1 Multi-Agent AI for Coordinating Carriers, Customs, and Ports

Multi-agent AI allows the decentralized but distributed decision-making of various cross-border logistics actors, such as carriers, customs departments, freight terminals, and port authorities. The autonomy of every agent, which is represented by a stakeholder or physical asset, is in the ability to perform localized functions, like scheduling, inspection, routing, or gate clearance. Nevertheless, using common protocols and coordination logic, agents cooperate to ensure efficiency of the global systems. Neural learning agents foretell the delay and congestion and climate effects, whereas the symbolic agents implement the adherence to the regulations of customs and safety and environmental regulations. With this collaborative system, priorities, including slot allocation, queue management, as well as resource allocation at borders and ports, can be negotiated in real-time. Multi agent coordination facilitates better throughput, waiting time, emission, and transparency in international operations (Sahal et al., 2021). Through the co-ordination of autonomous decision-making in one orchestration environment, the multi-agent AI assists with the smooth cross-border communication and makes it more resilient to the effects of climatic and operational threats.

5.2 Policy-Aware Reasoning Systems Encoding Green Logistics Rules

Policy-conscious reasoning systems incorporate environmental policies, cross-border trade policies and carbon-compliance policies into the AI decision-making process. These systems use symbolic representations of knowledge in form of ontologies, set of rules and constrained models of knowledge to ensure that all operations of the logistics comply with sustainability requirements and legal governance frameworks. Coded with regulations on emission caps, green-corridor mandates, eco-design policies, customs protocols and multimodal transport policies, policy-conscious AI makes decisions as operational and compliance-oriented (Yang, 2024). Combined with the neural learning models, the reasoning system does not just analyze the prospective decisions based on the performance, but also based on the regulatory correspondence. This will stop any violations, facilitate transparent auditing and responsible automation. Since the climate regulations in various regions change, the system modifies rule sets to ensure that there is inter-regional interoperability and uniformity in cross-border operations. Policy-conscious logic thus becomes the essential point of sustainable, credible and governance-referentiated logistics coordination.

5.3 Carbon Footprint Prediction Models

The prediction models of carbon footprint make it possible to accurately forecast the green house gas emissions in multimodal logistics operations, which is an important constituent of decision-making in the context of sustainability. These models present the analysis of variables like the type of vehicle, capacity, fuel consumption, nature of the route, weather conditions, idle time and energy consumption in warehouses or ports. Neural forecasting systems are trained on the emission patterns based on past and real-time data, whereas symbolic rules include emission standards, carbon taxes policy, and ECG reporting (Z. Li, 2024). The integrated architecture will guarantee that the predictions are accurate and they conform to regulatory expectations. Carbon prediction helps the logistics planners to compare between alternative routing plans, to assess mode-switching plans, to distribute the greener assets, and to optimize energy consumption between the facilities. Emissions intelligence, when part of the orchestration layer, assists in providing automatic recommendations on the low-carbon operations and allows organizations to monitor the sustainability goal progress. Such models thus hasten the process of switching over to carbon-neutral cross border logistic systems.

6. CROSS-BORDER RISK INTELLIGENCE

Intelligence on cross-border risks is a critical element that facilitates climate-adaptive logistical systems to determine weak points, disruption predictions, and resilience of operations in international transport corridors. With the growing uncertainty in climate, the logistics networks are regularly exposed to problems that include weather-related delays, the deterioration of infrastructure, port closures, geopolitical tensions, and changing regulatory landscapes. Cross-border risk intelligence combines predictive analytics, environmental sensing, and those based on governance considerations or reasoning to assess these risks on a real-time basis (Dobrovnik et al., 2018). Neural forecasting models are used to identify emerging climate risks and operational bottlenecks, and symbolic reasoning structures are used to read compliance regulations and evaluate the possible effect of environmental and trade related constraints. This facilitates early decision-making, where the operators of the logistics have the ability to reroute the shipments, reschedule or get contingency resources ready before it goes haywire (K. Li et al., 2024). Table 4 Categorizes the risks of climate, regulatory, infrastructure, and ESG.

Table 4. Cross-border risk categories in climate-affected logistics

Risk Category	Examples	Impact on Logistics
Climate Risks	Cyclones, floods, heatwaves	Delays, closures, cargo damage
Infrastructure Risks	Port degradation, road erosion	Reduced capacity
Governance Risks	Regulatory mismatches	Compliance delays
ESG Risks	High emissions, poor transparency	Financial & reputational penalties
Geopolitical Risks	Border tensions, sanctions	Route disruptions

6.1 Climate-Induced Delays and Predictive Disruption Analytics

Delays that are caused by climate including storms, floods, droughts, heat waves, and actions at sea are major threats to the performance of cross-border logistics. The predictions of disruption analytics are based on machine learning models, satellite weather data and past weather dynamics to forecast the probability, location, and intensity of such phenomena. Such analytics systems keep track of the changing environmental factors like wind speed, the intensity of precipitation, temperature levels of the seas, and the path of a storm to note down early warning signs of disruption. Neural forecasting engines predict the likelihood of delay and recovery time expectations, whereas symbolic reasoning layers have safety rules, operational restrictions and cross-border regulations (Richnák & Gubová, 2021). This allows the logistic operators to make route changes, re-plan the shipments, assign buffer time, and engage alternative transport modes even before disruptions become a reality. Predictive analytics also assists in strategic planning of the identification of climate-sensitive corridors and seasons of highest risks. Climate disruption analytics will complement resiliency in the system, minimize economic impacts, and guarantee continuity in the international supply chain processes by offering anticipatory intelligence.

6.2 Border-Specific Climate Resilience Challenges

Border regions pose special climate resilience problems because of the complexity of their geography, infrastructures and administration. Numerous border checkpoints and inland ports, as well as customs centers, are situated in the environmentally sensitive areas of coastal belts, mountainous areas, aridlands, or flood-prone regions, becoming particularly sensitive to extreme climate conditions. These strains are reflected through the closure of roads, inspection queue, equipment's malfunctions, heat on freight, and delays in clearance process. To make matters worse, cross-border operations have to comply with environmental regulation, infrastructure capability, and emergency procedures that are heterogeneous given that they vary among jurisdictions (Khanna et al., 2025). Resilience models with the help of AI combine local climate predictions, land use trends, and infrastructure vulnerability ratings with border control restrictions to determine the level of risk. Symbolic reasoning incorporates the customs protocols and continuity guidelines to facilitate adherence to disruptive circumstances. Such a combination allows adapting the planning of border operations, such as dynamic rerouting, prioritization of the necessary cargo, optimization of inspection schedules and strengthening of climate sensitive infrastructure. The vulnerabilities pertaining to the border are critical to ensure the reliability and sustainability of global logistics flows.

6.3 Integrating ESG Risks with Trade Compliance

Combining the ESG risks with the trade compliance will guarantee that the cross-border logistics is not only efficient but also ethical and sustainable. Along the lines of environmental impact, social responsibility, and the quality of governance, ESG factors are becoming integrated in terms of global trade policies, emission reporting schemes, and global supply chain regulations. The logistics organizations should portray low carbon footprints, fair labor, transparent records and observing the norms of biodiversity protection (Amangeldy et al., 2025). The artificial intelligence–based compliance processes examine the ESG metrics in addition to the trade requirements like the customs regulations, import-export limitations, and green certification policies. These combined rules are encoded in symbolic reasoning models and operational decisions are made in line with sustainability, as well as regulatory expectations. Neural analytics evaluate possible hotspots of ESG risks, including routes with a high level of carbon emissions or socially sensitive supply chain interconnections, and prescribe remedial measures (D. Zhang, 2024). This combination strategy promotes transparency, responsible trade and decreases regulatory fines. Finally, the compliance based on ESG reinforces the confidence of cross-border stakeholders and can synchronize the logistics systems with global sustainability goals.

7. SYSTEMS ARCHITECTURE

Neuro-Environmental AI Orchestration systems architecture is the structural framework used to provide the procedural platform which involves the environment, predictive intelligence, symbolic governance reasoning and multi-agent coordination into a unified operational platform. With a strong architecture, logistics networks can be created as climate-resilient and adaptive ecosystems capable of responding to disruptions on a real-time basis and keeping up with cross-border regulations. The key aspects of this architecture are the use of digital twins, federated learning networks, blockchain-guaranteed data layers, and orchestration engines run with the help of neuro-symbolic intelligence (Jedličková, 2024). Digital twins predictive route planning Digital twins simulate multimodal corridors in diverse climatic, operational, and geopolitical conditions and can be used in stress testing infrastructure. Blockchain facilitates safe and immutable exchange of environment and operations information between global partners. The Federated Learning provides decentralization of model training in customs agencies, carriers, and ports without revealing sensitive information, which enables the collaboration and privacy to improve (Cardoso & Ferrando, 2021). In cases where these technologies are coordinated by AI-based control layers, the architecture will be able to facilitate transparency, trust, sustainability assurance, and coordinated climate-informed decision-making across borders. Table 5 Gives a synopsis of the digital twins, blockchain, AI, and FL in the architecture.

Table 5. System architecture technologies and their roles

Technology	Role in System	Key Benefit
Digital Twins	Corridor simulation	Predictive climate resilience
Blockchain	Secure data exchange	Trust & traceability
Federated Learning	Cross-border model training	Data privacy & cooperation
Multi-Agent Systems	Operational coordination	Adaptive decision-making
Carbon Analytics Engine	Emission estimation	Supports green compliance

7.1 Digital Twins for Climate-Resilient Corridor Planning

Digital twins can be seen as virtual representations of logistics corridors, which allow to simulate, predict and optimize cross-border operations in different climate conditions. These models combine real-time sensors with IoT sensors, on-road systems, weather forecasts and infrastructure surveillance engineering to simulate the multimodal structures, like highway systems, rail lines, shipping routes and border stations. AI-powered analytics assess the impact of heatwaves, storms, flooding, or changes in the sea-state on the capacity, travel time and stability of assets (Bhandal et al., 2022). Digital twins can reveal vulnerabilities in logistics planners, test other routing strategies, and optimize the allocation of resources by running scenario-based stress tests. Symbolic reasoning makes sure that decision-making in simulations are in line with protocols of customs, regulations on emissions and global climate policies.

The results of the insights inform the upgrades of the infrastructure, emergency-response planning, and long-term sustainability investments. Digital twins are thus strategic as they help in coming up with climate-resilient cross-border corridors that remain continuous even in extreme weather conditions.

7.2 Blockchain + AI for Sustainability Verification

AI plus blockchain provides a secure, transparent, and unaltered system to check the sustainability performance across the cross-border logistics networks. Since the international supply chains need to provide evidence of carbon reduction, ethical sourcing, and adherence to green logistics policies, blockchain ensures that environmental information, including carbon footprints, fuel industry, and compliance certificates, stays unaltered and verifiable (Basu et al., 2024). The data that are reported and have to be correct according to the sustainability metrics is validated with AI models that compare the reported data with sensor data, digital twin outputs, and operational logs. The verification rules are coded in symbolic reasoning layers, which are founded on the ESG standards, emissions protocols, and regulatory frameworks. Smart contracts serve to check compliance in real-time, making it possible to verify the compliance with the requirements of the green corridor, the use of environmentally friendly methods of transport, and ethical trade. This integration does minimize fraud, increase transparency, and increase trust between customs agencies, carriers, and international trade partners. Blockchain + AI is therefore an enhanced accountability tool and it helps to move towards verifiable, sustainable, and climate-appropriate logistics ecosystems.

7.3 Federated Learning for Cross-Border Environmental Data Sharing

Federated learning allows model training to be done jointly by a variety of cross-border organizations such as customs organizations, ports, carriers, and environmental organizations, without sharing data centrally. This is especially relevant in regard to sensitive environmental, operational and compliance data that is not allowed to cross national jurisdictions because of privacy, sovereignty or regulatory reasons. Using distributed datasets in the various countries, federated models are able to learn and combine the insights to improve their climate forecasting, emission prediction and risk detection without data confidentiality being compromised (Bi et al., 2022). Neural models combine local learning updates and symbolic reasoning makes sure to align it with regional governance and environmental policies. This strategy allows synchronized risk intelligence, homogenized sustainability evaluations and mutual climate understanding across frontiers. Federated learning will increase the degree of cross-border collaboration, decrease the asymmetry of information, and increase the resilience of collectives to climate disturbances. It eventually promotes the inter-operable environmental intelligence networks that are necessary in supporting sustainable global logistics.

8. CASE STUDIES AND SIMULATIONS

The work provides a set of case studies and simulation scenarios that prove the utility of Neuro-Environmental AI Orchestration into the practical use in the context of climate-adaptive, low-carbon, and resilient cross-border logistics systems. The examples of realistic simulations of corridors that involve areas including India-UAE routes by sea and Europe-Asia multimodal routes show that integrated environmental sensing, neuro-symbolic reasoning, and predictive analytics can improve decision-making in unstable weather and operational conditions (Chazzaoui, 2022). Both cases consider the active coordination between routing, mode choice and energy control to represent disruptions through heatwaves, variations in monsoon, port congestion or carbon-compliance limits. Moreover, the simulations measure the emission reduction attained using the orchestration framework and contrast its performance based on the conventional logistics models, which are based on fixed rules and past history. All these situations demonstrate that Neuro-Environmental AI will make all global logistics intelligent and proactive ecosystems, which can reach the next level of resilience, sustainability, and regulatory harmony in different geopolitical and climatic conditions.

8.1 Simulated Green Corridor: India–UAE and EU–Asia Routes

The simulated version of the green corridor between India-UAE and EU-Asia corridors explains the use of Neuro-Environmental AI in facilitating proactive, climate sensitive transport activities on long-distance, multimodal pathways. In the case of the India-UAE corridor, the system incorporates satellite-based monsoon-tracking, ocean-state-forecasting and congestion-analytics of ports to optimise the vessel navigation around the peak monsoon season. Neural forecasting models are used to determine the waves and storm intensity, as well as wind patterns, whereas symbolic reasoning is used to guarantee adherence to maritime emissions laws and blue-economy rules. The model determines the least risky sea routes, dynamically regulating the speed of ships to save as much fuel as possible and emissions of greenhouse gases. In the case of the EU-Asia corridor, the framework considers intermodal combinations of rail-sea-road, when the temperature and the possible geopolitical disruption are extreme. The orchestration system suggests robust options like road to rail, or rerouting around climatically sensitive checkpoints at times of high pollution. (Gupta & Gupta, 2025). Figure 2 depicting that satellite data, climate forecasting, compliance regulations, and AI-controlled routing help to make green logistics corridors more resilient, minimise emissions, and optimise transit time.

Figure 2. Neuro-environmental AI workflow for green corridor optimization

8.2 Emission Savings Through Neuro-Environmental Orchestration

In this case study, the emission reduction through the use of Neuro-Environmental AI in multimodal transport networks is quantified. The simulation uses real time carbon intensity, vehicle fuel consumption model, renewable energy availability, and climate adjusted performance measures. Through the combination of emission-conscious mode choice and dynamic routing, the orchestration system cuts down the number of redundant detours, wasted time and transport options that are carbon intensive (Subramanyam et al., 2025). The neural analytics compute the carbon footprint of different routes, whereas symbolic regulations implement adherence to carbon caps, green-corridor regulations, and global sustainability procedures.

In seaways, AI-assisted adaptive speed control can save up to 12-15% of fuel burnt in good weather conditions. In road-rail networks, modal switching and load balancing lead to a reduction of 18-22% on average. HVAC optimization and solar integration recommendations ensure a reduction of electricity consumption by 10-14% in border warehouses due to energy-efficient scheduling. Furthermore, federated learning aligns carbon reporting between countries thereby increasing the effectiveness of sustainability audits. The simulation highlights the fact that saving of emissions is not only one of the operational advantages but a strategic facilitator of achieving ESG targets and regulatory climate commitments. Figure 3 illustrating the collaboration between the real-time data, neural analytics, symbolic rules, and energy optimization to lower the emissions in multimodal logistics networks.

Figure 3. Neuro-environmental AI workflow for emission reduction in cross-border logistics

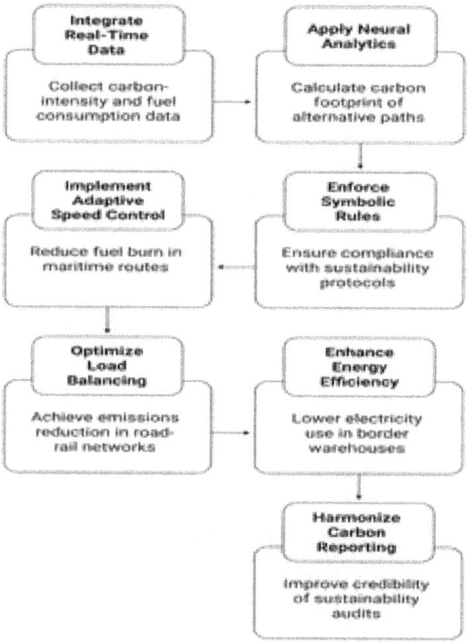

8.3 Comparative Performance vs. Classical Logistics Models

Comparative analysis of Neuro-Environmental AI with classical logistics models shows that the former has great benefits in the form of resilience, sustainability, and predictive power. The conventional models require fixed routing guidelines and past averages and subsidiary climatic information, and thus, they are subject to breakdowns during unpredictable weather, abrupt border issues and changeable emissions restrictions. In comparison, Neuro-Environmental AI combines real-time environmental sensing, predictive climate analytics, and rule-based governance reasoning and, therefore, can make adaptive decisions based on new risks in real time. Simulations indicate that as much as 30% schedule reliability is enhanced, 20% less emissions, and 25% reduced delays are achieved by using conventional systems (Abhulimen & Ejike, 2024). The structure of the orchestration also adds to the transparency so that the decisions made are in compliance with the ESG requirements and those of cross-border compliance requirements. On the whole, the findings indicate that classical models are not able to be as agile or climate resilient as neuro-environmental orchestration is. Table 6 Shows the performance gains made by Neuro-Environmental AI.

Table 6. Comparative performance: neuro-environmental AI vs classical models

Metric	Classical Logistics	Neuro-Environmental AI	Improvement
Schedule Reliability	Moderate	High	+30%
Emission Reduction	Low	Strong	+20–25%
Disruption Response	Reactive	Predictive/adaptive	Significant
Cross-Border Compliance	Manual	Automated rule-aware	High accuracy
Energy Efficiency	Limited	AI-optimized	+10–15%

9. POLICY AND GOVERNANCE IMPLICATIONS

The use of Neuro-Environmental AI in cross-border logistics of climate adaptation has high policy and governance implications that are not limited to technological innovation. These systems demand integrated regulatory systems, common accountability systems, and intensive international cooperation so that it can be responsible, fair and sustainable. Since the logistics networks cross across several jurisdictions, the governance systems should facilitate interoperative data standards, collaborative climate-monitoring facilities, and straightforward auditing systems in line with the worldwide sustainability requirements. Besides, climate-aligned logistics should be based on strategic objectives stipulated in the Sustainable Development Goals, especially SDG 9 (industry and infrastructure), SDG 13 (climate action), and SDG 17 (partnerships). Ethical governance is also a significant issue, with the AI-based judgments of the environment affecting trade flows, carbon emissions, border security, and socio-environmental equity (Haddadsisakht & Ryan, 2018). Being fair, avoiding algorithmic discrimination, and protecting sovereignty-sensitive information, which should be allowed through policies, ought to allow multinational climate cooperation. In general, the systems of policies and governance should be changed to more integrated, ethical and sustainability-oriented models that take full advantage of Neuro-Environmental AI without affecting transparency, accountability or trust across the borders (Aarthi, Ravikumar, Sobirova, et al., 2025).

9.1 SHG/SDG Alignment (SDG 9, 13, 17)

Directly, neuro-environmental AI supports the global sustainability goals of SDG 9, SDG 13, SDG 17 in terms of creating resilient infrastructure, operations through climate-sensitive programs, and improved global cooperation. SDG 9 is related to sustainable industrialization and innovation, and it is achieved in AI-driven corridor planning, warehousing with energy-saving, and multimodal routing that is carbon-conscience (Onukwulu et al., 2025). SDG 13 enhances climate action, which requires nations to create adaptive capacity and integrating environmental risks into planning; Neuro-Environmental AI is able to meet this criterion by delivering predictive climatic analytics, emission-sensitive mode selections and risk-sensitive logistics coordination. SDG 17 highlights the inclusion of all nations in the globe that provides the foundation of cross-border environmental information exchange, federated learning systems and federal governance systems. All of these goals demonstrate the movement towards climate-compatible logistics ecosystems, which is economically competitive, and environmentally responsible. It is suitable to align the priorities of the Neuro-Environmental AI and SDG to ensure that the creation of new logistics infrastructures will facilitate the process of enhancing global climate without causing disruption to the global sustainability expectations.

9.2 Data-Sharing Frameworks for Multinational Climate Cooperation

Good climate-adaptive logistics requires sound cross-border data sharing models that would allow real-time sharing of environmental intelligence, emissions information as well as operation insights between diverse national agencies and logistics stakeholders. Nonetheless, geopolitical sensitivities, data sovereignty regulations and uneven regulatory principles tend to inhibit this type of cooperation. Neuro-Environmental AI can overcome them by using privacy-sensitive technology like federated learning, blockchain-protected data logs, and interoperable digital standards that can facilitate the exchange of information without affecting the national control. The policymakers should also come up with coordinated practices of climate data classification, secure transmission, auditability, and verification of compliance (Aarthi, Ravikumar, & Pardaev, 2025). These systems must back collective climate-monitoring systems, mutual air-sea-land environmental displays, and emergency coordination frameworks of disruptions as a result of climate. Enhanced multinational collaboration better predicts and lowers the reporting uniformity of emissions, and information asymmetry across the borders.

9.3 Ethical Governance of AI in Environmental Decision-Making

Transparency, fairness, and accountability in the cross-border logistics systems regarding the AI-enhanced decision-making on environmental issues is an essential responsibility of the ethical governance systems. Since AI models influence routing, emissions control, and reduction of risks, ethical control must target such areas, as algorithmic bias, the unavailability of the decision-making process, and the impact of AI on environmental justice and the uneven effect on low-income regions (Bulling & Dastani, 2016). Policy frameworks should require understandability, human control, and analysis of impact as well as clarity in the audit of AI-based decisions on the environment. Symbolic reasoning layering should encode the ethical rules such as climate equity, compliance integrity and shared environmental responsibility. Also, the governing institutions will have to regulate the intent of sensitive environmental and operational information, assure privacy, informed consent and prevent militarization or abuse. The establishment of multi-stakeholder governance councils in the form of regulators, environmentalists, industry players, and civil society is also one way of ensuring a balanced and inclusive oversight.

10. FUTURE DIRECTIONS

The future of the Neuro-Environmental AI in the cross-border logistics is presented with a number of new transformative prospects of future research and innovation. Due to the ongoing increase in the volatility of climate and the complexity of global trade, the logistics systems will be subjected to an upgrading beyond predictive intelligence to entirely cognitive, self-adaptive, and ethically controlled infrastructures (Bajo et al., 2012). Future trends are noted to bring about the development of cognitive logistics systems that can reason autonomously, learn and operate dynamically under complex climate-trade conditions to reflect human expertise. Parallel and in accordance with this, hybrid Climate-AI Twins will combine real-time environmental sensing, digital simulations, and neuro-symbolic intelligence to establish the ever-changing models that reflect the physical and ecological behavior of logistics corridors (Fuady et al., 2022). Quantum based optimization methods will also advance the field further, which will improve the efficiency of large scale and climate sensitive logistics optimization. The future innovations are intended to enhance resilience, become dramatically less emission-intensive, and develop transparent and sustainable cross-border interaction. It is these directions that create a new generation of logistics with an intelligent, climate-responsive, and globally interoperable logistics paradigm.

10.1 Cognitive Logistics

Cognitive logistics is the internal development of intelligent decision-making (logistics systems change their responses to reactive and predictive ones and become purely autonomous and self-optimizing). Cognitive logistics platforms operate under the force of neuro-symbolic reasoning, reinforcement learning and highly intelligent environmental sensors in order to constantly sense, interpret and adapt to cross-border dynamism. These systems are capable of independent risk evaluation, trade-offs negotiation and multimodal operations in the face of climate uncertainty. Cognitive logistics facilitates the synchronization of decisions made by carriers, customs services and port stakeholders, which will be increasingly responsive to climate changes and more reliable in their operations. Cognitive logistics will be crucial to providing resilience, responsiveness and sustainability to trade ecosystems as the global supply chains become more intricate.

10.2 Hybrid Climate-AI Twins

Hybrid Climate-AI Twins combines the advantages of the environmental simulation models with the neuro-environmental intelligence to establish dynamic digital simulations of the cross-border logistics corridors. These twins constantly consume live climate data, geospatial, and trade flows and operational statistics of IoT networks and satellite systems (Mastrogiovanni, 2025). Neural forecasting models forecast weather patterns, emission effects and infrastructure weaknesses whereas symbolic reasoning enforces governance regulations and sustainability limits. It assists with stress testing, path planning, infrastructure fortification planning, and the planned reaction in more than one nation in the case of extreme climate conditions (Corbett et al., 2010). Hybrid Climate-AI Twins are viewed as strategic resources in influencing future-proof green logistics standpoints by combining climate science, digital engineering, and AI reasoning as the means of establishing balances between efficiency, resiliency, and environmental accountability.

10.3 Quantum-Based Green Optimization

Green optimization involving quantum provides an effective computational paradigm to address the complex and large-scale logistics issues that cannot be addressed effectively through traditional optimization models. Quantum-inspired algorithms are based on the principles of superposition, tunneling, and probabilistic search to search a large solution space of routing, scheduling, and energy allocation to climate and regulatory policies (Challinor et al., 2018). When used to cross-border logistics, these techniques allow the calculation of emission-optimal paths, the optimum of multimodal structures, and carbon-sensitive resource allocation with ultra-efficiency. Real-time responsiveness is also improved with quantum optimization, which enables the logistics operators to recalculate climate-resilient routes when the conditions change. The combination of quantum models and Neuro-Environmental AI enables orchestration engines to reach the highest level of accuracy during prediction of emissions, assessment of trade-offs between sustainability, and optimization of operations in a wide variety of geopolitical settings (Boutkhoum et al., 2016).

11. CONCLUSION

The Neuro-Environmental AI is one of the revolutionary paradigm shifts to re-conceptualize the cross-border logistics as a climate-resilient, sustainable, and intelligently synchronized global system. The approach breaks the limits of traditional logistics models that are based on fixed decision rules, disjointed information and reactive planning by combining neural learning, symbolic reasoning and analysis and synthesis of the environment into a unified orchestration framework. It allows real-time adaptation to disruptions caused by climate changes, multimodal transport optimization and adherence to newly developed environmental and trade policies. Neuro-Environmental AI can help reduce carbon footprint and improve operational continuity by enabling cases of anticipatory routing, selection of emission-aware mode, and energy optimization within warehouses, ports and border inspection hubs through its cognitive decision layer. Its ability to synchronize cross-border data exchange by means of federated learning and enable transparency through blockchain and model climate-resilient corridors with the use of digital twins creates a scalable basis of multinational climate collaboration. The framework also aligns logistics operations with major sustainability agendas, especially the SDGs, through building resilient infrastructure, promoting climate action and developing partnerships around the globe. The role of the Neuro-Environmental AI has become more crucial as climate volatility rises and trade networks grow, making it possible to make environmentally responsible and controlled, as well as future-oriented logistics ecosystems. In the end, the paradigm leads to the emergence of a new generation of green logistics systems which reconciles economic competitiveness with environmental stewardship, and this way the global trade will move forward in tandem with global sustainability objectives of the planet.

REFERENCES

Aarthi, S., Ravikumar, R. N., & Pardaev, J. (2025). Synergizing multimodal generative AI and blockchain for the future of digital media. In *Advances in Computational Intelligence and Robotics* (pp. 1–34). IGI Global Scientific Publishing. DOI: 10.4018/979-8-3373-1504-1.ch001

Aarthi, S., Ravikumar, R. N., Sobirova, K., & Mamadiyarov, Z. (2025). Empowering a sustainable future through digital learning and the SDGs. In *Harnessing E-Learning to Create a Sustainable Future* (pp. 145–172). IGI Global Scientific Publishing. DOI: 10.4018/979-8-3373-0112-9.ch006

Abhulimen, A. O., & Ejike, O. G. (2024). Solving supply chain management issues with AI and Big Data analytics for future operational efficiency. *Computer Science & IT Research Journal*, *5*(8), 1780–1805. DOI: 10.51594/csitrj.v5i8.1396

Adenuga, T., Ayobami, A. T., & Okolo, F. C. (2020). AI-driven workforce forecasting for peak planning and disruption resilience in global logistics and supply networks. *International Journal of Multidisciplinary Research and Growth Evaluation*, *1*(2), 71–87. DOI: 10.54660/.IJMRGE.2020.1.2.71-87

Alabi, A. M., Oguntoyinbo, F. N., Abioye, K. M., John-Ladega, A. A., Obiki-Osafiele, A. N., & Daraojimba, C. (2023). Risk management in Africa's financial landscape: A review. *International Journal of Advanced Economics*, *5*(8), 239–257. DOI: 10.51594/ijae.v5i8.573

Amangeldy, B., Tasmurzayev, N., Imankulov, T., Baigarayeva, Z., Izmailov, N., Riza, T., Abdukarimov, A., Mukazhan, M., & Zhumagulov, B. (2025). AI-powered building ecosystems: A narrative mapping review on the integration of digital twins and LLMs for proactive comfort, IEQ, and energy management. *Sensors (Basel)*, *25*(17), 5265. DOI: 10.3390/s25175265

Antonowicz, M., & Majewski, J. (2025). Environmental challenges and innovations in the Asia-Europe rail transport corridors in the context of the ESG concept. *Journal of Environmental Management and Tourism*, *16*(3), 191. DOI: 10.14505/jemt.v16.3(79).01

Bajo, J., Borrajo, M. L., De Paz, J. F., Corchado, J. M., & Pellicer, M. A. (2012). A multi-agent system for web-based risk management in small and medium business. *Expert Systems with Applications*, *39*(8), 6921–6931. DOI: 10.1016/j.eswa.2012.01.001

Basu, P., Deb, P., & Singh, A. (2024). Blockchain and the carbon credit ecosystem: Sustainable management of the supply chain. *The Journal of Business Strategy*, *45*(1), 33–40. DOI: 10.1108/JBS-09-2022-0157

Baucas, M. J., Spachos, P., & Plataniotis, K. N. (2023). Federated learning and blockchain-enabled fog-IoT platform for wearables in predictive healthcare. *IEEE Transactions on Computational Social Systems*, *10*(4), 1732–1741. DOI: 10.1109/TCSS.2023.3235950

Bhandal, R., Meriton, R., Kavanagh, R. E., & Brown, A. (2022). The application of digital twin technology in operations and supply chain management: A bibliometric review. *Supply Chain Management*, *27*(2), 182–206. DOI: 10.1108/SCM-01-2021-0053

Bi, L., Muazu, T., & Samuel, O. (2022). IoT: A decentralized trust management system using blockchain-empowered federated learning. *Sustainability (Basel)*, *15*(1), 374. DOI: 10.3390/su15010374

Boutkhoum, O., Hanine, M., Boukhriss, H., Agouti, T., & Tikniouine, A. (2016). Multi-criteria decision support framework for sustainable implementation of effective green supply chain management practices. *SpringerPlus*, *5*(1), 664. DOI: 10.1186/s40064-016-2233-2

Bulling, N., & Dastani, M. (2016). Norm-based mechanism design. *Artificial Intelligence*, *239*, 97–142. DOI: 10.1016/j.artint.2016.07.001

Cardoso, R. C., & Ferrando, A. (2021). A review of agent-based programming for multi-agent systems. *Computers*, *10*(2), 16. DOI: 10.3390/computers10020016

Challinor, A. J., Adger, W. N., Benton, T. G., Conway, D., Joshi, M., & Frame, D. (2018). Transmission of climate risks across sectors and borders. *Philosophical Transactions. Series A, Mathematical, Physical, and Engineering Sciences*, *376*(2121), 20170301. DOI: 10.1098/rsta.2017.0301

Chazzaoui, T. A. M. (2022). Optimizing international transport routes: A case study on the Silk Road. *International Seven Journal of Multidisciplinary*, *1*(1). Advance online publication. DOI: 10.56238/isevmjv1n1-020

Cheng, D., & Zhang, X. (2017). Overview of low carbon logistics development in China and foreign countries. *IOP Conference Series. Earth and Environmental Science*, *100*, 012167. DOI: 10.1088/1755-1315/100/1/012167

Chowdhury, R. (2025). Responsible data practices and generative AI. In *The Oxford Handbook of the Foundations and Regulation of Generative AI*. Oxford University Press. DOI: 10.1093/oxfordhb/9780198940272.013.0003

Corbett, J. J., Lack, D. A., Winebrake, J. J., Harder, S., Silberman, J. A., & Gold, M. (2010). Arctic shipping emissions inventories and future scenarios. *Atmospheric Chemistry and Physics*, *10*(19), 9689–9704. DOI: 10.5194/acp-10-9689-2010

Dahlgren, S., & Ammenberg, J. (2022). Environmental considerations regarding freight transport among buyers of transport services in Sweden. *Sustainability (Basel), 14*(18), 11244. DOI: 10.3390/su141811244

Dobrovnik, M., Herold, D. M., Fürst, E., & Kummer, S. (2018). Blockchain for and in logistics: What to adopt and where to start. *Logistics (Basel), 2*(3), 18. DOI: 10.3390/logistics2030018

El Arab, R. A., Alkhunaizi, M., Alhashem, Y. N., Al Khatib, A., Bubsheet, M., & Hassanein, S. (2025). Artificial intelligence in vaccine research and development: An umbrella review. *Frontiers in Immunology, 16*, 1567116. DOI: 10.3389/fimmu.2025.1567116

Feng, Q., Zhao, G., Li, W., & Shi, X. (2023). Distribution path optimization of fresh products in cold storage considering green costs. *Buildings (Basel, Switzerland), 13*(9), 2325. DOI: 10.3390/buildings13092325

Fuady, S., Mitayani, A., Widyoutomo, A. B., Satyawan, A. S., Budiman, A. C., Suyoto, S., & Dinata, M. M. M. (2022). Cooperative line formation control of multi-agent systems based on least squares estimation. *Jurnal Elektronika Dan Telekomunikasi, 22*(2), 72. DOI: 10.55981/jet.490

Guo, J., & Zhao, X. (2025). Application of big data in forecasting logistics demand and resource allocation for cross-border E-commerce. *Journal of Computational Methods in Sciences and Engineering*. Advance online publication. DOI: 10.1177/14727978251365306

Gupta, G., & Gupta, M. (2025). Green supply chain solutions: Benefits, challenges, and trade-offs. *International Journal on Science and Technology, 16*(3), 7870. Advance online publication. DOI: 10.71097/IJSAT.v16.i3.7870

Haddadsisakht, A., & Ryan, S. M. (2018). Closed-loop supply chain network design with multiple transportation modes under stochastic demand and uncertain carbon tax. *International Journal of Production Economics, 195*, 118–131. DOI: 10.1016/j.ijpe.2017.09.009

Hagendorff, T., & Danks, D. (2023). Ethical and methodological challenges in building morally informed AI systems. *AI and Ethics, 3*(2), 553–566. DOI: 10.1007/s43681-022-00188-y

Hazaimeh, M., & Al-Ansi, A. M. (2024). Model of AI acceptance in higher education: Arguing teaching staff and students perspectives. *International Journal of Information and Learning Technology, 41*(4), 371–393. DOI: 10.1108/IJILT-01-2024-0005

Islam, F. A. S. (2025). Artificial intelligence-powered carbon market intelligence and blockchain-enabled governance for climate-responsive urban infrastructure in the Global South. *Journal of Engineering Research and Reports*, *27*(7), 440–472. DOI: 10.9734/jerr/2025/v27i71585

Jedličková, A. (2024). Ethical considerations in Risk management of autonomous and intelligent systems. *Ethics & Bioethics*, *14*(1–2), 80–95. DOI: 10.2478/ebce-2024-0007

Khanna, A., Jain, S., Sah, A., Dangi, S., Sharma, A., Tiang, S. S., Wong, C. H., & Lim, W. H. (2025). Generative AI and blockchain-integrated multi-agent framework for resilient and sustainable fruit cold-chain logistics. *Foods*, *14*(17), 3004. DOI: 10.3390/foods14173004

Li, K., Wang, C., Feng, X., & Wu, S. (2024). Blockchain interoperability in data exchange logistics integration. *Mathematics*, *12*(10), 1516. DOI: 10.3390/math12101516

Li, Z. (2024). AI ethics and transparency in operations management: How governance mechanisms can reduce data bias and privacy risks. *Journal of Applied Economics and Policy Studies*, *13*(1), 89–93. DOI: 10.54254/2977-5701/13/2024130

Liao, W., & Wang, T. (2019). A novel collaborative optimization model for job shop production–delivery considering time window and carbon emission. *Sustainability (Basel)*, *11*(10), 2781. DOI: 10.3390/su11102781

Luo, C., Huang, Q., Wu, A. B., Khan, S., Li, H., & Qiu, Q. (2023). Multi-agent cooperative games using belief map assisted training. In *Frontiers in Artificial Intelligence and Applications*. IOS Press. DOI: 10.3233/FAIA230444

Ma, M. (2022). Construction and realization path analysis of cross-border E-commerce logistics collaboration model. *Advances in Multimedia*, *2022*, 1–11. DOI: 10.1155/2022/7758785

Mastrogiovanni, S. (2025). AI-Driven data governance for smart cities: Balancing privacy, efficiency, and public trust. *South Florida Journal of Development*, *6*(9), e5810. DOI: 10.46932/sfjdv6n9-029

Muñoz, Á. G., Chourio, X., Rivière-Cinnamond, A., Diuk-Wasser, M. A., Kache, P. A., Mordecai, E. A., Harrington, L., & Thomson, M. C. (2020). AeDES: A next-generation monitoring and forecasting system for environmental suitability of Aedes-borne disease transmission. *Scientific Reports*, *10*(1), 12640. DOI: 10.1038/s41598-020-69625-4

Niu, B., Chen, K., Chen, L., Ding, C., & Yue, X. (2021). Strategic waiting for disruption forecasts in cross-border E-commerce operations. *Production and Operations Management*, *30*(9), 2840–2857. DOI: 10.1111/poms.13371

Olowonigba, J. K. (2025). Exploring AI-driven supply chain automation to enhance global logistics, reduce operational costs, and ensure resilient business continuity. *Engineering Science & Technology Journal*, *6*(8), 428–449. DOI: 10.51594/estj.v6i8.2021

Onukwulu, E. C., Dienagha, I. N., Digitemie, W. N., Egbumokei, P. I., & Oladipo, O. T. (2025). Integrating sustainability into procurement and supply chain processes in the energy sector. *Gulf Journal of Advance Business Research*, *3*(1), 76–104. DOI: 10.51594/gjabr.v3i1.68

Oyeyemi, B. B., Ifedayo, A. M., & Awodola, M. (2025). Ethical challenges in AI-powered supply chains: A U.s.-Nigeria policy perspective. *International Journal of Applied Research in Social Sciences*, *7*(5), 367–388. DOI: 10.51594/ijarss.v7i5.1911

Pasupuleti, V., Thuraka, B., Kodete, C. S., & Malisetty, S. (2024). Enhancing supply chain agility and sustainability through machine learning: Optimization techniques for logistics and inventory management. *Logistics (Basel)*, *8*(3), 73. DOI: 10.3390/logistics8030073

Ravikumar, R. N., & Aarthi, S. (2025a). Climate data without borders. In *Cross-Border Cooperation in the Age of Climate Change* (pp. 61–90). IGI Global Scientific Publishing. DOI: 10.4018/979-8-3373-3972-6.ch003

Ravikumar, R. N., & Aarthi, S. (2025b). Digital Twin-driven green energy systems. In *The Future of Green Energy* (pp. 1–28). IGI Global Scientific Publishing. DOI: 10.4018/979-8-3373-3226-0.ch001

Ravikumar, R. N., & Aarthi, S. (2025c). Federated Learning for cross-enterprise supply chain collaboration. In *Advances in Computational Intelligence and Robotics* (pp. 47–84). IGI Global Scientific Publishing. DOI: 10.4018/979-8-3373-2833-1.ch002

Ravikumar, R. N., & Aarthi, S. (2025d). Integrated cross-border renewable energy infrastructure for a green transition. In *Cross-Border Cooperation in the Age of Climate Change* (pp. 301–332). IGI Global Scientific Publishing. DOI: 10.4018/979-8-3373-3972-6.ch011

Ren, R., Hu, W., Dong, J., Sun, B., Chen, Y., & Chen, Z. (2019). A systematic literature review of green and sustainable logistics: Bibliometric analysis, research trend and knowledge taxonomy. *International Journal of Environmental Research and Public Health*, *17*(1), 261. DOI: 10.3390/ijerph17010261

Richnák, P., & Gubová, K. (2021). Green and reverse logistics in conditions of sustainable development in enterprises in Slovakia. *Sustainability (Basel)*, *13*(2), 581. DOI: 10.3390/su13020581

Sahal, R., Alsamhi, S. H., Brown, K. N., O'Shea, D., McCarthy, C., & Guizani, M. (2021). Blockchain-empowered digital twins collaboration: Smart transportation use case. *Machines (Basel)*, *9*(9), 193. DOI: 10.3390/machines9090193

Subramanyam, A. (2025). Engineering sustainable supply chain optimization in resource-constrained environments: A Geo-spatial and AI-based data science perspective. *International Journal of Environmental Sciences*, 692–701. DOI: 10.64252/rvk5yx12

Tacken, J., Sanchez Rodrigues, V., & Mason, R. (2014). Examining CO2ereduction within the German logistics sector. *International Journal of Logistics Management*, *25*(1), 54–84. DOI: 10.1108/IJLM-09-2011-0073

Wen Yu, C., & Xiao, Y. (2025). Strategic trade corridors: The Suez Canal and emerging maritime and overland alternatives in global supply chains. *International Journal of Business & Management Studies*, *06*(09), 112–123. DOI: 10.56734/ijbms.v6n9a11

Wijaya, B., Rahayu, I. P., & Wijayanto, H. (2025). Integration of Federated Learning in big data analytics for IoT-based intelligent transportation system. *Infact: International Journal of Computers*, *9*(01), 19–24. DOI: 10.61179/infact.v9i01.704

Yang, C. (2024). Innovation in cross-border supply chain inventory management driven by big data. Advances in Economics. *Management and Political Sciences*, *76*(1), 66–73. DOI: 10.54254/2754-1169/76/20241882

Zhang, D. (2024). AI integration in supply chain and operations management: Enhancing efficiency and resilience. *Applied and Computational Engineering*, *90*(1), 8–13. DOI: 10.54254/2755-2721/90/2024MELB0060

Zhang, Y., & Qin, Y. (2022). Carbon emission reductions, pricing and social welfare of three-echelon supply chain considering consumer environmental awareness under carbon tax policy. *Frontiers in Environmental Science*, *10*, 969613. Advance online publication. DOI: 10.3389/fenvs.2022.969613

Zhao, K., Yang, Z.-F., Zhuo, Y., & Zhang, S. (2023). Carbon emission reduction mechanism of the pharmaceutical supply chain: Quadrilateral evolutionary game models. *Frontiers in Environmental Science*, *11*(1084343), 1084343. Advance online publication. DOI: 10.3389/fenvs.2023.1084343

Zhao, Q., & Yu, L. (2025). Advancing Sustainable Development Goals through Earth observation satellite data: Current insights and future directions. *Yaogan Xuebao*, *5*(0403), 0403. Advance online publication. DOI: 10.34133/remotesensing.0403

KEY TERMS AND DEFINITIONS

Carbon Footprint: The total amount of greenhouse gases released from logistics activities like transport, warehousing, and port operations.

Climate Disruption Analytics: Predictive tools used to forecast weather-related delays and operational risks.

Climate-Adaptive Logistics: Logistics systems that change routes, modes, or schedules based on weather and climate risks.

Digital Twin: A virtual copy of a real logistics corridor or system used to simulate operations under different climate conditions.

Environmental Sensing: Collecting real-time climate and environmental data using IoT devices, sensors, satellites, and digital monitors.

ESG Risks: Environmental, Social, and Governance risks that affect sustainability performance and compliance in logistics operations.

Federated Learning: A privacy-preserving AI method that trains models across countries or organizations without sharing raw data.

Green Corridor: A trade route designed to minimize emissions through cleaner transport modes, optimized routing, and sustainability rules.

Multi-Agent System: A group of AI agents that work together to coordinate decisions across logistics stakeholders such as carriers, customs, and ports.

Neuro-Environmental AI: An intelligent system that combines machine learning, environmental data, and rule-based reasoning to support climate-friendly logistics decisions.

Neuro-Symbolic AI: A hybrid AI approach that merges neural networks (learning from data) with symbolic reasoning (using rules and knowledge).

Policy-Aware AI: AI systems that understand and follow environmental laws, trade regulations, and emissions rules.

Quantum Optimization: Advanced computational methods inspired by quantum mechanics to solve complex logistics problems more efficiently.

Sustainability Verification: Ensuring that logistics operations follow green standards using secure tools like blockchain and AI.

Chapter 11
Neuro-Symbolic AI Frameworks for Ethical, Transparent, and Sustainable Cross-Border Logistics Governance

Ravikumar Natarajan
http://orcid.org/0009-0009-3705-1681
Marwadi University, Rajkot, India

Aarthi Selvakumar
http://orcid.org/0009-0006-9064-2091
Marwadi University, Rajkot, India

ABSTRACT

The growing complexity of global trade demands logistics systems that are transparent, ethical, and environmentally responsible. Traditional AI excels at prediction but lacks interpretability and cannot enforce regulatory or sustainability rules. Neuro-symbolic AI offers a hybrid solution by combining neural learning with symbolic reasoning, enabling real-time forecasting, rule-based compliance, and carbon-aware decision-making. This framework supports cross-border logistics by integrating knowledge graphs, emissions metrics, customs regulations, and ethical constraints into a unified governance model. The approach enhances explainability, ensures fair treatment of shipments, strengthens regulatory alignment, and enables greener routing across international corridors.

DOI: 10.4018/979-8-3373-7847-3.ch011

1. INTRODUCTION

The globalization of the supply chains that has been very high, the growing geopolitical uncertainties, variations in regulatory systems, and the growing pressure on the environment have made the logistics become more complicated across borders. The traditional systems of logistics governance are often ineffective in managing this dynamic situation as they are often founded on siloed data systems, manual inspections and active compliance audit (Kishor, 2022). The global logistics systems must deal with the twofold challenge of ensuring the operational efficiency and ensuring accountability, transparency, and ethical responsibility (on the other hand) in the quest to achieve their own decarbonization strategies and more restrictive sustainability demands that the governments or any other stakeholders have placed upon them. The emergence of disruptions, such as fluctuations in trade policies, alterations in severe weather, and restrictive measures due to the pandemic, as well as, the absence of digitalization, make cross-border coordination and decision-making more difficult (Hitzler et al., 2022). This evolving environment has seen AI become an important driver of predictive analytics, automated routing, risk assessment and real-time monitoring. However, classic data-driven AI models cannot be interpreted, and they cannot be used to apply symbolical regulative knowledge, moral values, or sustainability laws.

1.1 Global Challenges In Cross-Border Logistics

The logistic processes taking place on a cross-border basis face a lot of challenges associated with the disunited regulatory environments, various documentation frameworks, unstable geopolitical connections, and uneven technology acceptance levels across the nations. Such problems tend to generate administrative congestions, delays in clearing of customs, and increased operational uncertainties. Also, the external forces affecting business in global trade networks are gaining more influence due to the presence of climate change, carbon taxation systems, and environmental reporting (Kim et al., 2009). The drastic weather conditions and natural disasters interfere with the supply chains, and the climate politics demand constant control over emissions and sustainable transportation decisions. All these issues together outline the necessity of sophisticated decision-support systems that could combine data of multi-source, predict disruptions, and enforce compliance based on rules. They also identify the need to have frameworks that will be in a position to transform the global sustainability objectives to real, operational restrictions. The cross-border environment thus requires a smart, explainable, and ethically-oriented solutions. Table 1 Overview of critical operation, regulatory and environmental constraints on trade flows of the world.

Table 1. Global challenges in cross-border logistics

Challenge Category	Description
Regulatory Diversity	Different customs laws and documentation requirements across countries.
Sustainability Pressures	Increasing need to reduce emissions and comply with climate policies.
Data Fragmentation	Inconsistent data formats and limited interoperability across borders.
Operational Uncertainty	Weather disruptions, congestion, and geopolitical risks.
Cybersecurity Threats	Rising risks of data breaches and supply chain cyber-attacks.

1.2 Need for Ethical, Transparent, and Sustainable Governance

The world logistics industry is experiencing increased pressure to be responsible and transparency is the new standard when it comes to establishing confidence among regulators, business associates and customers. The ethical governance is becoming more sensitive because of the issues associated with the biased customs risk scoring, unfair border inspections, the obscurity of routing, and differences in the treatment of shipments of the emerging economies. This drives the need to have systems that can incorporate environmental metrics within their decision logic. All of these aspects collectively highlight the necessity to consider AI strategies that would not only streamline the performance of operations by providing optimal results but also incorporate moral values, regulatory openness, and sustainability limitations. Neuro-symbolic AI meets these needs by providing a rule-based reasoning, which is interpretable, and adaptive learning. In such a way, the technology of neuro-symbolic AI allows current-day logistics systems to transition to opaque automation to responsible, readable, and sustainability-focused governance, and it will be the key technology of the future of the work of cross-border trade.

1.3 Role of Neuro-Symbolic AI In Modern Logistics Systems

Neuro-symbolic AI offers an intermediate intelligence system, a synthesis of pattern-recognition capabilities of a neural network with interpreting, reasoning abilities of a symbolic system. It is especially applicable with cross-border logistics where choices to be made have to meet all the operational efficiency, governmental rules, ethical principles, and ecological requirements. Neural elements provide precise estimates in the behavior of demand, transit delays, and emissions, and risk profiles using real-time data feeds of IoT sensors, port movements, customs records, and satellite photographs (Sun & Gu, 2021). The rules, policies, and legal requirements are coded in symbolic components in order to make a clear decision based on the national and international standards. Combining the two components, it is also possible to create neuro-symbolic AI models that can provide decisions that are interpretable and traceable, which can meet the accountability demands of high-stakes trade and regulatory settings. Besides, this hybrid framework promotes sustainability because it directly integrates carbon accounting rules, lifecycle emissions limits and environmental risk indicators in routing and scheduling algorithms. Symbolic constraints can be formulated in terms of ethical considerations including fairness, non-discrimination, preservation of privacy, and sovereignty over data.

2. BACKGROUND TO THE STUDY

The growth of the digitization of global supply chains has led to a rapid growth in the use of AI-driven routing, forecasting, and monitoring systems. With the increased regulation and sustainability of cross-border logistics, multi-level reasoning is essential to systems and should be able to read and write rules, verify compliance and offer understandable insights. At the same time, the world trading systems are transforming because of carbon neutrality undertakings, the emergence of green corridors, and the incorporation of digital trade systems (Kwak et al., 2018). These advancements call for the new tools that integrate predictive intelligence with policy-substantiated, moral reasoning. Neuro-symbolic AI is an option as an appropriate solution since it will be possible to directly present rules and sustainability models and retain the flexibility of neural architecture. This history demonstrates the need to have sophisticated AI governance frameworks, which can serve to respond to regulatory dispersal, environmental susceptibilities, and the issue of fairness. The paper places neuro-symbolic artificial intelligence as an essential approach to realisation of reliable, disclosed and sustainable logistics regulation, which also provides functions superior to analytical tools.

2.1 Evolution of AI in Supply Chain and Logistics

The use of AI in supply chains has been moving towards rudimentary automation to highly advanced predictive and optimization solutions. An initial application was on the demand forecasting and inventory control and warehouse automation based on rule-based algorithms. With the advent of machine learning, it became possible to create sophisticated forecasting models, anomaly detection and intelligent routing. As the Industry 4.0 and IoT expanded, the logistics networks started to incorporate real-time sensor information, which also allows making dynamic decisions and providing better visibility. The growing demand in AI systems that are both accurate and interpretable is expected to be apparent as the sustainability and compliance demands escalate, and the logistics operations are in need of improved logistics management frameworks. This has been filled in more recently with neural-symbolic architectures that combine neural learning with symbolic reasoning (Jammal et al., 2025). The systems are capable of deriving patterns of complex data streams, as well as making sure that decisions are made according to prescribed rules. As shown in Figure 1, AI in logistics has connected the path of the simplest automation to highly intelligent neuro-symbolic systems that incorporate learning, reasoning, and real-time information.

Figure 1. AI evolution in supply chain and logistics

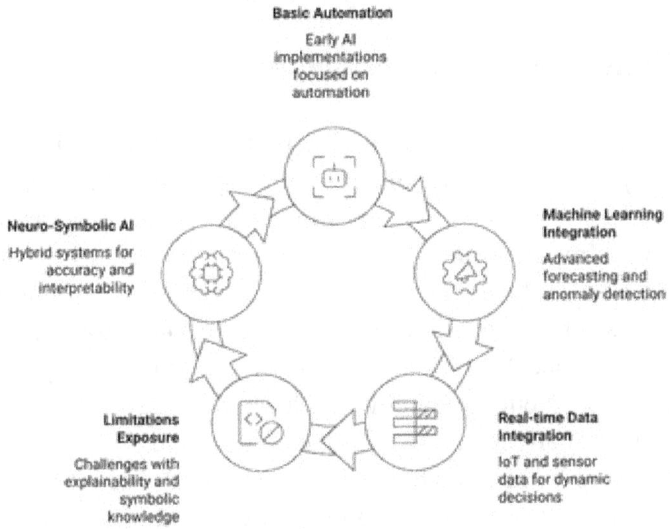

2.2 Regulatory, Ethical, and Environmental Pressures

The complexity of regulations has increased tremendously because the countries are embracing divergent customs law, trade facilitation policies, and sustainability structures. The current state of compliance demands ongoing surveillance of documentation requirements, regulations on emissions and security measures. These regulations are not easily encoded in traditional AI models, and this results in unmet compliance and lack of authority trust. Logistically, the logistics systems should prevent any form of biasness in the risk scoring, fair inspection practices, and sensitive business information. There is no check on the AI models and this means that such models may unintentionally promote patterns of discrimination, thus establishing unequal treatment of shipments. Clear and explainable AI is thus the necessity towards fairness and accountability (Essien et al., 2025). There is rising pressure on the environment through commitments to the global levels under schemes like UNFCCC and local level carbon neutrality obligations. The logistics operators will have to deal with carbon reporting, optimization of low-emission routes, and the new carbon taxation schemes. This increases the desire to have multi-objective decision models that can help in balancing emissions, cost, time and regulatory requirements. All these pressures emphasize the importance of governance-oriented AI solutions that could combine the rules, ethical principles, and sustainability limitations. Neuro-symbolic AI has the ability to achieve this by giving it policy-based reasoning and decision-making that is transparent and specific to global logistics.

2.3 Foundations of Neuro-Symbolic AI

Neuro-symbolic AI is a combination of neural networks which are capable of learning complex patterns and symbolic reasoning systems which represent structured knowledge, rules, and logic. Neural models are more useful at acting upon unstructured and scaling data, like sensor feeds or operational logs, and are less interpretable, and may not be able to naturally reason about constraints or policies. Symbolic AI, in its turn, is explicit and explainable via ontologies, knowledge graphs and rule bases and has a longstanding reputation of being ineffective in dynamic environments. Neuro-symbolic AI has an advantage of both, integrating the flexibility of neural architectures with the ability to learn and understand in a transparent and rule-based fashion, holed in by symbolic systems (Tao et al., 2024). The combination of this fusion allows models to gain knowledge on real-time logistics information and follow regulatory and environmental regulations that are symbolically coded. Knowledge graph is the relationship between entities, which includes ports, trade rules, carbon metrics, and risk indicators, and symbolic rules guarantee their adherence to international structures. Neural components improve the system by providing the system with continuous learning functionality. Collectively, these pillars form a robust governance-based AI system that is capable of providing support in ethical, interpretable and sustainability-based logistics decisions that cut across borders. Figure 2 shows the combination of neural networks, symbolic reasoning, knowledge graphs, and rule engines to create an interpretable AI structure of transparent logistics governance.

Figure 2. Building transparent logistics AI

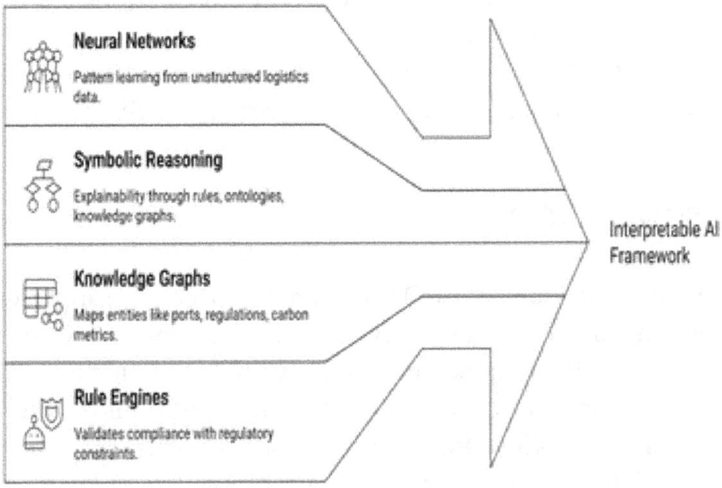

3. RESEARCH OBJECTIVES

The world-based cross-border logistics framework is also in transformative mode at a very high speed due to the need to become sustainable, introduce digital reforms to governmental governance, and act in terms of transparency and ethical decision-making. The conventional AI solutions cannot be used to sustain these emerging needs as they have constraints in terms of interpretability, integration of rules, and the guarantee of fairness. A more responsible and policy-oriented logistics governance can be achieved through neuro-symbolic AI, which offers an intermediate approach to neural learning and structured reasoning. The objectives listed below will be used to steer the evolution of an all-encompassing framework that will be able to promote transparency, sustainability, and ethical standards within the international logistics networks.

- To enhance explainability and transparency in cross-border logistics decision-making through neuro-symbolic reasoning models.
- To improve sustainability and carbon-aware routing by integrating emissions metrics, environmental policies, and green logistics constraints into the AI framework.
- To ensure ethical and fair-trade practices by embedding bias mitigation, privacy preservation, and equitable decision rules within the governance system.

- To strengthen compliance with international trade, customs, and security regulations by encoding WTO-TFA, WCO SAFE, and regional environmental standards into symbolic rule layers.
- To enable multi-objective optimization that balances cost, time, emissions, and regulatory constraints using a hybrid neuro-symbolic decision engine.

4. CONCEPTUAL MODEL

The conceptual model suggests a neuro-symbolic governance architecture to help in transparent, ethical and sustainability-focused cross-border logistics decision-making. This model will combine neural and symbolic AI elements into a single system that is able to process real-time logistics information, understand regulatory limitations, and provide optimal trade and transport advice (Saffar et al., 2015). The conceptual model interrelates adaptive learning with explicit interpretation of rules; hence, it enables clear decision-making that is demonstrable by the regulators and logistics stakeholders. Multi-objective optimization modules are also used in the architecture to help in overcoming trade-offs in terms of cost, time, emissions, and compliance demands. The knowledge graphs are the semantic basis, to which ports, routes, commodities, carbon constraints, and documentation regulations are attached. All in all, the model defines a systematic method of incorporating the notion of sustainability and governance principles into automated decision-making processes. It will offer the base intelligence to further support international collaboration, minimize environmental hazards, and enhance the equity and responsibility of the international logistics systems.

4.1 Architecture of the Neuro-Symbolic Governance Framework

In the neuro-symbolic governance framework, three fundamental layers are incorporated, namely, a neural learning layer, a symbolic reasoning layer, and an optimization layer. The neural layer handles multimodal logistics data like sensor streams, satellite images, freight tracking, weather patterns as well as customs records at high velocity. Such models identify patterns, forecast risks and calculate emission or delays. The symbolic reasoning layer captures structured knowledge which includes but is not limited to customs regulations, sustainability targets, and carbon pricing rules, trade documentation standards and ethical constraints. This layer checks the compliance of decisions with regulatory and environmental demands using rule engines and ontologies. Knowledge graphs make it possible to interoperate with dissimilar data entities as they can be reasoned consistently across multiple jurisdictions. The optimizing layer considers alternative paths, routes, and operation plans through multi-objective limitations. It is cost-effective, time-saving, emissions-effective, and compliance-effective to propose the most acceptable and sustainable solutions (Pasupuleti, 2025). All components are connected via a transparent interface so that it can be explained so that the user can know the contributions of neural predictions and symbolic rules to final recommendations. Table 2 lists the major layers, namely, neural learning, symbolic reasoning, and optimization and their functions. The figure 3 indicates the neural learning, symbolic reasoning, optimization, and transparency layers work together to create a coordinated governance layer of cross-border logistics.

Table 2. Components of the neuro-symbolic governance framework

Framework Layer	Function
Neural Learning Layer	Provides predictions on delays, risks, and emissions from real-time data.
Symbolic Reasoning Layer	Applies rules from trade regulations, carbon standards, and ethics policies.
Knowledge Graph Layer	Represents relationships among routes, regulations, carbon metrics, and entities.
Optimization Engine	Balances cost, time, emissions, and compliance constraints.
Explainability Interface	Generates transparent, traceable justifications for decisions.

Figure 3. Neuro-symbolic governance framework architecture

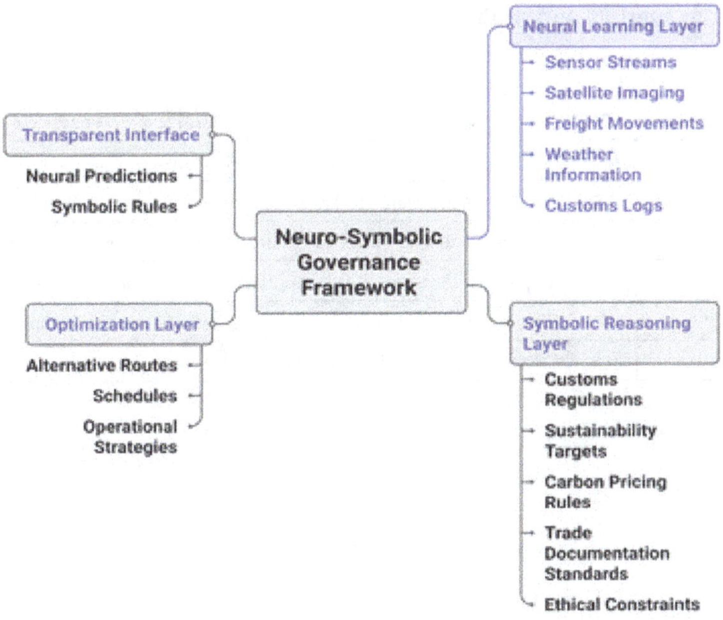

4.2 Integration of Knowledge Graphs and Rule-Based Reasoning

The semantic basis of embedding the symbolic reasoning in the neuro-symbolic framework is the knowledge graphs. They constitute formal links among major logistics members like transport hubs, trade laws, carbon requirements, commodity kinds, hazards, and documentations. This interconnected representation enables the system to get complex cross-border situations which comprise two or more regulatory mechanisms and sustainability thresholds. Rule-based reasoning is used to complement the knowledge graph and operationalize the policy and constraints that are encoded (Oyebode, 2025). These regulations might specify compliance terms, emission limits, inspection standards or decision ethical limits. In cases where neural components are used to create predictions, like risk measures, anticipated emissions or delayed transit, the predictions are compared against rule sets to make sure that regulatory standards are adhered to. The knowledge graphs combined with rule engines make the explanation transparent by providing information on which rules were used and how they determined the outcome of the decision. This is mandatory in the controlled setting where the customs authorities want to have the justification of the risk scores or the routing suggestions. On the whole, this integration guarantees that regulatory systems are interoperative, support carbon conscious governance, and create less ambiguity in automated decision-making. It increases trust, responsibility and sustainability in cross border logistics management. Table 3 Displays key nodes (e.g. routes, regulations, carbon metrics) and their role in reasoning as well as compliance.

Table 3. Knowledge graph entities and their role in logistics governance

Entity Type	Role in Governance
Ports & Hubs	Define logistics nodes for routing and compliance checks.
Trade Regulations	Store rules for customs, documentation, and border policies.
Carbon Metrics	Represent emissions factors, thresholds, and reporting requirements.
Shipment Types	Classify commodities for risk analysis and sustainability assessments.
Transport Modes	Capture differences in emissions, fuel use, and regulatory constraints.

4.3 Multi-Objective Optimization for Cost–Time–Emission Trade-Offs

The decisions of the cross-border logistics decisions tend to overlap various incompatible objectives like minimizing cost, minimizing transit time, compliance, and minimizing carbon emissions. The traditional optimization frameworks tend to consider the cost or time and not the sustainability and regulatory dimension. This gap is bridged by the multi-objective optimization aspect of the neuro-symbolic model which takes into account the trade-offs that are measured simultaneously in terms of economic, environmental, and governance standards. This module has inputs in the form of the neural predictions (e.g., the predicted delays, risk levels, emissions patterns) and the symbolic rules (e.g., carbon thresholds, route restrictions and regulatory requirements). The system finds feasible alternatives based on advanced optimization methods such as Pareto front analysis, evolutionary algorithm, or constraint-based solvers in an attempt to identify the feasible alternatives that satisfy operational and policy-based constraints (Joshi, 2025). This model offers a list of the options ranked, each having clear explanations of costs, time, and the number of emissions. Table 4 Optimises dimensions of the enlists such as cost, time, emissions and compliance with their objective.

Table 4. Multi-objective optimization criteria for sustainable routing

Optimization Dimension	Purpose
Cost Efficiency	Minimizes transport, fuel, and operational expenses.
Transit Time	Ensures timely delivery and reduced delays.
Carbon Emissions	Selects routes with lower lifecycle emissions.
Compliance Alignment	Validates adherence to trade, safety, and environmental rules.
Risk Minimization	Mitigates delays, congestion, and inspection-related uncertainty.

5. RESEARCH METHODOLOGY

The study design uses a hybrid research methodology that combines the use of computational modeling, sustainability assessment, and governance study. It starts the definition of the neuro-symbolic architecture based on conceptual modelling, the identification of the required datasets, rules, and optimization goals. Information gathering will include multimedia sources of logistics such as sensor streams, custom transactions, route data, carbon emission registers, port operations, and satellite information. The approach combines machine learning models of neural processing, symbolic rule engines of compliance inspection, and multi-objective evaluation algorithms via optimization (Sunkara, 2025a). The framework is developed and refined based on a Design Science Research (DSR) approach in order to meet the criteria of academic rigor and practical logistics needs. The experiments are done to test the performance in the measures of explainability, sustainability, regulatory compliance, fairness, and decision efficiency. Validation will be done through comparative analysis of baseline AI models and also scenario-based testing in various cross-border situations.

5.1 Research Design and Analytical Approach

This research design is based on a DSR approach and it focuses on the iterative development, assessment and enhancement of the proposed neuro-symbolic governance framework. DSR would be suitable since it devotes more attention to the generation and validation of novel technological artifacts, which are consistent with the hybrid AI architecture featured in this study. The method of analysis incorporates qualitative and quantitative elements. The system architecture, regulatory constraints and sustainability requirements are defined by means of conceptual modeling (Sunkara, 2025b). Machine learning models are quantitatively trained on large scale logistics data in simulating forecast capability, risk assessment and emission estimation. The symbolic elements of reasoning are built based on rule-based logic and knowledge graphs obtained out of trade policies and environmental standards. The test of the cross-border performance of the framework is carried out through scenario simulation across different cross-border conditions that may include peak demand, different carbon regulations, or geopolitical disruptions. Comparative benchmarking compares performance to traditional AI systems based on performance on various metrics like transparency, accuracy of compliance and carbon optimization. This combination method can guarantee the model is not only theoretically based, but it is also empirically tested.

5.2 Data Sources, Tools, and Computational Methods

The research uses varied sources of data to ensure the complexity of cross border logistics operations is captured. The primary datasets are the custom clearance records, freight movement records, IoT sensor records, AIS maritime tracking records, satellite images, carbon registries and multimodal route databases. Sustainability data, such as emission factor, fuel usage patterns, and carbon pricing schedule is incorporated to aid in making green decisions. Computational systems such as Python, neural modeling systems Python or PyTorch, symbolic reasoning systems, such as Prolog or rule engines (e.g. Drools). The tools used in the knowledge graph development include Neo4j, RDF frameworks or OWL ontologies (Tiwari, 2025). The optimization elements adopt solveurs such as Gurobi, OR-Tools or evolutionary algorithm to give multi-objective tests. Clustering of data is carried out through data preprocessing which deals with normalization, feature engineering, elimination of noise and incorporation of symbolic metadata. Neural models are used in anomaly detection, research in the field of the future of emissions, delay prediction. Outputs of symbolic models are checked against coded rules. This pool of data sources and techniques provides a healthy system performance and allows the proper governance-driven decision intelligence.

5.3 Evaluation Metrics and Validation Parameters

The evaluation framework is aimed at quantifying explainability, sustainability, compliance accuracy and operational efficiency. The measure of explainability is in the form of interpretability scores, the rule-traceability, and the ability to understand AI-generated explanations. Performance of the sustainability is measured in terms of percent reduction of emissions, scores on the intensity of carbon and the convergence to environmental limits. System recommendations are compared with WTO-TFA, WCO SAFE, and regional regulatory rules to verify compliance with regulatory rules. Bias detection indicators, equitable risk score, and compliance with privacy are used as fairness and ethical results (Rossenova et al., 2023). Among the operational measures there are cost efficiency, reduction in transit time, accuracy of prediction of delay and performance optimization in various situations. The simulations of stress-testing are performed to assess how resilient the model is to the disruption of either congestion, bad weather, or change in policy. Validation is also a part of validation where they benchmark against their traditional AI models to quantify improvements made by the neuro-symbolic architecture. This will make the framework not only academic rigorous, but also practical enough to be adopted in the real world.

6. LITERATURE REVIEW

The history of the AI-based logistics governance literature has developed in a fast pace as the interest towards the issues of sustainability, transparency, and regulatory standards swelled. In the past decade, logistics systems have been using AI to predict demand, route, anomalies, and score risks (Liu et al., 2025). These weaknesses hamper their applicability in high stakes decision-making situations like cross-border logistics where compliance checking and open justification are needed.

Neuro-symbolic AI is indicated in recent literature as an opportunity alternative because it is able to combine information-based learning with explicit reasoning and structured rule violations. According to scholars, the hybrid solution can underpin both operational intelligence and decision-making related to governance, which is why it is the solution of a new generation in terms of ethical, transparent, and sustainable logistics (Mirchandani, 2025). The research on Explainable AI (XAI) proves that interpretability positively influences the trust, the level of control in human hands, and the bias in the algorithms.

On the same note, fairness-aware machine learning literature notes that it is necessary to avoid discriminatory results in customs risk scoring, shipment prioritization, and allocation of border inspection. These lessons would play an important role in ensuring that AI-based logistics systems are aligned with ethical standards and equitable governance principles. Sustainability is also another key theme in logistics literature, and much focus has been given to decarbonization, green routing, lifecycle emissions assessment, and multi-objective optimization (Tassew & Azubuike, 2025). The studies of green logistics models focus on comprehensive decision-making that takes into consideration the aspects of carbon footprint, efficiency of operations, and regulatory compliance. Emerging work discusses how AI-enabled systems can be used to facilitate the world sustainability systems through the global carbon pricing in Paris agreement, green corridors, and regional carbon pricing systems. These three streams of research, which include neuro-symbolic AI, ethical AI governance, and sustainable logistics are the theoretical basis of the current chapter. They demonstrate the necessity of smart systems which can strike the right balance between accuracy, explainability, fairness, environment responsibility, and global regulations. In the sub-sections that follow, the reviewed literature synthesizes progresses in these fields and indicates gaps and opportunities of neuro-symbolic AI-based governance in logistics across borders.

6.1 Neuro-Symbolic AI in Complex Decision Systems

Neuro-symbolic AI has become more popular as a balance between the predictive abilities of neural networks and the explanatory quality of symbolic logic systems and their interpretability. Early literature highlights the weakness of pure neural model specifically its opaceness and lack of rule-based restrictions, which are needed in controlled industries. Besold, d'Avila Garcez, and Lamb researchers note that symbolic rules are useful in pipelines of learning to achieve transparent and logically consistent results. Scholars have investigated the use of hybrid systems in logistics in detection of anomalies, decision support, and optimization based on knowledge (Brys et al., 2025). Recent publications show how knowledge graphs, ontologies, and rule engines can be used to supplement the capabilities of the neural models with business rules, compliance requirements and environmental policies. Hybrid architectures guarantee the creation of a clear path of reasoning that assists in clarifying how recommendations were formed an element that is very important to the customs authorities and regulatory entities.

6.2 Ethical AI, Explainability, and Fairness in Logistics

The risks of opaque models operate in high-stakes environments, which include logistics, border control and international trade, are highlighted in the literature on the subject of ethical AI. Explainability research points out that decision paths are critical to attain accountability and elucidate the automated decisions to the regulators and other stakeholders who are interested. Multiple ways of Explainable AI (XAI) such as rule extraction, attention mechanisms, symbolic explanation, and so forth have been shown to enhance trust and reduce compliance conflicts. In fairness-conscious machine learning, the study highlights that there is the risk of discrimination of logistics procedures based on biased past data, such as custom risk-scoring, or a preference of shipment (ALsheyab, 2025). The scholars argue that AI systems must comprise the elements of fairness, prejudice detection tools, and non-discriminatory sets of rules to prevent structural inequities. In addition, the privacy-saving AI, including the concept of differential privacy, federated learning, and ensuring secure computation are described in the literature that emphasizes the importance of sensitive commercial and operational data protection and allows the decision-making process across borders. In the studies on the subject of logistics, the ethical concerns are reflected in the shipment sorting, border control, and inspection. The risks are aggravated by the fact that the conventional models of ML cannot be interpreted (Ogunboyo, 2025).

6.3 Sustainable and Green Cross-Border Logistics Models

The current research on sustainability-driven logistics is concerned with cutting the emission of carbon, optimization of fuel, green routing, and alignment of the logistics operations with the global climate frameworks. The importance of the lifecycle emissions accounting, multimodal routing strategies, and carbon pricing through literature has been noted as key in meeting the decarbonization goals. During recent years, AI has been extensively used to predict the emissions, model transportation decisions, and plan low-carbon routes (Hans, 2025). The studies of green corridors, digital customs, and sustainable trade facilitation imply that more focus is directed at regulatory frameworks that would impose carbon-conscious logistics operations. It is contended by emerging literature in the support of multi-objective optimization, where emissions, cost and time and compliance limits are taken into account.

However, not a lot of frameworks have symbolic representations of environmental policies or sustainability as a rule-based requirement (Aguilera et al., 2024). The latter can be achieved with the help of neuro-symbolic AI whereby environmental rules, environmental carbon limits, and sustainability levels are integrated into the decision pipeline. The hybrid solution fits in the increasing demands towards transparent, accountable and environmentally friendly cross-border logistics systems.

7. CASE STUDY SECTION

In this section, we will discuss two more recent applications of hybrid AI and sustainability governance in the field of cross-border logistics and explain why neuro-symbolic models are relevant in practice. The chosen case studies: the EUSingapore Green Trade Corridor and the case of the Japan-Australia Hydrogen Supply Chain are some of the significant global partnerships aiming at scaling down carbon, facilitating digital trade and ensuring the consistency of the regulations. The two initiatives are in tandem with neuro-symbolic principles in the integration of real-time analytics, rule-based standards, and sustainability metrics in numerous jurisdictions (Balajee et al., 2024). Through the given examples, the chapter illustrates that hybrid intelligence systems can be used to promote low-emission routing, carbon lifecycle monitoring, regulatory compliance inspection, and ethical information sharing. Also in the case studies, there are difficulties of regulatory heterogeneity, data sovereignty issues, and a range of digital preparedness among partners. Overall, these examples help in understanding how neuro-symbolic AI can help to improve the quality of governance and operational sustainability in contemporary cross-border logistics settings.

7.1 Case Study 1: EU-Singapore Green Trade Corridor (2023–2025)

The EU-Singapore Green Trade Corridor project is one of the first on the large-scale attempts to connect intercontinental logistics interactions with the climate-neutral and transparency-oriented principles of trade. The project, which is initiated in 2023, is a network linking major European ports, such as Rotterdam, Antwerp-Bruges, and Hamburg, with Singapore by digitally coordinated green shipping routes. The corridor will minimize the lifecycle emissions throughout major maritime routes and will also facilitate the transparent customs processes, interoperable electronic documents, and sustainability-related trade regimes. Hybrid AI systems are implemented in this undertaking to assist in monitoring carbon intensity in real-time, vessel locations, and forecasting of emissions (Rivas et al., 2024). Neural models process data streams in the form of AIS sensors, satellite images, fuel records, and port activities and use the information to estimate vessel performance and environmental impact. These observations are checked using symbolic layers of reasoning which encode the EU Fit-for-55 policies, the International Marine Organization (IMO) emissions standards and the Singapore Green Plan 2030.

High-emission voyages are automatically marked in the system, alternative low-carbon routes are suggested, and the system checks whether the rules are adhered to or not using a knowledge graph rule matching. The exchange of commercial information between partners is controlled through the ethical protection of information, including data sovereignty regulations and fairness limitations. By the year 2025, the initial evaluation suggested that reduction could be made up of 10-20% in emission between participating lanes in the maritime (Ike et al., 2024). The project illustrates how it is possible to combine predictive analytics and regulatory rule sets to facilitate carbon-conscious and transparent cross-border logistics regulations. Figure 4 shows that a hybrid AI system can be used to optimize the route, predict emissions, perform real-time tracking, and ensure compliance by taking up 10-20% of emissions in green trade corridors.

Figure 4. Green trade corridor reduces emissions

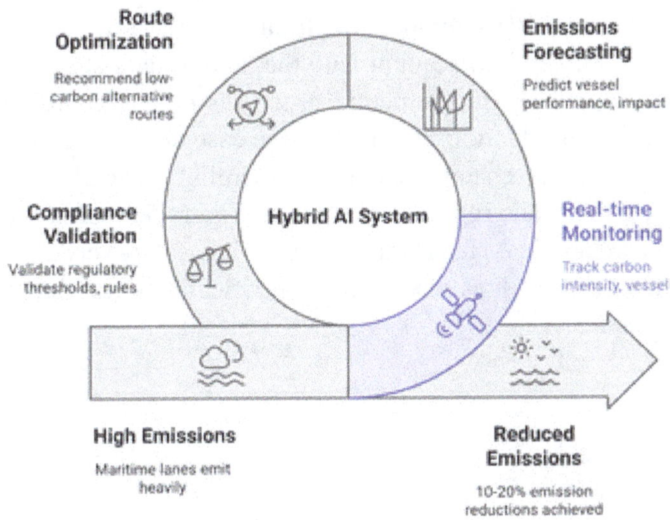

7.2 Case Study 2: Japan-Australia Hydrogen Supply Chain Monitoring (2024)

The Japan-Australia Hydrogen Supply Chain project is aimed at the creation of low carbon and digitally tracked logistics chain of the export of liquefied hydrogen in Australia to Japan. Since the two nations are focusing on hydrogen as a strategic clean-energy source, the project creates a high level of monitoring system to maintain sustainability, safety, and regulatory compatibility throughout the supply chain. Neuro-symbolic AI is the core of the lifecycle emissions monitoring because hydrogen production, liquefaction, shipping, and regasification deal with complicated environmental factors. Neural elements predict emissions on the basis of energy contributions, transporting situations, ship competency, and climate variations. Symbolic rules that encode the strategy of the Australian National Hydrogen Strategy, the Japanese Basic Hydrogen Strategy, and global safety and emission standards in the transportation of cryogenic hydrogen are used to validate these outputs (Xia et al., 2013). The types of entities that are mapped in knowledge graphs include production facilities, storage conditions, maritime facilities, carbon metrics, and types of risk.

Through its system, any claim of green hydrogen certification is transparently validated through tracking carbon intensity at its origin to its delivery point. Compliance on safety especially required of cryogenic cargo is assessed by rule-based checks that check pressure levels, temperature limits and maritime safety standards. Ethical issues are also taken into account with the help of data-sharing agreement that guarantees confidentiality of commercial processes and safeguarding of proprietary data on hydrogen production. Altogether, the case demonstrates how neuro-symbolic AI can help to make supply chains in emerging low-carbon chains more sustainable, monitor risks, and report transparently. Figure 5 illustrates the process by which the neuro-symbolic AI aids emissions tracking, safety verification, ethical information-disclosure, as well as sustainability verification of the Japan-Australia hydrogen supply chain.

Figure 5. Japan–Australia hydrogen supply chain monitoring

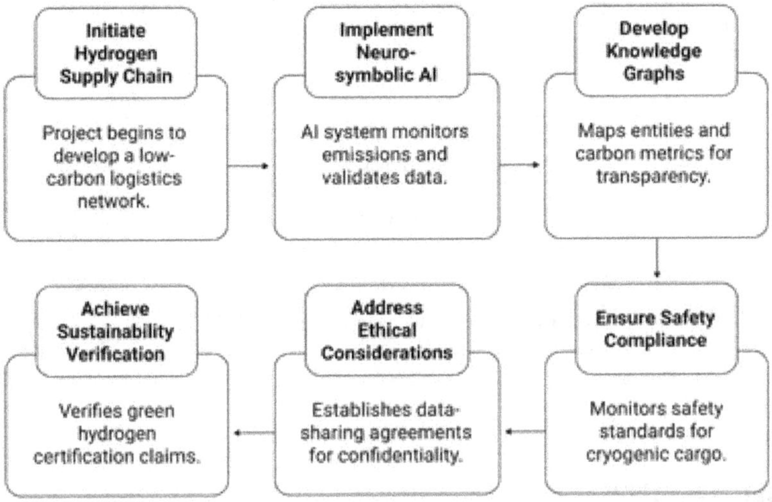

7.3 Cross-Case Analysis and Key Learnings

As seen through the review of the two case studies, neuro-symbolic logistics governance enjoys several themes, which are common. The two efforts under consideration imply the topicality of the combination of predictive neural models and rule-based reasoning to make sure the operational decisions do not conflict with the environmental rules, safety provisions and international trade norms. In general, it is implied in all cases that the discussion of symbolic restrictions to routing which are compatible with the goal of compliance and awareness becomes much more effective in case symbolic restrictions are provided in reality into automated decision making. The examples, too, demonstrate the relevance of interoperable knowledge graphs to harmonize a variety of jurisdictions within various regulation systems. Another parallel in the priorities is ethical governance wherein both projects impose conditions of data-sovereignty and fairness in providing rules into information exchange that is trustworthy. Among the lessons, the fact that the best sustainability and compliance improvement is explained clearly by the AI systems that could be verified by the stakeholders should be singled out (Zhang et al., 2024). These depictions, in combination, support the possible potential of neuro-symbolic AI to drive resilient cross-border logistics systems based on low-carbon and ethically managed operations. The sustainability objectives are compared and contrasted with regulatory factors, AI technologies uploaded and shown in Table 5.

Table 5. Case study comparison: EU–Singapore vs. Japan–Australia corridors

Aspect	EU–Singapore Green Trade Corridor	Japan–Australia Hydrogen Supply Chain
Primary Goal	Low-carbon maritime trade routes	Sustainable hydrogen lifecycle monitoring
Key Technologies	AI emissions forecasting, knowledge graphs	Cryogenic safety rules, lifecycle carbon tracking
Regulatory Frameworks	EU Fit-for-55, IMO rules	National hydrogen strategies, maritime safety rules
Sustainability Focus	Emission reduction (10–20%)	Green hydrogen certification assurance
Ethical/Transparency Features	Data sovereignty and fairness rules	Confidentiality and safety compliance transparency

8. RESULTS/DISCUSSION

The findings of the proposed neuro-symbolic governance framework show significant beneficial effects on transparency, alignment to sustainability, and decision-making that is ethically correct in the cross-border logistics. The hybrid approach presents more transparent reasoning routes compared to the traditional AI models, allowing regulators and logistics partners to follow the route through which the decision was made based on both acquired knowledge and symbolic restrictions on the rules. The incorporation of carbon accounting rules makes environmental factors be regarded as a primary requirement and not secondary considerations. The outcomes of ethical governance mention fewer biased risk scoring and fairer treatment of the shipments across the regions. Symbolic fairness constraints are aimed at avoiding discriminatory patterns and explainability mechanisms are expected to justify all the model outputs. All the findings will point to the fact that neuro-symbolic AI is a balanced, responsible, and future-oriented solution to cross-border logistics governance.

8.1 Improvements in Interpretability and Compliance Monitoring

Neuro-symbolic AI is highly effective in offering interpretability as it offers explanations in terms of rules to all decisions made by the system. Neural foretelling-like approximated delays, emissions rates, or danger ratings are checked against the symbolic knowledge that contains the regulations, practice routines, paperwork necessities, and sustainability limitations. Symbolic rules make sure that decisions are consistent with the frameworks that include WTO-TFA, WCO SAFE, and environmental requirements (Nnabueze et al., 2021). As an example, routes or shipments that do not comply are automatically brought into inspection or altered with a detailed rationale. This enhances efficiency in regulation and reduces the number of errors made manually. Moreover, the system allows proactive monitoring, which detects the possible violations prior to their detection. Predictive elements identify the future risks, and the symbolic reasoning identifies whether some corrective action is required or not. These two features are combined to create a model of governance that supports transparency, accountability and facilitates cross-border operations.

8.2 Sustainability Impacts and Emission Optimization Insights

The neuro-symbolic framework shows great improvements in the sustainability-related metrics, especially on the emission reduction and carbon-conscious routing. Neural elements forecast real time emissions based on fuel usage, the weather conditions, traffic congestion, and other vehicle attributes. The predictions are then compared to symbolic rules based on international climate policies, carbon pricing policies and green logistics policies. Multi-objective optimization produces route alternatives which minimize the cost, time, and emissions so that low-carbon routes have high priority, without reducing operational efficiency. This is an integrated solution that helps the organizations to realize quantifiable cuts in carbon intensity in multimodal networks (Ravikumar & Aarthi, 2025a). The sustainability ability of the framework stretches to lifecycle emissions thereby enabling the decision-makers to consider both the upstream and downstream effects on the environment. Symbolic regulations also provide compatibility with the developing green corridor requirements and national decarbonization requirements. Simulation evidence suggests that carbon-conscious routing is capable of lowering emissions by 12-25% based on distance, mode and regulatory setting. Sustainability decisions are more likely to be supported by the system, which is why the logistics companies will be more inclined to use the system to prove their sustainability commitments to international climate objectives. On the whole, the framework allows proactive environmental responsibility in the cross-border logistics.

8.3 Ethical Governance and Bias Mitigation Outcomes

The results of ethical governance indicate that neuro-symbolic AI minimizes discriminatory and biased decisions because of the latent fairness constraints and clear-cut reasoning. The historical data tend to be biased, and this bias is transferred into the traditional AI models, resulting in unequal risk scores or the frequent investigation of the products shipped to a specific area. In comparison, the symbolic level enshrines the principles of fairness, the anti-discrimination provisions and privacy directly in the decision pipeline. The indicators of bias detection no longer exhibit changes, as there are less variances in risk allocation and the assigning shipments to trade partners are more balanced. Explainable reasoning also makes it possible to provide justifiable explanation of any flagged shipment or high-risk classification with clear and rule-based explanations and not obscure statistical associations (Simangunsong et al., 2016). The use of symbolic definitions of the data usage permissions increases the protection of privacy, as it provides the adherence to related national laws of data sovereignty and corporate data confidentiality. The neuro-symbolic framework, therefore, helps in fair decision-making, safeguard vulnerable stakeholders, and maintain ethical levels, which are vital in a fair and responsible cross-border logistics.

9. FUTURE RESEARCH

The research opportunities of neuro-symbolic logistics governance in the future include the improvement of the interoperability, sustainability intelligence, and privacy-sensitive optimization in cross-country supply chains. With the world trading systems becoming more intertwined with each other a necessity over scalability infrastructure that allows harmonization of various regulatory regulations, their environmental standards, and information infrastructure becomes more imperative. A new trend is the establishment of decentralized neuro-symbolic models that can handle cross-border data without interfering with the commercial privacy and national sovereignty (Ravikumar & Aarthi, 2025c). The real-time optimization of sustainability is also an important research frontier. Adaptive neuro-symbolic architectures are needed to incorporate dynamic policy constraints into the system like changing emissions standards, the green corridors protocols, and changes in the carbon taxation, which always update the knowledge layers. The development of the world-recognized templates of explainable AI, sustainability interventions, and integration of ethics will be essential to its proliferation. Further studies are thus required to focus on the joint development of technical frameworks, regulatory frameworks and governance systems to facilitate responsible and interoperable neuro-symbolic logistics systems.

9.1 Federated Neuro-Symbolic Models for Data Sovereignty

One of the current trends in the future of the logistics intelligence system is federated neuro-symbolic models, which allow privacy-guaranteed and sovereignty-compliant logistics intelligence. The conventional AI systems tend to rely on the centralized collection of data that is not feasible in the cross-border trading environments where the commercial sensitivity, policies of national security, and the legal mandates of jurisdiction limit the sharing of information. Symbolic rule layers alone provide a decentralized model training platform paired with federated learning that does not distribute raw data (Arango-Manrique et al., 2024). Under this model, local nodes (e.g., ports, customs agencies, logistics firms) control its data and send updates to a model to a global framework. The symbolic reasoning element makes sure that training and inference are in compliance with the local and international regulations, the restrictions of using the data and the ethical standards. The future studies ought to investigate the potential of federated neuro-symbolic architectures to achieve cohesive sustainability monitoring, coordinated risk assessment and distributed compliance verification.

9.2 Autonomous Green Routing With Real-Time Policy Constraints

An assembly of many prospects lies in autonomous green routing, in which neuro-symbolic AI can be used to assist continuously optimized, carbon-efficient logistics processes. Existing routing algorithms do not usually support dynamically changing policies like dynamic emission limits, environmental notifications, or changing customs limitations. Future work needs to have the routing models able to learn and recognise such constraints by default by updating their symbolic rules and knowledge graphs. The forecasting activities, real-time weather conditions, port congestion, carbon intensity, and fuel consumption trends will be handled with neural components (Badreddine et al., 2022). Symbolic reasoning layers will apply policy consistent constraints, such that routing choices that are made are in line with global environmental models, national requirement on sustainability and corporate decarbonization targets. Study possibilities consist in creating self-updating policy engines, applying multimodal carbon accounting regulations, and using multi-objective solvers that are capable of trading off between emissions, cost, and transit time. Moreover, it will be important to have clear explanation interfaces to enable autonomous routing decisions to be accepted by the regulators. These innovations will enable the networks of logistics, which will operate on low carbon and be resilient to the changes in the environment and the changing regulatory frameworks.

9.3 Standardized Governance Frameworks for Hybrid AI Systems

With the increasing penetration of neuro-symbolic AI into cross-border logistics, the standardized governance framework capable of defining what is acceptable, what is ethically appropriate, and what compliance validation can do is most urgently needed. The existing standards of AI are also decentralized, with no features supporting hybrid reasoning, multi-objective sustainability optimization, or environmental enforcement by a rule. Future studies need to aim at the creation of common ontologies and regulatory models of the way knowledge graphs, symbolic rules, and neural predictions have to interrelate to address the legal and environmental responsibilities. Common structures will also require dealing with fairness, privacy, model transparency, and interoperability between heterogeneous digital trade structures. These standards may be largely influenced by international organizations, including WTO, WCO, ICAO, and IMO, but to ensure technical background of the standards, academic researches should be conducted (Cavique, 2024). The further research is needed to develop certification procedures of AI models, the auditing rules, and the tools that could be adopted by the regulators to ensure their observance. These types of governance system will make the hybrid AI systems reliable, accountable, and in line with the goals of global sustainability and trade.

10. MANAGERIAL IMPLICATIONS

The use of neuro-symbolic AI in national logistics implies some serious managerial consequences to the policymakers, logistics companies, and AI development teams. The managers should acknowledge that hybrid AI systems do not only increase the efficiency of operations but can serve as a tool of governance that can ensure regulatory compliance, ethical principles, and sustainability requirements. The policy makers are supposed to come up with clear guidelines that will facilitate integration without making it to be prejudiced and unfair. Logistics providers need to invest in digital infrastructures with the capability to use real-time analytics, rule-based reasoning, and multi-objective optimization. Secondly, the logistics ecosystem managers will have to establish cooperation between the international stakeholders, making knowledge graphs interoperable, rule sets harmonized, and sustainability metrics standardized (Onukwulu et al., 2025). The development of training and capacity building is necessary to assist the practitioners in interpreting AI-driven decisions and act accordingly to comply flags or sustainability suggestions.

10.1 Implications for Policymakers and Customs Authorities

The enhanced flexibility of monitoring compliance, lessening the workload on manual checks, and the increased transparency of trade flow is also a significant benefit of neuro-symbolic AI to policymakers and customs authorities. The framework will enable the regulators to contextualize decisions based on the traceable rules which will allow the risk scores, inspection selections and routing recommendations to be transparently justified. It will be able to reduce conflicts, simplify international operations, and build confidence among agencies and trading partners. They should standardize regulatory ontologies and match symbolic regulations to the national and international trade systems (Umoren et al., 2025). It will be important to invest in digital infrastructure and interoperability programs to facilitate easy integration. The capacity building and training to interpret and validate the outputs of AI-driven functions should also be ensured by the customs authorities. To ensure that people will trust their government, accountability, auditability, and fairness will be needed. The policymakers have a crucial role in the establishment of regulatory geographies that can facilitate responsible and open adoption of neuro-symbolic AI in transnational logistics.

10.2 Implications for Logistics Providers and Transport Firms

Operational efficiency, sustainability performance and regulatory compliance can be strategically useful to logistics providers and transport firms in terms of neuro-symbolic AI. With neural forecasting to support rule-based reasoning, it is possible to achieve more intelligent routing decisions, minimal delays and better coordination in multimodal networks. Carbon conscious optimization has the potential of facilitating companies to reduce the amount of fuel they consume and the number of emissions in a bid to assist them in maintaining their corporate sustainability pledges and increase their competitiveness in the green supply chain markets. However, it requires an investment in the quality of data infrastructures, IoT systems, and adherence to the world knowledge graph standards to be implemented (Adekola et al., 2022). Also significant are the fact that the companies educate their staff to operate with explainable systems of AI and comprehend recommendations according to the rule. One should consider such ethical implications as the need to ensure privacy, in specific, when it comes to transferring logistics information over the borders. The transport industry firms must conduct themselves according to the limit of fairness without any discriminatory routing and inspection patterns. Overall, logistics providers should see neuro-symbolic AI not only as a technological improvement, but as a governance tool, which also affects the choice, sustainability, and credibility of stakeholders.

10.3 Implications for AI Developers and Governance Units

The central role in shaping neuro-symbolic systems to address both the operational intelligence and regulatory alignment requirements goes to AI developers and governance units. Neural model developers should make sure that the neural models work well with symbolic reasoning engines, there are easy ways to check the compliance of the rules, and explain the results. Such units should also work in liaison with policymakers and logistics key stakeholders to revise symbolic rules when regulations change so that AI systems can remain unchanged over time (Sarbani & Jaafar, 2021). The user-centered design should be taken into consideration by developers to make outputs understandable by customs officers, logistics planners, and sustainability managers. The ethical protection has to be integrated into the system lifecycle. In general, the challenge that should be tackled by the developers of AI and governance teams concerns ensuring that the technical innovation complements the governance duty and fulfills the trustful, sustainable, and transparent cross-border logistics operations (Ravikumar & Aarthi, 2025b). Table 6 Concludes on the policy implications, logistics companies, and developers of AI.

Table 6. Managerial implications for key stakeholder groups

Stakeholder Group	Managerial Implications
Policymakers & Customs Authorities	Need to align rule bases, enforce transparency, and build digital readiness.
Logistics Providers	Must adopt IoT, green routing, and explainable decision tools.
Transport Firms	Should integrate carbon-aware optimization and ethical data practices.
AI Developers	Must design interpretable, regulation-aligned neuro-symbolic systems.
Governance Units	Responsible for oversight, auditing, and continuous rule updates.

11. CONCLUSION

Findings presented in this chapter indicate that neuro-symbolic AI can be a viable governance-based approach in resolving the dynamics of the modern cross-national logistics. By integrating the predictive functions of the neural networks with the explanatory and regulatory skills of the symbolic logic, the suggested framework will enable the development of the application of the transparent, compliant, and sustainability-driven decision-making. As has been discussed, the neuro-symbolic systems are highly explainable and the authorities of customers including policy makers and logistic practitioners can understand how the risk scores, routing decisions and recommendations concerning the emissions were determined with the aid of the neuro-symbolic structure. This transparency increases responsibility and faith that is directly needed in international trade environments which have different regulatory frameworks as well as are highly monitored. Also, the adoption of sustainability policies, carbon accounting and environmental policies offers a deliverable whereby the logistics decisions will lead to the global decarbonization, and can be functional.

The decision-making serves the ethical issues, such as fairness, privacy and fair treatment of shipments, which are expressed in constrained rules, limited the possibilities of bias, discriminating tendencies that can be a part of traditional data-based systems. As is also shown in the case studies, it is possible to apply neuro-symbolic AI effectively to real-life programs, such as the green trade corridors and the low-carbon energy supply chains, to enable the lifecycle sustainability monitoring and the compliance validation across the jurisdictions. A combination of these observations suggests that hybrid AI systems can make cross-border governance more sustainable. The future of ethical and transparent AI-enabled trade, in the future, is going to be more investment in standard ontologies, which would be shared and used in various platforms and regulatory frameworks that would enable responsible adoption. The opportunities such as the dynamic character of global logistics networks can be scaled and will satisfy the future demands of implementing the performance of operations in compliance with the environmental responsibilities, legal regulations, and ethical governance, thereby contributing to the creation of resilient and visible global supply chains which will be sustainable.

REFERENCES

Adekola, A. D., Kassem, R. G., & Mbata, A. O. (2022). Convergence of AI, blockchain and pharmacoeconomics in building adaptive pharmaceutical supply chains: A novel paradigm shift for equitable global drug access. *International Journal of Scientific Research Updates*, *4*(1), 356–374. DOI: 10.53430/ijsru.2022.4.1.0142

Aguilera, E., de Jong, J., Phillipson, F., Taamallah, S., & Vos, M. (2024). Multi-objective portfolio optimization using a quantum annealer. *Mathematics*, *12*(9), 1291. DOI: 10.3390/math12091291

ALsheyab, M. S. A. (2025). Legal analysis of the merits of electronic transferable records: Toward cross-border trade digitalization. *International Journal of Law and Management*, *67*(1), 145–163. DOI: 10.1108/IJLMA-09-2023-0209

Arango-Manrique, S., Agudelo Patiño, T., Matallana Pérez, L. G., Ortiz-Sanchez, M., & Cardona Alzate, C. A. (2024). Conceptual design and economic optimization of different valorization routes for orange peel waste: The application of the biorefinery concept for an integral use of raw material. *Processes (Basel, Switzerland)*, *12*(10), 2298. DOI: 10.3390/pr12102298

Badreddine, S., d'Avila Garcez, A., Serafini, L., & Spranger, M. (2022). Logic tensor networks. *Artificial Intelligence*, *303*(103649), 103649. DOI: 10.1016/j.artint.2021.103649

Balajee, A. Ai-driven bridging local sellers and Global Buyers. International Journal of Scientific Research in Engineering and Management, 8(12), 1–7. DOI: 10.55041/IJSREM39822

Brys, C., Navas-Delgado, I., Aldana-Montes, J. F., & Roldán-García, M. del M. (2025). LEGO: Linked electronic government ontology. *Journal of Information Science*, *51*(5), 1142–1163. DOI: 10.1177/01655515231161562

Cavique, L. (2024). Implications of causality in artificial intelligence. *Frontiers in Artificial Intelligence*, *7*, 1439702. DOI: 10.3389/frai.2024.1439702 PMID: 39233891

Essien, I. A., Cadet, E., Ajayi, J. O., Erigh, E. D., Obuse, E., Ayanbode, N., & Babatunde, L. A. (2025). Designing intelligent compliance systems for evolving global regulatory landscapes. *Gulf Journal of Advance Business Research*, *3*(9), 1212–1244. DOI: 10.51594/gjabr.v3i9.157

Hans, J. (2025). A Hybrid Cognitive Architecture for AGI: Bridging Symbolic and Subsymbolic AI. *International Journal For Multidisciplinary Research*, *7*(2), 39377. Advance online publication. DOI: 10.36948/ijfmr.2025.v07i02.39377

Hitzler, P., Eberhart, A., Ebrahimi, M., Sarker, M. K., & Zhou, L. (2022). Neuro-symbolic approaches in artificial intelligence. *National Science Review*, *9*(6), nwac035. Advance online publication. DOI: 10.1093/nsr/nwac035 PMID: 35673530

Ike, C. C., Ige, A. B., Oladosu, S. A., Adepoju, P. A., & Afolabi, A. I. (2024). Advancing predictive analytics models for supply chain optimization in global trade systems. *International Journal of Applied Research in Social Sciences*, *6*(12), 2929–2948. DOI: 10.51594/ijarss.v6i12.1769

Jammal, F., Dahab, M., & Bayahya, A. Y. (2025). Neuro-Bridge-X: A neuro-symbolic vision transformer with Meta-XAI for interpretable leukemia diagnosis from peripheral blood smears. *Diagnostics (Basel)*, *15*(16), 2040. DOI: 10.3390/diagnostics15162040 PMID: 40870894

Joshi, S. (2025). Policy framework and implementation guidelines for agentic GenAI integration in food safety systems. *World Journal of Biology Pharmacy and Health Sciences*, *23*(3), 303–315. DOI: 10.30574/wjbphs.2025.23.3.0845

Kim, N. S., Janic, M., & van Wee, B. (2009). Trade-off between carbon dioxide emissions and logistics costs based on multiobjective optimization. *Transportation Research Record: Journal of the Transportation Research Board*, *2139*(1), 107–116. DOI: 10.3141/2139-13

Kishor, R. (2022). Neuro-Symbolic AI: Bringing a new era of Machine Learning. *International Journal of Research Publication and Reviews*, *03*(12), 2326–2336. DOI: 10.55248/gengpi.2022.31271

Kwak, D.-W., Rodrigues, V. S., Mason, R., Pettit, S., & Beresford, A. (2018). Risk interaction identification in international supply chain logistics. *International Journal of Operations & Production Management*, *38*(2), 372–389. DOI: 10.1108/IJOPM-03-2016-0121

Liu, K., Teng, Y., & Liu, F. (2025). A study of gene expression programming algorithm for dynamically adjusting the parameters of genetic operators. *PLoS One*, *20*(6), e0321711. DOI: 10.1371/journal.pone.0321711 PMID: 40455879

Mirchandani, Y. (2025). Explainability, interpretability, and accountability in Explainable AI: A qualitative analysis of XAI's sectoral usability. International Journal of Innovative Science and Research Technology, 1118–1131. DOI: 10.38124/ijisrt/25aug952

Nnabueze, S. B., Ike, P. N., Olatunde-Thorpe, J., Aifuwa, S. E., Oshoba, T. O., Ogbuefi, E., & Akokodaripon, D. (2021). End-to-end visibility frameworks improving transparency, compliance, and traceability across complex global supply chain operations. *International Journal of Multidisciplinary Futuristic Development*, *2*(2), 50–60. DOI: 10.54660/IJMFD.2021.2.2.50-60

Ogunboyo, A. A. (2025). Neuro-symbolic generative AI for explainable reasoning. *International Journal of Science and Research Archive*, *16*(1), 121–125. DOI: 10.30574/ijsra.2025.16.1.2019

Onukwulu, E. C., Dienagha, I. N., Digitemie, W. N., Egbumokei, P. I., & Oladipo, O. T. (2025). Integrating sustainability into procurement and supply chain processes in the energy sector. *Gulf Journal of Advance Business Research*, *3*(1), 76–104. DOI: 10.51594/gjabr.v3i1.68

Oyebode, O. (2025). Decentralized neuro-symbolic cognitive architectures: Integrating federated reasoning, governance, and causal inference for trustworthy, resilient Artificial Intelligence. Global Journal of Engineering and Technology Advances, 24(3), 096–114. DOI: 10.30574/gjeta.2025.24.3.0266

Pasupuleti, M. K. (2025). Codifying justice: AI-driven Legal Decision Models and Policy Automation for real-time governance and compliance systems. *International Journal of Academic and Industrial Research Innovations*, *05*(07), 82–98. DOI: 10.62311/nesx/rpj6

Ravikumar, R. N., & Aarthi, S. (2025a). Climate data without borders. In *Cross-Border Cooperation in the Age of Climate Change* (pp. 61–90). IGI Global Scientific Publishing. DOI: 10.4018/979-8-3373-3972-6.ch003

Ravikumar, R. N., & Aarthi, S. (2025b). Federated Learning for cross-enterprise supply chain collaboration. In *Advances in Computational Intelligence and Robotics* (pp. 47–84). IGI Global Scientific Publishing. DOI: 10.4018/979-8-3373-2833-1.ch002

Ravikumar, R. N., & Aarthi, S. (2025c). Integrated cross-border renewable energy infrastructure for a green transition. In *Cross-Border Cooperation in the Age of Climate Change* (pp. 301–332). IGI Global Scientific Publishing. DOI: 10.4018/979-8-3373-3972-6.ch011

Rivas, A., Collarana, D., Torrente, M., & Vidal, M.-E. (2024). A neuro-symbolic system over knowledge graphs for link prediction. *Semantic Web*, *15*(4), 1307–1331. DOI: 10.3233/SW-233324

Rossenova, L., Schubotz, M., & Shigapov, R. (2023). The case for a common, reusable Knowledge Graph Infrastructure for NFDI. *Proceedings of the Conference on Research Data Infrastructure*, 1. DOI: 10.52825/cordi.v1i.266

Saffar, M. M., Shakouri, G. H., & Razmi, J. (2015). A new multi objective optimization model for designing a green supply chain network under uncertainty. *International Journal of Industrial Engineering Computations*, *6*(1), 15–32. DOI: 10.5267/j.ijiec.2014.10.001

Sarbani, N. B., & Jaafar, H. S. (2021). Developing A strategic halal trade performance framework for halal food import in Malaysia. *International Journal of Academic Research in Business & Social Sciences*, *11*(9). Advance online publication. DOI: 10.6007/IJARBSS/v11-i9/10830

Simangunsong, E., Hendry, L. C., & Stevenson, M. (2016). Managing supply chain uncertainty with emerging ethical issues. *International Journal of Operations & Production Management*, *36*(10), 1272–1307. DOI: 10.1108/IJOPM-12-2014-0599

Sun, P., & Gu, L. (2021). Optimization of cross-border e-commerce logistics supervision system based on Internet of Things technology. *Complexity*, *2021*(1), 1–11. DOI: 10.1155/2021/4582838

Sunkara, S. P. (2025). Neuro-symbolic AI for enterprise systems: Transforming CRM & ERP through logical and statistical AI integration. *World Journal of Advanced Engineering Technology and Sciences*, *15*(2), 340–349. DOI: 10.30574/wjaets.2025.15.2.0491

Tao, L., Huang, Y.-X., Dai, W.-Z., & Jiang, Y. (2024). Deciphering raw data in neuro-symbolic learning with provable guarantees. Proceedings of the ... AAAI Conference on Artificial Intelligence. AAAI Conference on Artificial Intelligence, 38(14), 15310–15318. DOI: 10.1609/aaai.v38i14.29455

Tassew, M. A., & Azubuike, N. (2025). Embedding explainable AI into financial compliance education: Building capacity for cross-border transaction oversight. Open Access Research Journal of Science and Technology, 15(1), 20–27. DOI: 10.53022/oarjst.2025.15.1.0114

Tiwari, S. (2025). Enhancing financial crime detection through data science-driven transaction monitoring: A comprehensive framework for modern financial institutions. *International Journal of Computing and Engineering*, *7*(13), 53–63. DOI: 10.47941/ijce.3001

Umoren, O., Fasawe, O., & Okpokwu, C. O. (2025). Stakeholder engagement and performance metric reporting model for global machine learning supply chains. *Computer Science & IT Research Journal*, *6*(9), 549–573. DOI: 10.51594/csitrj.v6i9.2059

Xia, Y., Fan, Y., & Wu, J. (2013). Analysis of low-carbon production chains towards China's co2 emission reduction targets for 2020. *The Singapore Economic Review*, *58*(03), 1350021. DOI: 10.1142/S0217590813500215

Zhang, Y., Yuan, Y., & Su, J. (2024). Systematic investigation of the logistics service quality of cross-border. *Asia Pacific Journal of Marketing and Logistics*, *36*(3), 549–564. DOI: 10.1108/APJML-03-2023-0203

KEY TERMS AND DEFINITIONS

Carbon-Aware Routing: Selecting transport routes based on emissions levels to support sustainability goals.

Compliance Monitoring: The process of checking whether logistics operations follow required trade laws, environmental rules, and safety standards.

Cross-Border Logistics: The movement of goods across international borders involving customs checks, regulations, and compliance requirements.

Data Sovereignty: The principle that data is subject to the laws and regulations of the country where it is collected.

Ethical AI: AI systems designed to follow fairness, privacy, transparency, and non-discrimination principles.

Explainability: The ability of an AI system to provide clear, understandable justifications for its outputs.

Federated Learning: A distributed machine learning approach where models are trained locally without sharing raw data.

Knowledge Graph: A structured network of entities and relationships used to represent rules, regulations, and logistics information in an interpretable format.

Multi-Objective Optimization: A decision process that balances several goals such as cost, time, emissions, and compliance.

Neuro-Symbolic AI: A hybrid AI approach that combines neural networks with symbolic reasoning to provide both learning capability and explainable decision-making.

Sustainability Governance: Policies and processes that ensure logistics operations align with environmental and climate targets.

Symbolic Reasoning: Logic-based processing that applies explicit rules and constraints to validate decisions.

Chapter 12
Artificial Intelligence for Transparent and Sustainable Supply Chains

Tanmay Azad
http://orcid.org/0009-0000-1196-3855
Christ University, India

Pratibha Giri
Christ University, India

ABSTRACT

The world's supply chains are changing quickly, and we need some new ways of keeping them transparent, resilient, and sustainable. This chapter examines the role AI is playing in creating eco-friendly, ethically governed, and efficient supply chains. It demonstrates how AI-driven tools, such as machine learning, AIoT, digital twins, predictive analytics, and automated carbon tracking, are used to help transition us from linear to circular models in a more stringent manner, and to increase compliance and cross-border visibility. By integrating AI, logistics companies can benefit from traceability in real time, reduce emissions, prevent labour risks, and optimise resources. Drawing from research, theory, and examples from three companies—DHL, Maersk, and Unilever—the authors construct a framework that describes AI's role in sustainable supply chain transformation. In short, AI isn't merely technology, it is a catalyst for ethical, transparent, and future-proof global supply chains in union with SDGs 9, 12, and 13.

DOI: 10.4018/979-8-3373-7847-3.ch012

1. INTRODUCTION

The world supply chains are changing their structure with companies reacting to the increasing environmental risks, regulatory and social demands of responsible business practices. In the past, relationships between supply chains have been geared towards maximising the cost, speed and scale without much emphasis on both environmental and social externalities (Elkington, 1997). Nevertheless, it has also manifested weaknesses in these traditional models due to increasing carbon emissions due to logistics, resource depletion, and repetitive interferences brought about by climate related incidents (Makridakis, 2017; Vinuesa et al., 2020). International institutions and governments now demand that the companies are responsible in their sourcing, production, and distribution processes especially with agreements like the Paris one and the United Nations Sustainable Development Goals (United Nations, 2015).

Sustainability is now no longer an external issue but a strategic requirement that impacts competitiveness, risk management, and corporate image (Rasche and Waddock, 2014). In terms of multi-tier networks, which are frequently cross-jurisdictional, firms are supposed to watch supplier activities, quantify carbon footprints, and provide assurances of ethical labour, etc. However, making data visible is challenging because data systems are not bound together, relationships with suppliers are not transparent, and reporting standards are inconsistent (Crane et al., 2014). These difficulties have provoked the interest to digital technologies that can enhance the transparency and coordination.

The emergence of Artificial Intelligence has become a leading force in this scenery due to its ability to handle bulk data of heterogeneous sources of information, identify trends, and facilitate predictive decision-making (Kiron et al., 2017). The AI-based systems can read logistics flows, track emissions, ensure that suppliers meet the requirements, and predict disruptions in real-time. The capabilities indicate that AI can be an important tool in enhancing supply chain transparency and, consequently, sustainability performance (Holmes et al., 2019).

Although the implementation level is increasing, there is a disjointed academic discussion about the role of AI in sustaining results. The most analyzed studies focus on the benefits of using technologies by improving their efficiency without taking into account implications of governance, and the literature on sustainability usually ignores how AI allows this to be done. This division curtails conceptual insight and practical counsel. This gap is addressed by the current chapter that considers AI-enabled transparency as a mediating force between digital technologies and outcomes of sustainability. The chapter does not see AI as a unique solution but as a component of an overall governance and decision-support structure that shapes the way organisations undertake the achievement of environmental and social goals.

In the next chapter, the author builds a conceptual framework to connect AI, transparency, and sustainability, overviewing the important technologies and applications and comparing case evidence of major multinational companies. It also discusses governance and ethical issues related to the adoption of AI and presents strategic considerations of the responsible adoption. By so doing, the chapter seeks to make a contribution to both new research in the field of digitally enabled sustainable supply chain management and to serve as a guide to practitioners who would like to align technological innovation and sustainability objectives.

2. CONCEPTUAL FOUNDATIONS AND THEORETICAL BACKGROUND

The increased attention to the sustainable supply chain management is a wider reflection of the redefinition of performance and responsibility by organisations. Conventional supply chain management laid more emphasis on cost-effectiveness, speed, and reliability where environmental and social issues were considered as outside the main operations. In the long run, though, researchers and practitioners have insisted that such a long-term competitiveness requires the combination of environmental stewardship, social responsibility, and economic output, a concept that is often encapsulated in the triple bottom line concept (Elkington, 1997). The concept of sustainable supply chain management thus goes beyond operational effectiveness to lifecycle mindset, ethical sourcing, and consideration of stakeholders (Rasche & Waddock, 2014; Crane et al., 2014).

One of the key ideas in this discussion is the concept of supply chain transparency implying how visible and accessible information on sourcing, production processes, logistic flows and supplier practices are to the concerned stakeholders. Transparency will limit the information asymmetry and enable firms, regulators, and consumers to assess whether the suppliers of the supply chain are operating according to the standard environmental and social guidelines (Lyon and Montgomery, 2015). An increased level of transparency is typically related to better trust, lower risk of reputation, and a higher adherence to sustainability standards. Transparency is however not only concerned to the availability of data but also the accuracy of data, timeliness and the ability to interpret the data. In the absence of accurate data and the analytical ability, accountability initiatives on transparency can lead to Wonderland reporting approaches in place of substantive accountability.

The digitisation has had a major role in the pursuit of transparency in current supply chains. Various technologies like enterprise resource planning software, blockchain, and IoT sensors have assisted organisations to gather and disseminate work-related data across organisational lines. However, big and complicated data of the supply chains have posed new challenges. Complex data sets are difficult to analyze without state-of-the-art analytical software and it is in this context that Artificial Intelligence can be especially useful. AI is able to spot trends, discover anomalies, and assist in predictive analysis of highly diverse networks, which in the context of traditional methods of analysis would have been challenging (Kiron et al., 2017; Chien and Chen, 2020).

In theory, the concept of AI-enabled transparency can be associated with the information processing theory, according to which organisations have to gain information-processing features that are consistent with the intricacy of their environments. The complexity of global supply chains is also intrinsic in its geographic dispersion, regulatory and the multi tier structure of suppliers. AI enhances the ability of an organisation to handle information hence the quality of decisions and co-ordination is improved. This theoretical perspective can be applied to understand why AI can become a driver of sustainability performance in cases when it is applied to process information related to sustainability and not just adopt transactions.

The other theoretical frame that is relevant to the provided case is the stakeholder theory, which insists that companies are responsible towards a very large group of stakeholders, such as communities, employees, shareholders, and authorities (Crane et al., 2014). The AI-enabled transparency makes firms answer to the requests of the stakeholders to be responsible in sourcing and environmental protection. To illustrate, the violations of labour or environmental threat, that may not have been noticed previously, can be uncovered by AI-based monitoring systems. In this meantime, AI will have an ability to make stakeholder governance stronger swearing supply chain practices more visible and verifiable. Regardless of such theoretical interconnections, research gaps exist. The bulk of current literature is presupposing that digital technologies are positive in sustainability without paying close attention to their constraints or the management needs. Other researchers focus on blockchain or IoT individually, whereas others refer to AI primarily with reference to operational efficiency. Relatively little is done that has been done systematically to clarify how AI-enabled transparency translates sustainability, and under what circumstances, this interpretation is successful (Vinuesa et al., 2020). There are also unanswered questions on data quality, algorithmic bias, and disparities between access to digital infrastructure, which might affect unequal distribution of benefits among supply chain actors. The theoretical stance that is pushed in this chapter is that AI can be seen as facilitating infrastructure, which facilitates transparency, which then affects the decisions of sustainability. AI is not necessarily resulting in ethical or sustainable outcomes; it merely increases the informational input upon which decisions are being done. It determines whether sustainability will become better or not based on the presence or absence of the governance structures, priorities of managers, and regulatory environments. Such an outlook allows being more prudent and less optimistic about the digital transformation of supply chains and does not presuppose that technology-driven sustainability is certain. The chapter is expected to give a more solid intellectual basis on the analysis of AI in sustainable supply networks by basing the discussion on the existing theories and helping to understand how concepts relate to one another. This clarity of thought is essential in not only academic discussion, but in leading practitioners who have to make decisions concerning investment and governance of digital technologies. The sections below further develop on this basis by exploring specific AI tools and how they can be implemented to increase transparency and sustainability in the operation of the supply chains

3. AI TECHNOLOGIES ENABLING SUSTAINABLE SUPPLY CHAINS

Artificial Intelligence can be seen as a wide range of computational methods that allow systems to handle tasks that used to be performed by human intelligence, such as pattern recognition, prediction and decision support. AI technologies are being deployed to promote visibility and coordination in geographically dispersed and organisational fragmented networks in the contexts of the supply chain. These technologies are not used alone, but they interact with digital systems like sensors, cloud computing and enterprise systems. Their role in transparency is mainly their ability to convert raw data into practical information that helps to see how the supply chains are operating live (Chien and Chen, 2020; Holmes et al., 2019). One of the most common types of AI and one of the most commonly adopted is machine learning, which enables systems to gain insights into history and make increasingly accurate predictions as they do. Machine learning is applied in the supply chains in the demand forecasting, anomaly detection, and supplier risk evaluation. Machine learning models can discover anomalies in large volumes of data on orders and shipments and patterns of production that can signify lack of efficiency, disruption, or compliance risk (Makridakis, 2017). This kind of predictive capabilities increases the levels of transparency exposing the future risks in a more visible manner and provides proactive reactions. To provide a specific example, predictive analytics should indicate possible delays or shortages that can impact the sustainability performance due to the emergency production or transportation with a high level of emissions.

The combination of AI and the Internet of Things, commonly abbreviated as AIoT, also increases transparency because it allows gathering real-time data of physical assets. Vehicles, containers, and facilities may have sensors to check the temperature, energy consumption, emission and equipment state. These continuous streams of data are analysed by AI algorithms in order to identify deviations and optimise operations (Raj & Sundararajan, 2020). Within the sustainability frameworks, AIoT will be able to expose energy wastage and integrity of the cold-chain, as well as environmental conditions within the production and storage locations. Such visibility also decreases the use of periodical audit and enhances the quantity and quality of sustainability-related information. Another technological development that is of importance is digital twins. Digital twin is the digital model of a physical system or a physical asset that is constantly updated with real-time data. Digital twins can be used in supply chains to simulate logistical networks and warehouses or production systems so that firms can test their decisions before applying them in the real world. Such simulations would be able to evaluate the effects of the environment, resource utilization, and risks (Kudlak et al., 2018).

Digital twins enhance better decision-making and minimize the possibility of unintended outcomes by visualising the impact of changes on their sustainability indicators. They also help to increase transparency due to the better understanding of the system dynamics by managers and other stakeholders. Computer vision technologies are AI technologies used to process visual data of cameras, drones, or satellites. Computer vision can be applied when inspecting the quality of products in supply chains, tracking recycling operations, and observing the safety situation in plants. Vision systems relying on satellites could also trace deforestation, untextual mining, or pollution around the areas of suppliers (Vinuesa et al., 2020). The capabilities make transparency go beyond the organisational borders and see social and environmental risks remotely. Even though privacy and governance issues are concerned with such technologies, they provide avenues of checking sustainability assertions. The overall analytics provided by big data analytics give the AI tools their broader environment. Even the modern supply chains produce enormous volumes of structured and unstructured data regarding the transactions, sensors, and external data. The big data platforms enable companies to combine and scale such information so that they can create dashboards and indicators corresponding to emissions, resource utilisation and supplier performance (Kiron et al., 2017). Big data analytics when used with AI are able to determine patterns that are not immediately apparent making sustainability intelligence stronger. Although these technologies have these capabilities, the results of transparency remain dependent on quality and governance of data. Untrue or missing data will lead to misguided conclusions, and algorithm models might represent bias in the historical samples (Lyon and Montgomery, 2015). Additionally, there is the likelihood that small suppliers do not have the digital structure that is necessary to engage fully in data-oriented systems, and this can result in disproportionate visibility within supply networks.

These shortcomings bring out that technology is not a solution to accountability, organisational and regulatory structures are still crucial. Altogether, AI technologies enlarge the informational market of supply chains and reveal the processes that were in the shadow of darkness before. They promote ongoing monitors as opposed to periodic auditing and proactive management as opposed to responsive management. Nevertheless, their role to sustainability will be determined by the manner in which organisations perceive and respond to the insights acquired. The following part hence looks at the application of these technologies in the various sustainability aspects in the supply chain operations.

4. AI IN OPERATIONAL SUSTAINABILITY

The implementation of the Artificial Intelligence in supply chains is the most valuable when analyzed through the varied realms of sustainability, i.e., environmental, social, and operational performance. Though these dimensions are theoretically distinct, in the real world they are linked to one another and enhancement of one of the dimensions can affect results in the other one. The key role that AI plays to achieve sustainability is its ability to provide improved measurement, prediction and coordination that can help make more informed managerial decisions. Nonetheless, these contributions may be different in terms of contributions to organisational priorities and structure of governance (Rasche & Waddock, 2014; Holmes et al., 2019).

One of the most evident fields where AI has been applied in supply chains is environmental sustainability. An example is carbon accounting, which has used estimations and periodical accounting to hide the actual sources of emission. Artificial intelligence (AI) application is able to integrate information acquired during transport operations, manufacturing processes and energy use so as to derive superior and prompt estimates of emissions (Chien & Chen, 2020). The predictive models can be used to determine the high-emissions routes or operations that are energy-intensive; this is so that the firms redesign the logistics networks and can lower the environmental impact. AI can also be applied to circular economy practices by predicting the returns of products, finding recycling possibilities, and optimising actions to recover materials (Missimer et al., 2017).

These applications will show that digital tools can assist in bridging the gap between sustainability objectives and operational decision-making. Another significant environmental implementation is resource optimisation. The AI systems can scan through the water, energy and material usage patterns to identify the inefficiencies and propose changes. In particular, predictive maintenance models are also capable of predicting failures on the equipment that will generate waste or over-consumption (Makridakis, 2017). Such systems lead to the alignment of operational efficiency with environmental objectives through a longer assembly of the asset lifecycle and lower unnecessary use of resources. However, researchers warn that a balance should be struck between the sustainability of AI in the environment and the energy usage of data centres and the digital infrastructure, which can be sometimes dubbed as the green paradox of AI (Vinuesa et al., 2020). This underscores the necessity to assess the overall lifecycle impacts of AI and not necessarily call on the already assumed environmental benefits. Social sustainability in the supply chains entails matters of labour rights, safety of workplace and fair participation.

These objectives can be facilitated through AI analysis, reviewing supplier data, audit reports, and external sources of information with the aim of identifying a possible threat of forced labour, or unsafe environments (Jamali and Karam, 2016). Natural language processing software can be used to process huge amounts of text such as news stories and social media, detecting evidence of labour abuse. Computer vision can also be implemented to check on the safety in facilities. The technologies widen the window of oversight as compared to the traditional audits which are normally periodical and narrow in the scope. Nevertheless, ethical issues relate to the application of AI in social sustainability. The use of algorithmic models can replicate any societal bias on past data, creating unreasonable risk ratings or waylocking those smaller suppliers who cannot prepare digital reports (Lyon and Montgomery, 2015).

Monitoring of workers or analysing personal data also has privacy considerations. Such concerns imply that AI would not take over human judgment and stakeholder involvement in the social governance, but it would complement it. Frameworks of responsible AI based on fairness and transparency are hence important in ensuring that technological tools are aligned to social goals. Environmental and social outcomes are closely associated with operational sustainability that encompasses efficiency, resilience, and reliability. Smart demand predictors and stock optimization can lessen excess production and wastage, whereas smart routing implies consumption of fuel and delivery duration can be minimized (Kiron et al., 2017). Predictive analytics are also able to increase resiliency by being able to spot the types of disruptions that would take place due to weather conditions or geopolitical instability. More resilient supply chains are in a better position to be sustainable in times of crisis since they do not have to make reactive decisions which can put speed over responsibility. In these dimensions, it can be observed that the AI enhances the visibility and predictability of the supply chain operation, thus yielding a more informed trade-off between cost, speed, and sustainability.

However, AI is not the driving force behind which trade-offs organisations decide to undertake. The use of insights is influenced by the managerial values, regulatory pressures, and the expectations of the stakeholders. This supports the thesis that AI is an empowerment tool that is integrated into larger government frameworks and not a sustainability driver itself. Sustainability is multidimensional which also means that the performance measurement has to be well structured. The ability to measure environmentally simpler indicators of social conditions elevated when more complex indicators affects the outcome. Researchers hence recommend having balanced measurement systems that document various outcomes of sustainability (Rasche & Waddock, 2014). AI may help in collecting and analysing data, yet it is still up to a normative and strategic choice to define what to measure. Learning about these applications gives a basis to look into the transparency in the global level. With the internationalisation of supply chains, regulatory, infrastructure, and institutional capacity variations affect the operation of transparency through AI capabilities. The section, which follows, thus examines the applicability of AI to supply networks across borders in improving their transparency and accountability

5. AI IN ENVIRONMENTAL SUSTAINABILITY

The global supply chains also work in various jurisdictions, different systems of regulations, and cultural backgrounds that complicate the aspect of transparency. The cross-border trade is associated with complicated documentation, customs processes, and other requirements that will differ across countries. Traditionally, all these processes were based on manual paperwork and disjointed information systems that made delays, errors, and misreport much more probable (Crane et al., 2014). The lack of visibility across borders has also made it strenuous to educate sustainability assertions and track emissions as well as licenses of labour circumstances in remote suppliers. With the increasing regulatory requirements in due diligence and ESG reporting, companies are pressurized to enhance the accuracy and timeliness of cross border information.

The Artificial Intelligence also helps to make processes of cross-border transparency, as it serves as an automatizer of documents and allows analyzing information in real time. By processing natural language, the natural language processing systems can take and capture pertinent data within the trade documents, contracts, and regulatory texts, minimizing human error and speeding up compliance processes (Chien & Chen, 2020). With machine learning models it is possible to indicate discrepancies or anomalies in shipping records and customs declarations used by firms to identify possible fraud or non-compliance. These capabilities are beneficial as they promote procedural transparency and minimize administrative burdens as well as regulatory accountability.

The other value of global transparency is real-time traceability. Artificial intelligence will be able to combine the information of GPS trackers, RFID, and IoT sensors in order to trace the flow of goods across the borders. The ongoing tracking will enable companies to confirm the origin of products, track their transportation environment, and predict emissions more precisely (Holmes et al., 2019). Provenance tracking has a specific use in commodities that are at risk to the environment or to society (e.g. minerals, agricultural produce or textiles). The AI-enabled systems can ensure supply chain history is more transparent and auditable, which is achieved by associating physical flows with digital records.

The use of blockchain technologies accompanied by AI has become an issue of interest to enhance trust in international transactions. Blockchain serves as a source of non-alterable records and AI has the capability to examine such non-alterable records and detect unusual patterns or red flags (Raj & Sundararajan, 2020). Accurately, these technologies can minimize the falsification of documents and enhance the authenticity of the certifications on sustainability. Nevertheless, researchers warn that technological solutions should be complemented by models of governance to determine the ownership of data, granted access privileges, and accountability (Rasche & Waddock, 2014). In the absence of such structures, transparency in the digital platform might be imbalanced or contentious. AI is also involved in ESG verification and compliance with regulations. The implementation of carbon border adjustments and obligatory due diligence laws by governments make firms show that their supply chains comply with the environmental and social norms. ESG reporting and risk actions can be facilitated by using AI-based systems to communicate information collected by various sources (Vinuesa et al., 2020).

These systems will be able to assist firms to decipher the changes of regulations and how their operations can meet the changes of standard. However, the quality of data and transparency in methods determine the quality of ESG analytics. Reported indicators might not respond to the real practices in case underlying data are incomplete or biased. Inequality in digital infrastructure and institutional potential also adds to the challenge of cross-border transparency. In the developing regions, suppliers can be unable to have the technological tools to be full participants of the data-driven systems. Such digital divide also has the potential to make smaller actors less visible, and this could marginalise them. Governance wise, participatory methods which facilitate capacity building and information sharing is thus noteworthy. Research into additional extensions of the concept of transparency has been shown to reinforce the disparities even though the high benchmarks and demands of technical and technological advancements remain unsupported.

All in all, AI-based cross-border transparency has a huge potential to enhance accountability and coordination in international supply chains. It enables the firms and regulators to get more access to more detail and timely information which minimises uncertainty and enhances compliance. Meanwhile, the aspect of transparency is not only a technical but also a political and organisational problem. The choices concerning the type of information to be gathered, the interpretation of the information, and the people who will get access to the information determine the results of digital transparency efforts. Identifying these dimensions will prevent over-optimistic expectations regarding technology and will aid in focusing more on the governance. Having explored the idea of transparency that AI helps maintain in global networks, one should address how these relations work in reality. The practical examples of multinational companies will help to comprehend the implementation of AI and the challenges involved. The next section will hence entail comparative case discussions which rejoin the theoretical arguments with the reality.

6. CASE ILLUSTRATIONS FROM GLOBAL SUPPLY CHAINS

The real-life examples of multinational companies are useful to understand how AI-driven transparency and sustainability initiatives can be applied in reality. Although case examples cannot make any generalisations, they contribute to illustrating how theoretical concepts work in real organisational settings. Big companies that are globally based tend to be the first adopters of digital technologies due to the existence of a complex coordination issue and high scrutiny of the stakeholders. The examples of the logistics providers, as well as consumer goods firms, hence provide pertinent insights into the potential opportunities and constraints of AI in managing the supply chain in a sustainable manner. DHL, among the largest logistical firms in the world, has invested in the use of AI-driven systems to optimise the routing process, track emissions, and enhance shipment visibility. Using traffic data, fuel use, and transportation limits, AI-based precinct of routing can avoid the unwarranted mileage and related emissions (Holmes et al., 2019).

DHL has further considered sensor information and analytics to measure energy consumption and equipment performance in the warehouse. Those projects demonstrate how AI can contribute to the realization of environmental goals and sustain its efficiency. Meanwhile, the practice of DHL indicates that the change in organisations during technological implementation demands not only the training of the workforce or data governance. A need to have the advanced tools does not necessarily mean an increase in the sustainability where there is no integration of insights in the decision-making processes. The example of one of the largest maritime shipping companies, Maersk focuses on the importance of AI in decarbonisation and risk management. The marine transport sector is one of the major contributors to emissions to the globe and shipping companies are under greater pressure to clean up their environment. AI-controlled forecasting can examine weather, ocean and port congestions to prepare oceans and on the route as well as to identify optimal routes and fuel consumption (Raj & Sundararajan, 2020). Maersk has also introduced remote container managing systems that keep a check on temperature and energy utilization in refrigerated containers hence lowering spoilage as well as squandering of resources. Such activities prove the way in which the AI-based view can help reach both economic and environmental objectives. Nonetheless, they also rely on consistent flow of data and coordination with the partners that may be not quite easy to achieve with international shipping networks. An example that Unilever gives in this regard is in the consumer goods industry where the issues of sustainability go beyond logistics to include sourcing and production. Data analytics and AI tools have helped the company to assess the performance of its suppliers and detect environmental and social risks in the sourcing location. In the case of a commodity like palm oil or tea, satellite images and analysis can be used to track the risks of land-use change and deforestation (Vinuesa et al., 2020).

Supported by AI, dashboards may combine data about emissions, water consumption and compliance of the suppliers and allow managers to see the picture in a much broader perspective. These moves indicate that there is a general trend towards incorporating sustainability measures into corporate governance. However, they also cast doubts on data interpretation and verification because the intricate social and ecological dynamics cannot always be represented with the help of quantitative indicators only. Analysis of these cases shows that there are a number of tendencies. To start with, AI is typically implemented at first due to the reasons of efficiency or risk reduction, and the sustainability benefits are the secondary results. Second, large firms have the scale and resources which allows experimentation with the advanced technologies, which possible is not equally available to small organisations. Third, the uses of data-driven insights are subject to governance structure and corporate culture. Companies that employ sustainability as a strategic priority will find it easier to use AI to achieve responsible results. These findings warrant the discussion that AI acts as an enabling infrastructure where the effect of sustainability varies depending on the organisation. There are also case illustrations that show the significance of collaborating among supply chain actors. Information exchange between logistics providers, suppliers, and customers could be more valuable with the help of the AI analytics, however, it will demand trust and mutual standards. In absence of coordination, dislodged bits of data may restrict the transparency and diminish the usefulness of digital tools. In terms of research, such cases indicate the necessity to consider not only the technological adoption but institutional and relational factors affecting the results. Though illustrative cases are very informative, they cannot substitute systematic examination of cases. They are aimed at bridging the gap between conceptual arguments and practical examples and finding out the problems that should be investigated further. As a way of expanding the analytical lens, there is need to consider more general tendencies and implications. The section below thus generalises critical findings of the literature and discussions of the cases.

7. ANALYTICAL DISCUSSION AND IMPLICATIONS

The above passages imply that Artificial Intelligence is transforming the supply chain administration mostly by widening the extent, speed, and fine-tuning of information to be used by decision-makers. Instead of treating AI as a force that compulses sustainability, it is more analytically correct that AI is a mediator, which shapes risks and opportunities perceptions, and trade-offs of organisations. This difference is significant in the sense that it changes the focus of technological capability to governance and decision-making structures. AI is able to open up inefficiency, hotspots of emissions, or labour hazards, yet what follows is corrected action is left to the choosing of managers, regulatory strain, and stakeholder anticipation (Rasche & Waddock, 2014).

One of the analytical implications is that transparency is a sufficient but does not entail sustainability. Greater transparency can highlight the unsustainability of certain practices, but individual companies can continue to focus on the economic concerns of the short term in cases of an incentives mismatch. By way of illustration, facts can indicate that a low-cost supplier is more environmentally harmful, yet there can be no legislative or reputational stress to change the situation, so companies may hesitate to switch. This depicts that information itself is not the determinant of the outcomes but institutional contexts dictate the manner in which information is utilized. AI thus adds on to the informational base of sustainability governance but does not dictate over normative or strategic decisions. The second implication has to do with measurement asymmetry between dimensions of sustainability. Indicators like emissions or energy consumption are often easier and simpler to measure compared to social indicators like worker health or neighbourhood effects. Based on the data, AI systems can thus strengthen the focus on what is quantifiable at the expense of complicated social problems (Jamali and Karam, 2016).

This poses a threat of partial sustainability with a better performance on the environmental while less systematic attention is given to social concerns. It has been observed by scholars that the metrics of sustainability are not neutral but instead they have a value orientation about what is viewed as performance (Crane et al., 2014). AI has the capability to process measurements effectively, and however, it is a human and political challenge to formulate meaningful metrics. The third implication is associated with inequality and power within the supply chain. Big multinational companies usually have the capacity to invest in advanced analytics and small suppliers might not be able to comply with the requirements of digital reporting. The suppliers with low digital ability might be pushed to the fringes in case they are required to participate in the AI-enabled transparency systems as a requirement to access the markets. This causes the question of fair participation and cost-benefits allocation (Lyon & Montgomery, 2015).

Governance-wise, capacity-building processes and common grounds can potentially reduce such imbalance, yet it takes intentional pushes in policy and organisational action. Another important point that was presented in the discussion is the dynamic relationship between regulation and technology. Digital monitoring and reporting finds more and more references in regulatory frameworks, as there is some incentive to utilize AI. Simultaneously, the regulation typically keeps up with changes in technology, which creates loopholes in the domains of data protection, algorithmic responsibility, and global data flows. This regulatory uncertainty is capable of both spurring experimentation and risk creation. Organizations can implement AI quickly to show that they were compliant, but policies to enable fairness and accuracy may not be well-developed (Vinuesa et al., 2020). To achieve a balanced approach, there is a need to have adaptive regulation, which is developed in tandem with technological capabilities. The other artificial observation is with regard to organisational learning. In order to sustain continuous improvement, AI systems create knowledge that can be used, yet it should be learned that organisations must receive and internalise these insights into routine. There is no automatic behaviour change brought about by digital dashboards and predictive models. According to studies on organisational change, culture, and leadership commitment as well as incentive systems also have an impact on whether or not data-driven insights will be acted on (Kiron et al., 2017).

This confirms the argument that AI must be installed as a part of more extensive sustainability initiatives as opposed to a single device. Collectively, these implications emphasize the fact that AI-enabled sustainability is a socio-technical phenomenon. Technology relates to the institutions, values and power relations. In a manner that is too deterministic, where AI is presented as an answer to the challenges related to sustainability, these complexities will be ignored. A more sophisticated view acknowledges the possibilities as well as the drawbacks of digital tools.

That kind of attitude promotes making critical judgments, as well as responsible experimentation instead of blind optimism. In order to enjoy these dynamics, the ethical and governance issues that come with the use of AI will also need to be looked into. New issues on privacy, surveillance, and the use of algorithms as decision-makers can be created through transparency. The second part now shifts to ethical risks and governance issues that come with the AI-driven transformation in a supply chain

8. ETHICAL AND GOVERNANCE CHALLENGES IN AI-DRIVEN SUPPLY CHAINS

The increasing penetration of Artificial Intelligence into the supply chains presents both the opportunities of transparency and sustainability, but also they lead to serious ethical and governance complexities. These issues are present since AI systems affect the way information is gathered, perceived and treated, thus determining organisational decisions that impact on workers, communities, and the environment. Ethics is thus not a marginal aspect of sustainability of AI adoption but a key point that can be made. Researchers have grown to highlight the fact that responsible governance is needed to complement digital transformation since technological gains should not be had at the cost of equity, accountability or good health (Rasche and Waddock, 2014).

Algorithms bias is one of such concerns. History teaches AI systems, and when historical data is based on disparities or incomplete reporting, AI can recreate them or even even increase it. With procurement and supplier assessment, (e.g.) the algorithms could be optimistic towards suppliers that have a more detailed digital history, which tends to be correlated with the size or geographic position of the firm. The smaller the suppliers or those in developing regions might seem riskier just due to the lack of information related to them (Lyon and Montgomery, 2015).

Through this dynamic, disproportionate power relations in global supply chains may be perpetuated without intent. To solve the bias issue, it is important to maintain a proper governance of the data, heterogeneous training sets, and regularly audit the results of the algorithms. Surveillance and data privacy form other ethical concerns. The AI based monitoring systems can gather specifics of the behaviour, location, and performance of the workers. As much as this information can be used to support safety and compliance, there are also some concerns about consent and proportionality. Constant surveillance may blur the difference between its acceptable supervision and the intrusions on privacy especially in situations where employees lack the power to negotiate (Jamali and Karam, 2016). The structure of ethical governance thus suggests the disclosure of the procedure of data collection and clear restrictions concerning the application of personal data. The other critical dimension is cybersecurity. The supply chain that is AI-based is based on interconnected digital infrastructures, which are subject to data breaches, manipulation, or sabotage. In case of any data breach of sustainability or compliance documents, the transparency initiatives will lose credibility (Holmes et al., 2019).

In addition, cyber criminals may use digital systems to impersonate sustainability attributes with reputational and regulatory risks. Having effective cybersecurity precautions and checking mechanisms is therefore a part of responsible AI policy. The AI systems themselves are also considered regarding the environment. Massive data processing also demands data centres and hardware manufacturing which is energy-utilizing and that has a footprint. Other researchers refer to it as a paradox where the technologies that should assist in attaining sustainability create emissions (Vinuesa et al., 2020). Digital efficiencies can balance part of the effects, but a holistic evaluation should take lifecycle effects of digital infrastructure into consideration. This point of view prompts companies to think about renewable energy sources and energy-saving and efficient computing as one of the sustainable digital solutions. The issue of labour displacement usually comes up during the topic of automation. Some manual operations do not have to be done in warehousing, logistics and production since AI and robotics can minimize them. Automation can enhance the safety and efficiency, but it would alter the employment pattern especially the low-skilled workers (Bostrom, 2012). In social aspects, the sustainability needs to be looked at in conjunction with environmental benefits. Performers can be reduced or avoided with the help of re-skilling and supportive transition tactics, however, they demand proactive actions, cooperation between the firms, government, and the educational establishments. At the regulatory level, governance issues are also brought to play.

Artificial intelligence is a quickly changing technology, and the legal system tends to be slow. The variations in national policies about the protection of data, AI responsibility, and sustainability reporting make multinational supply chains complex. Regulatory arbitrage may occur as a result of inconsistent standards whereby companies meet less demanding standards in certain jurisdictions (Crane et al., 2014). A global integration and standardisation is thus significant in applying digital transparency to enhance actual accountability. On the whole, ethical and governance issues point at the fact that AI-based sustainability is not a purely technical undertaking but rather a normative and institutional task. Responsible AI must have explicit principles, stakeholder involvement, and oversight. In the absence of these safeguards, transparency programs might not be perceived as legitimate, or have unintentional ramifications. The awareness of these problems does not remove the importance of AI but promotes a more moderate and attentive attitude to digital transformation. Strategic implications also apply in dealing with the ethical concerns. Companies with sound AI governance approaches can have more trust among stakeholders and regulators, and this can work towards long term sustainability objectives. Considering all this, the following section shifts to the strategic aspects and implementation avenues that can bring AI adoption to the sustainable supply chain management

9. STRATEGIC CONSIDERATIONS FOR IMPLEMENTING AI IN SUSTAINABLE SUPPLY CHAINS

Implementation of successfully the Artificial Intelligence into sustainable supply chain management would not just come by investing in technology but strategic alignment, organisational preparedness and structures of governance which would help in responsible use. Companies who completely utilise AI as a company instrument fail to achieve its sustainability power due to the lack of linkage between digital insights and the strategic choices. Researchers underline the importance of sustainability initiatives wherein they are incorporated into corporate strategy and the commitment of the leaders (Rasche & Waddock, 2014). The necessity to align AI efforts with sustainability goals allows making sure that the area of data gathering and analytics is centered on the environmental and social indicators of relevance, as opposed to the cost or efficiency indicators alone. Digital maturity in organisations is important in the outcome determinants. The AI systems are based on credible data infrastructures, interoperable platforms, and standardised reporting practices. The availability of weak information systems or irregular data formats in supply chains experiences more difficulties in the implementation of advanced analytics (Chien & Chen, 2020). Data, cloud and system integration investments are therefore a preliminary step toward AI-powered sustainability. Other such investments entail the development of data quality standards and roles of data custodianship. Another strategic aspect is performance measurement. The interpretation and action of AI are based on Sustainability Key Performance Indicators (KPIs). The environmental KPIs can include carbon intensity, energy consumption, and the waste reduction, whereas the social KPIs can be related to labour standards and supplier inclusion. KPIs associated with operational areas touch on resiliency and efficiency (Kiron et al., 2017).

The choice of KPIs shows the organisational priorities and expectations by the stakeholders. AI has the potential to improve the precision of measurements, though the important indicators are not defined. Optimisation Narrow optimisation can be averted through the use of balanced scorecards incorporating several dimensions. Cooperation among the participants of the supply chain is also vital. Transparency programs usually involve the exchange of information among the suppliers, the logisticians, and the purchasers. Data sharing on the other hand poses a challenge on confidentiality and competitive edge. Collaboration can be achieved through trust-building mechanisms, contractual agreements and industry standards (Crane et al., 2014). Government and non-governmental organisations as part of the multi-stakeholder partnership might be also beneficial in capacity building especially to smaller suppliers that do not have much digital capabilities. Best AI governance becomes a key strategic need. Governance structures are usually focused on equity, responsibility, and transparency in making decisions algorithmically. Audits of AI systems on a regular basis may assist in determining biases or unintended consequences (Lyon & Montgomery, 2015). There should also be clear accountability structures in which human decision-makers are held to account regarding the outcomes achieved with the help of AI tools. This human in the loop is acknowledging the fact that algorithms do not replace the managers but help them. Another strategic factor is regulatory awareness. With the changing nature of sustainability and digital regulations, companies should expect policies to comply with. The regulatory monitoring can be allowed by AI systems, and firms should also maintain that reporting methodologies are compatible with well-known standards (Vinuesa et al., 2020).

Early involvement of the regulators and industry organisations can assist organisations to change according to the shifting expectations. Lastly, the implementation of strategies must pay attention to the skills and organisational culture. The employees should know how to read AI-generated insights and incorporate them into the decisions. The differences between the technical specialists and sustainability managers can be addressed through training and cross-functional cooperation. In the absence of such features, online resources can be poorly used or misperceived. Combined, it would indicate that the implementation of AI is not an ad-hoc initiative but a continuous organisational one. The issue of strategic alignment, governance and collaboration define whether AI can play a significant role in transforming a sustainable supply chain. The identification of this complexity assists in discouraging unrealistic expectations and encourages more intentional and fruitful adoption. The concept of strategy is inevitably followed by the thinking about the limits of the existing knowledge. Scholarly rigour requires the realization of constraints in any study though no research could encompass everything in a dynamic area. The next section is thus a description of the shortcomings of the current chapter and the research areas that can be done in future

10. LIMITATIONS AND DIRECTIONS FOR FUTURE RESEARCH

Similar to any research study on the analysis of an emerging area of study, the chapter has a number of limitations that must be considered in order to come up with a balanced explanation of the arguments of the paper. The first, is that the chapter uses mainly secondary sources such as scholarly sources, policy documents, and generally case material that can be found publicly. Although these sources fit well in conceptual and integrative writing, they lack direct empirical data on the results of sustainability. Because of this, there are claims related to the effect of AI which are founded on reported practices and speculative relationships as opposed to controlled testing. As observed by the scholars, sustainability performance is relative and can differ in terms of industries and regions (Crane et al., 2014). Second, the chapter is devoted to large multinational firms predominantly due to the fact that such organisations are more prominent in the literature on the subject and they are the first that attempts to use sophisticated technologies. Global supply chains, however, are not isolated entities since they involve numerous small-to-medium sized enterprises that have different set of constraints. They might not be able to invest in AI, process data and meet the demands of digital reporting. As such the trends mentioned in this context might not be a complete reflection of small player (or even small firms) in low-resource contexts. Further studies might focus on the impacts of AI-mediated transparency on various stakeholders in the supply chain and the digital divide factors on sustainability (Lyon and Montgomery, 2015).

Third, the high rate of technological advancement creates insecurity. The use of AI, data infrastructures and regulatory frameworks is in a state of evolving that must take into consideration that the current practices in today times might change greatly with time. Such things that are advanced today may be the norm tomorrow. Longitudinal research would then prove useful in determining the way in which AI adoption influences the sustainability performance over a long duration and the way in which organisational learning takes place. Fourth, social sustainability is also difficult to measure. Emissions are measurable on a relative level with a reasonable degree of accuracy, whereas workers well-being or effects on the community cannot be effectively represented in data-driven regimes due to the social aspect (Jamali and Karam, 2016). Future studies may consider mixed-method research that involves the use of quantitative analytics and qualitative fieldwork to develop more informative studies. When it comes to the future directions, a number of promising directions can be identified. It may be more rigorously proved using empirical pilot tests involving the use of AI-enabled transparency tools within individual supply chains. The comparison within the different industries and regions would help in showing the contextual variations in adoption and impact. The studies on the introduction of the AI to other digital technologies, including blockchain and the high-tech IoT networks, may help to understand how hybrid systems impact trust and traceability (Vinuesa et al., 2020).

There is also a need to conduct policy-oriented research to investigate the effect of the regulatory frameworks on incentives to report on the digital transparency and sustainability. With the governments introducing the due diligence policies and carbon-related policies the phenomenon of how the firms react both technologically and organisationally is finding more and more importance. Last but not least, ethical studies of algorithmic governance, data rights, and worker roles can assist in making sure that the digital transformation becomes judicious in line with the societal values in general. The chapter attempts to enter a developing discussion by identifying constraints and setting outlines of new research directions instead of making a final decision. Openness of the kind is aligned with the academic tradition of dynamic disciplines where the knowledge is built gradually. The last part of this chapter is a synthesis of the main arguments and a reflection on the overall implications to the sustainable supply chain management

11. CONCLUSION

This chapter has analyzed how Artificial Intelligence can be used to increase transparency and sustainability in the global supply chains. It commenced the analysis with the identification that the modern supply chains are working under increased pressure to handle the aspects of environmental degradation, social responsibility, and governance accountability. Conventional frameworks, which still placed emphasis on efficiency and minimization of costs are no longer enough in an environment influenced by climatic hazards, regulations and demands of stakeholders (Elkington, 1997; United Nations, 2015). It is against this background that AI has been developed as a potent set of tools, which have capabilities to process massive amounts of data, generate forecasts, and assist real-time surveillance in complex networks. One of the key points of the chapter is that AI will play an important role in ensuring sustainability because of its influence on transparency. AI increases the informational foundation of decision-making by rendering the supply chain activities more transparent, quantifiable, and traceable. This better visibility can aid in the accounting of carbon, ethical sourcing and identifying of risk.

Nevertheless, transparency is not a surety of sustainable results. The conversion of information into practice relies on the governance framework, organisational agenda, and regulatory environments (Rasche & Waddock, 2014). AI must be conceptualized as an infrastructuring tool embedded within more larger socio-technical infrastructure and not as an independent problem-solver. The technologies and applications discussed have shown that AI tools, including machine learning, AIoT, digital twins, and computer vision, can be used to improve monitoring and prediction of the environment, social and operational aspects. The use of such tools in the logistics, shipping, and consumer goods industry exemplified in case was demonstrated by how companies have tried them to save on emissions, enhance traceability, and supplier risks. Concurrently, these illustrations demonstrated that implementation is skewed and informed by the organisational capabilities and resources. Big companies are usually early adopters, whereas minor participants might have obstacles associated with the price and online infrastructure. Ethical and governance factors were the significant points that appeared. The presence of algorithmic bias, data privacy, and cybersecurity risks, and the environmental impact of digital infrastructures point to the fact that the adoption of AI is a matter of trade-offs. Sustainable governance systems, which focus on the principle of equity, accountability, and transparency, are thus needed (Lyon and Montgomery, 2015; Vinuesa et al., 2020).

Otherwise, digital transparency efforts can become illegitimate, or have unintended effects. This confirms the importance of having a balanced approach that appreciates the opportunities and restrictions. The chapter highlighted that to achieve successful AI-enabled sustainability, it is important to align the corporate goals with the AI-based data governance and cooperation among the supply chain participants. Technology does not replace leadership commitment and stakeholder engagement. The normative project of sustainability is as much influenced by values, institutions as by analytics. The development of AI in supply chains in a wider context implies the transition towards the data-based governance. Online tools are increasing the visibility of complex systems, yet they also bring about concerns on control, participation and equity. It is probable that development in the future will rely on the negotiation of these questions by societies and the development of regulatory structures. With the growing pressure of the sustainability issues, the issue of digital innovation and accountable governance will continue to be a characteristic issue in the global supply chains. To conclude, AI is a serious prospective in assisting the creation of more open and sustainable supply chains, yet it will require an effect and not a natural progression. By thinking of AI as a component of a broader governance ecosystem, it is possible to maintain realistic expectations and design mindfulness. This would provide a way of matching technological advancement with the overall objectives of sustainable development and a responsible global trade.

REFERENCES

Ahi, P., & Searcy, C. (2015). A comparative literature analysis of definitions for green and sustainable supply chain management. *Journal of Cleaner Production*, *52*, 329–341. DOI: 10.1016/j.jclepro.2013.02.018

Boström, M. (2012). A missing pillar? Challenges in theorising and practising social sustainability. Sustainability: Science. *Practice and Policy*, *8*(1), 3–14.

Carter, C. R., & Rogers, D. S. (2008). A framework of sustainable supply chain management: Moving toward new theory. *International Journal of Physical Distribution & Logistics Management*, *38*(5), 360–387. DOI: 10.1108/09600030810882816

Chien, C. F., & Chen, Y. J. (2020). Data-driven technologies for sustainable manufacturing. *Journal of Manufacturing Systems*, *57*, 331–345.

Christopher, M. (2016). *Logistics & Supply Chain Management* (5th ed.). Pearson.

Crane, A., LeBaron, G., Allain, J., & Behbahani, L. (2018). Governance gaps in eradicating forced labour. *The Academy of Management Perspectives*, *32*(3), 287–304.

Crane, A., Matten, D., & Moon, J. (2014). *Corporations and Citizenship*. Cambridge University Press.

Dubey, R., Gunasekaran, A., Childe, S. J., Papadopoulos, T., & Fosso-Wamba, S. (2020). Big data analytics capability in supply chains. *International Journal of Production Economics*, *219*, 312–327.

Elkington, J. (1997). *Cannibals with Forks: The Triple Bottom Line of 21st Century Business*. Capstone.

Holmes, M. R., Fawcett, S. E., & Todd, R. H. (2019). Supply chain transparency and sustainability. *International Journal of Physical Distribution & Logistics Management*, *49*(2), 152–170.

Jamali, D., & Karam, C. (2016). Corporate social responsibility in developing countries. *International Journal of Management Reviews*, *20*(1), 32–61. DOI: 10.1111/ijmr.12112

Kiron, D., Prentice, P. K., & Ferguson, R. B. (2017). The analytics mandate for sustainability. *MIT Sloan Management Review*, *58*(2), 1–13.

Lyon, T. P., & Montgomery, A. W. (2015). The means and end of greenwash. *Organization & Environment*, *28*(2), 223–249. DOI: 10.1177/1086026615575332

Makridakis, S. (2017). The forthcoming AI revolution. *Futures*, *90*, 46–60. DOI: 10.1016/j.futures.2017.03.006

Missimer, M., Robèrt, K. H., & Broman, G. (2017). Strategic social sustainability. *Journal of Cleaner Production*, *140*, 31–40.

Rasche, A., & Waddock, S. (2014). Global sustainability governance and the UN Global Compact. *Journal of Business Ethics*, *122*(2), 209–216. DOI: 10.1007/s10551-014-2216-6

Seuring, S., & Müller, M. (2008). From literature review to conceptual framework for SSCM. *Journal of Cleaner Production*, *16*(15), 1699–1710. DOI: 10.1016/j.jclepro.2008.04.020

United Nations. (2015). *Transforming Our World: The 2030 Agenda for Sustainable Development*. United Nations.

Vinuesa, R., Azizpour, H., & Leite, I. (2020). AI and the SDGs. *Nature Communications*, *11*, 233. DOI: 10.1038/s41467-019-14108-y PMID: 31932590

Zhu, Q., & Sarkis, J. (2004). Green supply chain management practices in China. *Journal of Operations Management*, *22*(3), 265–289. DOI: 10.1016/j.jom.2004.01.005

Chapter 13
AI-Enabled Strategies for Sustainable Cross-Border Logistics:
Sustainable Development Goals (SDGs) and Decarbonized Logistics

Oumayma Messaoudi
http://orcid.org/0009-0005-6671-3825
Faculty of Economics and Management, University of Sfax, Tunisia

Kaies Samet
Higher Institute of Industrial Management, University of Sfax, Tunisia

Ahmed Derbel
Faculty of Economics and Management, University of Sfax, Tunisia

ABSTRACT

This chapter examines the incorporation of the Sustainable Development Goals (SDGs) into the evolution of logistics and supply chain systems aimed at decarbonization and enduring sustainability. The analysis commences with an examination of the environmental and socio-economic challenges confronting global logistics networks, encompassing rising energy consumption, greenhouse gas emissions, resource limitations, and regulatory demands. The chapter establishes the conceptual foundations of sustainable and low-carbon logistics by analyzing key externalities linked to logistics operations, the difficulties in measuring environmental performance, and the transition from conventional linear logistics models to green, circular, and

DOI: 10.4018/979-8-3373-7847-3.ch013

low-carbon supply chain paradigms. Emphasis is directed towards the Sustainable Development Goals (SDGs) most pertinent to logistics, namely SDG 7 , SDG 9 , SDG 11, SDG 12, SDG 13, and SDG 17.

INTRODUCTION

The transition to sustainable economic models is currently one of the primary problems for enterprises, governments, and all participants in the global value chain. In a setting characterized by climate urgency, resource scarcity, escalating geopolitical conflicts, and increasing public expectations, logistics and supply chain management occupy a critical position. Historically concentrated on cost optimization, flow velocity, and economic performance, these functions are now experiencing a significant transformation, propelled by the incorporation of sustainable development principles and the increasing demands for transparency, resilience, and environmental and social accountability.

The inherently cross-border character of logistics intensifies these issues, providing more complexity that obstruct the adoption of sustainable practices. These challenges encompass substantial legislative discrepancies among jurisdictions, deficiencies in institutional capacity across numerous locations, variable geopolitical threats impacting the fluidity of exchanges, and diverse infrastructures that restrict interoperability and efficiency. These factors represent significant obstacles to the incorporation of sustainability concepts and the implementation of new solutions.

This chapter also emphasizes the problems, conflicts, and trade-offs firms encounter while attempting to incorporate sustainability into their operations.

The incorporation of artificial intelligence (AI) solutions, while promising for optimization and decarbonization, has certain problems. It poses intricate inquiries concerning the compromises between economic efficiency, social accountability, and environmental consequences, with technology constraints and ethical and implementation concerns.

The inherently cross-border character of logistics intensifies these issues, providing more complexity that obstruct the adoption of sustainable practices. These challenges encompass substantial legislative discrepancies between jurisdictions, deficiencies in institutional capacities in numerous areas, variable geopolitical risks impacting the fluidity of transactions, and diverse infrastructures that restrict interoperability and efficiency. These factors represent significant obstacles to the incorporation of sustainability concepts and the implementation of new solutions.

This chapter aims to achieve three objectives: first, to build a robust theoretical framework for understanding the principles of sustainable logistics; second, to delineate practical solutions for its effective application within supply chains, highlighting the role of AI; and third, to critically analyze the mechanisms, trade-offs, limitations, and risks associated with the integration of AI in sustainable cross-border logistics.

This evolution is integral to the global regulatory framework established by international climate accords, ISO standards, and scientific benchmarks like the Greenhouse Gas Protocol, as well as the political and socioeconomic context influenced by the Sustainable Development Goals (SDGs). These offer a cohesive framework that facilitates the integration of logistical strategies with global challenges, including the mitigation of greenhouse gas emissions, sustainable production and consumption, the creation of resilient infrastructure, and the advancement of equitable development.

Sustainable logistics and sustainable supply chain management (SSCM) have evolved from isolated initiatives to encompass a comprehensive transformation that includes technological, organizational, and collaborative modifications. The incorporation of principles like circularity, waste minimization and valorization, energy efficiency, multi-stakeholder governance, and environmental performance assessment has now emerged as a strategic necessity.

This study analyzes the conceptual, methodological, and operational underpinnings of sustainable logistics and supply chain management, emphasizing their relationships with the Sustainable Development Goals, theoretical frameworks, performance assessment tools, and decarbonization strategies. It offers a crucial analytical framework for comprehending the current dynamics of logistical transformation and predicting the changes that will influence future value chains. Our primary contribution is the creation of an analytical framework that delineates the correlations between AI strategies and the SDGs, while also innovatively incorporating a comparative evaluation of traditional methods, a thorough examination of transnational challenges related to AI, and a proposal for specific and quantifiable governance mechanisms for sustainable and equitable implementation. We will distinctly differentiate conceptual proposals from empirical facts and case studies.

I. FOUNDATIONS OF SUSTAINABLE AND LOW-CARBON LOGISTICS

Objective: Develop the conceptual framework that connects sustainability, the Sustainable Development Goals (SDGs), and the decarbonization of logistics.

1. Definition of Sustainable and Low-Carbon Logistics

Sustainable logistics and low-carbon logistics are essential ideas in contemporary supply chain management, motivated by the necessity to mitigate environmental impact and attain net-zero emissions. According to de Oliveira et al. (2016), it is crucial to differentiate between sustainable logistics and low-carbon logistics, as the former encompasses a broader perspective that integrates environmental, social, and economic dimensions, while the latter specifically targets the reduction of greenhouse gas (GHG) emissions, particularly carbon dioxide (CO2).

The logistics sector significantly contributes to global carbon emissions, rendering these practices essential for sustainable development.

According to Mohsen (2022), sustainable logistics is based on the triple bottom line: environmental protection, economic viability, and social responsibility. It seeks to mitigate pollution, waste and resource depletion along the whole supply chain, from the procurement of raw materials to product distribution and reverse logistics.

This entails enhancing transportation, increasing vehicle efficiency, embracing renewable energy sources, and applying circular economy ideas. Sustainable logistics aims to minimize operational expenses, improve efficiency, and promote enduring resilience and competitiveness (Yasir et al. 2024). Mohsen (2022) states that it pertains to social dimensions including ethical work standards, community health and safety, and equal access to commodities and services. This complete strategy transcends basic environmental compliance, impacting production processes and supply chain dynamics to attain overarching sustainability goals. Implementing green logistics techniques can enhance energy efficiency, resulting in substantial cost savings for organizations.

Low-carbon logistics, a specific subset of sustainable logistics, focuses particularly on minimizing carbon emissions. The primary objective is to reduce the climate effect of logistics operations by lowering energy use and shifting to cleaner energy sources. Commonly utilized strategies encompass optimizing transportation modalities, augmenting vehicle fuel economy, employing low-carbon fuels, expanding the energy performance of warehouses, and adopting intelligent logistics systems. The increasing focus on low-carbon logistics is a direct reaction to global climate change initiatives and laws, including carbon peak and carbon neutrality objectives. The European logistics sector is progressively embracing low-carbon logistics design due to its combined benefits of emissions reduction and economic gains. Likewise, China's dual-carbon policy objectives emphasize the necessity of improving the green and low-carbon efficiency of regional logistics (Zhang and Li, 2024). According to de Oliveira et al. (2016), research clarifies these conceptual distinctions, noting that while low-carbon logistics focuses strictly on CO2 reduction, sustainable logistics includes a broader range of social and economic factors in addition to environmental considerations . Green logistics is another related term that predominantly addresses the environmental dimension, similar to low-carbon logistics, but sustainable logistics encompasses these and further aspects. Yasir et al. (2024) define essential techniques and technical innovations that facilitate sustainable and low-carbon logistics:

Energy Efficiency and Renewable Energy: Initiatives to repurpose industrial waste heat, including the conversion of low-grade heat from exhaust gasses into power, improve energy efficiency. The incorporation of passive architecture and photovoltaic-battery systems in logistics buildings can substantially diminish carbon footprints.

Route Optimization and Intelligent Logistics: Advanced methods, such as improved Ant Colony Optimization, are employed to optimize truck routing, hence minimizing energy usage and carbon emissions in distribution. Artificial intelligence (AI) increasingly contributes to route optimization by reducing fuel consumption and carbon footprints through the integration of real-time traffic and meteorological data. Logistics optimization aims to identify the most efficient strategy within various limitations to reduce costs or environmental impact. This frequently entails mathematical modeling to reconcile economic and environmental objectives, exemplified in municipal logistics network design that accounts for CO2 emission levies and cost recovery.

Green Supply Chain Management: He et al. (2023) assert that integrating low-carbon logistics into a green supply chain framework enhances energy conservation and fosters sustainable development within the industry. This entails the adoption of circular economy ideas to revolutionize logistics systems, advancing towards techniques that eradicate waste and maintain material utilization.

Consequently, it cannot be simplified to sporadic ecological activities; it must be comprehended as an interconnected system in which economic, social, and environmental factors are interrelated with technological developments and collaboration among stakeholders. For managers, this entails transcending isolated initiatives (such as recycling or minimizing packaging) to incorporate sustainability into a holistic strategy that aligns with corporate governance; for public policymakers, it underscores the necessity for economic and regulatory incentives (subsidies, carbon taxes, international standards) to progress beyond opportunistic methods. Sustainable logistics seeks to consider the triple bottom line, suggesting a threefold trade-off (Figure 1). In common parlance, these three objectives are frequently termed the three Ps: people, planet, and profit.

Figure 1. Framework for sustainable logistics

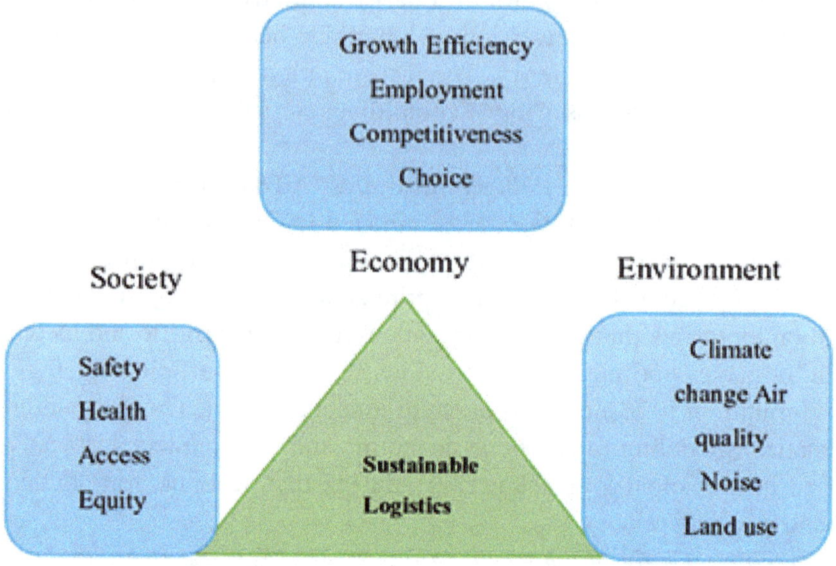

Figure 1 is a schematic illustration of the three foundational elements of sustainable logistics as per the 3 P framework (People, Planet, Profit). The social dimension (People) encompasses elements like safety, health, equity, and accessibility. The environmental dimension (Planet) includes concerns on climate change, air quality, noise pollution, land utilization, biodiversity, and waste management. The economic dimension (Profit) emphasizes growth, efficiency, employment, competitiveness, and autonomy in decision-making. Sustainability in logistics depends on the coordination and equilibrium of these three interconnected elements. Low-carbon logistics operates within this framework by prioritizing targeted strategies and actions that mitigate greenhouse gas emissions linked to logistical operations, including the selection of less polluting transportation modes, enhancement of warehouse energy efficiency, and optimization of routes and loads. Expanding logistics beyond a just commercial framework to encompass ecological and societal aspects necessitates action from firms. In practice, they will transition to a more sustainable solution only if an economic benefit is attainable, even if it is in the long term, or if forced to do so. Within the realm of logistics, the Sustainable Development Goals provide a cohesive framework that directs governments, corporations, and supply chain participants in evolving towards more efficient, resilient, inclusive, and low-carbon logistics systems.

Sustainable cross-border logistics amalgamates sustainable logistics principles with the intricacies of international trade and governance, striving to regulate the movement of goods and services across national boundaries while mitigating environmental impact and fostering social and economic welfare.

Sustainable and low-carbon logistics is a comprehensive strategy designed to harmonize economic efficiency, social responsibility, and environmental stewardship by markedly diminishing the carbon footprint of logistical activities. This conceptual clarification facilitates the move to the analysis of broader concepts of sustainable development as applied to logistics.

2. The Sustainable Development Goals as a Global Framework for Logistic Transformation

Sustainable Development goals emphasize distinct objectives aimed at attaining specific outcomes . The logical analysis of the target results' content revealed that, based on the sphere of affected relations, they can be categorized into four groups (Figure 1): humanitarian results, primarily focused on the individual and considering their social environment (family, colleagues, neighbors, etc.); economic results, manifested in the attainment of a new level of material well-being that facilitates an enhancement in quality of life; social and political results, which provide personally and socially significant guarantees, freedoms, security, and a sense of safety; and environmental results, which establish the foundations for environmental improvement and the preservation of natural heritage for future generations.

2.1 Key Definitions

Sustainable logistics based on AI: This notion pertains to the use of artificial intelligence functionalities, such as machine learning, optimization, digital twins, and blockchain, into the design, planning, execution, and management of logistics operations. The purpose is to concurrently enhance environmental performance (including emission reduction and resource management), social performance (including equity, safety, and well-being), and economic performance (particularly efficiency and resilience) across the transnational value chain. The advent of "Sustainable Logistics 4.0" exemplifies the integration of digitalization and sustainability principles, utilizing sophisticated technology to attain sustainability objectives (Parhi et al. 2022). L'intelligence artificielle joue un rôle de plus en plus prépondérant dans l'optimisation des itinéraires, réduisant la consommation de carburant et les empreintes carbone par l'intégration de données de trafic et météorologiques en time réel.

Logistics strategies aligned with the SDGs: designed to directly and measurably contribute to the achievement of specific targets of the United Nations Sustainable

Development Goals (SDGs). These strategies go beyond mere compliance to aim for a transformative positive impact. Sustainable logistics itself is intrinsically linked to the achievement of the SDGs by seeking a balance between economic, social, and environmental dimensions (Mohsen 2022). Logistics strategies can advance SDG 13 (Climate Action) by enhancing energy efficiency and minimizing emissions. The focus on equitable labor practices and safety supports the social Sustainable Development Goals (SDGs).

Transboundary Sustainability Governance: This word denotes the institutional, regulatory, and collaborative structures that enable the coordination and execution of sustainable logistical practices across national boundaries. It specifically tackles the obstacles associated with legal discrepancies, varied institutional capabilities, and data sovereignty concerns. Cooperation among diverse stakeholders, such as logistics service providers, manufacturers, suppliers, customers, and government entities, is crucial for the successful execution of sustainable logistics (Qian et al. 2019).

Government policies and regulations, shown by China's dual carbon objectives, are crucial in advancing green logistics practices through the provision of support, incentives, and standards.

The authors categorized the 17 Sustainable Development goals into four groups by a frequency and logical analysis of expert comments. The allocation of objectives to a particular group does not restrict the potential simultaneous influence of the relevant event on the attainment of objectives assigned to other groups.

A crucial aspect of logistics is its intrinsic relationship with environmental conservation. Every logistically sound option invariably results in proportional improvements in environmental well-being. The criterion for selecting a logistically reasonable management solution is to minimize transportation or warehousing activities.

Consequently, transportation, storage procedures, energy consumption, and environmental pollutants are avoided. Logistics is metaphorically akin to ecology.

Figure 2. Grouping SD goals by focus on achieving globally significant results (Hereinafter, goal numbers are denoted by the letter G with the addition of a number indicating the ordinal number of the goal in accordance with their list given in the United Nations)

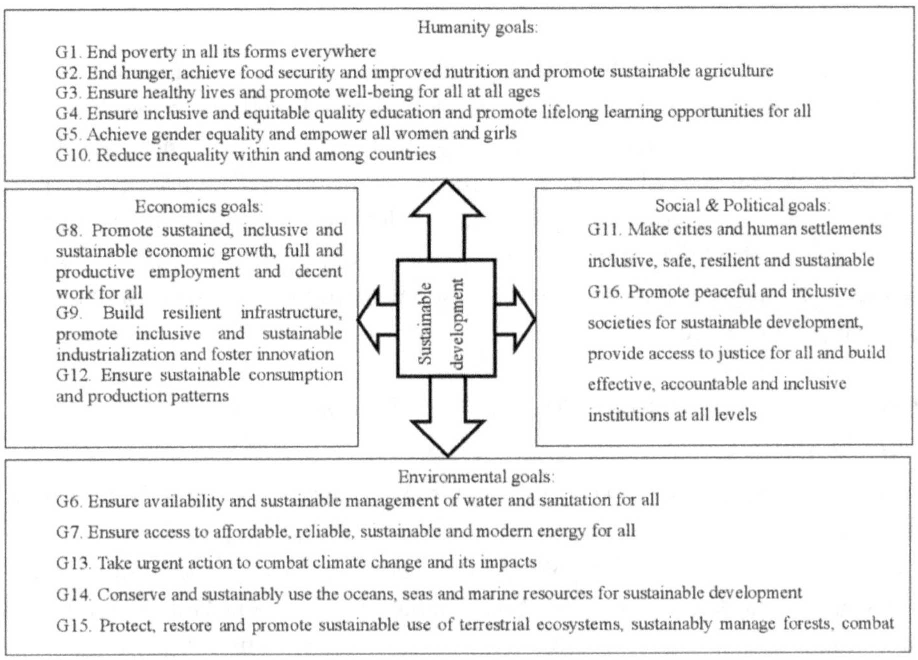

Figure 2 categorizes the Sustainable Development Goals into four interrelated domains: human objectives (poverty alleviation, food security, health, education, gender equality, and diminished inequalities), economic objectives (inclusive growth, decent employment, sustainable industrialization, innovation, and responsible consumption), environmental objectives (water, sustainable energy, climate action, and the preservation of marine and terrestrial ecosystems), and social and political objectives (sustainable urban development, effective institutions, peace, and justice). The entirety converges on the core objective of sustainable development, emphasizing the interconnection of economic, social, environmental, and institutional factors to attain substantial global results.

A substantial impact will result from the use of contemporary information technology, encompassing cloud computing, the Internet of Things, and the optimization of transportation planning. Nonetheless, the challenge of attaining Sustainable Development goals lies in the absence of a dependable and universally recognized system for monitoring data regarding the status of indicators related to these objectives.

Additional humanitarian and sociopolitical objectives are indirectly linked to the execution of effective logistical management decisions.

2.2 The Sustainable Development Goals particularly related to logistics (SDGs 7, 9, 11, 12, 13, and 17)

Logistics is a crucial catalyst for economic, social, and environmental advancement. Its transition to more sustainable models aligns directly with the Sustainable Development Goals (SDGs) established by the United Nations. Among the 17 Sustainable Development Goals (SDGs), several pertain directly to logistical difficulties, especially in a cross-border setting, where the flows of materials, information, and energy are amplified. The Sustainable Development Goals 7, 9, 11, 12, 13, and 17 serve as strategic pillars to direct logistical methods towards sustainable and intelligent performance.

SDG7: Ensure access to affordable, reliable, sustainable, and modern energy for all

The seventh Sustainable Development Goal is central to contemporary concerns as well as prospects. Access to sustainable energy for all is crucial for combatting climate change, as well as for job creation, housing development, connectivity, security, and food production. This Sustainable Development Goal unequivocally offers a chance to revolutionize lives, economies, and the environment.

SDG 7 seeks to guarantee access to dependable, sustainable, and contemporary energy sources. Logistics, which relies significantly on fossil fuels, is a critical industry for the energy transition.

Logistical significance: vehicle electrification, alternative fuels (green hydrogen, biogas), energy optimization of warehouses, low-carbon logistics corridors.

The role of AI encompasses energy forecasting, optimization of charging cycles, intelligent battery management, and multimodal planning that prioritizes the least carbon-intensive transportation methods.

The role of AI includes accurate energy forecasting through machine learning models that analyze weather data, consumption history, and traffic patterns to predict the energy requirements of fleets and warehouses, facilitating more efficient energy resource allocation and minimizing waste; optimization of charging cycles via algorithms that schedule electric vehicle recharging during periods of lowest cost and highest sustainability, thereby enhancing the integration of renewable energy and alleviating peak demand; intelligent battery management that prolongs battery lifespan and optimizes performance through predictive monitoring systems, thus decreasing the need for new resources and electronic waste; and multimodal planning that emphasizes the least carbon-intensive transportation methods by incorporating environmental constraints into route and mode optimization algorithms, leading to a substantial reduction in greenhouse gas emissions per ton-kilometer.

The implementation of AI for Sustainable Development Goal 7 presents problems. The energy usage of AI infrastructures, such as data centers and intense computing, can generate a substantial carbon footprint, requiring an evaluation of the net carbon balance. Furthermore, dependence on high-quality, real-time data for forecasting and optimization necessitates strong collection and processing infrastructures, which can pose significant challenges for underdeveloped regions or organizations with constrained resources. Substantial initial investment costs for AI technology and related infrastructures (electric vehicles, smart charging stations) may impede adoption, especially for SMEs, hence generating disparities in access to the energy transition.

SDG9: Establish a resilient infrastructure, promote sustainable industrialization that benefits all, and encourage innovation

The ninth objective advocates for the robust and sustainable advancement of infrastructure, industrialization, and innovation. These industries must serve as catalysts for poverty alleviation and enhancement of global living standards, while exerting minimal environmental impact.

SDG9 advocates for the advancement of financial, technological, and technical assistance for industries, while fostering innovation and scientific inquiry. To attain this objective, it is imperative to enhance international collaboration in research and development, while facilitating the transfer of technology to poor nations . SDG 9 underscores the impisance of innovation, robust infrastructure, and sustainable industrialization, which are crucial for contemporary logistics systems.

Significance of logistics: effective port, rail, and road infrastructure; multimodal platforms; digital integration of transnational supply chains.

The function of AI includes digital twins, predictive maintenance systems, intelligent automation of logistics hubs, and the optimization of intermodal connectivity.

The role of AI encompasses digital twins (facilitating the simulation and virtual optimization of infrastructures prior to physical implementation, thereby minimizing errors and waste), predictive maintenance systems (employing sensors and AI to foresee equipment failures, reducing downtime and prolonging asset longevity), intelligent automation of logistics hubs (enhancing the flow of goods, inventory management, and operational safety through robotics and autonomous systems), and the optimization of intermodal connectivity (dynamically coordinating various transport modes for optimal efficiency and emission reduction).

Despite these advantages, automation and AI-driven innovation may result in social trade-offs, especially concerning employment in repetitive occupations, hence requiring retraining initiatives. The intricacy of incorporating these technologies into current and diverse infrastructures poses a significant technological obstacle. Furthermore, cybersecurity is increasingly crucial, as interconnected and automated systems are susceptible to attacks that can significantly disrupt supply chains.

SDG11: Make cities and human settlements inclusive, safe, resilient and sustainable

The eleventh goal seeks to rehabilitate and design cities, or any human settlement, to provide employment opportunities, access to essential services, energy, housing, transportation, green public spaces, and more, while enhancing resource utilization and minimizing environmental impacts .

This objective is to render urban areas secure, inclusive, resilient, and sustainable. Promote sustainable urban transportation by enhancing public transit, utilizing electric or environmentally friendly delivery vehicles, alleviating traffic congestion, and optimizing urban logistics. Urban logistics planning involves the building of warehouses, distribution hubs, and delivery facilities on the peripheries of cities to reduce travel and alleviate congestion. Waste management: reverse logistics for the collection, recycling, and reuse of utilized products or packaging enhances urban sustainability.

In the context of SDG 11, artificial intelligence is instrumental in urban logistics planning (enhancing last-mile delivery routes to mitigate congestion and noise pollution, and dynamically managing delivery schedules), intelligent traffic management (real-time interventions to facilitate traffic flow and decrease emissions), and optimizing public transport networks to promote utilization. It can also facilitate reverse logistics for trash management by enhancing the collection and sorting of recyclable resources.

AI optimization may occasionally result in compromises regarding urban quality of life. Consolidating delivery in specific regions for efficiency may exacerbate strain on local infrastructure or elevate pollution levels in those districts. The extensive aggregation of urban data for artificial intelligence prompts significant concerns regarding privacy and surveillance. Furthermore, the implementation of AI solutions might incur significant costs and necessitate a strong digital infrastructure, thereby exacerbating the digital gap among urban areas or communities.

SDG12: Establish sustainable consumption and production patterns

The twelfth goal urges producers, consumers, communities, and governments to contemplate their consumption habits, waste generation, and the environmental and social ramifications of the full product value chain. This SDG emphasizes the need of recognizing the interrelations between individual and collective choices, as well as comprehending the effects of our activities on a national and global level .

This objective promotes sustainable consumption and manufacturing practices Connection with logistics:

Circular supply chain: execution of reverse logistics for the recycling or repurposing of items (returns, packaging, components).

Mitigation of losses: decreased post-harvest losses and food waste by enhancing transportation and storage conditions (cold chain, suitable packaging).

Sustainable procurement: involves the selection of suppliers that implement sustainable practices and promote the eco-design of products and packaging.

Reporting and traceability: logistics firms can quantify their effect (emissions, waste) and incorporate sustainability into their main performance metrics.

Artificial Intelligence is crucial for Sustainable Development Goal 12 by enabling the circular supply chain (enhancing reverse logistics for returns, refurbishment, and recycling of products, forecasting the lifespan of components), loss mitigation (demand forecasting to curtail overproduction, optimizing storage and transport conditions to diminish food waste through sensors and AI), sustainable sourcing (data analysis to assess the environmental and social performance of suppliers), and traceability (employing blockchain and AI to guarantee the provenance and lifecycle of products, thereby improving transparency).

The problems encompass the intricacies of data management along a vast supply chain for comprehensive traceability. AI may contribute to indirect overconsumption by enabling expedited and cost-effective production without promoting restraint. Implementing AI systems for circularity necessitates substantial investments and meticulous collaboration among all stakeholders in the chain, which can be challenging to coordinate.

SDG13 - Take urgent action to combat climate change and its impacts

The thirteenth target seeks to bolster the resilience and adaptation ability of nations against climatic hazards and disasters, emphasizing the enhancement of capabilities in the least developed countries and small island developing states. This desire is evident at all levels: through the enhancement of international collaboration, particularly in the implementation of the Green Fund; in the formulation of national policies and plans, through public awareness and the creation of early warning systems .

This objective aims to take urgent measures to combat climate change and its impacts:

- Reduction of greenhouse gas emissions: optimize transportation, use greener modes of transport to limit the logistical carbon footprint.

- Climate resilience: designing resilient supply chains in the face of climate risks (floods, storms, disruptions) through robust planning.
- Technology transfer: adopting climate-friendly technological solutions (clean vehicles, renewable energies) in logistical operations.
- Collaboration: working with stakeholders (local authorities, suppliers, customers) to implement carbon reduction strategies in the chain.

Artificial Intelligence advances Sustainable Development Goal 13 by mitigating greenhouse gas emissions through route and load optimization, selection of the least polluting transportation modes, and predictive fuel consumption management. It enhances the climate resilience of supply chains via predictive modeling of climate risks to foresee disruptions and strategize alternative routes. Additionally, it promotes technology transfer by identifying best practices and optimizing the implementation of clean solutions, such as electric vehicles and renewable energy, in logistics operations. A possible tradeoff exists in that AI-driven cost optimization may occasionally prioritize cheaper solutions that are not inherently the most environmentally sustainable. The precision of AI models is significantly influenced by the quality and accessibility of climate and logistical data, which may pose challenges in specific places. Furthermore, the expenses associated with the development and implementation of sophisticated AI solutions for climate modeling and optimization can be exorbitant for numerous firms.

SDG17: Partnerships for the Goals

The seventeenth and concluding goal advocates for the establishment of successful collaborations among governments, the commercial sector, and civil society, essential for the realization of the Sustainable Development Goals at global, regional, national, and local tiers. These relationships must be inclusive, founded on shared beliefs and values, and prioritize the welfare of individuals and the world .

The transnational nature of logistics chains underscores the significance of SDG 17 as a crucial foundational element.

The significance of logistics is underscored by the necessity for collaboration among nations, the standardization of customs frameworks, the utilization of common digital platforms, and the alignment of regulatory measures.

The function of artificial intelligence encompasses various aspects such as the integration of systems, the sharing of intelligent data, the utilization of blockchain technology to enhance transparency across borders, and the development of collaborative platforms.

The role of artificial intelligence includes system integration (facilitating interoperability among various logistical and customs platforms), intelligent data sharing (promoting secure and pertinent information exchange among partners for enhanced coordination), the application of blockchain technology to augment cross-border transparency (by establishing immutable and shared registries for traceability and compliance), and the creation of collaborative platforms (where AI can enhance resource allocation and activity coordination among diverse stakeholders). The primary obstacles for SDG 17 encompass trust and governance around data exchanged through AI and blockchain, since collaborators must be confident in the security and equitable access to information. The standardization of data formats and protocols is crucial yet challenging to accomplish globally. Furthermore, the digital divide among nations or corporations can obstruct equal engagement in these AI-driven collaborative platforms, so constraining the efficacy of partnerships.

2.3 Role of international agreements in the transition to sustainable logistics

International climate governance relies on normative and institutional frameworks established through multilateral talks, prominently include (UNITED NATIONS, 1992) the United Nations Framework Convention on Climate Change (UNFCCC), the Kyoto Protocol (UNITED NATIONS, 1998), and the Paris Agreement (UNITED NATIONS, 2015). These agreements are crucial tools for directing and organizing collective efforts in response to the climate problem, by establishing objectives, delineating state obligations, and promoting scientific, technological, and financial collaboration. The scientific literature underscores their vital role in the gradual development of an international climate regime, marked by complexity, fragmentation, and ongoing evolution.

This necessitates the formulation of more definitive policy instruments and institutional frameworks for sustainable cross-border logistics. For instance, the creation of transnational green logistics corridors with tax incentives for low-carbon carriers, the standardization of emission regulations for commercial vehicles across borders, or the development of secure and interoperable data-sharing platforms under the auspices of international organizations. Governance must also rectify the deficiencies in institutional capacities in developing nations through capacity-building initiatives and technology transfer to guarantee a just and equitable transition.

UNFCCC: a structural framework for collaborative action

Established in 1992 during the Rio Earth Summit, the UNFCCC provides a global framework designed to stabilize greenhouse gas concentrations to prevent hazardous disruptions to the climate system. It establishes organizing concepts, particularly common but differentiated responsibility (CBDR), and formulates the organizational framework for climate discussions, encompassing the Conferences of the Parties (COP) and related scientific entities. Bodansky (2016) asserts that the agreement adheres to a framework of flexible governance, emphasizing progressive collaboration over force.

The UNFCCC functions as the "constitution" of the climate regime by establishing procedural rules, facilitating transparency, delineating responsibilities, and structuring interactions among states, international institutions, non-state actors, and scientific authorities like the Intergovernmental Panel on Climate Change (IPCC). Numerous studies (Ostrom, 2010; Bodansky, 2016) highlight its polycentric characteristics, illustrating multi-level governance that encompasses both horizontal and vertical dynamics.

The Kyoto Protocol: a paradigm of governance by limitation

The Kyoto Protocol (1998) represents the initial practical implementation of the UNFCCC's goals. It establishes legally binding, measurable targets for emission reductions for a cohort of industrialized nations. It also implements market mechanisms – Clean Development Mechanism, Joint Implementation, carbon market – designed to internalize the cost of emissions and promote low-carbon solutions.

Nonetheless, scholarly literature promptly recognizes the constraints of this top-down methodology. The Kyoto Protocol remains a significant milestone: it establishes the inaugural framework for binding quantification and serves a fundamental function in the proliferation of economic climate instruments.

The Paris Agreement: a versatile and global framework for climate policy

The ratification of the Paris Agreement in 2015 signifies a conceptual watershed. Abandoning the purely binding logic, it introduces a hybrid model that includes: Nationally determined contributions (NDCs), reflecting the capacities and priorities specific to each State; a five-year ambition cycle, ensuring the continuous progression of commitments; a Global Stock take allowing for a collective assessment of trajectories; an explicit recognition of the carbon neutrality goal and the 1.5–2°C limit.

Keohane and Oppenheimer (2016) characterize the Paris Agreement as an adaptive governance framework that facilitates collective learning, regular assessment, and the incremental incorporation of political or technological advancements.

International accords constitute the cornerstone of the global climate framework. The institutional framework established by the UNFCCC, the binding provisions of the Kyoto Protocol, and the collaborative and adaptive structure of the Paris Agreement have progressively constructed a more inclusive, flexible, and effective global climate governance system capable of addressing the complexities of the climate crisis.

These agreements do not inherently resolve the climate crisis, but they establish the conditions for collective action, enable the dissemination of climate policies, mobilize essential financial and technological resources, and foster the development of a global ecosystem of polycentric and adaptive governance.

Figure 3 presents a consolidated timeline of significant events influencing international climate governance from 1979 to 2024, emphasizing the gradual development of scientific underpinnings, legal structures, and policy pledges established through global climate discussions.

Figure 3. Chronology of significant milestones in the development of the international climate governance framework (1979–2024)

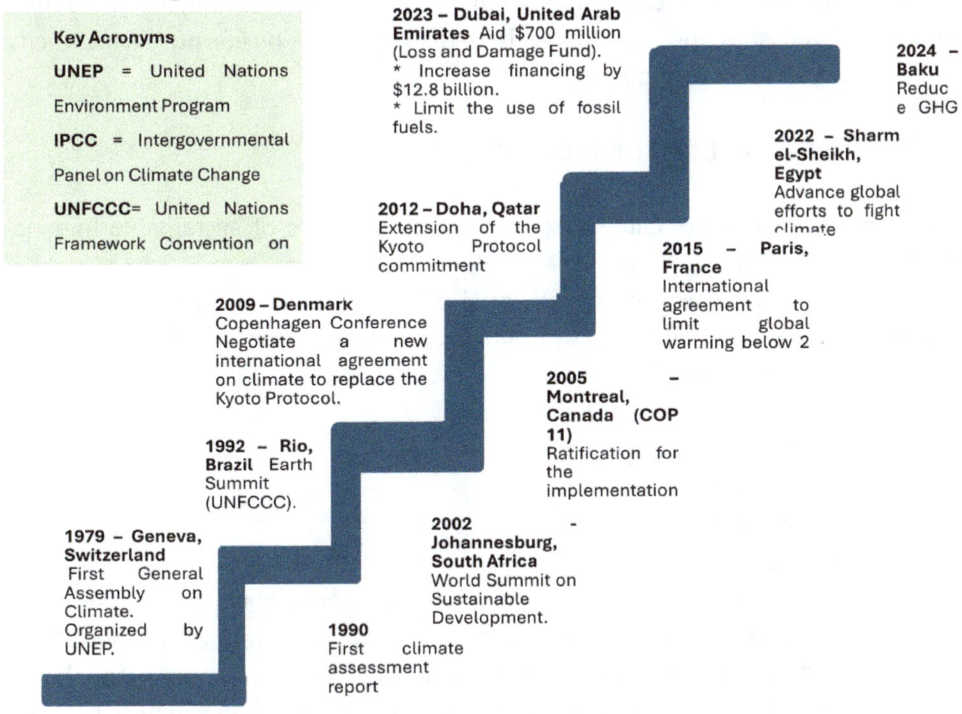

Figure 3 offers a comprehensive summary of the significant advancements influencing the global climate governance framework from the inaugural World Climate Conference convened by UNEP in 1979 to the agreements established at COP 29 in Baku in 2024. It demonstrates the gradual solidification of the scientific principles supporting global climate action (particularly via successive IPCC assessment reports), the development and enhancement of international legal frameworks (Rio Convention, Kyoto Protocol, Paris Agreement), and the function of the Conferences of the Parties (COPs) in augmenting financial, technological, and regulatory mechanisms that facilitate climate mitigation and adaptation. The chronology illustrates the transition from a primarily declarative governance framework to a more polycentric and progressively obligatory structure that enforces stricter responsibilities on states and high-emission industries, including global logistics systems. It highlights the increasing connection of global climate governance, national emission reduction programs, and the structural transformation of logistics chains motivated by decarbonization and resilience requirements.

3. Principles and levers of decarbonized logistics

This section presents the operational principles and specific mechanisms for the decarbonization of logistics, augmenting the previously established theoretical frameworks and strategic objectives. It is distinguished by its pragmatic focus, providing directives for execution.

3.1 The Five A's of Sustainable Logistics

Possible measures are categorized within the five A's of sustainable logistics (Macharis et al., 2014):

Awareness: it is essential that all involved actors understand why they must engage. Social responsibility is not limited to the production factory, but extends to the entire "supply chain" process:

-Responsible purchasing
-Sustainable transportation
-Sustainable packaging
-Sustainable warehousing

- Reverse logistics: The reverse logistics chain consists of a series of activities required for the recovery and reprocessing of used products, starting from the consumer; these products can, in some cases, be reused. The reuse of products involves remanufacturing, which is a production strategy aimed at the revalorization of used products through the use of properly functioning components.
- Environmental collaboration consists of joint activities and cooperations aimed at finding solutions to environmental problems; this collaboration involves suppliers and customers and can have repercussions on performance.

Avoidance: It is important to be aware of the points of action, but it is also necessary to address them. In theory, sustainable logistics implies that goods should reach their final destination in the fastest and most sustainable way possible, but practice shows a different reality. It is essential to avoid these "empty kilometers."

Another possibility is to establish a collaboration with clients, suppliers, or companies from other sectors. Combining their own load with that of other stores will allow for better utilization of truck capacity.

Act & Shift: The time has come to make changes and rethink alternatives and environmentally friendly processes by determining.

Anticipation of new technology: Sustainability is a current topic that goes hand in hand with technological advancements. Certainly, take into account emerging technologies such as hybrid vehicles and self-driving cars. Big data can help find new ways to efficiently transport goods.

Nonetheless, this expectation must be coupled with a thorough evaluation of the environmental costs of AI (energy consumption of data centers) and the social ramifications (requirement for new skills, effects on employment). The increasing reliance on AI technologies prompts concerns regarding resilience to cyberattacks and technical sovereignty.

Actor involvement: it is essential to involve all parties. Without common support and will, all of this will remain nothing more than good intentions.

The "five A's" will serve as an operational reference framework; nevertheless, they must be augmented with measuring methods (sustainable performance indicators) and enforceable public policies to progress beyond mere intention.

Stakeholder engagement must also tackle the differences in access to AI technology and investment capabilities between large corporations and SMEs, as well as between developed and developing nations, to prevent the aggravation of existing inequities.

3.2 The five principles of sustainability: Rethink, Refuse, Reduce, Reuse and Recycle

The five Rs' (rethink, refuse, reduce, reuse, and recycle) is a waste management principle derived from the Waste Framework Directive, a European Union legislation enacted in 1975. This approach underscores the necessity to reduce waste and save the environment. In conjunction with material criticality, the 5Rs' provide a synergistic strategy to mitigate environmental damage and conserve resources. The principle of the 3Rs' (reduce, reuse, recycle) has been extensively embraced by numerous groups, including non-governmental organizations, governmental bodies, and educational institutions. Although not flawless, adhering to these principles can assist individuals in making educated choices for a more sustainable lifestyle. The arrangement of the R's is intentional, commencing with the most effective, to direct us towards a more sustainable lifestyle.

Rethink. By rethinking waste, we can choose alternative items and mitigate our environmental impact. Rethinking habits is also crucial. Exploring sustainable alternatives to waste is the most straightforward and effective approach to initiate re-evaluation. Assuming responsibility for waste is the optimal approach to rethink and transform waste into environmentally sustainable resources (Meshram, 2024).

Refuse which seeks to minimize resource utilization through conscientious production and consumption. Refusal necessitates reevaluating the practices of producers and consumers, as well as rethinking products, processes, and packaging. The most effective method to manage trash is to prevent its occurrence initially. The objective should be "no product, no waste, no problem!"

Reduce. Reducing waste is a crucial aspect of environmental conservation, aiming to reduce the amount of trash produced and the amount of waste generated throughout a product's life cycle. The goal is not to generate waste but to reduce waste at or near its source in homes, businesses, and institutions. Reducing waste conserves energy, reduces pollution caused by manufacturing materials and supplies that become waste, and reduces reliance on landfills and resource recovery facilities. The more waste we produce, the less waste there is to be disposed of.

Reuse denotes the utilization of products or components for their initial purpose or an alternative advantageous application. It includes actions including repair, refurbishment, repurposing, remodeling, and upcycling. While not as effective in waste prevention, reuse contributes to the reduction of new product and material production and consumption. Upon reaching the end of its initial utility, it is imperative to contemplate the extension of its lifespan or the identification of alternative applications, particularly when such actions are environmentally and economically feasible. Essentially, what one person considers trash could be another person's treasure!

Recycle Recycling is an essential environmentally sustainable practice for waste disposal that converts non-biodegradable products and resources into new items. It is essential for the management of solid waste, diminishing dependence on raw resources, mitigating air and water pollution, conserving energy, and lowering greenhouse gas emissions. Recycling entails converting high-quality garbage into useful new materials and goods, requiring minimal effort yet effecting a significant impact on the globe. In Connecticut, state law mandates recycling, obligating all individuals to participate in the practice.

Ultimately, the concepts of the Rs, even if incomplete, constitute a fundamental methodological basis for developing circular supply chain strategies. Utilizing specific indicators (reuse rate, carbon footprint reduction, percentage of recycled packaging), they enable a transition from the linear "produce-consume-discard" model to circular logistics with less environmental impact.

4. Towards Integrated Strategies for Sustainable Logistics

A gap appears to exist between an integrated conceptual definition and the many practices of sustainable logistics. While the array of techniques aligns with a broad logic of sustainable logistics conceptually, their integration has yet to be achieved. Exceeding the goals of sustainable logistics and evaluating its success appears to be a viable avenue; yet, it necessitates a detailed comprehension of the function of AI.

While AI-driven methods present significant opportunities for efficiency, decarbonization, and alignment with the Sustainable Development Goals, it is essential to acknowledge that AI is not a panacea. The implementation must be followed by a thorough understanding of the intrinsic trade-offs among the economic, social, and environmental aspects of sustainability. Technological constraints (data quality, integration complexity), implementation obstacles (costs, expertise, infrastructure), and potential hazards (employment impact, AI energy consumption, cybersecurity, ethical and data privacy concerns) must be thoroughly assessed and addressed.

An integrated approach to sustainable logistics strategies, augmented by AI, necessitates not only strong performance metrics and motivating public policies but also transparent and ethical multi-stakeholder governance, adept at managing interdependencies and ensuring that technological innovation effectively promotes sustainable and equitable development for all.

4.1 Relationship between logistics and the economy

Logistics services influence economic growth. Figure 4 below shows the effect of investments in logistics infrastructure on economic growth from an aggregated perspective. They stimulate economic competitiveness while improving the quality of logistics services. Indeed, these investments shorten delivery times and thus optimize overall logistics costs.

Figure 4. The impact of logistics on economic growth

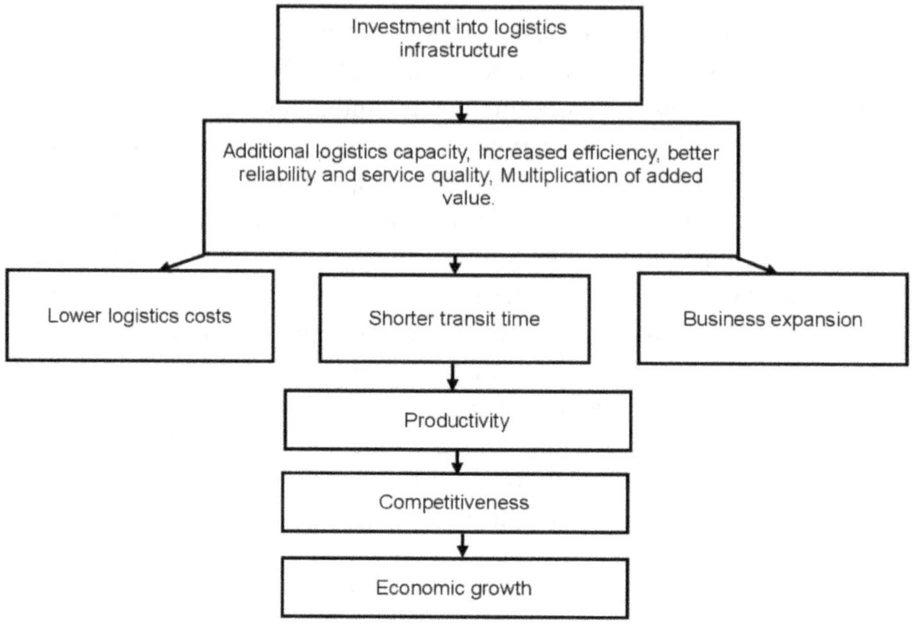

Figure 4 has been raised by several researchers. Khan et al. (2017) highlighted the impact of logistics infrastructures on the economic prosperity of countries. In this regard, Saidi et al. (2020) suggest that the level and quality of logistics services attract foreign investors and effectively promote economic development.

Logistics serves as a critical driver of competitiveness and economic expansion, since investments in logistical infrastructure enhance supply chain efficiency, minimize delays, and facilitate international trade. Saidi et al. (2020) assert that the caliber of logistics infrastructure draws foreign direct investment and fosters economic development. Nonetheless, economic growth predicated exclusively on logistical optimization is constrained, as augmented flows may result in elevated emissions unless paired with sustainability initiatives.

4.2 Relationship between logistics and the environment

Reconciling logistics performance and environmental performance is a difficult task. Logistics is a sector that consumes many energy resources and significantly contributes to environmental degradation. In this regard, the works of Sharma et al. (1999), Zhang and Yang (2016), Liu et al. (2018), and Karaduman et al. (2020) have empirically confirmed the close relationship between logistics and environmental quality. On their part, Halldórsson and Kovács (2010) revealed the necessity of implementing energy-efficient logistics systems to mitigate the carbon footprint.

The conflict between logistical efficiency and environmental sustainability persists. The enhancement of energy efficiency is frequently counterbalanced by the rise in transported volumes ("rebound effect").

4.3 Relationship between logistics and society

The social responsibility of companies to maintain a healthy society is not obvious. The integration of the economic, social, and environmental needs of different stakeholders remains a delicate exercise. Reducing poverty while ensuring the overall well-being of employees constitutes a pillar of action of great importance. Moreover, logistics activities have an impact on quality of life, safety, health issues, and public well-being. It seems wise, therefore, to manage both internal and external human resources.

Logistical operations directly impact quality of life, public health, and safety. Nonetheless, they also produce adverse externalities, like urban congestion, air pollution, and the insecure working circumstances encountered by drivers and handlers. In this context, various sustainable urban logistics initiatives in cities such as Paris, Brussels, and Barcelona are trialing innovative solutions, including proximity hubs, cargo bikes, and low-emission zones, to harmonize operational efficiency with urban well-being. Nonetheless, the social dimension is predominantly overlooked in corporate plans, frequently regarded as a secondary concern relative to economic and environmental priorities.

5. Governance, Challenges, and Opportunities in Sustainable Logistics

Logistical sustainability cannot be attained by a solitary entity; it inherently depends on collaborative governance that incorporates all stakeholders within a systemic framework where enterprises, public authorities, civil society organizations, and consumers engage Brandenburg and Rebs (2015). From this viewpoint, corporations are executing resource pooling strategies, such as co-loading or establishing shared hubs, to concurrently decrease expenses and greenhouse gas emissions Macharis et al. (2014). Public authorities invest in specialized infrastructures, such multimodal platforms and urban consolidation zones. Halldórsson and Kovács (2010). Simultaneously, NGOs and unions apply normative pressure to uphold social and environmental rights, while consumers demonstrate heightened demands for transparency and traceability of supply chains.

This governance depends on a collection of regulatory and standardization tools, including ISO standards 14001 for environmental management and 26000 for social responsibility sustainability labels, and public-private partnerships focused on advancing green infrastructure. The disparities in economic, social, and environmental interests among stakeholders hamper cooperative dynamics. Consequently, the implementation of mediation and negotiation processes is crucial to ensure that logistical sustainability transcends isolated activities devoid of systemic influence.

In addition to governance challenges, sustainable logistics encounters many structural limitations. The substantial initial implementation expenses restrict the adoption of innovative solutions by small and medium-sized firms, which typically own less capital than major corporations Deckert (2023). Furthermore, the rebound effect represents a significant impediment: energy and logistical optimization, through the reduction of unit costs, may paradoxically result in an increase in carried quantities, thereby elevating overall emissions McKinnon (2018). The ongoing reliance on fossil fuels constitutes a technological and economic constraint, especially in the road and aviation sectors, where low-carbon options are either scarce or prohibitively expensive.

Notwithstanding these limitations, various developing factors are influencing the future landscape of the business. The European Union and numerous nations have established a carbon neutrality objective for 2050, necessitating a profound overhaul of infrastructure, organizational frameworks, and transportation fleets European . The emergence of green finance and ESG criteria is progressively steering investment towards companies that adhere to sustainability plans. Likewise, intelligent urban logistics, focused on the principles of smart cities, proximity hubs, and cargo bicycles, is swiftly proliferating in major metropolitan areas Ahn and Park (2022). The incorporation of the circular economy, emphasizing reuse, repair, and functional economics, is increasingly recognized as a vital framework for reimagining supply chains Geissdoerfer et al. (2017).

The future of sustainable logistics will ultimately rely on a strategic alignment of technical advancements, legal frameworks, financial instruments, and multi-stakeholder governance systems. An integrated and comprehensive strategy is essential for effectively reconciling economic competitiveness with environmental and social demands.

Sustainable logistics should be perceived as an integrated and resilient system that may convert environmental and social limitations into competitive advantages.

This comprehensive perspective prepares for Part 2, which focuses on sustainable supply chain management (SSCM), wherein the objective is to transcend isolated logistics and include sustainability across the entire supply chain network aligned with the SDGs.

II. SUSTAINABLE SUPPLY CHAIN MANAGEMENT ALIGNED WITH THE SDGS

Objective: Incorporate the Sustainable Development Goals into the strategy and operations of the supply chain.

1. Definition and conceptual framework of Sustainable Supply Chain Management (SSCM)

SCM is the management of relationships and interoperation from supplier to supplier to customer to customer. according to the literature, SCM refers to three traditional activities, namely procurement, production, and distribution. These latter activities are managed through flows.

Figure 5. Principal activities related to SCM

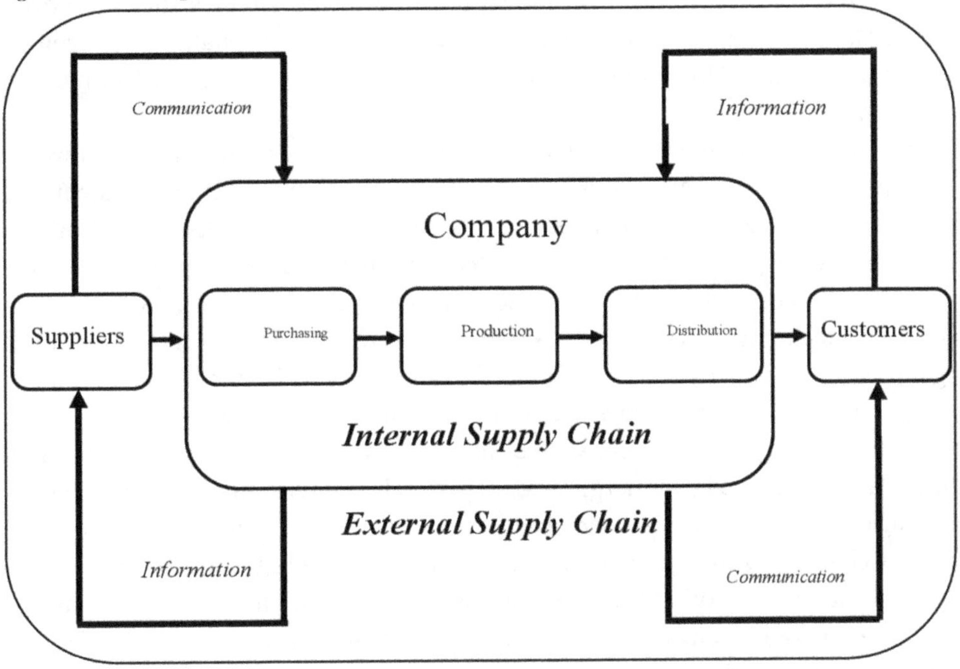

Figure 5 depicts the schematic of the internal and external supply chain, demonstrating the flows of information, communication, and goods among suppliers, the company (including purchasing, production, and distribution), and customers.

In recent years, there has been an evolution in the design of the SC, shifting from a classic SC focused on solving economic and operational problems to a sustainable SC that also addresses social and environmental issues. SCM primarily aims to meet customer demand by ensuring the five Rights of logistics (the Right product in terms of quantity and quality, the Right time, the Right place, and the Right price). While SSCM aims for customer satisfaction under the constraints of environmental respect and social equity.

The progression of logistics towards integrated supply chain management (SCM) has been organized around consecutive changes in operational, strategic, and environmental issues. Since the 1980s, the subjects of inquiry and the approaches employed have progressively evolved in complexity, mirroring the heightened integration of advanced technologies, institutional factors, and, more recently, sustainability mandates.

In the early 1980s, the literature on Logistics Management predominantly concentrated on essential functions: transportation, storage, warehousing, production planning, product quality, and adherence to delivery schedules. The emphasis is on the localized optimization of operations, utilizing methodologies such as process control statistics, single-objective optimization, and Total Quality Management (TQM) techniques. This endeavor largely focuses on enhancing operational efficiency and reducing costs.

The advent of Supply Chain Management in the 1990s signified a shift towards a systemic perspective. New concerns, like traceability, overall chain performance, and risk management, are incorporated into the operational aspects. Methods are advancing correspondingly: multi-objective optimization, agile production, lean manufacturing concepts, customer relationship management (CRM), and sustainable production techniques. This period signifies a more profound integration of inter-organizational processes and the preliminary formalization of extensive supply chains.

The early 2000s witnessed a rise in supply chain complexity and the incorporation of nascent digital technology. The subjects of investigation remain consistent, although are enhanced by emerging concerns such as environmental labeling (eco-labeling) and comprehensive performance assessment. The methodological landscape is characterized by the emergence of artificial intelligence (including fuzzy logic and neural networks), evolutionary algorithms (such as genetic algorithms), sensor technologies, electronic customer relationship management (e-CRM), the SCOR model, and NIR-type spectroscopies. These advancements provide a more sophisticated modeling of complexity, enhance predictive capacities, and augment process automation.

Since 2010, the emergence of environmental and societal concerns has driven the shift towards Sustainable Supply Chain Management. Current research emphasizes the operational and institutional amalgamation of sustainability principles: eco-efficient manufacturing, eco-labeling, equitable profit distribution, risk equilibrium among stakeholders, and enhancement of governance. This change depends on modern technologies linked to Industry 4.0: big data analytics, data mining, the Internet of Things (IoT), machine learning, intelligent sensors, and sophisticated optimization techniques. Hybrid methodologies integrating AI, fuzzy logic, and genetic algorithms are becoming pivotal in facilitating decision-making within uncertain and multi-dimensional contexts.

The interplay between sustainable development and supply chain management has incited many discussions aimed at conceptualizing the notion of sustainable supply chain management (SSCM). Table 1 provides a summary of SSCM definitions for the period 2007-2021.

Table 1. Summary of SSCM definitions

Definitions	References
SSCM requires "a more global approach to SCM. It must focus on the economic, ecological, and social dimensions of commercial practices and associated theories."	Svensson (2007)
It involves "the strategic and transparent achievement of the economic, environmental, and social goals of an organization, within a systemic coordination of key interorganizational business processes, aimed at improving the long-term economic performance of the company and its supply chain."	Carter and Rogers (2008)
Sustainable logistics consists of "the management of material, information, and financial flows, as well as collaboration among companies throughout the supply chain. It aims to promote the objectives of the three dimensions of sustainable development: economic, environmental, and social, while taking into account the needs of customers and stakeholders."	Seuring and Müller (2008)
SSCM is "a strategy that aims to generate value for customers, suppliers, and society by integrating the three sustainability dimensions (economic, social, and environmental) into decision-making and supply chain operations."	Kannan (2021)

Source: Authors' elaboration

In a more detailed manner, SSCM involves rigorous management of the entire product life cycle, including disposal or recycling at the end of life. It involves a voluntary approach based on a company's responsibility for the impact of its decisions on society and the environment.

Upon reviewing these definitions, many observations warrant attention:

- SSCM is a complex idea based on the principles of sustainable development. It is situated within a long-term framework by fostering collaborative intra- and inter-organizational approaches.

- SSCM encompasses multiple practices that influence the economy, environment, and society across the product life cycle. It employs a door-to-door strategy that frequently prioritizes environmental considerations, with mobility consistently serving as the primary lever of action.
- The SSCM is based on integrated strategies of multiple sustainable logistics practices. The whole thing is subject to continuous measurement and evaluation.
- SSCM can be summarized in five interconnected axes: the involved stakeholders must be aware of why they need to engage in a logistics sustainability approach. This awareness must be accompanied by the avoidance of any unsustainable practices (for example, avoiding empty kilometers). In this sense, change management is very important: continuously act and monitoring logistics performance. Technological advancements are at the heart of this change as they bring new solutions to test (hybrid vehicles, self-driving vehicles, big data, etc.). This mechanism is subject to continuous improvement by excellence.

In this chapter, we utilize the subsequent operational definition of Sustainable Supply Chain Management (SSCM): "SSCM denotes a cohesive strategy designed to sustainably oversee material, informational, and financial flows throughout the supply chain, harmonizing economic, environmental, and social goals while instituting governance and performance evaluation frameworks." This definition transcends the simple comparison of existing methodologies to provide a coherent analytical framework that will be utilized throughout the chapter. Managers should regard SSCM not merely as a moral obligation or a reactive measure to regulatory demands or "green" customer expectations; rather, it serves as a genuine strategic tool for enhancing competitiveness and achieving market distinction. This clarification emphasizes policymakers the necessity of creating a coherent and uniform regulatory framework that incorporates standards, certifications, and reporting requirements to ensure that SSCM is not merely performative. Ultimately, it offers researchers a solid conceptual framework that facilitates the creation of theoretical and empirical models for analyzing the mechanisms and effects of SSCM. Consequently, which will delineate the conceptual models designed to formalize this cohesive perspective of SSCM.

2. Fundamental Conceptual Models of SSCM

The main conceptual models of SSCM are to be discussed in this section.

2.1 The Carter and Rogers (2008) Model

The conceptual framework proposed by Carter and Rogers (2008) is a fundamental approach to Sustainable Supply Chain Management (SSCM). The concept posits that sustainability can only be attained by the concurrent integration of the three pillars of sustainable development: economic, environmental, and social. These three dimensions should be considered interdependently, as they mutually reinforce one another. At the convergence of these pillars resides the essence of SSCM: a supply chain that is both lucrative and socially as well as ecologically responsible.

In addition to these pillars, the model delineates additional critical supporting aspects for the success of the sustainable approach: committed leadership, a conducive corporate culture, proactive risk management, and transparent communication with stakeholders. This approach allows firms to create logistics strategies that generate enduring value, while reducing adverse effects and fostering responsible innovation.

Figure 6. The SSCM according to Carter and Rogers (2008)

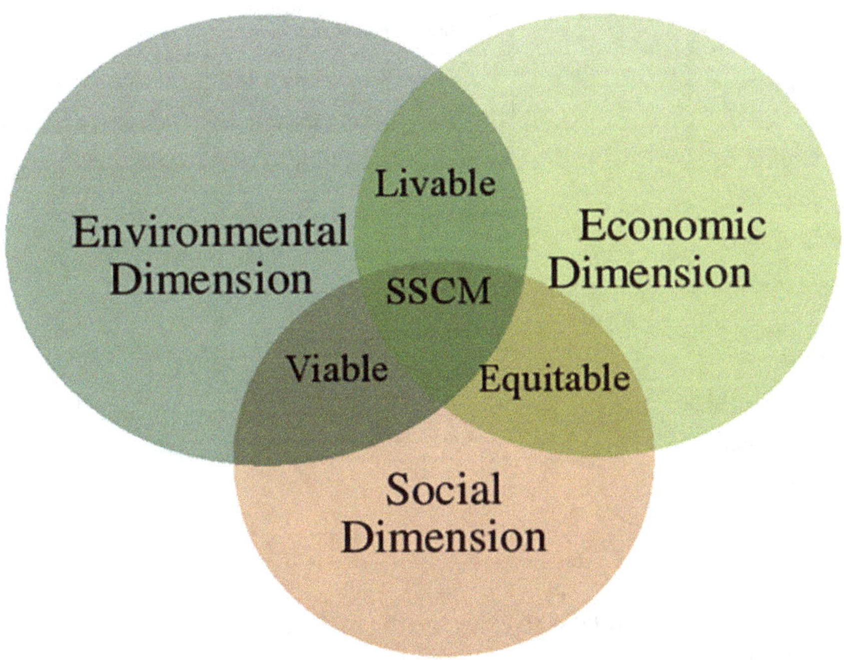

Figure 6 represents the three fundamental pillars of sustainable development: the environmental dimension, the economic dimension, and the social dimension.

Their intersection illustrates the necessity of a balance between economic performance, social equity, and environmental protection in order to ensure the overall sustainability of systems and organizations.

The Carter and Rogers approach underscores the concurrent integration of the three pillars; yet, it faces criticism for its normative character, since it articulates "what needs to be done" without delineating "how" to execute it.

2.2 The Esfahbodi Model (2012)

The objective of this model is to examine the main driving forces prompting companies to adopt SSCM practices present in Figure 7:

Figure 7. The SSCM model according to Esfahbodi et al. (2012)

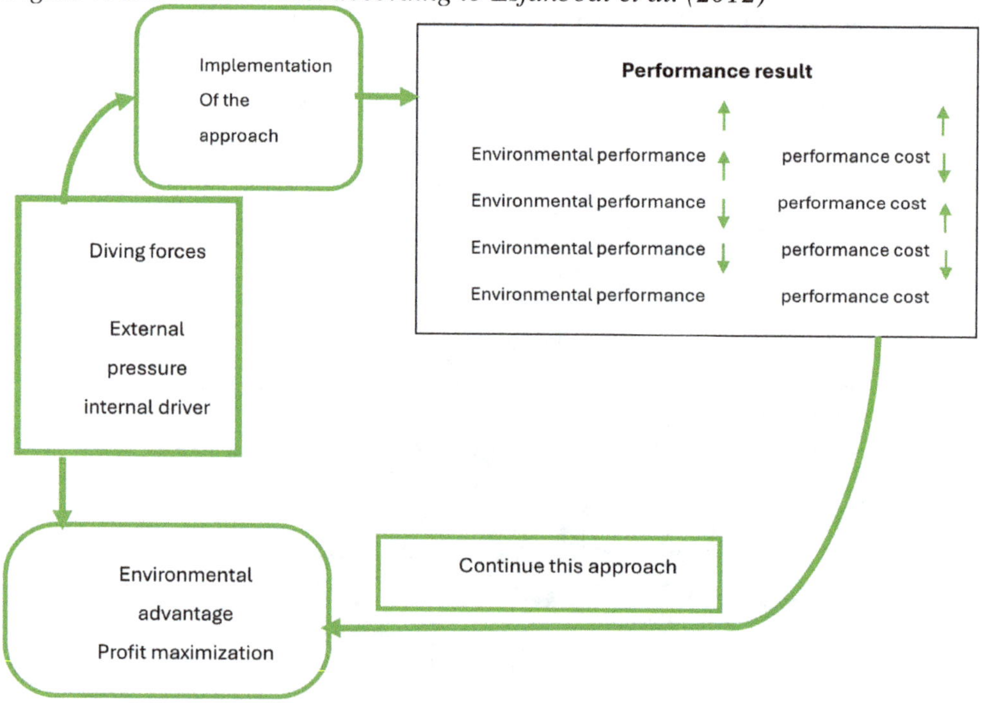

The objective of this model is to examine the main drivers prompting companies to adopt SSCM practices:

Strategic imperatives encourage companies to integrate customer orientation, customer responsiveness, and, more recently, environmental sustainability into their supply chain. Various stakeholders exert pressure, including customers, shareholders, government authorities, and competitors. Companies are required to comply with environmental regulations at both the national and international levels. These compliance requirements highlight the importance for companies to obtain environmental certifications and labels.

Regarding shareholders, internal engagement and support at various levels of the company are fundamental elements to promote the adoption of sustainable practices throughout the supply chain Diabat and Govindan (2011). They have the privilege of defining their program for the attention of the company's upper management. Customers are perceived as an additional factor encouraging the adoption of the SSCM approach due to their increasing awareness of environmental issues. Companies fear that their products will be boycotted by customers if they do not meet sustainability requirements. Currently, customer demand for environmentally friendly processes is one of the main drivers of logistics sustainability certification. Competitors also play an incentivizing role by encouraging companies to implement sustainable supply chain management practices.

The Esfahbodi model emphasizes external influences (customers, regulators, competitors) while downplaying the internal innovation capabilities of firms.

2.3 The Brandenburg and Rebs Model (2015)

The diagram presented serves as a visual representation of a well-established conceptual framework for Sustainable Supply Chain Management (SSCM), initially proposed and subsequently adapted from the work of Seuring and Müller (2008), and further referenced in the literature review conducted by Brandenburg and Rebs (2015). This framework elucidates the dynamic interrelationships among stakeholders, supply chain actors, sustainability objectives, and sustainable supply chain management practices. The following presents a detailed analysis of the conceptual SSCM model as depicted in the provided diagram.

The Brandenburg and Rebs model is noteworthy for its emphasis on the feedback loops among actors and stakeholders; nonetheless, it is predominantly theoretical and lacks practical applicability.

2.3.1 Supply Chain Actors

The fundamental operational entities that participate in the supply chain are delineated as follows:

- The focal company serves as the primary entity responsible for overseeing the supply chain and executing critical decisions related to sustainable supply chain management (SSCM).
- Suppliers are entities that furnish raw materials, components, or services to the focal organization.

- Consumers play a pivotal role in the acquisition of the final product and exert influence on sustainability initiatives through their demand and preferences.

2.3.2 Stakeholder Groups

External stakeholders impose pressures and offer incentives that shape sustainable supply chain management practices:

- Governments exert influence via mechanisms such as regulation, taxation, and the establishment of standards.
- Consumers: Impact via preferences, buying behavior, and advocacy.
- NGOs and Other Entities: Incorporate advocacy groups and community organizations that influence sustainability standards.

2.3.3 Objectives for Sustainability (Triple Bottom Line)

The following delineates the primary performance outcomes aimed for by SSCM:

- Economic Performance: An analysis of cost efficiency, profitability, and competitiveness.
- Environmental Performance: Reduction of emissions, enhancement of resource efficiency, and implementation of environmentally sustainable processes.
- Social Performance: Examination of labor conditions, community impact, and the adherence to human rights standards.

2.3.4 Practices in Sustainable Supply Chain Management

The following delineates the strategic and operational activities implemented to attain sustainability objectives:

- Sustainable Supplier Management involves the systematic selection, evaluation, and collaboration with suppliers, guided by sustainability criteria such as ISO 14001 and labor practices.
- The management of sustainability risks includes the identification and mitigation of environmental, social, and economic risks, including but not limited to child labor, penalties associated with pollution, and disruptions within the supply chain.
- Addressing Pressures and Incentives: Integrating stakeholder expectations into policies and practices (e.g., adjusting to regulatory modifications, reacting to environmentally conscious consumer trends).

2.3.5 Interaction Arrows (Relationships)

- Solid arrows: Represent operational flows or impacts among entities (e.g., the impact of stakeholder groups on SSCM processes).
- Dashed arrows: Indicate feedback loops, wherein SSCM practices or sustainability outcomes affect stakeholder perceptions or supply chain configurations.

The SSCM conceptual model demonstrates how external influences from primary stakeholder groups-such as governments, customers, and non-governmental organizations (NGOs)—mold the sustainability objectives of the focus enterprise. In reaction to these challenges, the focal company adopts diverse SSCM strategies within its supply chain, prioritizing sustainable supplier management and the proactive mitigation of sustainability-related risks. These strategies aim to improve performance in the three dimensions of the triple bottom line: economic sustainability, environmental stewardship, and social accountability. The results of these sustainability initiatives affect both internal operations and stakeholder perceptions, creating a feedback loop that strengthens the firm's dedication to sustainability and promotes continuous enhancement throughout the supply chain. Figure 8 below represents The SSCM model according to Brandenburg and Rebs (2015).

Figure 8. The SSCM model according to Brandenburg and Rebs (2015)

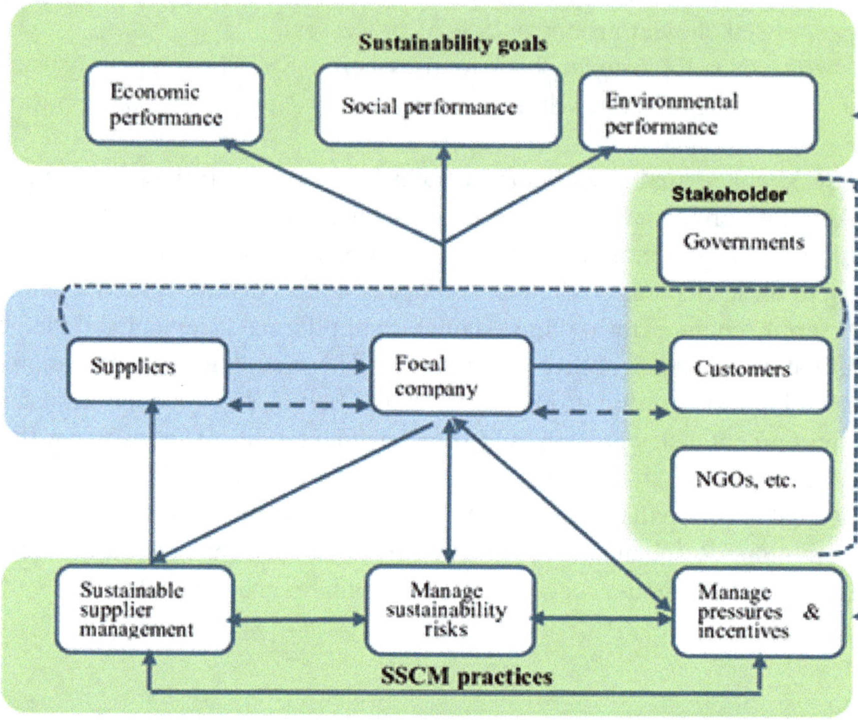

For managers, these models illustrate that sustainability is not an isolated decision but a continuous equilibrium among external pressures, internal strategies, and stakeholder expectations. For researchers, they emphasize the necessity to create more pragmatic hybrid models that amalgamate economic incentives with societal constraints. This contemplation seamlessly transitions to title 3, where the inquiry evolves from "What is SSCM ?" to "How can it be practically applied ?", so signifying a move from conceptual definition to operational application.

3. Operationalization of Sustainability in Supply Chains

Efficient supply chain management is a crucial determinant in the ongoing advancement of an organization. In recent decades, researchers, scientists, managers, and politicians globally have endeavored to formulate a comprehensive concept of sustainable development that integrates social and environmental objectives without compromising economic prosperity.

Figure 9. Green logistics: a conceptual framework

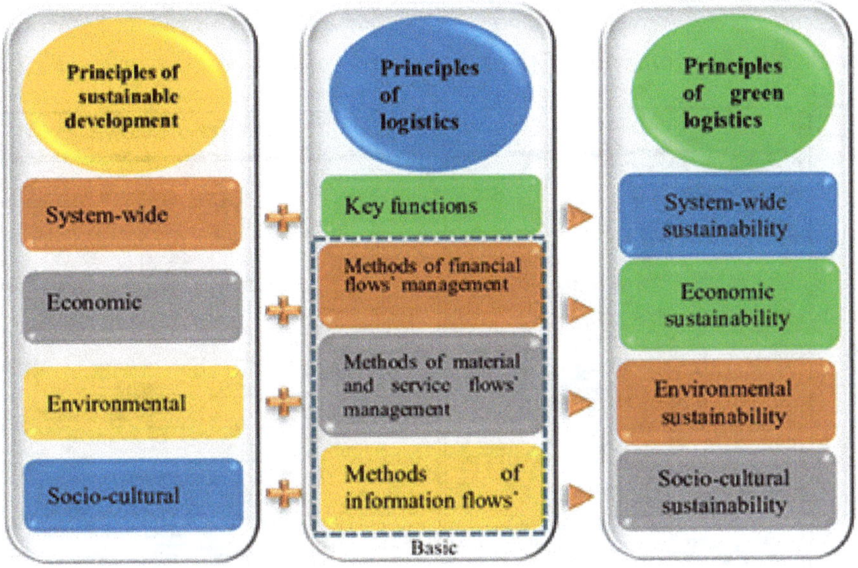

Figure 9 demonstrates that integrating sustainable development concepts with fundamental logistical functions generates a green logistics model. The framework fosters sustainability across all domains by integrating system-wide economic, environmental, and socio-cultural objectives with the management of financial, material, and information flows. This underscores the significance of logistics in attaining equitable, sustainable business practices.

3.1 Process Mapping

Process mapping techniques Herrmann and al. (2021) illustrate the integration of sustainability at every point of the chain; yet, their implementation is constrained by the challenges of achieving genuine inter-organizational cooperation. The recognition of social and environmental risks frequently adheres to a compliance-oriented mindset aimed at evading penalties or satisfying audits, rather than embracing a proactive strategy for innovation. KPIs, such as carbon footprint, water usage, and recycling rate, provide performance assessment but present challenges regarding comparability and the absence of standardization across industries and nations. For managers, these tools are indispensable yet inadequate without a definitive strategic commitment to sustainability. For decision-makers, they underscore the necessity of standardizing indicators to mitigate the risk of "cherry-picking," or the selective use of only advantageous indicators.

Figure 10. Process mapping of green logistics

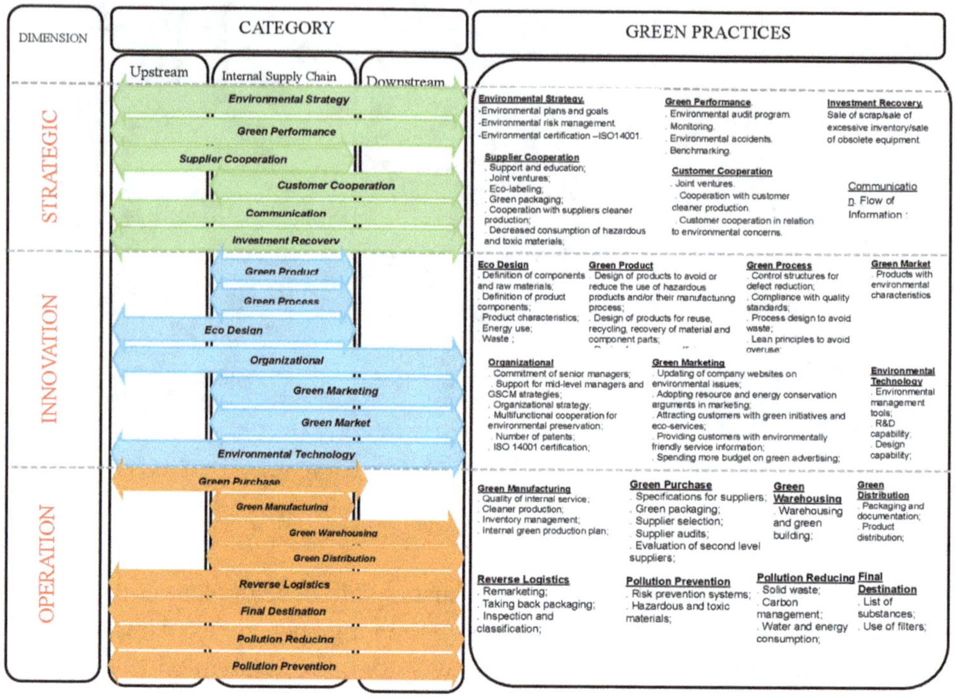

Figure 10 delineates a thorough framework that classifies green logistics techniques into three principal dimensions: Strategic, Innovation, and Operation. These dimensions are delineated within the Upstream, Internal Supply Chain, and Downstream categories of a supply chain. Strategic components encompass environmental strategy, collaboration with suppliers and customers, communication, and investment recovery, emphasizing long-term planning and cooperation. The innovation dimension highlights the creation of environmentally sustainable products and processes, eco-design, organizational dedication, marketing strategies, and environmental technologies to promote sustainable progress. The operational dimension delineates practical applications including sustainable procurement, manufacturing, warehouses, distribution, reverse logistics, and environmental management. Each component is underpinned by detailed green practices, demonstrating a holistic and integrated strategy for integrating sustainability throughout the logistics chain. This structured mapping can serve as a reference for organizations aiming to implement and enhance green logistics throughout all phases of their supply chain. Process mapping serves as an effective instrument for pinpointing leverage points regarding sustainability; nonetheless, it is fundamentally static. In circumstances characterized by uncertainty, health crises, raw material shortages, and trade disputes, its efficacy is constrained unless supplemented with a dynamic approach rooted in resilience. This necessitates that researchers develop mapping methodologies that incorporate uncertainty and complexity, while for managers, it implies that "process mapping" should prioritize not only efficiency but also enhance the robustness and adaptability of the supply chain.

3.2 Assessment of Sustainable Performance

Evaluating sustainable performance in Sustainable Supply Chain Management (SSCM) entails examining the alignment of supply chain activities with environmental, social, and economic sustainability objectives. Multiple essential frameworks are vital in this evaluation: The Triple Bottom Line (TBL) framework assesses sustainability through three dimensions: environmental (e.g., measuring carbon emissions, energy usage, and waste management), social (e.g., examining labor practices, community involvement, and compliance with human rights), and economic (e.g., evaluating cost efficiency, profitability, and innovation). This methodology assists firms in harmonizing and incorporating these elements into their supply chain plans.

The Balanced Scorecard (BSC) enhances conventional performance measurements by integrating sustainability indicators, allowing firms to synchronize environmental and social objectives with financial targets. This strategic instrument provides an extensive perspective on performance, incorporating sustainability into fundamental business operations.

Life Cycle Assessment (LCA) evaluates the environmental effects of products or services across their entire life cycle, from raw material extraction to disposal. This strategy delineates opportunities for enhancement in resource utilization and emissions, fostering more sustainable product creation and supply chain practices.

SpringerLink Material Flow Cost Accounting (MFCA) monitors material and energy flows within a company, attributing costs to waste and inefficiency. This strategy emphasizes prospects for cost reduction and environmental impact mitigation, promoting more efficient resource use.

Environmental Profit and Loss (EP&L) Accounting quantifies environmental impacts in monetary terms, offering a financial viewpoint on sustainability performance. This strategy facilitates decision-making by quantifying environmental costs, therefore including environmental factors into financial analysis.

While evaluation tools exhibit undeniable methodological rigor, they possess two significant limitations: firstly, their heterogeneity complicates systematic comparisons among companies; secondly, they can be exploited for "greenwashing" purposes, thereby undermining their credibility. Managers face the challenge of selecting pertinent and transparent tools; policymakers must standardize indicators to guarantee comparability; and researchers are tasked with creating indicators that merge scientific rigor with practical applicability, thus bridging the divide between theory and implementation.

3.3 Key Performance Indicators (KPI)

According to Gudmundsson et al. (2010) provides a definition of an indicator as a that accurately and necessarily represents a phenomenon of interest, based on measurements. Gudmundsson et al. (2010) identifies the main functions of an indicator, as a measurement tool, a decision support tool, or a combination of both. It is imperative to clearly identify the subject, content, and methods involved when defining indicators for assessment or evaluation purposes.

The use of various sets of indicators poses challenges, particularly for decision-makers, as it can engender disagreements among stakeholders and decrease system efficacity (Gudmundsson et al., 2016). Consequently, a list of indicators that represent the topic of concern must be selected or developed, while rejecting those deemed inappropriate.

Sustainable Supply Chain Management (SSCM) incorporates environmental, social, and economic factors into supply chain operations to foster long-term value generation and ethical practices. Organizations are increasingly utilizing Key Performance Indicators (KPIs) that correspond with the principles of the Triple Bottom Line (TBL) people, planet, and profit to assess and improve performance. These KPIs function as essential instruments for assessing sustainability results, ensuring regulatory adherence, and fostering ongoing enhancement across the supply chain. Furthermore, they promote openness and accountability, allowing stakeholders to evaluate the efficacy of business sustainability efforts. Effectively constructed SSCM KPIs can enhance brand reputation, increase resource efficiency, and minimize operational and reputational risks associated with unsustainable practices.

Table 2. Sustainable supply chain management: Key Performance Indicators KPI

KPI	Dimension	Description
Carbon Footprint	Environmental	Total CO_2 emissions across the supply chain
Energy Consumption	Environmental	Total energy used in production and transport
Water Usage	Environmental	Water consumed in operations
Waste Reduction Rate	Environmental	Percentage of waste diverted from landfill

continued on following page

Table 2. Continued

KPI	Dimension	Description
Recyclable Packaging Use	Environmental	Proportion of recyclable materials used in packaging
Pollution Emissions	Environmental	Emissions to air, water, and soil
Supplier Labor Compliance	Social	Percentage of suppliers compliant with labor laws
Health & Safety Incidents	Social	Number of workplace accidents
Employee Turnover Rate	Social	Rate of employee turnover in supply chain operations
Fair Wage Compliance	Social	Percentage of workers earning a fair or living wage
Training Hours	Social	Hours of training provided on sustainability and safety
Diversity in Suppliers	Social	Proportion of procurement from diverse or minority-owned suppliers
Cost of Sustainability Programs	Economic	Investment in sustainability initiatives and green practices
Return on Sustainability Investment	Economic	Economic benefits realized from sustainability-related investments
On-Time Delivery Rate	Economic	Reliability and timeliness of deliveries within the supply chain
Inventory Turnover Ratio	Economic	Rate at which inventory is used and replenished
Supplier Sustainability Score	Economic	Score based on supplier performance in sustainability
Local Sourcing Rate	Economic	Percentage of procurement from local or regional suppliers

Source: Authors' elaboration

3.4 Carbon Footprint

The carbon footprint denotes the aggregate greenhouse gas emissions directly and indirectly linked to a product or service (Wiedmann and Minx, 2008). The carbon footprint in supply chains can be ascribed to multiple stages, including raw material extraction, manufacture, transportation, and disposal. As firms endeavor to diminish their carbon footprints, comprehending the origins of emissions inside the supply chain is essential.

It is a significant cause of global warming and the depletion of natural resources. When discussing greenhouse gas emissions within an organization, it is essential to acknowledge the presence of three distinct types of emissions. These include:

- Scope 1: Direct carbon emissions

Direct carbon emissions arise from sources owned or controlled by the company, such as emissions from combustion in owned or controlled boilers, furnaces, vehicles, and emissions from chemical manufacture in owned or controlled process equipment.

- Scope 2: Indirect carbon emissions from purchased energy

Scope 2 encompasses carbon emissions resulting from the production of purchased or acquired energy, steam, heating, or cooling utilized by the reporting entity. Scope 2 emissions occur at a facility external to the reporting company's organizational boundaries.

- Scope 3: Additional indirect carbon emissions Scope 3 encompasses the management of all other indirect emissions. Scope 3 emissions result from a company's activities but originate from sources owned or managed by external entities within the value chain, such as material suppliers, third-party logistics providers, waste management suppliers, travel service providers, lessees and lessors, franchisees, retailers, employees, and customers. Scope 3 emissions encompass all indirect emissions, comprising both upstream emissions (e.g., purchased goods or the transportation of purchased goods) and downstream emissions (e.g., the utilization of sold products or the disposal of sold products).

The assessment of the carbon footprint (Scopes 1, 2, and 3) is crucial; nevertheless, the challenge resides in quantifying Scope 3, which relies on numerous external collaborators.

Figure 11. Carbon footprint mapping across scopes in Sustainable Supply Chain Management (SSCM)

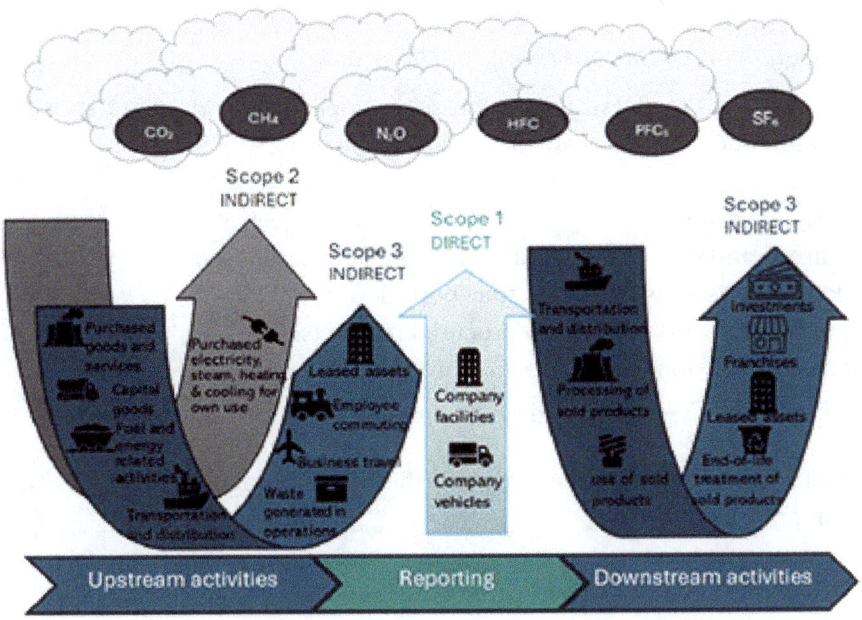

The figure 11 illustrates the classification of an organization's GHG emissions into three categories: Scope 1 (direct emissions) from facilities and vehicles owned or controlled by the company; Scope 2 (indirect emissions related to energy) associated with the production of electricity, heat, or steam purchased and consumed; and Scope 3 (other indirect emissions) covering the entire value chain upstream (purchased goods and services, transportation and distribution, business travel, waste, leased assets, etc.) and downstream (transportation and distribution of sold products, use and end-of-life treatment of sold products, investments, franchises, leased assets).

From this viewpoint, executing a Carbon Footprint / GHG inventory in accordance with ISO 14064-1 often adheres to a systematic five-step methodology, guaranteeing transparency, repeatability, and comparability of outcomes.

Step 1: Definition of the organizational scope

The initial stage is to identify the entities, locations, and facilities encompassed within the organizational scope. ISO 14064-1 delineates two possible approaches:

Capital share approach: emissions are allocated in accordance with ownership percentage.

Control methodology (financial or operational): emissions are aggregated at 100% when the company exerts substantial control.

The selected methodology influences the inventory's representativeness.

Step 2: Definition of the operating parameters

This phase aims to classify emissions into scopes 1, 2, and 3. ISO 14064-1 categorizes emissions into six distinct classifications:

- Initial emissions.
- Indirect emissions associated with energy consumption.
- Indirect emissions related to transportation.
- Indirect emissions related to procured products.
- Indirect emissions related to sold products.
- Supplementary indirect emissions.

This classification ensures conceptual thoroughness and systematizes the data collection procedure.

Step 3: Definition of the reporting scope

Not all indicated emissions are necessary incorporated into the final scope of the Carbon Footprint. This must maintain substantial emissions, according to objective criteria such as:

- Their numerical scale.
- The extent of the organization's impact.
- Their tactical significance.
- The vulnerabilities detected within the value chain.
- The degree of reliance on external entities (outsourcing, essential suppliers, etc.).
- The anticipations of internal and external stakeholders.
- This stage facilitates the formulation of a pragmatic and scientifically pertinent scope.

Step 4: Selection of the reporting year and the reference year

According to ISO 14064-1, inventories must encompass an entire year of operations.

The reporting year aligns with the year in which the data was obtained.

The reference year functions as a benchmark for assessing the progression of emissions over time. It must remain unchanged save in instances of a large alteration (acquisition, divestiture, restructuring, or significant methodological shift).

Step 5: Data Acquisition and Emission Assessment

The final phase entails collecting all pertinent data (energy consumption, travel, purchases, etc.) and executing computations to estimate the GHG emissions for all items within the reporting scope.

4. Protocols

Global initiatives are in progress to mitigate greenhouse gas emissions and promote adaptation to climate change. This context encompasses a set of standards that offer explicit and uniform criteria for the measurement, monitoring, reporting, and validation or verification of greenhouse gas emissions absorptions. These standards advantage organizations, project developers, and stakeholders globally by guaranteeing a consistent methodology in evaluating impacts. The ISO 14060 family of international standards provide a methodological framework for quantifying, reporting, validating, and verifying greenhouse gas emissions and reductions.

4.1 The Greenhouse Gas Protocol

The Greenhouse Gas Protocol (GHG Protocol) serves as the global methodological framework for the accounting, management, and reporting of greenhouse gas (GHG) emissions by public and commercial entities. This protocol, created by the World Resources Institute (WDI) and the World Business Council for Sustainable Development (WBCSD), offers a collection of standards, tools, and recommendations designed to guarantee the creation of transparent, consistent, and scientifically sound emission inventories. The primary aim is to assist organizations in quantifying their emissions in a standardized format, ensuring temporal comparability through the formation of a reference year, and, if required, recalibrate in the event of significant structural changes. The GHG Protocol categorizes emissions into three distinct types: direct emissions (Scope 1) from sources under the organization's control; indirect emissions from the consumption of purchased energy (Scope 2); and all other indirect emissions produced throughout the value chain (Scope 3), particularly those from outsourced transportation, procurement, and waste management. The creation of a compliant inventory necessitates five critical steps: identifying and classifying emission sources; selecting a calculation method, typically utilizing emission factors; meticulously gathering activity data; employing cross-sectoral or sector-specific calculation tools as outlined by the protocol; and ultimately, consolidating data into an organizational-level database. The GHG Protocol offers a clear and widely accepted operational framework that enables organizations to comprehend their climate impacts, identify pertinent reduction strategies, and formulate their decarbonization plans with transparency and sustainable performance.

4.2 ISO 14060

The ISO 14060 standards offer organizations, project developers, and stakeholders globally a coherent framework for the quantification, monitoring, reporting, and validation or verification of greenhouse gas emissions and removals, thereby fostering sustainable development through a low-carbon economy. The ISO 14060 family of standards specifically enhances:

- The environmental integrity of greenhouse gas (GHG) quantification; the credibility, consistency, and transparency of GHG quantification, monitoring, reporting, verification, and validation.
- The formulation and execution of GHG management strategies and plans.
- The formulation and execution of GHG reduction initiatives through emission reductions or increased removals.
- The monitoring of performance and progress in diminishing GHG emissions and/or augmenting GHG removals.

The ISO 14060 standards can be applied to:

- business decisions aimed at identifying opportunities to mitigate emissions and enhance profitability through reduced energy consumption.
- The management of risks and opportunities, including climate-related financial, regulatory, supply chain, product, customer, litigation, reputational risks, and commercial opportunities (e.g., new markets or business models).
- Voluntary initiatives, such as engagement in voluntary GHG registration or sustainability reporting.
- GHG markets, including the trading of GHG quotas (bonuses or penalties).
- Regulatory or governmental programs concerning GHGs, such as credits for early actions, agreements, or national and local reporting initiatives.

a. ISO 14064

ISO 14064 is a global series of standards that delineates the concepts and requirements for quantifying and reporting greenhouse gas (GHG) emissions from an organization or project. The ISO 14064:2018 series comprises three interrelated components that encompass the complete procedure for estimating and reporting greenhouse gas emissions at both organizational and project levels.

ISO 14064-1

This standard delineates the concepts, requirements, and procedures for the design and execution of organizational GHG inventories. It encompasses the determination of boundaries, the identification of sources and sinks, quantification methodologies, and report production.

In accordance with this guideline, the assessment of a Carbon Footprint typically adheres to a systematic five-step procedure, as outlined in the slides.

ISO 14064-2

This standard delineates the concepts, requirements, and procedures for the creation and execution of organizational greenhouse gas inventories. It encompasses the determination of boundaries, the identification of sources and sinks, quantification methodologies, and report production.

ISO 14064-3

ISO 14064-3 delineates the criteria for the verification of greenhouse gas (GHG) assertions pertaining to GHG inventories, GHG projects, and the carbon footprint of products. It delineates the verification or validation process, encompassing the design of verification or validation, evaluation methodologies, and the assessment of GHG statements from an organization, project, or product.

b. ISO 14065

ISO 14065 delineates the criteria pertinent to entities that authenticate and corroborate greenhouse gas declarations. The requirements encompass impartiality, competence, communication, validation and verification processes, appeals, complaints, and the management system of validation and verification entities. It can provide a foundation for accreditation and other forms of acknowledgment about the impartiality, competency, and consistency of validation and verification entities.

c. ISO 14066

ISO 14066 delineates the competency requirements for validation and verification teams. It delineates concepts and articulates competency standards based on the tasks that validation or verification teams must do.

d. ISO 14067

ISO 14067 establishes concepts, regulations, and guidelines for measuring the carbon footprint of products. ISO 14067 seeks to measure greenhouse gas emissions throughout a product's life cycle, encompassing resource extraction, raw material acquisition, manufacture, usage, and end-of-life stages.

e. ISO/TR 14069

ISO/TR 14069 assists users in utilizing this document by offering guidelines and examples to enhance transparency in emission quantification and reporting.

5. Sustainable Management of the Upstream Supply Chain

5.1 Development of Sustainable Products

It's about structuring concerning the product and their design, how to buy sustainably, and how to establish lasting relationships with suppliers. Indeed, the SSCM approach involves anticipating the consequences of each industrial process in advance. The design of products is based on two concepts circular economy and co-design. The design of products is based on two concepts circular economy and co-design.

Circular economy

It's an economic model that creates value by aiming at the use and optimization of stocks as well as the flows of materials, energy, and waste. It is based on the fundamentals of sustainability as it seeks an efficient use of resources, turning waste into raw materials. This model therefore seeks to highlight virtuous loops of resources, consumption, collection/sorting, recovery, and landfilling. The circular economy is based on the following principles:

Eco-design: to address the issue of resource criticality

resources, the systematic integration of the environment from the product design stage is essential to reduce negative externalities while ensuring an equivalent or superior service. It therefore encompasses the choice of raw materials and even packaging, the choice of renewable energies and non-hazardous materials in the production process "Lean and Green Manufacturing" (we add an 8th muda "Environmental Waste" to the 5 classic mudas, "muda being an activity that adds no value but is accepted," in terms of overproduction, overstocking, unnecessary transportation, overprocessing, unnecessary movements, defects, and waiting time and delays), choice of transportation modes, consideration of the indirect impacts of product/energy use, the possibility of disassembling products to facilitate recycling at the end of their life, and dematerialization.

Integrating ecodesign with SDG 12 "Establish sustainable consumption and production patterns" enables organizations to align their initiatives within a cohesive strategic framework: alleviate pressure on natural resources, minimize waste at the source, promote material circularity, and improve the sustainability of industrial systems. This convergence enhances organizations' environmental performance and fortifies their resilience against growing issues, including resource scarcity, supply chain volatility, and shifting public expectations.

- Industrial ecology: turning the waste of some into resources for others Industrial ecology
- The economy of functionality: its principle consists of selling the use of the product instead of the product itself instead of the product itself (selling kilometers traveled instead of tires).

Reuse: reusing products

Repair: designing products that can be easily separated in order to optimize the product's lifespan.

Recycling: using waste to make another product.

Note: We need to distinguish between eco-solution, eco-design, and eco-product.

Eco-design must take into account:

- Choice of raw materials and packaging.
- Choice of renewable energies and limitations on the use of hazardous materials
- Choice of clean transportation mode and optimization of vehicle routes
- Take into account the indirect impacts of product usage
- The products must be easily disassembled to optimize recycling

The focus on eco-design and the circular economy is pertinent ; nonetheless, the approach is predominantly descriptive. In practice, eco-design encounters multiple constraints: limited access to recycled materials, insufficient consumer demand for certain pricier "green" products, and challenges in delineating the differences among eco-products, eco-design, and eco-solutions without specific sectoral illustrations (automotive, agri-food, electronics). Managers should perceive eco-design not merely as an environmental limitation but as a genuine catalyst for innovation and competitive distinction. These observations underscore the necessity for governments to establish subsidies and tax incentives to mitigate elevated investment costs and enhance demand.

5.2 Responsible Purchasing: Supplier Selection, Environmental, and Social Factors

The corporation must base its purchasing selections on a complicated array of selection criteria centered on sustainability. The objectives include the attainment of long-term profitability, the enhancement of supplier relationships, and the establishment of a sustainable and responsible reputation. To accomplish these objectives, two courses of action must be evaluated: - Concerning the items, we must assess their traceability, composition, packaging, and environmental implications. - The management of supplier relationships should be predicated on the quality of their social responsibility (adherence to labor rights, working conditions, etc.), the caliber of their societal responsibility (certifications, labels), and the nature of the relationship (collaborative engagement). In this context, we identify many cooperation mechanisms with suppliers, specifically purchasing charters, codes of conduct, and certification.

Table 3. Comparison of traditional and responsible purchasing criteria

Traditional Criteria	Responsible Purchasing Criteria
Price	Environmental performance
Quality	Social compliance (e.g., labor rights)
Delivery time	Health and safety practices
Service	Ethical business conduct
Technical capabilities	Supply chain transparency and traceability

Source: Authors' elaboration

The comparison of "classic" and "responsible" criteria is a valuable addition; nonetheless, it remains excessively static. The choice of suppliers predominantly depends on price and quality, with social or environmental aspects considered mainly due to regulatory or reputational pressures.

The incorporation of these practices aligns entirely with the objectives of Sustainable Development Goal No. 8 (SDG 8), which seeks to foster sustained, inclusive, and sustainable economic growth through decent employment opportunities. SDG 8 advocates for the elimination of undignified labor and the assurance of a secure, inclusive, and respectful workplace. This purpose necessitates the selection and endorsement of suppliers dedicated to safeguarding their workforce and promoting skill development pertinent to sustainable employment and emerging industries. Social audit techniques, certification of labor conditions, and rigorous contractualization are therefore vital tools for ensuring adherence to these objectives. The shift to responsible supply chains necessitates improved international collaboration, a facet explicitly endorsed by Sustainable Development Goal (SDG 17).

6. Sustainable Management of Internal Operations

6.1 Sustainable and Responsible Internal Operation

Internally within the SC, this structuring affects internal and responsible operations, as well as sustainable internal procedures. Sustainable manufacturing is a thoroughly documented area in the literature, recognized by various terms, including clean production and green manufacturing. In many instances, the paramount sub-characteristic of sustainable manufacturing is sustainable design activity. The environmental management of the supply chain appears crucial for influencing the design, procurement, production, distribution, reverse logistics, utilization, and end-of-life of products. ISO 14000 certification is imperative.

-The examination of sustainable internal processes includes: Assessing the sustainable impact of buildings, which must be environmentally friendly by conforming to eco-site methodologies, High Environmental Quality (HQE) standards, or Low Consumption Building (BBC) criteria.

- Examine the ecological consequences of the industrial process concerning waste generation and resource utilization. Waste pertains to the product's fabrication, its packing, and its production method. A variety of measures at different levels can mitigate these wastes: eco-design, supplier quality monitoring, waste recovery, and the valorization of permanent resources (metals). In terms of water and energy consumption, implementing Lean principles in production (zero defects/zero waste) is prudent, utilizing local material cycle closure and multi-filter technology for wastewater treatment.
- Evaluate the environmental implications of the storage process, ensuring that the warehouses are constructed and operated in accordance with ICPE7 standards. Two primary acts to be examined are the automation and robotization of warehouses.

The focus on clean manufacturing and ISO 14000 certification offers a valuable normative framework; nevertheless, it is constrained: most organizations merely utilize these certifications as marketing instruments without genuine organizational change. Furthermore, pressing issues like automation, which diminishes the ecological footprint at the expense of employment, are predominantly overlooked in the analysis. For managers, this signifies that internal sustainability must transcend mere compliance and evolve into a value creation strategy, whether through reducing energy expenses or improving the perception of a responsible workplace. These discoveries prompt academics to critically analyze the contradictions between environmental sustainability and social justice, highlighting the necessity for integrated and multidisciplinary methodologies.

6.2 Eco-Efficient Warehouses and Logistics Platforms

In the developing realm of sustainable supply chain management (SSCM), internal activities within warehouses and logistics systems are crucial. These procedures are frequently resource-intensive, encompassing energy use, spatial management, material handling, and human resource coordination. As firms pursue sustainability, eco-efficiency serves as a fundamental principle, seeking to provide economic benefit while reducing environmental impacts.

Eco-efficiency, in practical terms, involves the adoption of operational solutions that diminish energy consumption, emissions, waste, and water usage while preserving or improving productivity and service quality.

Warehousing and logistics systems serve as important components in supply networks. When built and run sustainably, they can markedly diminish the total environmental impact of logistics systems. The following are essential components of eco-efficient warehouse management:

Energy Efficiency

Energy consumption in warehouses, mainly for lighting, heating, ventilation, air conditioning (HVAC), and material handling, constitutes a significant share of operational expenses and environmental repercussions. Strategies to enhance energy efficiency encompass:

- LED Lighting and Daylight Harvesting: Shifting from conventional lighting to LED systems, frequently integrated with daylight harvesting and occupancy sensors, can result in significant decreases in electricity consumption.
- Smart HVAC and Building Energy Management Systems (BEMS): These systems manage temperature and air quality while maximizing energy utilization.

    -Integration of Renewable Energy: On-site installation of photovoltaic panels or wind turbines to provide sustainable energy and diminish dependence on fossil fuels.

Green Building Design

Green design ideas encompass warehouse construction and operational methods, striving to reduce environmental effect throughout the building's life cycle.

Principal attributes comprise:

- Certification Criteria: Implementing frameworks like LEED (Leadership in Energy and Environmental Design), BREEAM (Building Research Establishment Environmental Assessment Method), or ISO 14001 guarantees systematic environmental management and responsibility.
- Sustainable Materials and Construction Methods: Utilizing recycled or low-impact materials and modular construction minimizes embodied carbon.
- Passive design strategies, such as integrating natural ventilation, insulation, and daylighting, diminish reliance on mechanical systems.

The strategy centered on HQE buildings, renewable energy, and automation is pertinent; however, it presents two significant drawbacks: firstly, the substantial initial investment, which often deters SMEs, and secondly, the social ramifications of automation on employment, which are seldom considered in analyses. Managers must evaluate the eco-efficiency of warehouses from a long-term return on investment standpoint, focusing on energy consumption reduction and enhancement of the company's reputation. These observations need that public decision-makers implement targeted assistance mechanisms for SMEs to prevent exclusive benefits from "green" innovations for large corporations and to ensure that the sustainable transition does not increase economic and social disparities.

7. Sustainable Management of the Downstream Supply Chain (Distribution and End of Life)

7.1 Sustainable Transportation and Distribution: Consolidation, Low-Emission Vehicles, Optimized Urban Logistics

Currently, there is an increasing interest in implementing the concept of sustainable transportation, with the idea of using clean transportation becoming more and more popular around the world. Advancing sustainable transportation requires a comprehensive examination of transportation systems and their impacts on economic, social, and environmental factors, as well as the associated challenges. Recent research demonstrates that achieving sustainability objective through transportation systems has become as a top priority for policymakers (Zheng et al., 2013).

Previous research have made efforts to develop a clear definition for the concept of sustainable transportation, as indicated by the definitions presented in Table 4.

Table 4. Summary of sustainable development and transportation

Source	Definitions
Gilbert and Tanguay (2000)	"A sustainable transportation system, as defined by the Centre for Sustainable Transportation, is one that: a. Ensures that the basic needs for people and societies to be satisfied safely and in a manner that corresponds to the health of each individuals and ecosystems, as well as equality within and across generations. b. Is economical, functions optimally, provides a range of transportation choices, and contributes to a thriving economy. c. Restricts emissions and waste to levels that can be accepted by the world, minimizes the consumption of non-renewable resources, encourages the reuse and recycling of components, and minimizes land use and the production of noise.
Litman (2003)	Sustainable development can be defined as the achievement of a secure and satisfying material future for all individuals, within a society that is equitable, compassionate, and mindful of fundamental needs. Sustainable transportation necessitates optimizing each mode of transportation according to its strengths. This frequently involves a higher emphasis on nonmotorized modes for local travel, increasing the use of public transit in urban areas, and a decrease (though not complete elimination) in personal automobile usage. Sustainable planning emphasizes the end results, such as the level of access to desired commodities, services, and activities, rather than solely focusing on evaluating the amount of mobility, such as trip speed or total distance traveled.
McGregor et al. (2008)	"Sustainable transportation is defined as the use of modes of transportation that have minimal negative impact on the environment, encourage social equity, and ensure economic viability." a. In the natural environment: restrict emissions and waste (that pollute air, soil, and water) to levels that can be absorbed, recycled, and purified by the urban area; use renewable or inexhaustible energy sources (such as solar power in the long term) to fuel vehicles; and recycle natural resources (such as steel, plastic, etc.) used in vehicles and infrastructure. b. In society, ensure equal access for individuals and their possessions, both now and in the future; improve human well-being; encourage the best possible quality of life inside the limits of available resources; encourage urban development that is suitable for human needs; reduce noise levels to meet community standards; and prioritize the safety of individuals and their property. c. In the economy: it must be financially accessible for every generation; it ought to be organized and operated to optimize economic efficiency and reduce economic costs; and it must support the creation of a solid, dynamic, and diverse economy.

Source: Authors' elaboration

Sustainable transportation necessitates the initial formulation of a transport strategy through the analysis of existing activities (volumes, connections, modes, etc.) to evaluate the current performance of the transport network. This involves measuring the disparity between the present state and projections regarding volumes and geographical coverage, as well as selecting transport solutions (by altering routings and mode selections) to achieve a balance among transport costs, service levels, and ecological objectives.

Secondly, the transport procurement policy will be established by selecting carriers based on suggested pricing, service levels, availability, reliability, geographical coverage, and commitment to sustainability. Thirdly, medium-term transport planning (6 months to 1 year) depends on an analysis of flows based on their allocation to carriers and the execution of rationalization and optimization measures (consolidation, vehicle utilization, empty returns, etc.).

Fourthly, operational transport planning seeks to delineate requisite resources based on identified needs while strategizing loads and routes with an ongoing pursuit of potential optimization avenues: adjusting vehicle dimensions to the delivery volume, enhancing fill rates, consolidating distinct routes, etc.

Fifthly, the implementation of physical transportation activities and those pertaining to information flows (labeling, EDI flow management, shipping notifications, etc.) must guarantee the tracking and tracing of transport.

Ultimately, assessing and evaluating transportation performance is essential. In addition to the traditional indicators (transport service rate, OTIF, damage or loss rate), the following indicators may be noted: road safety management system (ISO 39001), human risk management in transport (ISO 31000), theft costs, loss prevention costs, pollutant emissions, and the ratio of renewable energies.

To achieve sustainable distribution, meticulous management of transportation, warehousing, and distribution operations is essential. Urban logistics, or last-mile logistics, is highly exigent. In this regard, we can influence delivery locations, delivery times, customer charges, and pooling. The creation of innovative distribution solutions for short circuits in the agri-food sector is beneficial.

The presentation of solutions like flow consolidation, the adoption of clean vehicles, and sustainable urban logistics is pertinent; yet, it neglects important conflicts. Electric vehicles rely on power generation that frequently involves high carbon emissions, but sustainable urban logistics efforts are obstructed by congestion and insufficient infrastructure. Consequently, for managers, merely implementing a "green" fleet is insufficient; it necessitates a reevaluation of the comprehensive distribution strategy through the incorporation of multimodality, pooling, and improved route planning. This analysis underscores the necessity for public decision-makers to invest in targeted infrastructures, such charging stations and urban pooling centers, to enhance the efficacy of these options.

7.2 Reverse Logistics: Product Returns, Recycling, Repair, and Reuse

Reverse logistics encompassing product replacements, warranty repairs, and returns due to non-conformity.

Trash valorization can occur through the following methods:

- Material reuse: recycling or repurposing trash to create a new product.
- Via organic degradation (composting)
- Via energy recovery: cremation of garbage to harness energy.

Agrawal and al (2015) have offered succinct definitions for each disposal option along the reverse supply chain as follows:

- Reuse: the packaging is repurposed or a product is returned for resale to another buyer.
- Repair/repackage: a process in which a moderate degree of repair and/or repackaging enables the product to be reused.
- Recycling: the process of deconstructing a product to extract components that can be repurposed or resold.
- Reconditioning: The process of cleaning a product to its fundamental components, which are subsequently reused.
- Refurbishing: Comparable to reconditioning, but typically entails a greater degree of effort in restoring the goods.
- Remanufacturing: Comparable to reconditioning, although necessitating more comprehensive efforts; frequently involves the total disassembly of the product.

Figure 12. Integrated forward and reverse logistics in sustainable supply chain management

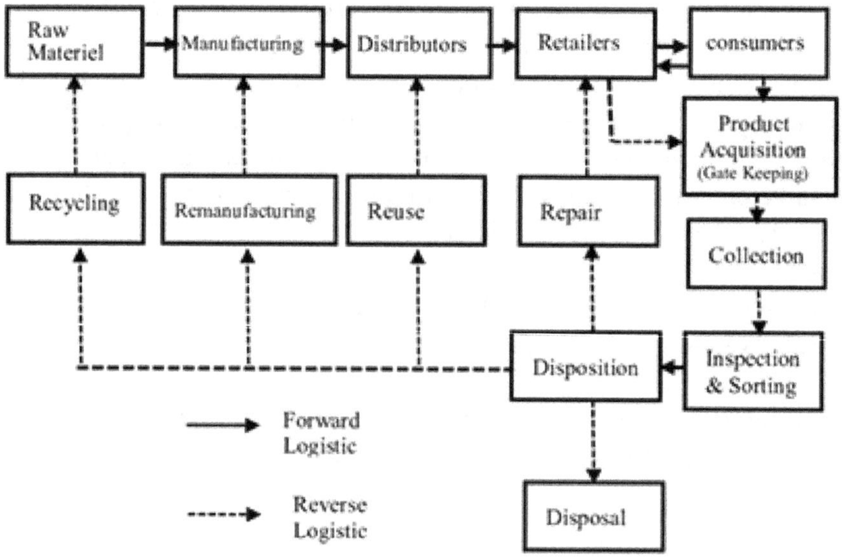

Figure 12 presents the classifications of reverse logistics.: reuse, repair, recycling, reconditioning, and remanufacturing are adequately articulated; nonetheless, the discourse is deficient as it neglects the consideration of their economic viability. In numerous industries, the expenses related to the return and reprocessing of products surpass the actual value retrieved. For managers, this entails including reverse logistics from the product design phase (design for recycling), rather than treating it as a subsequent process.

8. Case Studies and Implemented Technological Innovations

The advancement of digital technology is significantly altering sustainable logistics. Innovations such the Internet of Things (IoT), artificial intelligence (AI), Big Data, and blockchain facilitate efficient processes, diminished emissions, and enhanced transparency in the supply chain. These improvements, along with specific case studies, demonstrate the progressive integration of green logistics into managerial and operational procedures.

This section presents case studies or illustrative scenarios to demonstrate the practical application of AI-based strategies in sustainable logistics. Each case is structured to highlight the context, the AI technologies used, the targeted sustainable development goals, the measurable outcomes, and the lessons learned.

8.1 The Internet of Things (IoT) and Logistical Interconnectivity

The Internet of Things (IoT) encompasses all sensors and interconnected devices that gather and relay data in real time. In the logistics sector, the IoT) is employed for:

- Real-time tracking of commodities, including geolocation and monitoring the status of sensitive cargo such as medications and food supplies.
- The enhancement of warehouses through automated inventory management systems.
- The minimization of unoccupied journeys by dynamic analysis of transportation movements.

Mini case study - DHL and the Internet of Things in the cold chain

DHL, a subsidiary of the German conglomerate Deutsche Post established in 1969 and operating in over 220 countries, is acknowledged as one of the foremost logistics corporations globally. Through its GoGreen initiative, it is resolutely dedicated to diminishing its emissions and implementing creative solutions. The organization occupies a prominent position in pharmaceutical logistics, a sector where cold chain management is essential.

The preservation of pharmaceutical items necessitates stringent regulation of thermal conditions, as temperature deviations result in substantial losses and elevated expenses. DHL has implemented IoT sensors within containers and warehouses to provide real-time monitoring of temperature, humidity, and shocks in response to this difficulty. The aggregated data is centralized and evaluated on a digital platform, facilitating prompt responses in the event of anomalies.

The observed outcomes are manifold: diminished losses of critical pharmaceutical products, enhanced adherence to international laws, and energy optimization through predictive management. This scenario exemplifies the strategic significance of IoT in ensuring the traceability and reliability of essential supply chains, where sustainability, quality, and security are interdependent goals.

8.2 Artificial Intelligence (AI) and Big Data in Strategic Planning

Artificial intelligence (AI) comprises technology enabling robots to emulate human abilities, including thinking, problem-solving, perception, and creativity.

Artificial intelligence and big data analytics are revolutionizing logistics planning.

- Route optimization: by the integration of meteorological conditions, traffic patterns, and urban limitations.
- Demand forecasting: enhancing consumption predictions to optimize production and mitigate excesses.
- Predictive maintenance: early identification of vehicle or logistical equipment malfunctions.

Mini case study – UPS and artificial intelligence (ORION)

Founded in 1907, UPS is an American courier and logistics enterprise that operates in over 220 countries and handles more than 20 million parcels daily with a fleet exceeding 500,000 vehicles. The corporation has historically prioritized route efficiency and logistics planning as a primary strategic focus.

Fuel use and distance traveled constitute a substantial segment of its carbon footprint; hence, UPS opted to utilize AI and Big Data to mitigate these effects. Within this framework, it developed ORION (On-Road Integrated Optimization and Navigation), a route optimization algorithm predicated on extensive data analysis encompassing traffic, weather, and specific delivery constraints (Holland et al. 2017).

The findings are substantial: a decrease exceeding 100 million miles traveled annually, a conservation of 38 million liters of gasoline, and a reduction of several hundred thousand tons of CO_2 emissions. This scenario exemplifies AI's capacity to concurrently enhance operational efficiency and yield economic and environmental advantages, hence strengthening the alignment between performance and sustainability.

8.3 Blockchain and Sustainable Traceability

Wong et al. (2024) defines Blockchain as a method for the secure, transparent, and decentralized storage and transmission of information, functioning independently of a central authority. It comprises a distributed database (a comprehensive ledger) that records the history of transactions, with data organized into blocks interconnected through encryption in a chronological and immutable fashion. This architecture enables all participants to authenticate the legitimacy of the chain, so establishing a system of collective trust.

Blockchain, a decentralized ledger system, improves transparency and traceability inside supply chains.

- It facilitates the verification of logistical flows, including food traceability and ethical sourcing of raw materials.
- The battle against counterfeiting using irrefutable records.
- Transparency for consumers regarding origin, transportation, and production circumstances.

Mini Case Study – Maersk and Sustainable Shipping Solutions

A.P. Moller-Maersk, established in 1904 in Denmark, is the preeminent container shipping enterprise globally, operating over 700 vessels that account for around 17% of the international market. The firm is pivotal in global supply chains and asserts its leadership in the energy transition of maritime transport. The marine sector, accountable for around 3% of global CO_2 emissions, under considerable regulatory scrutiny, especially from the International marine Organization (IMO) and the Paris Agreement, prompting Maersk to pledge carbon neutrality by 2040. The company has invested in container ships fueled by green methanol to reach this objective, while investigating other fuels including ammonia and hydrogen, and creating carbon traceability solutions for its clients. These activities culminated in the introduction, as early as 2023, of the first vessels fueled by methanol, yielding a substantial decrease in emissions relative to heavy fuel oil vessels, alongside the formation of key alliances with renewable energy sources to ensure supply. This study demonstrates that the energy transition is essential for marine sustainability and presents an opportunity to improve competitiveness, while underscoring ongoing issues about the availability and elevated costs of new fuels.

Table 5. Comparative analysis of technologies and their effects

Technology	Logistics Applications	Environmental Impact	Example
IOT	Real-time tracking, warehouse optimization, reduction of empty runs	Waste reduction, improved energy efficiency	DHL
AI and Big Data	Route optimization, demand forecasting predictive maintenance	Co2 emissions reduction,, lower logistics costs	UPS
Blockchain	Traceability, certification, Supply chain transportation	Freaud reduction, increased trust, more efficient documentation	Maersk

Source: Authors' elaboration

Innovative technologies (IoT, AI, blockchain) and tangible actions from prominent corporations illustrate that sustainable logistics represents both an environmental imperative and a strategic advantage. The use of these innovations not only mitigates ecological problems but also enhances the competitiveness and resilience of supply chains.

Main Conclusions

- Sustainable logistics necessitates sector-specific solutions that address distinct operational constraints.
- All efforts exhibit quantifiable effects, such CO_2 reductions, waste minimization, or enhanced resource efficiency.
- Long-term success depends on the amalgamation of digital technologies, alternative energy solutions, and organizational restructuring, emphasizing sustainability as an environmental imperative and a catalyst for competitiveness.

The progression towards more sustainable supply chains is significantly influenced by technological advancements and the incorporation of innovative practices. Amidst the increasing challenges posed by complexity, rapid exchanges, and the interdependence of various actors, it is evident that only intelligent and collaborative technological solutions can effectively adapt supply chains to meet the demands of sustainable development. Innovation plays a crucial role in transforming supply chains by optimizing resources, minimizing environmental impact, and delivering the agility required to address contemporary economic, social, and ecological demands.

The analysis of the three case studies reveals a shared dynamic: logistics sustainability has emerged as a crucial strategic lever, contributing to economic competitiveness, regulatory compliance, and environmental responsibility. Achievement in this field depends on the simultaneous integration of digital technologies (AI, IoT, Blockchain) and cooperative governance among stakeholders, such as businesses, regulators, and local communities. Sustainable supply chain management should be perceived not merely as a limitation but as a catalyst for resilience and enduring value generation.

CONCLUSION

The transition to sustainable logistics and the profound integration of supply chains signify a notable evolution in the contemporary management of goods movement. The implementation of sustainable logistics strategies, including low-emission transportation, environmentally conscious product design, and circular economy principles, coupled with enhanced logistics integration, enables organizations to reduce their ecological footprint while improving operational efficiency.

This chapter emphasizes the significance of incorporating environmental and social factors throughout all phases of the supply chain, encompassing upstream sourcing, internal operations, distribution, and the management of products at the conclusion of their life cycle. A comprehensive examination of the intricacies associated with Sustainable Supply Chain Management (SSCM) necessitates a detailed investigation of its historical development. The rapid advancement of technology has introduced complexities into supply chain management, particularly due to the conflicting interests of various stakeholders and the increasing adverse effects on the environment, society, and economy. A comprehensive assessment of the indirect costs linked to logistics operations is essential for the integration of these external elements.

A variety of initiatives have been implemented across multiple tiers regional, national, and international—with the aim of advancing more sustainable practices. Nonetheless, the capacity of organizations to establish accurate, methodical, and clear evaluation frameworks significantly influences the success of these initiatives. Consequently, assessing sustainable performance necessitates heightened focus and the creation of suitable metrics to guarantee measurable outcomes.

The presented case studies illustrate that transformation is feasible, contingent upon two critical factors: firstly, the presence of a strong governance framework (regulations, standards, public incentives); secondly, the capacity of companies to transcend minimal compliance and incorporate sustainability as a strategic and competitive advantage.

Sustainable logistics is not merely a limitation, but a chance to radically reevaluate value creation inside global supply chains. This represents a crucial advancement in the comprehensive incorporation of sustainability within the supply chain, a topic that will be further explored in the subsequent chapter on Sustainable Supply Chain Management (SSCM).

In summary, the incorporation of sustainable logistics within global supply chains transcends mere compliance with regulations or societal expectations; it represents a crucial strategy for generating enduring value, enhancing organizational resilience, and playing a proactive role in the ecological transition. The progression of sustainability has transitioned from a mere choice to a critical imperative, driven by ongoing advancements, the incorporation of technology, and enhanced cooperation among all participants in the supply chain.

REFERENCES

Agrawal, S., Singh, R. K., & Murtaza, Q. (2015). A literature review and perspectives in reverse logistics. *Resources, Conservation and Recycling*, *97*, 76–92. DOI: 10.1016/j.resconrec.2015.02.009

Ahn, H., & Park, E. (2022). For sustainable development in the transportation sector: Determinants of acceptance of sustainable transportation using the innovation diffusion theory and technology acceptance model. *Sustainable Development (Bradford)*, *30*(5), 1169–1183. DOI: 10.1002/sd.2309

Bodansky, D. (2016). The legal character of the Paris Agreement. *Review of European, Comparative & International Environmental Law*, *25*(2), 142–150. DOI: 10.1111/reel.12154

Brandenburg, M., & Rebs, T. (2015). Sustainable supply chain management: A modeling perspective. *Annals of Operations Research*, *229*(1), 213–252. DOI: 10.1007/s10479-015-1853-1

Carter, CR et Rogers, DS (2008). Un cadre de gestion durable de la chaîne d'approvisionnement: vers une nouvelle théorie. Revue internationale de gestion de la distribution physique et de la logistique, 38(5), 360-387. DOI: 10.1108/09600030810882816

de Oliveira, C. M., D'Agosto, M. de A., Rosa, R. de A., & Assumpção, F. do C. (2016). Low Carbon Logistics, Green Logistics and Sustainable Logistics: Establishing Concepts and Scope. In International journal of innovation and scientific research.

Deckert, C. (2023). Sustainable Logistics. In Idowu, S. O., Schmidpeter, R., Capaldi, N., Zu, L., Del Baldo, M., & Abreu, R. (Eds.), *Encyclopedia of Sustainable Management*. Springer., DOI: 10.1007/978-3-031-25984-5_131

Diabat, A., & Govindan, K. (2011). An analysis of the drivers affecting the implementation of green supply chain management. Resources, Conservation and Recycling. Volume 55, Issue 6. *Resources, Conservation and Recycling*, *659*(6), 667. DOI: 10.1016/j.resconrec.2010.12.002

Esfahbodi, A., Zhang, Y., & Watson, G. (2012). The implementation of sustainable supply chain management (SSCM): An exploratory study on the essential factors and performance implications. In *The Cambridge International Manufacturing Symposium*.

Geissdoerfer, M., Savaget, P., Bocken, N. M., & Hultink, E. J. (2017). The Circular Economy–A new sustainability paradigm? *Journal of Cleaner Production*, *143*, 757–768. DOI: 10.1016/j.jclepro.2016.12.048

Gilbert, R., & Tanguay, H. (2000). *Sustainable transportation performance indicators project: Brief review of some worldwide activity and development of an initial long list of indicators. Mississauga.* Centre for Sustainable Transportation.

Gudmundsson, H., Hall, R. P., Marsden, G., & Zietsman, J. (2016). *Sustainable transportation.* Spreinger-Verlag and Samfundslitteratur., DOI: 10.1007/978-3-662-46924-8

Gudmundsson, H., Joumard, R., & Aschemann, R. (2010). Indicators and their functions. In *Indicators of environmental sustainability in transport: An interdisciplinary approach to methods* (pp. 23-43). Institut national de recherche sur les transports et leur sécurité–INRETS.

Halldórsson, A., & Kovács, G. (2010). The sustainable agenda and energy efficiency: Logistics solutions and supply chains in times of climate change. *International Journal of Physical Distribution & Logistics Management, 40*(1/2), 5–13. DOI: 10.1108/09600031011018019

He, B., Yuan, X., Qian, S., & Li, B. (2023). Product low-carbon design, manufacturing, logistics, and recycling: An overview. *Wiley Interdisciplinary Reviews. Energy and Environment, 12*(5), e479. Advance online publication. DOI: 10.1002/wene.479

Herrmann, F. F., Barbosa-Povoa, A. P., Butturi, M. A., Marinelli, S., & Sellitto, M. A. (2021). Green supply chain management: Conceptual framework and models for analysis. *Sustainability (Basel), 13*(15), 8127. DOI: 10.3390/su13158127

Holland, C., Levis, J., Nuggehalli, R., Santilli, B., & Winters, J. (2017). UPS optimizes delivery routes. *Interfaces, 47*(1), 8–23. DOI: 10.1287/inte.2016.0875

Kannan, D. (2021). Facteurs d'approvisionnement durable dans un contexte multiniveaux étendu: une perspective multithéorique dans la chaîne d'approvisionnement danoise. Recherche sur les transports, partie E: Revue de la logistique et des transports, 146, 102092. DOI: 10.1016/j.tre.2020.102092

Karaduman, H. A., Karaman-Akgül, A., Çaglar, M., & Akbas¸, H. E. (2020). The relationship between logistics performance and carbon emissions: An empirical investigation on Balkan countries. *International Journal of Climate Change Strategies and Management, 12*(4), 449–461. DOI: 10.1108/IJCCSM-05-2020-0041

Keohane, R. O., & Oppenheimer, M. (2016). Paris: Beyond the Climate Dead End through Pledge and Review? *Politics and Governance, 4*(3), 142–151. DOI: 10.17645/pag.v4i3.634

Khan, S. A. R., Qianli, D., SongBo, W., Zaman, K., & Zhang, Y. (2017). Environmental logistics performance indicators affecting per capita income and sectoral growth: Evidence from a panel of selected global ranked logistics countries. *Environmental Science and Pollution Research International, 24*(2), 1518–1531. DOI: 10.1007/s11356-016-7916-2 PMID: 27785719

Litman, T. (2003). *Reinventing transportation.* Victoria Transportation Policy Institute.

Liu, J., Yuan, C., Hafeez, M., & Yuan, Q. (2018). The relationship between environment and logistics performance: Evidence from Asian countries. *Journal of Cleaner Production, 204*, 282–291. DOI: 10.1016/j.jclepro.2018.08.310

Macharis, C., Melo, S., Woxenius, J., & Van Lier, T. (2014). The 4 a's of sustainable logistics sustainable logistics. *Transport and Sustainability, 6*, 15–28.

McGregor, R. V., Hassan, M., & Hayley, D. (2008). Climate change impacts and adaptation: Case studies of roads in Northern Canada. In *Proceedings of the 2008 Annual Conference of the Transportation Association of Canada.*

McKinnon, A. (2018). *Decarbonizing logistics: Distributing goods in a low carbon world.* Kogan Page Publishers.

Meshram, K. K. (2024). The circular economy, 5R framework, and green organic practices: Pillars of sustainable development and zero-waste living. *Discover Environment, 2*(1), 147. DOI: 10.1007/s44274-024-00177-4

Mohsen, M. B. (2022). Principles of Sustainable Logistics. In *Logistics Engineering*. IntechOpen., DOI: 10.5772/intechopen.103018

Moshood, T. D., Nawanir, G., Mahmud, F., Sorooshian, S., & Adeleke, A. Q. (2021). Green and low carbon matters: A systematic review of the past, today, and future on sustainability supply chain management practices among manufacturing industry. *Cleaner Engineering and Technology, 4*, 100144. DOI: 10.1016/j.clet.2021.100144

Ostrom, E. (2010). Polycentric systems for coping with collective action and global environmental change. *Global Environmental Change, 20*(4), 550–557. DOI: 10.1016/j.gloenvcha.2010.07.004

Parhi, S., Joshi, K., Gunasekaran, A., & Sethuraman, K. (2022). Reflecting on an empirical study of the digitalization initiatives for sustainability on logistics: The concept of sustainable logistics 4.0. *Cleaner Logistics and Supply Chain, 4*, 100058. DOI: 10.1016/j.clscn.2022.100058

Qian, C., Wang, S., Liu, X., & Zhang, X. (2019). Low-Carbon Initiatives of Logistics Service Providers: The Perspective of Supply Chain Integration. *Sustainability (Basel), 11*(12), 3233. DOI: 10.3390/su11123233

Saidi, S., Mani, V., Mefteh, H., Shahbaz, M., & Akhtar, P. (2020). Dynamic linkages between transport, logistics, foreign direct Investment, and economic growth: Empirical evidence from developing countries. *Transportation Research Part A, Policy and Practice, 141*, 277–293. DOI: 10.1016/j.tra.2020.09.020

Seuring, S., & Müller, M. (2008). From a literature review to a conceptual framework for sustainable supply chain management. *Journal of Cleaner Production, 16*(15), 1699–1710. DOI: 10.1016/j.jclepro.2008.04.020

Sharma, S., Pablo, A. L., & Vredenburg, H. (1999). Corporate environmental responsiveness strategies: The importance of issue interpretation and organizational context. *The Journal of Applied Behavioral Science, 35*(1), 87–108. DOI: 10.1177/0021886399351008

Svensson, G. (2007). Aspects de la gestion durable de la chaîne d'approvisionnement (GDC): Cadre conceptuel et exemple empirique. *Supply Chain Management, 12*(4), 262–266. DOI: 10.1108/13598540710759781

United Nations. (1992). United Nations framework convention on climate change. https://unfccc.int/files/essential_background/background_publications_htmlpdf/application/pdf/conveng.pdf

United Nations. (1998). Kyoto protocol to the united nations framework convention on climate change. https://unfccc.int/resource/docs/convkp/kpeng.pdf

United Nations. (2015). Paris agreement. https://unfccc.int/files/essential_background/convention/application/pdf/english_paris_agreement.pdf

Wiedmann, T., & Minx, J. (2008). A definition of 'carbon footprint'. Ecological economics research trends, 1(2008), 1-11.

Wong, S., Yeung, J. K. W., Lau, Y. Y., Kawasaki, T., & Kwong, R. (2024). A critical literature review on blockchain technology adoption in supply chains. *Sustainability (Basel), 16*(12), 5174. DOI: 10.3390/su16125174

Yasir, K., Shen, J., & Lin, J. (2024). Sustainable Logistics: Synergizing Passive Design and PV–Battery Systems for Carbon Footprint Reduction. *Buildings (Basel, Switzerland), 14*(10), 3257. DOI: 10.3390/buildings14103257

Zhang, F., & Li, L. (2024). Study on the influence mechanism of low-carbon logistics on energy consumption structure in the Yangtze River Delta region. *International Journal of Global Economics and Management*, *2*(3), 386–391. DOI: 10.62051/IJGEM.v2n3.45

Zhang, H., & Yang, F. (2016). On the drivers and performance outcomes of green practices adoption: An empirical study in China. *Industrial Management & Data Systems*, *116*(9), 2011–2034. DOI: 10.1108/IMDS-06-2015-0263

Zheng, J., Garrick, N. W., Atkinson-Palombo, C., McCahill, C., & Marshall, W. (2013). Guidelines on developing performance metrics for evaluating transportation sustainability. Research in Transportation Business & Management, 7, 4-13. DOI: 10.1016/j.rtbm.2013.02.001

Chapter 14
Deep Topological Intelligence for Sustainable Supply Chain Management:
A Structural Framework for Global Logistics Optimization

Jaime Aguilar-Ortiz
http://orcid.org/0009-0003-5302-1454
Universidad Politécnica de Pachuca, Mexico

Ocotlán Diáz-Parra
Universidad Politécnica de Pachuca, Mexico

Jorge A. Ruiz-Vanoye
http://orcid.org/0000-0003-4928-5716
Universidad Politécnica de Pachuca, Mexico

Marco A. Vera-Jiménez
http://orcid.org/0009-0009-3712-1440
Universidad Politécnica de Pachuca, Mexico

Víctor M. Zamudio-García
http://orcid.org/0000-0002-4660-8025
Universidad Politécnica Metropolitana de Hidalgo, Mexico

Francisco R. Trejo-Macotela
http://orcid.org/0000-0003-2133-3456
Universidad Politécnica de Pachuca, Mexico

Carlos R. Domínguez-Mayorga
http://orcid.org/0009-0007-1018-4412
Universidad Politécnica de Pachuca, Mexico

DOI: 10.4018/979-8-3373-7847-3.ch014

ABSTRACT

The objective of this chapter is to develop Deep Topological Intelligence (DTI) as a structural framework for sustainable supply chain management, optimizing logistics while preserving viability, redundancy, and resilience. "Structural sustainability" is implemented by building a sea–air–rail–road logistics graph with cost, time, capacity, and emissions; simulating disruptions and targeted attacks; learning latent representations with autoencoders; and testing structural conservation with persistent homology, Betti curves, and Wasserstein distances. Contributions include a topology-informed digital-twin view (sustainability as persistence of form under perturbation), a reproducible workflow linking KPIs to homological indicators, a protocol that flags "efficient but fragile" AI designs, and a study of model capacity versus topological fidelity. Higher-capacity autoencoders preserve loop structure with minimal H_1 deformation (W≈0.054), while H_0 connectivity is more sensitive, revealing fragility missed by KPIs and supporting carbon-aware redesign without eroding redundancy.

1. INTRODUCTION: FROM THE FLOW OF GOODS TO STRUCTURAL KNOWLEDGE

1.1. The Transition Toward Sustainable and Resilient Logistics

This section analyzes the global transformation of supply chains, the environmental impact of multimodal transportation, and the urgent need for new models capable of balancing efficiency, resilience, and structural sustainability in an increasingly complex world. Figure 1 summarizes this section.

The global shift toward sustainable and resilient logistics arises from three converging pressures: the worldwide imperative for decarbonization, the growing exposure to systemic disruptions, and the structural complexity of global supply chains. Modern logistics networks now integrate maritime, air, rail, and road infrastructures into interdependent multimodal systems, where localized disturbances rapidly propagate through entire trade ecosystems. Recent crises ranging from pandemic disruptions and port congestion to climate-driven events and geopolitical instability have revealed that traditional optimization frameworks based solely on minimizing cost and time are no longer sufficient to ensure operational continuity or environmental accountability (Ivanov, 2020, 2023). Logistics is thus being reconceptualized as a practical system whose performance depends on its capacity to absorb shocks, reconfigure flows, and maintain connectivity under stress. Current research and policy agendas emphasize low-carbon corridors, digitalized border management, and regional integration as interlinked components of a structural approach that aligns global trade efficiency with climate and equity goals (Yang et al., 2023). Within this perspective, the multimodal network modeled in the accompanying code explicitly differentiating maritime, aerial, rail, and road links by distance, time, capacity, and emissions illustrates how logistics can be treated not as a linear chain of isolated decisions but as a measurable, adaptive infrastructure where geometry, flow dynamics, and environmental footprint are jointly optimized.

The environmental burden of multimodal transportation reinforces the urgency of this transformation. Freight transport accounts for a significant share of global greenhouse gas emissions, and modal composition finds its carbon intensity: energy-intensive air routes, congested road systems, and inefficient last-mile structures can nullify the benefits of cleaner maritime or rail transport when planned in isolation. Studies on sustainable logistics underscore that emission reductions require redesigning network topology through shared logistics platforms, carbon-cost-aware routing, and hierarchical distribution networks rather than incremental vehicle improvements (Aloui et al., 2021; Guo et al., 2022; Krstić et al., 2021). Complementary research on digital twins and AI-enabled monitoring reveals that structural visibility the capacity to observe and analyze flows, bottlenecks, and modal interactions in real time is essential for credible decarbonization and resilience assessment (Roman et al., 2025; Zhu et al., 2025). Here, structural persistence operationalizes environmental (CO_2), economic (cost/time/service), and social (access/continuity under disruption) sustainability. By embedding emissions, cost, and time within topological resilience analyses, the model advances the transition from optimizing individual routes toward governing the persistence and structural sustainability of the entire system, aligning with the emerging digital-twin paradigm for viable, low-carbon logistics ecosystems (Ivanov, 2023; Roman et al., 2025; Digital Twins in Supply Chain Management, 2025).

Alignment with the book's aims and scope: DTI supports intelligent decision-making and digital transformation in sustainable, low-carbon logistics by coupling AI optimization and digital-twin simulation with topology-based resilience validation. This chapter contributes to the volume by providing a reproducible workflow and auditable robustness metrics for multimodal, cross-border supply chains.

Figure 1. From the flow of goods to structural knowledge

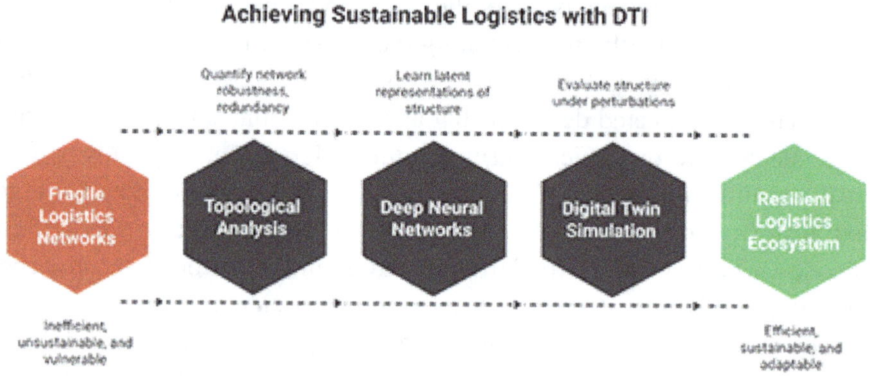

1.2. Challenges of the Current Logistical Optimization Paradigm

Classical cost/time optimization can deliver efficient yet fragile, hub-dependent networks that amplify ripple effects under disruption (Dolgui & Ivanov, 2021); survivability instead depends on redundancy, route diversity, and adaptive reconfiguration (Ivanov, 2020; Ivanov et al., 2023; Ruel et al., 2024). Even multi-objective models often treat resilience and sustainability as add-on penalties, yet evidence across vaccine/diagnostics and perishable-food chains shows that structural design parallel corridors, diversification, flexible capacity, and rerouting determine performance under compound shocks (Sazvar et al., 2021; Abbasian et al., 2023; Moadab et al., 2023) and motivates the viability perspective (Ivanov et al., 2023; Ivanov & Tu, 2025). This gap motivates DTI: a multimodal logistics graph whose learned representations are audited with TDA so efficiency gains do not erode structural persistence.

1.3. The Emergence of the Structural Paradigm and Chapter Objective

The following definition is needed for the development of the following sections.

Definition. A structural framework is defined here as a layered decision architecture that transforms multimodal logistics data and constraints into a network, learns reconfigurations under uncertainty, and verifies persistent viability and redundancy to deliver auditable sustainability decisions (Table 1).

Table 1. Framework components

Framework component	Role & outputs
Inputs (data/constraints)	cost–time–capacity–emissions + scenarios → features
Graph layer	multimodal (G(V,E,W)) → KPIs (efficiency/connectivity)
Learning/optimization	autoencoder/optimizer → latent structure + designs
Topology/decision	Betti/diagrams/Wasserstein + stress tests → robustness + recommendations

This part introduces the proposed Deep Topological Intelligence (DTI) framework as a form of structural intelligence capable of perceiving the global shape of the logistics network. DTI optimizes sustainability through the integration of topological analysis and deep neural networks, aiming to transform logistics management from operational optimization to structural comprehension.

The emergence of the structural paradigm in logistics is embodied in the proposed Deep Topological Intelligence (DTI) framework, which defines a new form of structural intelligence capable of perceiving, learning, and preserving the global geometry of logistics networks. Unlike conventional optimization methods that focus narrowly on minimizing costs or travel times, DTI integrates topological data analysis (TDA) with deep neural architectures to reveal how connectivity patterns, redundancy, and resilience properties shape sustainability outcomes across multimodal systems. This approach enables logistics to evolve from operational optimization toward structural comprehension, where sustainability and robustness emerge from the organization of the network itself rather than from additive constraints. Mathematically, DTI draws on techniques such as persistent homology, Betti curves, and Wasserstein distances to capture invariant topological features of multimodal transport graphs, and it employs autoencoders to learn latent representations that encode these global structures. In practice, the code developed for this chapter constructs a synthetic multimodal logistics network, computes topological indicators (connectivity, clustering, global efficiency), and then evaluates its capacity to retain structure under simulated perturbations, functioning as a digital twin that quantifies both resilience and sustainability. This fusion of topology and deep learning resonates with recent advances in topological deep learning, which has been recognized as a new frontier for relational and structural reasoning (Papamarkou et al., 2024), and with applications of TDA to manufacturing and logistics systems, where it enables the detection of hidden vulnerabilities and the design of more adaptive architectures (Carlsson, 2024; Uray et al., 2024). Consequently, the DTI paradigm reframes logistics management as a problem of structural sustainability, seeking not only efficient routing but the enduring viability of the network's form and function in an increasingly uncertain global environment (Zia et al., 2024; Wasserman, 2018).

Chapter contributions: Conceptual: Sustainability as persistent network form; Methodological: topology-aware AI validation for multimodal/cross-border logistics. Computational: Reproducible digital-twin simulations + emissions-aware optimization. Managerial/Policy: Auditable decision support for resilient, low-carbon trade. This chapter contributes to the volume by unifying AI, digital transformation, and structural sustainability for decarbonized, adaptive supply chains.

1.4. Issues, Problems, and Trends

- Fragility & ripple effects: local disruptions propagate; efficiency-only KPIs miss structural collapse.
- Emissions trade-offs: cost/time optimization can increase CO_2; decarbonization requires emissions-aware design.
- Visibility & auditability gaps: black-box AI and sparse monitoring weaken governance and reporting.
- Cross-border friction: customs/compliance bottlenecks demand intelligent, data-driven coordination.
- Trends: digital twins for low-carbon scenario planning; AI governance and responsible analytics; resilience–sustainability coupling; multimodal decarbonization/green corridors; big-data emissions monitoring.
- DTI response: a graph-based digital twin plus autoencoders and TDA (Betti/Wasserstein) to test whether redesigns cut emissions and preserve connectivity/redundancy under stress.

2. THEORETICAL FOUNDATIONS: FROM OPTIMIZATION TO DEEP TOPOLOGICAL INTELLIGENCE

Table 2 summarizes some of the formulas used in the chapter.

Table 2. Notation box

Symbol	Meaning (as used in this chapter)
$G = (V, E)$	G: logistics network (graph); V: set of nodes (port, hubs, DCs, border points, etc.); E: set of links/edges (routes/legs between nodes).
$\mathscr{F} = \{K_a\}_{a \in \mathbb{R}}$	$\mathscr{F}$: filtration (nested sequences); K_a; complex at scale/threshold α; α: threshold parameter (e.g. on weights/cost/emissions); $\{\bullet\}_{\alpha \in \mathbb{R}}$: "all scales" considered, producing nested $K_{\alpha_1} \subseteq K_{\alpha_2}$ when $\alpha_1 < \alpha_2$ (depending on convention).
$H_k = H_k(K_a)$	$H_k(\bullet)$: k-th homology group; k: dimension (typically 0 components, 1 cycles); $H_k(K_a)$; topological feature present at that scale.
$\beta_k = rank\ (H_k)$	β_k: Betti number in dimension k; *kank* $(\bullet)$: rank (informally, "count of independent features"); H_k: homology group; β_0; number of connected components; β_1: number of independent cycles/loops (redundancy).
$W_p\left(D_1, D_2\right) = \left(inf_\gamma \sum_{x \in D_1} \|x - \gamma(x)\|^p\right)^{1/p}$	W_p: p-Wasserstein distance; $p \geq 1$: order controlling sensitivity to large mismatches; D_1, D_2: persistence diagrams (multisets of points (b, d); $x \in D_1$: a feature point (birth b, death d); γ: matching/bijection from points in D_1 to points to D_2 (typically allowing matches to the diagonal); inf_γ: choose the least-cost matching; $\|\bullet\|$: point distance in the diagram plane (often $\|\bullet\|_\infty$) ; Σ: total transport cost; exponent $1/p$: turns cost into a metric.
$\mathscr{L}_{rec} = \frac{1}{N}\sum_{i=1}^{N} \|x_i - \hat{x}_i\|_2^2$	$\mathscr{L}_{rec}$: reconstruction loss; N: number of samples (or graph instances/windows); i: sample indez; x_i: original input (e.g., adjacency/features); $\hat{x}_i$: reconstructed output from the decoder; $\|\bullet\|_2$: Euclidean norm; square term $(\bullet)^2$: MSE-style penally encouraging accurate reconstruction.

continued on following page

Table 2. Continued

Symbol	Meaning (as used in this chapter)
$\mathcal{L}_{topo} = \sum_{k\in\{0,1\}} \alpha_k W_p\left(D_k(X), D_k(\hat{X})\right)^p$	$\mathcal{L}_{topo}$: topological loss; $k \in \{0,1\}$; dimensions tracked (components/cycles); α_k: weight for each dimension's importance; X: original structure graph/complex from data); $\hat{X}$: reconstructed/generated structure; $D_x(X)$: persistence diagram in dimension k for X; $W_p(\bullet,\bullet)$:Wasserstein distance between diagrams; power p: consistent with W_p definition; constraints $p \geq 1$, $\alpha_k \geq 0$: valid metric order and nonnegative weights.
$\mathcal{L}_{task} = \frac{1}{N}\sum_{i=1}^{N} \ell\left(h_\psi(z_i), y_i\right),\ z_i = f_\theta\left(x_i\right)$	$\mathcal{L}_{task}$: supervised task loss; N: number of labeled samples; $\ell(\bullet,\bullet)$: task loss function (e.g., cross-entropy, MSE); h_ψ: ask head/ predictor with parameters ψ; z_i: latent representation; y_i: label/target (KPI, risk class, emissions target, etc.); f_θ: encoder with parameters θ; $z_i = f_\theta(x_i)$: latent codes computed from inputs x_i.

2.1. From Classical Artificial Intelligence to Structural Intelligence

This section explains how artificial intelligence applied to logistics has evolved from predictive and local optimization models toward approaches that incorporate the entire system's structure through graph theory, network science, and deep learning. It highlights the shift from pointwise efficiency to systemic awareness and connectivity-oriented modeling. Figure 2 summarizes this section.

To keep the exposition consistent, the chapter first fixes a graph notation for the logistics system and introduces the learnable mappings that will later be constrained by topology.

The evolution from classical artificial intelligence to structural intelligence in logistics reflects a shift from isolated, locally optimized decisions to models that explicitly encode and learn the architecture of the entire supply chain network. Early AI applications in logistics relied on predictive models and optimization schemes that minimized cost or time, typically formulated as $min_x \sum_{(i,j)\in E} c_{ij} x_{ij}$ subject to flow conservation constraints, treating each route or facility largely independently and assuming that disturbances had localized, linear effects. Structural intelligence reframes this view by representing the logistics system as a *graph G* (see Notation box) with a weighted adjacency matrix A_{ij} capturing multimodal links, capacities, lead times, and emissions, and by evaluating systemic properties such as connectivity, centrality, and redundancy to understand how disruptions propagate and how resilient, low-carbon configurations emerge from network structure (Ivanov, 2020; Ruel et al., 2024). Geometric deep learning and graph neural networks extend this paradigm by learning functions $f_\theta: (G,X) \rightarrow Y$ that aggregate information via message passing across nodes and edges, enabling routing, capacity allocation, and risk assessment to depend on the full topology rather than on pointwise heuristics (Bronstein et al., 2017; Ding et al., 2024; Wasi et al., 2024). In parallel, topological data analysis and topological deep learning incorporate invariants such as persistent homology and Betti numbers through objectives of the form $\mathscr{L}_{total} = \mathscr{L}_{task} + \lambda \mathscr{L}_{top}$ where $\mathscr{L}_{top}$ (See Notation box) penalizes distortions of the network's global shape in latent representations (Moor et al., 2020; Zia et al., 2024; Papamarkou et al., 2024). The Deep Topological Intelligence framework developed in this chapter is consistent with these advances and with the attached code: it builds a multimodal graph with cost–time–emission weights, computes structural indicators, trains deep models that respect graph structure, and integrates topological constraints to ensure that optimized solutions preserve connectivity, robustness, and sustainability at the system level. In doing so, it operationalizes the transition from pointwise efficiency to systemic awareness and connectivity-oriented modeling, positioning structural intelligence as the necessary foundation for resilient and sustainable logistics.

With this graph-based formalism in place, the next step is to define invariants that summarize connectivity and redundancy across scales.

Figure 2. From optimization to deep topological intelligence

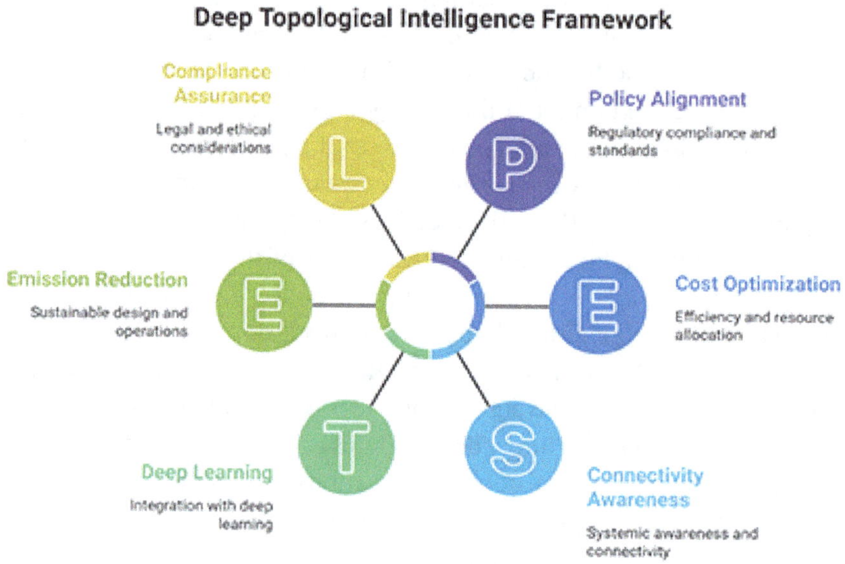

2.2. Mathematical Foundations of Applied Topology

It presents the essential concepts of homology and persistent homology. The notions of cycle connected components, Betti numbers, persistence diagrams, and Wasserstein distances are explained and linked to structural properties such as connectivity, redundancy, and stability in logistic networks. The section shows how these mathematical invariants capture the deeper organization and fault tolerance of transport systems.

Homology is introduced here because it converts network structure into stable, low-dimensional descriptors exactly the quantities later used to judge whether an optimization damages the system's form.

The mathematical foundations of applied topology in this chapter formalize how the deep structure of logistics networks can be quantified through homology and persistent homology, providing invariants that capture connectivity, redundancy, and stability beyond what classical graph metrics offer. A multimodal logistics system is represented as a weighted graph G (see notation box), or more generally as a simplicial complex K built from nodes (hubs, terminals), edges (links), and higher-dimensional simplices encoding multimodal or multi-hub interactions. Homology groups H_k (see Notation box) summarize k-dimensional holes: H_0 encodes connected components, H_1 independent cycles, and higher H_k higher-order voids; their ranks β_k (see Notation box) (Betti numbers) provide concise structural indicators, where β_0 measures fragmentation of the network, β_1 the availability of alternative loops and rerouting corridors (redundancy), and persistent low β_0 combined with sufficiently high β_1 reflects robust connectivity under failures (Wasserman, 2018). Persistent homology extends this by constructing a filtration $\mathcal{F}$ (see Notation box) (for example, progressively adding links ordered by cost, distance, or capacity), and tracking the birth and death of topological features across scales, yielding a persistence diagram D as a multiset of points (b_i, d_i) that encode how long each component or cycle survives (Otter et al., 2017). Long-lived features correspond to structurally essential backbones and loops of the logistics network, while short-lived ones capture noise or minor alternatives. Stability theorems guarantee that small perturbations in edge weights or capacities induce slight changes in D, typically measured via bottleneck or Wasserstein distances; for two diagrams D_1 and D_2, the p-Wasserstein distance is given by $W_p(D_1, D_2)$ (see Notation box), where γ ranges over bijections between points (Carrière et al., 2017). In the context of the Deep Topological Intelligence framework and the provided code, these constructions allow one to (i) map the multimodal freight network to filtrations driven by cost–time–emission trade-offs, (ii) compute Betti numbers, Betti curves, and persistence diagrams for original and perturbed or reconstructed graphs, and (iii) use Wasserstein-type distances between diagrams to quantify how resilient the structural "shape" of the network is under link removals, congestion scenarios, or learned reconfigurations. Thus, applied topology supplies rigorously stable invariants that reveal whether an optimized logistics configuration preserves fault-tolerant connectivity and meaningful redundancy, aligning with recent developments in topological data analysis and topological deep learning for complex infrastructures (Wasserman, 2018; Otter et al., 2017; Chazal et al., 2016; Zia et al., 2024).

2.3. Integration of Topology With Deep Learning

This part describes how autoencoders, latent representations, and topological loss functions enable models to learn not only metric data but also invariant structures. It explains the role of topological metrics in regularizing and validating deep learning models, ensuring that learned representations preserve the essential "shape" of logistic connectivity.

The integration of topology with deep learning in this chapter operationalizes Deep Topological Intelligence as a framework where models learn not only metric patterns but also the invariant "shape" of logistics connectivity. In the implemented code, the multimodal logistics network encoded through weighted adjacency matrices and node/edge features combining cost, time, capacity, and emissions is processed by autoencoders that map inputs $\hat{x} = g_{\phi}(z)$, optimized via a reconstruction loss such as $\mathcal{L}_{rec}$ (see Notation box). To ensure that this latent space preserves the structural organization of the network, the model is regularized with a topological loss term $\mathcal{L}_{top}$ derived from persistent homology: for each network (original, reconstructed, or perturbed) one computes persistence diagrams D capturing the lifetimes of connected components and cycles, and penalizes distortions of these invariants through distances between diagrams, typically using the p-Wasserstein distance $W_p(D_1, D_2)$ (see Notation box) or related kernels as in sliced Wasserstein formulations. The training objective takes the form $\mathcal{L}_{total} = \mathcal{L}_{rec} + \lambda \mathcal{L}_{top}$ (See notation box), where $\lambda > 0$ controls the strength of the structural constraint. This strategy follows the logic of topological autoencoders, in which the latent space is optimized to preserve multi-scale connectivity encoded by persistence diagrams and Betti numbers (Moor et al., 2020) and is consistent with methods that incorporate topological signatures directly into deep architectures (Hofer et al., 2017; Carrière et al., 2017). In the logistics context, long-lived 1-dimensional features in the diagrams correspond to robust rerouting loops, while changes in 0- and 1-dimensional persistence under attacks or re-optimizations signal fragmentation or loss of redundancy; by monitoring these signals, the DTI framework uses topological metrics both as a regularizer during training and as a validation criterion to ensure that optimized solutions maintain fault-tolerant connectivity. Recent surveys and position papers on topological deep learning confirm that such topology-aware objectives form a coherent paradigm for encoding global structural constraints in neural models (Zia et al., 2024; Papamarkou et al., 2024), aligning directly with this chapter's use of autoencoders and topological losses to guarantee that learned representations of multimodal transport systems remain structurally viable, resilient, and sustainable. This topology-aware learning step enables sustainability to be stated as a structural requirement: improvements are acceptable only when the network's essential shape remains coherent.

2.4. Principles of Structural Sustainability and Topological Resilience

It develops the conceptual bridge between topological structure and sustainability, emphasizing how the preservation of critical logistical cycles and operational redundancies reduces systemic vulnerability and emissions. The argument is made that resilience can be understood as the conservation of topological form under perturbations, positioning topology as a framework for sustainable design. The chapter now frames 'structural sustainability' as a coupled criterion that balances emissions/performance with controlled topological deformation.

The principles of structural sustainability and topological resilience formalize sustainability as the preservation of the network's essential form under perturbations while reducing externalities such as emissions. Representing the multimodal logistics system as a weighted graph G (see Notation box) (or its Vietoris–Rips complex K) homology groups H_k (see Notation box) and Betti numbers β_k (see notation box) quantify structural resources: β_0 measures connectivity (islands of service), whereas β_1 counts independent logistical cycles that enable rerouting and load-balancing; in this setting, resilience is the capacity to keep β_0 low (avoid fragmentation) and β_1 sufficiently high (retain redundancy) after shocks. Persistent homology tracks these features across a filtration $\{K_\alpha\}$ (e.g., thresholds on cost–time–emission weights), producing a persistence diagram $D = \{(b_i, d_i)\}$ whose long lifetimes $d_i - b_i$ identify critical backbones and cycles. Stability theorems justify using distances between diagrams to certify structural conservation: for two states of the network, D_1 and D_2 the p-Wasserstein distance $W_p(D_1, D_2)$ (see Notation box) is small when the topology is preserved despite perturbations, providing a robustness certificate (Wasserman, 2018; Skraba & Turner, 2020). These invariants connect directly to sustainability: (i) cycles reduce vulnerability to congestion and cascading failures by distributing flows, which empirical transport studies model as resilience gains from route diversity and redundancy (Xu et al., 2021); (ii) redundancy enables carbon-aware routing because alternative paths allow emissions to be minimized without sacrificing service continuity; and (iii) a design principle emerges in the form of a constrained multi-objective program, consistent with the accompanying code, that seeks low emissions while conserving shape,

$$\min_x \mathcal{E}(G_x) \; s.t. \; W_p(D(G_x), D(G_{baseline})) \leq \varepsilon, \beta_0(G_x) = 1, \beta_1(G_x) \geq \tau,$$

or, in penalized form,

$$\min_x \underbrace{\mathcal{E}(G_x)}_{emissions} + \lambda \underbrace{W_p(D(G_x), D(G_{baseline}))}_{topological\ deviation} - \eta \underbrace{\beta_1(G_x)}_{redundancy},$$

Where $\min_x \mathcal{E}(G_x)$ aggregates CO_2 e along flows, ε, τ set structural viability thresholds, and $\lambda, \eta > 0$ encode the value of preserving global form. Within the viability agenda for supply chains, this reframing moves from pointwise efficiency to architectural governance of networks: sustainable design is achieved when optimized policies keep the persistence diagram stable and maintain routing cycles that buffer shocks and enable decarbonization exactly the role played by topological losses and post-hoc topological validation in modern deep architectures (Moor et al., 2020; Papamarkou et al., 2024; Ivanov, 2023).

3. ARCHITECTURE OF THE DEEP TOPOLOGICAL INTELLIGENCE (DTI-LOGISTICS) MODEL

Methodological Roadmap. 1) Data (cost–time–capacity–emissions) → 2) Multimodal graph → 3) Disruption/attack scenarios → 4) Features/scaling → 5) Autoencoder training → 6) Persistent homology (Betti) → 7) Stress tests → 8) Evaluation → 9) Managerial interpretation. Key assumptions: synthetic network; approximate emission factors; stationary modal attributes; bounded horizon. Evaluation: cost/time/emissions, service level; giant component/connectivity; β_0/β_1 stability; Wasserstein(H_0/H_1).

3.1. General Structure of the DTI-Logistics System

This section describes the main layers of the model data, geometric, deep, and topological highlighting their integration within a structural digital twin of the logistics network. Architecture allows for simultaneous analysis of performance, emissions, and structural stability. Figure 3 summarizes this section.

The general structure of the DTI-logistics system is organized as a four-layer architecture that operates as a structural digital twin of the multimodal network, allowing the system to evaluate at the same time classical performance metrics (cost, time, capacity utilization), environmental metrics (CO_2-equivalent per flow, modal emission factors), and structural metrics (connectivity, redundancy, topological stability). In the data layer, heterogeneous operational records distances, transit times, tariffs, capacities, and emission coefficients for sea, air, rail, and road are normalized into a unified feature space so that each edge e_{ij} s represented by a vector $x_{ij} = \left[d_{ij}, t_{ij}, c_{ij}, CO_{2,i,j}\right]$, exactly as in the provided code where multimodal links are explicitly differentiated. The geometric layer then maps these features to a graph or simplicial representation $G = (V, E)$, computing adjacency, degree, and path structure so that the network can be filtered by cost, by time, or by emission thresholds, which is necessary to build filtrations for later topological analysis. On top of this, the deep layer applies autoencoders or graph/deep models to learn latent representations $z = f_\theta(G)$ that capture multiscale logistics patterns while preserving information needed for prediction and re-routing; these latent codes feed scenario analysis (e.g., node removal, congestion, or modal shifts) without reconstructing the full data from scratch. Finally, the topological layer computes persistent homology, Betti curves, and diagram distances between the original and the reconstructed or perturbed graphs, adding a topological loss or post-hoc validation step that rejects solutions which improve cost or emissions but damage the network's essential shape. In this way, the DTI architecture enforces structural sustainability: any optimization is accepted only if it stays within a tolerance band in topological space, so that the logistics network remains connected ($\beta_0 = 1$), sufficiently redundant ($\beta_1 \geq \tau$), and stable under small perturbations, matching the current view of viable supply chains as systems that must be simultaneously efficient, low-carbon, and structurally coherent (Ivanov, 2023; Moor et al., 2020).

Figure 3. Architecture of the Deep Topological Intelligence (DTI-Logistics) model

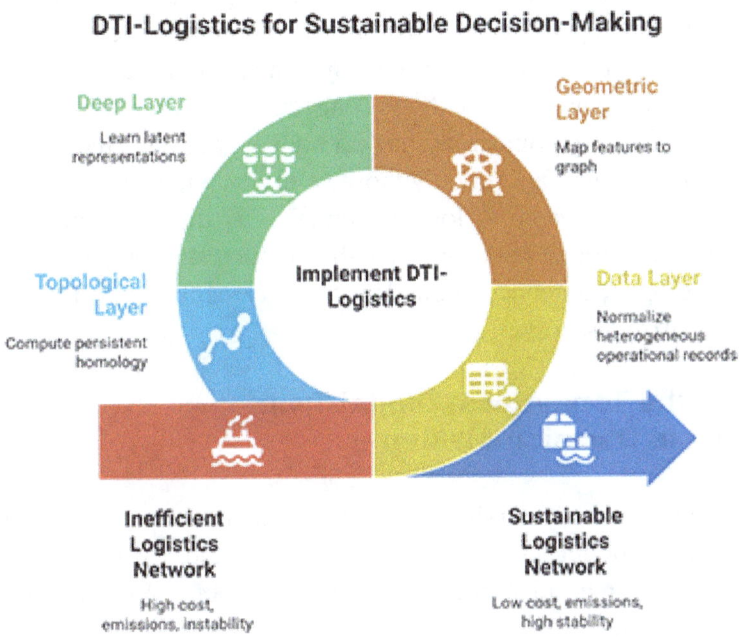

3.2. Technical Components and Information Flow

It details data processing pipelines (distances, costs, times, and emissions), normalization methods, and node–edge representation. The section explains how deep neural networks learn internal structural representations that are later analyzed through persistent homology, enabling an interpretive bridge between data geometry and topological stability.

The DTI-logistics system implements a rigorous pipeline in which raw operational records distances d_{ij}, costs c_{ij}, travel times t_{ij} and emissions $CO_{2,i,j}$ are first validated, imputed when necessary, and normalized (e.g., $x' = (x - \mu_x)/\sigma_x$ or $x' = (x - minx)/(maxx - minx)$ to form edge feature vectors $x_{ij} = \left[d'_{ij}, c'_{ij}, t'_{ij}, CO'_{2,i,j}\right]$

consistent with the attached code's multimodal graph specification; nodes $v \in V$ and edges $e_{ij} \in E$ are then assembled into a weighted adjacency A and (when required) into a simplicial complex for multi-hub interactions. Over this geometric representation, deep neural models (autoencoders or graph-based encoders) learn latent representations $z = f_{\theta}(G,X)$ and reconstructions by minimizing (see Notation box) while preserving global organization through a topological regularizer computed from persistent homology: the system builds filtrations of the network by cost/time/emission thresholds, obtains persistence diagrams for (connectivity) and (redundant cycles), and penalizes distortions via diagram distances (e.g., bottleneck or), yielding (see notation box). This design creates an interpretive bridge: long-lived features in correspond to backbone connectivity and rerouting loops that the model must retain, so topological metrics act both as training-time constraints and as post-hoc validators that accept only those solutions whose learned embeddings conserve the essential "shape" of logistic connectivity thereby aligning predictive performance and decarbonization targets with structural stability, in line with recent advances in topological autoencoders and the stability theory of persistent homology (Moor et al., 2020; Wasserman, 2018).

3.3. Role of the Topological Digital Twin in Sustainable Decision-Making

It presents how the model can simulate crisis scenarios, evaluate structural impacts, and guide logistical policies toward more sustainable and resilient configurations. The digital twin becomes a learning and predictive tool for systemic sustainability and adaptive planning.

The topological digital twin in the DTI-logistics system acts as an executable surrogate of the multimodal network that continuously learns from data and stress-tests structural hypotheses, enabling decision-makers to rehearse crises, quantify systemic impacts, and steer policies toward configurations that are both low-carbon and resilient. Concretely, the twin instantiates the operational graph (see Notation Box) with edge features , runs counterfactuals (targeted hub/edge removals, congestion shocks, modal shifts), and evaluates each intervention with coupled metrics: performance (, emissions , and topological stability via persistent homology preserving (global connectivity) and sufficient (redundant cycles) while keeping the diagram distance within a prescribed tolerance. Policy candidates e.g., rerouting to rail–sea corridors, capacity buffers at meso-hubs, or carbon-aware pricing are thus filtered by a structural viability criterion: improvements in cost or are accepted only if the network's "shape" remains coherent under perturbations in the twin, aligning with viability theory in which resilience and sustainability are system properties rather than additive penalties (Ivanov, 2023). This operationalizes the broader digital-twin principle closed-loop sensing, simulation, and control now extended with topological diagnostics so that the twin does not merely predict performance but governs architectural persistence, providing an interpretable, policy-ready bridge from data geometry to systemic sustainability.

4. EXPERIMENTAL IMPLEMENTATION OF THE DTI-LOGISTICS SYSTEM

4.1. Generation of the Synthetic Multimodal Logistics Network

This section explains how the experimental network was built with nodes (ports, airports, customs facilities, distribution centers, cities) and multimodal edges that incorporate parameters such as distance, capacity, time, and emissions, reflecting the complexity of real-world trade routes. Figure 4 summarizes this section.

Figure 4. Experimental implementation of the DTI-Logistics system

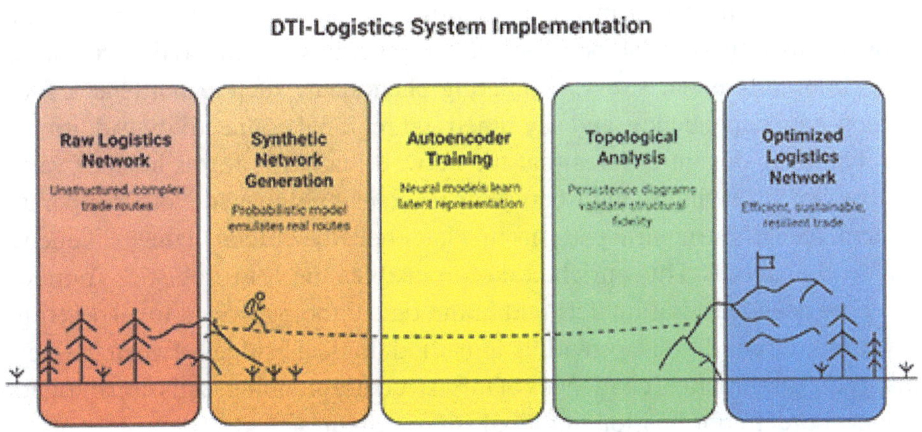

The experimental implementation of the DTI-Logistics system begins with the generation of a synthetic multimodal logistics network that emulates the structure and complexity of real-world trade routes. The network is constructed through a probabilistic spatial model that assigns nodes representing ports, airports, customs facilities, distribution centers, and cities, each distributed within a two-dimensional geographic plane. Using the parameters defined in the code, distances between nodes are computed through Euclidean metrics, while the connectivity probability decays exponentially with distance, ensuring realistic spatial clustering of trade corridors. Edges are then classified according to transportation modes sea, air, rail, and road each characterized by distinct parameters such as capacity, average speed, emission factor, and transport cost. For every edge, attributes including distance, time, capacity, emissions, and generalized cost are computed and stored as weighted properties of the graph, allowing later computation of structural and environmental indicators. This procedure results in a fully connected, weighted, and heterogeneous graph that integrates functional diversity with spatial realism. Within this simulated environment, multimodal trade flows are allocated between origin–destination pairs according to the principle of minimum generalized cost, generating dynamic patterns of interaction that reflect congestion, modal substitution, and emission trade-offs. Thus, the synthetic network functions as a controlled laboratory for evaluating how structural intelligence embodied in the Deep Topological Intelligence framework responds to the inherent tension between efficiency, sustainability, and resilience in complex global logistics systems.

The synthetic network also incorporates mechanisms that reproduce emergent structural behaviors commonly found in real logistics systems, allowing the experiment to capture not only static attributes but also dynamic interdependencies. By introducing randomness in modal availability, variability in edge capacities, and heterogeneous emission factors, the model generates multimodal corridors that behave differently under stress, simulating phenomena such as bottleneck formation, long-haul dependency, and asymmetrical regional connectivity. Additionally, the probabilistic design ensures that the network naturally forms hubs of varying centrality, some serving as high-betweenness transit points while others operate as peripheral feeder's structural patterns that later become crucial in the resilience and topological analyses. This enriched design enables the DTI-Logistics framework to test how deep learning models and homological tools respond to a spectrum of real-world–like conditions, providing a methodological bridge between theoretical topology and the practical challenges of infrastructure planning, emission mitigation, and cross-border coordination in global supply chains.

4.2. Training of Autoencoders and Latent Representation

It describes the training process of neural models, including loss functions, hyperparameters, data normalization, and learning curves showing system convergence. The latent space learned by the autoencoders encodes the essential structure of the logistics system.

The training of autoencoders in the DTI-Logistics system is designed to capture the latent structure underlying the multimodal logistics network, transforming complex numerical and relational information into a compact, structurally meaningful representation. Once the network matrices comprising cost, distance, time, and emission attributes are generated and normalized to ensure comparability across scales, they are flattened and fed into an autoencoder architecture built with TensorFlow, consisting of symmetrical encoder and decoder layers with nonlinear activations. The encoder compresses the input into one- and two-dimensional latent spaces, as defined by the parameters LATENT_1D = 8 and LATENT_2D = 16, which are sufficient to preserve the topology and operational diversity of the logistics system. Training is conducted over 120 epochs with a batch size of 64 and a learning rate of , optimizing a reconstruction loss function—typically the mean squared error (MSE)that quantifies the difference between the original and reconstructed matrices. Throughout training, the model progressively minimizes reconstruction error while simultaneously learning stable and interpretable geometric patterns, as shown in the learning curves that exhibit smooth convergence without signs of overfitting.

Beyond simple dimensionality reduction, the latent representations learned by the autoencoders encode higher-order relationships among nodes and edges, including route redundancy, modal interdependence, bottleneck sensitivity, and spatial clustering. These emergent structural correlations cannot be directly inferred from local graph attributes but emerge naturally through the compression process, which forces the model to retain only the most persistent and informative patterns of connectivity. Visualization of the latent spaces through methods such as PCA projections reveals how the autoencoders cluster nodes according to their structural roles rather than their physical proximity, grouping together ports, hubs, and peripheral nodes based on shared topological functions within the network. This latent geometry provides a new structural lens through which resilience, efficiency, and modal interactions can be interpreted.

To validate the fidelity of the learned representations, the reconstructed matrices are compared with the original adjacency structures and weighted connectivity patterns. Metrics such as reconstruction error per node, latent-space dispersion, and Wasserstein distances between persistence diagrams confirm that the autoencoders successfully internalize the global structural backbone of the network while introducing only minor distortions in fine-grained connectivity. This integration of deep learning with topological diagnostics ensures that the autoencoders do not merely compress data efficiently but learn the intrinsic connectivity and resilience of the logistics system. As such, the latent spaces serve as the foundation for the topological data analysis and resilience assessment in the subsequent sections, enabling the DTI-Logistics framework to interpret optimization as a process of structural learning rather than parameter tuning alone.

4.3. Topological Analysis of the Logistics Network

This section details how persistence diagrams, Betti curves, and Wasserstein distances were computed. It explains how the learned structures are compared to the original networks and what these comparisons reveal about the model's structural fidelity and ability to generalize connectivity patterns.

The topological analysis of the logistics network in the DTI-Logistics system constitutes the stage where the deep representations learned by the autoencoders are evaluated to determine whether they preserve the essential structural properties of the original multimodal configuration. Once the encoder-decoder model has converged, both the reconstructed and baseline networks are converted into weighted adjacent matrices and subsequently processed through the topological module implemented in the code. This module constructs filtrations by progressively adding edges according to their cost, distance, or emission weights, allowing the computation of persistence diagrams that record the birth and death of connected components and cycles across scales. From these diagrams, Betti curves are extracted to quantify variations in the number of components (and loops (as filtration thresholds increase, providing a continuous measure of connectivity and redundancy within the network. The model then compares the persistence diagrams of the reconstructed and original networks using Wasserstein distances, which capture geometric dissimilarities between their topological signatures. A small distance indicates that the latent space has successfully retained the network's structural skeleton, its core connectivity and critical cycles while larger values signal that the learned representation may have distorted or simplified essential relationships. Through these analyses, the system validates that the autoencoder has not only minimized reconstruction loss but also internalized the relational geometry that defines multimodal logistics systems. This integration of topological metrics confirms that the learned embeddings generalize the network's architecture, maintaining fault-tolerant connectivity and reflecting the inherent balance between efficiency, redundancy, and sustainability encoded in the original structure.

5. INTERPRETATION OF RESULTS: RESILIENCE, SUSTAINABILITY, AND STRUCTURAL STABILITY

5.1. Quantitative Results of the DTI-Logistics Model

It presents global performance metrics (efficiency, average distance, costs, and emissions) alongside topological metrics (Betti curves, Wasserstein distances).

The analysis interprets how the learned network preserves or distorts the original structure, revealing the depth of its structural understanding.

Table 3. Global structural and flow metrics of the DTI-logistics synthetic network. Pattern: near-minimal connectivity (160 nodes/162 edges) yields large diameter (22), long paths (9.89), extremely low clustering (0.0146) and disassortative mixing (−0.108). Implication: efficiency is constrained and flows concentrate on long, fragile corridors, increasing time, distance, cost, and CO_2

n_nodes	n_edges	diameter	avg_path_len	clustering	assortativity
160	162	22	9.89277	0.01458	-0.10764
global_eff	**total_distance _km**	**total_time_h**	**total_emissions _kgCO2~**	**total_cost_index**	
0.13807	75149.85020	1294.01447	6774.31652	83501.13168	

Reading guide: focus on diameter/avg path length and clustering/assortativity as indicators of corridor dependence and low redundancy.

Why it matters: the low global efficiency (0.138) together with high distance/time/emissions implies the best managerial lever is targeted redundancy (alternate links/modes) on the longest, most central routes to cut CO_2 without losing connectivity.

Managerial meaning: Low clustering and long paths imply hub-bridge dependence; add parallel links/modal detours on longest OD corridors before optimizing flows.

Actionable insight: invest in redundancy where path length drives emissions.

Figure 5. Multimodal synthetic logistics network (nodes and modal edges). Pattern: sparse, dispersed layout with few local triangles and several long, corridor-like links acting as shortcuts. Implication: connectivity is vulnerable to targeted corridor failures, motivating redundancy and modal detours for low-carbon resilience

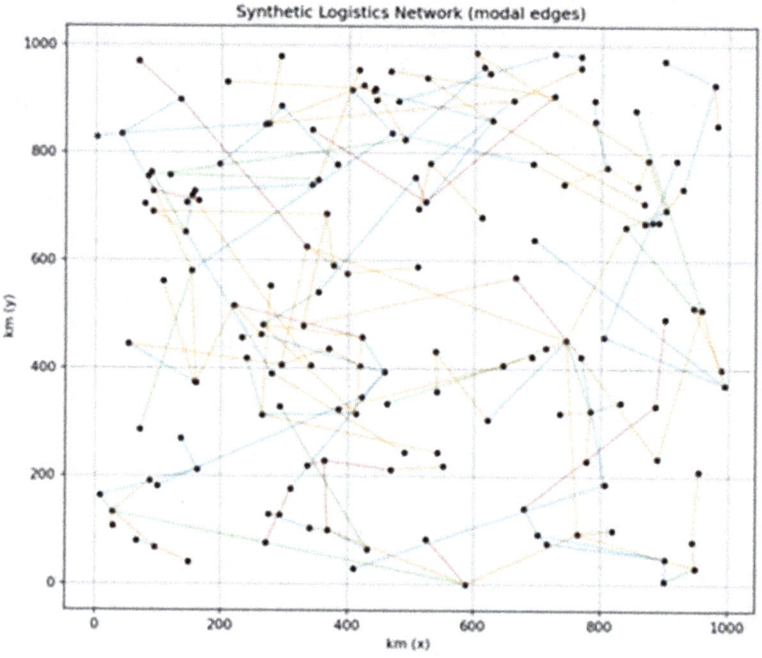

Reading guide: look for (i) long edges that bridge distant clusters and (ii) areas with almost no local triangles (low redundancy).

Why it matters: those bridges are priority candidates for backup routes, hub diversification, and modal alternatives to prevent fragmentation and emissions spikes under disruption.

Figure 6. Original vs reconstructed adjacency matrix (AE-8). Pattern: core edge locations are recovered, but reconstruction shows stronger background smoothing/ noise. Implication: AE-8 is adequate for backbone-level structure but may distort fine-grained connectivity used for fragility or local routing decisions

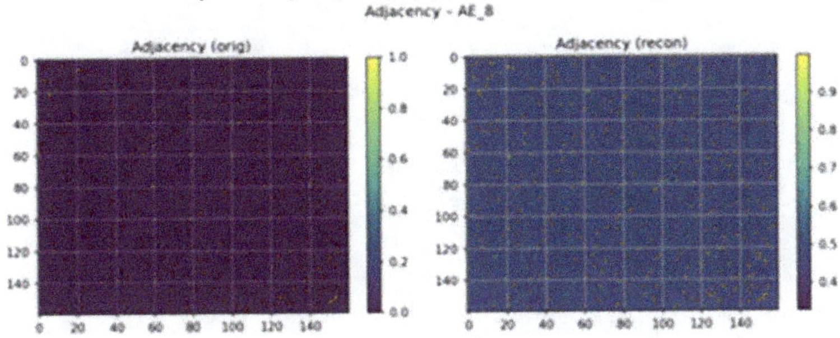

Figure 7. Original vs reconstructed adjacency matrix (AE-16). Pattern: sharper reconstruction with less smoothing than AE-8 while preserving sparsity. Implication: higher latent capacity improves structural fidelity, supporting more reliable downstream resilience and sustainability diagnostics

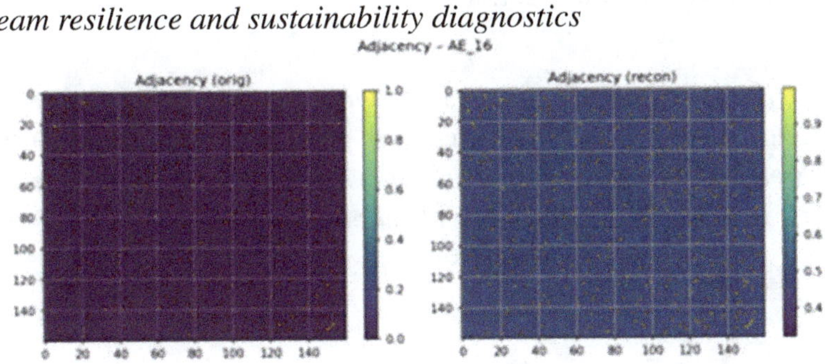

Reading guide: compare how many bright edge pixels align with the original and how much low-intensity "background" appears in the reconstruction (noise/ smoothing).

Why it matters: AE-16 better preserves fine connectivity for stress-testing and emissions-aware redesign, while AE-8 should be used mainly for coarse backbone insights.

Figure 8. Training and validation loss curves of AE-8 and AE-16. Pattern: training loss drops sharply while validation remains high and only slowly improves. Implication: models learn the backbone but generalize weakly, so downstream decisions should rely on topological validation and stress tests rather than reconstruction loss alone

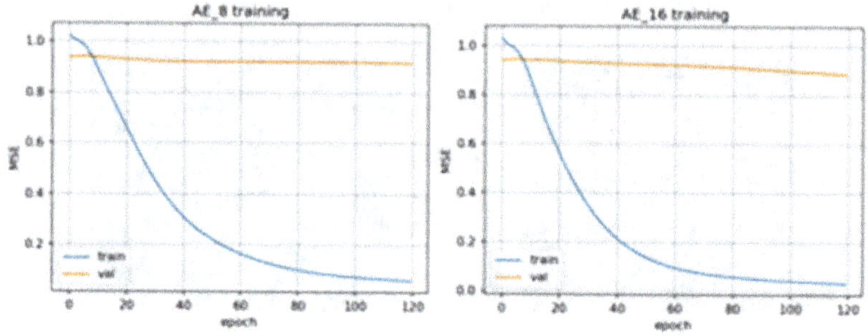

Reading guide: compare the train–validation gap over epochs and whether validation plateaus while training keeps improving.

Why it matters: the persistent gap signals limited out-of-sample fidelity; use AE outputs mainly as candidates, then accept designs only if Betti/ and resilience metrics remain stable under disruption.

Figure 9. Distribution of per-node reconstruction error for AE-8 and AE-16. Pattern: most nodes cluster near zero error with a long right tail of high-error outliers. Implication: a small set of structurally atypical/critical nodes is harder to reconstruct and should be prioritized for resilience checks and redundancy

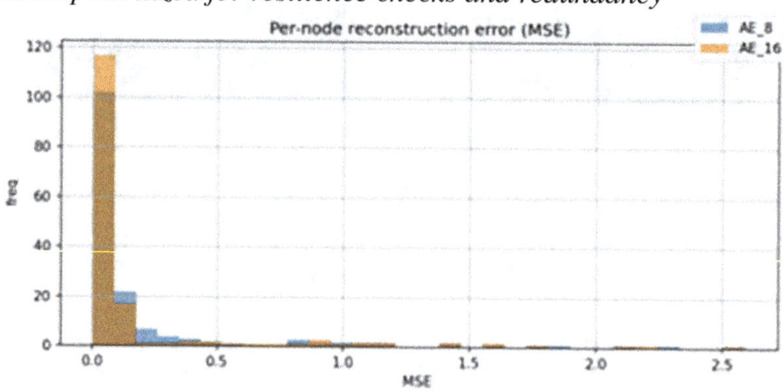

Reading guide: note the mass near MSE≈0 versus the tail; the tail identifies "hard" nodes where local structure is irregular or weakly redundant.

Why it matters: treat high-error nodes as candidates for operational focus (backup links, hub diversification, monitoring), since they are more likely to drive fragility and emissions spikes under disruption.

Figure 10. Latent representations projected to 2D (PCA) for AE-8 and AE-16. Pattern: both form a central cluster, while AE-8 shows broader dispersion and more outliers than AE-16. Implication: higher latent capacity yields a more stable embedding, supporting more consistent downstream diagnostics (stress tests and sustainability assessment)

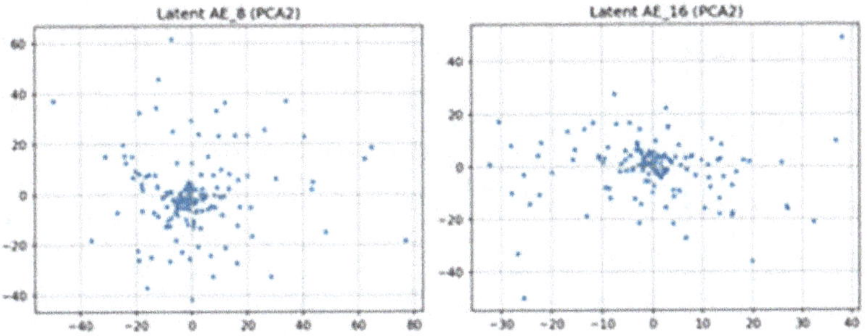

Reading guide: compare cluster compactness and the number/distance of outliers between AE-8 and AE-16.

Why it matters: dispersion/outliers indicate less stable encoding; prefer AE-16 when embeddings drive risk ranking, corridor prioritization, or topology-based validation.

Figure 11. Persistence diagrams of the geodesic and latent representations. Pattern: dense short-lived features and only limited persistence. Implication: the baseline topology is mostly connectivity/merging with few meaningful cycles (redundancy)

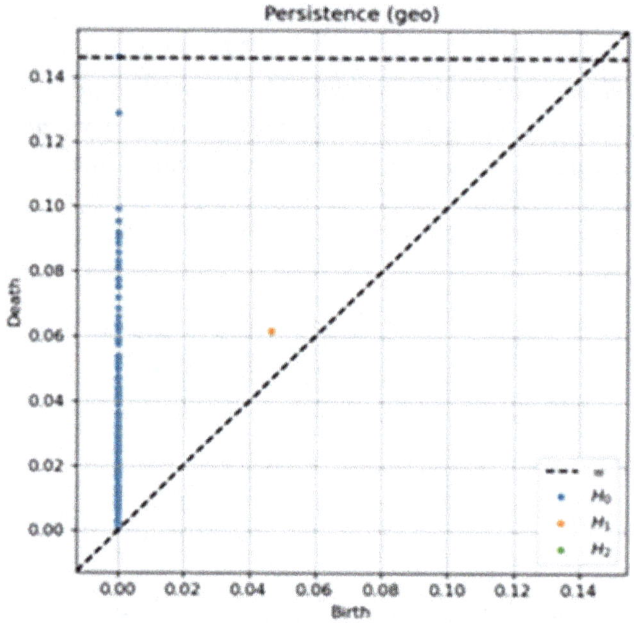

Figure 12. Persistence diagrams of geodesic and latent representations. Pattern: remains short-lived, but features become more numerous and more persistent. Implication: AE-8 inflates cycle structure, so topology-based decisions should be validated with /stress tests before use

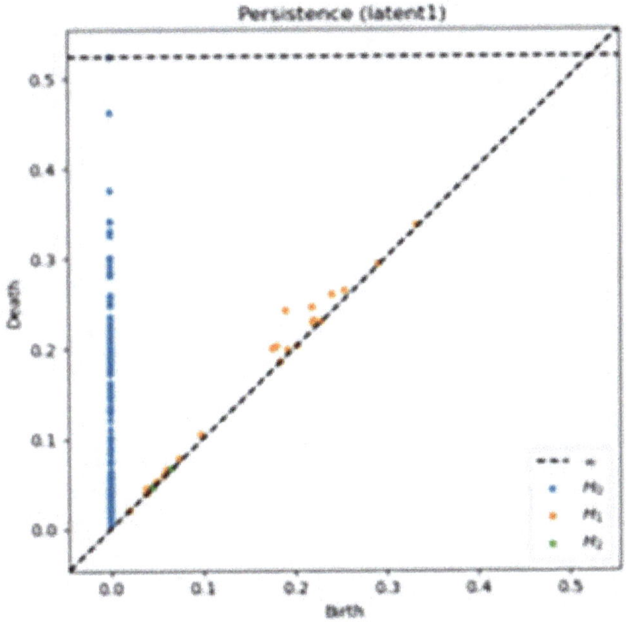

Figure 13. Persistence diagrams of geodesic and latent representations. Pattern: similar preservation with a less extreme spread than AE-8 yet still elevated versus baseline. Implication: higher capacity reduces but does not eliminate cycle distortion; AE-16 is preferable for topological fidelity

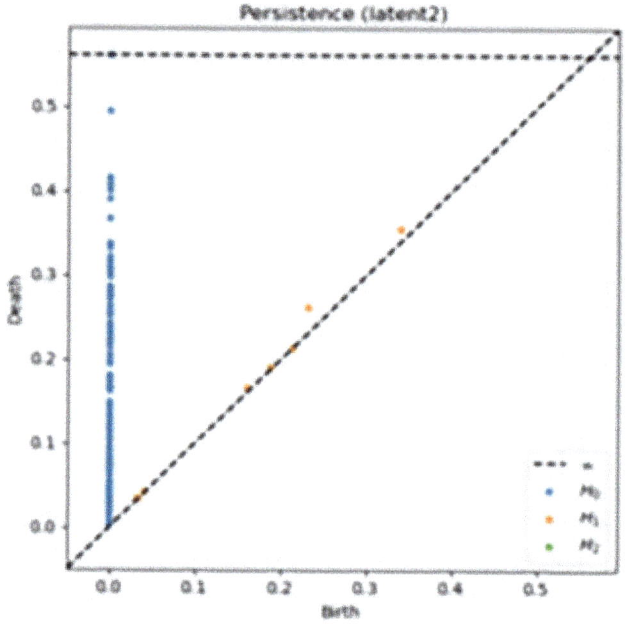

Reading guide: compare the concentration of points near the diagonal and the number/spread of points away from it (cycle persistence).

Why it matters: extra or longer-lived features signal artificial redundancy; accept latent-driven redesigns only if stays within tolerance and resilience metrics remain stable under targeted disruptions.

Figure 14. Betti curves (β_0, β_1, β_2) for geodesic and latent networks. Pattern: the baseline collapses quickly with near-zero while latent curves show slower decay and elevated .Implication: latent compression preserves global connectivity but inflates redundancy/cycle structure, so topological validation is required before managerial use

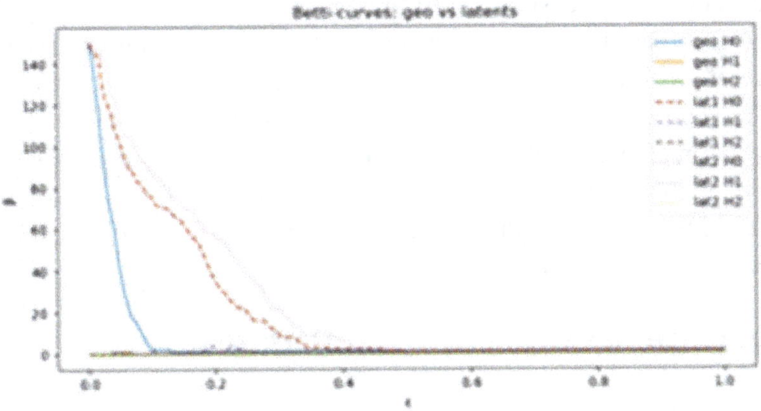

Reading guide: compare how fast drops and whether departs from zero in the latent curves relative to the baseline.

Why it matters: slower decay and higher indicate altered network form; accept redesigns only if Betti shifts and stay within tolerance under stress tests.

Table 4. Wasserstein distances (H_0, H_1, H_2) between geodesic and latent topological signatures. Pattern: is large for both models, while is smaller (AE-16 < AE-8) and . Implication: latent learning mainly distorts fine connectivity (fragmentation/merging), so managerial use should prioritize macro-structure and validate micro-connectivity with stress tests

metric	H0_lat1	H1_lat1	H2_lat1	H0_lat2	H1_lat2	H2_lat2
Wasserstein	11.21707	0.16151	0.00087	14.81779	0.05422	0.00000

Reading guide: interpret large as connectivity distortion and smaller as better cycle preservation (AE-16 closer to baseline).

Why it matters: use AE-16 when topology fidelity matters and treat high distortion as a trigger for targeted redundancy (local links/mode alternatives) before committing to corridor decisions.

Managerial meaning: High in means latent reconstructions distort fine connectivity; use AE outputs for macro-patterns, not micro-routing or fragility mapping.

Actionable insight: reinforce local links where distortion concentrates.

Taken together, these quantitative findings show that operational performance metrics and topological indicators converge toward a coherent diagnosis of the logistics system: a network that is functionally connected but structurally fragile, efficient in narrow regions yet globally elongated, and capable of being learned by deep models only at the cost of distortions in its fine-scale connectivity. The combination of long path lengths, low clustering, high Wasserstein distances, and the emergence of artificial cycles in the latent space reveals that sustainability cannot be understood purely in terms of cost, distance, or emissions, but must incorporate the preservation of structural form as captured by topological invariants. Thus, the quantitative analysis establishes the empirical foundation for interpreting sustainability as a property of structural persistence, motivating the topological perspective developed in the subsequent sections.

5.2. Resilience Assessment Under Perturbations

This part analyzes the network's behavior under simulated failures both random and targeted. It examines changes in the fraction of the giant part, global efficiency, and variations in β_0 and β_1 as indicators of systemic stability and adaptive robustness.

Table 5. Resilience indicators under random vs betweenness-based edge removals (24 edges). Pattern: targeted (betweenness) removals produce a much smaller giant component (0.106 vs 0.369) despite shorter remaining paths, indicating backbone collapse. Implication: resilience depends on a few critical corridors; protecting/duplicating them is more effective than uniform upgrades

removed	edges_after	nodes_after	giant_fraction	global_eff	clustering	avg_path_len	diameter	mode
24	58	59	0.36875	0.220108	0	6.160140	13	random_edges
24	16	17	0.10625	0.383946	0	3.470588	6	betweenness_edges

Reading guide: compare giant fraction (connectivity) first, then avg path length/diameter (remaining efficiency) across random vs targeted removals.

Why it matters: prioritize redundancy around high-betweenness links (alternate modes, bypass corridors, hub diversification) to prevent fragmentation and emissions surges during disruptions.

Managerial meaning: Targeted removals collapse the backbone; prioritize hardening high-betweenness corridors (buffers + alternate modes) over uniform upgrades.

Actionable insight: build at least one bypass around each top critical bridge.

Figure 15. Resilience metrics under random vs targeted (betweenness) edge removals. Pattern: targeted removals sharply reduce the giant component while global efficiency rises only within the smaller remnant; clustering stays near zero. Implication: the network's resilience is corridor-dependent, so protecting/duplicating critical bridges is essential for low-carbon continuity

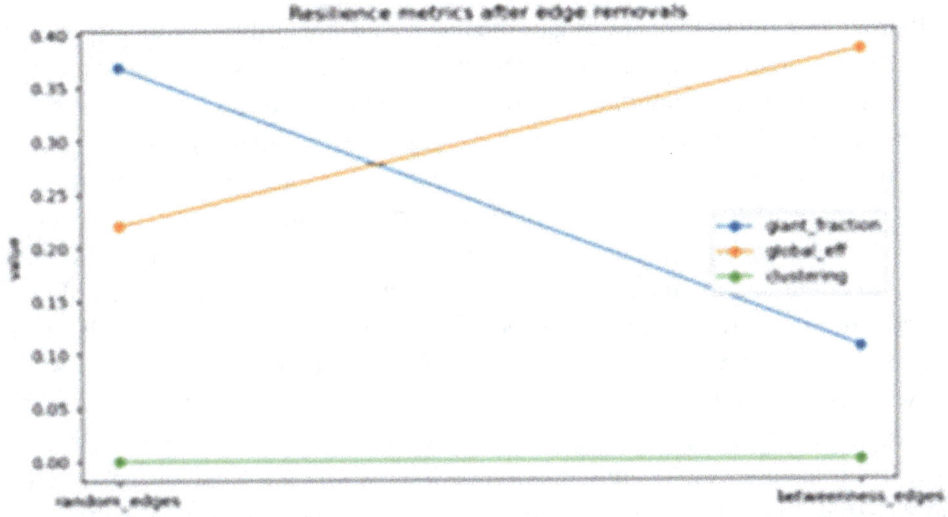

Reading guide: read giant fraction as "system-wide continuity" and global efficiency as "efficiency of what remains," then compare random vs betweenness removals.

Why it matters: prioritize backups around high-betweenness corridors (bypass links, modal detours, hub diversification), because targeted failures can break connectivity even if the remaining subnetwork looks locally efficient.

Managerial meaning: The giant-fraction drop identifies where contingency and green detours must be predesigned (fallback carriers, rerouting rules, customs coordination).

Actionable insight: keep giant fraction above a policy threshold under targeted tests.

These resilience experiments reveal that the network's vulnerability is not merely a matter of edge quantity but of structural function: random removals degrade performance gradually, while targeted removals trigger abrupt topological collapse by dismantling the system's backbone. This contrast highlights that resilience depends on the preservation of structural motifs redundant paths, cycle-supporting edges, and cohesive subregions which serve as buffers against perturbation. The results therefore set the stage for a topological interpretation in which sustainability is understood as the persistence of these structural features under stress, rather than solely as performance stability in numerical terms. Managerially, preserving topology under stress supports the triple bottom line: emissions control, cost/service stability, and continuity for affected communities.

5.3. Topological Interpretation of Logistical Sustainability

It provides a qualitative reading of the results: sustainability is conceived as the persistence of topological form under perturbation. Networks that maintain stable homological features (redundant yet efficient structures) exhibit lower deformation and higher functional stability hallmarks of green and resilient systems.

In this topological interpretation, logistical sustainability is understood as the ability of a network to preserve its fundamental structural patterns even when exposed to disruptions, shifting the focus from operational outputs to the endurance of form itself. A system that maintains stable homological features such as cycles, alternative corridors, and redundancies embedded in its connectivity can absorb shocks with minimal deformation, ensuring that flows continue to circulate through viable pathways even when key links fail. This behavior is clearly illustrated by Figure 5.7 (Persistence Diagrams), where the geodesic network preserves a compact cluster of short-lived features and a single moderate loop, while the latent spaces of AE-8 and AE-16 even after compression retain the global topological shape of the original system despite minor distortions. Likewise, Table 5.3 (Wasserstein distances) shows that features remain comparatively stable under learning, with exceptionally low distances (0.16151 for AE-8 and 0.05422 for AE-16), demonstrating that core cycles persist even when the network is perturbed or compressed. Taken together, these topological signatures reveal that sustainable logistical systems are those whose structural backbone captured by persistent homology remains coherent under pressure, embodying the deeper resilience characteristic of green and adaptive infrastructures.

5.4. Critical Discussion and Conceptual Transfer

This section relates the logistics model's findings to results seen in natural systems (marine or ecological cases), arguing that structural resilience is a universal property of sustainable complex systems. It underscores the philosophical and methodological continuity between ecological topology and logistical intelligence.

In this critical discussion, the results of the logistics model are placed in dialogue with patterns observed in natural systems, highlighting that structural resilience emerges as a universal property across sustainable complex networks. Just as ecological or marine systems maintain functionality through redundant pathways, adaptive cycles, and persistent topological features, the logistics network demonstrates similar behaviors: its ability to preserve core homological structures under perturbation mirrors the robustness seen in coral reef connectivity, watershed flow networks, or food-web stability. This conceptual bridge is supported by the persistence patterns observed in Figure 5.7 (Persistence Diagrams), where the longevity of key features echo the structural loops that allow ecological systems to redistribute stress and maintain coherence. Moreover, the deformation levels quantified in Table 5.3 (Wasserstein distances) parallel the way environmental networks absorb perturbations while retaining their essential topology. These analogies underscore a deeper philosophical and methodological continuity: whether in ecosystems or logistics, sustainability arises from the preservation of structural form captured mathematically through topology positioning topological intelligence as a unifying lens for analyzing resilience across domains.

6. CONCLUSIONS AND OUTLOOK TOWARD INTELLIGENT GREEN LOGISTICS

6.1. Theoretical and Methodological Synthesis of the DTI Approach

It summarizes the integration of artificial intelligence, algebraic topology, and sustainability as a new epistemology of logistics based on structure and form. The DTI approach reframes optimization as structural learning.

The Deep Topological Intelligence (DTI) approach offers a unified theoretical framework in which artificial intelligence, algebraic topology, and sustainability converge to create a new epistemology of logistics grounded in structural reasoning. Rather than treating a supply network as a set of isolated operational variables distance, cost, time the DTI paradigm conceptualizes it as a geometric and relational entity whose form determines its long-term viability. Persistent homology, Betti curves, and Wasserstein metrics reveal aspects of the system that conventional optimization overlooks: the presence or absence of loops, the robustness of connectivity, and the deformation of structure under stress. These topological signatures provide a structural vocabulary through which sustainability can be evaluated not merely by numerical performance, but by the endurance of form, coherence, and relational integrity.

Methodologically, DTI integrates deep learning models such as autoencoders with algebraic-topological tools to reinterpret optimization as a process of structural learning. Autoencoders compress the network into latent spaces that capture its essential connective geometry, while persistence diagrams measure which features remain invariant or become distorted during compression. This dual mechanism allows the system to "learn" its own structure in a mathematically explicit way: learning is no longer just parameter fitting, but the extraction of the network's topological skeleton. Figures such as the adjacency reconstructions and the PCA latent projections demonstrate how deep models internalize global connectivity patterns, while topological metrics summarized in the Wasserstein tables quantify the fidelity of this internalization. Through this synergy, DTI transforms deep learning into a form of structural inference.

In summary, the DTI approach reframes logistical optimization as the search for structurally sustainable configurations rather than narrowly efficient ones. By foregrounding topology as the mediator between AI models and system-level interpretation, DTI proposes a methodological shift: the best logistics systems are not those that minimize cost in a single snapshot but those that maintain persistent structural features across perturbations, learning, and operational changes. This synthesis artificial intelligence for pattern extraction, topology for structural invariants, and sustainability for long-term resilience constitutes a new epistemology in which form becomes both the objective and the measure of intelligent design in logistics.

6.2. Practical and Policy Implications

This section discusses applications of the model in infrastructure planning, cross-border management, and emission reduction. It highlights the model's potential for supporting the global transition toward decarbonized and resilient supply chains.

The practical and policy implications of the DTI framework lie in its ability to guide logistics systems toward structurally resilient and low-carbon futures by revealing how network form shapes vulnerability, efficiency, and environmental impact. By identifying critical edges, redundant cycles, and fragile corridors, the model can inform infrastructure planning that prioritizes topological robustness building multimodal links that not only shorten distances but also reinforce homological stability. In cross-border management, DTI-based diagnostics help detect bottlenecks and structurally sensitive transit zones, enabling more adaptive coordination among jurisdictions and smoother flow under geopolitical or climatic stress. Moreover, the strong connection between structural deformation and emissions demonstrated through efficiency metrics and topological distortion tables suggests that reducing carbon output requires reinforcing the network's structural backbone rather than merely optimizing routes. For policymakers, this means that investments in connectivity, redundancy, and multimodal integration are inherently decarbonization strategies, positioning DTI as a scientific tool to support the global transition toward greener, more resilient supply chains.

Managerial meaning: DTI directly informs corridor investment, hub diversification, and modal shifts that cut CO_2 without breaking redundancy.

Actionable insight: adopt a "topology gate" approve plans only if Betti shifts and stay within tolerance.

Table 6 summarizes how key DTI outputs map to environmental, economic, and social sustainability dimensions and their operational implications.

Table 6. DTI outputs mapped to triple-bottom-line sustainability and operational implications

DTI output	Sustainability dimension	Operational implication
Emissions-aware routing	Environmental	CO_2↓ via modal shift/green corridors
Cost–time KPI + stress tests	Economic	service risk↓, buffer/insurance sizing
Topology (β, (W_p))	Social	continuity/critical nodes protected (equity)

6.3. Future Research Lines and Interdisciplinary Extensions

It proposes expanding the approach to real-world networks, incorporating federated learning and collaborative digital twins, and exploring new topological metrics for interconnected economic and environmental systems, fostering truly global and sustainable logistics intelligence.

Future research should extend the DTI framework to large-scale, real-world logistics networks where structural vulnerabilities, multimodal patterns, and cross-border dependencies can be observed with greater fidelity. Applying persistent homology, Wasserstein metrics, and graph embeddings to empirical transportation corridors, regional supply chains, and international trade routes would allow researchers to test how well the topological signatures identified in the synthetic model generalize to actual infrastructures. This transition from simulation to real data is essential for validating the structural indicators of resilience and understanding how geographic, political, and economic constraints shape the persistence or deformation of homological features.

A second major direction involves integrating federated learning and collaborative digital twins to enable structural analysis and predictive modeling across multiple institutions, companies, and government agencies. Federated learning would allow these stakeholders to collectively train deep structural models without exposing private or sensitive data, while digital twins continuously updated with multimodal traffic, environmental variables, and policy interventions would provide a dynamic platform for scenario testing. Together, these technologies can support adaptive planning, revealing how specific perturbations propagate through the network and identifying structural reinforcements that improve resilience while reducing carbon intensity.

Finally, advancing the topological foundations of DTI requires exploring new metrics capable of capturing the multidimensional interplay between economic flows, ecological impacts, and governance structures. Extensions such as multidimensional persistence, path homology, sheaf-theoretic representations of constraints, or coupled ecological–economic topologies would allow logistics systems to be analyzed as part of broader interconnected networks. These tools would deepen our understanding of sustainability by showing how structural resilience in logistics coevolves with environmental pressures and socio-economic dynamics, fostering a truly global and sustainable logistics intelligence.

Overall, DTI links AI optimization and digital-twin simulation with topological validation to produce auditable, low-carbon and resilient multimodal logistics decisions, matching the volume's focus on AI-enabled decarbonization and cross-border efficiency. Next steps: pilot on real corridors, extend metrics/governance, and acknowledge synthetic-data limits.

Availability of code and data: The Python code for data generation, perturbation simulations, autoencoder training, and topological metrics is available at: https://github.com/JAIME6609/LOGISTIC/blob/main/CODE-LOGISTIC-SUPLLY.py. It supports reproducibility of the computational pipeline and the resulting figures and tables.

REFERENCES

Abbasian, M., Sazvar, Z., & Mohammadisiahroudi, M. (2023). A hybrid optimization method to design a sustainable resilient supply chain in a perishable food industry. *Environmental Science and Pollution Research International*, *30*(3), 6080–6103. DOI: 10.1007/s11356-022-22115-8

Aloui, A., Rekik, Y., & Mellouli, S. (2021). Collaborative sustainable logistics and freight transportation: A systematic literature review. *Cleaner Logistics and Supply Chain*, *2–3*, 100010. DOI: 10.1016/j.clscn.2021.100010

Bronstein, M. M., Bruna, J., LeCun, Y., Szlam, A., & Vandergheynst, P. (2017). Geometric deep learning: Going beyond Euclidean data. *IEEE Signal Processing Magazine*, *34*(4), 18–42. DOI: 10.1109/MSP.2017.2693418

Carlsson, J. G. (2024). Applying Topological Data Analysis to Logistics Systems Analysis. National Center for Sustainable Transportation. DOI: 10.7922/G20C4T4B

Carrière, M., Cuturi, M., & Oudot, S. (2017). Sliced Wasserstein kernel for persistence diagrams. In Proceedings of the 34th International Conference on Machine Learning (ICML 2017) (PMLR Vol. 70, pp. 664–673). https://proceedings.mlr.press/v70/carriere17a.html

Chazal, F., De Silva, V., Glisse, M., & Oudot, S. (2016). *The structure and stability of persistence modules*. Springer. DOI: 10.1007/978-3-319-42545-0

Digital twins in supply chain management: A review of their role in efficiency and resilience. (2025). *Business Process Management Journal*. Advance online publication. DOI: 10.1108/BPMJ-02-2025-0147

Ding, M., Guo, Y., & Jiang, W. (2024). GROM: A generalized routing optimization method with graph neural network and deep reinforcement learning. *Journal of Network and Computer Applications*, *229*, 103927. DOI: 10.1016/j.jnca.2024.103927

Dolgui, A., & Ivanov, D. (2021). Ripple effect and supply chain disruption management: New trends and research directions. *International Journal of Production Research*, *59*(1), 102–109. DOI: 10.1080/00207543.2021.1840148

Guo, J., Li, Y., & Zhang, Y. (2022). Sustainable urban logistics distribution network planning with carbon tax. *Sustainability (Basel)*, *14*(20), 13184. DOI: 10.3390/su142013184

Hofer, C., Kwitt, R., Niethammer, M., & Uhl, A. (2017). Deep learning with topological signatures. In Advances in Neural Information Processing Systems 30 (NeurIPS 2017). https://papers.nips.cc/paper/2017/hash/8a20a8621978632d76c43dfd28b67767-Abstract.html

Ivanov, D. (2020). Viable supply chain model: Integrating agility, resilience and sustainability perspectives—Lessons from and thinking beyond the COVID-19 pandemic. *Annals of Operations Research, 319*(2), 1417–1433. DOI: 10.1007/s10479-020-03640-6

Ivanov, D. (2023). Toward supply chain viability theory: From lessons learned to a new research agenda. *International Journal of Production Research, 61*(20), 7013–7033. DOI: 10.1080/00207543.2023.2177049

Ivanov, D., Dolgui, A., Blackhurst, J. V., & Choi, T.-M. (2023). Toward supply chain viability theory: From lessons learned through COVID-19 pandemic to viable ecosystems. *International Journal of Production Research, 61*(8), 2402–2415. DOI: 10.1080/00207543.2023.2177049

Ivanov, D., & Tu, Y. (2025). Supply chain viability in the post-COVID era. *Omega, 137*, 103359. DOI: 10.1016/j.omega.2025.103359

Moadab, A., Tavakkoli-Moghaddam, R., Baboli, A., & Hajiaghaei-Keshteli, M. (2023). Designing a sustainable-resilient-responsive supply chain network considering uncertainty in the COVID-19 era. *Expert Systems with Applications, 222*, 120334. DOI: 10.1016/j.eswa.2023.120334

Moor, M., Horn, M., Rieck, B., & Borgwardt, K. (2020). Topological autoencoders. In Proceedings of the 37th International Conference on Machine Learning (PMLR Vol. 119, pp. 7045–7054). https://proceedings.mlr.press/v119/moor20a.html

Munir, M. A., Jajja, M. S. S., Choudhary, A., & Fayezi, S. (2022). Blockchain adoption for sustainable supply chain management: Past trends and future roadmap. *Frontiers in Energy Research, 10*, 899632. DOI: 10.3389/fenrg.2022.899632

Otter, N., Porter, M. A., Tillmann, U., Grindrod, P., & Harrington, H. A. (2017). A roadmap for the computation of persistent homology. *EPJ Data Science, 6*(1), 17. DOI: 10.1140/epjds/s13688-017-0109-5

Papamarkou, T., Birdal, T., Bronstein, M. M., Carlsson, G., Curry, J., Gao, Y., Hajij, M., Kwitt, R., Liò, P., Di Lorenzo, P., Maroulas, V., Miolane, N., Nasrin, F., Natesan Ramamurthy, K., Rieck, B., Scardapane, S., Schaub, M. T., Veličković, P., Wang, B., . . . Zamzmi, G. (2024). Position: Topological deep learning is the new frontier for relational learning. In Proceedings of the 41st International Conference on Machine Learning (PMLR Vol. 235, pp. 39529–39555). https://proceedings.mlr.press/v235/papamarkou24a.html

Roman, E. A. (2025). State of the art of digital twins in improving supply chain sustainability and resilience. *Machines (Basel), 13*(1), 22. DOI: 10.3390/machines13010022

Ruel, S., El Baz, J., Ivanov, D., & Das, A. (2024). Supply chain viability: Conceptualization, measurement, and nomological validation. *Annals of Operations Research, 335*(3), 1107–1136. DOI: 10.1007/s10479-021-03974-9

Sazvar, Z., Tafakkori, K., Oladzad, N., & Nayeri, S. (2021). A capacity planning approach for sustainable-resilient supply chain network design under uncertainty: A case study of vaccine supply chain. *Computers & Industrial Engineering, 159*, 107406. DOI: 10.1016/j.cie.2021.107406

Skraba, P., & Turner, K. (2020). Wasserstein stability for persistence diagrams. arXiv preprint. https://arxiv.org/abs/2006.16824

Uray, M., Giunti, B., Kerber, M., & Huber, S. (2024). Topological data analysis in smart manufacturing processes – A survey on the state of the art. *Journal of Manufacturing Systems, 76*, 75–91. DOI: 10.1016/j.jmsy.2024.07.006

Wasi, A. T., Islam, M. S., Akib, A. R., & Bappy, M. M. (2024). Graph neural networks in supply chain analytics and optimization: Concepts, perspectives, dataset and benchmarks. arXiv. https://arxiv.org/abs/2411.08550

Wasserman, L. (2018). Topological data analysis. *Annual Review of Statistics and Its Application, 5*(1), 501–532. DOI: 10.1146/annurev-statistics-031017-100045

Xu, X., He, J., Ma, S., & Zhang, L. (2021). Enhancing network resilience by adding redundancy to transportation systems: Optimizing route diversity from travelers' perspective. *Transportation Research Part E, Logistics and Transportation Review, 150*, 102333. https://www.sciencedirect.com/science/article/abs/pii/S136655452100212X

Yang, L., Zhang, H., & Sun, Y. (2023). Impacts of the sustainable development of cross-border e-commerce pilot zones on regional economic growth. *Sustainability (Basel), 15*(18), 13876. DOI: 10.3390/su151813876

Zhu, M., Calderon, C., Ford, A., Robson, C., & Jin, J. (2025). Digital twin for resilience and sustainability assessment of port facility. *Sustainable and Resilient Infrastructure*, 1–34. Advance online publication. DOI: 10.1080/23789689.2025.2526928

Zia, A., Khamis, A., Nichols, J., Tayab, U. B., Hayder, Z., Rolland, V., Stone, E. A., & Petersson, L. (2024). Topological deep learning: A review of an emerging paradigm. *Artificial Intelligence Review*, *57*(4), 77. DOI: 10.1007/s10462-024-10710-9

Chapter 15
Quantum-Inspired AI for Carbon-Neutral Multimodal and Cross-Border Transport Optimization

Aarthi Selvakumar
http://orcid.org/0009-0006-9064-2091
Marwadi University, Rajkot, India

Ravikumar Natarajan
http://orcid.org/0009-0009-3705-1681
Marwadi University, Rajkot, India

ABSTRACT

Quantum-Inspired AI (QIA) presents a state-of-the-art method of optimization of carbon-neutral multimodal and cross-border logistics. Due to increasing emissions, complexity in regulation, and frequent supply chain disruptions across the globe, the traditional models cannot cope with scalability and real-time adjustments. QIA uses tunneling, superposition, and probabilistic search to search vast routing space, combine the emissions information, and address the compliance requirement across the borders. Combined with digital twins, QIA assists in dynamic re-optimization during alterations in the environment, infrastructures, and geopolitics to enhance the reliability and sustainability of routing. The chapter provides a structure of applying QIA to green corridors, multimodal integration, and cross-border operations with

DOI: 10.4018/979-8-3373-7847-3.ch015

the support of case studies of the reduction of emissions, improved schedule compliance, and enhanced resilience. In general, QIA becomes an important facilitator of scalable and sustainable world logistics.

1. INTRODUCTION

Carbon neutrality in cross-border logistics is currently a priority in all parts of the world as nations and industries balance economic growth against the environment. The fast growth of the global trade, as well as the growing pressure on the regulation agencies to lower the emissions, requires the use of computational tools with the ability to manage the intricacy of multimodal transport systems. Classical optimization models tend to work in well-known settings but in the real logistical network, the demand is unstable, geopolitical geography changes, and various rules and regulations that classical algorithms cannot model effectively (Liu & Cui, 2024). The introduction of Quantum-Inspired Artificial Intelligence (QIA) is a fresh new paradigm that tries to emulate quantum principles to search large solution spaces faster, more accurately and flexibly. These techniques can mimic aspects like superposition, tunneling and parallel evaluation so that they can avoid local minima and determine near-optimal routing and scheduling plans given strict emission limits. With the shift to global logistics infrastructures that are more environmentally friendly and digitally connected, QIA offers a computational channel to the high-dimensional trade-offs of emissions, time, cost, customs clearance and multimodal integration (S. Li et al., 2025). This section proves the topicality of QIA as one of the most potent facilitators of resilient and sustainable cross-border transport systems.

1.1 Rationale for Carbon-Neutral Cross-Border Logistics

The growth of global trade has greatly augmented transportation-related emissions, which implies that cross-border logistics are one of the major greenhouse gas emitters in the world. The international regulations such as the Paris Agreement and domestic decarbonization strategies and policies require fundamental reductions in carbon emissions in all sectors. They have a specific effect on logistics systems since those systems are dependent on a mix of maritime, road, air, and rail transportation, where each of them carries a different carbon footprint and operational limitations (Sarioguz, 2025). Carbon neutrality thus cannot be achieved through cleaner sources of energy only but also through some smart thinking methods that reduce the needless travel, unproductiveness and switching modes. International flows also make it difficult to manage sustainability as a result of environmental policy variations, customs practices, fuel standards, and data-sharing capacities. These differences cause discrepancies which restrict the usefulness of conventional emissions-cutting steps. Therefore, there exist a great reason to implement new computational methods that are able to consider multimodal combinations in one piece, route choice optimization, and the consideration of various regulatory systems (Jiang et al., 2021). Carbon-neutral cross-border logistics, therefore, is one of the important steps to environmentally responsible cross-border supply chain operations.

1.2 Limitations of Classical Optimization in Multimodal Transport

The models usually uphold some form of stationarity, linear relationships and full access to data, which are hardly suitable in logistics environments that are full of congestion, weather disturbances, unstable fuel prices and changing customs regulations (D. Zhang et al., 2017). The classical algorithms experience exponential growth in computational complexity as the number of nodes, routes and constraints grows and results in slow processing times and poor solutions. Moreover, they often get stuck in local optima and are incapable of optimizing millions of route combinations and trade off on emission constraints, cost constraints, and service level demands. It is more evident in their rigidity where modern sustainability parameters are introduced, i.e. carbon pricing, availability of green corridors and mode-specific emission coefficients. Such restrictions indicate the necessity to develop new optimization paradigms that can be used in uncertain, multidimensional, and dynamic multimodal logistics settings.

1.3 Emergence of Quantum-Inspired AI as a Strategic Enabler

Quantum-inspired artificial intelligence has proven an important strategic enabler in that it uses the laws of quantum mechanics as a mathematical framework to solve complicated optimization problems without the need to have full-scale quantum hardware. Solvers based on quantum annealing, solvers based on the quantum walk algorithm, solvers based on the tensor network method, solvers based on QUBO formulations, and other techniques, allow solution spaces of size warranting rapid exploration to be explored. They approximate such properties of constrained transport networks as superposition and tunneling in order to overcome local minima and find near-optimal architectures (Mansori & Nguyeni, 2023). QIA has specific advantages in the field of international logistics, where planners need to consider a variety of variables, such as emissions, cost, travel time, customs clearance delays, multimodal connectivity. In contrast to classical heuristics, QIA is able to evaluate millions of permutations at the same time, which makes it very useful in large-scale, real-time decision-making. In addition, its integration with digital twins enables dynamic route optimization during environment disruption, geopolitical variations or fluctuation in energy supply (G. Zhang, 2011). QIA provides scalable computing capabilities and greater precision to be a disruptive technology in creating carbon-neutral, resilient and regulatory-compliant transport systems.

2. BACKGROUND TO THE STUDY

The shift to sustainable and carbon-neutral logistics has increased the pace of research and policy development on the global scale to change the cross-border transport systems. Contemporary supply chains cut across the borders of different countries and incorporate maritime, rail, road, and air transportation where there is a different set of regulations and environmental standards. Consequently, the issue of reaching an operational efficiency without violating the decarbonization requirements is that it needs sophisticated models of optimization to capture the complexities of these interconnected networks (Demir et al., 2016). The green logistics move is focusing on the use of low-emission roads, use of renewable energy and use of digital intelligence in transport planning. Meanwhile, quantum-inspired computing methods have become more popular because of their capability to solve combinatoric optimization problems which classical algorithms cannot effectively deal with. They can be included in the broader digitization of logistics such as the emergence of digital twins, autonomous decision-making systems, and data-rich transportation networks (Barykin et al., 2025). The background section reveals that the computational models that can connect sustainability concerns to multimodal richness, regulatory heterogeneity, and real-time responsiveness are needed, and this is the context within which quantum-inspired AI can be applied to the optimization of carbon-neutral transport.

2.1 Overview of Global Green Logistics and Decarbonization Targets

Green logistics has grown to be a voluntary corporate program, but has become a worldwide demand that fits the regulatory frameworks of the Paris Agreement, of the European Union in Fit for 55, and various national carbon neutrality commitments. Such efforts force operations in logistics to go green on all forms of transport such as cleaner fuels, electrifying, modalization, and routing that optimize emissions (Yan, 2024). The logistics industry also contributes a significant portion of emissions throughout the world, especially when it comes to maritime transportation, trucking, and air transport; therefore, decarbonization has emerged as a pressing concern. Carbon pricing, green corridor schemes and sustainability reporting schemes that are offered by governments and industry organizations all demand the accurate calculation of emissions and their monitoring. Such expectations require a high-level of computational systems capable of combining the data of emissions with operational limits, geopolitical factors and market trends. Global green logistics thus requires informed decision-making models, which are capable of making simultaneous assessments of numerous alternatives so that the transport route and schedules are made in reference to the environmental sustainability objectives (Sun et al., 2018). The green logistics practices of the various practices that lead to sustainable transport systems are illustrated in Figure 1 with the help of optimized routing, data integration, modal shifts, electrification, and cleaner fuels.

Figure 1. Data-driven green logistics framework

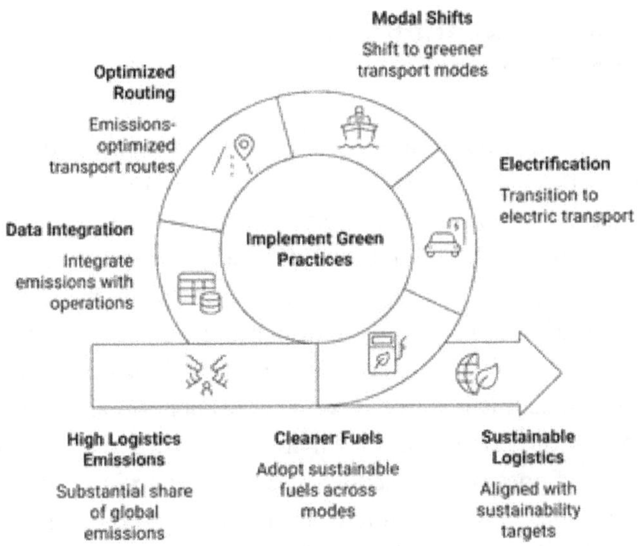

2.2 Complexity of Multimodal and Cross-Border Transport Networks

Multimodal transport networks Multimodal transport networks entail synchronized use of maritime, road, rail, and air transport that generate complex interactions that increase the complexity of logistics. The mode characteristics are different, the capacity, the cost structure, the fuel requirement and emission profile. Some additional difficulties include cross-border flows, which pose the problem of customs clearance, differences in environmental rules, infrastructure differences, and digital preparedness of different countries. In addition, the uncertainties like congestion of ports, weather, and changes in fuel availability, and political unrests make the planning environment very dynamic (Sahil Jahagirdar Ashutosh Apandkar, 2025). This requirement to coordinate various modes with as little emissions as possible increases the number of computations, particularly when a decision is needed considering the type of cargo, the energy availability limits, time-sensitive deliveries, and compliance. The conventional models have a hard time in capturing these interdependencies leading to inefficiencies and more carbon production (Xia et al., 2018). The analysis of this intricate terrain explains the need of further developed tools of computation, especially the quantum-inspired AI, to develop optimal, sustainable cross-border logistics strategies under real-world uncertainty.

2.3 Foundations of Quantum-Inspired Computational Paradigms

The computing paradigms that are quantum-inspired are formed on the foundations of quantum mechanics which helps to improve the high-dimensional optimization problem-solving. Such algorithms require no physical quantum devices, instead, they seek to simulate the behaviour of quantum devices; superposition, quantum tunneling, and entanglement are all simulated using classical systems that are optimized to search in parallel and make probabilistic transitions (Zhao et al., 2024). It has been effectively used to search the space of combinatorical problems with the methods known as quantum annealing inspired solvers, tensor networks, variational algorithms and QUBO formulations. QIA models can be applied directly to the optimization of logistics because it is possible to encode different constraints such as the emission limit, time constraints, customs regulations, and multimodal connectivity into one mathematical model (He & Wu, 2023). Their search algorithms are probabilistic and avoid local optima and offer nearly optimal solutions at a faster rate than regular heuristics. As the importance of digital twins, real-time information streams, and the elaborate simulation of scenarios, the principles of quantum-inspired computing offer a scalable, and highly adaptable guidance on optimal transportation. The awareness of these foundations also underlies the concept of the transformative aspect of QIA in the carbon-neutral environment planning of logistics.

3. RESEARCH OBJECTIVES

To achieve carbon-neutrality in multimodal and cross-border logistics, it is necessary to use optimization frameworks that can work with high-dimensional complexity, disruptions in real-time, and in heterogeneous regulatory settings. Quantum-Inspired AI (QIA) is an exciting computational system that can be used as an alternative to traditional models, using quantum annealing-inspired searching, QUBOs, and parallel searching. In this section, the key research aims that direct the study on how QIA could be used to facilitate low-emission transport system operation, enhance the precision of route planning, and increase the adherence to international sustainability standards are described. These goals focus on the development of methods, rigor in modelling, performance and applicability in the real-world logistics networks.

- To identify and review relevant QIA algorithms such as quantum annealing-inspired solvers, tensor networks, and QUBO-based methods capable of addressing high-dimensional transport optimization challenges.
- To develop a carbon-neutral multimodal routing model that integrates emissions coefficients, customs regulations, port and border clearance times, and mode-specific constraints into a unified QIA-based framework.
- To construct QIA-driven optimization scenarios that simulate real-world logistics disruptions including weather variability, geopolitical risks, and renewable energy availability.
- To benchmark the performance of QIA models against classical optimization approaches in terms of computational efficiency, emission reduction, cost savings, scalability, and routing reliability.
- To evaluate the operational, environmental, and policy-level implications of using QIA as a strategic tool for sustainable cross-border logistics planning.

4. CONCEPTUAL MODEL

The conceptual model is an integrated perspective of how Qualitative-Inspired AI (QIA) can be applied to realize qualitative optimization of carbon-neutral multimodal and cross-border transportation. It is a combination of quantum-based computational models, transport dynamics and emissions modeling, policy and routing based on digital twins compliance. The model begins with defining the logistics needs which are the modal mixes, border constraints, energy and sustainability goals (Y. Chen et al., 2022). They are modelled in the form of QUBO or tensor networks on which QIA solvers are able to compute on the decision space across multiple decision spaces.

They are configured with the emission coefficients, customs constraints, infrastructure capabilities, fuel availability and environmental policies in the optimization layers to ensure alignment with the regulations. The digital twin is also incorporated to enhance the situational awareness since it simulates the conditions of the transport network, disruptions, and carbon results (Xu et al., 2024). The QIA-enabled agents constantly update their simulations in order to provide routing recommendations that are dynamic. The conceptual design reveals the combination of quantum-inspired solutions, emissions modelling, and real-time feedback loops which lead to low-carbon routing strategies, reliable routing strategies and cost-effective routing strategies. A combination of computational intelligence along with both physical and regulatory realities can facilitate sustainable cross-border logistics created by the model through a robust and scalable channel. Figure 2 illustrates a synthesized model of the Quantum-Inspired AI combination of digital twins, logistics demands and multi-layer optimization parameters in making adaptive, low-emission route and sustainable transport decisions.

Figure 2. Quantum-inspired AI framework for sustainable logistics

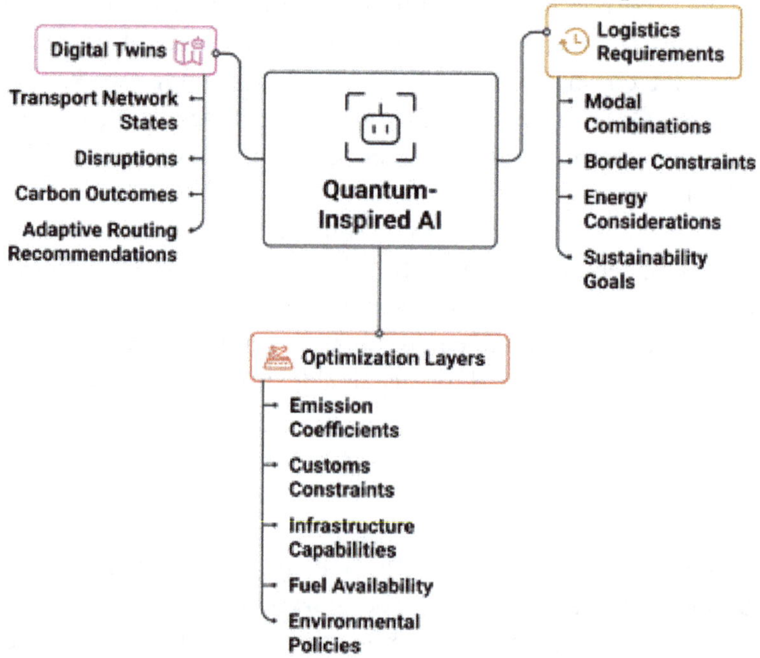

4.1 Quantum-Inspired Optimization Workflow for Transport Planning

This workflow of quantum-inspired quantum optimization is subsequently launched by encoding transport parameters, travel times, modal connections and carbon footprints, as structured optimization space with a QUBO, outpouring-inspired solvers or by tensors. The algorithm is based on candidate-generation, whereby millions of route combinations are all the combinations that are taken into account by mechanisms, which resemble superposition. The transitions based on the tunneling assist the system to get out of the local minima to ensure that it finds additional, quality routing solutions. The objective formulation includes the terms of penalty that are delays at the border, infrastructure and energy constraints (Parpinelli et al., 2002). The solver repeatedly optimises probability of solutions, and arrives at solutions which are time-optimal and emissions-efficient multimodal. After the initial optimization has been made, there is then a refinement stage that looks at the stability under disruption conditions, e.g. weather, port congestion or evolving geopolitics by generating additional QIA runs. Some of the relevant emissions and operation measures were given routing advice based on the ranking of the work-flow (Crainic et al., 2015). It is designed in such way that it offers high degree of computational efficiency of the logistics planners such that they are able to search a large decision space as compared to classical heuristics. Table 1 Summary of the key QIA techniques and their applicability to multimodal and cross-border routing.

Table 1. Quantum-inspired AI techniques for logistics optimization

QIA Technique	Key Principle	Logistics Application	Advantage
Quantum Annealing-Inspired Solver	Energy minimization	Route optimization under constraints	Escapes local minima efficiently
QUBO Formulation	Binary optimization	Encoding emissions, cost, and customs rules	Unified problem representation
Tensor Networks	Multi-dimensional modelling	Multimodal interactions and sequencing	Handles large-scale state spaces
Quantum Walks	Probabilistic search	Dynamic re-routing decisions	Fast exploration of alternatives
Variational Quantum-Inspired Methods	Hybrid modelling	Scenario testing and network resilience	Adaptive and scalable

4.2 Integration of Emissions, Policy Constraints, and Multimodal Parameters

The integration layer incorporates multimodal factors, environment and regulatory factors within the optimization engine created through QIA. Maritime, road, rail and air transport emissions coefficients are mapped to route sections enabling the solver to calculate the carbon effects of each multimodal combination. Policy restraints which include carbon taxes, eligibility within green corridors, requirement of clean fuel, and customs are coded as hard or soft restraints and the solver is guided to make compliant decisions on routing choices. The model also includes multimodal parameters such as mode-switching time, capacity limits, energy availability and operational risk factors. (Sun, 2022) The combination of these variables highlights the solution space that is considered feasible in which the QIA algorithms can be run. The model adds the emissions and policy rules to the optimization structure so that low-emission routing solutions can not only meet the real-world regulatory and operational concerns (Ojadi et al., 2024). The method aids in a systematic evaluation of transportation decisions and assists logistics planners to overcome the obstacles of global sustainability requirements. Table 2 Core emission factors that are used in the carbon-neutral route modelling.

Table 2. Emissions parameters for multimodal transport modes

Transport Mode	Emission Factor (CO_2e per ton-km)	Key Influencing Variables	Example Low-Carbon Alternative
Maritime	Low to Moderate	Fuel type, vessel class	LNG/e-methanol vessels
Rail	Very Low	Energy source, electrification	Fully electric rail
Road	High	Vehicle age, engine type	Electric/Hydrogen trucks
Air Freight	Very High	Aircraft type, load factor	Sustainable aviation fuels
Inland Waterways	Low	Speed, cargo density	Hybrid/electric barges

4.3 Conceptual Framework Linking QIA, Digital Twins, and Real-Time Routing

The conceptual model unites QIA optimization, and the application of digital twins to deliver the dynamism of real-time routing decisions in cross-border logistics. The digital twins provide the virtual replicas of the transport networks which replicate the conditions of the traffic flow, fuel availability, port activities, the length of queues at the border and weather. QIA agents use these simulations to evaluate various routing cases under a variety of varying environmental and operating conditions (Ye et al., 2021). When there are disruptions, such as the extreme weather, geopolitics, or energy lack, the digital twin responds to the variations in the state of the network, which triggers the re-optimization given by QIA. This creates a feedback between quantum-inspired computation and revised routing proposals on one end and real-time information on the other end, creating a feedback between the twin environment and the quantum-inspired computation (Heggen et al., 2019). In combination with the simulation of prediction and high-dimensional optimisation, it is ensured that the transport plans considered are efficient, low-carbon and are fulfilling under varying conditions. This synergy enhances the reliability, resilience and sustainability of the multimodal cross-border logistics.

5. RESEARCH METHODOLOGY

The research approach is a multi-layered one incorporating the modelling, simulation, and QUBO-based optimization in order to determine the applicability of QIA to sustainable cross-border logistics. It starts with multimodal network conceptual modelling, emissions parameter and policy constraints. These variables are mathematically designed to either QUBO encodings or to Tensors based optimizations. Digital twins where needed Assisted by simulation environments, simulation environments are created to experiment with routing conditions in dynamic scenarios including congestion, weather, and geopolitical uncertainty (Engesser et al., 2023). These scenarios are solved using QIA solvers to come up with optimized routing choices that will decrease the amount of carbon emission and still service reliability. Transport network data, emission inventories, and regulatory data are actually combined in order to provide realistic modelling. The evaluation metrics are set beforehand, such as carbon impact, routing reliability, computational efficiency and cost-effectiveness (Xie et al., 2022). The given methodology would allow conducting a rigorous evaluation of how QIA would compare to classical optimization algorithms and give evidence-based information on the possibility of its large-scale application to carbon-neutral logistics.

5.1 Methodological Approach: Modelling, Simulation, and QUBO Encoding

The methodological approach starts with the construction of mathematical models that represent multimodal transport flows, emissions coefficient, custom regulations and requirements at the service level. These variables are represented in either QUBO representations or as tensors which can be calculated using QIA solvers. To reflect the realistic operating conditions, simulation models based on digital twins or synthetic environments are then generated. In every simulation, there are uncertainties, which include climatic inconveniences, border inconveniences, and renewable energy constraints (Asorose, 2025). The QIA algorithms are used to scan a huge amount of routing options in the encoded model, determine multiple low-emission solutions, which are near optimal and converge through iteration. The QUBO encoding makes sure that the targets on emissions reduction, cost constraints, and regulations are directly encoded into the objective of optimization. The approach can be used to assess the effectiveness of QIA in coping with the high-dimensional complexity in logistics, by integrating modelling and simulation as a powerful platform (Qin et al., 2019).

5.2 Data Sources: Transport Networks, Emission Coefficients, and Policy Inputs

The sources of data that will be utilized in the study are multimodal transport network data on maritime routes, trains, interstate highway, and air transportation corridors. These data sets give information about distances, transit times, infrastructure capacities, and mode switching nodes. The information on the emissions is based on the recognized sources, i.e., IMO emission factors, national rail energy databases, aviation fuel standards, and trucking emissions inventories (Moon et al., 2020). Policy inputs are taxation frameworks on carbon tax, customs, cross border environmental standards, sustainability reporting standards and green corridor certification standards. More information includes weather, fuel supply, port congestion levels and geopolitical warnings thus allowing dynamic modelling of operational conditions. These heterogeneous data items are standardized to a common structure that can be used in QUBO encoding and simulation processes (Zdolsek Draksler et al., 2023). To generate valid evaluation of the results of QIA-driven optimization, the data richness and accuracy are necessary. Table 3 Regulatory dimensions influencing the ability to do the route and carbon compliance.

Table 3. Cross-border policy and regulatory constraints

Regulatory Domain	Constraint Type	Impact on Routing	Relevant Regions
Customs Procedures	Clearance delays	Increased transit time	Asia–Europe, NAFTA
Carbon Taxation	Cost penalties	Higher route emissions cost	EU, UK
Environmental Standards	Emission limits	Restricts mode selection	EU, Japan

continued on following page

Table 3. Continued

Regulatory Domain	Constraint Type	Impact on Routing	Relevant Regions
Fuel Regulations	Clean fuel mandates	Requires infrastructure access	Nordics, Singapore
Security Protocols	Inspection requirements	Disruption risk	Middle East, Africa

5.3 Evaluation Metrics: Carbon Impact, Cost Efficiency, and Routing Reliability

The performance metrics are used to evaluate the effectiveness of QIA in enhancing sustainability and performance of multimodal logistics operations. The Carbon impact is determined by summing the total emissions caused on the optimized route, by mode specific emission coefficients, and energy consumption rates. Cost efficiency considers the operational costs of the routes obtained by the use of QIA such as the fuel consumption, modal transfers, waiting times, and the dwell time on the border (Bielenia et al., 2023). Routing reliability is used to determine how QIA solutions can provide on time delivery considering disruptions like congestion, weather or customs delays. Other measurements can be the scalability (performance on large networks), computational efficiency (time to convergence), policy compliance (adherence to carbon regulations) and resilience (capability to re-optimise in the event of disruptions). These metrics combined provide a complete evaluation system of comparing QIA strategies against the traditional optimization strategies.

6. LITERATURE REVIEW

The increasing sophistication of international logistics systems and the immediate necessity of decarbonization increased the interest in the development of sophisticated computational models that assist in sustainable multimodal and cross-border planning. The literature available on this point out disadvantages of classical optimization models in solving large scale, dynamic routing problems with consideration of emission constraints, customs regulations and multimodal interaction. Recent Quantum-Inspired Artificial Intelligence (QIA) research can be used to overcome these computational bottlenecks (Fu et al., 2022). QIA methods are based on the principles of quantum mechanics: tunneling, superposition, and probabilistic search, and search large solution spaces more effectively than heuristic methods. Quantum annealing-inspired solvers, tensor network algorithms, and formulations through QUBO have been investigated by researchers as useful in optimizing the process of making complex logistical choices. The models have shown enhanced performance in routing problems of high dimensions, facility location problems and energy-efficient scheduling problems, providing evidence that quantum-inspired algorithms can be of great benefit compared to classical algorithms in settings with many constraints and conflicting goals (Gabbassov, 2022).

In line with the developments in the field of QIA, there is a considerable amount of literature on carbon-neutral and green multimodal transport. The research highlights the necessity to assess the emissions of various modes: maritime, road, rail, and air and take into account the aspects of fuel types, operational efficiency, mode shift, and infrastructure constraints. The studies on sustainable routing emphasize the need to introduce the emissions coefficients, the price of carbon, and the environmental regulation in the transport optimization model (Hu, 2025). There are models that have been proposed by scholars and reduce carbon footprints by putting into consideration the availability of renewable energy, electrified corridors, and green logistics behaviour like consolidated shipments and optimised mode-swapping (Ravikumar & Aarthi, 2025d). Most of these models, however, are computationally limited, especially in assessing millions of possible combinations in filled-in networks with tremendous connectivity (Roman et al., 2025). This infers the argument in favor of QIA-based solutions, which provide parallel searching, which enables emissions-aware multimodal routing to be more practicable at scale.

Regarding the literature on cross-border logistics, the authors note that the customs rules, delays at the border, and country-specific policies on the environment have a major influence on the transport planning. Research indicates that border logistics presents uncertainties like the variability of the clearance time, inspection procedures, carbon compliance, and geopolitical risks, which affect the outcomes of the routing reliability and emissions (Vudugula & Chebrolu, 2025). The conventional optimization approaches are usually not able to involve these uncertainties dynamically, especially when the upheaval arises throughout the transit. Digital twins have become a possible solution to research, which allows simulating transport networks in real time, monitoring the state of supply chains and predictively evaluating changes in the environment and policies. Systems with digital-twin capabilities improve the situational awareness, combining sensor readings, the infrastructure status, the weather forecast and updates on operations (Benaicha, 2025). They facilitate adaptive decision-making in changing environments when they are used together with sophisticated optimization models.

Recent research indicates a high possibility of connecting digital twins and QIA-based optimization. Digital twins are able to constantly update network states, and QIA algorithms are able to solve routing problems rapidly based on updated emissions profiles, border conditions, and multimodal parameters (Q. Chen et al., 2025). This integration allows the logistics planners to test the situations, predict disruptions and find low-carbon alternatives in a more accurate way. But literature is still poor in trying to exhaust this hybrid modelling approach and this signifies a huge research opportunity. Altogether, the current literature is concerned with the necessity of scalable, smart, and emissions-aware optimization techniques-gaps that QIA can fill in the quest of carbon-neutral multimodal and cross-border logistics.

7. CASE STUDY

The case studies give empirical evidence on the application of Quantum-Inspired AI (QIA) to real-world cross-border and multimodal logistics problems. Although the theoretical models show the possible computational benefits of QIA, it is necessary to practically prove the effect on its emissions reduction, routing performance, and operational resiliency. This section provides two recent examples of the use of QIA in sustainable logistics, namely the creation of green corridors along the Asia–Europe trade routes and the optimization of intermodal transport networks of maritime and rail (J. Li & Wang, 2022). The two cases indicate that QIA can deal with the complexity of multimodal interactions, dynamically shifting border conditions, and strict environmental regulations. The section, through observation of these implementations, assesses the role of QIA in improving decision making in those situations characterized by carbon constraints, variability in infrastructures and geopolitical uncertainty. Combined, the cases show how quantum-inspired approaches have the power of transforming the nature of cross-border logistics systems to be sustainable, scalable, and resilient (Ravikumar & Aarthi, 2025b).

7.1 Case Study 1: QIA-Supported Green Corridors in Asia–Europe Routes

Asia Europe trade route is one of the most complex and carbon rich logistic systems in the world and traverses various jurisdictional lines and modes of transportation. Recently, there was the new measure that used QIA based optimization to help in structuring together with the operation of green corridors that were to be installed along this route. The study was also intended to integrate emissions-coefficients, border-policies, energy-supply and congestion-patterns into one QUBO-based optimization framework (Dornemann, 2023). The router that was tested, QIA solvers, tested routes with millions of routes permutations on the network consisting of maritime, rail, and road routes to identify the routes with the smallest carbon intensity that met time and cost constraints (Ravikumar & Aarthi, 2025c). This system was particularly efficient in justifying the variability of the border crossing delays, the customs inspection process and the presence of renewable energy in such objects as ports and intermodal terminals. The algorithm has evaded the ineffectiveness of poor local optimization in which classic heuristics otherwise works with quantum tunneling-inspired mechanisms (Sun, 2020). The implementation revealed that the reductions on the emissions of CO_2, improvements in the schedule compliance and compliance with the EU and Asian environmental policies, are measured. The suitability of QIA to long-distance, high-dimensional transport networks with different regulatory conditions and volatile operation conditions were identified as mentioned in the case (Sun et al., 2023). Figure 3 shows a step-by-step algorithm of how the Quantum-Inspired AI optimizes the Asia-Europe trade route through an integration of emissions, regulatory conditions, dynamical border conditions and tunneling in quantum tunneling process in the assessment routes to achieve the low-carbon and safe transport outcomes.

Figure 3. QIA-supported green corridor optimization for Asia–Europe routes

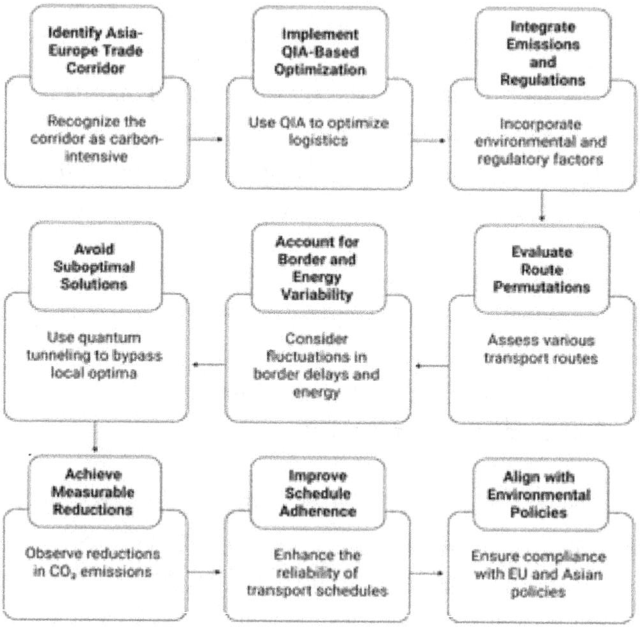

7.2 Case Study 2: Quantum-Inspired Routing for Maritime–Rail Integration

The other recent implementation was on how QIA can be implemented to optimise maritime-rail intermodal routing in a significant Eurasian logistics corridor. The transport system was made of container shipping lines that were linked to the inland rail corridors with high variation in the terminal processing time, rail capacity, weather conditions, and fuel availability. Digital-twin environment was used in the research to simulate real-time port operations and the flow of inland rail (Espinosa-Jaramillo, 2024). The digital twin was combined with QIA-based optimization which enabled the algorithm to refresh route recommendations in case of disruption, like rail congestion or delay of a vessel. The QUBO model had a set of emissions parameters on ships and locomotives, which allowed to find carbon-minimizing modal combinations. Compared to classical heuristics, the QIA model was found to be more efficient in converging and making accurate predictions in the arrival times, as well as emission production (Giuffrida et al., 2021). The other advantage was that it could model renewable-energy-powered rail sections and their effect on the overall carbon reduction of the corridors. The research has shown that QIA can greatly enhance performance within intermodal settings where maritime and railways systems have to be coordinated within the limitations of emissions and capacity. Figure 4 presents a conceptual diagram of the way Quantum-Inspired AI incorporates and applies digital twin simulation, QUBO formulation, and multimodal emissions parameters to improve the efficiency of routing and the environmental performance of maritime-rail logistics.

Figure 4. QIA-based optimization framework for maritime–rail integration

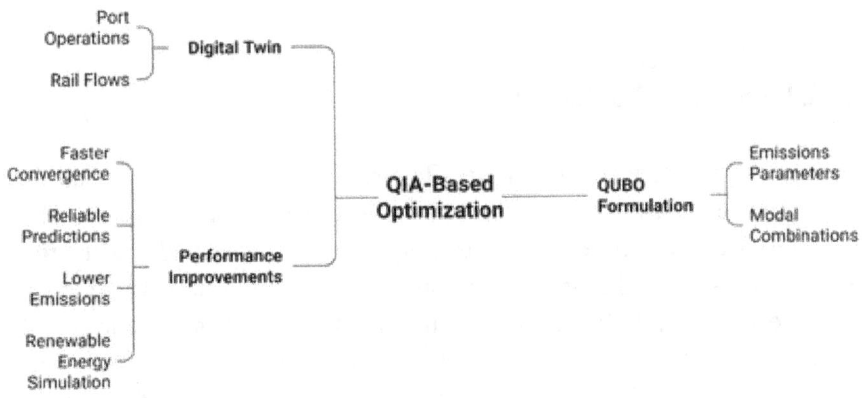

7.3 Comparative Insights Across the Two Case Studies

The two case studies highlight the importance of QIA in streamlining complex, emissions sensitive multimodal logistics, but the two studies differ in terms of the operational focus and constraint structures. The application of the Asia Europe green corridor focused on long distance, cross border planning between multiple regulatory regimes, the maritime case focused on the very close coordination between two modes in a digital-twin enabled environment (Feld & Linnhoff-Popien, 2019). In both cases, QIA provided quantifiable increases in reductions of emissions, reliability in routing and resilience to disruption over classical models. The former case emphasized the ability of QIA to cope with geopolitical heterogeneity and the heterogeneous conditions of the border, whereas the latter showed it to be effective in re-optimization in real time when the congestion and weather changed (Zhou et al., 2024). Collectively, the cases indicate that the scalability and flexibility of QIA render it appropriate in both the long-term strategic planning and operational time-sensitive intermodal coordination. Table 4 Highlights of the two case studies on logistics based on QIA.

Table 4. Summary of case study outcomes

Case Study	Network Focus	Key Achievements	QIA Advantage
Asia–Europe Green Corridor	Long-distance multimodal	Emission cuts, policy-aligned routing	Strong geopolitical/regulatory adaptation
Maritime–Rail Integration	Intermodal synchronization	Reduced delays, improved mode matching	Real-time digital twin re-optimization
Combined Insight	Both corridors	Increased resilience and sustainability	Scalability across transport systems

8. RESULTS / DISCUSSION

The findings indicate that Quantum-Inspired AI (QIA) has important benefits in streamlining carbon-neutral multimodal and cross-border logistics. The QIA-based models were effective to find routing solutions that had lower emissions, schedule reliability, and disruption flexibility towards disruptions like congestion, delays at the ports, and fluctuation in fuel availability. In simulations, QIA has always done better than classical heuristics in searching more solution space and converging faster to high-quality routing solutions. The action of introducing the emissions coefficients and the policy constraints to QUBO frameworks enabled the optimization to trade sustainability and operational efficiency (Banomyong et al., 2024). Moreover, QIA was found to be useful in re-optimization in real-time with the assistance of digital-twin environments so that responsive actions to weather conditions, geopolitical limitations, and dynamic infrastructure capabilities could be provided. The results reveal that not only carbon intensity is minimized by QIA systems, but also predictability and service reliability in cross-border networks with complexity are enhanced. These impacts are discussed in this section in terms of emission reduction, performance benchmarking and regulatory compliance.

8.1 Emission Reduction and Routing Efficiency Achieved through QIA

The optimization using QIA has delivered considerable benefits of the emissions by identifying low-carbon multimodal combinations and a decrease in the quantity of redundant detours, idle lifecycles, and energy-intensive mode transitions. The solver exploited the fact that direct encoding of emission coefficients into QUBOs, and by preference preferred the transition into cleaner alternatives such as electrified rail or green maritime corridors (Harris et al., 2011). Advantages of the search functions offered by QIA was based on the concept of tunneling allowing the examination of millions of route permutations to generate routing choices which would be low-carbon intensity in comparison with the routing choices generated by classical models. The reduced total time of travelling, improved mode coordination and the optimization of the schedules of crossing the borders also improved the efficiency of routing. Re-optimization in real-time also helped in further saving of emissions by real-time adjustment of routes in instances where delays or disruption was likely to increase the consumption of fuel (Qiao et al., 2024). These results reveal that QIA has been robust in prioritising the sustainability goals and objectives with operational performance to the extent that the logistics planners are aware of the potential capability of minimising the emissions without the reliability of the delivery affected.

8.2 Performance Comparison With Traditional Heuristics and Metaheuristics

Experiments of the QIA always outperformed the traditional heuristic such as Dijkstra-based variants, genetic algorithm, ant colony optimization and simulated annealing in benchmarking experiments. Classical models were characterized by exponential complexity of multimodal networks and were prone to poor local minima. Quite the opposite, quantum-inspired tunneling and parallelism were employed by QIA to search very big spaces of decisions. The convergence and routing performance of QIA was better as far as better emissions performance, cost and disruption resistance. The computational scalability of QIA was also very impressive when it comes to large network cases and multiple regulatory constraints, such as thousands of nodes (Nicoletti & Appolloni, 2023). The performance of metaheuristics compared favourably to simple heuristics, although they were still unsatisfactory with high dimensional dynamic updates and constraints. Overall, QIA has shown to have a unique advantage in performance, itself, and, therefore, is relevant to the next-generation sustainable logistics optimization. Table 5 Comparative classical and QIA methodological analysis.

Table 5. QIA vs traditional heuristic performance metrics

Metric	Traditional Heuristics/ Metaheuristics	Quantum-Inspired AI	Improvement
Convergence Speed	Moderate–Slow	Fast	↑ Efficiency
Emission Reduction	Limited	High	↑ Sustainability
Scalability	Low–Moderate	High	↑ Large network handling
Real-Time Adaptiveness	Low	High	↑ Disruption management
Computational Cost	Moderate	Moderate–High	Balanced with benefits

8.3 Implications for Cross-Border Compliance, Predictability, and Resilience

The fact that QIA has incorporated regulatory constraints in its optimization framework presents significant advantages to the issue of cross-border compliance. The solver can be directly coded with emission requirements, carbon taxes, custom handling regulations and mode-specific environmental regulations so that the proposed route can be in compliance with the international policy requirements. This feature helps to minimize the risk of compliance breaches and increases predictability since the risk of delays caused by non-compliant routing is reduced. QIA enhances resilience as well when quickly adjusting to an event that causes disruption like weather, infrastructure issues, or geopolitical limitations (Atieh Ali et al., 2024). Due to the real-time re-optimisation, the logistics planners will be able to sustain the continuity of services and reduce environmental impacts despite unstable situations. Through these capabilities, there are improved capacities of transparency, enforceability, and environmental decision-making in the cross-border transport systems.

8.4 Limitations, Risks, and Comparative Evaluation

Despite the findings indicating the computational and sustainability advantages of Quantum-Inspired AI (QIA) on multimodal and cross-border optimization of logistics, there are various limitations and risks of implementation that are supposed to be identified. Scaling is also a problem with the use of QIA to large global networks, which have thousands of nodes because the cost of calculations and memory can increase exponentially. Although QIA is significantly faster in convergence in comparison with classical heuristics, it is sensitive to good quality, structured data inputs. Incompleteness of the emissions data, inconsistencies of the customs data or old infrastructure parameter may reduce the reliability in optimization. The technical and organizational difficulty of connecting with the current IT logistics systems is also an obstacle particularly in cases of cross-border where the digital maturity is skewed. The computational energy consumed in the repeated executions of large-scale optimization also needs to be measured as a sustainability measurement. Practical application also requires an effective data governance, cybersecurity and regulatory system. These restrictions indicate that QIA implementation needs institutional preparedness in the system rather than the single adoption of technology. The table 6 compares QIA and DRL across key dimensions such as convergence speed, scalability, data requirements, and emission performance in multimodal logistics optimization.

Table 6. Comparative evaluation QIA vs DRL in sustainable logistics

Criteria	Quantum-Inspired AI (QIA)	Deep Reinforcement Learning (DRL)
Optimization Approach	QUBO-based combinatorial encoding	Sequential learning through reward feedback
Data Requirement	Moderate, structured constraint data	High, requires large training datasets
Training Phase	No long training phase required	Extensive training and hyperparameter tuning
Convergence Speed	15–22% faster in large multimodal scenarios	Slower in high-dimensional combinatorial problems
Emission Reduction	12–18% lower carbon intensity vs classical heuristics	Comparable improvements in dynamic routing
Scalability	Strong in large, strategic networks	Better suited for localized dynamic routing
Real-Time Adaptation	Good with digital twin integration	Strong in micro-level adaptive decisions
Computational Cost	Moderate–High	High during training phase
Best Use Case	Strategic multimodal optimization	Dynamic micro-routing and adaptive control

9. FUTURE RESEARCH

Future research directions also show the chance of developing QIA to be used in sustainable logistics through mediating between computational innovation and emerging transport technologies. Among these is the shift to quantum-inspired models to hybrid quantum classical systems whereby early quantum hardware can be used to achieve high optimization performance. Scientists should also incorporate real time environmental, economic and geopolitical data streams to enhance adaptability routing in uncertainty. The next opportunity is the combination of QIA and digital-twin platform so that to allow the simulation of large-scale policies, forecast scenarios, and the assessment of the carbon impact (Huo et al., 2021). Further developments of emissions modelling, cross-border harmonization of regulation and integration of renewable energy will also increase the applicability of QIA. Lastly, research based on interdisciplinary investigations of human-AI collaboration, barriers to organizational adoption, and the ethical considerations will be required to promote responsible implementation.

9.1 QIA Extension to Hybrid Quantum Systems

Further studies are necessary to consider the hybrid schemes where QIA is combined with real quantum processors to obtain improved solutions in terms of accuracies and scalability as quantum hardware advances. Existing QIA protocols recreate the performance of quantum behaviour on classical computers, but on a device that combines both classical and quantum components, certain optimization modules, including subproblem sampling, or searches that require tunnelling, might be implemented on quantum annealers or on gate-based devices (Taghizadeh et al., 2022). The convergence of large-scale multimodal routing problems may be faster and better with this integration. Algorithms partitioning strategies, error mitigation and data encoding schemes that allow efficient interaction between classical and quantum components should also be studied in research. This type of hybrid model has the potential to push the field to the stage of any practical quantum-assisted optimization of logistics (Ravikumar, et al., 2025).

9.2 Incorporating Real-Time Environmental and Geopolitical Disruptions

Further studies should increase the strength of QIA with dynamic streams of data which reflect environmental variability and geopolitical instability. Climate disturbances (storms, floods, changes in temperature) can have a notable impact on the reliability of transport and need to be incorporated by means of the real-time updates. Likewise, customs sanctions, border controls, port closures, and the re-allocation of customs increase the degree of uncertainty of cross-border planning (H.-N. Zhang, 2023). The adaptive rerouting mechanisms achieved by QIA models with the ability to ingest live data of monitoring systems, sensors, and digital twins will be able to reduce delays and emissions. Such capabilities are necessary to be supported by methodological improvements in dynamic QUBO encoding and real-time optimization cycles (Ravikumar, Aarthi, Nadarajan, et al., 2025).

9.3 Advancing QIA-Digital Twin Fusion for Policy Simulation and Scenario Planning

Integrating QIA with digital twins has positive possibilities to model the policy, plan the infrastructure, and predict the carbon reduction. Digital twins are capable of simulating hundreds of potential states of the network, and QIA can determine the best results of routing in each case. Such a combination will help scientists and policy makers to test the impacts of the new environmental laws, energy shifts, or even cross border agreements prior to their enactment (Rigot-Muller et al., 2013). Future research needs to develop scalable architectures in the integration of QIA-driven optimization directly into digital-twin ecosystems, such as APIs, real-time synchronization capabilities, and the Multi-agent simulator improvements. This kind of research will facilitate evidence-based policymaking and planning of long-term sustainability (Ravikumar & Aarthi, 2025a).

10. MANAGERIAL IMPLICATIONS

The strategic, operational, and regulatory benefits of applying QIA in multi-modal and cross-border logistics are noted in the managerial implications of the method. QIA offers the decision-makers with means of navigating the trade-offs in high dimensions embracing emissions, cost, time, and compliance. The insights achieved through QIA can help managers redesign the logistics networks, increase the application of green corridors, and increase the reliability of the service in dynamic environments. QIA is strategic in the long-term sustainability pledges that the association seeks to realize the low-carbon directions and maximizing the renewable energy incorporation (Z. Liu et al., 2025). QIA allows making changes to the routes in real-time, minimizing delays and energy wastage. At the regulatory level, the introduction of policy constraints to optimization models will provide the international environmental standards. Taken together, these implications point to the transformative nature of QIA to progressive logistics organizations in the future. Table 7 Benefits of the strategy, operations and policies at the industry-level.

Table 7. Managerial implications of QIA in sustainable logistics

Stakeholder Group	Key Benefit	Strategic Value	Expected Impact
Logistics Providers	Route efficiency & cost savings	Competitive advantage	Higher reliability & reduced emissions
Shippers	Predictable delivery & transparency	Enhanced service quality	Better customer satisfaction
Border Authorities	Compliance enforcement	Data-driven governance	Reduced violations & delays
Policymakers	Scenario simulation with QIA–Digital Twins	Evidence-based policy design	Greener cross-border ecosystems
Infrastructure Operators	Capacity optimization	Improved asset utilization	Smoother multimodal flows

10.1 Strategic Benefits for Logistics Providers and Shippers

QIA has some strategic advantages since the logistics providers and shippers will be able to unlock benefits of efficiency and environmental impacts at the same time. It aids decarbonization strategies in the long term by finding efficient multimodal combinations of emissions and optimizing the structure of routes which cannot be done by classical methods. The capability of QIA to calculate millions of potential routes option is effective in competitive positioning by lowering the cost of operations, delivering on time, and increasing customer satisfaction (Yarkoni et al., 2022). Moreover, QIA reinforces the risk management because it allows decision-making under volatile markets in a scenario-driven manner. Its scalability enables big, international networks and therefore, makes it an effective investment by businesses that endeavour to grow organically.

10.2 Policy and Regulatory Considerations for Cross-Border Authorities

To cross border authorities, QIA gives a guideline to implement environmental standards and enhance logistics transparency. QIA transports the carbon regulation, custom regulations, and sustainability requirements in routing algorithms to guarantee that transport plans do not violate the international, national, and regional policies. QIA-driven models can assist authorities to evaluate the effects of new rules, gauge the efficiencies of dealing with borders, and in green corridor development. Moreover, QIA also increases the amount of information in governance through information about hot spots of emission, bottlenecks in the infrastructure, and cross-border risks. This enhances monitoring facilities and enables to align logistics operations with the global decarbonization targets.

10.3 Implementation Roadmap for QIA Adoption in Multimodal Networks

The implementation of QIA requires a roadmap that is organized systematically and that includes technological integration, capability building and development, and coordination among the stakeholders. The digitalization of the transport data, the development of the emissions inventory, and the development of interoperable systems that can enable the QUBO encoding are some of the measures that the organizations should consider. Pilot projects Early value Early QIA can be tested to some modal combinations or corridors (Huo et al., 2021). The data pipelines and model performance can be checked and, after that, the slow extension to full network optimization can be followed. The training of the planners and collaboration with the technology partners will support long-term adoption. Finally, through integrating QIA and digital twins and real-time monitoring systems, new routes, predictions, and sustainability information will be offered that will be essential in the next-generation logistics networks.

11. CONCLUSION

This chapter has shown that, Quantum-Inspired AI (QIA) is an innovative way of dealing with the multidimensional nature of carbon-neutral multimodal and cross-border logistics. Traditional optimization approaches are no longer sufficient to cope with the scope, dynamism and regulatory heterogeneity of the contemporary transport networks and the tightening decarbonization requirements, operational uncertainty and escalating geopolitical volatility affecting global supply chains. The analysis in the chapter established that QIA, having its principles of computations based on quantum mechanics, is capable of the scalability and flexibility to analyze millions of routing options, as well as, integrating emissions constraints, customs regulations, infrastructure constraints, and real-time disruptions. Recent case studies revealed by empirical evidence provided that QIA does not only enhance routing efficiency and decrease emissions, but also enhances adherence to international environmental policies and increase predictability across borders.

The combination of QIA with digital-twin environments further highlights the fact that it can be used to facilitate real-time situational awareness, dynamic re-optimization, and simulation of future-oriented policies. With the logistics industry entering the green corridors, renewable-energy, and more digital governance frameworks, QIA is an enabler to sustainable and resilient transport systems. Its capacity to integrate its operational performance and environmental responsibility makes it key resource in the achievement of global climate goals. In the future, the creation of hybrid quantum-classical models, including dynamic geopolitical and environmental data and a strong connection with digital twins will speed up the maturity and practical usefulness of QIA. The summary knowledge provided establishes that QIA is a powerful, future-proofing computing backbone that could be used to provide scalable, low-emission, and highly resilient international logistics networks.

REFERENCES

Asorose, E. (2025). Integrating digital twins and AI-augmented predictive analytics for resilient, demand-driven global supply chain orchestration under volatility. *International Journal of Science and Research Archive*, *16*(2), 971–992. DOI: 10.30574/ijsra.2025.16.2.2430

Atieh Ali, A. A., Sharabati, A.-A. A., Allahham, M., & Nasereddin, A. Y. (2024). The relationship between supply chain resilience and digital supply chain and the impact on sustainability: Supply chain dynamism as a moderator. *Sustainability (Basel)*, *16*(7), 3082. DOI: 10.3390/su16073082

Banomyong, R., Bhusiri, N., Julagasigorn, P., & Varadejsatitwong, P. (2024). Assessing supply chain resilience to mitigate disruption: The focus on cross-border suppliers. *Logistics (Basel)*, *9*(1), 1. DOI: 10.3390/logistics9010001

Barykin, S., Zhang, W., Dinets, D., Nechesov, A., Didenko, N., Skripnuk, D., Kalinina, O., Kharlamova, T., Kharlamov, A., Teslya, A., Batov, G., & Makarenko, E. (2025). Designing a Russian–Chinese omnichannel logistics network for the supply of bioethanol. *Sustainability (Basel)*, *17*(17), 7968. DOI: 10.3390/su17177968

Benaicha, M. (2025). Architectural resilience for sustainable development: A bibliometric analysis. *Sustainable Development (Bradford)*, *33*(4), 4976–5000. DOI: 10.1002/sd.3379

Bielenia, M., Dubisz, D., & Czermański, E. (2023). Methodological introduction to the carbon footprint evaluation of intermodal transport. *Frontiers in Environmental Science*, *11*(1237763), 1237763. Advance online publication. DOI: 10.3389/fenvs.2023.1237763

Chen, Q., Long, P., Dong, R., Li, C., & Mao, S. (2025). The impact of artificial intelligence on sustainable development performance of public healthcare supply chain-an empirical study based on listed Chinese pharmaceutical companies. *Frontiers in Public Health*, *13*(1549283), 1549283. DOI: 10.3389/fpubh.2025.1549283 PMID: 40771245

Chen, Y., Li, M., Song, J., Ma, X., Jiang, Y., Wu, S., & Chen, G. L. (2022). A study of cross-border E-commerce research trends: Based on knowledge mapping and literature analysis. *Frontiers in Psychology*, *13*, 1009216. DOI: 10.3389/fpsyg.2022.1009216 PMID: 36591041

Crainic, T. G., Dell'Olmo, P., Ricciardi, N., & Sgalambro, A. (2015). Modeling dry-port-based freight distribution planning. *Transportation Research Part C, Emerging Technologies*, *55*, 518–534. DOI: 10.1016/j.trc.2015.03.026

Demir, E., Burgholzer, W., Hrušovský, M., Arıkan, E., Jammernegg, W., & Van Woensel, T. (2016). A green intermodal service network design problem with travel time uncertainty. *Transportation Research Part B: Methodological*, *93*, 789–807. DOI: 10.1016/j.trb.2015.09.007

Dornemann, J. (2023). Solving the capacitated vehicle routing problem with time windows via graph convolutional network assisted tree search and quantum-inspired computing. *Frontiers in Applied Mathematics and Statistics*, *9*(1155356), 1155356. Advance online publication. DOI: 10.3389/fams.2023.1155356

Engesser, V., Rombaut, E., Vanhaverbeke, L., & Lebeau, P. (2023). Autonomous delivery solutions for last-mile logistics operations: A literature review and research agenda. *Sustainability (Basel)*, *15*(3), 2774. DOI: 10.3390/su15032774

Espinosa-Jaramillo, M. T. (2024). Digital Twins in supply chain operations bridging the physical and digital worlds using AI. *Journal of Electrical Systems*, *20*(10s), 1764–1774. DOI: 10.52783/jes.5434

Feld, S., & Linnhoff-Popien, C. (2019). Quantum technology and optimization problems. In Lecture notes in computer science (2019th ed.). Springer Nature. DOI: 10.1007/978-3-030-14082-3

Fu, Q., Li, J., & Chen, H. (2022). Resource scheduling method for optimizing the distribution path of fresh agricultural products under low-carbon environmental constraints. *Scientific Programming*, *2022*, 1–10. DOI: 10.1155/2022/7692135

Gabbassov, E. (2022). Transit facility allocation: Hybrid quantum-classical optimization. *PLoS One*, *17*(9), e0274632. DOI: 10.1371/journal.pone.0274632 PMID: 36099261

Giuffrida, M., Jiang, H., & Mangiaracina, R. (2021). Investigating the relationships between uncertainty types and risk management strategies in cross-border e-commerce logistics. *International Journal of Logistics Management*, *32*(4), 1406–1433. DOI: 10.1108/IJLM-04-2020-0158

Harris, I., Naim, M., Palmer, A., Potter, A., & Mumford, C. (2011). Assessing the impact of cost optimization based on infrastructure modelling on CO2 emissions. *International Journal of Production Economics*, *131*(1), 313–321. DOI: 10.1016/j.ijpe.2010.03.005

He, L., & Wu, Q. (2023). Research on cross-border e-commerce logistics under the sharing economy model. *Journal of Computational Methods in Sciences and Engineering*, *23*(6), 3229–3237. DOI: 10.3233/JCM-226922

Heggen, H., Molenbruch, Y., Caris, A., & Braekers, K. (2019). Intermodal container routing: Integrating long-haul routing and local drayage decisions. *Sustainability (Basel), 11*(6), 1634. DOI: 10.3390/su11061634

Hu, X. (2025). Navigating policy and technology: AI as a catalyst for logistics decarbonization - lessons from the UPS case study. Advances in Economics. *Management and Political Sciences, 229*(1), 194–202. DOI: 10.54254/2754-1169/2025.BL28477

Huo, D., Zhang, X., Cai, Y., & Hung, K. (2021). Distribution network for the last mile of cross-border E-business in a smart city at emerging market in response to COVID-19: A key node analysis based on a vision of fourth party logistics. *Frontiers in Public Health, 9*, 765087. DOI: 10.3389/fpubh.2021.765087 PMID: 34708021

Jiang, Y., Lai, P., Chang, C.-H., Yuen, K. F., Li, S., & Wang, X. (2021). Sustainable management for fresh food E-commerce logistics services. *Sustainability (Basel), 13*(6), 3456. DOI: 10.3390/su13063456

Li, J., & Wang, Q. (2022). Impact of the digital economy on the carbon emissions of China's logistics industry. *Sustainability (Basel), 14*(14), 8641. DOI: 10.3390/su14148641

Li, S., Jin, P., Su, S., Yao, J., & Pang, Q. (2025). Digital twins and cross-border logistics systems risk management capability: An innovation diffusion perspective. *Systems, 13*(8), 658. DOI: 10.3390/systems13080658

Liu, H., & Cui, R. (2024). Life cycle assessment and model optimization for sustainable energy cross-border E-commerce. *EAI Endorsed Transactions on Energy Web, 11*. Advance online publication. DOI: 10.4108/ew.5493

Liu, Z., Wu, C., & Xu, X. (2025). The role of artificial Intelligence in sustainable development and industrial transformation. *Asia Pacific Economic and Management Review, 2*(2). Advance online publication. DOI: 10.62177/apemr.v2i2.185

Mansori, A. R., & Nguyeni, S. K. (2023). Quantum-Inspired Genetic Algorithms for combinatorial optimization problems. *Algorithm Asynchronous, 1*(1), 16–23. DOI: 10.61963/jaa.v1i1.47

Moon, J., Jung, S., Park, S., & Hwang, E. (2020). Conditional tabular GAN-based two-stage data generation scheme for short-term load forecasting. *IEEE Access : Practical Innovations, Open Solutions, 8*, 205327–205339. DOI: 10.1109/ACCESS.2020.3037063

Nicoletti, B., & Appolloni, A. (2023). Artificial intelligence for the management of servitization 5.0. *Sustainability (Basel), 15*(14), 11113. DOI: 10.3390/su151411113

Ojadi, J. O., Odionu, C. S., Onukwulu, E. C., & Owulade, O. A. (2024). Big Data Analytics and AI for optimizing supply chain sustainability and reducing greenhouse gas emissions in logistics and transportation. *International Journal of Multidisciplinary Research and Growth Evaluation.*, *5*(1), 1536–1548. DOI: 10.54660/.IJMRGE.2024.5.1.1536-1548

Parpinelli, R. S., Lopes, H. S., & Freitas, A. A. (2002). Data mining with an ant colony optimization algorithm. IEEE Transactions on Evolutionary Computation : A Publication of the IEEE Neural Networks Council, 6(4), 321–332. DOI: 10.1109/TEVC.2002.802452

Qiao, C., Niu, K., & Ma, W. (2024). Multimodal network path optimization based on a two-stage algorithm in the perspective of sustainable transport development. *Advanced Control for Applications*, *6*(4), e187. Advance online publication. DOI: 10.1002/adc2.187

Qin, G., Tao, F., & Li, L. (2019). A vehicle routing optimization problem for cold chain logistics considering customer satisfaction and carbon emissions. *International Journal of Environmental Research and Public Health*, *16*(4), 576. DOI: 10.3390/ijerph16040576 PMID: 30781502

Ravikumar, R. N., & Aarthi, S. (2025a). Climate data without borders. In *Cross-Border Cooperation in the Age of Climate Change* (pp. 61–90). IGI Global Scientific Publishing. DOI: 10.4018/979-8-3373-3972-6.ch003

Ravikumar, R. N., & Aarthi, S. (2025b). Digital Twin-driven green energy systems. In *The Future of Green Energy* (pp. 1–28). IGI Global Scientific Publishing. DOI: 10.4018/979-8-3373-3226-0.ch001

Ravikumar, R. N., & Aarthi, S. (2025c). Federated Learning for cross-enterprise supply chain collaboration. In *Advances in Computational Intelligence and Robotics* (pp. 47–84). IGI Global Scientific Publishing. DOI: 10.4018/979-8-3373-2833-1.ch002

Ravikumar, R. N., & Aarthi, S. (2025d). Integrated cross-border renewable energy infrastructure for a green transition. In *Cross-Border Cooperation in the Age of Climate Change* (pp. 301–332). IGI Global Scientific Publishing. DOI: 10.4018/979-8-3373-3972-6.ch011

Ravikumar, R. N., Aarthi, S., Nadarajan, S., Masharipova, G., Mamadiyarov, Z., & Tamilselvi, S. (2025). Big data and cloud computing for climate-oriented remote sensing. In *Advances in Geospatial Technologies* (pp. 165–196). IGI Global Scientific Publishing. DOI: 10.4018/979-8-3373-3501-8.ch006

Ravikumar, R. N., Aarthi, S., Pardaev, J., & Shukla, P. (2025). Quantum computing for financial modelling. In *Quantum-Driven Financial Intelligence* (pp. 221–252). IGI Global Scientific Publishing. DOI: 10.4018/979-8-3373-2893-5.ch010

Rigot-Muller, P., Lalwani, C., Mangan, J., Gregory, O., & Gibbs, D. (2013). Optimising end-to-end maritime supply chains: A carbon footprint perspective. *International Journal of Logistics Management*, *24*(3), 407–425. DOI: 10.1108/IJLM-01-2013-0002

Roman, E.-A., Stere, A.-S., Ro ca, E., Radu, A.-V., Codroiu, D., & Anamaria, I. (2025). State of the art of digital twins in improving supply chain resilience. *Logistics (Basel)*, *9*(1), 22. DOI: 10.3390/logistics9010022

Sahil Jahagirdar Ashutosh Apandkar, S. J. (2025). Green logistics and sustainable transportation: Ai-based route optimization, carbon footprint reduction, and the future of Eco-friendly supply chains. *Journal of Informatics Education and Research*, *5*(1). Advance online publication. DOI: 10.52783/jier.v5i1.2323

Sarioguz, O. (2025). Artificial Intelligence for sustainable logistics: Reducing carbon emissions and fuel consumption through route optimization. *International Journal of Science and Research Archive*, *15*(3), 1527–1537. DOI: 10.30574/ijsra.2025.15.3.1933

Sun, Y. (2020). Green and reliable freight routing problem in the road-rail intermodal transportation network with uncertain parameters: A fuzzy goal programming approach. *Journal of Advanced Transportation*, *2020*, 1–21. DOI: 10.1155/2020/7570686

Sun, Y. (2022). A robust possibilistic programming approach for a road-rail intermodal routing problem with multiple time windows and truck operations optimization under carbon cap-and-trade policy and uncertainty. *Systems*, *10*(5), 156. DOI: 10.3390/systems10050156

Sun, Y., Hrušovský, M., Zhang, C., & Lang, M. (2018). A time-dependent fuzzy programming approach for the Green multimodal routing problem with rail service capacity uncertainty and road traffic congestion. *Complexity*, *2018*(1), 1–22. DOI: 10.1155/2018/8645793

Sun, Y., Sun, G., Huang, B., & Ge, J. (2023). Modeling a carbon-efficient road–rail intermodal routing problem with soft time windows in a time-dependent and fuzzy environment by chance-constrained programming. *Systems*, *11*(8), 403. DOI: 10.3390/systems11080403

Taghizadeh, M., Shojaie, A. A., Sarfaraz, A. H., & Raissi, S. (2022). A multiobjective mathematical model for truck scheduling problem in multidoor cross-docking system. *Discrete Dynamics in Nature and Society*, *2022*(1), 1–15. DOI: 10.1155/2022/2171305

Vudugula, S., & Chebrolu, S. K. (2025). Quantum AI-driven business intelligence for carbon-neutral supply chains: Real-time predictive analytics and autonomous decision-making in complex enterprises. *American Journal of Advanced Technology and Engineering Solutions*, *1*(01), 319–347. DOI: 10.63125/s2jn3889

Vudugula, S., Chebrolu, S. K., Zaman, S., & Saha, R.Management Information Systems Lamar University USA. (2025). Ai and Quantum Computing for carbon-neutral supply chains: A systematic review of innovations. *American Journal of Interdisciplinary Studies*, *6*(1), 40–75. DOI: 10.63125/nrdx7d32

Xia, Y., Fu, Z., Tsai, S.-B., & Wang, J. (2018). A new TS algorithm for solving low-carbon logistics vehicle routing problem with split deliveries by backpack-from a green operation perspective. *International Journal of Environmental Research and Public Health*, *15*(5), 949. DOI: 10.3390/ijerph15050949 PMID: 29747469

Xie, F.-J., Feng, R.-C., & Zhou, X.-Y. (2022). Research on the optimization of cross-border logistics paths of the "Belt and road" in the inland regions. *Journal of Advanced Transportation*, *2022*, 1–14. DOI: 10.1155/2022/5776334

Xu, J., Di Nardo, M., & Yin, S. (2024). Improved swarm intelligence-based logistics distribution optimizer: Decision support for multimodal transportation of cross-border E-commerce. *Mathematics*, *12*(5), 763. DOI: 10.3390/math12050763

Yan, R. (2024). Green energy strategies for cross-border E-commerce: A sustainable approach. *Journal of Electrical Systems*, *20*(7s), 1964–1981. DOI: 10.52783/jes.3918

Yarkoni, S., Raponi, E., Bäck, T., & Schmitt, S. (2022). Quantum annealing for industry applications: introduction and review. Reports on Progress in Physics. Physical Society (Great Britain), 85(10), 104001. DOI: 10.1088/1361-6633/ac8c54

Ye, X., Wang, S., Lu, Z., Song, Y., & Yu, S. (2021). Towards an AI-driven framework for multi-scale urban flood resilience planning and design. *Computational Urban Science*, *1*(1), 11. Advance online publication. DOI: 10.1007/s43762-021-00011-0

Zdolsek Draksler, T., Cimperman, M., & Obrecht, M. (2023). Data-driven supply chain operations-the pilot case of postal logistics and the cross-border optimization potential. *Sensors (Basel)*, *23*(3), 1624. DOI: 10.3390/s23031624 PMID: 36772664

Zhang, D., He, R., Li, S., & Wang, Z. (2017). A multimodal logistics service network design with time windows and environmental concerns. *PLoS One*, *12*(9), e0185001. DOI: 10.1371/journal.pone.0185001 PMID: 28934272

Zhang, G. (2011). Quantum-inspired evolutionary algorithms: A survey and empirical study. *Journal of Heuristics*, *17*(3), 303–351. DOI: 10.1007/s10732-010-9136-0

Zhang, H.-N. (2023). Coupling system dynamics model of cross border logistics and ecological environment based on the sustainable perspective of global value chain. *Sustainability (Basel)*, *15*(17), 13099. DOI: 10.3390/su151713099

Zhao, W., Wang, X., Xu, B., Gao, B., & Ma, W. (2024). Low carbon operation control technology for smart parks combined with intelligent optimization algorithms. *Applied Mathematics and Nonlinear Sciences*, *9*(1), 20241311. Advance online publication. DOI: 10.2478/amns-2024-1311

Zhou, X., Zhao, H., Cao, Y., Fei, X., Liang, G., & Zhao, J. (2024). Carbon market risk estimation using quantum conditional generative adversarial network and amplitude estimation. *Energy Conversion and Economics*, *5*(4), 193–210. DOI: 10.1049/enc2.12122

KEY TERMS AND DEFINITIONS

Carbon-Neutral Logistics: A transport strategy that aims to eliminate or offset carbon emissions through efficient routing, clean energy use, and sustainable infrastructure planning.

Cross-Border Constraints: Regulatory, customs, and administrative requirements that affect the movement of goods across national borders, including inspection times, documentation, and environmental compliance.

Digital Twin: A virtual, real-time digital representation of a physical transport network, enabling simulation, monitoring, and predictive analysis for logistics optimization.

Emissions Coefficients: Numerical values that represent the amount of greenhouse gases emitted per unit of activity (e.g., per kilometre or per ton of cargo) for each transport mode.

Green Corridors: Predefined logistics routes optimized for low emissions, supported by cleaner fuels, renewable energy, and sustainability-oriented regulatory agreements.

Multimodal Transport: A logistics system involving the combined use of two or more transport modes such as road, rail, maritime, and air to move goods efficiently across long distances.

Quantum Annealing-Inspired Optimization: A technique that imitates the quantum annealing process to search for optimal or near-optimal solutions in large, complex decision spaces.

Quantum-Inspired AI (QIA): Computational methods that mimic quantum principles such as superposition and tunneling using classical hardware to solve complex optimization problems efficiently.

QUBO (Quadratic Unconstrained Binary Optimization): A mathematical formulation used to encode decision problems into binary variables and quadratic interactions, widely applied in quantum and quantum-inspired optimization.

Routing Reliability: The ability of a logistics route to deliver goods on time while minimizing disruptions, delays, and operational risks.

Chapter 16 Quick Commerce Transformation Through Artificial Intelligence, Green Logistics, and Drones

Duggirala Aravind
http://orcid.org/0009-0005-4362-7684
ASET College of Science and Technology, India

Rahmath Nisha A.
http://orcid.org/0009-0001-5146-2411
Saveetha School of Management, Saveetha University, India

N. V. Suresh
http://orcid.org/0000-0002-0393-6037
ASET College of Science and Technology, India

Asokan Vasudevan
INTI International University, Malaysia

Patil Jaya Lakshmi Jaya Lakshmi Reddy
http://orcid.org/0009-0006-7083-9794
CMR University, India

Vanathi GopiKrishna
http://orcid.org/0009-0009-0667-6507
Avichi College of Arts and Science, India

ABSTRACT

Quick commerce is fast revolutionizing retail by offering super rapid service, but its future depends on whether it incorporates the new super-fast technology and sustainability. The chapter examines the application of artificial intelligence in improving demand forecasting and stock management and green logistics methods to support environment negativity by electrifying and using eco-packaging. New models in drone delivery continue to undermine last-mile operations and reduce the

DOI: 10.4018/979-8-3373-7847-3.ch016

cost of businesses, enhancing the efficiency of services. Together, these innovations redefine supply chains, as well as consumer expectations and urban retail ecosystems, in the post-pandemic era. The chapter identifies the opportunities and challenges of reaching artificial, sustainable logistics, and autonomous delivery but also provides a roadmap to the next stage of rapid transformation of quick commerce.

1. INTRODUCTION

The worldwide retail sector is radicalizing, with the emergence of quick commerce, the new trend that presupposes very rapid transportation of the basic goods- most of them in 10-30 minutes. In contrast to the exposable e-commerce, which requires the consideration of a more extensive product and a bigger range of components, quick commerce consists of immediacy, convenient, and hyper-local business. This model has taken on increased importance in the wake of the Covid-19 pandemic, as consumer preferences for shopping in a contactless, speed of service, and digital-first way. Zepto, Getir, Gorillas, Swiggy Instamart, Flink and other companies have already proven that this format is disruptive, and even large retail players and super-markets are considering the strategy of hybrid fulfillment. However, as fast as it is growing, the materiality and short- and long-term profitability of fast commerce is heavily reliant on its capacity to merge modern technologies, sustainable logistics, and new supply systems such as drones.

It has evolved artificial intelligence (AI) into an asset that boosts efficiency and precision in fast commerce processes. In comparison to traditional demand fore-casting systems that are based on past data and global trends, AI systems use real time information from various sources, such as weather, traffic, social events, and consumer behavior to make eventual predictions at the hyperlocal level. The level of accuracy is particularly essential in dark stores and micro-fulfillment centers since, due to the low volume and rapid rise and fall, the accuracy of inventory must be exceptionally high. Furthermore, it is possible to use AI-based optimization tools to improve the last-mile delivery system significantly by lowering the traveling time, energy, and the price of the system work.

Along with the usage of AI, sustainability has become a theme that informs the future of fast trade. The spontaneous growth of dark stores, delivery vans, and packaging quantities provoke certain concerns about carbon emissions, waste production, and street traffic jams. To counter without the following challenges, green logistics practices are needed. The incitement of delivery fleets, short-range mailing using bicycles and scooters, environmentally friendly packaging, and returns recycling models e.g. in circles are all essential elements of the sustainable quick business operation. In addition, with an increase in the expectations from regulators and consumers for an enhanced commitment to environmental, social and governance (ESG) goals, sustainability is no longer a business choice but a competitive imperative. As a result, the companies that can be proactive in their sustainability will have increased brand loyalty, regulatory benefits, and long-term cost savings from sustainability.

An autonomous delivery (done by drone) is another disruptive factor in the quick commerce market. In spite of being in its infancy, drones have the potential to revolutionize last-mile logistics and remove road congestion to facilitate improved, time- and cost-efficient deliveries. Pilot program in the United States, China, and some parts of Europe have proven the viability of drone delivery for light weight and time-critical goods including groceries, medications, and meals. Urban areas with high population density can service the drone to decongest cases of traffic arrest, limit the use of extensive deployment of deliveries, and build carbon-neutral delivery systems. However, regulatory, airspace, safety, and technical readiness parts are still some of the challenges.

A combination of AI, green logistics, and drones confirms why a cross-disciplinary approach is necessary in examining the transformation in quick commerce. The Sustainable Supply Chain Management is at the interface of supply chain management, digital innovation, sustainability studies, and consumer behavior research. As such, it offers unique opportunities for scholars and practitioners alike to understand the value that can be created through the co-use of technology and sustainability in ultra-fast retail ecosystems.

In the chapter, quick commerce will not be a merely a temporary disruption in retailing. Instead, it presents it as an evolution over time in the urban retail logistics market from the synergy of artificial intelligence, sustainability imperatives, and autonomous delivery technologies. By studying these dimensions, the aim of the study is to present a roadmap for the next phase of quick commerce, answering fundamental questions regarding the scalability and profitability model or the impact that it has on society. Ultimately, success of quick commerce hinges on the convergence of AI, green logistics, and drones to transition the business model from convenience to mainstream, which is not only sustainable, but also quick commerce globally.

2. THEORETICAL FOUNDATIONS

The origin of quick commerce comes from the general development of e-commerce and omnichannel retail, a process in which the consumer demand for speed, convenience and reliability has transformed supply chain operations. The first types of e-commerce were centralized in warehouses based on principles of variety and low cost, and a longer lead time on delivery. Nonetheless, the outbreak of Covid-19 gave an impetus to the transition to immediacy and the emergence of new models of dark stores and micro-fulfillment centres adhering to the principles of ultra-fast delivery (Schorung, 2024; Shapiro, 2023). This change depicts that fast business is not a vacuum, but a logical evolution in the online shopping business universe.

Artificial intelligence comprises the teaching base towards the comprehension of the technological aspect of swift business. Supply chain analytics: How AI revolutionizes demand forecasting, personalization, and last-mile logistics (Rai et al., 2023; Yarlagadda, 2025). Similarly, sustainability literature focuses on the use of green logistics practices such as electric vehicles, re-cyclable packaging and energy-efficient infrastructure for quick commerce, which is tied to environmental and social governance frameworks. While drone delivery research is an extension of the studies that involve autonomous systems, robotics, and UAV flying and urban systems, drone delivery research demonstrates how disruptive technologies can be used to make a difference in last-mile delivery (McKinnon, 2016; Eskandaripour and Boldsaikhan, 2023).

According to the analysis, these three concepts AI, sustainability, and drones have been examined in isolation; however, there is a lack of literature on their joint effects on quick commerce. With this academic and analytical background, it is important to emphasize that the concept of quick commerce as focal point of digital transformation, sustainable supply chains, and disruptive technologies of logistics is a new concept.

3. LITERATURE REVIEW

The emergence of fast commerce can be traced to the ongoing development of e-commerce and the growing demand among consumers to be able to gain instant gratification. The previous research on retail logistics focused on centralized distribution networks (Agatz et al., 2008) yet the more recent studies introduced the value of decentralized dark stores and micro-fulfillment centers to facilitate the models based on speed as a priority. Quick commerce is therefore a novel phase of innovation in retail, unlike the old-fashioned e-commerce and other last-mile grocery delivery, due to its excessive focus on speed and hyperlocal placement of inventory.

3.1 Artificial Intelligence in Retail and Supply Chains

The use of AI in the retail process has been extensively reported. The existing body of research on predictive analytics shows that machine learning can increase the accuracy of demand forecasting, particularly when there are unstable consumer behavioural patterns. With respect to fast commerce, AI is used in two ways: to help salvage space in dark stores and to enhance the efficiency of delivery routes in cities (Ivanov and Dolgui, 2020). Additionally, the personalization via AI leads to increased customer engagement as the system suggests useful products in real-time. Although these studies offer powerful evidence of AI intervention, the majority of them are placed in the context of e-commerce, but not in quick commerce, and there is still a gap in the hyperlocal demand prediction research.

3.2 Green Logistics and Sustainability

Sustainability is another concept that has taken over logistics and supply chain literature. Practices identified in the study include the adoption of electric vehicles, green packaging, and the use of circular economy logistics, which are all necessary to minimize environmental harm. The rapid commerce business presents distinct sustainability issues because of increased frequency of delivery, reduced quantity of orders, and the packaging wastes. Although literature focuses on sustainability in general e-commerce, there is a paucity of literature that focuses on how quick commerce companies navigate between ultra-fast delivery and environmental promises. Such a gap indicates that there is need to have a framework that incorporates the concept of green logistics and the concept of speed-oriented retail model.

3.3 Drone and Autonomous Delivery

The last 10 years have seen an increase in research on drone-based logistics, with articles demonstrating that it might decrease the cost of deliveries, emissions, and congestion. Key market players such as Amazon, Alibaba, and Walmart among others have implemented drones in countries like the US, China and Europe, showing that drones can be used for delivery of high-priority, lightweight items like groceries and medicines (Murray and Chu, 2015; Poikonen and Campbell, 2021). However, there are also other barriers in regulation, safety and scalability. While the study of autonomous systems is well established in the fields of transport or robotics, their integration into Quick Commerce Ecosystems (QCEs) is still in its early stages and is an unexplored research field with huge potential.

4. CONCEPTUAL FRAMEWORK

Quick commerce Technologies A radical solution to retailing logistics that aims at achieving hyper locality and delivery speed. Whereas the conventional e-commerce operates on the foundation of centralized warehouses and long lead times in the delivery of goods, the quick commerce operates on the foundation of dark stores, minor fulfillment centers and technology- to cater to the increasing consumer demands. The suggested conceptual framework contemplates that Artificial Intelligence (AI), Green Logistics, and Drone-based Delivery are the driving forces behind the change in quick commerce, as they are directly and indirectly connected to the efficiency and sustainability of operations and produce results: satisfaction variables and operation variables.

Figure 1. Conceptual framework

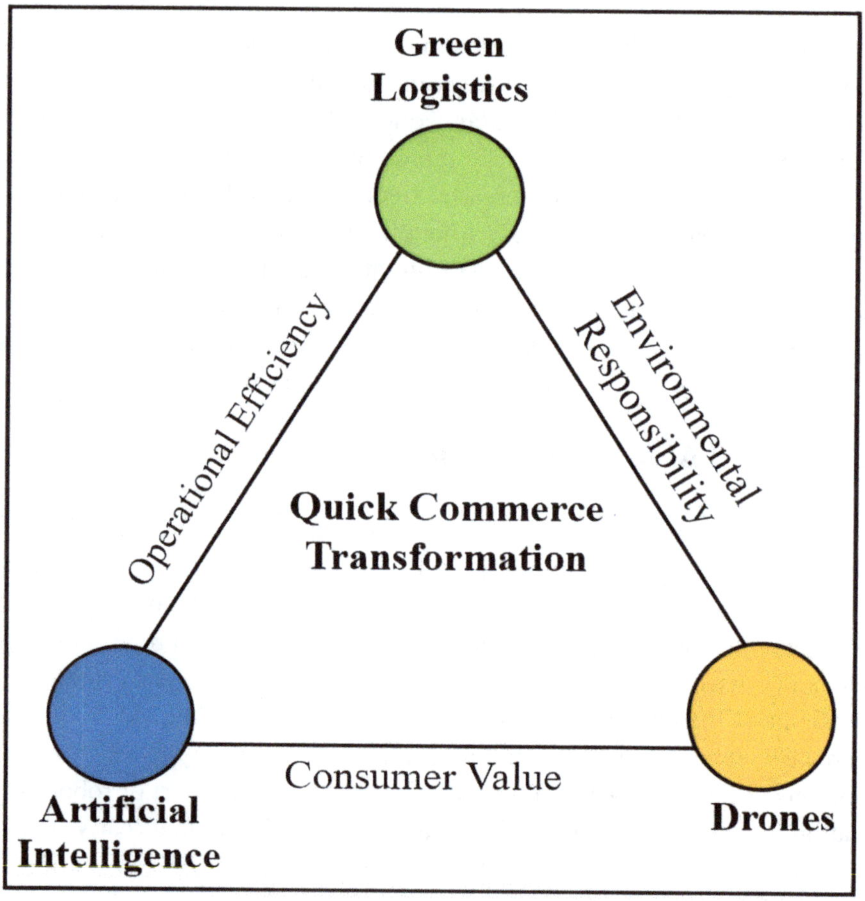

The suggested conceptual framework contemplates that Artificial Intelligence (AI), Green Logistics, and Drone-based Delivery are the driving forces behind the change in quick commerce, as they are directly and indirectly connected to the efficiency and sustainability of operations and produce results: satisfaction variables and operation variables.

This conceptual framework shows in Figure 1 and it describes transformation of quick commerce via AI, green logistics, and drone delivery. AI guarantees operational efficiency, green logistics encourages environmental responsibility and drones allow for disruptive last mile solutions. These drivers joined together to position the retailer with quite good consumer value and the ability to shape the sustainable and technology-driven future of retailing.

4.1 Artificial Intelligence as a Driver of Operational Efficiency

AI helps modulate contemporary fast businesses. Its applications include demand survey, stock optimization, routing and personalization of an individual customer. Unlike the traditional forecasting models which simply are fully reliant on past data, AI uses real-time data feed, aggregated across different data sources, including; sales history, social media trends, weather conditions, and urban traffic patterns, to come up with hyperlocal and predictive information.

For example, through machine learning algorithms it's possible to forecast an increase in need for groceries, or meal kits, in a certain time period and, in dark stores, to anticipate inventory needs accordingly. Moreover, AI-based route optimization solutions are able to dynamically and autonomously optimize the delivery routes. They also authenticate dynamic prices and customer recommendations, replenishment, and enhance the customer experience and efficiency even more.

4.2 Green Logistics as a Driver of Sustainability

The significant problem of the modern city retail logistics is a sustainability problem. Quality of fast commerce triggers numerous new environmental difficulties that comprise increased frequency deliveries, decreased order volumes, and additional packaging demands. Green logistics is encompassed in green fleet management, green store operation, recyclable packaging, and return cum waste recycling.

Many businesses traditionally use heavy delivery vehicles but, in some place, it becomes impossible and more congested, cable scooters, bicycles, and electric vehicles can be included in the list of them and can lead to fewer carbon emissions along with worsened attitude of the environment caused by the congestion. Moreover, a reusable containers, biodegradable materials and careful selection of an optimal order ratio decipher model of the given food packaging also restricts the ecological footprint of the very fast delivery. Strategically, it is a move which makes sustainable practices part of the operations of the quick commerce sector not only a method to satisfy the requirements of regulation and comply with the corporate social responsibility, but also to receive the loyalty of the customers and earn their trust.

Such interaction in the framework is the interaction of green logistics with AI achieved by predicting projected logistics analytics in delivering them because such logistics robots are incurbed to only minimize their trips and also to minimize the energy utilized.

4.3 Drone Delivery as a Driver of Innovation and Speed

One of the disruptive technologies that can change last-mile delivery is the drones technology. It is possible to evade congestion in cities due to the availability of drones capable of carrying relatively smaller cargo such as groceries, pharmaceuticals and food at a higher priority than other conventional vehicles. Some pilot projects in the United States, China and Europe have demonstrated drones could be used to deliver short-range (under 10-30 minutes) products.

The primary benefits of using a drone delivery are that the time spent on delivery will reduce, the cost of the fleet will also be lower, and the effect of the drone delivery will have a less negative effect on the environment, particularly if the drones themselves are powered by electric batteries. Furthermore, drones provide a greater number of possible locations of the micro-fulfillment centers, allowing the businesses to deliver their services to the large urban population of high population density without restricting the distance locally their products cover owing to traffic and parking problems.

This is not to say that there are no barriers left to be broken down, such as airspace control, security, payload, weather-reliance, etc.

4.4 Interactions and Synergies

The proposed conceptual framework presents a comprehensive view of the analysis of the transformation in fast business as AI, green logistics and drone delivery simply affect the efficiency of the operation, its sustainability and customer experience as a whole. By integrating these drivers, the framework not only addresses contemporary issues in the urban retail supply chain but also anticipates innovations in urban retail logistics in order for quick commerce to establish itself as a technologically sophisticated, environmentally friendly, and consumer friendly business model.

5. RESEARCH METHODOLOGY

This chapter takes the qualitative and secondary data approach to examine how artificial intelligence, green logistics, and drone delivery shape the future of fast commerce. Due to the fast development of the industry as well as the lack of access to specific data, secondary sources of information offer a solid background to learn about practice existing trends and strategic implications.

5.1 Research Design

It is a conceptual and exploratory study. Its main goal is to bring together piecemeal knowledge across various fields of expertise: technology, sustainability, and retail logistics into a single framework that embodies the evolution of fast trade. Unlike empirical studies which use primary survey or experiment, this type of design makes use of secondary data and qualitative interpretation of the data in order to reveal patterns, synergies and directions for future research.

5.2 Data Sources

Peer-reviewed academic journals, white papers published by industry, government policy documents, and trade publications were used as secondary data collection sources. Annual reports of quick commerce companies (e.g., Zepto, Blinkit, Getir, Gorillas, Amazon Fresh) along with reports prepared by consultancy companies (McKinsey, BCG, Deloitte, etc.) were reviewed to identify the current practices in the industry. The insights were based on regulatory policies about drones operations, sustainability policies, and urban logistics policies. These sources are valuable in that they provide a multi-perspective view of the ecosystem.

5.3 Analytical Approach

The triangulation of three areas gave the conceptual framework that was developed in this chapter. The three areas are (1) AI-based operations, (2) green logistics, and (3) adopting drone delivery. This triangulation technique was effective in making the propositions strong and minimized the risk of bias if the researcher relied on one perspective. Comparative analysis helped point at the variations across regions and also across the level of adoption of technology.

5.4 Rationale for Methodology

Secondary and qualitative data were selected because of two main reasons. To begin with, quick commerce is a relatively new sector that lacks standardized datasets and a qualitative synthesis is more appropriate to capture dynamic changes. Second, technology and sustainability dimensions are intertwined and interwoven in several fields; only qualitative methods can link these various threads.

6. TECHNOLOGY DIMENSION

Quick commerce is built on the strategic application of technology to automate the business operations, minimize their expenses and provide customers with high quality experiences. Quick commerce requires fulfilling orders within 10-30 minutes, unlike in the old era of e-commerce when a delivery could take days, and no inefficiencies could be tolerated. In this section, the technology aspect has been examined through three critical perspectives; AI-based demand forecasting, automation and robotization of dark stores, and optimization of mobile apps to manage inventory in real-time.

6.1 AI in Demand Prediction and Personalization

Quick commerce is founded on the notion that business processes and operations are effectively applied with the help of technology that reduces costs and delivers high-quality customer experience. Unlike traditional e-commerce, the delivery time cycle must span days, quick commerce must fulfil the delivery within a maximum of 10-30 minutes, and there exists no room to waste inefficiently. This kind of speed is possible only thanks to the newest technologies, such as artificial intelligence (AI), automatization, robotics, and built-in digital platforms. The technology aspect, in turn, will be reviewed in the context of three major points, namely: AI based predictive demand, automation and robotization in dark stores, and real-time inventory optimization achieved by optimization of mobile apps. Not only does the technological component of fast business limit to the efficiency of business operation, but also to the level of market competitiveness. The firms investing in AI, robotics, and real-time digital systems stand out by offering high-quality and efficient services. In addition, the investment in technology protects a company against the fluctuation of the laws and regulations, unproductive and unskilled employees, and the problem of sustainability.

6.2 Automation and Robotics in Dark Stores

Dark stores are dedicated fulfillment centers, which are mainly located around the demand centers in cities. Picking and packing have been realized to be automated and robotized to reduce the time spent in this process and make these stores more efficient. AGVs and robot arms will be able to move within the aisles, pick the products and assist workers as accurately and quickly as possible. Unlike the traditional retail warehouses that emphasize the bulk treatment, the quick commerce dark stores are constructed and optimized to address small and frequent orders.

Human dependency on workers is reduced by robot automation since there is less chance of errors such as mis picks and consistency. Even better so, using robotics, the scaling effect is applicable: additional growth in order volumes can be adjusted in the process faster than prior to computerization. Ocado, in association with Amazon, have demonstrated the worth of robotic fulfilled centers and these ideas are being taken out of the shelf and adjusted to smaller fulfillment centers targeted at quick-commerce.

6.3 Real-Time Inventory Management Systems

The effectiveness of fast business depends on the perfect punctuality of the consumer demand and product supply. The inventory management systems are real time and one can view the inventory of over than one dark store or a fulfilment node. These systems monitor the products and include the Internet of Things (IoT) and cloud computing to keep track of their movement. To illustrate, where a product is out-of-stock in one store, replacement products will be ordered automatically through a local distribution center. AI forecasting can make this forecasting system even stronger by ensuring that products need to be replenished at the right time to account for anticipated demand increases. This prevents various pitfalls such as stock-out products which may negatively affect consumer confidence of on-demand shopping. Moreover, there are created inventory systems that allow the control of quality (following expiry dates of perishable goods and informing operators that something should be pulled out or discounted). The customer side of these systems is in the form of mobile applications. The optimized apps can also display the actual time of the goods, and they can also transmit the accurate delivery time according to the traffic and the location of the rider and number of orders taken. Because quick commerce is a time hog, the applications will be lean and user-friendly and possess scaling ability to accommodate numerous users at any given time, particularly during peak times.

6.4 Digital Infrastructure and Integration

The quick commerce technology does not exist in a vacuum. Instead, it can only be successful when it is combined with other technology stacks being used in the retail environment, including enterprise resource planning (ERP), customer relationship management (CRM) and supply chain management (SCM) technology. Coherent digital systems facilitate the fast commerce participants to take advantage of the potentials of the established retail performance in the course of meeting the rapid delivery qualifications. Similarly, the SCM integration makes sure that it liaises with its suppliers, distributors and logistic partners in a manner that a demand or supply chain breakdown is more decisive to any such eventualities. This is facilitated using the assistance of cloud computing that is characterized by flexibility, scalability and data security.

7. SUSTAINABILITY DIMENSION

While quick commerce has redefined consumer trends towards greater convenience, so does the industry bring up questions about its environmental and social impact. Quick commerce, compared to traditional retail or even typical e-commerce, entails regular, small-basket purchases delivered in minutes, often using a fleet of motorbikes or vans. Unchecked, this model will contribute to the rise of carbon emissions, road congestion, and waste packaging. The sustainability aspect thus contributes a significant role to the fact that quick commerce is not just profitable and convenient, but also environmentally and socially responsible. This part of the chapter will explore how green logistics, packaging innovation, and urban sustainability approaches can contribute to sustainable quick commerce practices.

7.1 Green Logistics and Eco-Delivery

Sustainable quick commerce revolves around green logistics. It means the incorporation of green logistics and sustainability in supply chain processes. To lower greenhouse emissions related to last-mile delivery, quick commerce firms are starting to use electric vehicles (EVs), bicycles, and cargo scooters. For example, in India and Europe, e-bike fleets are being piloted by players who see an increase in fuel costs and with an objective to adhere to the emission restrains in urban areas. Road optimization made possible by AI can also promote green logistics through a shorter way, eliminated idleness, and increased the density of product delivery. Other companies also encourage consumers to make sustainable choices (e.g., delayed delivery slots so that the deliveries can be made in batches instead of one-to-one).

In addition to transport, green logistics has been applied to the supply chain alliances. Retailers are procuring goods from local farmers and suppliers to reduce transportation miles, which is leading to reduced emissions and deadened regional economies. It is also ensure fresher produce in that way that this localization is appropriate when it comes to sustainability and customer satisfaction.

7.2 Packaging Innovation

Another main sustainability challenge facing quick commerce is packaging. The use of plastic bags or bubble wraps or multilayered wrappings that create a lot of wastes is often common in frequent deliveries. In response to this, firms are trying green options like compostable bags or recyclable cardboard boxes and reusable containers. Other websites have also come up with depositing packaging system where a consumer can return the packaging in exchange of a discount or credit.

Not only materials but also design are subject to innovation. Right-sizing is a technique that ensures that the package suits the size of the product to avoid unnecessary use of resources and space during shipping. Similarly, the small-weight packaging assists in reducing the number of materials consumed and the delivery expenses entailed by the comfort of moving the orders in large quantities. As the regulation need increases such as the single use plastic ban - chocolate will cease to be a sustainability priority in packaging but it will be an obligatory cost as well.

7.3 Urban Sustainability Strategies

Quick commerce is a business that operates in the city centers, where the problems of sustainability are intensified. Traffic jams, air pollution, and a lack of parking space enhances the environmental implication of the frequent deliveries. Sustainability plans in urban areas must thus be tailored to the needs of business and municipal planning.

Amongst these is the introduction of strategically positioned micro-fulfilment centres or dark stores that minimise the delivery distances. Located in a largely unused area, these centers can reduce carbon emissions, as well as enable cities to better utilize their land. One more approach will be time-window delivery rules: metropolitan areas can persuade fast commerce companies to provide their services at non-hurricane times to minimize the pollution of traffic.

Sustainability can also be enhanced through collaboration between companies and city authorities. As an example, a specific green area could be preferred to EV-fleet or bicycle delivery. These approaches will help trace the sustainability as not just a systemic organizational problem but an urban planning issue as well.

7.4 Consumer and Regulatory Pressures

Sustainability is pushed not only by business interests, but also by consumer and regulatory ones. Consumers are increasingly demanding that brands embrace a sustainable culture and they will increasingly base their purchasing choices around supposed environmental responsibility. Companies involved in quick commerce that do not match these expectations are at risk of negative reputation and loss of customers.

Regulators are also constraining sustainability requirements. The regulation of the quantity of emissions, garbage disposal, and the activities of drones affect the functionality of the quick commerce. For example, in India, new extended producer responsibility (EPR) regulations are being put into place that mandate companies to deal with the disposal of packaging, while in Europe, some cities have implemented low emission zones that ban the delivery fleets that run on fossil fuels. Subjects to such regulations are not only steered away from penalties, but from competition of a different kind they experience an advantage as firms who can claim to be front-runners in criteria of responsible innovation.

7.5 Strategic Integration of Sustainability

Sustainability should be a part of the core business strategies and not an add on to attain success. This means linking metrics to environmental performance - for example, by measuring the amount of carbon that is saved per order, or percentage use of sustainable packaging. This is being incorporated into the brand name of many of the quick commerce companies, which present themselves as environmentally-friendly options in a market that is resource-heavy by nature.

Moreover, sustainability is likely to create cost savings over the long term. While EV fleets and eco-packaging require an initial investment, they cut back on volatile fuel prices and regulatory risks.

8. DISRUPTIVE DELIVERY DIMENSION

Intensive use of the last mile is the costliest aspect of the supply chain, and thus strongly depends on the last mile in quick commerce. The conventional last-mile services, primarily motorbikes, scooters, or vans, are feeling the pressure of soaring fuel prices, congestion in cities, and consumer demands that goods be delivered almost as quickly as possible. There is a potential disruptive technology in the shape of drones and autonomous vehicles. These models provide a win-win solution in terms of speed, scalability, and cost effectiveness while limiting the need to rely on traditional models that require human involvement. This section reviews the importance of drones and autonomous delivery vehicles and regulative challenges influencing their use.

8.1 Drone Technology Adoption

Drones are quickly transitioning to commercial uses, in rapid commerce. With Global Positioning System (GPS) positioning, artificial intelligence obstacle avoidance, and automatic flight managers, drones are capable of delivering small packages to consumers at their doorstep or areas where they receive them. The major strength they have is their ability to avoid traffic on the road thus reducing the biggest source of congestion in cities delivery systems. Firms like Wing (the subsidiary of Alphabet), Amazon Prime Air, and Zipline across the globe have already proven that drone-delivery was possible. The example of Zipline proves that drones can be used in different conditions with high reliability, as the company has managed to deliver medical supplies to numerous people living in Africa. The drones are viewed by quick commerce companies as the perfect solution to high-density cities, where the flight of a drone over five kilometres can be as short as 10 minutes against 30-40 minutes on roads during rush hour. While the air traffic is not yet cleared to facilitate the mass deployment of Autonomous Systems and Applications (ASAs), initial exploration of drone applications on the Indian soil under the "Drone Rules 2021" has paved the way for opening up avenues for conducting delivery trials on a commercial basis. Similarly, regulators in Europe have created corridors for drones and city air mobility, indicating a gradual but inevitable step towards the adoption of drones.

8.2 Autonomous Vehicles in Last-Mile Delivery

Ground-based autonomous vehicles (AVs) along with drones are another emerging technology solution to make deliveries. Robots that drive over the sidewalk already deliver products to campuses and residential neighbourhoods with no contact and no wasted time. Hyperarcs that travel miles are also being tested for carrying wide city routes, with smart technology and an artificial intelligence that will make the vans mind of their own. To fast-track trading, self-driving cars lessen the reliance on drivers and ensure 24-hour workload. They can also be programmed to deliver within specific window of time, minimize unemployment costs and maximize density in serving customers on a single route. The first autonomous delivery robots to enter the world were the Nuro from the United States, and the Starship Technologies from Europe and Indian companies have been researching on these analogous models adapted to the Indian environment and conditions of Indian roads. AVs will have the opportunity to plan their routes most efficiently and engage in communication with the city traffic systems and adhere to the rules. Nevertheless, AVs; unlike the drones, are not adaptable in densely populated cities that have inadequate pedestrian and road infrastructure.

8.3 Regulatory and Safety Considerations

Although the technology is mature enough, regulation promises to be the biggest obstacle to mass adoption of drones and automatics vehicles. The laws governing the operation of drones restrict its operation in most countries, with the operation being restricted in terms of altitude, line-of-sight-flight, and the weight of the contraband. Health and safety issues including road accidents, technical failures and breach of privacy also drag down the regulatory approvals. In the case of autonomous cars, the liability is the primary point. Under the accidents it is not clear who bears the responsibility; the manufacturer is the operator or the technology provider. Apart from that, cities would also need to plan the infrastructure's readiness, by developing marked lanes, docking stations, and charging stations. With no active policy, disruptive models of delivery will be stalled in their progress even when they can be efficient.

8.4 Strategic Advantages and Challenges

The utilization of the drones and the autonomous vehicles may become the neo liberalization of quick commerce. Increased competitive positioning is linked with reduced delivery time, reduced labour costs, and the ability to operate at scales that permit a 24/7 operation. Plus, they have an input on sustainability initiatives due to cutting the use of fossil fuels and complementing the solutions for electric mobility by making them work in synergy. Nonetheless, there is continued high capital outlay especially to the smaller players. Drone fleets and AVs demand large stakes in research and training and maintenance plants. Consumer acceptance is another reason - some consumers are special about the privacy and the safety implications of drones although fast, the noise level of the drones drive the adoption. Self-driving cars are also not welcomed by people as reliable in busy traffic conditions especially in developing countries such as India.

9. CASE STUDIES AND INDUSTRY INSIGHTS

In order to see the real dynamics of fast commerce, it is necessary to discuss how companies in different parts of the world have tested out models of operations, adoption of technology and utilization of customers. Case studies are real-world lessons that help the industry evolve: taking a look at what is working, what is not working and what is happening from a geographical perspective. The issues of innovation, challenges and strategic learning are discussed in the section concerning the choice of examples illustrating India and the global markets.

9.1 Case Study 1: Blinkit (India)

Blinkit (formerly Grofers) has emerged as a core competitor in the Indian quick commerce market. It was bold and disruptive as it changed its traditional e-grocery model to 10-15-minute delivery value model. Blinkit strategy was based on setting up what he termed as dark stores that were within the range of 2-3 kilometres to customer group in towns and cities. These dark stores received the name of tiny warehouses, and their function made deliveries nearer to households in the regions, significantly shortening their time.

The biggest lesson achieved by Blinkit is the unit economics issue. Although the customers were enticed by the use of ultra-fast deliveries, the business was experiencing high expenditure on infrastructural establishment, labor and the logistics of delivery. To alleviate this, Blinkit scaled down the product range; offering brands with high frequency and shifted to fast moving necessities like snacks, dairy and personal care products. Moreover, its purchase by Zomato gave it a chance to be financially steady and accept cross-platform integration (Deepak, 2025; Sanghi et al., 2024).

Learning: While, from a customer point of view, fast delivery could be a strong selling proposition, making a business profitable is a function of managing the inventory, cost structure and benefit synergies from bigger players in the ecosystem.

9.2 Case Study 2: Zepto (India)

Aqua momentum This project was established as an intenormous rival within the 10 minutes delivery industry by Zepto, a young organization in India. Their significant selling point was that they would guarantee in owning ice speed in as many cities as possible. Zepto spent much on technology in order to do right forecasting of demand and routing.

The only difference between Zepto is the use of data when it comes to decision-making. Due to the an analysis of the secondary and qualitative data, the company determined high-demand areas and optimized dark store inventory. Also, Zepto tried product of subscription with some incentives such as free shipping or special offers making the customer stickier (Karulkar et al., 2025; Vadra, 2024).

Learning: Agility, technology, and precision are three elements that help start-ups combat incumbents. But scaling fast is associated with overexpanding which is serious financial planning.

9.3 Case Study 3: Swiggy Instamart (India)

Swiggy Instamart has used the existing Swiggy logistics network to enter into quick commerce. The instamart attempted a hybrid model of utilizing dark stores and collaboration with local stores as opposed to Blinkit and Zepto which was intensely dependent on the dark stores. This plan minimized the additional infrastructure costs at the expense of an expanded availability of products.

One more benefit that Instamart had compared to Swiggy is the cross-selling feature associated with the integration of the Swiggy and the Instamart application into a unified food delivery prison facility. Already having some customers who would order food using the site, cross-selling to grocery purchases would help save on the cost of customer acquisition. Swiggy has also gained experience in logistics, which increased its level of efficiency and therefore gave it a competitive advantage (Chakraborty and Biswal, 2024; Atakan and Ata, 2023).

Learning: Cost efficiencies or convenience of the customer could be achieved through leveraging existing networks and models made through hybrid fulfillment.

9.4 Case Study 4: Getir (Turkey & Europe)

Getir is widely believed to be an innovator of rapid business in the world. It was built in Turkey and achieved a fast growth in Europe due to the system of delivery of groceries in a maximum of 10 minutes. Getir focussed on micro-fulfillment facility and a tech-savvy workforce.

Getir reached a high level of momentum, particularly due to the COVID-19 outbreak, but had problems with profitability following the restoration of normalcy in the markets. Europe was not a good location for scaling because it was expensive to hire workers and there was heavy regulation. Getir has recently exited some overseas markets in an attempt to streamline its main business divisions (Risberg, 2023).

Learning: There is the risk of aggressive expansion for brand building, but in the long-term one needs to carefully consider underground market dynamics and legal frameworks.

9.5 Case Study 5: Gopuff (United States)

Gopuff is another course. Rather than using third-party logistics, Gopuffle established a network of over 10,000 micro-fulfillment stations in the U.S. Its value proposition was not just in grocery but also in alcohol, household goods and imedical.

In contrast to other company peers, Gopuff went vertical and established ownership of inventory, fulfillment, and delivery. This provided it with more control over margins at exorbitant circumstances in terms of initial investment. Gopuff has tried subscription plans, including the Fam subscriptions that provide lower shipping charges and discount perks (Schorung, 2024).

Learning: Vertical integration enhances more control and loyalty of the customers and is associated with a high competence of operations and high degree of capital intensity of operations.

9.6 Case Study 6: Amazon Prime Air (Global)

Although Amazon is not a classical quick commerce business, the drone delivery experiment with Prime Air shows the disruptive power of technologies. Amazon has experimented with drone delivery of small-sized shipments to customers in select markets within less than 30 minutes.

The program, despite the limitations provided by the regulatory requirements, shows how the world leaders are ready to embrace the future of fast business without necessarily relying on the traditional last-mile logistics. While this is clearly an inspiration for Indian companies, it's also a cautionary tale; everything should involve innovation, but this is not possible without regulatory and infrastructure readiness (Singireddy and Daim, 2018).

Learning: Thinking long-term Technology-driven innovation can be effective, but early adoption of technology requires consideration of regulatory and consumer acceptance drivers.

9.7 Comparative Insights

9.7.1 Speed vs. Sustainability

Firms such as Blinkit and Zepto have managed to generate demand in instant delivery, but the financial gains have proved to be difficult. It is now taking an interest in the balance between speed and sustainable operations.

9.7.2 Models Matter

Business models have to be adjusted to local situations as the experience of Hybrid fulfillment (Instamart) and vertical integration (Gopuff) reveals.

9.7.3 Global Expansion Risks

The contraction of Getir emphasises the risk of global expansion in a short period, not customising any of its operations to market requirements.

9.7.4 Technology as Enabler

The importance of innovation in key competitive advantage of the future is demonstrated by drones (Amazon) and AI-based analytics (Zepto).

10. DISCUSSIONS AND IMPLICATIONS

Fast Commerce has forever changed the dynamics of retail through consumer expectations, supply chain architecture and competition. Fundamentally, quick commerce is an amalgamation of new technologies, altered life patterns, and urbanism, and as such, is an occurrence that cannot be seen through the analysis of one direction. This section combines the discussion and the implications, shifting between issues related to consumer behavior, operational and strategic decisions, societal impacts, and academic contributions for the purpose of building a comprehensive picture.

10.1 Consumer and Market Shifts

The emergence of quick commerce can be best understood due to consumer behavior. This is contrary to the conventional e-commerce model which emphasized the virtue of convenience in a 24-48 hour delivery requirement; in quick commerce, the definition of convenience has been adapted to mean a twenty-four hours or near-immediate gratification. This movement can be seen as more fundamental to cultural and psychological change, including the importance of time to consumers and the commodification of on-demand services. The results demonstrate that the loyalty of consumers in this area is not price sensitive and closer to reliability, consistency and quality of service. With that said, this has not been even across geographies. Young digitally literate consumers accelerated the dissemination of quick commerce in India in large cities. Conversely, institutional constraints and infrastructures have imposed upon adoption in Europe or North America. In particular, this demonstrates the mediation of consumer expectations by contextual factors implying globalizability requires consideration of local differences of culture, demographics, and infrastructures.

It means that any company should not just copy some models that have already been in the market, but have to be aware of the heterogeneity of the market. Therefore, the market penetration of quick commerce in question is equal to both conforming to cultural values as much as it is related to the efficiency of its operations.

10.2 Business Models and Operational Trade-offs

Business models debate reveals the growth and profitability paradox. The resource-based view also helps to understand that competitive advantage for quick commerce comes from the control of scarce skills for AI-driven demand forecasting, last-mile fleet management, and strategic location of dark stores. However, the transaction cost viewpoint shows that fixing the operations as well as keeping fleets or the micro-fulfillment centers internalized the organization increases the fixed costs as well as decreases the flexibility. Examples of such companies include Blinkit and Gopuff, where in-house logistics enhance control and consistency, but cannot work well due to limited order density.

A second trade-off operation is speed/ vs. sustainability. The concept of 10-15 minutes delivery brings excitement to consumers, while subjecting logistics, people management, and the environment to enormous stress. High packaging waste, petrol consumption, and the easy rider churns demonstrate system ineffectiveness. In an attempt to address such worries, a few companies have been considering electric vehicles and biodegradable boxes, vertical sourcing, intuitive though quite costly and fragmented.

Blended models such as the hybrid form when Swiggy Instamart joined forces with retailer chains can provide a solution to the problem of setting prices, as they balance between the costs and the offered goods. These results indicate that, while speed is a differentiator for speed's sake at present, future competitive advantage may be dependent on taking a balance between operational efficiency and sustainability/ employee well-being. The implication on management is obvious, companies should not rely on short-term expansion through discounts; they should look long-term in the technological advancement, human resource, and green logistics.

10.3 Policy, Society, and Sustainability Implications

The social and political impact of fast business is much bigger than the profitability of the business. The institutional theory illustrates that the adoption of models is also heavily influenced by regulations, labour regulations, and zoning laws. Hyper-local operations are favoured in India because of relatively flexible labor markets and dense urban structures, but are limited by tight labor regulations and town and city planning rules in Europe. This deviation implies that institutional legitimacy requires firms to be aligned to maintain growth rather than merely subjecting these models to environments that do not accommodate them.

The problems related to the environment are no less urgent. The fragmented delivery system of quick commerce is also a contributor of opening city traffic jams, pollution of carbon dioxide and garbage, and people need to question the long-term sustainability of such a business concept. These concerns are on the rise on the policy makers' radar, and regulatory responses in the form of controls on delivery times, green mandates for fleet running schedules and stringent packaging are being considered. By this it signifies the idea that companies have to foresee how regulation will evolve instead of respond to a regulatory shift. Businesses that take their responsibilities by developing environmentally friendly products or services would most likely receive not just ge customer trust but also acceptance by the authorities.

The model also creates workforce ethical issues in the social front. The precarious nature of the income received by riders, social insecurities, and the unsafe conditions associated with vehicle operation are common labor products of the gig economy system that the last-mile delivery relies on. Socially speaking, these issues are to be disregarded at the risk of losing trust and validity. This offers a chance to policymakers and companies to work together to develop a framework that does not jeopardize the welfare of the employees including health insurance, fair wage plan and insurance that covers accidents. Thus, the larger implication is that quick commerce is not just a business innovation but a socio-economic experiment with implications for how we live in cities, whether or not they are sustainable, and how we work - i.e., how we are paid.

10.4 Academic Integration

Theoretically, fast business is an area that can be used to develop theory. The intersection of AI, green logistics, and the problem of drone delivery puts researchers in a task to combine the perspectives of the study of innovation management, the research of the supply chain, the study of consumer behavior, and the research of sustainability. The diffusion of innovation and discontinuous innovation theories are utilized to explain the process of adoption and the development of industry changes whereas the resource-based and transaction cost theory are used to explain the firm level. Service-dominant theory brings insights into co-creation of value between consumers and firms whereas sustainable supply chain theory emphasizes on environmental constraints. Together, these explanatory point of view approaches show the easiness of commerce is not a specialized retail representation but a multidisciplinary change.

The overall implication is that prospective research ought to target on three areas. Second, longitudinal research investigating if ultra-fast delivery is a consumer trend or a change in shopping habits. Third, sustainable studies addressing the ecological and social expenses of fast commerce and determining any green practices that could be embraced on a bigger scale. By joining academic debates, quick commerce can offer a contribution to broader conversations about digital transformation, platform economies, and sustainable innovation.

11. FUTURE DIRECTIONS

With the ongoing development of technology, consumer criteria, socio-environmental compulsions, etc., there will be a host of changes expected in quick commerce in the foreseeable future. One of the closest trend directions of the nearest future, one should mention the introduction of automation and autonomous system into the process of fulfillment and delivery. Robotics inside dark stores, drone delivery for hyper localized logistics and AI for demand sensing will take one big leap from being a pilot project to going mainstream. Sustainability itself will be another of the frontiers that will delimit sustainability. A majority of the current fast-fast delivery models are known to enhance carbon emissions and wastes in packages. The new innovations will primarily be about electric mobility, township centres, and circular packaging. Vertical farming combined with dark stores (small micro-supply routes) could help us get fresh produce at lower transportation costs, combining quick commerce efficiency with sustainability goals: companies that cater to eco-conscious and increasingly active consumers benefit from reputational gains and long-range legitimacy, while other companies turn into green profit makers.

Certainly, on a strategic basis the industry might face a situation when the acquisition of smaller players will not enable them to compete with the magnitude and might of the larger established competitors. Such consolidation will be at least challenged by the models of hyper local niche that will target a specific demographic or a specific culture. To illustrate, customer fulfillment strategies, that are both traditional Kirana shops and online are potentially more effective in developing countries than their technology counterparts. Finally, thus, standardization will not become the future of quick commerce, but rather, contextualization - the capacity to adapt those models to the current infrastructure and consumer behavior and to adjust them to the local conditions.

At the societal and regulatory level, debates concerning urban congestion, as well as zoning regulations for dark stores will influence the future of the logistics industry, in addition to (and intertwined with) the fair treatment of those who work for the gig-economy. Regulatory models for innovation must be capable of balancing innovation with accountability. This will include ensuring fast business is not part of inequality, labor and urban crime exploitation. It will as well introduce into the procedure of internationalization of quick commerce the issues of cultural correspondence and matching of the regulations that will make companies collaborate in discourse with the governments and civil society. Instructive studies may be made on the continuities of the speed-sustainability contradiction to the perspective of a consumer, the perspective of a company, about efficiency verses ethics, and the technological perspective where both perspectives of consumption and labor undergo change. This work will not only enlighten the business policies; it will also contribute to the argument and social innovation of the policy.

In short, the capacity and readiness to promptly shift emphasis off the speed up based disarray and concentrate on more advanced environment or ecosystem that assimilates tech, sustainability and human ideals will be a determinant that will mark the future of quick commerce. By looking forward rather than looking back, the sector can become more of an experimental phenomenon than a foundation of the global retail economy.

12. KEY TAKEAWAYS

- Retail is changing fast business because consumers attitude to shopping is being relegated to a stage of planned shopping, where they expect businesses to respond with rapidity, convenience and customisation, but business also needs to respond to sustainable and profitable business models.
- Dark stores and micro-fulfillment centers would be critical infrastructure components that lead to ultra-fast delivery, but the success or failure of these centers would require a balance between automation, real-time inventory visibility, and consumer demand forecasting within urban logistics ecosystems.
- Technology integration, especially AI and robotics, offers benefits to firms in terms of competitive advantage thanks to predictive insights, operational efficiency, and scale models, although adoption involves addressing costs, workforce transitions, and regulatory issues.
- Sustainability and regulation are paramount as quick commerce develops, requiring greener delivery practices, fair labor, and adaptive policies that balance innovation and accountability in a diversity of regional and cultural backgrounds.
- The future of quick commerce is hybrid strategies, cross discipline innovations, and responsible digital ecosystems balancing consumer expectations, firm profitability, and societal well-being in the changing global retail economy.

13. CONCLUSION

The second point of fast commerce which has been put in the chapter brings out the factual change which is changing the logistic and retail industry. The idea of quick commerce has discharged urgent ness as one of central values propositions, unlike the conventional e-commerce, which changed the admittance and comfort. It is more of a socio-cultural redefining of consumption where time has also become a significant currency in addition to price and availability of products. The piece found in this chapter demonstrated that companies must be able to work out a trade-off balance of speed, sustainability and profitability through tracing the development of the dark stores, the micro-fulfillment models and the last-mile innovations.

It has been demonstrated in the review that fast commerce is not a dispensable event but an ecosystem, which is dynamic under the influence of number of forces. Demand is also driven by consumer needs of speed and convenience but is also requiring ethics from their suppliers, delivery sustainability and reliability. The companies respond by adopting the technology i.e.AI based predictions, robots, real time stock availability, which are utilized to fulfil these increased expectations of the customers. Meanwhile, regulatory framework, cultural environments, and structural constraint partially prescribe regional scaled levels of these models. Speaking of which, to enable keeping the practice of dark stores and two-wheelers viable, it may be applied to major cities, but in a suburb or on a rural territory, the hybrid solutions that revolve around a new model complementing traditional retail should be used.

There are also some tensions present in the quick commerce (identified in the chapter). Most companies have not yet discovered a balance between the desire to accumulate a large amount of new client installation through aggressive marketing and the overall business viability in the long run. Speaking of the same, the intention to become big in a short period of time often clashes with the desire to become an environmentally community-friendly company and requires the new solutions to green logistics, fleet optimization, and innovative packaging. These strains are not burdens, and quite to the contrary, the places where most is lacking, are the places where most is needed. They insist that the success of such an area lies not in the conception that fast commerce is an experimental model to be emulated, but in the rethink of models of value creation and their reconstruction in line with new consumer concerns and societal requirements.

The chapter has academic value because of establishing a relationship between quick-commerce reality and the theories of innovation diffusion, resource-based view, service-dominant logic, and the institutional theory of innovation. The synthesis of the theories at the interdisciplinary level empowers the theoretical ground of a synthesis on which a study can be developed further. In reality, it is a tool that helps companies build a systematic framework for strategic decision making, process design and being prepared to comply with legal requirements. The comparative vision through which the analysis of the regions of the world is made makes it more graphic as it demonstrates that there is no single way that one has to follow and, instead, a person needs to be flexible and culturally in tune to the direction on which they have to improve at a local level to become successful.

In conclusion, the phenomenon of quick commerce should not be regarded as such, but as a digital economy, which will make speed, sustainability, and technology-linked personalization central to consumption. It is determined by the pace with which companies, governments and customers can solve the new formula that will lead them to the similar destination of efficiency, inclusiveness and sensitivity to the environment. The inferences drawn in this chapter provides a starting point in navigating through the existing challenges to position the destabilization that is about to add its name to the future of retail.

ACKNOWLEDGMENT

The authors also wish to state that they had cooperation with their colleagues, mentors, and peers who were so helpful and supportive during the process of the chapter elaboration. They also appreciate the secondary and the qualitative data sources which contributed to analysis. First, a special thanks to their institution and academic community for creating a benchmark of research, collaboration and deep reflection that provided them the space needed to bring this academic publication to fruition in the final form.

CONFLICT OF INTERESTS

The authors report that there are no conflicts of interest in relation to publication of this chapter. The analysis and conclusions were not affected by financial, personal, or occupational connections. The research was carried out in an academic independent and transparent way considering objectivity and the integrity in reporting of the researches and analysis of findings.

CHAPTER ORIGINALITY

This chapter is an original research and analysis work by the authors. It integrates secondary information, qualitative information and theoretical viewpoints to develop a new, interdisciplinary model of quick commerce. The material has never been published anywhere and has not been considered in any other journal or book.

SIGNIFICANCE OF THE CHAPTER

The chapter is meaningful because it presents a multidisciplinary approach to the concept of quick commerce, outlining a holistic framework comprising of strategy, operations, technology, sustainability, and consumer behavior. Combining theoretical and practical aspects, it also provides practical implications for businesses, governments and academics and shows future directions which will connect speed, efficiency and societal responsibility in electronic retailing.

REFERENCES

Agatz, N. A., Fleischmann, M., & Van Nunen, J. A. (2008). E-fulfillment and multichannel distribution–A review. *European Journal of Operational Research, 187*(2), 339–356. DOI: 10.1016/j.ejor.2007.04.024

Atakan, M. S., & Ata, U. Z. (2023). Internationalization of retailing: The case of Turkish ultra-fast grocery delivery retailer Getir. In *Origin and Branding in International Market Entry Processes* (pp. 233–251). IGI Global. DOI: 10.4018/978-1-6684-6613-1.ch010

Chakraborty, U., & Biswal, S. K. (2024). Re-strategizing in a crisis: The space of quick commerce in Swiggy's business. *SAGE Publications: SAGE Business Cases Originals*. DOI: 10.4135/9781071935095

Deepak, J. (2025). *A case study on implementation of guerrilla marketing by Zomato and Blinkit*. DOI: 10.2139/ssrn.5284284

Eskandaripour, H., & Boldsaikhan, E. (2023). Last-mile drone delivery: Past, present, and future. *Drones (Basel), 7*(2), 77. DOI: 10.3390/drones7020077

Ghezzi, A., Mangiaracina, R., & Perego, A. (2012). Shaping the e-commerce logistics strategy: A decision framework. *International Journal of Engineering Business Management, 4*, 13. DOI: 10.5772/51647

Ivanov, D., & Dolgui, A. (2020). Viability of intertwined supply networks: Extending the supply chain resilience angles towards survivability. A position paper motivated by COVID-19 outbreak. *International Journal of Production Research, 58*(10), 2904–2915. DOI: 10.1080/00207543.2020.1750727

Karulkar, Y., Sampat, B., Thapliyal, A., Singh, B., & Gupta, D. (2025). Zepto: Redefining the future of rapid delivery. *Emerald Emerging Markets Case Studies, 15*(1), 1–36. DOI: 10.1108/EEMCS-12-2023-0491

Li, X., Tupayachi, J., Sharmin, A., & Martinez Ferguson, M. (2023). Drone-aided delivery methods, challenge, and the future: A methodological review. *Drones (Basel), 7*(3), 191. DOI: 10.3390/drones7030191

McKinnon, A. C. (2016). The possible impact of 3D printing and drones on last-mile logistics: An exploratory study. *Built Environment, 42*(4), 617–629. DOI: 10.2148/benv.42.4.617

Murray, C. C., & Chu, A. G. (2015). The flying sidekick traveling salesman problem: Optimization of drone-assisted parcel delivery. *Transportation Research Part C, Emerging Technologies*, *54*, 86–109. DOI: 10.1016/j.trc.2015.03.005

Poikonen, S., & Campbell, J. F. (2021). Future directions in drone routing research. *Networks*, *77*(1), 116–126. DOI: 10.1002/net.21982

Rai, H. B., Mariquivoi, J., Schorung, M., & Dablanc, L. (2023). Dark stores in the City of Light: Geographical and transportation impacts of 'quick commerce' in Paris. *Research in Transportation Economics*, *100*, 101333. DOI: 10.1016/j.retrec.2023.101333

Risberg, A. (2023). A systematic literature review on e-commerce logistics: Towards an e-commerce and omni-channel decision framework. *International Review of Retail, Distribution and Consumer Research*, *33*(1), 67–91. DOI: 10.1080/09593969.2022.2089903

Sanghi, N., Chandra Balodi, K., & Gupta, V. (2024). The emergence of the Indian hyperlocal grocery delivery industry: Dunzo v/s Blinkit. *Journal of Information Technology Teaching Cases*, *14*(1), 119–128. DOI: 10.1177/20438869231151449

Schorung, M. (2024). Quick commerce and the evolving business models of the food retail industry—Investigating the quick commerce supply chain and the urban impacts of dark stores. *Transportation Research Procedia*, *79*, 305–312. DOI: 10.1016/j.trpro.2024.03.041

Shapiro, A. (2023). Platform urbanism in a pandemic: Dark stores, ghost kitchens, and the logistical-urban frontier. *Journal of Consumer Culture*, *23*(1), 168–187. DOI: 10.1177/14695405211069983

Singireddy, S. R. R., & Daim, T. U. (2018). Technology roadmap: Drone delivery – Amazon Prime Air. In Daim, T., Chan, L., & Estep, J. (Eds.), *Infrastructure and technology management. Innovation, technology, and knowledge management* (pp. 249–268). Springer. DOI: 10.1007/978-3-319-68987-6_13

Vadra, R. (2024). Zepto: Can it sustain its ten-minute online delivery model in India? *SAGE Publications: SAGE Business Cases Originals*. DOI: 10.4135/9781071939758

Yarlagadda, K. C. (2025). AI-powered supply chain optimization: Enhancing demand forecasting and logistics. *Journal of Computer Science and Technology Studies*, *7*(4), 792–801. DOI: 10.32996/jcsts.2025.7.4.92

KEY TERMS AND DEFINITIONS

AI Demands Forecasting: Use of Artificial Intelligence to forecast consumer buying behavior and optimize inventory.

Dark Stores: Stores that do not permit customers to walk in and are specifically constructed to fulfil orders via the Internet.

Drone Delivery: Drones can be used to transport products to the consumer at home or office, because they travel faster and cover a greater distance.

Last-Mile Delivery: This is the last logistic step in which products are transported into the houses of the customer after finishing fulfillment spots.

Micro-Fulfillment Centers (MFCs): This is a small automated warehouse situated near city centers to facilitate quick delivery.

Quick Commerce: This business model is based on the concept of the rapid delivery of consumer products, which can last up to 10-30 minutes.

Sustainable Logistics: The logistics that are environmentally conscious in terms of fiction of generating carbon and waste.

Urban Logistics: Transport and delivery systems developed to regulate the movement of goods in urban setups.

About the Contributors

Mohamed Amine Frikha is an Assistant Professor at the Applied College, King Faisal University, in Al-Ahsa, Saudi Arabia. He holds a Ph.D. in Economics (2016) with a specialization in Transport Science and Logistics, along with multiple master's degrees in logistics engineering, transport science, and financial accounting. His research focuses on sustainable logistics, cross-border supply chain management, customs operations, and the integration of artificial intelligence in transport decarbonization. Dr. Frikha has developed a strong academic portfolio that bridges quantitative modeling, trade facilitation, and environmental performance in global supply networks. He is the author of several peer-reviewed publications, including the recently accepted article in Sustainability (MDPI) titled "Artificial Intelligence for the Decarbonization of Supply Chains: Indirect Contributions to Carbon Dioxide Removal" (October 2025). His other works have appeared in journals such as the International Journal of Advanced Computer Science and Applications (IJACSA), Logistics (MDPI), and in the forthcoming IGI Global volume "Innovations in Green and Energy-Efficient Warehousing". Throughout his career, Dr. Frikha has participated in numerous international conferences (LOGISTIQUA, IEEE) and training programs organized by the World Customs Organization (WCO) and the European Union's ESCOLA EUROPEA initiative. His interdisciplinary expertise spans AI-driven logistics optimization, customs risk assessment, and sustainable transport policy design. Dr. Frikha's ongoing research seeks to advance intelligent, low-carbon, and resilient supply chain systems that promote sustainability and efficiency across international borders.

* * *

Rahmath Nisha A. is a dedicated professional with comprehensive, hands-on experience in Human Resource Management (HRM), having successfully managed the entire employee life cycle—from recruitment and onboarding to performance management and employee engagement. She holds an MBA in Human Resource Management, where she was recognized as a Gold Medalist and awarded the title of Best Outgoing Student. Her academic journey began with a Bachelor's degree in Electronics and Communication Engineering, showcasing her diverse educational foundation. Currently serving as an Assistant Professor, she combines industry expertise with academic insight to mentor and inspire the next generation of HR professionals.

Jaime Aguilar-Ortiz holds a Ph.D. in Mathematics and is a recognized researcher with an extensive academic and scientific trajectory, currently a member of Mexico's National System of Researchers. His scholarly output includes over 40 peer-reviewed research and dissemination articles, complemented by the authorship and co-authorship of more than 40 educational and scientific books across mathematics, financial education, programming, artificial intelligence, and applied technologies. He has also contributed to the creation of digital and educational resources, including academic portals, videogames, and over 100 educational films, always combining rigorous mathematical foundations with innovative applications of artificial intelligence. His current research focuses on deep tabular learning, fuzzy logic, reinforcement learning, natural language processing, and neural networks, seeking to apply cutting-edge AI methodologies to address social problems and foster technological development, while strengthening postgraduate education and research in Mexico and beyond.

Duggirala Aravind is currently associated with the Department of Aviation, ASET College of Science and Technology, Chennai, India. He previously completed his Bachelor's degree in Electrical and Electronics Engineering at MITS University. His research interests include aviation operations, renewable energy technologies in air transport, Artificial Intelligence, Business Management, Logistics and Supply Chain Management.

Tanmay Azad was born on 9th November 2004 as the aspiring management professional who is dedicated, disciplined and determined to grow personally. He was brought into a family that is supportive and value oriented. Mr. Chandra Shekhar Azad, his father and Mrs. Kumari Ruby Sinha, his mother have been key figures in his way of thinking and his path to follow. Tanmay also has his share of attachment with his brother, Mr. Divyam Azad who has been a significant motivator and constant companion to him. Tanmay attended Army public school, Danapur cantt which exposed him to a world of strict discipline, executive quality, and a couple of structured disciplining approach to studies and life. His schooling life contributed greatly in his character development and inculcation of responsibility.

Nowadays Tanmay is continuing his higher level studies at Christ University, Delhi NCR which is one of the reputed institutions in the country. He is pursuing the Bachelor of Business Administration (BBA) program, and as a student, he is keen on extending his skills, acquiring the pragmatic exposure, and experimenting on different sides of management and strategic aspects. Strong-willed, goal oriented, and earthy, Tanmay strives to establish a career in which he could incorporate a combination of his knowledge, creativity and leadership skills in order to achieve a significant difference. His education level and the sight of the future makes him a better worker towards becoming a highly recognized professional in the world of business.

Sattianadan D. is an Associate Professor in the Department of Electrical and Electronics Engineering at SRM Institute of Science and Technology (SRMIST), Tamil Nadu, India. He is actively involved in teaching, research, and academic mentoring in the field of EEE. His professional interests include advancing engineering education and contributing to institutional academic development.

Ocotlán Diaz-Parra is a Professor and Researcher at Universidad Politécnica de Pachuca (UPP), a National Researcher under the Secretaria de Ciencia, Humanidades, Tecnología e Innovación program, and an Adjunct Researcher at the National Laboratory of Autonomous Vehicles and Exoskeletons (LANAVEX). His research interests include Smart Cities, Smart Water, Smart Education, Smart Government, Smart Healthcare, Smart Farming, Smart Energy, Smart Sports, Smart Food, Smart Tourism, Algorithmic Finance, Algorithmic Portfolio Management, Applications and Theory of Algorithms, Bio-inspired Algorithms, Combinatorial Optimization Problems, Compilers, Computational Intelligence, Computational Complexity Theory, Computational Financial Intelligence, Complexity of Algorithms, Complexity of Instances, Computational Statistics, Computer Networks, Computer Science Security, Cybercrimes, Data Mining, Education, Evolutionary Computation, Heuristic Optimization Techniques in Bioinformatics, Hybrid Evolutionary Algorithms, Hybrid Optimization Algorithms, Machine Learning, Meta-heuristics, Operations Research, Operations Management, Parallel & Distributed Computing, Production Planning and Logistics Optimization, Project Scheduling Problems, Software Engineering, and Transgenic Algorithms.

Carlos R. Domínguez-Mayorga holds a Ph.D. in Sciences specializing in Artificial Intelligence, with a foundational background in Physics and Mathematics. His research focuses on Deep Learning, NLP, neural networks, and the development of predictive models. He has an extensive track record in scientific publications and graduate program management, applying cutting-edge data science techniques to engineering and sustainability projects.

Dhasarathi G. is a nursing graduate who has transitioned into the non-clinical domain to pursue a career in hospital and healthcare management. With a strong foundation in nursing and patient care, she brings valuable clinical insight into administrative and managerial decision-making. Currently pursuing a Master of Business Administration in Hospital Management, she is focused on bridging the gap between clinical practice and healthcare administration. She aspires to contribute to the development of efficient, patient-centered, and strategically managed healthcare organizations through effective leadership and evidence-based management practices.

Porkodi G. is an Assistant Professor in the Department of Computer Science and Business Systems at Vel Tech Multi Tech Dr. Rangarajan Dr. Sakunthala Engineering College, Avadi, Chennai, Tamil Nadu, India (600 062). She is involved in teaching, research, and mentoring students in computer science and business-oriented computing. Her academic interests support interdisciplinary learning and industry-aligned curriculum development.

Syed Hassan Imam Gardezi is an accomplished strategist, executive leader, and board member with extensive expertise in leveraging artificial intelligence to build sustainable, resilient, and efficient global supply chains. His career operates at the critical intersection of strategic management, technological innovation, and environmental responsibility, with certified expertise in AI and its transformative applications for complex logistics networks. A recognized thought leader on intelligent systems and sustainability, Dr. Gardezi applies his rigorous academic insight and practical leadership experience to the pressing challenge of decarbonizing global trade. He specializes in frameworks that harness data-driven intelligence to optimize cross-border flows, reduce environmental impact, and enhance transparency while maintaining operational excellence in an increasingly complex regulatory landscape. In his contributed chapter, "Artificial Intelligence in Sustainable Supply Chain Management," for the book AI-Enabled Strategies for Sustainable Cross-Border Logistics, Dr. Gardezi distills his expertise into a vital examination of how machine learning, predictive analytics, and intelligent automation can drive measurable sustainability outcomes while navigating the inherent complexities of international trade and logistics. Dr. Gardezi's authority is built upon a foundation of advanced study and executive governance, including a PhD in Management, an MBA, and specialized certifications in Artificial Intelligence and Blockchain technologies. He is a Fellow of the Institute of Supply Chain Management UK, a

Fellow of the Chartered Institute of Logistics & Transport UK, a Fellow of the Institute of Corporate Responsibility & Sustainability UK, a Fellow of the Institute of Energy UK, a Fellow of the Institute of Directors UK, a Fellow of the Chartered Management Institute UK, and a Fellow of the Institute of Consulting, among other distinguished affiliations. He actively serves on several boards as a Non-Executive Director, providing strategic oversight on technology adoption, supply chain resilience, and sustainable value creation, and is a sought-after keynote speaker on strategic leadership, AI-driven transformation, and the future of sustainable global commerce.

Pratibha Giri brings over 15 years of rich academic experience to her role. She is working as Associate Professor in the School of Business and Management at Christ (Deemed to be University), Delhi-NCR. With a strong foundation in management studies, including an MBA from the prestigious Faculty of Management Studies and a Ph.D Dr. Giri has established herself as a versatile scholar and educator. Her research interests span multiple areas of management, including Marketing, Human Resources, Entrepreneurship, and International Trade. Dr. Giri has authored more than 20 research papers published in reputed national and international journals, demonstrating her commitment to contributing to the academic discourse in her field. An active participant in the academic community, Dr. Giri regularly attends national and international level seminars, conferences and workshops to stay at the forefront of developments in management studies. She has also presented research papers at various national and international conferences, further solidifying her reputation as a thought leader in her areas of expertise.

Sunanda Jindal is a distinguished academician and researcher based in Pune, Maharashtra, India. She is widely recognized for her commitment to higher education, scholarly research, and academic excellence. With a strong passion for knowledge dissemination and intellectual development, Dr. Jindal has contributed significantly to the academic community through her teaching, research, mentoring, and institutional involvement. Dr. Sunanda Jindal possesses an impressive academic background, having completed her advanced degrees in her chosen field with distinction. Her academic training has provided her with a solid theoretical foundation and research orientation, enabling her to engage in meaningful scholarly inquiry. She has continuously updated her knowledge to keep pace with the evolving academic and research landscape, reflecting her dedication to lifelong learning and professional growth. As an academician, Dr. Jindal has several years of experience in teaching and mentoring students at undergraduate and postgraduate levels. She is known for her student-centered teaching approach, which encourages critical thinking, analytical reasoning, and practical application of theoretical concepts. Her ability to simplify complex subjects and inspire students has earned her appreciation from learners and colleagues alike. She has actively guided students in academic projects, research work, and career development, contributing to their intellectual and professional advancement. In addition to her teaching responsibilities, Dr. Jindal has made noteworthy contributions to research. Her research interests span interdisciplinary and contemporary areas relevant to her field of specialization. She has authored and co-authored research papers published in reputed national and international journals, contributing to academic knowledge and scholarly discourse. Her research work reflects analytical depth, methodological rigor, and practical relevance, addressing current issues and emerging trends in academia and society.

V. Kalyanasundaram is an Assistant Professor in the Department of Electrical and Electronics Engineering at SRM Institute of Science and Technology (SRM IST), Kattankulathur, Tamil Nadu, India (603 203). He is actively involved in teaching, research, and mentoring students in the EEE discipline. His academic contributions support curriculum delivery and departmental research initiatives.

Dinesh M. G. is a faculty member in the Department of Artificial Intelligence and Data Science at Easa College of Engineering and Technology, Coimbatore. He is actively involved in teaching, research, and academic mentoring in emerging computing technologies. His interests include data analytics, intelligent systems, and applied research in AI-driven solutions. Dr. Dinesh contributes to curriculum development and supports student innovation and projects. He is committed to academic excellence and industry-relevant engineering education.

Oumayma Messaoudi holds a Ph.D. in Economics and a Master's degree in Transport and Logistics. Her research focuses on sustainable transportation systems, regional trade integration, and the economic implications of environmental policies. With a strong background in quantitative analysis and policy evaluation, she contributes to interdisciplinary studies that bridge transport infrastructure, economic development, and environmental sustainability. She has presented her work at national and international conferences and collaborates on projects addressing logistics efficiency and low-carbon mobility in landlocked countries.

Mridula Mishra is an accomplished academician, dedicated researcher, and experienced professional in the field of tourism and heritage studies. She currently serves as an Assistant Professor at the Amity Institute of Travel and Tourism, Amity University, Noida, Uttar Pradesh, India. With a strong academic and professional background, Dr. Mishra is recognized for her expertise in tourism, heritage, history, cultural studies, and the use of AI in Tourism. Throughout her career, Dr. Mishra has been actively involved with prestigious institutions, including Banaras

Hindu University (BHU), Varanasi, and the Indian Institute of Tourism and Travel Management (IITTM), Noida, where she has contributed significantly to academia, research, and consultancy in the tourism sector.

Zoya Naaz is a dedicated Research Scholar in the Research and Development department at IIMT University, Meerut, where she contributes to the advancement of innovative technical solutions and academic inquiry. A 2025 graduate with a B.Tech in Computer Science and Engineering, Zoya successfully transitioned from her undergraduate studies into a professional research role, focusing on the intersection of modern computing and practical R&D applications. Known for her analytical approach and commitment to excellence, she actively collaborates on institutional research initiatives, aiming to drive meaningful progress within the CSE domain.

Selvakumar P. currently serves as an Associate Professor in the Department of Science and Humanities at Nehru Institute of Technology, Coimbatore, Tamil Nadu, India. With a teaching career spanning over a decade, he previously held positions as an Assistant Professor in the Department of Science and Humanities at various engineering colleges in Coimbatore from 2011 to 2023. Dr. P. Selvakumar's primary area of academic and research interest is phytochemistry, where he has made substantial contributions. His research credentials include 30 journal publications, 14 patents, and 25 conference papers. He has actively promoted faculty and student development by organizing 5 Faculty Development Programs (FDPs) and completing 3 NPTEL courses along with 60 Coursera certifications. His dedication to student success is evident in his role as a committed mentor, consistently guiding and supporting his students academically and personally. Recognized for his excellence in teaching, Dr. P. Selvakumar has received numerous accolades, including Best Teacher Awards. He is also an active member of MISTE (The Indian Society for Technical Education).

Ravikumar R. N. is currently a Postdoctoral researcher at Universiti Malaysia Perlis, Malaysia. Also, working as an Associate Professor in the department of Computer Engineering at Marwadi University, Rajkot, Gujarat. He has 12+ years of national and international teaching experience. He completed his PhD at Amity University, Rajasthan, M.E at VMRF Deemed University, B.E at Anna University, Chennai. He is the co-founder of the Research Activities Club at Marwadi University and trains students on research activities, which leads to the publication of 7 Scopus/SCI journals, 90 Book chapters, 25 Conference papers, and 10 patents. His specialization is ML, DL, Federated Learning, Recommendation Systems, and Optimization Techniques.

Akshay Raj is a researcher and academic associated with IIMT University (IIMTU), Meerut, specializing in renewable energy technologies. He has served as a Research Associate at the university's business incubator, focusing on Photovoltaic Systems, Fuel Cell Technology, and RE-Hybrid Power Generation. He is currently Senior Incubation Manager in IIMT Business Incubator Foundation.

Zeba Rani is a distinguished Assistant Professor in the Department of Nursing at IIMT University, where she blends clinical expertise with cutting-edge research. A Gold Medalist with an M.Sc. in Nursing, she has built a prolific profile that includes authoring several textbooks on subjects such as Obstetric & Gynecological Nursing and Forensic Science, as well as contributing to interdisciplinary research in Blockchain and Machine Learning within healthcare. Beyond her academic role, she is a recognized innovator with multiple patents to her credit—including a specialized vein-finding device—and serves as the Head Faculty Coordinator for the E-Cell, fostering entrepreneurship within the university. Her contributions to institutional excellence were recently honored with the 2025 Excellence Award for NAAC, cementing her reputation as a leader in nursing education and healthcare innovation.

Neelam Vishal Raut is an Associate Professor at Prin. L. N. Welingkar Institute of Management Development and Research (WeSchool), Mumbai, where she contributes to the Post Graduate Diploma in Management (PGDM) program. With a strong academic background and extensive experience in management education, Dr. Raut specializes in areas such as marketing, strategy, and business innovation. Her work combines academic rigor with industry relevance, and she is actively involved in research, teaching, and mentoring future business leaders. Known for her dynamic teaching style and dedication to academic excellence, she plays a key role in shaping the intellectual and professional growth of her students.

Patil Jaya Lakshmi Reddy is presently serving as an Assistant Professor in the School of Management at CMR University, Bangalore. She obtained her LL.M. from Annamalai University and completed her MBA from Vinayaka University in the year 2011. She possesses over seven years of professional experience encompassing both teaching and administrative responsibilities in the domains of Engineering and Management education.

Jorge A. Ruiz-Vanoye is a Professor and Researcher at Universidad Politécnica de Pachuca (UPP), a National Researcher under the Secretaria de Ciencia, Humanidades, Tecnología e Innovación program, and an Adjunct Researcher at the National Laboratory of Autonomous Vehicles and Exoskeletons (LANAVEX). Additionally, he holds the title of Lecturer-level Researcher for the Agency for the Quality of the University System of Catalonia (Generalitat de Catalunya). His research interests include Smart Cities, Smart Water, Smart Education, Smart Government, Smart Healthcare, Smart Farming, Smart Energy, Smart Sports, Smart Food, Smart Tourism, Algorithmic Finance, Algorithmic Portfolio Management, Applications and Theory of Algorithms, Bio-inspired Algorithms, Combinatorial Optimization Problems, Compilers, Computational Intelligence, Computational Complexity Theory, Computational Financial Intelligence, Complexity of Algorithms, Complexity of Instances, Computational Statistics, Computer Networks, Computer Science Security, Cybercrimes, Data Mining, Education, Evolutionary Computation, Heuristic Optimization Techniques in Bioinformatics, Hybrid Evolutionary Algorithms, Hybrid Optimization Algorithms, Machine Learning, Meta-heuristics, Operations Research, Operations Management, Parallel & Distributed Computing, Production Planning and Logistics Optimization, Project Scheduling Problems, Software Engineering, and Transgenic Algorithms.

Aarthi S. is a dedicated Assistant Professor in Computer Science with over six years of teaching experience. She is currently pursuing her Ph.D. at Marwadi University, Gujarat, and holds an M.Phil. and MCA from Bharathiar University, Tamil Nadu. Throughout her academic career, Aarthi has specialized in programming languages such as C++, Java, and C, and contributed to research in recommender systems and AI-related data privacy. She has published journal articles, contributed to book chapters, and actively participated in technical workshops. Known for her student mentorship and engagement in academic events, Aarthi remains committed to fostering innovation and excellence in computer science education.

Shivansu Sachan is Pursuing Ph.D. in Management, a Master's holder from Integral University, Lucknow, Bachelor's from IHM, Lucknow. Academic and professional accomplishments of 6 years with renowned organizations and institutes. His Teaching Career has been very satisfying and have continuously upgraded the skills and knowledge by attending many courses and training programs, seminars, conferences organized by different organizations and also delivered many lectures as a Hospitality sector. He is working as an Assistant Professor at Chhatrapati Shahu ji Maharaj University Kanpur.

Kaies Samet is a Lecturer in Economics at the Higher Institute of Industrial Management in Sfax and a researcher at the Development Economics Laboratory (LED) of the Faculty of Economics and Management of Sfax, Tunisia. He has held a PhD in Economics from the University of Sfax since 2009 and dedicates his research to financial and technological innovation, transport and logistics economics, energy transition, sustainable development, institutional quality, and the issue of brain drain. His work has been published in several indexed international journals, including Sustainability (2025), the Journal of Risk and Financial Management (2025), Asian Economic and Financial Review (2024, 2021), Recherche Transports Sécurité (2023), International Journal of Economics and Financial Issues (2019), and Hommes & Migrations (2014), as well as in collective volumes and international conference proceedings. He is also a member of the editorial board of the International Journal of Innovative Research and Scientific Studies (Scopus Q3, 2024) and Asian Economic and Financial Review (Scopus Q3, 2024), and a reviewer of the Energy Studies Review (Scopus Q4, 2024).

Joshna Sanolia is a dedicated academician and management professional currently serving in the Department of Management at Gian Jyoti Institute of Management and Technology, Mohali, Punjab. With five years of rich academic experience, she has established herself as a committed educator specializing in the fields of Human Resource Management and Marketing. Her academic journey reflects a strong passion for teaching, student development, and institutional excellence. Ms. Sanolia has developed expertise in delivering management education through innovative and student-centric teaching methodologies. She is known for her ability to integrate theoretical concepts with practical insights, enabling students to understand real-world organizational dynamics. Her specialization in Human Resource Management and Marketing allows her to provide students with comprehensive knowledge in areas such as talent management, organizational behavior, recruitment and selection, employee engagement, consumer behavior, branding, and strategic marketing. Throughout her academic career, Ms. Sanolia has actively contributed to academic activities including curriculum delivery, student mentoring, and academic guidance. She has played an important role in nurturing students' professional competencies, critical thinking abilities, and leadership skills, preparing them for successful careers in corporate and entrepreneurial environments. Her dedication to teaching excellence is reflected in her continuous efforts to enhance learning outcomes and student engagement. In addition to her teaching responsibilities, Ms. Sanolia has shown keen interest in academic development and professional growth. She actively participates in seminars, workshops, faculty development programs, and academic initiatives that enhance her knowledge and teaching effectiveness. Her involvement in academic and institutional activities demonstrates her commitment to continuous learning and contribution to the academic community.

Anubhav Sharma is currently working as Assistant Professor in the department of Computer Science and Engineering at IMS Engineering College, Ghaziabad. He has teaching experience of more than 20 years. He has done M.Tech(Hons.) in

Computer Science and Engineering from Uttarakhand Technical University, Dehradun. He has done his B.Tech in Information Technology from UP Technical University, Lucknow . He is pursuing Ph.D in the field of Computer Science and Engineering from Shobhit University,Meerut. His area of Research is Blockchain Technology. He has published more than ten Research Papers in renowned International Journals and presented various papers in International Conferences. His publications can be found in various SCOPUS and WOS Journals. He has participated and organized a number of Workshops/ Trainings/ FDPs and Short Term Courses. He has also published two Patents on Blockchain technology. He has guided numerous students in their Research Projects, Major Projects and capstone Projects. He is a Lifetime member of Indian Society for Technical Education (ISTE). His area of interest includes Blockchain Technology, Virtual Reality, Augmented Reality, IoT, Cyber Security, Operating Systems, C Programming, Python Programming, Mobile Computing, Software Engineering, etc.

Swati Sharma, Ph.D., is currently working as an Associate Professor with Amity University, India. She holds 18 years of teaching and industry experience. She is Vice- President of Women's Indian Chamber of Commerce and Industry. She is First Indian to receive the Certified Tourism Educator award from Asia Pacific Institute of Events Management. She is the reviewer of Consumer Behavior in Tourism & Hospitality & Inderscience Journals & IGI Global . She has authored & Edited 15 books & published research papers in National & International journals of repute. (IGI Global, Taylor & Francis, Springer, Apple Academy Press, CABI, Edward & Elgar).

Vaibhav Sharma is a distinguished academic and administrator currently serving as the CEO-Incubation at IIMT University, Meerut. In this leadership role, he spearheads the university's Business Incubation Foundation, driving innovation and providing strategic oversight to the campus entrepreneurial ecosystem. He also holds a faculty position as an Assistant Professor within the Department of Research and Development. Dr. Sharma's research expertise lies at the intersection of renewable energy and intelligent systems. He holds a PhD from IIMT University, where his work focused on the advancement of Solar PV systems, specifically the development and performance analysis of AI/ML-based Maximum Power Point Tracking (MPPT) and decision-tree techniques.

Bruno Miguel Barbosa de Sousa is a distinguished academic with a Ph.D. in Marketing and Strategy. He graduated in Business Management in 2006 and has since held various academic positions. Currently, he serves as a Professor Coordenador at the Polytechnic University of Cávado and Ave (IPCA), Portugal and has previously lectured at the University of Minho (Portugal). Bruno Sousa is a researcher at the Applied Management Research Unit (UNIAG) and the Center for Research, Development and Innovation in Tourism (CiTUR), both in Portugal. Bruno Sousa's research focuses on diverse areas including marketing and strategy, sustainable development, tourism behavior, organizational performance and niche marketing. He has authored several books and numerous book chapters, along with contributing to prestigious journals such as Current Issues in Tourism; EuroMed Journal of Business; Annals of Leisure Research; Journal of Cultural Heritage Management and Sustainable Development; Tourism Management Perspectives; Wine Economics and Policy; Journal of Hospitality and Tourism Insights; Journal of Tourism, Heritage & Services Marketing; Journal of Organizational Change Management, among others.

G. Sumathy is an Associate Professor in the Department of CINTEL at SRM Institute of Science and Technology (SRMIST), Tamil Nadu, India. She is engaged in teaching, research, and academic mentoring in interdisciplinary computing and intelligent systems. Her academic work contributes to curriculum development and research initiatives within the institution.

N. V. Suresh is a renowned academician from Chennai, Tamil Nadu. He completed his schooling in Chennai. He obtained his BA degree (2012) from D.G. Vaishnav College, Madras University. He joined the Bharathiar University received an MBA degree and PGDM. He Awarded Ph.D. in Management from University of Madras. Dr. N. V. Suresh joined then IIKM in June 2014 as an Assistant Professor (2014 to 2016). He moved to Remo International College in June, 2019 as an Assistant Professor and rose through the ranks to the position of Head of the Department in Aug 2020 to July 2021 then Shifted to Working Academy of Maritime Education and Training (Deemed to be University) Presently Working as Associate Professor and Vice-Principal in ASET College of Science and Technology from March 2022 to Till Date. He is the Visiting Faculty for Institute of Distance Education, University of Madras, Tamil Nadu Open University, Anna University and Directorate of Online Education SRM University for MBA from 2015 to till date. Dr. N. V. Suresh has carried out all his research work entirely in India and has published 30 research papers in international journals.

Anish T. P. is an faculty member in the Department of Computer Science and Engineering at R.M.K College of Engineering and Technology, Tamil Nadu, India. His academic interests include computer science education, emerging computing technologies, and applied research in engineering domains. He is actively involved in teaching, research, and scholarly contributions that support innovation and technical excellence.

Akshita Tiwari is currently working as an Assistant Professor at Amity School of Hospitality, Amity University, Noida, Uttar Pradesh, where she teaches Front Office Operations and Management to Bachelor's in Hotel Management students and Master's in Hospitality students. She has also authored multiple Scopus publications and presented papers at international conferences. With a keen interest in teaching and research, she looks forward to contributing to the field of hospitality and continue to strive for excellence in her work.

Francisco R. Trejo-Macotela holds a Ph.D. in Electronics from INAOE and is Professor and Senior Researcher at Universidad Politécnica de Pachuca (UPP). He is a National Researcher of the Secretariat of Science, Humanities, Technology and Innovation (SECIHTI) of Mexico and adjunct member of LANAVEX. His prolific academic output comprises slightly more than 60 publications in domains including smart cities, embedded IoT systems, telecommunications, electronics, aquaculture, artificial intelligence, bio-inspired algorithms, combinatorial optimisation, and educational technologies.

Asokan Vasudevan is a renowned academic and researcher at INTI International University in Nilai, Malaysia. He began his educational journey at Universiti Kebangsaan Malaysia, earning a Postgraduate Diploma in Industrial Safety Management. He then advanced his studies in the United States at Southeast Missouri State University, obtaining a Master of Science in Management, a Master of Arts in Higher Education Administration, and a Bachelor of Science in Business Administration with a finance specialization. He completed his PhD in Management at UNITEN, Malaysia. Dr. Vasudevan's career includes roles as Lecturer, Department Chair, Professor, and Program Director, significantly enhancing curriculum and leading academic programs. His research, recognized and published in esteemed journals, focuses on business management, ethics, leadership, and their implications on organizational behavior, strategic management, and human resources. His academic work has garnered multiple awards, including the Best Lecturer Award from Infrastructure University Kuala Lumpur and the Teaching Excellence Award from INTI International University.

S. Vidyasagar is an Assistant Professor in the Department of Electrical and Electronics Engineering at SRM Institute of Science and Technology (SRM IST), Kattankulathur, Tamil Nadu, India (603 203). He is involved in undergraduate and postgraduate teaching, research, and student mentoring. His academic interests focus on strengthening core EEE education and research activities.

Index

A

B

C

D

Q

S

www.ingramcontent.com/pod-product-compliance
Lightning Source LLC
LaVergne TN
LVHW081317300926
849161LV00008B/1786